ISBN 978-0-364-65019-6
PIBN 10518321

A HISTORY OF FRENCH LITERATURE

FROM THE EARLIEST TIMES
TO THE GREAT WAR

BY

WILLIAM A. NITZE

AND

E. PRESTON DARGAN

PROFESSORS OF FRENCH LITERATURE
IN THE UNIVERSITY OF CHICAGO

NEW YORK
HENRY HOLT AND COMPANY
1922

PREFACE

THE present *History of French Literature,* intended both for
the general reader and for students, does not aim to be exhaustive. It is divided into three parts: Medieval, Renaissance
and Modern; and within these parts it emphasizes in turn the
chief literary movements and writers, leaving minor tendencies
and figures out of consideration or mentioning them only incidentally. Mere lists of names and dates, valuable as they are
for reference, belong rather to bibliography than to literary history as such. Thus our aim has been to give a connected account of the " main currents " of French literature from the
earliest times down to the present day.

In this attempt we have had several further considerations
to guide us. In the first place, the book is written primarily for
American and English readers. The one key to literary
treasures is not erudition but sympathy. Needless to say, we
would instill in our readers a liking for French literature;
but such sympathy will come only through an appreciation of
the French, as distinguished from the Anglo-Saxon, point of
view. Hence the introductory chapter on the " Spirit of French
Letters " and, in the body of the book, the frequent references
to what appear to be dominant French traits. Another result
of this method is the attention we give to the historical and
social background. Whether we have succeeded or not, we
have consistently tried to depict for each age the historical and
social elements that produced it; briefly of course, with the expectation that the reader will complete the outline by reference
to works dealing directly with these subjects.

In the second place, the authors are convinced that a literature must be learned — if learned is the proper word — by the
stimulus of suggestion rather than by any dogmatic method.
The opinions we state are by no means new. They necessarily
reflect the views of others on the subject; in fact, for each particular movement and author, we have tried to discover the best

authorities, from a scholarly and critical point of view, and to incorporate their conclusions in the text and the titles of their treatises in the bibliography. Yet in each case we have stated these opinions in our own way, with reference to our general plan of treatment, and we have not shunned the expression of an original opinion when circumstances justified it. We make no claim for the absolute value of these views, but we venture to hope that they will rouse the reader's interest and lead him to formulate ideas of his own on the authors and books we have considered. If our book wins new readers for French literature itself, our main purpose will have been achieved.

Again, the authors are well aware that in a work of condensation such as a history of literature the statement of " facts " is necessarily difficult to make. One reason is that the facts in a given case are not always ascertainable. We have, as far as we have been able, given the correct dates for both writers and works of literature. With regard to other facts, such as literary sources and influences, we have — especially in doubtful cases — cited and even quoted the best authorities on the subject. But truth in literary matters, depending as it does on interpretation and taste, is of course relative; and we have no doubt that many readers, more competent than ourselves, will regard much of our material as open to question or in need of correction. We do not cling to the determinism of Taine, nor do we deny that it expresses a great truth. The French may not be a " race," but they are certainly a "nation " with a distinct civilization of their own; and it is the history of the literary manifestations of this civilization that we have attempted to write. If our critics will take the same pains to correct our mistakes as we have taken to avoid them, they will earn our gratitude and, what is even better, help us to mend our ways.

As for matters of detail, it may be pointed out that the collaborators have divided their task in such a way that the responsibility for the treatment of the Middle Ages and the Renaissance (through French Classicism) belongs to W. A. Nitze, and for that of Modern Times to E. P. Dargan. Provençal literature is not treated by us, nor is the rich Latin literature of the Middle Ages, except as these incidentally affect French literature in one of its own stages. The substance as well as the structure of our book owes much, of course, to the admirable treatises of Gaston Paris, Lanson and Brunetière, and in the Medieval and Renaissance periods to the works of Suchier and Morf. In the field of criticism, Saintsbury's important work has again and again been laid under contribution. For Modern Times, the essays of Sainte-Beuve and Brunetière, the treatises of Villemain and Taine have been found particularly valuable. To these and to our numerous special authorities we here acknowledge obligation. For all titles we refer the reader to the selected bibliography at the end of the work.

As regards the question of proportion, a word remains to be said. The increasing number of chapters and authors in Part III is due to the increasing complexity or "heterogeneity" of French literature in the last two centuries. Since our intention is to stress both ideas and form, a full treatment has been accorded to the liberalism of the eighteenth century and to the various artistic currents of the nineteenth. This has been done, it is hoped, without detracting from the importance of previous periods, especially the great Classical Age.

The illustrations have been chosen to symbolize the spirit of each epoch. They are masterpieces dating, in each case, from the period under consideration.

In conclusion, we most sincerely thank those friends and colleagues whose guidance and criticism have been at our disposal. Professors Jenkins and Pietsch of the University of Chicago have assisted us materially with their knowledge of the Middle Ages. In particular, our selections from the *Chanson de Roland* have had the benefit of Professor Jenkins' revision. Our colleague, Professor Coleman, has been gracious enough to revise the chapters on the early seventeenth century. Professors Lancaster, Lovejoy and Chinard of Johns Hopkins University have performed a similar service for portions of the eighteenth and nineteenth centuries; and Professor Guérard of the Rice Institute has been unsparing in his help on matters concerning modern French thought. For additional services, willingly and carefully rendered, we are indebted to Professors Albert Schinz of Smith College, Henri David of the University of Chicago, B. E. Young of Vanderbilt University and Henry M. Dargan of the University of North Carolina. Obviously none of these friends are responsible for the errors and imperfections of our book. It is owing to them, to their generous suggestions and criticisms, that its sins of omission and commission are not more numerous. On the other hand, if our book has — as we hope — points to commend it, their assistance should not be forgotten:

Secundas res splendidiores facit amicitia.

W. A. N.
E. P. D.

CHICAGO, *September*, 1921.

NOTE.— In spelling French words, our aim has been to modernize the titles of important works. The titles of less well-known works are often given in their archaic forms. Citations of text, however, are not modernized until we reach the seventeenth century. At the same time, Montaigne's *Essais* are cited in a modernized form according to Jeanroy's *Principaux chapitres et extraits de Montaigne.*

vii

CONTENTS

ILLUSTRATIONS

INTRODUCTION

THE SPIRIT OF FRENCH LETTERS

> " L'histoire de la littérature d'un peuple, j'ai eu occasion de vous le dire souvent déjà, est l'histoire de sa vie morale, et particulièrement de sa conscience nationale." Gaston Paris, *La Poésie du moyen âge*, I, 94.

IT is said that distinctions are invidious. But surely only for the unintelligent or uneducated. If we find pleasure in Shakespeare, this does not prove that we must dislike Racine. On the contrary, a thorough understanding of both authors should lead us to like both — but for different reasons. The qualities we admire in the Englishman are not and cannot be the traits we find in the Frenchman, quite aside from the fact that each is a different individual and not the same person. Thus every literature, so-called, is an embodiment of the national life. And while certain writers, and especially certain literary epochs, are less clearly national than others, yet it remains true that no author can divorce himself from his people and represent a point of view that is really alien to them. Indirectly, at least, he will reflect their type of emotion, their brand of ideas, their particular way of viewing and expressing things — in a word, their psychology or *vie morale*,[1] as Gaston Paris says in the quotation made above. Hence literature is not only a matter of individuals but of groups; and not the least of its functions is to portray the interactions between the poet and the social consciousness of the nation to which he belongs.

If, then, French literature has certain essentials or fundamental traits, they are not always easy to define, since national characteristics appear only by contrast with those of other peoples. At the same time, as far as they can be ascertained, they are seen in the selection French writers make of their materials and in the tendencies they follow in working them out. It will be the object of this introductory chapter to state what are some of the distinguishing features of French literature.

[1] Let us note, at the outset, that the French word *moral* means "psychological."

The remark has been repeatedly made that the French value truth more than beauty — not that they scorn the beautiful, but **Reason** their attachment to truth is stronger. To quote one of their modern critics: " Ce qu'il nous faut, c'est le vrai dans l'art *encore* plus que le beau." As early as the seventeenth century Boileau crystallized this ideal when he wrote:

> Rien n'est beau que le vrai, le vrai seul est aimable;
> Il doit régner partout, et même dans la fable.

If we substitute the word " rational " for the word " true " in these quotations,[2] we shall come nearer to the French point of view; for French art, and especially French literature, is largely a product of the human reason. With English literature it thus offers an interesting contrast.

We of English tradition are accustomed to look upon a literary work as " holding the mirror up to nature " — to use Shakespeare's phrase. We see life as an endless complexity, and by nature we mean not only man but man in his surroundings, as part of the natural world that enfolds him. To a greater degree than the French, we are conscious of the fact that the universe holds us in its grip; and we struggle to be " free," to make ourselves felt for what we are as " individuals." But whatever the problem may be with which man contends, to us the human being is never separated from the background of reality in which life is passed. So that Dickens, like Wordsworth, like Milton, like Chaucer, deals with the setting of human character as a matter of prime and essential importance. " Character," said Emerson, " is nature in the highest form." Thus English literature is primarily the record and the product of individuals, in their manifold surroundings. It is varied rather than homogeneous. It deals with things rather than with ideas. It is imaginative rather than logical; concrete rather than abstract. It tends to embrace creation and not merely the life of man.

In comparison, French literature is essentially a reflection of the mind. Not only the treatment of life but the French conception of it is intellectual. Types, not individuals, appeal to the logical sense of the French; and types are not direct obser-

---

[2] French distinguishes between the two types of truth, rational truth and truth to fact, by the two expressions *le vrai* and *la vérité.*

vations of life but deductions or classifications we make from it.
The Frenchman views life primarily as idea, secondarily as fact.
His chief interest lies not so much in character or nature as in
the permanent traits of humanity and the universality of their
application. Hence his method is analytic and comparative,
whereas ours is empirical and absolute. He works from the surface of life inward, not from the kernel to the surface. Metaphysics is not his forte — that " art de s'égarer avec méthode,"
as Michelet called it. The French have no counterpart to a
great lyric genius like Shelley, who takes his own visions for
reality, who hopes

> till Hope creates
> From its own wreck the thing it contemplates.

Yet England has no equivalent to Voltaire: the embodiment of
the pure reason and the sworn enemy of all illusion. The following selection from Montaigne might be taken as a general definition of the French point of view, so widespread is its application to the French:

> I propose à life mean and without luster, but 'tis all one;
> all moral philosophy is applied as well to a private life as to
> one of the greatest employment. Every man carries the entire
> form of the human condition. Authors have hitherto com-
> municated themselves to the people by some particular and
> foreign mark; I, the first of any, by my universal being, as
> Michel de Montaigne, not as a grammarian, a poet or a
> lawyer. If the public complain that I speak too much of
> myself, I complain that they do not think exclusively of
> themselves.

French literature, therefore, is _social_. " La critique étrangère
et la critique française se sont accordées à le proclamer," said

Sociability
Gaston Paris. The public, whose approval Montaigne craves, is always in a French writer's confidence. He writes to the public, for the public, about public
questions generally. Discussion is the breath of French life, as
conversation is one of its greatest arts. Even so individual a
writer as Pascal addresses his _Pensées_ to an unseen companion;
and Pascal said, " the ego is hateful." The dialogue is a favorite form in French, from the medieval _débat_ down to the
confidente rôle in Classical French drama. Descartes defined

reading as " a conversation with the best people of bygone ages."
And one of the most personal of modern poets, Musset, liked
poetry because " it is intelligible to the world, though spoken by
the poet alone."

As a consequence, French writers choose their themes broadly
with reference to their application. They seem to ask not only:
is this my problem? but also, is it your problem? because, in
Montaigne's words, it is a fundamentally human problem, as well
as the problem of a grammarian, a poet or a lawyer. Look
at any representative French work and you will see how
generally true this is. The author makes an abstraction
of his experience and then views it in the form of action. He
exploits his idea or emotion to the full extent of its social
value.

This accounts for the hospitality of French art, to which in a
very real sense nothing human is inacceptable. " The [French]
cathedrals," says Mr. Brownell, " are not feudal. They are the
products of a spirit partly ecclesiastical, partly secular, but
always social — the true Gallo-Roman spirit which, great as
was the perfection attained by German feudalism in France,
constantly struggled against and finally conquered its foreign
Frankish foe." The same thing is true of French letters. Time
and again, the French have borrowed an idea from without: it
is they who socialize the idea, widen its application, standardize
it, and thereupon send it broadcast over the world to bear
fruit in a larger, more extended form. Thus during the Middle
Ages France took over the Germanic idea of obligation and,
through the efforts of her scholars and her poets, made it dominant over Europe; likewise in the Renaissance she chose the
Italian idea of formal perfection or *virtù*, and in the later
eighteenth century the northern idea of personality, and worked
them over into their broadest, most social expression. France
has been, and still is, the intellectual clearing-house of Europe.

A literature that is social is necessarily a literature of *form*
fully as much as of content. To be sure, the sense of form
Form has grown in France since the sixteenth century,
owing to the cult of antiquity. But the trait is
nevertheless inherent in French culture. Kant once said: " The
French may have the flowers of the tree of knowledge but they

rarely possess its roots," and sweeping as the generalization is, there is this truth in it: that to them the form is often as important as the idea. By form the French mean technique; that is, the observed principles or laws of form rather than the ethos of form itself, which is always individual, as it is in the *Divine Comedy* or in Goethe's *Faust*, or in most of Shakespeare's tragedies. A French play or novel is a very conscious product: the author is an adept in the laws of the genre, and his work is generally the best that training and talent can produce. At least, a minimum is left to chance or individual inspiration; the maximum is artistry, schooling, the interaction of critical power and the creative mind. The result is a high average: general proficiency in place of sporadic preëminence. "La France est en tout un pays de moyennes," said a distinguished Russian in a spirit of praise. Probably no literature has been so productive or so continuous as that of France. Certainly none is so rich in criticism, in reflections on the manner of life. Thus, in a very real sense, it is possible to speak of the " schools " of French literature, in which the critics play an important rôle. And the highest literary expression in France is, as Anatole France says of the landscape about Florence, *une parfaite et mesurée œuvre d'art*. On the other hand, idiosyncrasy of genius has never flourished there as it has elsewhere, and it would be useless to look in French literature for a *Hamlet*, an *Iliad* or a *Don Quixote*.

It is clear that whatever the French may lack in range, they make up in homogeneity and poise. Witness their language with its strong Latin tradition toward balance and unity. The few words which the Roman conquerors of Gaul took over from the Celts did not perceptibly affect the word-stock of French. Even the Franks, whose conquest of Gaul in the fifth century gave to France her name and many of her institutions, did not alter the language except by the addition of a few hundred new words. So that in structure and even vocabulary French is an offspring of Popular Latin as it was spoken by Caesar's soldiers in Gaul, supplemented from time to time by other elements, one of which is Literary Latin. Here again, England presents an interesting contrast. There the Germanic form of speech, Anglo-Saxon, triumphed; until in the eleventh century (after

1066) it was temporarily thrust aside and French became the
language of the higher classes, and consequently of literature.
Hence English is dual in nature; at once Teutonic and Latin,
a mixture of two opposing tendencies, which manifest themselves again and again in English writing; whereas, comparatively speaking, French is a unit, and the literature as well as
the language is informed throughout with the Latin genius of
clarity and precision. " Ce qui n'est pas clair, n'est pas
français," said Rivarol in a famous essay on the universality
of French. To state a thing in French is to state it well; that is,
with accuracy and distinction. Renan affirmed that " truth lies
in a shading " (" la vérité est dans une nuance "). The shadings,
those subtle boundaries of truth, rarely escape a French writer's
eye.

At the same time, there is a tendency in French to overstate an
idea or emotion, to make it more pressing and effective than it
really is. An excellent example is the French drama, where the
difficulty presented so often leads to a logical but not to a very
convincing conclusion. Hervieu's Le Dédale and Bernstein's
Samson, to cite only modern instances, are dramatic but they
are inconclusive: the cases depicted are too special to warrant
a general inference such as the dramatist would have us make.
The best literature proves nothing since demonstration is not
its function. Or take Maupassant in the realm of fiction. As
an expression of irony, of human stupidity, his Necklace (La
Parure) is perfect, but as a picture of reality, this story is an
argumentum in vacuo. It assumes a mistake — the necklace is
" paste," not genuine — and it carries this mistake to an abstract
conclusion. Thus the love of argument, so strong in the French,
is also a limitation; granting that logical precision makes for
clearness and intelligibility, it satisfies the mind but not the
imagination.) Yet, in the hands of a genius like Racine, this
very control intensifies the emotion and achieves effects of flaw-
less and inevitable beauty.)

Such an attention to form and method has given to French
poetry a tendency which the Anglo-Saxon may find hard to
grasp. France has had many wonderful poets: Hugo, Musset,
Vigny, Chénier, Ronsard, Villon; and her collected poetry fills
volumes. Nevertheless, French poetry has the externality of a

fine art. The Gallic spirit is inventive. It is too critical, too self-conscious, too mathematical and logical to be deeply lyrical. The social instinct works havoc with the world of illusion and mystery in which the great lyrist moves. At all events, the French illusions are short-lived. They are the illusions of the market-place, they affect the masses more than the individual: honor, vanity, glory, equality — rather than loyalty, ambition, immortality, freedom. And the loneliness of genius, while it is seen in such a writer as Vigny, is rare in France. So, too, the French poet's attachments are to the visible world — the world of light and sunshine. It has been said that no verses express more clearly this side of the French temper than Régnier's *Le Secret:*

> Car la forme, l'odeur et la beauté des choses
> Sont le seul souvenir dont on ne souffre pas.

Racine, the poet of deep feeling and with a vision turned inward, manages to externalize his emotions in the most tangible of forms: " Il rase la prose," observes Lamaitre, " mais avec des ailes." Or take Hugo, who has sweep and sustained utterance, and a gift of imagery such as few poets can equal: again it is the artist in him that dominates the lyrist; his power of execution is greater than his inspiration, and his verse is oratorical and brilliant far more than it is passionately deep and sincere. If, then, the " lyric cry " is rare in France, and the quality of French verse is prevailingly temperate and moderate in comparison with ours, let us not forget that French poetry is formally the more artistic. There are " gems " of French verse which as regards technical perfection it would be difficult to match in other literatures. The French are apt at seizing the fleeting and transitory aspects of man's nature, at immortalizing a mood or whim, at endowing not only the humble but the commonplace with the eternity of art. The much-quoted line of Musset:

> Mon verre n'est pas grand, mais je bois dans mon verre,

well expresses the crowded experience which French verse can portray, and Musset for all his technical imperfections is a great French poet.

On the other hand, while French poetry is often like prose, it must not be forgotten that French prose is in a class by itself. There are pages of Pascal, Flaubert, Rabelais, Chateaubriand, Anatole France, which are superior to anything else that has ever been written.   Here the national genius for expression comes to full fruition.   Rarely does one find in French prose an idea that is obscure, a character whose psychology is not intelligible, a situation the outlines of which are not visible to the inner eye.   Of Flaubert, Henry James says: " To be intensely definite and perfectly positive, to know so well what he meant that he could at every point strikingly and conclusively verify it, was the first of his needs."   Moreover, style to the French is at once the garment and the method of thought. The control the French show in their writing is proverbial. Limpid, descriptive, harmonious, suave, picturesque, as the case may be, French prose is the elaboration of thought, the presentation of the idea in action, the concrete realization of the impression the author *wishes* to convey.   " Le style est l'homme même," said Buffon, and deflected as this phrase has been from its original meaning, the statement is often literally true.   It is frequently in style, rather than in newness of idea, that the individuality of the French writer triumphs; and the personal accent we look for in literature the French manifest not in what they say but in the way they say it.   Hence, of the two kinds of prose, *la bonne prose* and *la belle prose,* France exemplifies the latter.

II

To sum up: the dominant traits of French literature are poise, harmony, reason, sympathy; a sense of structure and a sense of delicacy; a preference for ideas over things, but for active social ideas, not metaphysical personal ones. **Summary** French literature is an immediate reflection of the *esprit gaulois:* brilliant, vivacious, good-natured, ironic, curious of everything essentially human; as M. Lanson has said: " more sensible than sensuous, but more sensuous than ethical."   A race singularly conscious of itself, firm in the conviction that:

all the world's a stage
And all the men and women merely players.

Consciously to play a part in life, to be an actor and at the same time an observer and a critic, never to take life too seriously nor yet to neglect it; this is the touchstone of the French point of view, and when all is said, French literature is its expression.

Many readers will therefore find in French authors a marked uniformity; or rather they will fail to see that variety must be sought in elaboration and detail, and not in background or theme. They will miss the more pronounced display of personality, the greater emphasis on idiosyncrasy, to which English literature has made them accustomed — often overlooking the fact that they have been blind to the swift analysis, the careful distinctions, the exquisite sense of form wherewith the greatest French writers have set forth life. Thus, little can be gained by reading a French writer hastily or with insufficient knowledge of the language. The reader must weigh the phrases, evaluate the words, institute comparisons, take account of the fact that the highest art is apparently the most simple; otherwise the literature of France will remain to him, in large measure, a book sealed with seven seals.

Further, the intellectual and emotional relations of the French are not primarily moral, in the English sense of the word. This could hardly be expected of a nation which views life so clearly as contact with humanity or to which living itself is an "art." "Montaigne," says Emerson, "is the frankest and honestest of men." You cannot deal with the social ideas on a large scale and not be outspoken. On the whole, the French would rather boast of imaginary crimes than pose as more virtuous than they are. With us conduct is personal and therefore inviolate; with the French it is conventional and thus more easily shifted to others' shoulders. Moral lapses in the strict sense are more easily pardoned in France than lapses in good form or etiquette, since the former affect the individual and not society directly. Molière remarks: "On veut bien être méchant; mais on ne veut point être ridicule" — a distinctly social attitude, in harmony with his conception of comedy and its flaying of the social vices: affectation, hypocrisy, avarice and misanthropy. For Molière's *Le Misanthrope* is a "comedy," however tragic its chief character may seem to Anglo-Saxon eyes. On the other hand, in our workaday world nothing is a safer guide than *le bon sens* — and *bon sens*, as the social reason is called, has generally been uppermost in French character.

Lastly, the doctrinaire attitude of trusting to ideas is what the person of Germanic traditions finds hardest to understand. We are the children of expediency. We react more readily to impulse or sentiment — to the " inner fact of things," as Carlyle used to say — and we distrust logic. Centuries of struggle with the material universe have impressed on us the fact that theory and practice are two very different things, and we would follow our instinct rather than reason the thing out.

Not so the French. The one definite link between the Gauls whom Caesar describes and the modern French is their passion for ideas. Being and thinking may be at variance, therefore it is the duty of man to make them one — that is, to identify facts with logic. In short, the problem of humanity is to make the universe rational. A dream, we should say. To this the French reply in the phrase of Descartes: " je pense, donc je suis "; and in its length and breadth their literature is a conscious striving to realize this ideal. In general, English literature is more lyrical and varied, Italian literature possesses a richer and more voluptuous sense of beauty, Spanish literature is closer to the well-springs of popular inspiration in the ballad and the epic — but French literature is by all odds the most broadly *human:* it speaks to the large audience of *les honnêtes gens* the world over, and for him who has mastered the French language it does so in terms that are at once stimulating to the mind and satisfying to the artistic sense.

PART I

THE MIDDLE AGES

Illustration from a *Graal-Lancelot* Manuscript

BOOK I

FEUDALISM AND CHIVALRY

CHAPTER I

THE MIDDLE AGES AND THE EPIC

THE Middle Ages in France extend from the treaty of Verdun in 843 to the expedition of Charles VIII into Italy in 1494. The first date represents the earliest recognition of the French as a nation, and the second their appearance as a world-power vying with other nations, notably with Spain and England, for the political control of Europe. Between these dates lies an interesting and significant development which, however transitional it may seem on the surface, has a distinct character of its own.

The ruling features of this era are: the Christianization of culture, with its emphasis on man's sinful nature — the redemption of which is considered essential; the feudalization of society and the rise of chivalry as an expression of the new social order; and, finally, the growth of city life under the control of a bourgeois class. The last division is coincident roughly with the Middle French period (fourteenth and fifteenth centuries) as distinguished from the Old French or medieval period proper. If we add to these features the growing importance of Paris as a political and intellectual center, the chief elements of the entire epoch lie before us.

The collapse of the Empire of Charlemagne marks the beginning of France. With all his enthusiasm for Latin culture, Charlemagne was virtually a Teutonic monarch; so that when in 843 the country west of the Meuse, the Saône and the Rhône fell to the sceptre of Charles the Bald, it was the birth of a new nation that men witnessed. The language of this territory had received formal recognition a year earlier. The dialect of Popular Latin spoken by Charles' subjects was no longer the same speech that the Franks had found when they invaded Gaul. It had undergone changes in structure and especially in vocabulary, which, while in no sense identifying it with the *lingua teutonica* of the Germanic tribes, yet distinguish it sharply from the *lingua romana* as spoken in the South. Some of these differences appear in the *Serments de Strasbourg* of 842. Here, Louis the German and Charles the Bald pledge themselves in each other's language to maintain their respective interests against their brother Lothaire. Louis' part of this covenant is the earliest document extant in the *langue d'oïl* or French, and although it has no literary value it is important evidence of the fact that a national speech is being formed.

But the kingdom of Charles is only partly France. The destinies of the country are henceforth distinct from those of the rest of continental Europe, but they are not yet strictly under French control. The imperial régime is weakened, notably by the spread of feudalism in the ninth century; its power, however, is definitely broken only with the death of Louis V in 987. With the accession of Hugh Capet, Count of Paris, in that year the Carolingian epoch ends completely, and the history of France proper, of her institutions, her culture, her art and her literature, begins.

It is not our purpose to trace that history except as it is reflected in literature. At the same time, it may be useful to recall that the Duchy of France, or the territory immediately surrounding Paris, is the nucleus from which the national development spread. Although Hugh Capet was nominally King of France, his real power extended little beyond his own domain and those fiefs whose obedience he could command. Thus, broadly viewed, the history of medieval France was a struggle of the monarchy against feudal aggression on the part of the great barons. It was a struggle waged with varying fortunes until one by one the great provinces are brought under the rule of the crown: Normandy in 1204, Anjou and Languedoc shortly after, Champagne in 1274, Provence in 1486; and, finally, a highly centralized state is established. In this nation the three dominant races of Europe are represented — the Nordic in Normandy and the northeast, the Alpine in Savoy and Auvergne, and the Mediterranean in the south. The French, therefore, are a racial epitome of Western Europe.

Cultural Aspects

Turning now from this hasty glance at history to the conditions of medieval society in general, we may note first: that in place of a uniform language for the whole territory each province develops its own dialect. The main dialects are: Norman and Picard in the north, Champenois and Burgundian in the east, Angevin in the west, with Francian or the dialect of the Duchy of France in the center. While these dialects belong to the *langue d'oïl* or Old French, just as the *langue d'oc* or Old Provençal consists of the various forms of southern speech, none of them is supreme during the medieval period. Each has its official and literary monuments — the *Vie de Saint-Alexis*, Wace's *Brut*, the *Lais* of Marie de France are in Norman; a masterpiece like the *Aucassin et Nicolette* is in Picard; the romances of Crestien de Troyes are partly in Champenois, and so on. Not until the end of the twelfth century does Francian assume the leading rôle. And even then it is still far from being the sole literary speech, although the tendency is more and more in that direction. In 1173 Garnier de Pont-Sainte-Maxence (near Paris) is able to boast:

> Mis langages est buens, car en France fui nez;

and the recognition of Paris in the thirteenth century as the intellectual capital of Europe does much to establish Francian — especially the speech of Paris — as standard French. Whoever knows his Chaucer will recall the famous quip on the Prioress in the *Canterbury Tales:*

> And Frensch sche spak ful faire and fetysly —
> After the scole of Stratford atte Bowe,
> For Frensch of Parys was to hire unknowe.

But important as it is, the question of language is secondary to the cultural aspects of the age. And in these the laity were not the prime movers. Latin, not French, was the language of the clergy, and the Middle Ages are primarily an ecclesiastical epoch. When Hugh Capet relinquished the rich abbeys of Saint-Denis, Saint-Germain-des-Prés, Saint-Riquier and Saint-Valéry to the clergy, he received in exchange the title of " Defender of the Church," and France became, if not the focus, at least the mainstay of Roman Christianity.

The influence of the church shows itself on every hand: in the development of new lands and out-of-the-way districts, in the building of monasteries and churches, in giving impetus to the movement which leads to the crusades in Spain and in the East, but above all in the spread of such learning and culture as the age allowed. It was the clergy who composed the music, developed the arts of MS illumination, of woodcarving and the like, and it is to them we owe much of the classical literature that survived the destruction of Rome by the barbarians.

It is but natural that they gave to their work, secular as well as sacred, an ecclesiastical interpretation. Alone responsible for man's spiritual guidance, they reinterpreted — as every age has done — the past in terms of the present. But they had no sense of history, or rather their history was the history of the " soul," as revealed in the Bible and the writings of the Church Fathers. Thus they saw life mainly from one angle, that of salvation; and all created things, including Nature herself, assumed a symbolic, theological value. To them Aristotle was no longer an independent thinker, a philosopher who had sought the boundaries of truth, but the inventor of the laws of reason; and reason was given man, they thought, to apprehend the faith. Through faith alone, it was thought, the human being attained to complete knowledge, the wisdom of God which passeth understanding. *Credo ut intelligam* (" I believe in order that I may understand "), said St. Anselm, a statement that we may contrast with the *Cogito ergo sum* (" I think, therefore I am ") of Descartes.

Thus the medieval method is exegesis. The sage is he who can interpret the divine order in things by discovering their underlying *sensus* or " meaning " — the idea recurs in the Old French romances (see Ch. II). And the dominant philosophical idea is that of " fixity." For the church taught that the universe, in its narrow scope as men then knew it, according to the Ptolemaic system, was limited. There is no conscious effort to change it, to widen its horizons, to better its conditions materially. The highest aim is the liberation from sin, its avoidance or its expiation. But since the age is at once too sophisticated and too childlike to grasp in full measure the spiritual side of Christianity, it conceives of it picturesquely, in terms of a material

Heaven, a material Hell and a material Purgatory, in hierarchies of saints and demons, in pilgrimages, fastings and physical suffering. He who gave alms, gave them primarily to redeem himself, not to benefit his neighbor. A crucified Saviour, a Christ victorious through physical pain, is the quintessence of the mystical, medieval spirit.

But if the church dominates society in its outlook upon life, the forms of the church are themselves the product of social forces. These are of course feudal. The guiding force of feudalism is obligation. The freeman and small proprietor, unable to guard his own interests, " commended himself " to his more powerful neighbor, and thereupon received back his property in the shape of a " fief," for the loan of which he promised service or money, or both. That is, feudalism is a mutual guarantee of person and property in an age of weak government. It flourished in France from about the ninth to the fourteenth century, and it gave to medieval life its distinctive hierarchal form.

The result was that, while in the tenth and eleventh centuries the political power of the church is still great and that of the king — in reality little more than a tribal leader — is weak, the twelfth century witnessed a notable change. Not only does feudalism become a national institution but society itself conforms to its ideals, and the distinctions between noble and serf, knight and yeoman, *courtois* (" courtly ") and *vilain* (" vulgar ") are definitely worked out. Thus four great classes or castes arise: (1) the nobles, (2) the clergy, (3) the townsfolk or bourgeois and (4) the peasantry. In addition, the crusades begin and chivalry as a military and social organization spreads over Europe. In short, polite or *courtois* society comes into being. All this gives to the twelfth and thirteenth centuries a cultural florescence in which art and literature share. But, like everything else, human institutions decay; by degrees the monarchy allies itself with the lower classes, especially the bourgeoisie, the power of the great nobles wanes and feudalism disintegrates. Finally, with the fall of the feudal order, the medieval " fixity " is broken and the Renaissance sets in. The fourteenth and fifteenth centuries mark the beginning of this change.

The literature of such an epoch is necessarily one-sided. For the emphasis is on one ideal, faith in the established order, and on the expression of one dominant emotion, that of honor or obligation to one's trust. The knight does homage to his liege, the courtier to his lady, the cleric to his God, in much the same manner and in about the same terms. But because of this restriction the literature is vivid and intense, poetic and imaginative rather than real, and, like all mystical literature, it is fraught with personal longings and with the aspiration, in the words of St. Augustine, "to grasp the infinite within the vessel of the finite." In the second place, it is didactic and formalistic. It moralizes on life, lays down a code for human conduct, even in the affairs of the heart, and neglects the intrinsic values of life itself, such as beauty, individual happiness and justice. Nothing could be more significant than the numerous bestiaries, lapidaries and astrologies *(computi)* in which the Middle Ages sought to reveal the symbolic or ethical meaning of Nature herself. When the reaction begins, the note that is heard is satire and irony, a reflection of Gallic common-sense, voicing its protest in the *fabliaux* and the beast-epic.

Thus the divisions of medieval literature are mainly these:
(1) The saints' legends, the epics or *chansons de geste,* didactic treatises of various kinds, and the serious drama. These are mostly clerical; at least, their source of inspiration is the church, directly in the saints' legends and the drama, or indirectly in the epic.
(2) The various forms of the lyric, — largely an importation from Provence — the romances of chivalry and the allegory. Here the inspiration comes largely from aristocratic feudal society, or what we may call by the generic name of courtly or *courtois.*
(3) The increasing current of bourgeois expression, appearing first in the *fabliaux* and the beast-epic, then in the second part of the *Roman de la Rose,* and finally in various productions of the fourteenth and fifteenth centuries.

In October, 878, the discovery of the supposed bones of a Christian saint was made in Barcelona, Spain. This event led to the composition in French of the church "sequence" of *Sainte Eulalie* — so far as we know, the first French work of literary merit. It inaugurates the large literature in the vernacular, inspired by the passion of piety, of which the saint's lives of *Saint Léger* (tenth century) and *Saint-Alexis* (about 1050) are early, and to some extent illustrious, examples. A short poem on the Passion (tenth century) should be added to these as showing the beginnings of French literary composition. But whatever incidental interest these works may have, they do not yet reflect a truly national spirit. To find this we must turn to the French epic, or *chansons de geste.*

The Epic

The title *geste* (Lat. *gesta*) originally meant deeds, and the "songs of deeds" are the products of the race which Hugh Capet and his successors were called upon to govern. As the number of epic poems increased, the *jongleurs* or "minstrels" who sang them arranged them in families or "cycles," each headed by the name of an ancestor. Thus the poems concerned with Charlemagne and his family went under the name of Pepin, or the *geste du roi;* others treating of the south of France and its struggle with the Saracen invaders, under the names of Garin de Monglane or Guillaume d'Orange; while those relating the deadly strife of the feudal barons among themselves were classed under the name of Doön de Mayence. But this classification, probably made long after the composition of the actual epic, is conventional rather than real. The various groups are inter-related, and other groups besides those mentioned existed. A separate cycle is that of the crusades. To it belong such poems as the *Chanson de Jérusalem* and the *Chanson d'Antioche,* and linked to the crusade-cycle are romantic compositions like the *Chevalier au cygne* — the story of Lohengrin — and *Godefroi de Bouillon,* the ancestor of the House of Brabant. In the fourteenth century this last group became the object of burlesque and parody, a fate that awaited all epic and chivalric expression at the close of the Middle Ages.

In form the *chansons de geste* consist of *laisses* or stanzas, composed at first on one vowel-rime or assonance, and later on one rime, for each *laisse,* the whole being set to music. The stanzas are of unequal length and are written, generally but not always, in ten-syllable verse, which is the heroic verse of the French until Ronsard's time, when it was superseded by the twelve-syllable, or Alexandrine.

Since the epic celebrates heroes for the most part contemporaneous with Charlemagne, who himself is the focus of a group of poems, the theory early arose that the epic is Germanic in origin and inspiration. Of this theory there are several variations. One view is that the Frankish invaders of Gaul sang epico-lyric songs or *cantilenae* — somewhat like our English ballads — and that, although none of these is extant in the original form, the epic itself is due to a combination of them made by the *jongleurs*. Another hypothesis is that there existed a sort of " poetic history " constructed out of the legendary remnants of the Germanic past, and that this, transmitted either by writing or by word of mouth, inspired the extant poems, none of which antedate the close of the eleventh century.

The modern view combats these earlier theories by affirming that the French epic is virtually contemporaneous in origin with the twelfth-century *chansons*. In other words, the epic — it is now thought — was the immediate product of the warlike conditions of the eleventh and twelfth centuries in France: the period of pilgrimages to holy places, of expeditions against the Saracens in Spain, and of the wars of the crusades. The part that Charlemagne has in it is a recollection of the past, but a conscious one, supplied by proselyting monks from monastery chronicles and shreds of oral tradition for ecclesiastical and national ends. Thus the *chansons de geste* would have originated at the hands of some poet along one of the great pilgrimage routes leading to St. James of Compòstella in Spain, St. Peter's in Rome, or some shrine within the borders of France. In any case, French feudalism and the Christian church combine to make the epic what it is, and whatever view we take as to its ultimate origin, the actual epic belongs to the twelfth century.

The greatest and probably the earliest example of the epic is the *Chanson de Roland*, in 4002 assonanced verses. Found in **The** this form in a manuscript of the end of the twelfth **" Roland "** century (now in the Bodleian library at Oxford), the work itself must be nearly a century older. The poet Wace (in 1160) affirms that the minstrel Taillefer chanted a *Song of Roland* at Hastings in 1066. Later versions occur in the Latin prose *Pseudo-Turpin*, which is part of a pilgrimage guide to Compostella, and in the *Carmen de proditione Guenonis*, emphasizing the treachery of Ganelon. In its French form, however, the *Roland* stands at the threshold of a literature of which it is one of·the most inspired and characteristic expressions.

The story is simple and fairly commonplace. For seven years Charles "the king, our mighty emperor" has battled against the Saracens in Spain. Bereft of his strongholds, Marsile, the Saracen — who differs from a Christian only by being a pagan — sends delegates to Charles to promise peace falsely. The embassy is headed by Blancandrin, a wise pagan, who conspires with Ganelon for the death of Roland, nephew of Charles and bravest of the French. Ganelon is no coward, but he hates Roland for the obvious reason that Roland, rich in worldly possessions, is his step-son:

> "Ço set hom bien que jo sui tis padrastres."

Thus Ganelon's hatred becomes the ruin of the French.

Won by the promises of Marsile, Charles withdraws his main army across the Pyrenees to celebrate Michaelmas at Aix, the minster-town. Roland, left behind in Spain with the rearguard of 20,000, including the flower of French knighthood (the Twelve Peers), is attacked at Roncevaux near the defiles of the Pyrenees by an overwhelming host of Saracens. Oliver, his boon companion, who personifies wisdom as Roland does bravery —

> Rodlanz est proz et Oliviers est sages
> Roland is brave and Oliver is wise —

scents the danger and pleads with his friend, but in vain, to summon the Emperor's aid. The French are massacred. One by one they fall until of the Twelve Peers only two or three are left. Then, at last, Roland blows his horn and, with his failing strength, summons Charles:

> Rodlanz at mis l'olifant a sa boche,
> Empeint lo bien, par grant vertut lo sonet.
> Halt sont li pui e la voiz ert molt longe,
> Granz xxx. liwes l'odirent il respondre.

> Unto his lips he raised the ivory horn,
> And from his breast drew forth a mighty blast;
> High are the hills the soaring strain breaks o'er
> And thirty leagues the answering echoes roll.

In a last effort to break his sword in order to save it from the pagans, Roland sacrifices himself for his king, his country and his honor.

Charles braves Ganelon's scorn to hasten to the rescue. But, although the Almighty arrests the sun in its course to grant him time for vengeance, when Charles arrives Roland is dead. Absolved of his sins by Turpin of Rheims, the archbishop, he lies amid his fallen companions, with his face turned toward France:

> Deus i tramist son angele cherubin
> E saint Michiel de la Mer del Peril,
> Ensembl'od els sainz Gabriël i vint;
> L'anme del conte portent en paredis.

> God sent to him His angel cherubim,
> Saint Michael of the Peril of the Sea,
> Together with them came holy Gabriel.
> To Paradise they bear the Count's soul home.

Having crushed the Saracens, Charles returns to France with the bodies of his beloved knights. Alde, Roland's betrothed, falls dead at Charlemagne's feet. Ganelon is brought to justice and torn to pieces by four stallions, while the Emperor under the weight of his sorrows, and despite his two hundred years, lives wearily on.

Historically the poem rests on the slightest of foundations — the expedition of Charles into Spain in 778, an episode of which was the destruction of his rear-guard by the Basques in the Pyrenees. Among the slain, according to the chronicler Einhard, who reports the event, was *Hruodlandus, Britannici limitis praefectus;* that is, Roland prefect of the March of Brittany.

Concerning the author we know next to nothing, save that he may be identical with the Turoldus mentioned at the end of the last *laisse:*

> Ci falt la geste que Turoldus declinet.

> Here ends the poem which Turoldus relates.

But whoever he was (whether or not an archbishop of Bayeux by that name), his poetic gift was of the highest; to this his poem bears ample testimony.

In the first place, the poem is a unit in subordinating details to the theme of Christian feudal valor. Religion and patriotism are one; the knights of Charles fight for the greater glory of Christian France: *la dolce France, la Tere major.*

> Paien ont tort e Chrestien ont dreit
>
> Wrong the pagans, right the Christians are —

this idea, in one form or another, runs through the whole poem. The narrative consists of three parts: the treachery of Ganelon, the pride and loyalty of Roland, the vengeance and sorrow of Charles. Clear as crystal, these motives emerge from the mass of episode and control the action. Thus the poem has an obvious kinship with French Classical tragedy, showing that clarity of outline and a sense of proportion are characteristic of French literary art from the beginning.

In the second place, the characters are ideal contrasts. The fact that Roland has the typical epic motive of *desmesure* or "lack of measure" renders the work intensely dramatic. When the pagan messengers have spoken, Roland designates Ganelon as the return-messenger to Marsile. But Ganelon is equal to the part; enraged at his step-son's presumption, he singles him out for vengeance. Ganelon is no commonplace traitor: he does not directly betray the French; he not only braves Marsile, he defies him, as any follower of Charles would; but he cannot forgive Roland, and in his passion he makes Marsile believe that the destruction of the rear-guard will destroy the French. Again, Oliver, who represents reason, remains reasonable to the end. In the eleventh hour his logic tells him that Roland is responsible for the French defeat, and in his affection for his friend he mingles the cruelty of a reproach, for thus his conscience compels him to do. One of the most poignant scenes in the poem is when Roland and Oliver, in the face of death, speak the words of their hearts:

> Ço dist Rodlanz: "Por quei me portez ire?"
> E cil respont: "Com proz vos lo feïstes,
> Kar vasselages par sens nen est folie:
> Mielz valt mesure que ne fait estoltie.
> Franceis sont mort par vostre legerie."

> Then Roland said: "Why do you bear me ill?"
> And he replied: "Bravely you fought for us,
> Yet fealty's not courage uncontrolled
> But measure which through madness goes not blind.
> The French are slain: your folly is to blame."

Thus each character is true to his nature; Roland to his unmeasured prowess, Oliver to his calm, cool reason, Ganelon to his insensate hatred, and Charles, most to be pitied of all, to his sense of solitary grandeur amid the warring factions of his race. To this extent has the poet seen in legend the working out of human character and fate — and this is the acme of epic art.

The style of the *Roland* is of a piece with its elemental character. The thought does not flow, it comes in leaps and bounds, or, as Gaston Paris has said, " par une suite d'explosions successives, toujours arrêtées court et toujours reprenant avec soudaineté." The lyric mood, intensely simple and overpowering, dominates the whole; yet separate lyric passages are few and generally conventional. Transitions from one episode to another are abrupt, as befits their dramatic quality, but this again is the abruptness of detail, " like a broken sea with a larger wave moving under it." So, too, the language of the poem is lapidary; each verse, if possible, is a unit. Metaphors are rare; when used they designate an act, as when the dying Roland proffers his gauntlet to the angel Gabriel. In short, the language is action rather than description; like the trumpet-call of Roland it speaks to the ear, since the *Roland* was to be sung, not read. When, however, the poet does depict, as in giving the setting, he uses simple, bold strokes. To the pagan messengers Charles appears thus:

> Desoz un pin delez un aiglentier
> Un faldestoel i out, fait tot d'ormier,
> La siet li reis ki dolce France tient;
> Blanche at la barbe e tot florit le chief,
> Gent at le cors e lo contenant fier:
> S'est qui'l demandet ne'l estoet enseignier.

> Beneath a pine, beside a wild white thorn,
> An armchair stands, inlaid with mother-of-pearl;
> There sits the king who governeth sweet France;
> White is his beard, all hoary is his head;
> Graceful is he and proud his countenance.
> Who asks his name? He needs no pointing out.

Or if we turn to the background of the battle, the pass above Roncevaux, its bleak outlines are revealed in:

> Halt sont li pui e li val tenebros,
> Les roches bises, li destroit merveillos.

> High are the hills, the valleys filled with gloom;
> Gray-brown the cliffs, and wonderful the passes.

As for the social aspects of the work, these are clearly feudal. The characters are "barons," even Turpin, the archbishop, being a vassal of Charles. But the feudalism depicted is early, reaching back possibly to the tenth century. The *Roland* is not *courtois* in the sense we defined above. The manners of the knights are crude, the tribal or family bond is strong; Roland is a typical "sister's son" (a frequent character in primitive literature in general, and the Twelve Peers represent an institution known as *compagnonnage*, which hardly extended beyond the eleventh century. When not fighting, these paladins of France play warlike games; the old men play chess and the young men fence or joust:

> E escremissent cil bachelier legier.

Of the refining influence of women there is scarce a trace. Says Oliver to Roland in their final interview:

> "Se puis vedeir ma gente soror Alde,
> Vos ne jerreiz ja mais entre sa brace."

> "If I could see my lovely sister Alde,
> Thou should'st ne'er lie within her arms' embrace."

And Charles can think of no gentler consolation for the grief-stricken Alde than to offer his son Louis as a substitute for Roland. Surely the *Roland*, with its fighting bishops and its Valkyrie-like angels, ready to carry the souls of the valiant to Paradise, has no place for the sophisticated emotions we associate with a cultivated form of society.

Thus the *Roland* is not lacking in art; indeed, technically it shows remarkable artistry, as we have seen. But the point of view it represents is simple, at times fairly naïve; the emotions it breathes are elemental, and its plane of life is primitive and direct. In this it shows the influence of the Latin works on the First Crusade.

The atmosphere of elemental contrast pervades all except the latest forms of epic. In the *Pèlerinage de Charlemagne à Constantinople* (before 1150) the serious tone of the *Roland* gives way to a spirit of braggadocio and rollicking fun. Incidentally the work, which is written in twelve-syllable *laisses*, accounts for the presence at Saint-Denis of the relics of the Passion. Charles,

Other epics who wears the crown at Saint-Denis, asks the Queen whether there can be a more imposing monarch than himself. Rashly she names Hugo of Constantinople. At once Charles and the Twelve Peers journey to the Orient for the purpose of disproving the Queen's assertion. In Jerusalem, which they visit first, they occupy the chairs formerly used by Christ and the apostles, and the sight of them thus seated so overwhelms a Jew that he straightway seeks baptism. And in Constantinople, where they linger on the return, the relics which they had acquired enable them to execute a series of preposterous boasts or *gabs*. Thus King Hugo, majestic as he is, gladly does homage and admits that a *Français de France* is no ordinary mortal. The poem epitomizes its particular note of vanity in the verse:

> Ja ne vendrons en terre, nostre ne seit li los.

> Never shall we come into a land where renown is not ours.

The *Pèlerinage*, then, is a popular counterpart to the more inspired *Roland;* it is a market place epic addressed to the populace of a great church fair, the *Endit* (Lat. *indictum*) of Saint-Denis, near Paris, and it aims to amuse rather than to uplift.

But, in general, the epic muse is tragic, " reiterating and reinforcing the heroic motives," and glorifying France and the

Second Group church. This can be seen in the second or William of Orange cycle, the central theme of which is the exaltation of Christianity: *essaucier la sainte crestienté*. Linked to this motive is the idea of loyalty to the Carolingian dynasty, tottering to its fall in the successors of Charles. For instance, the *Couronnement de Louis* (about 1130) shows us William hastening to the aid of Charles' son, Louis, who is too timid to grasp the reins of power single-handed. William takes the feeble King under his protection, kills off the usurpers and marries Louis to his own sister. Yet Louis, characteristically weak, is ungrateful:

> En grant barnage fu Looïs entrez;
> Quant il fu riches, Guillelme n'en sot gré.

> In great domain had Louis been installed;
> When he was strong, to William he bore no love.

Again, in the *Aliscans* (close to 1150) the Saracen host is victorious and the battle-field is strewn with Christian dead (a fiction suggested by the Graeco-Roman cemetery at Arles). William, who despite his heroism is unable to rescue his favorite nephew, Vivien, is forced to seek refuge at Orange, where Guiborc, his wife, fails to recognize him, partly because she cannot believe that William would have fled. On hearing of the slaughter of all his companions, she persuades him to seek the King's aid at Saint-Denis. At first the latter turns a deaf ear to his appeal, until cowed by William's wrath Louis finally yields, as he always does, and sends assistance. William's final victory is due to the help of a burlesque creature, Renouart — the Morgante of the French epic — and the second half of the work is a mock heroic, in which the inspiration flags. The story of William survives also in an early form, the *Chançun de Guillelme* — which some scholars place above the *Roland* in merit. This is rather the "draft of an epic," interesting because of its vigor and primitive traits, but hardly the literary equal of the *chansons* proper.

The third division of the epic, the cycle of Doön de Mayence, deals with the feuds between the great barons and the crown, **Third** and is rich in the delineation of character. Excel-**Group** lent examples are *Raoul de Cambrai* and *Girard de Roussillon* (extant in versions composed after 1150).

A "sister's son" like Roland, Raoul has strong attachments to his imperial uncle. But Louis, unlike Charlemagne, forsakes his nephew's cause. Grown to manhood, Raoul is driven to demand of Louis his just inheritance. Louis promises and then wavers in favor of another. This act of perfidy so infuriates the hero that he destroys the town of Origini and its cloister of nuns, although in true medieval fashion he refuses to eat meat on Friday. Among the innocents who perish is the mother of Bernier, the "boon companion" of Raoul. Bernier breaks his bond of companionship in order to kill Raoul, and the vendetta that ensues between the families of the two heroes lasts for years. Finally a reconciliation is effected, in which the King also pays a forfeit. In mere force of conception this story is perhaps unique among the *chansons de geste*. Although it fails to depict any imaginative passion, it is supremely tragic in its realism and the barbaric truthfulness of its utterance. The character of Bernier, " dull, expostulatory, helpless," is an excellent example of the hero marked by fate.

The church and the pilgrimage routes again play a rôle in *Girard de Roussillon*. Here the strife is between Charles the Bald and his most powerful vassal in the east, for Roussillon is placed by the poet near Vézelay, famous for its shrine of Mary Magdalen. Charles and Girard had married sisters, but Charles' wife was once the betrothed of Girard, who had yielded her to his liege as an act of fealty, in return for which service the King gave Girard certain property rights. These Charles violates, and a long and bitter struggle follows. In the end Charles triumphs, Roussillon is razed to the ground, and Girard and his faithful wife flee into the forest of the Ardennes. Through the influence of a hermit, Girard now renounces the world and becomes a charcoal-burner, while Bertha, his wife, earns a pittance by sewing. But the sight of her husband's degradation moves Bertha to appeal to the Queen, and a reconciliation with Charles is brought about. Once more Girard's wrath (his *desmesure*) flares up and he holds the King at bay. At last, however, his proud spirit is broken, and both he and Bertha devote the remainder of their lives to building churches (Vézelay and Pothières), in honor of her who at Bethany washed the Saviour's feet. Here we see clearly the process whereby chronicle-history, saint's legend and monastic foundation combine to produce a literary work of enduring human interest. The *Girard de Roussillon* is typical of the composition of many a French epic, and the ecclesiastical and feudal ideas on which it rests are on the whole the controlling ideas of the first half of the twelfth century, when king and baron, castle and monastery, were struggling with one another for the possession of the land.

Out of the welter of this striving the great cultural upheaval of the second half of the century was to come. Monastic schools and feudal castles arose on every hand. Polite society took form in definite molds. Women began to play a part in the affairs of state and gave tone to the ideals of which they themselves were the object. The new era is still warlike, yet war is no longer an opposition of popular forces, the conflict of rival clans, but a social game, waged according to fixed rules: those of chivalry. In this period epic *desmesure* or " excess of character " is no longer the inspiration of narrative. The heroic gives place to the sentimental and adventurous; and gradually epic poetry dies out or becomes merged with a new genre, the " romance." Thus *Huon de Bordeaux* (about 1220), with its main theme of the story of Oberon, is an example of the heroic followed by the purely fanciful or magical; whereas *Aiol* (before 1250) transfuses an epic background with romantic *motifs* and a vein of real humor. Finally, after 1250, heroic motivation disappears altogether, and the *chansons de geste* translated into prose become a part of the romantic narrative lore of Europe.

CHAPTER II

THE LYRIC AND THE ROMANCE

As the epic was set to music and sung, so also there were in twelfth-century France songs of personal or " lyric " inspiration. An essential feature of these songs is that originally they were written as accompaniments to the dance (*la carole*), so that " the leader would sing the successive lines, while the rest of the dancers holding hands all joined in the refrain." Of this custom our modern May-dances, with the crowning of the May Queen, are a survival. In the Middle Ages, however, such festive gatherings were popular in a wide sense, and lyric songs set to the dance were the diversion of castle and bower fully as much as of the people. In principle, then, we may say that the lyric originates with the folk — provided we bear in mind that the individual poet or singer (the *jongleur*) was capable of using it for his own ends and of infusing it with a spirit that was anything but popular. A dividing line is hard to draw; and the term " folk-poetry " often implies no more than that the particular lyric deals with traditional themes, dating from a time when there was no formal division between polite society and the people as such.

At the same time, the Old French lyric undoubtedly owes more to the influence of Latin models than has commonly been admitted. Such an influence would be especially strong in the south of France, where the juxtaposition of springtide, the nightingale and love is a recurrent feature of Latin verse. Observe, as an example, the last quatrain of a Latin song (eleventh century) from one of the manuscripts of St. Martial's at Limoges:

> Jam nix glaciesque liquescit,
> Folium et herba virescit,
> Philomela jam cantat in alto,
> Ardet amor cordis in antro.

Now are melted ice and snow,
Trees and grass their verdure show,
Philomela sings on high,
Loving hearts burn secretly.

Thus there arise two classes of twelfth-century French lyrics: those in which the emotion is presented objectively as part of a popular dramatic setting; and those in which a fixed subjective experience determines the burden and the form of the song.

The first class embraces the northern French types: the *chanson à toile* or *d'histoire*, the *reverdie*, the *chanson de mal mariée*
Northern Types and the *pastourelle*. As a rule, these are independent of southern, Provençal influence. While often intended for sophisticated audiences, they betray their popular origin by the use of dance refrains, and they are addressed to society at large, ʋithout any expressed distinction of caste. Their form is narrative, the love experience being told as a story.

Thus the *chanson à toile* is virtually a ballad, a spinning or weaving song adapted to women at their work. The theme is a maiden's love for a knight, Doette's for Doön, Gaiette's for Gerard, Eremborc's for Renald — notice the alliteration of names — and the whole is presented as a kind of miniature drama in stanzas of ten-syllable lines, ending in a refrain of one, two or three shorter verses. The beginning of *La belle Doette* may be regarded as typical:

> Bele Doette as fenestres se siet,
> Lit en un livre, mais au cuer ne l'en tient;
> De son ami Doön li ressovient
> Qu'en autres terres est alez tornoier,
> E or en ai dol.

> Fair Doette at the casement sat,
> Read in a book, but in her heart is sad;
> To Doön her thoughts turn back
> Who's gone away to fight, alack!
> How sorrowful am I.

Closer to the dance in movement are the *reverdies* and the *chansons de mal mariée*. The former, as the title indicates, have reference to the spring-tide, the season of love and joy;

whereas the latter, pungent and cynical in tone, embody the lament of those wedded unhappily. Here, as elsewhere in this early work, the protagonist is a woman — who in the *chansons de mal mariée* usually consoles herself by taking a lover.

With the *pastourelle* we approach a type more complicated indeed but having considerable inherent charm. It has, moreover, a corresponding southern form in the Provençal *pastorela* or *pastoreta*. The name refers to the " shepherdess " whose graces the poem celebrates. But again the popular origin is remote, since the extant *pastourelles* all have an aristocratic tinge. The poet, generally a knight, while riding through the country meets a shepherdess whose love he implores. When she remains obdurate to his entreaties, it is because Marion — the name of the rustic belle — wishes to remain true to Robin or Perrin or Guiot; indeed, the latter at times comes to her rescue and attacks the importunate nobleman, frequently to the regret of the girl. A typical setting is the following, though most *pastourelles* have a more involved stanza form:

> L'autrier me chevalchoie
> Toute ma senturelle,
> Trovai en mei ma voie
> Cortoise pastourelle;
> Lou cors ait bel et avenant,
>   La color vermeillete.
> Ausi tost come je la vi,
>   E je li prix a faire.

> As I rode forth the other day,
> I found, what would you guess?
> Upon the winding country-way
> A charming shepherdess.
> Her shapely form brought joy to me,
> Her glowing color too;
> And stopping there, her close to see,
> I straightway 'gan to woo.

The knight wins his suit. Despite the fear of her relatives the lady succumbs to his *beau parler* and forgets her rustic Robin in the arms of the new lover. The delightful *Jeu de Robin et Marion* by Adam de la Halle (thirteenth century) dramatizes the main situation of the *pastourelle.*

By degrees, and almost simultaneously with the objective lyric, a new spirit manifests itself. In 1150, signs of a great **Southern** cultural change are everywhere evident. The rise **Types** of chivalry, noted above (Ch. I), and the development of a *courtois* state of society, attended by the growth of great school centers like Le Bec, Chartres and Paris, and encouraged, along artistic lines, by the rivalry of the courts of Champagne, Blois, Flanders and England — all of this gave to the new age a distinction second only to that of the later Renaissance. The century which follows, the thirteenth, represents the florescence of the Middle Ages, in many ways as complete an expression of the French national genius as the Classical age of Louis XIV.

The quickening impulse came from the region associated with Provençal or the *langue d'oc*, whose dominion had reached as far north as Poitou. From Poitou came William IX (1087-1127), the earliest known *trobador* (the Provençal form for *trouvère*, meaning " poet ") and the grandfather of the light-hearted Eleanor, successively queen of Louis VII of France and Henry II of England, and mother of Marie of Champagne and Alice of Blois. Thus the avenue northward was established, and the Provençal lyric was the literary baggage of the poets who travelled over it: in the suite of Eleanor, the troubadours Bernart de Ventadorn and Bertran de Born, and in that of Marie, Rigaud de Barbézieux. But these noble ladies were themselves adepts in the *gai saber*, as the new poetic art was called; and Marie herself suggested topics to Crestien de Troyes (see below), while in her behalf André le Chapelain (Andreas Capellanus) wrote the new Ovid of the age, the *Tractatus Amoris* or *De Amore*.

In this way the subjective lyric was a poetry of " art " in our modern sense of the word. Its point of departure is the identification of love and religion: *Omnia vincit amor*. Only in place of the purely sensuous ideal of antiquity, the Provençal lover mingled with the reactions of sense the conviction of the unattainable, and like the mystic before his God he humbled himself before his lady. The result was a philosophical interpretation of love as the sovereign or infinite good, and the development of a system whereby the lover became the perfect worshipper of his unattainable mistress. This system had its precepts, its laws, its remedies — in a word, its code — complex in the extreme and administered by Love, whom Dante called " the Lord of Terrible Aspect."

With such an ideal, poetry becomes subtilized and thoroughly conventional. Conceits and euphuisms abound. Every natural note is banished as dishonorable and vulgar, or *vilain*. The true *courtois* glows only with an illicit passion, for love and marriage are regarded as inimical. On the other hand, the gain in poetic expression is considerable. The psychology of emotion is worked out in detail and with some variety; and it is noteworthy that the emotion depicted is not without a real background in aristocratic circles, for the Provençal lyric is not of the people. But the greatest triumph of the new genre was in artistic form, and the best known varieties of Provençal verse were adopted almost without a change by the rest of cultured Europe. The German Minnesong is largely an importation from Provence.

Of the southern forms which found favor in French the most popular are: the *chanson* (Prov. *canson*), the *tenson* (Prov. *tenson*) and the *jeu-parti* (Prov. *joc partit*). The first of these is a lyric of five or six stanzas, usually with the rime-scheme abab-baba, and ending in a half stanza, called *envoi* (Prov. *tornada*), in which the poet draws his conclusions and apostrophizes his lady or his patron. The themes of the *chanson* vary, some being suggested by the crusades. Thus Conon de Béthune (1180), who was a well known *trouvère* and also a crusader, begins one of his *chansons* as follows:

> Ahi, amors, com dure departie
> Me covient faire a perdre la millor,
> Qui onques fust amée ne servie!
> Deus me ramainst a li par sa dolçor,
> Si voirement com j'en part a dolor!
> Deus! qu'ai-je dit? ja ne m'en part je mie:
> Se li cors va servir Nostre Signor,
> Toz li miens cuers remaint en sa baillie.

> Oh, Love! how hard it is to sever
> Myself from her whose sweet embrace
> I fondly woo, forsaking never:
> God bring me back, I beg this grace

> As truly as I part in sorrow.
> What did I say? I do not part:
> My body serves the Lord tomorrow,
> But with my love remains my heart!

Gracefully as it is used here, this conceit of the wandering body (*cors*) and the captive heart (*cuers*) is characteristic of courtly literature, and shows how easy it was for the poet to glide from the facts of life into the subtleties of the mind and turn art into rhetoric.

The acme of this tendency is reached in the *tenson* and the *jeu parti*. These are debates or contests in verse on some problem of love casuistry; such as, should a lover prefer the marriage or the death of his beloved? which lover has the greater chance, one who is blind, or one who is deaf and dumb? In form these types resemble the *chanson*, except that in the *tenson* different persons, feigned or real, sing alternate stanzas, while in the *jeu parti* one poet offers to another the alternate side of a debate. Here poetry degenerates and becomes a foster child of scholasticism, with which these types are contemporary. Gace Brulé, Thibaut de Navarre (the royal lover of Blanche of Castille), and the Châtelain de Coucy (in legend the lover of the Dame de Fayel), are among those who plied this difficult art. Their game was to toy with ideas, and in them we have the forerunners of the preciosity and Petrarchizing of a later day.

Fortunately not all of the courtly poetry moved in these artificial channels, nor was lyric expression henceforth confined **Other Lyric Types** to *courtois* circles. For poetry is ever ready to draw on popular sources, just as the people are willing to adopt courtly forms and modify them. Thus the *aube* (Prov. *alba*) or "morning song" maintains the externals of a set type with some freedom of expression, so that the situation it embodies is still apparent in *Romeo and Juliet:*

> " Wilt thou be gone? it is not yet near day:
> It was the nightingale and not the lark,
> That pierced the fearful hollow of thine ear:
> Nightly she sings on yon pomegranate tree:
> Believe me, love, it was the nightingale."

More varied in form than its Provençal model is the *salut d'amour*, a verse epistle, beginning with a greeting to the lady

for whom the poet writes. An adept in this type was the celebrated Philippe de Beaumanoir (1250), known widely for his
code of laws, the *Coutumes du Beauvaisis*. Other measures,
like the *motet, descort* and *lai lyrique* are musical in origin,
deriving from the sequences of the church, although the *lai
lyrique*, which had a notable practitioner in Colin Muset, a
jongleur who moved in the courtly world (thirteenth century),
may have arisen from the musical accompaniment of the Breton
contes (see p. 52).

Finally, a freer spirit breathes in those forms which, while
based once more on popular dance refrains, later become courtly
in tone. Such are the *rondels*, from which the more modern
triolet and *rondeau* descend; and especially the *ballete*, subsequently known by the name *ballade*. The *rondeau* remains
essentially a one-strophe composition, while the *ballade* consists
of three strophes having the same rimes and ending in the same
refrain), to which there was later added an *envoi*. With the
rise of the literary guilds or *puys* (from the Latin *podium* or
" hill ") in Arras and other northern cities, the *ballade* and the
rondeau become the dominant lyric forms, especially in the
hands of the fourteenth-century poets, Guillaume de Machaut
and Eustache Deschamps (see Bk. II, Ch. 1). And so they remain until displaced, in the Renaissance, by the sonnet. In
them the characteristic grace of French verse appears anew,
and there is something almost national in the suspensive phrasing in which these forms excel. A modern *triolet* by Austin
Dobson reproduces this quality well:

> I intended an ode
>   But it turned into triolets,
> It began à la mode,
> I intended an ode;
> But Rose crossed the road,
>   With a bunch of fresh violets.
> I intended an ode
>   But it turned into triolets.

From the courtly lyric it is but a short step to the lyricism
of narrative. The *courtois* ladies who were enamored of the
The Rise of art of Provence also reacted to the wonder of the
the Romance Orient, now made accessible by the crusades, and
to the tales of marvels and enchantments the crusaders brought

back to France. It was with a new interest that they heard the legend of Troy, the adventures of Aeneas, and all that ancient story had made illustrious. Thus by degrees the past seemed contemporaneous and actual, and a genuine renascence set in — in which, however, antiquity was dressed up in chivalric garb. Hector became a knight in medieval armor, Alexander a princely patron — incidentally the symbol of *largesse* or bounty — and Troilus a fate-stricken lover. Above all, and here the *courtois* spirit is obvious, the women of the past assumed a new value, and to be matchless like Helen, tragic like Dido, or bewitching like Medea, was the aim of most twelfth-century heroines.

The monasteries play an important part in this innovation. Here, according to the method of exegesis outlined in Chapter I, the past was exploited as to its *sensus* or "meaning"; and as culture became secular, and the clerks depended more and more on the favor of the great, they drew from their manuscripts ever fresh examples of worldly fame and grandeur. In this process not only the *Aeneid* but also Statius' *Thebaid*, Lucan's *Pharsalia*, and especially Ovid's *Metamorphoses* and *Heroïdes* were laid under contribution. But the monks studied other works of a more doubtful origin as well. Owing to their ignorance of Greek, Homer was practically unknown except as a name; and so they took their account of Troy from Latin versions of Dares Phrygius and Dictys Cretensis, erroneously reputed to have been eye-witnesses of Ilion's fall. For the monks were themselves compilers, and any authority with the sanction of age was accepted as reliable. With the help of this material they then fashioned the instruments of a new narrative style. Incidents were elaborated by the use of metaphor and hyperbole. Physical traits are "catalogued" as preliminary to character drawing. But particularly, the eight-syllable couplet, with its tendency to "overflow," replaces the ten-syllable line as a vehicle of expression, and poetry gains almost the freedom of prose. The result is that by the year 1160 a whole literature "drawn from the Latin," as the phrase is, begins to appear in the vernacular. And to this literature, irrespective of its derivation, the name *roman* or Romance (from the fact that it is translated from Latin into a Romance tongue) is attached. It is this form which gradually assumes the function of a distinct genre, independent of any Latin origin, and becomes the prototype of our modern " novel."

The Middle Ages classified its narrative literature under the head of *matière*, according to its derivation. There was the

Types of Romances Matter of France or the National Epic, which we treated in Chapter I; the Matter of Rome, deriving from classical and pseudo-classical sources; and the Matter of Britain or what we call today the Arthurian romances. Differ as they may in derivation, the last two divisions show very much the same method (*sens*) of narrative treatment.

Chief among the works of the Matter of Rome are the *Alexandre*, the *Thèbes*, the *Enéas* and the *Troie*.

The life of the great Alexander, always the beau ideal of generosity to the Middle Ages, is the theme of the first work men-

The Matter of Rome tioned. It survives in three forms, of which the earliest (about 1100) is a fragment, in monorime *laisses*, by a certain Albéric de Besançon or Briançon. Written near the Provençal border, this version incorporates the idea, attributed to Solomon, that " all is vanity," which it applies to the career of the hero. The second or ten-syllable version, by a poet from Poitou (twelfth century), has been praised for its style; whereas the last or French form proper (1177) is the work of three poets from the vicinity of Paris and employs the twelve-syllable line, whence the well-known *vers alexandrins* of French Classical poetry. This finished form makes a strong appeal to the reader's love of the fanciful: Alexander's campaigns become the exploits of an adventurous knight-errant; strange animals and amphibious men beset his path, he visits Valleys from which None Return, he and his hosts are rejuvenated in a Fountain of Youth, and speaking trees foretell his doom. For all this the authors had Latin sources, derived ultimately from a Greek romance, by a certain Callisthenes, written in Alexandria, Egypt (about A.D. 200). But it is they who popularize the work as the Wonder-book of the East by reason of their spirited style and their richly flowing narrative.

The *Thèbes* (after 1150), is the medieval interpretation of the legend of Oedipus, as its derivation from Statius would imply. Formally it differs from the *Alexandre* by being written in eight-syllable couplets; but in spirit the work is still close to the *chansons de geste.* Accordingly, the fate of Oedipus is conceived as epic *desmesure,* and while the grief of Jocasta and her maidens is graphically depicted — when they learn the terrible truth of Oedipus' crime — the position of woman in this romance is still subordinate to that of man. This last feature of exalting woman becomes the distinctive trait of the *Enéas* and to a greater degree of the *Troie.*

In the *Enéas* (probably later than the *Thèbes*) the *courtois* element manifests itself in the handling of the source. Imagine an *Aeneid* with the founding of Rome all but forgotten. In the six thousand lines of the Old French poem, the hero does little else but circle about Dido and Lavinia, as the moth plays about the flame; through Dido he becomes uxorious and neglectful of chivalry, and through Lavinia, more skilled in the artifices of love, he regains his prowess and accomplishes the high emprise of defeating Turnus — and, incidentally, of founding Rome. This emphasis on the " love-sickness " of Aeneas made the work popular with other romancers and also shows the growing influence of Ovid on the narrative literature of the time. Although the language of the *Enéas* is often shockingly unrefined, the style is marked by the deft and vivid handling of dialogue — a notable innovation.

Finally, with the appearance (about 1165) of the *Roman de Troie* by Benoît de Sainte-More, the Matter of Rome loses its anonymity and scores its most lasting success. Benoît, a younger contemporary of the poet Wace (see below) — whom he replaced in the favor of Henry II of England — wrote his poem of thirty thousand verses in honor of Eleanor of Poitou. For this expansion of the Troy theme his sources, Dares and Dictys, furnished only the background and the main characters; medieval elaboration, largely by Benoît himself, furnished the rest. Thus the fall of Troy becomes a typical twelfth-century military exploit, with knights in armor and ladies in castles and bowers, and behind it all the trials and tribulations of courtly lovers. A prominent position among the latter is given to the un-Homeric Troilus and the lady of his dreams, the lovely Briseida (later Cressida). As Professor Saintsbury justly says, " Helen was too puzzling, as well as too Greek; Andromache only a faithful wife; Cassandra a scolding sorceress; Polyxena a victim "; whereas Briseida had a fairly clear record. Benoît undoubtedly has his *longueurs*, but he knew his public and he did for the Middle Ages what Virgil had done so majestically for imperial Rome: he gave feudal society an ancestry in the halls of Ilion. In some respects he did not himself harvest the full reward of his achievement. His romance was put into Latin by an Italian, Guido delle Colonne, and in this later form was diffused all over Europe. In this general way it became the source of Boccaccio and then of Chaucer, whose *Troilus* is one of the masterpieces of medieval English fiction:

> In which ye may the double sorwes here,
> Of Troylus, in loving of Criseyde,
> And how that she forsook him er she deyde.

Benoît lacks the insight of this prince of story-tellers; indeed, he has a mere suggestion of Chaucer's masterly conception of Criseyde as a character. Yet his narrative has both flow and charm, and Benoît is not without a sense of the picturesque. As late as the sixteenth century it was the medieval concept of Troy that inspired Jean Lemaire de Belges, from whose version Ronsard drew material for the *Franciade*.

The Norman Conquest (1066) had brought the French into contact with Celtic stories: in England through Wales and **The Matter** Cornwall, and on the continent through Armorica **of Britain** or Brittany — for there were Breton knights in the army with which William conquered England. It would not repay us to discuss whether the Matter of Britain came into French literature by the one or the other channel. Suffice it to say that both were open, and that commerce, and therefore literature, could travel over either route. Moreover, the rich literature of ancient Ireland contains many a parallel to Arthurian material, and Irish monks were frequent visitors to England, as they had been to continental Europe. But the spread of Celtic stories was undoubtedly facilitated by the Breton *conteurs,* who. to a musical accompaniment on the " rote " or the harp told their tales (see below, the *lais*) in the French court circles. Much of this material was of a folklore character. Thus the romantic fancy of the Celts is brought into contact with the artistic ideals of Provence and the storied memories of antiquity.

The fountain-head for the history of King Arthur is the *Historia regum Britanniae* (1136) by the Welsh monk, Geoffrey of Monmouth. Written in Latin, this work furnishes a parallel to the classical sources mentioned above. As the title states, the *Historia* is an account of the kings of Britain, with whose lineage Geoffrey wishes to link the Norman régime. But he deals with his subject romantically — in the spirit of his times. He traces the genealogy of the kings back to Troy through a certain Brutus (eponymic of Britain), grandson of Aeneas, and he elaborates Arthur's career with the aid of oral and written tradition; so that Arthur appears as the exemplar of chivalry, the *courtois* British counterpart of the French Charlemagne. In general, the story is the one familiar to us from the paraphrase of Sir Thomas Malory and the *Idylls* of Tennyson. But Geoffrey does not mention the Round Table, Mordred — not Lancelot — is the lover of Guinevere, and no reference is made to Tristan or to the Holy Grail. On the other hand, Arthur himself is still a " leader in battles," and his court at Caerleon-on-Usk is a center of " politeness, which people of other countries thought worthy of imitation " — thus speaks the Welshman in Geoffrey. Most interesting of all, for its influence on the romances, is the idea that " love " inspires " knighthood." This is the crux of a discussion ending in the conclusion that " the women of Arthur's court esteem none worthy of their love who have not given proof of their valor in three days' battle."

To Geoffrey is also attributed a *Vita Merlini*, written probably in 1148. In 1155 the *Historia* was put into French verse by the Norman poet Wace. In this somewhat elaborated form, known as the *Roman de Brut*, — Wace adds an account of the Round Table — it became the framework for later Arthurian story.

The legend of Tristan is one of the greatest tragedies of love in literature. Here the Celtic " magic " has wrought a combination of human passion, primitive adventure and custom, which is unique in French romance. As Gaston Paris has said:

> Qui aurait pu, en dehors des Bretons de Cambrie, de Cornouailles ou d'Armorique, concevoir ce théâtre multiple et y dérouler librement les épisodes du vaste drame?

Unlike the story of Arthur, the Tristan romances apparently come straight from the vernacular. The lost *Estoire* to which the extant versions refer was presumably written in England, in Norman French. This work told of Tristan's expedition to Ireland to fetch the blond-haired Isolt for his maternal uncle, King Mark of Cornwall. One need hardly recall how by a fatal mistake Tristan drains with Isolt the " love-philter " intended for the bridal pair; how Tristan, stung by repentance on account of his passion for his uncle's lawful wife, again and again endeavors to renounce Isolt; how in fact he flees to Brittany and marries a second Isolt, her of the White Hands; and how, deceived by the false report that the boat which was to bring the true Isolt from Cornwall carries a black sail· (instead of a white one, as he had hoped), Tristan falls dead. All this is familiar to most modern readers.

But Béroul, who came from Brittany, and Thomas, who wrote in England (about 1165), dealt with the story in the manner of their contemporaries. In particular, they represent the two forms which the legend takes with subsequent writers. Béroul still clings to primitive traits, such as Mark's Midas-like ears, concealed under a cap; the cunning of the dwarf Frocin, who reveals Tristan's guilt to Mark; Tristan's leap to freedom from the chapel window at Tintagel, and Isolt — called by the older form *Iselt* — handed over to a band of lepers. Nevertheless, he shows insight into character and a subtle sense of humor, and he connects the legend with Arthur, from whom the *Tristan* was originally quite distinct. On the other hand, Thomas moves in another world. He does not narrate, he psychologizes on the basis of a narrative already familiar. He dwells on the genealogy of his hero as a knight of Brittany; in true scholastic fashion he treats Tristan's *désir* (which binds him to Isolt) and his *volonté* (which tears him from her), and he develops the conceit of Isolt's *cuers*, which is Tristan's, and her *cors*, which to his and her shame Tristan shares with Mark. Thus he lays the foundation for a theme popular in his day, the *ménage à trois*, and his work foreshadows that of his great contemporary, Crestien de Troyes. But Thomas was also a poet. He penetrates the tragedy of Mark's life, and his lyricism appears in lines like:

"Iseut ma drue, Iseut m'amie,
En vus ma mort, en vus ma vie! "

addressed by Tristan to Isolt after drinking the love-philter and
symbolizing the triumph of love over death.

In Germany, the version according to Béroul was the source
of a long poem by Eilhart von Oberge (1190–1200), whereas
Thomas was the model for the more poetic work of Gottfried
von Strassburg (about 1200). In France, a later *Prose Tristan*,
taken from a source perhaps independent of the other versions,
was also popular. Finally, the story according to Thomas was
current in Old Norse (in 1226) and served as a source for the
English strophic poem, *Sir Tristan* (between 1294 and 1300).
From all these sources, and from the so-called *Folie Tristan*
— wherein Tristan appears disguised as a " fool " — Professor
Bédier has reconstructed the tale in Modern French.

With such models as a guide, the Romance enters upon a fruitful career. To " read " romances now became the fashion, and
Crestien this inevitably led to an improvement in technique
de Troyes and to the evolution of a fixed form. In this connection Crestien de Troyes is of supreme importance. Says
Gaston Paris:

> On pourrait citer tel morceau de Chrétien de Troyes qui ne le
> cède pas en vérité, en ingéniosité, parfois en subtilité, aux plus
> célèbres monologues de nos tragédies, aux pages les plus fouillées de
> nos romans contemporains.

This is perhaps high praise for one who still lacks the fullness of life, whose plots are often imperfect and wearisome,
and whose style, clear as it is, in places seems affected and
trifling. But his age thought otherwise and accorded him
the greatest honor.

Of Crestien's life we know next to nothing. As he hailed from
Troyes and wrote in a dialect which shows many local traits,
he evidently was in contact with the aristocratic circles that
surrounded Marie of Champagne. It was she who gave him
the *matière* and the *sens* of one of his romances, while Philip
of Alsace (before 1191) — better known as ruler of Flanders —
provided him with the source for another. At one time he may
have resided at Beauvais, from the cathedral library of which

he derived the source of his *Cligès*. Beyond this we have no facts, and it is idle to speculate on his station in life. But he was well educated and he glories in *clergie*, which, he declares, is now domiciled in France:

> Par les livres que nos avons
> Les fez des anciens savons
> Et del siecle qui fu jadis.

His point of view is courtly; in fact, in the *Ivain* he prefers *un cortois mort* to *un vilain vif*. Nevertheless, he was an observer and a psychologist, and he makes distinctions. Love and marriage are not necessarily inimical but can be reconciled — this is his great thesis. The only work which controverts this idea is precisely the work for which Marie of Champagne gave him the theme, and this romance Crestien did not complete.

In addition to his translations from Ovid (one of which may be the *Philomela*, attributed to him by some scholars) and a lost poem on King Mark and Isolt, Crestien wrote five romances, possibly six, in case the *Guillaume d'Angleterre*, a somewhat colorless version of the legend of St. Eustace, is really by him. These five all center more or less about the court of Arthur and, with the exception of the *Cligès*, belong to the Matter of Britain.

The *Erec*, which is still close to the older epic in style, brings up at once the conflict between chivalry and love. Can Erec be a lover and also an active knight? Can Enid be an *amie* and also a dutiful and long-suffering *femme?* So Crestien would have it. After the adventures in which Erec, avenging an insult to Guinevere, wins the matchless Enid, he falls a prey to sloth and in his uxoriousness neglects his knighthood. As Tennyson says in the idyll drawn from the Welsh version of this story, the hero became

> Forgetful of the tilt and tournament,
> Forgetful of his glory and his name,
> Forgetful of his princedom and its cares.

It is on this account that Enid weeps and, weeping over her sleeping lord, rouses him to his sovereignty as a knight and a husband — for the second part of the romance is one long perilous adventure, in which Enid's part is to play the rôle of a

Griselda. But all's well that ends well, and the romance closes with the crowning of the reconciled pair at Nantes in Brittany, attended by the entire Arthurian court. The "matter" out of which this story is constructed is thoroughly romantic: Erec originally wins Enid as the prize of a "sparrow-hawk contest"; Arthur and his knights go on a hunt for a mysterious "white stag"; Erec destroys the enchantment of a "magic garden" in which his opponent, Mabonograin, leads a charmed life. All these incidents bear the impress of an original fairy tale, Celtic at least in concept, and recalling in the garden episode the Irish Otherworld into which heroes were thought to stray when lured by love and adventure.

With the *Cligès* the poet comes closer to the polite world. An Eastern story connected with the legend of Solomon's wife, the *Cligès* becomes in Crestien's hands a remodeled *Tristan*, in which the heroine's virtue is saved by a trick practiced on Cligès' usurping uncle. Thus does Crestien gratify *courtois* sophistry and please the fashionable people of his day, who took delight in the thought that an Athenian Greek should go to Arthur's court, and who liked the Ovidian sentiments which the characters express. The heroine, Fénice, is a typical young *rusée*, the ancestor of the Angès and Célimènes of a later day. What saves the romance from the taint of the unnatural is its occasional appeal to real sentiment, as in the lines reëchoing the *Erec:*

> De s'amie a feite sa fame,
> Mes il l'apele amie et dame,
> Ne por ce ne pert ele mie,
> Que il ne l'aint come s'amie.[1]

The sophisticated *Cligès* was followed by the still more artificial *Lancelot* or, to use the correct title, the *Chevalier de la charrete*, for Crestien now affects the pseudonym for his heroes. The background of the story is the abduction of Guinevere to the Otherworld and her rescue by Lancelot — a Celtic theme similar to the Persephone myth. But Marie of Champagne obviously influenced the poet to subordinate the plot to the Provençal

---

[1] Compare the words of Chaucer in the *Franklin's Tale:*

> Sith he hathe bothe his lady and his love,
> His lady, certes, and his wyf also,
> The which that lawe of love accordeth to.

conception of love. Thus Lancelot — whose relationship to the Lady of the Lake is barely mentioned — rides in a very unchivalric cart and otherwise lowers himself by playing the coward in a three days' tournament (see Geoffrey of Monmouth), all for the sake of Guinevere's illicit love. Clearly the Lancelot legend, which is known from a later *Prose Lancelot,* is here diverted from its true channel and made to serve a special *courtois* purpose. In general, the *Lancelot* is not so well written as Crestien's other works; moreover, he left the romance to be completed by a certain Godefroi de Leigni. Yet few love stories have enjoyed a greater vogue than that of Lancelot and Arthur's Queen. The flame that sweeps through Paolo and Francesca in the *Divine Comedy* ultimately has this source — for it was a prose version of the Lancelot story that these lovers found, and reading it read no more:

> Quel giorno più non vi leggemmo avante.

In the *Ivain* or *Chevalier au lion* we return to the land of faery and adventure. A storm breaks over the fountain of Broceliande when water is poured on a rock at its brim, and a combat ensues in which Ivain slays the fountain's defender. He then woos and weds the latter's widow, since the truth is

> Que fame a plus de mil corages.

Vergil and Ovid said so before Crestien, and Shakespeare after him; the ironies of life change little. At least Crestien's heroine has the excuse that by nature she is a fairy-mistress, whose fountain, like Diana's at Nemi, needs a protector, and that the valiant and gracious Ivain is fitted for this rôle. It is true he subsequently revisits Arthur's court and overstays the leave granted him by the imperious Laudine. The result is that love drives him mad and he wanders distraught until finally, with the aid of a helpful lion — which like Androcles he befriends — he wins his way back to the fountain and to the favor of Laudine. As firmly conceived as the *Erec,* this romance excels it as to style and expression of sentiment; in fact, Crestien never wrote better narrative than in the picturesque lines of the *Ivain.*

Crestien died before he could complete the *Conte del graal* or *Perceval;* this a continuator of the work affirms. But he composed some ten thousand lines in which inspired by a *livre* given him by Philip of Flanders, he gave the earli-

The Holy Grail

est literary expression to the world-famed legend of the Holy Grail. What the Grail originally was no one knows, although explanations have not been lacking. To Crestien the word was still a common noun, *graal* meaning a dish or platter ordinarily used in the houses of the wealthy. Yet he himself speaks of it as *une sainte chose* and gives it qualities which are marvelous and in part mystical. When the dish is carried in a procession, the "gleam" of the Grail is beheld by hundreds of knights; and a single wafer on it sustains the life of a century-old king. What makes it, however, the central motive of Crestien's story is the question the hero should ask with respect to it, failing in which he neglects the cure of a wounded Fisher King and inflicts harm and suffering on the land and people of Logres, or Britain.

For such a part the naïve and uncultured Perceval the Welshman is dramatically well chosen. Brought up as a fatherless boy, Perceval escapes from a too vigilant mother and makes his way to Arthur's court and finally to the Castle of the Grail. He then learns the bitterness of failure, is cursed by the Grail messenger, and like so many of Crestien's heroes roams madly through the forest. From this plight he is rescued by a hermit uncle, who on Good Friday gives him a lesson in humility as another uncle had previously instructed him in chivalry. Then the action starts anew: Perceval resumes his quest for the Grail, in which other knights now join, especially the courtly Gawain — whom Crestien treats as the exemplar of bravery and *sens* — until suddenly the story breaks off in the middle of a phrase.

Those who continued it (to the extent of some fifty thousand verses) were three: Wauchier de Denain, otherwise known as a translator of saints' legends, a certain Manessier, and Gerbert de Montreuil, the author also of the *Roman de la violette*. Wauchier, who like Manessier wrote for Joanna of Flanders, varies from Crestien by giving a Gawain-quest in which the Grail is described as *riche*, not holy, and its food-providing qualities are connected in some special way with the reproductive, vegetative forces of nature — so that most scholars have seen in Wauchier's continuation a more primitive form of the legend than that of Crestien. On the other hand, Manessier represents a more advanced stage of the story: the Grail has become Christianized into the vessel in which Joseph of Arimathea caught the Saviour's blood, and the lance, which accompanies the Grail in most versions, is that with which Longinus pierced the Saviour's side. Lastly, Gerbert fluctuates between these two accounts, although both he and Manessier end the story with Perceval's final achievement of the quest.

But none of these continuations has the literary merit of the original *Perceval*. Not only does Crestien write well, he penetrates the human relationships of his chief character; with him Perceval is the untrained youth brought through the experience of life to the fulness of wisdom. Crestien's romance abounds in touches of naïve wonder at the terrible splendor of life; a romantic attachment of Blanchefleur for the hero is portrayed with a simplicity that Crestien lacks in his more sophisticated *Cligès* and *Ivain;* and all the episodes emerge from the general background of adventure with great vividness. How mighty the contemporary appeal of the *Perceval* was can be seen from the warning a pious monk gives Blanche of Navarre, a later Countess of Champagne:

> Laissiez Cligès et Perceval
> Qui les cuers perce et trait a val,
> Et les romans de vanité.

Crestien's *Perceval* is not the only form which the Grail legend had in France. Near the close of the twelfth century a certain Robert de Boron (probably from Burgundy) wrote the so-called *Metrical Joseph*, a much-confused poem on the career of Joseph of Arimathea. This connects the Grail definitely with the cup of the Last Supper and relates how the followers of Joseph brought the Grail to England. Thus the foundation is laid for an entire Christianization of the legend and a general remodeling of the Grail quest, which is largely the work of the first quarter of the thirteenth century.

Later Versions of the Grail Legend

Early in the century the prose *Perlesvaus* added Lancelot to the questers and brought the legend into connection with Glastonbury Abbey. For Glastonbury had come to be regarded as the Avalon from which King Arthur was some day to return; and to this claim it had added the other of being the primate church of Great Britain. Meanwhile, Robert de Boron's *Joseph*, together with a fragmentary *Merlin* — also by Robert — had been remodeled in prose; and thereto was joined a new *Prose Perceval* — the whole constituting a trilogy on the subject of the Grail. In this way, by successive accretions, there arose (about 1215) the huge *Grail-Lancelot Cycle*, in which Galahad, the ascetic son of the sinful Lancelot, replaces Perceval as the successful Grail hero. Attributed to Walter Map, for a reason that no one has been able to discover, this combination of Arthurian material in prose has continued to fascinate the imaginations of Europe down to the present day. It furnished the matter and much of the spirit of Sir Thomas Malory's *Morte Darthur* in the fifteenth century; and this in turn inspired Tennyson and the Victorian poets. Thus was Lancelot's sin fated to destroy the Arthurian order, while the pure and blameless Galahad follows a Grail " clothed in white samite, mystic, wonderful " and devoid of all material attributes. In the words of Tennyson's Sir Percivale:

> " Lo, if I find the Holy Grail itself
> And touch it, it will crumble into dust."

At the same time, Crestien's own poem was to inspire a masterpiece in Germany — the Middle High German *Parzival* (1215) by Wolfram von Eschenbach. Although Wolfram claims to remodel Crestien with the help of a version by an unknown Kiot (apparently a Frenchman), in reality he makes Parzival an exemplar of German *treue* or fidelity of character; and in so doing he creates a type second only to Faust, allowing always for the differences of time and circumstance.

The Middle English *Sir Percyvelle*, a fourteenth-century poem in tail-rime strophes, relates the Perceval tale in bare outline, making the hero, however, a sister's son of King Arthur and never once referring to the Grail or to the characters associated with it.

The themes of Crestien's three romances, *Erec, Ivain* and *Perceval*, are also treated in the famous Welsh *Mabinogion*, a delightful collection of partly indigenous Celtic tales of the Middle Ages. But the relationship between the Welsh and the French romances is still a matter of controversy among scholars.

The genre so ably illustrated by the Champagne poet continues to flourish in Europe throughout the medieval period, **Later History of the Romance** until it receives its *coup de grâce* in the undying pages of *Don Quixote* — although the last statement applies mainly to the exaltation of chivalry and not to the romances as such.

Next to Crestien, the best-known wielder of the Matter of Britain is Raoul de Houdenc (after 1200). His *Méraugis de Portlesguez* accords the prize of beauty to Idoine, a superior Enid, and lets the hero accomplish impossible tasks in the pursuit of prowess, while Raoul's *Vengeance de Raguidel* is one of the numerous tales in which Sir Gawain plays the chief part. But these stories have little to hold the reader except the thrill of adventure; and of this the *Chevalier as deus espées* and the justly popular *Bel Inconnu*, by Renaud de Beaujeu, are better examples. Yet none of these stories contains the character-drawing we find in the Middle English *Sir Gawain and the Green Knight* (about 1370). Here the romance of chivalry produced one of its fairest blossoms. Written on a theme that goes back to Old Irish — the so-called jeopardy whereby the green enchanter proffers his head provided the hero will accept a " return-stroke " — the motivation of the story is thoroughly French, Gawain's bravery and courtesy are nowhere better developed, nor does any Arthurian romance show more humor and fancy.

Meantime, the genre had an offshoot that goes under the somewhat misleading name of *romans d'aventure* or fate-romances. **The Romans d'aventure** Chivalry having become a thing apart, the courtly " love adventure," treated with more and more realism as time passed, was allowed to pursue its own path. Thus love is considered for its own sake, as an expression of the *droit de vivre;* in a word, as fate. Another trait is the mingling of Eastern and Arthurian matter, as in Crestien's *Cligès*. The charming *Partenopeus de Blois* (before 1188), from the region north of Poitou, combines a motive related to the story of Cupid and Psyche with an Arthurian setting and names taken from the *Thèbes*. But the earliest exponent of the new form is Gautier d'Arras, a contemporary and in a sense the rival of Crestien. Attached to the court of Thibaut of Blois, who had married Alice of France, another daughter of Eleanor of Poitou, Gautier first wrote an *Eracle* (about 1160), where historical and Eastern features are blended in a love intrigue, and then his better known *Ille et Galeron*. This tale deals with the theme of the husband and two wives by elaborating a point discussed in courtly circles; namely, the extent to which blindness is an obstacle in love. In much the same way, the anonymous *Amadas et Idoine* (before 1200) contains the triangular arrangement of the *Tristan*, with the important difference that the heroine acts conventionally and seeks a divorce.

Thus the *romans d'aventure* approach realism, and characters as well as motives and incidents are drawn from contemporary life. Crestien's pseudonyms of the Knight of the Lion and the Knight of the Cart, so widely imitated, now make room for actual personages, such as *Joufroi* (Geoffrey), the *Comte de Poitiers*, the *Châtelain de Coucy* and the touching *Châtelaine de Vergy*, who dies because her lover stupidly betrays their secret. And, lastly, the background itself becomes real and *courtois* society is analyzed in detail. An excellent example of this is the sensuous but very artistic *Guillaume de Dole*. The plot of this story belongs to the widespread "cycle of the wager" involving a woman's honor, of which the *Roman de la violette* by Gerbert de Montreuil and Shakespeare's *Cymbeline* are later and better examples. But the plot of the *Guillaume* is secondary; what makes the romance so readable today is the vigor and beauty of its descriptions, the picture we get of a ripe and joyous existence which no care can darken for long. The masterpiece, however, of the realistic genre is the Provençal *Flamenca*. Again it is the background, a tourney at the Baths of Bourbon, that gives the author his opportunity. We see the gathering of the princely guests, the splendor of their apparel and their worldly pursuits; and we listen to their intrigues, great and small, grouped about the central affair of the lady Flamenca. Bound to a jealous and insupportable husband, this heroine cleverly deceives him and thereby not only cures his jealousy but retains her own lover. The Provençals called this story a *novas*. Except for its metrical form, the *Flamenca* differs but little from a modern novel.

But narrative fiction also had a " short-story " form in the twelfth century. This went under the name of *lai*. And the **The Narra-** counterpart to Crestien, in this field, was Marie **tive Lais** de France, who spent most of her life in England and may have been the half-sister of Henry II. Written for the same *courtois* society as the romances, the *lais* are artis-tic presentations of a simple situation, based generally on a widespread folklore *motif*. Their art, if not their substance, is perpetuated in the later *fabliau* and, as respects prose, in the *novella* (see Ch. IV).

There is little doubt that Marie de France derived her ma-terial from the *contes* which the Bretons told in the Norman and French courts to the accompaniment of their songs (Irish *lôid* or *laid*) — whence she took the name for her stories. What determined her preference, she says, was that others were writ-ing romances and she regarded this field as preëmpted. Marie was also the author of a collection of *Fables*, modeled on a medieval *Romulus* — as such fable collections were then called — and under the title of *L'Espurgatoire de Saint Patrice* she paraphrased in French a medieval Latin " vision " by Henry of Saltrey. These works are presumably later than the *Lais*, with which she seems to have begun her literary career (about 1165).

Her subjects are the love of a fairy for a luckless knight, compelled by a jealous queen to reveal his secret (*Lanval*); the metamorphosis of a knight in the one case (*Yonec*) into a hawk, and in the other (*Bisclavret*) into a were-wolf whom a faith-less wife betrays; the self-effacement of a wife (*Eliduc*), in another case of a maiden (*Fraisne*), for the man she loves; the love-tryst of Tristan and Isolt (*Chèvrefeuille*), symbolized by the honeysuckle twining about the hazel bush, and so on. Like Crestien, Marie exploits the rich mine of Ovid, and of her own she adds a strong romantic sentiment which gives her tales a wistful, meditative tone. Best of all, perhaps, is her simple, translucent style: the narrative of the *Lais* flows easily, and the various situations stand out clearly and dramatically without the clumsy interruptions which mar the narrative of many romances.

Few French *lais* are equal, and none superior, to Marie's. Several anonymous ones treat Breton subjects; notably *Graelent*, *Tydorel* and *Tyolet*. The *Lai du Cor* and the *Manteau mal taillé* are written on the theme of the fidelity of women. *Guiron* tells the story of the husband who forces his wife to eat the heart of her lover — a motif that is incorporated in the romance of the *Châtelain de Coucy* (see above). One of the best survives in the form of the Middle English *Sir Orfeo*. Here the classical tale of Orpheus and Eurydice is retold as a typical Breton lay: the tone and the atmosphere are made courtly, the motivation is built up on the basis of a Celtic fairy-tale, the sad ending is changed to a happy one, and the poet cleverly places his own interest in the foreground — Sir Orfeo is a minstrel. This *lai* is as complete a reduction to *type* as medieval literature has to offer. Derived from a French source, it may be referred to as a standard, " to show " — says Professor Ker — " what can be done in the medieval art of narrative, with the simplest means and the smallest amount of decoration."

One important narrative, however, defies classification. This is the charming story of *Aucassin et Nicolette* (about 1200). In matter it resembles the *Floire et Blanchefleur*, one of the earlier types of *romans d'aventure*. But since it is written in alternating prose and verse, an arrangement found in Arabic and Old Irish, its form is unique in France and may have been the invention of the unknown author. The verse portions are in seven-syllable assonant lines.

The "Aucassin et Nicolette"

To judge by the single extant manuscript, the author composed his work in the Picard dialect, but he laid its scene in the south of France, in the country near Beaucaire. Here Aucassin, the count's son, is desperately in love with Nicolette, a Saracen captive, the daughter of the " King of Carthage." The deep love of the youthful pair, their flight from the stern parent who is planning a loftier match for his son, their separation by pirates and their final reunion, effected by Nicolette disguised as a *jongleur:* these are the principal episodes of the action, and show the kinship of the plot with such tales as the *Apollonius of Tyre* and its derivatives. But again the plot is secondary

to the author's insight into human passion, his faith in the beauty
of life and his great gift of expression. Thus he fastens our
attention on his characters, whom he describes as taken from his
own observation and experience. He knows that his tale is
"noble and courtly," that no man, "sick as he may be," will
not rejoice to hear it. Having said this, he lets his characters
reveal themselves. "Nicolette," says Aucassin, "were she empress of Constantinople, or of Germany, or Queen of France or
England, 'twould be little enough for her, so noble is she and
gracious and well-bred and compact of all good qualities." Or
take the famous passage in which Aucassin denounces the colorless Christian Paradise and concludes: "But to Hell will I go.
For to Hell go the fine clerks and the fine knights, who have
died in tourneys and in great wars. . . . And there go the
gold and the silver, and the vair and the grey; and there go too
harpers and minstrels and the kings of this world." Could
youthful enthusiasm speak plainer? Moreover, romantic as it
is, the story does not lack contrasts with the darker side of life.
Witness Aucassin's conversation with the ploughboy who, having lost one of his oxen, dares not to enter town where he will
be cast into prison — and who yet worries most because his
mother is sick at home and would have no support. In this
way does the poet set the love story over against the real world
of fact, and by his sense of values raise his narrative to an epic
plane. Stereotyped phrasings, courtly conceits, snatches of incident from this tale or that, bits of burlesque out of some legend
of a land of Cockayne — all these the poet has gathered into his
web and fused with his narrative. *Aucassin et Nicolette* is
the idyll of medieval literature; the polished jewel of its best
narrative art. The story has been admirably translated into
English by Andrew Lang.

CHAPTER III

THE ALLEGORY AND THE EARLY DRAMA

LOVE of abstraction, which appears in thirteenth-century "learning" and, indeed, in Gothic art after 1200, is also seen in the rise of literary allegory. Allegory, that peculiarly clerical product which places the imagination in the service of the reason, is not merely a personification but the conscious representation of one action in terms of an entirely different action. Thus "the book of life, without ceasing to be a true story, becomes a volume of symbols."

This is not the place to examine the origins of allegory in detail. Suffice it to say that, aside from Biblical interpretation or *sensus*, which is of course allegorical, independent allegorizations are current early. Examples in Latin are the *Concilium Amoris* (about 1100) and the influential *De Phyllide et Flora* (shortly after), types of debate which symbolize the comparative merits of clerical and chivalric life. And French instances are to be found in the various visions and dreams reflecting the state of the soul when freed from the body, which go back to the *Psychomachia* of Prudentius and to Cicero's *Somnium Scipionis* as well as to the rich "vision" literature of the medieval church. Moreover, such treatises as the *De Amore* of Andreas Capellanus, together with the influence of Ovid, lead authors to personify moral and physical traits and to discuss the love motive in abstract forms.

In the *Dit de la Rose*, a short poem of the close of the twelfth century, a rose figures as the symbol of the heroine; and in **The "Roman de la Rose"** Raoul de Houdenc's *Songe d'Enfer* (see above, Ch. II) consistent allegory in the form of a dream expresses a personal experience. The combination of these two features is characteristic of the *Roman de la Rose*, except for the *Divine Comedy*, which it foreshadows, the greatest allegory of European literature.

55

The *Roman de la Rose,* in some twenty-two thousand eight-syllable verses, falls into two parts. These are so different in concept and execution as to constitute two separate works, although the plot is continuous throughout. The first part, by Guillaume de Lorris, comprises four thousand and sixty-eight verses of the poem, and was written before 1234, probably between 1225 and 1230. The second and in some respects the more important part, by Jean Clopinel from Meun on the Loire, did not appear until close to 1270. Thus the work bridges the thirteenth century and represents, in its contrasting elements, the passage from the *courtois* to the *bourgeois* point of view. In Guillaume the courtly ideal reaches its apogee, and in Clopinel, aptly called the Voltaire of the century, the hard common-sense of the " third estate " scores its earliest victory. The first part is a poem on the psychology of love, the second a philippic against the evils of medieval society in general.

Guillaume relates that in the spring-time of life he had a dream, which has since come true. At the command of the God of Love he has put it into verse, for the delight of his readers and in honor of her

> Qui tant est digne d'estre amée
> Qu'el doit estre Rose clamée.

The dream is as follows: In May, when Nature weaves her chaplet of leaves and flowers and joy reigns supreme, the lover strolls " cousant ses manches " (a curious fashion) toward the bank of a river. Having washed his face in the river's clear waters, he comes to a high wall, surrounding a spacious garden. On its outer side the wall is decorated with ten wonderful paintings in gold and blue colors. The art with which they are fashioned arrests his eye (obviously Guillaume is a connoisseur), and he lingers to describe them. They represent respectively, Hatred and her boon companions, Felony and Villainy, and surrounding this central group on the one side, Cupidity, Avarice, Envy and Sorrow, and on the other, Old Age, Hypocrisy (*Papelardie*) and Poverty. In spite of these significant figures, the lover knocks at the " door " of the garden and is admitted by a noble lady, called Idleness (*Oiseuse*). Her friend is Delight (*Deduit*), who had built the garden in order to enjoy it with her. Led by Idleness over paths scented with fennel and mint and shaded by trees from Saracen lands, the lover reaches a lawn where Mirth (*Liesse*) is dancing with Delight. Courtesy asks him to join in the " carole," an invitation he accepts. The other couples in the dance are: Cupid who leads Beauty, Riches who showers favor on Bounty (*Largesse*), and Candor and Youth, each with an appropriate partner. Passing on through groves of domestic and foreign trees of various descriptions, the lover arrives at the Fountain of Youth, the water of which is of crystalline purity and on the border of which stands the inscription:

Here died the handsome Narcissus.

Looking down into its depths, he sees reflected in a mirror

— C'est li mireors perilleus —

amidst a multitude of lovely objects some rose-bushes in bloom. The beauty of one particular rose fascinates him, and willingly he would have picked it were it not for the brambles and thorns which protect it. In the meantime, unseen by him, Cupid has approached, and seeing the lover lost in rapture, he pierces his heart with the arrows of Beauty, Simplicity and Courtesy. By the use of further arrows Cupid then completes the capture, and the lover declares himself his vassal. Thereupon, Cupid locks the lover's heart with a golden key, and instructs him in the rules of love, its trials and tribulations, and the support to be derived from Hope, Sweet Thoughts, Sweet Speaking and Sweet Looks.

After this exposition of the Art of Love, Cupid disappears. But presently the gracious figure of Welcome invites the lover to approach the Rose. This summons he follows with avidity, but when he grows bold and proclaims that as the servant of love he intends to pick the Rose, Welcome cries out, and Danger forces the lover to retreat. In despair the lover now laments, and is reproached by Reason — descending from her lofty tower — for foolishly associating with Idleness and Delight. Better for him, she says, if he had never listened to Cupid. It is needless to say, Reason's advice falls on deaf ears, and the lover seeks consolation of Friendship (*Ami*), who teaches him how to appease Danger. The result is that he is again allowed to see the Rose, and encouraged by the intercession of Venus, Welcome grants him permission to kiss it.

Unfortunately, Slander (*Malebouche*) sees the kiss, and by sending the news broadcast arouses Jealousy, who after chiding Shame (*Honte*) for her indifference, builds a wall about the Rose and locks up Welcome in a tower, guarded by an old woman. The lover, his grief increased by the remembered savor of the Rose —

> Car je suis a greignor meschief
> Par la joie que j'ai perdue,
> Que s'onques ne l'eusse eue,
>
> For I am in greater trouble,
> Through the joy which I have lost,
> Than if never I had had it, —

is left helpless outside.

It is obvious that Guillaume did not intend to have his poem end quite so abruptly, and in fact Jean de Meun states that Guillaume's death prevented its completion. But what was the end to be? Most of the manuscripts — and there are some two hundred — contain the continuation by Jean de Meun. Two alone have the separate ending of about eighty verses. According to the latter, the lover is finally put in complete possession of the Rose. Granting that Guillaume considered his work as almost finished, it is clear that little remained to be said except to explain the dream in terms that all would understand. Thus, allowing for this addition, we may conclude that Guillaume's poem is practically a unit.

"To comprehend a Gothic cathedral," says Professor Saintsbury, "the *Rose* should be as familiar (to us) as the *Dies Irae*. For the spirit of it is indeed, though faintly 'decadent,' even more the medieval spirit than that of the Arthurian legend, precisely for the reason that it is less universal, less of humanity generally, more of this particular phase of humanity." It is true, the *Rose* is typical of an age and a civilization. But what distinguishes Guillaume de Lorris' work from that of his contemporaries is its art. Guillaume has caught the vividness of the dream experience. His personifications are alive; they act within their rôles; there are no tiresome digressions, no scholastic *jeux de mots*. So, too, the various aspects of the garden are well depicted; we are made to see the paths traversed by the lover and we scent the flowers.

> " L'odour des roses savorées
> M'entra ens jusques es corées —"

> " The odor of the perfumed roses
> Penetrated to the depths of my being,"

exclaims the impassioned poet. All critics are agreed that the portraits on the wall are remarkable for their delineation. In a different genre Guillaume de Lorris approaches the virtuosity of Botticelli, and the noble distinction of the latter is also his. As for his plot, it is firmly conceived from start to finish; far superior in this respect to his continuator, Guillaume makes his action rapid, well-proportioned and consecutive. More than once the poet has drawn on Ovid, especially when dealing with the rules of Love, but he borrows with measure and always adapts his imitations to the spirit of his age and the exigencies of his composition. In short, few works of the Middle Ages show more careful planning or a richer and more poetic technique.

Turning now to the continuation by Jean de Meun, we at once perceive the change from a poetic to a philosophic and satiric attitude. The general narrative is carried through but the " values are all transvalued." The lover is reproved, indeed scorned, for his attachment to his lady (the Rose) because

> Amours, ce est pais haïneuse,
> Amours est haïne amoureuse.
> C'est loiauté la desloial,
> C'est la desloiauté loial.

> Love is peace full of hate,
> Love is hate full of love.
> It is loyalty most disloyal,
> Disloyalty that proves loyal.

These words — and there are sixty verses of them — borrowed by Jean de Meun from the *De Planctu Naturae* of Alain de Lille, are placed in the mouth of Reason, whom the lover in his misery has invoked. But the lover would prefer an outright definition.

Reason replies by citing Andréas Capellanus: " Love is an affection of the soul which draws together two people of different
sex." For some the object of love is pleasure, and this object
is base; for others it is the continuation of the race, and this
Reason approves. But, retorts the lover, one must love or hate,
and hatred is worse than love. This leads Reason to define
friendship, with its obligations — an imitation of Cicero. Friendship she recommends, provided it does not mean association
with the rich; for Fortune is fickle, she says, and the rich are
not happy, whether they be merchants, lawyers, physicians or
preachers:

> Maint ribaud ont les cuers si bauz,
> Portant sas de charbon en Grieve,
> Que la poine riens ne lor grieve —

> Wretches often have joy in their hearts,
> Carrying coal to the public place,
> For the trouble they have does not smart.

Far happier are they than kings with their treasures and servants, since no king can call these his own. But there are other
forms of love; namely, the love of humanity and the love of offspring. Neither of these, however, interests the lover, and
finally Reason offers herself as a worthy mistress.

All these arguments do not convince the lover, who further
dislikes Reason because she has used an indecent word. This
leads Reason to attack the prudery of women, and to defend
frankness of speech with a citation from Plato's *Timaeus*.

The lover now seeks out Friendship (*Ami*) and is instructed
in the Ovidian method of treating women. A description of the
Golden Age — also from Ovid — develops the idea of equality,
which man has long since lost:

> Un grant vilain entre eus eslurent
> Le plus ossu de quant qu'il purent,
> Le plus corsu et le graignour,
> Si le firent prince et seignour.

> A powerful serf men elected,
> The strongest they could ever find,
> The heaviest and the tallest:
> Him they made prince and lord.

Nowadays women must be bought, and Ovid's precepts show us how to dupe without being duped. Thus the lover turns to Extravagance (*Trop Donner*), but Riches blocks his path — again with a long disquisition.

This brings us back to Cupid and the main thread of the narrative. Cupid gathers his troops, and divided into four groups they lay siege to the tower. Fearing a defeat, he sends messengers to Venus, the avowed enemy of Chastity. Finding her hunting with Adonis, they win from her a promise that henceforth Chastity shall be banished from women. Then follows perhaps the most striking passage in the whole poem: Nature is depicted as laboring at her forge against death, who strives to destroy the race which Nature has produced. Art imitates Nature, but in vain, for the artist cannot give life, movement, sensation and speech to his creations. Nature complains bitterly to her companion Genius, who recalls to her

> Les figures representables
> De toutes choses corrompables.

> The representative forms
> Of all corruptible things.

This complaint summarizes the entire physical, geographic and astronomical knowledge of Jean de Meun (twenty-six hundred verses). Of all of Nature's creatures, Man alone does not observe her laws. Genius seeks to absolve Man but is ordered by Nature to join Cupid's army. Genius first sermonizes the combined forces on the vices of Man, and then exhorts them in the quest of natural love. Thus the tower is taken; a maid, more beautiful than Pygmalion, appears; Welcome, set free, grants the Rose to the hero, and the latter picks it.

Such is the substance of Jean de Meun's work: an encyclopedia of views on every possible subject, supported by great learning, and revealing a master-mind. Some of the ideas are astonishingly bold, and one wonders that the poet dared express them. To be sure, in a long description of Faux-Semblant, as a member of Cupid's army, Jean is careful to distinguish hypocrites from

ome vivant
Sainte religion siuant,
Ne qui sa vie use en bone uevre,
De quelque robe qu'il se cuevre.

any living man
Following holy religion,
Or who employs his days in noble works,
To whatever class he may belong.

Nevertheless, the animus against the church is clear, and Jean's hatred of class privilege breathes in every line he writes. As to his views on women we shall hear more later; suffice it to say here that his scorn of the fair sex helped to keep his work alive at a time when many of his other ideas were out of date or inappropriate. On the positive side, it is interesting to note that Boethius' *Consolation of Philosophy* was so to say his handbook, that he admired the writings of Roger Bacon, and that he never fails to uphold science against superstition — another reason for comparing him to Voltaire. Lastly, Jean's style is energetic, imaginative (his account of a storm is almost the equal of Rabelais') and often eloquent, a number of his lines having become proverbial.

As an artist, however, Jean de Meun is inferior to his predecessor. His continuation lacks harmony, emotional unity and a dominating idea, to say nothing of its prolixity. Apparently he wrote the " continuation " in his youth, but his other works of a later date — a *Testament* and a *Codicille* — while showing unabated energy, are scarcely more artistic. Thus, while Jean de Meun made the *Roman de la Rose* a vehicle of philosophic thought, as a work of literature it owes most to Guillaume de Lorris.

The vogue of the poem was almost as great in foreign countries as in France. As early as 1300 it was translated into Flemish by Hein van Aken. An adaptation in sonnet form, called *Il Fiore,* and an imitation in rimed couplets, *Il Detto d'Amore,* probably both by a certain Durante (who is perhaps identical with Dante Alighieri), were made in Italy. Two translations into English verse, the one by Chaucer, the other anonymous, are extant in fragmentary forms. Petrarch considered the romance the greatest French

Influence of the " Rose "

poem and sent a copy of it to Guido di Gonzaga, Duke of Mantua.

In addition to its many manuscripts, various tapestries illustrating scenes from the poem testify to its popularity in France. In 1290 Gui de Mori reworked it by making various changes, but his *rifacimento* had little success. On the other hand, a much later prose version, in which the allegory has been made religious, by Jean Molinet — the *rhétoriqueur* poet — was published in several editions. And in 1526, Clément Marot, who calls Guillaume de Lorris the French Ennius, modernized the language of both parts for an edition which was very popular.

There is little doubt that the *Rose* furnished inspiration to other poets. It is mentioned as a source in the *Dit de la Panthère* by Nicole de Margival and in the *Cour d'Amour* by Mahieu Poriier, works of the end of the fourteenth century. But allegory was then in fashion, and a direct influence, except in general idea, is hard to trace. In the Middle French period (especially the fifteenth century) Jean de Meun's attack on woman led to a debate which shows how important was the influence of the *Rose*. The debate began with the *Pèlerinage de la vie humaine* by Guillaume de Digulleville, written about 1335. This allegory, which was to enjoy great popularity — Chaucer translated selections from it and John Bunyan modeled his *Pilgrim's Progress* on it — is prefaced by the remark that Jean de Meun was inspired by lust (*luxure*). But the question does not become acute until some fifty years later Christine de Pisan and Gerson, chancellor of the University of Paris, lock arms against Jean de Montreuil (Bk. II, Ch. II), one of the earliest French humanists and apologist of Jean de Meun. This "grant guerre" lasted three years, the most important document in the quarrel being Gerson's *Tractatus* (1402) — also an allegory. And even at the end of this discussion the strife does not cease, for men continued to take sides for or against Jean de Meun until interest in the position of women abated with the triumph of the Renaissance. The poets of the Pléiade (1550), in spite of their neglect of the Middle Ages, look upon the *Rose* as a work of which every Frenchman should feel proud.

Another great allegory, the *Roman de Renard*, derives its method from a genre known in antiquity, namely, the Aesopic fable. Differing from the *Rose* in the use of animals instead of personified human traits, the *Renard* resembles it in allegorizing the animal world. While parts of the *Renard* doubt-less go back to the twelfth century, the body of the work (arranged in "branches") was composed after 1200 — a time when courtly idealism was disintegrating and bourgeois irony scored its first victories.

The Aesopic Fable and the "Renard"

The Aesopic fable had reappeared in Old French under the title of *Ysopet*. Such was the name of the fable collection of Marie de France (see Ch. II), and in the thirteenth century there was an *Ysopet de Lyon*, and so on. These works, however, were not derived from Greek but from medieval collections called *Romuli*, which also included fables by the Latin writers Phaedrus and Avianus, and which owed their name to the erroneous belief that a certain Romulus, son of Tiberius, had composed them. In the hands, then, of the medieval rhetorician the fable underwent considerable expansion. Any tale, whether strictly animalistic or not, having a *moral* to preach could be told as a fable; and oriental apologues (including *exempla* of Sanskrit origin) were often incorporated in the genre. In general, says M. Sudre, "les fables médiévales les meilleures n'offrent que des qualités secondaires: clarté d'exposition, rapidité du récit, parfaite appropriation de la morale à l'action." True as this is, the fables of Marie are gracefully and deftly told, and the trait of making the fable reflect contemporary manners is seen in Marie's defense of feudalism as a system. It is from a complete identification of the animal world with society, in the manner of an epic or a romance, that the *Roman de Renard* sprang.

In this direction, too, there were antecedents. As early as the tenth century, the *Ecbasis captivi* allegorized society in the guise of animals — the wolf appears as a hypocritical priest, the story of the Sick Lion is told with all the byplay of an epic action, and the flight of the calf from its stable is made to represent the escape of a monk from his cloister. It needed but the appearance of the Latin *Ysengrimus* (1150), by Nivard, a monk of Ghent, to add the characteristic names of Renard, Ysengrin, Noble, etc., by which the animals are henceforth known — and the best-epic is born. To this Latin work the French *Renard* is indebted for much, if not most, of its material.

In its complete form the *Roman de Renard* consists of some thirty thousand eight-syllable verses, divided into twenty-seven branches, sixteen of which antedate the rest and give the main thread of the narrative.

The sixteen branches relate how Renard, the Fox, and Ysengrin, the Wolf, wage a hard-fought struggle of cunning and strength until, apparently vanquished, the Fox is carried forth in funeral procession by the court of Noble, the Lion. But Renard's death is only feigned, and before the end of the would-be burial, he is in full flight to the amazement and terror of the other animals. Thus Renard is really immortal — ever ready, at the beck of the medieval romancer to begin his tricks anew. These are the subject of the various branches or *contes* that comprise the *Renard*.

Some embody a well-known fable, such as the Sick Lion (X), the Cock and the Fox (II), the Crow and the Cheese (II). Others are probably of folklore origin, as, for example, the League of the Weak (VIII) or the amusing account of How the Wolf lost his Tail (III), a story found also in our American Brer Rabbit collections. The names of the animals are either personified traits, like Noble the Lion; or they are traditional names, such as Renard (German *Raginhart*) himself, Brichmer the Stag and Bernard the Ass. Hence, although typical, the animals are treated as individuals, with distinctive traits of their own, and the structure of feudal society is carried over into their world. Renard is the *compère* of Ysengrin, he resides in *chastel Renard;* and both animals are heroically conceived.

Nevertheless, it is the Fox who occupies the center of the stage. He is the light-footed and ingenious rogue, a " furred Jonathan Wild," whose cunning triumphs constantly. His main exploit, that which gives epic texture to the cycle, is the rape of Ysengrin's wife, Dame Hersent. This event forms the climax of branch II, about which the other branches can be grouped. Thus an attempt is made to bring Renard to justice; it fails because Noble, with characteristic weakness, himself impugns the reliability of Hersent as a witness. What sensible man, argues Brichmer, would not doubt her word since Hersent is clearly an interested party. And so the reader is treated to an exquisite example of the miscarriage of justice — a masterful satire on social conditions.

But the best rendering of the feudal world is found in branch I, the *Plaid* or Judgment of Renard. Here the irony of the situation rises to a climax, both in idea and in style. Renard is now accused by Ysengrin before the assembled court of Noble. His acquittal seems assured, when enter Chantecler and his four wives carrying upon a litter the body of a member of their family, killed by the Fox. The body is prepared for burial, the prayers for the dead are recited, and Renard is remanded for justice. He tries lie after lie, and when these fail to win his judges, he audaciously pretends to have a contrite heart and asks leave to undertake a pilgrimage *outre mer.* Sainte-Beuve has pertinently asked " si le hasard seul a pu produire une parodie si fine qu'elle ressemble à la vie même? " Not chance, assuredly, but a great poet. Yet we do not know who the author of the *Renard* was. Some of the branches have been attributed to a certain Pierre de Saint-Cloud. The only fact we have is that the main part of the *Renard* was written in the northeast of France, not far from Flanders.

As for the influence of the French romance, the earlier sections of it inspired the Middle High German *Reinhart Fuchs* (1180), by Heinrich der Glichezâre. On the other hand, Goethe's famous *Reinecke Fuchs* is derived from a Dutch version of the French poem, the *Reinaert,* made in the thirteenth century by a certain Willem. In France the character of Renard gradually lost much, if not all, of its charm. Whatever was base and cruel in humanity was associated with the Fox's name, and almost any contemptible act was called a *renardie.* Such is the spirit of the *Couronnement de Renard,* written in Flanders about 1260. More cynical still is the *Renard le nouvel* by Jacquemard Gelée of Lille — an out-and-out allegory, of the close of the thirteenth century. Here Renard is the enemy of Noble, symbolizing the struggle between evil and good in the bosom of the church. The poet Rutebeuf wrote a *Renard le Bestourné,* a short satiric piece with obscure allusions. Finally, the encyclopedic *Renard le Contrefait,* by an unknown poet of the fourteenth century, contains a history of the world which throws many interesting side lights on social customs. All these works show how popular this form of satirical allegory became in the latter Middle Ages. It afforded an opportunity to speak plainly, and it stimulated the French love of ridicule — as the original *Renard* had stated:

> tel chose dire
> Dont je vos puisse fere rire,
> Quar je sai bien, ce est la pure.

> such things to tell
> Whereby, I know, laugh you may,
> For that forsooth is the way of truth.

The drama in France does not reach its florescence until the later Middle Ages, in the fifteenth century. It waited for a public which came with the development of the great in-

The Early Drama

dustrial centers and the rise of the bourgeoisie to a place of prominence. Henceforth the drama filled the gap left by the decline of the national epic.

Before this time, however, drama had existed in several well-known and on the whole distinct forms, comprised under the generic name *jeu*. There was the liturgical play, having its origin in the ceremonies and festivals of the church and later developing into the so-called *mystère* or Mystery-play (1374); the *miracle* or Miracle-play, which applies the dramatic method to the life of a saint; and the secular, comic *jeu*, peculiar to Adam de la Halle, a poet of Arras. Of these types, the first two represent the real dramatic tradition of the Middle Ages. The Middle Ages had lost the distinction between tragedy and comedy as applied to the theater, and while pure comedy forms were plentiful, being found, for example, in the *farce* and the *sottie*, these have no connection with the literary comedy of antiquity.

Thus, the French drama is primarily of religious origin. The point has often been made that in this respect it offers an analogy to the dramas of Greece and India. And, in fact, the Christian mass contains the essential elements of dramatic action: (1) as to content or idea, in that the mass symbolizes the sacrifice of the Saviour's body for the sinful world; and (2) as to form, in the dialogue by recitation and song (*responsorium*) between the priest and the choir. On this foundation it was easy to build, especially as the life of the time centered so largely in the church.

The first step in the dramatic evolution was the introduction into the mass of a brief dialogue, called a "trope," and the

use of antiphonal song in the accompanying music. Thus
we find the Easter service adorned with a trope on the Resurrection — the *Quem quaeritis in sepulcro, ô Christicolae?*
(Whom seek ye in the tomb, O Christians?) — and presently
the Christmas mass is similarly expanded. But these are
only the beginnings. Finally the Holy Script itself is taken
over into the dialogue, in which the vulgar tongue then appears
by the side of Latin, and we get (early in the twelfth century)
a genuine liturgical play in the form of the *Sponsus* or Bridegroom. Derived from the story of the Wise and Foolish Virgins,
this " drama " consists of ninety-four verses, arranged in
strophes, part of which are in Latin and the remainder in French.
The action, which is extremely simple, begins with the prediction
by the choir of the advent of the Bridegroom, who at the close
pronounces the doom of the Foolish Virgins. The *Sponsus* was
composed in Angoûmois, near the Provençal border.

The next stages in the growth of drama include the enlargement of the central theme, the complete vulgarization into
French, and lastly the separation of the play from the mass.
An important advance in these respects is found in the *Représentation d'Adam*, of the middle of the twelfth century. Here
the text is almost entirely French and the scene is laid on the
parvis or square in front of the church doors. But this work
has also a distinct merit of its own. In form of a trilogy, it summarizes for the Christmas service various aspects of Christian
dogma, as seen in the fall of Adam, the murder of Abel by Cain
and the prophecy of Christ. Unequal as these parts are, some
of the characters are well delineated — especially Eve, strikingly
described as " faiblette et tendre chose " — and an element of
realism pervades the action. The third and principal part of
the *Adam* is the most interesting. This is a version of the famous sermon falsely assigned to St. Augustine (known separately
as the *Prophètes du Christ*), in which a long line of prophets
from Adam to Nebuchadnezzar foretell the coming of the Saviour. Theme and method are thus alike significant, for while
the subject is of the highest dramatic import the opportunity for
character-drawing is excellent. Of interest, too, are the stage
directions. These call for Paradise on a " raised place " in front
of the church door and for the abduction of the prophets into

"hell," the location of which, however, is not stated precisely. It requires no stretch of the imagination to see how from this simple setting later playwrights pass to the elaborate scenery, with various booths or " mansions," such as we shall find in the *mystères*.

The *Représentation d'Adam* is in Norman dialect and was presumably written in England. The Miracle-play (*miracle*), which The "Miracle" is the chief dramatic form of the thirteenth century, brings us back to France proper. Its first and best example is the *Jeu de Saint Nicolas*, by Jean Bodel of Arras, best known as a writer of epic. In origin the *miracle* is a dramatized saint's life. Its connection with the liturgy is therefore slight. Indeed, its beginnings have recently been traced to " musical services as an un-ecclesiastical feature of St. Nicholas' feast day celebration (Dec. 6)." Thus, when Bodel wrote, he followed an established tradition. Because of its personal touches his play has often been termed the "first romantic drama." With great freedom Bodel sketches a battle between Christians and Saracens, and when the former are all dead but one, he allows the saint to perform the " miracle " whereby the survivor's life is spared. A scene between thieves in a tavern is made almost as striking as the main action. Evidently Bodel was no respecter of sources. His play abounds in lyrical passages and in realism of detail. Incidentally, the first thieves' slang — later called *argot* — is found there.

Another early example of the same genre is the *Miracle de Théophile* (thirteenth century) by Rutebeuf. This embodies the theme later found in the Faust stories: a monk has bartered his soul to the Devil and finally, having grown repentant, he recovers it through the intercession of the Virgin. Rutebeuf was a *jongleur*, a satirist of considerable power, who counted among his patrons the eldest daughter of Louis IX, Isabella of Navarre. For her he composed a Life of St. Elizabeth and a *Complainte* on Thibaut V, her husband, who died in 1270. He also had a hand in writing allegory; but his shorter poems, especially the *Dis des Jacobins*, are among his best productions. In these his individualism has a free rein and he approaches Villon as a singer of the outlaw class. His *Théophile* is the first dramatization of a miracle of the Virgin. The plot follows the Greek legend (Theophilus is a priest of Cilicia) and the action is distributed over eight " mansions " — as the booths designating the place of the action were called — extending from Heaven to Hell. While the play as a whole is tedious, the lyric parts throb with genuine emotion.

It is in the fourteenth century, however, that the Miracle-plays reach their apogee. The *Quarante Miracles de Notre Dame* of that period form a kind of cycle, which in volume exceeds the entire extant drama of the early period. But their chief value today is sociological rather than literary. Written for a *puy* or literary guild of Notre Dame, probably located in Paris, they throw a side light on manners and customs of the age such as few other works do. Thus they differ as to style and structure; some are preceded by short sermons in prose, some contain *serventois* — a lyric form — in honor of the Virgin, a recurrent feature is the use of the *rondel* to celebrate her approach, and so on. But all agree in introducing the Virgin as a sort of *Dea ex machina*. A favorite theme is that of a wife slandered by a revengeful lover — occurring in the *Miracle de Notre Dame de la Marquise de la Gaudine* and in a host of other examples, including one of the *Mystères de Notre Dame de Liesse* (sixteenth century). The authorship of the *Miracles de Notre Dame* is unknown. In modern times, the type has been revived for the stage by Maeterlinck in his version of the Legend of Sister Beatrice.

As indicated above, the dramatic work of Adam de la Halle or Adam Le Bossu stands in a class by itself. The attempt to **Adam de** connect his name with the *puy* or guild of Arras (his **la Halle** home town) fails because it cannot be shown that this *puy* occupied itself with the drama. The probability is that Adam wrote for a company of friends who had no official function. In any case, we now come to the most independent dramatic form of the Middle Ages: the secular, comic *jeu*.[1] It is Adam himself who has the chief part in the *Jeu de la Feuillée* (between 1255 and 1264), the title of which refers to the arbor (*feuillée*) beneath which the May-festivals took place.

---

[1] In origin Adam de la Halle's *jeux* doubtless go back to folklore sources. They have parallels in the wooing plays, jigs and "mummings" found in northern Europe, especially England. Of such survivals there is a delightful account in Thomas Hardy's *The Return of the Native*.

The action begins with Adam's wishing to leave Arras and his wife Maroie, who wearies him, in order to become a clerk in Paris. But one cannot travel without money, and his father, on the score of his own maladies, refuses to provide any. A physician tells the father that his disease is avarice and mentions others similarly afflicted. This leads to a tirade against the abuses of the times, in which a blind boy, an itinerant monk and others take part. It happens to be the first of May, and Morgan the fairy is expected. She arrives to the wild notes of the *maisnie Hellekin* (Harlequin), a fairy-king resembling the German Erlkönig. Among the fairies present is Maglore. She feels slighted, and while her companions promise Adam fame as a poet she condemns him to forget his desire for learning in the arms of his hated wife. The play closes with the monk's surrender of his relics to his host as bail. The analogy with Aristophanes is clear, while the similarity to *A Midsummer-Night's Dream* is striking. The *Jeu de la Feuillée* is at once poetic and gross, purely fanciful and harshly satiric. Certainly, in the extant literature of the time, it is unique.

Of Adam's other play, the *Jeu de Robin et Marion*, the most characteristic feature is the obvious adaptation of a *pastourelle* (see above, Ch. II) to a musical, dramatic form. Thus it is spoken of as a forerunner of comic opera. Robin loves Marion, and together they ward off an importunate knight. This occurs amid scenes of merry-making and frolic; a wolf is driven from the flock attended by the two shepherds, and the play ends in a dance which carries the company off to the woods. The beauty and grace of the entire composition has often been noted. Certain lines breathe the spring-time of life, although many of the *motifs* are commonplaces — for example, the refrain

> Robins m'aime, Robins m'a,
> Robins m'a demandée, si m'ara,

is found in a *pastourelle* of Perrin d'Angecourt (1250 and after). From the *Jeu du Pèlerin*, by another author, though it was added to Adam's work as a kind of " filler," we learn that Adam died in Naples. It is probable that his comedy was performed there before the court of Charles of Anjou in 1283 or 1284.

With the dramatization in 1395 of the story of the patient Griselda — the so-called *Estoire de Griseldis* — the early drama in France may be said to close. Although a secular work, the *Estoire de Griseldis*, consisting of two parts, forms a kind of *miroir des dames* exalting the unnatural rôle of the long-suffering wife. In the fifteenth century the drama enters the more definite channels of the *mystère*, the *moralité*, the *sottie* and the *farce*. These types involve a consideration of the drama as an organized social product, toward which the preceding age had been feeling its way.

CHAPTER IV

HISTORY, DIDACTIC LITERATURE AND STORIOLOGY

ARTISTIC prose is always a late arrival in the literary field. To this France is no exception. It is not until the close of the twelfth century that Pierre de Beauvais, translator of the *Pseudo-Turpin* (see Ch. I), chooses prose, he says, because " rime requires the addition of words not found in the Latin." About the same time, as we have seen, many of the Arthurian romances appear in prose, and the *Aucassin et Nicolette* employs prose in most of its narrative portions.

But it is chiefly in the domain of history that prose-writing was to flourish. The vernacular histories of the twelfth century were exclusively rimed chronicles. Like Wace's *Brut*, the *Estoire des Engleis* by Geoffrey Gaimer is an expanded paraphrase in verse of the *Historia regum Britanniae* (Ch. II). Wace himself also wrote a *Roman de Rou* or *Geste des Normans* (1174); and Benôit de Sainte-More carried his *Chronique* of the Norman kings down to the death of Henry I. But the only approach to modern historical writing — in this early period — is a biography. This is the *Vie de Saint Thomas Becket* by Garnier de Pont-Sainte-Maxence, which we have mentioned before as the earliest document in the Francian dialect. Garnier still writes in verse and his outlook is strictly clerical; but he shows a sense of historical fact and he is impartial enough to condemn the arrogance of Henry II without mincing the hypocrisy of the Roman church. He wrote in 1173, just thirty-six years before the appearance of Villehardouin's *Conquête de Constantinople*. With this work historical prose-writing is born.

Geoffrey de Villehardouin (1160 to about 1212) was a knight of Champagne and planned his work primarily as an apologia of the Fourth Crusade. The success of the expedition had been jeopardized by rival political interests, in

**Ville-
hardouin**

73

which those of Venice (then mistress of the Mediterranean) had
a paramount rôle. An emissary on behalf of Philip of Champagne in 1199, Villehardouin had committed himself to the
Venetian policy. The consequence was that the crusade was
divided between those who went directly to the Holy Land and
others who, like Villehardouin, accompanied the Venetians to
Constantinople. The latter, after besieging Zara (on the Dal-
matian coast), twice captured Constantinople and then founded
the so-called Latin Kingdom, with Baldwin of Flanders at its
head.

In this campaign it was Villehardouin's part to act as a special
pleader. He was both brave and astute; and besides rescuing
a band of French knights from annihilation by the Bulgarians
at Adrianople, and otherwise winning distinction in military exploits, he seems to have been the guiding mind of the expedition.
In his castle at Messinople he wrote his book for his friends in
France. His real motives have been often impugned. In fact,
many historians doubt his sincerity, but his ability as a politician and as a writer is admitted by all critics.

In prose which is remarkable for its austere simplicity he
dwells on the merits of his case. He solemnly states that " bien
fust la crestiëntés hauciée et la terre des Turs abaissiée " if all
parties had been united. For the aged doge, Henry Dandolo, he
has unbounded admiration, and throughout his work the feudal
sense of obligation to his trust runs high. The tone of the Conquête is aristocratic, the whole being cast in the epic mold of restrained statement and noble aims. But despite its interesting
subject the work is poor in picturesque details. Villehardouin
rarely describes; whenever he does, as in the account of the blind
doge or the siege of Constantinople, he paints in outline on a
large canvas and leaves it to the reader to fill in the sketch.
Hence the writer dominates his material. We see the expedition
stripped of its vagaries, in broad outline, coldly but clearly, as
Villehardouin wishes us to see it.

The warmth which Villehardouin lacks is seen in the works
of his contemporaries, Robert de Clari and Henri de Valenciennes. The first describes the Fourth Crusade from the standpoint of the simpler folk, " la menue gent," whom the great
barons scorn. Here all is detail — the reverse of the Conquête.

We hear the camp-fire talk, the recital of individual deeds of bravery, the author's rapture at the wonders of St. Sophia, and so on. He wrote his work in the Picard dialect but on French soil, whither he returned soon after 1210. On the other hand, Henri de Valenciennes was a poet, the *Histoire de l'empereur Henri* — successor to Baldwin of Flanders — which is found in many of the Villehardouin manuscripts being a marred prose redaction of an original poem. Unfortunately this poem is lost, but such glimpses as we get of it in the prose show that it possessed considerable literary value.

Another knight of Champagne, Jean de Joinville (1224-1317), accompanied Louis IX on the Sixth Crusade. After an adventurous experience, in which he took part in the ill-managed campaign along the banks of the Nile (1248), was captured by the Saracens, and later shared in various exploits in Syria, Joinville returned to France in 1254, not yet thirty years of age, and spent the rest of his life in peaceful pursuits. Years later, at the advanced age of eighty, he composed for his sovereign, Jeanne, Countess of Champagne and Queen of France, a *Livre des saintes paroles et des bonnes actions de Saint Louis*. On this work, which is more of a memoir than a consecutive history, his fame rests.

Joinville is above all a *causeur*. Though he professes to have a plan, Joinville gives us a chaplet of anecdotes strung about the career of the great King and his relations with him. Thus the *Livre* offers a strong contrast to the work of Villehardouin. Joinville has a bent for the picturesque and even the trivial. He relates that on the island of Lampedusa the crusaders found plenty of rabbits and two skeletons in a cave, that at Cyprus the King received many foreign delegations, that Louis sent to the Tartar princes a tent of woolen cloth (*escarlate*), adorned with an image of the Annunciation and other Christian mysteries — but as to the political side of the campaign he leaves us in the dark. Nevertheless, his failure as a historian is amply redeemed by his vividness as an artist. Joinville is never at a loss for the proper expression to fit the characteristic feature which his eye catches. In particular, the noble figure of Louis, with his strong temper but his innate sense of justice and excessive bounty, emerges into the clearest possible light; and by his side the far more material character of Joinville himself wins us by his sincerity and his frank interest in "life." We learn that he was *courtois*, well-read, and never recoiled from what he considered his duty; but we are told also that he revolted at the idea of washing the feet of the poor and that a *vilain* did not enter into his scheme of salvation. A crusader's prejudice breathes in the lines he pens on the Bedouins: "De touailles sont entorteilliées (wrapped) leur testes qui leur vont par dessous le menton, dont laides gens et hisdeuses sont à regarder." On the whole, his work is a most valuable cultural document of the time.

But it remained for Jean Froissart (1337–1404 ?), chronicler of the Hundred Years' War, to glorify individual prowess as no one else had glorified it. In the preface to his *Chroniques* he warns us:

Froissart

> Vous verés et trouverés en ce livre comment pluiseur chevalier et escuier se sont fait et avanciét plus par leur proëce que par leur lignage. Li noms de preu est si haus et si nobles, et la vertu si clere et belle que elle replendist en ces sales et en ces places où il a assamblée et fuison de grans signeurs, et se remoustre dessus tous les autres.

Thus prowess is his theme — prowess which advances men irrespective of their country and birth. In its bearing on Froissart, the remark is significant.

He was born at Valenciennes, in French Flanders. In 1361 he went to England to offer his services to Queen Philippa and obviously in order to *faire fortune*. Here he soon became the intimate of the great and won for himself the title and functions of royal historiographer. Apparently he took the post seriously, as much so as his vain and childlike nature permitted. "Se je disoie," he remarks, "ainsi et ainsi advint en ce temps, sans ouvrir n'esclaircir la matiere, ce seroit cronique et non pas histoire." Fortunately, his patron allowed him to travel. He visited Scotland, where he knew Robert Bruce; he went to southern France in the suite of the Black Prince; he journeyed to Italy for the marriage of Lionel, Duke of Clarence. He had met Chaucer; at Milan he saw Petrarch; at Ferrara he came into contact with Pierre de Lusignan, King of Cyprus. For a person of Froissart's observant eye these were fruitful years.

But in 1369 Philippa died, and the reaction against her party at the court of Edward III drove Froissart back to Hainault in Flanders. Here he won in 1373 the curacy of Lestinnes and for the next ten years devoted himself to writing the first book of his *Chroniques,* the first version of which, composed from the "English point of view," covers the period of 1325–1377.

A change of heart now brings him under the influence of Gui de Blois, whose family and sympathies were French. The curacy at Lestinnes is exchanged for a canonship at Chimai, and about 1390 Froissart becomes Gui's private chaplain. Under the latter's inspiration he published a "French revision" of his *Chroniques;* and to this he soon added a second book, embodying the disturbances in Flanders, which he himself had witnessed. Once more he sets his sail to the wind, and provided with letters from his new patron he visits the court of the renowned Gaston de Foix in Gascony. This visit, recorded about 1390 in the third book, is the most vivid of Froissart's many experiences. At the same time he is busy on his fourth and last book. However, in 1394 the truce signed between France and England arouses in him the desire to revisit the scenes of his youthful triumphs, and he readily accepts the invitation of Richard II to pass three months at the English Court. Although flattered by the reception given him, Froissart is not blinded to Richard's misrule and leaves England abruptly in order to complete his fourth book. This recounts the beginning of the Civil Wars and ends abruptly with the abdication and death of the English King.

During his last ten years Froissart revised once more the first book of his *Chroniques,* adding an attack on the English people and an elegy on Richard. His own death is wrapped in mystery — the tradition is that he died at Chimai, destitute and bereft of friends.

Obviously, Froissart is an historian, "doublé d'un romancier" as the French say. With his poetry we shall deal elsewhere; it shares in the learned sophistications of his contemporaries. But it may be said of all his work that the pageantry of life made a far deeper impression upon him than did the hidden motives of human action. It is characteristic that in England the translation of the *Chroniques* in 1523–1525 became a rich source of dramatic inspiration. Froissart has the "curiosity" of the French, but he lacks their attachment to ideas. At bottom he is a Fleming, artistic, fond of color, sensual and essentially unmoral. His divided allegiance may be pardoned since he depended on the favor of patrons and was neither French nor English by birth. Moreover, his social background was, so to speak, Arthurian; and the tilt and tournament were part of the atmosphere he breathed. What is harder to understand is " his incurable optimism, his innate contentment in the face of so much shame and suffering, of so many crimes and outrages left unpunished " (Lanson). Persuaded that all heroism and virtue consist in " adventure," Froissart represents his century in terms of an interminable feat of arms, the brilliant facets of which delight the eye but confound the reason. If this be chivalry, then chivalry has come to a sad pass: a tinkling cymbal and an empty name.

Nevertheless, the stream of life flows strong in the pages of this prince of chroniclers. The battles of Crécy and Poitiers will live forever in the glowing colors in which he has set them forth. In prose that was then unmatched for its lucidity and flow he gave to the great families of Europe the first worthy narrative of their illustrious deeds. That the English, on the whole, fare better in his pages than the French is due to fortune, not to prejudice. With due allowance for his aristocratic leanings he had genuine admiration for those " povres brigans," who " s'en allant par voies couvertes " waylay the rich and gain their lives by pillaging castles and cities, for their valor is the equal of any. And who, having read them, can forget the admirable speech of Aymerigot Marchés on the adventurous life of the past or the insolent words of Jean Chandos challenging his adversary? Froissart had a good ear, a retentive memory and the gift of drawing men out. He wished to be an echo, says Gaston Paris, " mais il est le plus sonore et le plus fidèle des échos."

The writing of history, however, is only one of the manifestations of the " learned " thirteenth century. The monastic schools **Didactic** of the preceding age were now followed by the rise **Literature** of the universities (by 1200, Orleans is competing with Paris, Bologna and Toledo), and this in turn led to the vulgarization of a vast body of didactic literature. We have the great Dante's word that because of her " easier and more agreeable vulgar-tongue " France is also the home of works of a learned character. Witness the Italian, Brunetto Latini, who in 1265 wrote his famous *Trésor* in French prose. But the didactic spirit is abroad among the French long before this date. And here it was the Normans (many of them in England), with their practical sense, caring more for fact than for poetry, who took the lead. It was among the Normans that the *Physiologus*, used as a text-book on natural history, was first put into French, that parts of the Bible were translated, and that the learned spirit generally was fostered and promulgated. On this foundation the thirteenth century built. In numerous " lapidaries," " bestiaries " and " calendars " the allegorizing method is applied to the realm of Nature. In compendia of various kinds, *sommes, bibles, images du monde* or *mappemondes*, information of every sort, fantastic and real, is arranged and codified. In the form of *chastiements, doctrinaux* or *enseignements*, the age embodies its laws of behavior and its views on education.

Plentiful as these works are, few of them reveal any superior talent or can be ranked as literature. Rarely do they give an insight into the larger questions of human life. The great problem of scholastic philosophy — the relation of ideas (*universalia*) to facts (*res*), on which the master minds of Anselm and Abelard were engaged — does not get down into the vernacular, for not until Descartes (seventeenth century) is philosophy written in French. The sources of scientific knowledge were of course books: treatises which like Aristotle's *Organon*, Solinus' *Geography*, the Latin versions of the late Greek *Physiologus*, had survived the blight of the early Christian era, to be overlaid with a mass of commentary. Boethius' *Consolation of Philosophy*, translated into Provençal as early as the tenth century, was a stock theme of exegesis down to the threshold of the Renaissance. The books of travel due to pilgrims and crusaders, however rich in detail, were insignificant as to matter or based on hearsay and therefore fanciful. But the greatest obstacle to enlightenment was the church dogma (see Ch. I) that since truth is " revealed " it is the purpose of science to " understand," not to " investigate," the universe.

Let us not forget, however, that Latin, and not French, was the medieval language of scholarship. Thus, if we include theology, the greatest of the medieval " sciences," the minds of the time were not only active — they were encyclopedic. Here, as elsewhere in matters of culture, France was the leader as well as the disseminator. In the *Summa Theologia* of her "universal doctor," St. Thomas Aquinas [1] (1225–1274), she gave to the medieval fixity its final form. In this way, the implements of the reason (if not reason itself), logic, grammar, rhetoric, are sharpened and controlled as never before. So, too, a fresh impulse is given to mathematics, together with its complementary art, music. All this made for expression, in the vernacular as well as in Latin; but for its formal or dialectic elements, structure and style, not content or thought.

How sophisticated and yet naïve medieval science could be is seen in the works of Philippe de Thaon, an Anglo-Norman writer **Natural** of the court of Henry I (early twelfth century). **History** In six- and then eight-syllable verse Philip wrote a *Comput,* a *Bestiaire* and a *Lapidaire.* His style, says M. Langlois, " est d'une indigence, d'une nullité et d'une gaucherie sans pareilles." Yet Philip aims to instruct the clergy, whose ignorance moves him to compassion. In the *Comput* he treats after Bede and John of Garlande the ins-and-outs of the ecclesiastical calendar: the days, months, church festivals, equinoxes, solstices, and so forth. For all these arid themes he points a moral lesson. For instance, he derives the word August from Lat. *gustus,* and since God is " pur gustement " it follows that August signifies God. The same kind of reasoning is typical of the *Bestiaire* and the *Lapidaire.* The former follows the *Physiologus* in allegorizing animals: the lion with his large head and comparatively small body represents " Jhesu filz de Marie"; if the pelican opens her breast to feed her young this action is symbolic of the Saviour:

> par le sanc precius
> que Dés (Dieu) laissat pur nus

—- as centuries later Musset made it a symbol of the poet. The *Lapidaire* puts into French the Latin version of a work by Damigeron, a first-century Greek. Here Philip dwells on the curative value of certain minerals and gives short directions for their use — another testimony to medieval credulity.

Other bestiaries were composed in the Middle Ages. In the thir-

---

[1] Thomas Aquinas (d'Aquino) was an Italian, but he studied and taught in Paris.

teenth century, Richard de Fournival, Chancellor of Amiens, had the fantastic idea of celebrating his lady in a *Bestiaire d'amour.* Richard's subtleties are in prose, but they were easily turned into verse. As for lapidaries, numerous translations into various European languages testify to the vogue of a Latin lapidary by Marbode, Bishop of Rennes (eleventh century). All of these works, however, vary in character but slightly from Philip's, which may thus be considered typical of the genre.

A good illustration of the medieval encyclopedia is the *Image du monde* (about 1245) by Gautier de Metz. Preserved in many **Encyclo-** manuscripts with handsome miniatures, this poem of **pedias** eleven thousand verses aims to embrace all creation, including geography and astronomy. Here the sensation-loving layman would receive food for his imagination, together with considerable moral edification. The work gives some facts, but on the whole it abounds in descriptions of fanciful lands, unheard-of monsters, and treasures of stupendous value. The majority of *images* were a similar bait for the unwary. One, however, has a distinct literary and cultural value. This is the *Livre du Trésor* (1265), by the Florentine Brunetto Latini, master of Dante. As we have said, he wrote his treatise in French because (to quote his exact words) this " parleure est plus delitàble et plus commune à toutes gens." Knowledge, which Brunetto compared to the small change which we daily spend, is, he says, necessary in life. Accordingly, in three long books he runs through the gamut of the knowable. Today the interesting part of the treatise is the section on politics. Here Brunetto has collected some real information, with finely drawn distinctions, on national and civil government in France and Italy. But it is the language which constitutes the noteworthy trait of the *Trésor.* Brunetto, whom Alain Chartier later compared to Livy, writes better French than many a native Frenchman. His style is clear and succinct, and remarkably idiomatic. The *Trésor* enjoyed a long and merited popularity and was twice translated into Italian.

Moral precepts, akin to the type still current in the " Letters **The Chas-** of a Father to his Son," are embodied in the *chastie-* **tiements** *ment.* This genre began with the *Chastiement d'un père à son fils,* which is a twelfth-century verse translation of the *Disciplina clericalis* by the Spanish Jew, Petrus Alphonsus. The educational features of the work are secondary, however, to the tales or *exempla* with which the discussion is illustrated. Indeed, this feature is what saved much medieval edification from oblivion. In the course of time, a large body of such tales, derived chiefly from the Orient, found their way into the vernacular and served not only to instruct but also to entertain and amuse. We have observed the fact in dealing with the " fable " (Ch. III) and we shall have occasion to mention it again.

A *chastiement* of genuine educational value is the prose work, *Des quatre d'aage d'home* (about 1270), by Philippe de Novaire (Novara). Here the moralizing tone yields to the mellow reflections of old age. Philip wrote at the close of an adventurous career. His *Gestes des Chiprois,* giving an account of the tragic struggle of Cyprus against Frederick II, was in the nature of a memoir; this is followed by the *chastiement* as an essay on wisdom. Philip deals at some length with the various " ages " of man, but dwells particularly on the age of childhood, about which he makes several telling observations.

On the other hand, the *Chastiement des dames* (about 1250), by Robert de Blois, is filled with a didacticism of a purely worldly type. Written in verse, this work is a veritable manual on courtesy for the noble ladies of Robert's time. Many of the instructions given are of course commonplace; others, however, are quite characteristic — as, for example, the precept that a lady should always love secretly (*celéement*) or her reputation will be at stake. In exalted, almost religious verse, Robert intones the praise of *courtoisie, bien parler* and *douce acointance,* which are the sterling traits of a woman's education. Obviously, he follows Ovid, but never slavishly.

A more serious type of moral treatise is inaugurated by the *Livre des manières* of Etienne de Fougères (1170) — at one time chaplain of Henry II of England. The anonymous *Poème moral* (thirteenth century) incorporates in its moralizing the legend of Thaïs. For the most part, however, such works are satirical. Their animus against certain classes grows more and more violent until in the so-called *Roman de charité,* by Barthélemy de Molliens (thirteenth century), the somberness of the author's picture holds out little hope for the ideals for which the Middle Ages once stood.

We may fittingly close this section on didactic literature with a glance at the *Bataille des sept arts* (after 1235) by the cele-

**The "Ba-
taille des
sept arts "**

brated *trouvère*, Henri d'Andeli. In form this work belongs to the genre of verse-dispute or *débat* de-rived from late Latin literature. A typical example is the *Débat de l'hiver et de l'été*, which embodies the im-memorial theme of the conflict of the seasons. The appellation *bataille* — and there are other works of this name — was inspired by the *Psychomachia* of the poet Prudentius (fourth century), in which a battle of the virtues and vices is narrated. But Henry's poem transcends the limits of a mere genre. Henry is one of the enlightened spirits of the thirteenth century. He has individuality, grasp and variety of idea, and skill in statement. Like the later seventeenth century, the medieval period had its quarrel as to the relative merits of the ancients and moderns. It was Henry's distinction to stand up for the classics and de-fend Orleans against Paris, where, he says, " students care for naught except to read books on nature":

> Et li arciens n'ont mès cure
> Lire fors livres de nature.

In eight-syllable couplets Henry marshals the representatives of " literature " (*grammaire*) against the converts to " dialectics " (*logique*). But in vain; the former are worsted, and the poem closes on the despairing note that " the times are given to empti-ness " and only a new generation can restore culture to its true status. Henry was over-sanguine; the culture he had in mind had to await the appearance of Petrarch, and even then the new humanism made its way slowly in France. But through its emphasis on the classics Henry's poem heralds the Renaissance. From every point of view it is a cultural document of the first rank.

No picture of the thirteenth and fourteenth centuries could be complete without a reference to the vast body of floating *contes,*

Storiology

dits, fabliaux and *lais* in which the age delighted. Moralizing and instructive, or purely imaginative or ironical, these stories often have no special hall-mark, are addressed to no particular class, and must be assigned to the field of general European folklore. This, however, does not preclude the fact that many such tales may be of individual French inven_tion; nor does the group embrace the large class of Oriental stories which came into Western Europe directly through the crusades and the Saracen domination in Spain.

The " fable " and the romantic *lai* we treated above (Chs. II and III). As for the *fabliau* or *fablel*, it is defined by M. Bédier as a " conte à rire en vers." The shortest has eighteen verses, the longest thirteen hundred.

The Fabliau, Dit and Conte

Essentially anecdotes by nature, the *fabliaux* are akin to the *gabs* or boasts which are told in some forms of the Old French epic. The *fabliau* of *Barat et Haimet,* which a certain Jean Bodel set to verse in the thirteenth century, has also been recorded in Armenia and Albania.

Thus, universal and perennial as stories, the *fabliaux* flourished particularly in the thirteenth century, when they supplanted more and more the *lais* of the preceding age. Reflecting the ironic, bourgeois spirit, they were well fitted to make a person while away an idle moment on a long journey or at an inn.. In fact, one of the most amusing, *Les deux bordeors* (jesters) *ribauz,* recounts the " half-clumsy, half-satiric boasts of two members of the order, who misquote the titles of their répertoire, make by accident or intention ironic comments on its contents " and thus show that their wit cuts both ways.

In short, the *fabliau* ridicules society. It is brief, to the point, and effective. It strikes at the priestly class, as title after title shows, dethrones the lofty heroine of romance, and pictures the " real and practical, not the ideal or sentimental." One of the earliest and best examples of the genre is *Richeut.* This is the story of a courtesan who together with her son and servant plies her unsavory trade among various classes and in this way furthers her own and her offspring's career. Certain traits remind the modern reader of *Manon Lescaut* — except that the unknown author is neither a sentimentalist nor a cynic but a cool observer of brutal fact. Most *fabliaux,* however, deal less with a situation than with a traditional theme. Such is the so-called *Lai d'Aristote,* by Henri d'Andeli, which repeats the age-old plot of the scholar duped by a woman; or the *Vilain Mire,* which furnished the basis of Molière's comedy, *Le Médecin malgré lui;* or *Le Mari qui fist sa femme confesse,* whence La Fontaine extracted his *Chevalier confesseur*, and so on. Thus by means of the *fabliau* the "real world" in the Middle Ages jostles and elbows the courtly and the fanciful. Many a story of Boccaccio is but a *fabliau* retold; and how lacking in contrasts would be the *Canterbury Tales* if Chaucer had not seen fit to make use of the genre!

But not all *fabliaux* are ironical or satirical. Or rather the genre is not always distinguishable from the *dit* and the *conte.* The *dit*, in particular, is supposed to point a moral lesson. It is characteristic of all these compositions, however, that they deal with "ordinary life" and are to the point. Thus *La Housse partie* (" The Saddlecloth Divided into Portions,") — a *fabliau* — has an ethical purpose; namely, to show the dangers of filial ingratitude. A special class is perhaps the *contes dévots*, similar in spirit to the pious *Miracles* (in this case, legends) *de la sainte vierge* by Gautier de Coincy. Such a one is the *Dit dou vrai aniel* (" The Parable of the True Ring"), an eastern tale retold by Boccaccio and later embodied in Lessing's drama, *Nathan der Weise;* or the charming *Tombeor Nostre Dame*, which Massenet has put into opera. In the first of these the theme is philosophical; in the second it is lyric — in the best sense.

Finally, the edifying spirit reigns in the Latin *exempla* or parables with which the medieval preacher embellished his ser-**The Exempla** mons. These are mainly of Arabic — indirectly, **and Oriental** of Sanskrit — origin and are preserved in such col-**Tales** lections as that of Jacques de Vitry (before 1240) or the *Disciplina clericalis*, mentioned above. The *Arabian Nights* did not reach France until the eighteenth century, yet the Oriental plan of setting a group of stories in a framework is found as early as 1155 in the *Roman des sept sages* — which existed in a host of European versions. This work was planned to set forth certain traits which the Brahmins thought youth should guard against. Here a young prince is rescued from the treachery of his step-mother by seven wise men, each of whom delays the prince's execution by telling a story. In a similar way, an account of the Buddha, turned into a Christian Greek legend in the sixth century, found its way into Latin and thence into French. Of this *Barlaam et Josaphat* there are three French rimed-versions (the last about 1250), which tell how

Barlaam (originally the Buddha) converts Josaphat to Christianity, largely through the influence of Oriental stories skillfully adapted for the purpose.

Here our sketch of medieval storiology ends. As to form, be it noted that by the fifteenth century the French verse-tale disappears, on the one hand, into the prose *conte,* and on the other, into the *farce,* a type of the drama. The *Cent Nouvelles nouvelles* (1461) show the influence of the Italian *novella* and are the direct forerunners of our modern short-stories. As we observed in the case of the *Flamenca* (Ch. II), the Provençals had used the word *novas* for narrative fiction, but without any distinction between its longer and its shorter forms.

que nobles faitz
mes et honourable
uenues par les
terres de france et
oit notablement
ouablemet enre

vucille treer et mettre en n
sens et entendemt si vertue
ce liure que iay encommer
Je puisse continuer et pr
en tele maniere que tous
qui le siuont seront et o

Illustration from Froissart's *Chroniques* (Fifteenth Century Manuscri

BOOK II

THE BOURGEOIS INFLUENCE

CHAPTER I

THE LYRIC POETS OF THE SCHOOL OF MACHAUT AND DESCHAMPS

WE have now come to the fourteenth and fifteenth centuries, which, as we noted above (Bk. I, Ch. I), represent the Middle French period, as distinguished from the Middle Ages proper.

Politically this was an age of hesitation, not to say, of disintegration. The Valois princes, who came to the throne in 1328, have the trappings of chivalry, but their love of display and luxury is out of all keeping with the real misery of the times. The retinue of minor kings and nobles surrounding them is often brilliant; especially in such persons as John of Luxemburg who, though ruler of Bohemia, kept open house in Paris, where his gaiety became proverbial. The fact is that feudalism is tottering, and such examples are prophetic of its fall. The political security it once gave is lost in the Hundred Years' War (between France and England), and as in the case of Froissart, " fealty " has become a matter of convenience, to be treated lightly according to one's self-interest. The great nobles still respond to the glamour of feudal life, but they have long wearied of its obligations. The terrific struggle (1405–1421) for the control of the crown, between Louis of Orleans and John Without-Fear, of Burgundy, is indicative of this fact. At last the monarchy is forced to seek other means of support; and these it finds in the great cities among the rapidly rising merchant class. Here Artois and Flanders, centers of the textile arts, Lyons at the head of the Rhone Valley, and Rouen with the commerce of the Seine at her feet, were of

The Middle French Period

great importance. With an instinct close to genius, Louis XI (1461–1483) worked for the future of France by his control of the feudal barons. And, finally, with the Renaissance, when national unity is achieved, its mainstay is an enterprising and self-reliant bourgeoisie.

The effect of this period on literature is reactionary rather than progressive. Here and there the gleam of a new humanism shines forth, especially during the reign of. Charles V, in the works of Pierre Berçuire and Nicolas Oresme, in imitations of Boccaccio and to a less degree of Petrarch. But, in the main, the attempts at innovation are abortive or in any case super-ficial; and the older literary forms continue, mannered and flam-boyant in response to Italian and Flemish influences, but other-wise changing little. One fact, however, is noteworthy. The great lord who has his own library, and the bourgeois now a client of the *jongleur,* insist on the portrayal of their opinions and their emotions; and these are anything but poetic. The result is a sharp contrast between form and thought; the poets consume their efforts in seeking new and striking effects, and to represent an idea by the image most foreign to it becomes the rule of rules. A *Songe du Vergier* clothes a treatise on politics; *Le roi Modus et la reine Racio* is a manual on falconry. Hence, most of the poetry is a labyrinth of allegory framed to a purpose for which it was never intended. And it is significant that the art of poetry — the technique of which now becomes the serious con-sideration of the *puys* (see above) — is officially termed *rhéto-rique* and the poet assumes the ominous name of a *faiseur.* In this way, the formal elements of the Middle Ages survived long after the time when the spirit that produced them had fled.

Meanwhile, the French language itself is undergoing a marked change. Many learned words derived from the classics come to enrich the vocabulary. Not at once, but certainly by the close of the fifteenth century, the feminine *e* ceases to be sounded before other vowels: *veü* is reduced to *vu;* further, the diph-thong *oi* acquires the sound of *wè* or *è* or *wa,* and most of the final consonants become silent. Above all, the language loses all but the last vestige of case-forms in the merging of the nominative and the oblique (thus *on* and *homme,* both derived from Latin *homo,* continue not as separate cases but as distinct words); and the sentence structure of Modern French, less flexible but far clearer than that of Old French, is inaugurated.

In short, the fourteenth and the fifteenth centuries are the bridge between the Middle Ages and the Renaissance, between the age of faith and the age of reason. On the political and cultural side, the period is marked by the decay of feudalism and by the rise of the township and the bourgeois spirit. Intellectually, the beginnings of humanism are apparent; sporadically, however, and then only as a veneer. As for literature, it flows prevailingly in the former channels; where there is a revival, as in the lyric, the tendency is toward a polished and involved form — the *ballade* and the *rondeau* are supreme, like the sonnet later on — and poetic expression is artificial, complicated, or only " graceful," like the Gothic architecture of the time. On the other hand, the point of view is more and more personal and autobiographic, and as regards the one genius of the age, François Villon, it is strikingly modern.

The founder of the poetic school of the fourteenth century is Guillaume de Machaut (about 1300–1377). In acknowledging **Machaut** this fact, we need not go the length of René of Anjou, who gave him a place above Petrarch and Boccaccio, although Chaucer's imitation of him in the *Book of the Duchess* is in itself high praise. He was born in Champagne and early entered the service of John of Luxemburg, who took him to Germany, Austria, Italy and even Russia. After John's death on the field of Crécy, Guillaume found a new patron in the Dauphin, the future Charles V, and had leisure for literature. Others who supported his pen were Charles of Navarre, for whom he wrote a *Jugement* and the *Confort d'ami*, and the famous Pierre de Lusignan, whose exploits he celebrated in the *Prise d'Alexandrie*.

But Guillaume's true vein lay in the shorter genres, the *ballade* and the lyric *lai*. Artificial as these are in his treatment, their preciosity is redeemed by the alliance of verse to music, a feature which Guillaume developed, and by marked dexterity in the detail of expression. In the *Livre du voir-dit* (about 1363) Guillaume has collected the best of his lyric experience.

Made up of the shorter forms, such as *ballades, lais, rondels,* this work purports to be the amorous exchange of the aging poet and the young and charming Péronelle d'Armentières. In fact, the work has been called the "journal amoureux du quatorzième siècle," but for all that the exchange may have been a poetic fiction. In any case, the *Voir-dit* reveals to perfection the gallant love-making of the time. Guillaume plays gracefully with his passion until the inevitable happens: Péronelle deserts him for another, and the poet consoles himself with an avowal of friendship. Thus the work has the outward semblance of a novel.

Guillaume's best remembered short poem is probably the following *rondel* or triolet:

> Blanche com lys, plus que rose vermeille,
> Resplendissant com rubis d'oriant,
> En remirant vo biauté non pareille,
> Blanche com lys, plus que rose vermeille,
> Suy si ravis que mes cuers toudis veille
> Afin que serve, à loy de fin amant,
> Blanche com lys, plus que rose vermeille,
> Resplendissant com rubis d'oriant.

> White as a lily, rosier than the roses red,
> Outshining far the ruby of the East!
> To see your peerless beauty being led —
> White as a lily, rosier than the roses red —
> So charmed am I straightway my heart is sped
> Humbly to serve you where true love holds feast.
> White as a lily, rosier than the roses red,
> Outshining far the ruby of the East!

Guillaume's pupil and friend was Eustache Deschamps (about 1340–1405), who bewailed the former's death in harmonious
Deschamps   words:

> Tous instrumens l'ont complaint et plouré,
> Musique a fait son obseque et ses plours,
> Et Orpheus a le cors enterré.

Deschamps, who wrote some eleven hundred *ballades,* was the ·lawgiver of the school and composed an *Art de dictier et fere chansons*, etc., the first treatise of its kind (in French) that has come down to us. Yet he differed much from Guillaume in character and temperament. A frequenter of taverns and the common people, Eustache had an aversion for the rich and high-placed. This attitude led him to write a *Miroir de mariage* in which he jeers at women and the abuses of the courtly world. But he was not courageous enough to abjure the artificiality of verse and write in the more suitable medium of prose. Deschamps lacked taste, and voluminous as his output was, it is often dull and incoherent. At the same time, he is capable of occasional lapidary effects and a manly and personal accent that does him credit. He stood in personal relations with Chaucer, to whom his sturdy character appealed and to whose genius Deschamps does homage in a well-known *ballade*, with the refrain:

> Grant translateur, noble Geoffrey Chaucier.

Another poet whom Chaucer imitated is Froissart. Justly famous for his prose *Chroniques* (see above, Bk. I, Ch. IV),
Froissart Froissart also composed various light forms of verse, as well as the *Paradis d'amour* — the work which Chaucer used — and the tiresome Arthurian romance, *Méliador*. Passing through Avignon, he was stupid enough to allow himself to be robbed of two florins given him by Gaston de Foix. This untoward event he bewails gracefully in the *Dit dou florin*, which thus remains a good index of his lighter verse. A courtier by instinct, Froissart is less stilted than most of his contemporaries, and he achieves greater unity of thought and expression. One of his characteristic *rondels* — *On doit le temps ensi prendre qu'il vient* — has been charmingly translated by Longfellow:

> Take time while yet it is in view,
> For fortune is a fickle fair:
> Days fade, and others spring anew;
> Then take the moment still in view.
> What boots to toil and cares pursue?
> Each month a new moon hangs in air.
> Take, then, the moment still in view,
> For fortune is a fickle fair.

As we approach the fifteenth century, the outstanding figures in poetry are Christine de Pisan, Alain Chartier and the royal poet, Charles d'Orléans.

Time has dealt rudely with the fame of Christine de Pisan. An Italian by birth, she yet was once considered one of the **Christine de Pisan** glories of France. In general, she is remarkable for her knowledge and her ideas, and the tragedy of her life again and again infuses her writing with lyrical feeling — although she cannot escape the allegorizing fashion of her age.

Christine was born in Venice (1364) and not, as her name might suggest, in Pisa or Pezzano. Her father, Thomas de Pezano, a scholar of Bologna, took his family to France, whither he had been called as physician and astrologer to Charles V. While Charles lived the family fortunes of the Pezanos flourished, Christine received an excellent education and was married young and advantageously to a Picard gentleman, Estienne de Castel. But fortune plays strange tricks, and after a few years of happiness Christine lost not only her husband and her father but through litigation and debt much of her property. With a fortitude unusual in her youth and sex, she braved the insolence of law-courts and the injustice of the world, and rescued what little she could from the family disaster. Her real help, and incidentally her consolation, was her writing. After the battle of Agincourt she retired more and more from the world, and finally took religious orders. She died in 1429, shortly after celebrating in song Joan of Arc, whose triumph she had lived to see.

Besides her early lyrics and the poems in which she defended her sex against the attack of Jean de Meun (Bk. I, Ch. III), Christine left three poems of a meditative nature: the *Mutacion de Fortune*, the *Chemin de long estude* and a so-called *Vision*. She also wrote a prose Life of Charles V for his successor, in which her hero's *courage*, *chevalerie* and *sagesse* are proved by illustration.

All of these works (barring perhaps the last) have a marked personal touch; a good part of them indeed is out-and-out autobiography. Of the shorter lyrics, the *ballades*, forming a kind of sequence in the manuscripts, are among the best. Note the *ballade* beginning:

> Seulete sui et seulete vueil estre,
> Seulete m'a mon douz ami laissiée;
> Seulete sui, sanz compaignon ne maistre,
> Seulete sui. dolente et courrouciée.

Seulete sui, en langueur mesaisiée,
Seulete sui, plus que nulle esgarée,
Seulete sui, sanz ami demourée.

Alone am I, alone I wish to be,
Alone my sweetest friend hath left me here,
Alone am I, in my sole company,
Alone in sorrow bent, and without cheer.
Alone am I in languorous disgrace,
Alone far more than wanderer from God's grace,
Alone, without a friend, the world I face.

Or another, which reveals Christine's classical reading:

Ovid relates a messenger there is
Who sleeping bears his tidings unto men,
Making them dream, and in their dreams, I wys,
See joy and sorrow to the full again, etc.

Taking her title from Dante — *Vagliami il lungo studio* — she relates in the *Chemin de long estude* how Almathea, the Cumean sibyl, leads her after various wanderings to the fifth heaven. Thither Earth has sent a messenger to ask Reason where the perfect man can be found. Nobility, Riches, Chivalry and Wisdom take part in the discussion, and the question — unanswerable as it is — is left for a decision to the King of France to whom Christine is dispatched as an ambassador. Thereupon Christine awakes to find that she has been dreaming. The other two philosophical poems are of the same general character as the first. The *Mutacion de Fortune* throws light on the author's early life and education, while the third part of the *Vision*, inspired largely by Boethius, abounds in philosophizing on life and stresses a strict adherence to duty as the only road to happiness.

Thus Christine's traits are a firm grasp of moral values, a quick and broad sympathy, and a learning quite out of the ordinary. In her day Christine was an enlightening force which slowly but emphatically cleared the way for the Renaissance.

Compared to this " virile " woman, the so-called " father of French letters " at first seems a weakling. Son of a bourgeois **Alain** of Bayeux, who was a pillar of the state, Alain **Chartier** Chartier (1394–1440) early prepared for a life at court and for literature. In the *Espérance des trois vertus* he mentions Homer, Virgil, Livy, Horace, Statius and Lucan. To this substantial knowledge must be added Cicero and Seneca — whose vogue Alain began — and among the moderns, Brunetto Latini, Dante and Boccaccio. The legend, circulated in the sixteenth century, that Margaret of Scotland, finding the poet asleep, kissed the lips that had framed such beautiful verse, is probably an invention. But Alain was skillful, and besides maintaining himself in the royal favor — Charles VI sent him on diplomatic missions — he wrote in the court manner.

In one of his early works, the *Livre des quatre dames*, each of whom had lost a suitor at Agincourt, Alain shows how vapid was the period in its hopeless neglect of the real woes of France. Similarly, the *Lay de Plaisance* and the famous *Belle Dame sans merci* reveal the same indifference to the horrors wrought by Orleanists and Burgundians. It has often been said that this callousness is conventional. In any case, the *Belle Dame* fulfills all the sophisticated rules of gallantry. Can one die of love? The heartless lady thinks not; the lover dies and thus disproves her point. Could stilted artifice go further? Yet the poem was translated into English by a follower of Chaucer, in part as follows:

> Full oftentimes to speak himself he pained,
> But shamefasteness and drede said ever nay,
> Yet at the last, so sore he was constrained
> When he full long had put it in delay,
> To his lady right thus than gan he say,
> With dredeful voice, weeping, half in a rage;
> "For me was purueyed an unhappy day,
> When I first had a sight of your visage!"

Fortunately, Alain's fame does not rest on his verse. It was his prose, modeled on that of Seneca, which dazzled his contemporaries and made him a classic to the sixteenth century. Among other admirers, Etienne Pasquier speaks of " les mots dorez et belles sentences de Maistre Alain Chartier." Marot also mentions him with praise.

Le Quadrilogue invectif (1422) is the most important of Alain's prose works. The three estates, the nobility, the clergy and the people, debate with France on the crying abuses of the time. The clergy, acting as judge between the other orders, is particularly severe on the nobles and accuses them of sacrificing the country to their own lawlessness. Alain's style is grave, periodic, sententious. In an argument rising occasionally to eloquence he preaches the destruction of feudalism and pleads for a national army in which royalty and people shall unite. The *Quadrilogue* is the earliest work to treat feudalism unsparingly. A satire on the life of the courtier, *Le Curial,* is less convincing in its invective; but the *Espérance des trois vertus* — composed in the tenth year of Alain's exile from the capital (1429), whence he had been driven by the Burgundian faction — again strikes a clarion note. Here the poet blames the church openly for her temporizing attitude: the triumph of evil on earth is to a large extent her work. Nevertheless, the poet is confident that France will some day rise against her foes, foreign and domestic, and crush them. This work, in which prose and verse are intermingled, contains some of Alain's best imitations of Seneca and approaches the *prose oratoire* of a later day.

> Within this book of my thought
> The tale of my heart is related,
> The grief of my soul can be sought
> With tears illuminated!

So sang Charles d'Orléans (1391–1465), the last exponent of the graces and refinements of chivalry. His life falls into three

Charles d'Orléans

periods of almost equal length. The son of Louis of Orleans and Valentine of Milan, from both of whom he inherited the love of art and letters, his first twenty-five years were spent amid the ruin of the Hundred Years' War and the enmity of Burgundy and Orleans. He was educated at Blois and married (at the age of fifteen) his cousin, Isabella of France, the widow of Richard II of England. In 1407 his father was murdered at the instigation of John Without-Fear, and his mother and his wife died barely a year after. For seven years, with the aid of the Armagnacs, he waged continuous warfare against the Burgundian faction, relieved by occasional but momentary truces. In 1415 he was captured by the English at Agincourt and taken to England a prisoner. The next twenty-five years — his second period — he languished in captivity. It was then that most of his poetry was written. Released on condition that he make peace with Burgundy — and the grace with which he accepted these terms lives in the words he addressed to the Duchess of Burgundy:

> Madame, vu ce que vous avez fait pour ma delivrance,
> il est juste que je me rende votre prisonnier —

he married Marie de Clèves and settled down to a life of artistic enjoyment at Blois. During this, his third, period he gave to the poetry of chivalry a brief but brilliant afterglow, and he died gladdened by the thought that his infant son was destined to mount the throne of France as Louis XII.

As his recent biographer points out, there is in the poetry of Charles d'Orléans a note that recalls at once Petrarch and Heine. Of the one he has the longing, of the other the intimacy, while he has the tenderness of both. But he undoubtedly lacks their penetration and force, and despite his own experience the tragedy of life affected him little. To rank him with Villon — his contemporary and friend — is to compare a reed with an oak.

His poems fall into two groups: those written in captivity — of which a number were translated into English — and those composed after Charles' return to France. The first group, the so-called *Livre de la Prison*, imitates, in narrative interspersed with *ballades*, the allegory of the *Roman de la Rose*. The second, containing the standard lyric forms, again celebrates " love," but it also represents the progress of the poet's experience: daily occurrences, anniversaries, May-festivals, and so on. Charles excels in crystallizing such details, in making the fleeting permanent. The famous *rondeau:*

> Le temps a laissié son manteau
> De vent, de froidure et de pluye,

is in all anthologies and has been beautifully rendered by Andrew Lang:

> The year has changed his mantle cold
> Of wind, of rain, of bitter air;
> And he goes clad in cloth of gold,
> Of laughing suns and seasons fair;
> No bird or beast of wood or wold
> But doth with cry or song declare
> The year lays down his mantle cold.

> All founts, all rivers, seaward rolled,
> The pleasant summer livery wear,
> With silver studs on broidered vair;
> The world puts off its raiment old,
> The year lays down his mantle cold.

But again, Charles was indifferent to the misery of his time, and charm and grace are the main assets of his verse. In one *ballade*, rather freely translated by Longfellow,[1] the longing for France is at least genuine; it begins:

> En regardant vers le pays de France,
> Ung jour m'avint, à Dovre sur la mer. . .

By a singular fate, the poems of Charles d'Orléans remained virtually unprinted until the seventeenth century.

---

[1] See Longfellow's *Poetry of Europe.*

CHAPTER II

THE UNIVERSITY AND THE HUMANISM OF THE FOURTEENTH CENTURY

AMID the political and social turmoil of the fourteenth and fifteenth centuries the University of Paris represents one of the few elements of stability. In upholding the medieval point of view and thus assuming more and more a reactionary rôle, it nevertheless served the cause of learning (see especially Oresme's vulgarization of Aristotle) and it championed the rights of the people against the nobles. The outstanding figure of the University group was the great chancellor, Jean Gerson. We know him already, along with Christine de Pisan, as an opponent of Jean de Meun in the " grant guerre " concerning the *Roman de la Rose*. But he was also a fighter for " justice against political interests, a reformer of the inner life of the church, a steadfast worker for church unity, and — above all — the greatest religious writer and preacher of his age in France." [1]   In this last respect he is a parallel to Bossuet.

But Gerson had his intellectual forbears, and with these we shall deal first. An important scholar and translator of the middle of the fourteenth century is Pierre Berçuire. **Early Humanists** He lived for a while at Avignon (1320–1340) and there met Petrarch in retirement at Vaucluse. Aptly the latter calls him " vir insignis pietate et litteris." In 1342 Berçuire was busy at Paris on a large encyclopedia in three parts: the *Reductorium, Repertorium et Breviarium morale*. He then became secretary to John the Good, and like Vincent de Beauvais (the translator of the *Legenda aurea* and other widely-read books), he set himself the task of translating Livy into French. The *Rommans de Titus Livius* (completed in 1356), as the title is, deals only with the better known portions of Livy's history. But it does so in vivid, forceful language, which won the work

[1] D. H. Carnahan, *University of Illinois Studies*, III, p. 11.

readers beyond the borders of France, in Spain and in Italy. The translation, which is addressed to those " qui vouldront savoir l'art de chevalerie et prendre exemple aux vertus anciennes," is still strictly medieval; at the same time, Roman heroism is exalted and a differentiation as to classical traits is already apparent. In a less degree than Oresme, but to a considerable extent certainly, Berçuire enriched French by the introduction of words of a learned character.

The greatest impetus to learning, however, at this date was given by the circle surrounding Charles V (1364 – 1380), justly surnamed the Wise. Charles' own part in this movement was preëminently that of a Maecenas. The most noteworthy among those he encouraged was Nicolas Oresme. Of Norman birth, Oresme studied in Paris and was subsequently *maître* and *grand maître* in the University; in 1361 he became dean of the Church of Rouen, and in 1377 he was appointed bishop of Lisieux. An intimate of Charles, he yet enjoyed the privilege of voicing his own convictions; and when the King became deeply interested in astrology — an art which the French borrowed from the Arabians — he had the boldness to write *Des Divinations* (1370), an attack on the futility of such superstitions. Encouraged by the King, Oresme was the first to translate Aristotle into French — to be sure, from a Latin version derived from the Arabic. Slight as is the merit of this translation, since Oresme wrote Latin far better than French, the work was an innovation and thus paved the way for future students of the Stagirite. Oresme himself remarks prophetically: " Ou temps advenir pourra estre baillée par autres en françoys plus clerement et plus complectement " — a criticism which we admit and admire. The Latinism of his style, in which such words as *industrie, cure, fortitude, constance, architectonique* occur, is indicative of a new strain in the language and shows that humanism,[2] astir in Italy, is having some effect in France.

One writer, but only one, is indeed frankly humanistic. This is Jean de Montreuil (1354–1418), secretary to Charles VI and to the Dukes of Burgundy and Orleans. Although his writing was mainly Latin, he deserves mention here because of his defense

[2] On humanism, see Part II, Bk. I, Ch. I

of Jean de Meun against the attack of Christine de Pisan. He also undertook various embassies for Charles: to England, to Germany and to Italy. Later, in 1418, he fell a victim to the fury of Armagnacs because he refused to flee from Paris. What characterizes him, however, in both his life and his writings is his overt paganism. He inscribed the ten laws of Lycurgus on the portico of his house in bold defiance of the church. Thus he presents the dilemma of the Renaissance: divided between faith and reason.

This brings us back to Gerson, who admitted the need of greater enlightenment, especially as regards justice, but found the **Jean Gerson** solvent for the conflicting currents of the age in the Universal Church. Jean Le Charlier was a native of Gerson in Champagne (1363) — hence the name. Of peasant stock, he had it in him to enter the Collège de Navarre and work his way to the *doctorat en théologie* (1392). He then taught theology and became court preacher to Charles VI. In 1395 he succeeded his former teacher, Pierre d'Ailly, in the chancellorship of the University of Paris. In this rôle he became conspicuous as a reformer and a thinker, and his eloquence appeared in the great number of brilliant sermons which bear his name. But the " great schism " in the Church (1378–1449) was a source of deep sorrow to this ardent unifier; further, the courageous part he played in having the University condemn the murder of the Duke of Orleans made his position as chancellor difficult. After the Council of Constance he went into voluntary exile in Austria, and his last years were spent in meditation at Lyons. He died in 1429, when the clouds hung heavily over France.

Gerson united in his work the subtlety of scholasticism and the qualities of a brilliant but somewhat uneven orator. His masters were Saint Bernard, of whom he had the simplicity; Saint Bonaventura, whose conciliating and mystical theology was more to his liking than the more abstruse thinking of Thomas Aquinas; and Cicero, who was his model in style. His great traits are sincerity, simplicity of language, and a profound love of the people. Was not Christ a carpenter's son and he, Gerson, the son of a peasant? Thus he encouraged teaching in French and sought to make truth, as he saw it, accessible to all.

Some sixty of his sermons are extant in their French forms.

Many of these have the devices of the medieval genres. A sermon on the Immaculate Conception is a *débat* between Nature and Grace; another, on the Sins, is a *bataille des vertus et des vices*. Allegory of course is frequent: the apostles are armed with the sword of true wisdom and protected by the shield of faith, and so on. But his greatest *discours*, the *Vivat Rex*, delivered before the King, is laden with classical allusions. Yet he addresses the monarch in accents as bold and striking as Bossuet's:

> Le pauvre homme n'aura pain à manger, sinon par advanture aucun peu de seigle ou d'orge; sa pauvre femme gerra, et auront quatre ou six petits enfans au fouyer, ou au four, qui par advanture sera chauld, demanderont du pain, crieront à la rage de faim. . . . Or, devroit bien suffire cette misère . . . viendront ces paillars qui chergeront tout . . . tout sera prins et happé; et querez qui paye.

The same graphic power is seen in the famous sermon on the Passion, the *Ad Deum vadit*, delivered before the court in 1402. The picture Gerson gives of the streets of Jerusalem as Christ is led away from Pilate is so vivid that the reader has a convincing impression of being there himself.

Or taking the *Tractatus contra Romantium de Rosa*, written (in 1402) in the form of a " vision," we note the same forceful traits in Gerson's Latin style:

> Quis succendit magnam Trojam crudeliter igni et flamma? *Stultus amator.* Quis tum interire fecit plures quam centum mille Nobiles: Hectorem, Achillem, Priamum, et alios? *Fatuus amor.* Quis expulsit urbe Tarquinium Regem et ejus sobolem? *Fatuus amor.*

Gerson, somewhat differently from Christine, saw in the *Roman de la Rose* a work subversive of private and public morality; in fact, in his *Sermon contre la luxure* (1399) he had condemned the poem to be burnt. Thus to him ethical standards outweigh other considerations, and he challenges those who, like Jean de Montreuil and Pierre Col — canon of Paris — see in Jean de Meun the apostle of freedom and social betterment.

In short, the chancellor remains the representative of his time: a traditionalist with a sense of political justice and an enthusiasm for formal learning but withal a subservient son of the church. On the whole, he retarded the enlightenment of the spirit more than he aided it. At the same time, his championship of the masses and his cult of Cicero were not without significance. The fifteenth century was to see the appearance of the printing press. Not the least influence of this abortive humanism was to increase the reading public, by making new material accessible and encouraging the use of French for erudite purposes. Its great defect is that it also inaugurated *la verbocination latiale* (the abuse of Latinism), from which both prose and poetry were to suffer.

It must not be thought, however, that in the fourteenth and fifteenth centuries the University of Paris enjoyed the literary distinction it had had during the Old French period proper. To be sure, the Sorbonne, founded in 1250 for poor students in theology, continued to number important persons among its graduates, and the Collège de Navarre, its rival in importance, fulfilled as in the case of Orseme the rôle of providing scholars for the court. Both of these colleges were to maintain their hold until well into the Renaissance; while the Sorbonne, though no longer a church institution, is, of course, even today, an important part of the University. Nevertheless, as we saw above, in 1236 Henry d'Andeli bewailed the passing of the arts students in Paris and the increasing attention given to logic and dialectics. As regards education, the current of the thirteenth century was in the direction of science. Contact with the Orient, and especially with the Mohammedan world, had spread the knowledge of Aristotle's treatises on natural philosophy, and thus the " New Aristotle " became the controlling factor in educational affairs. Again it was to be part of the work of the Renaissance to dethrone this narrow interpretation of Aristotle in favor of Plato and the Aristotle of the *Poetics*. Thus, one emphasis succeeds another.

On the whole, then, the study of the classics declined in this period, while that of medicine and the law rose. This was not true of all French universities; the southern ones, among them Toulouse, continued to have a lingering regard for classical learning. But the decline was sufficient to enable Petrarch, in a letter (1367) to Pope Urban V, to deride the French " as bar-

[margin note: Education in general]

barians among whom there could be no orators or poets." The original Seven Arts had consisted of the *trivium,* that is grammar, rhetoric and dialectic; and the *quadrivium,* or arithmetic, geometry, astronomy and music. This was the program of the lesser medieval schools, upon which the university was built; either by elaborating these subjects, as for instance dialectic, or by adding others, such as law or theology. After the stimulating twelfth century, the general development was as follows: for the time being the *quadrivium* flourished in accordance with the new interest in natural philosophy — we must not forget that Roger Bacon was a student at Paris before 1240; then this influence lapsed, and the subjects of the *trivium,* originally connected with the classics or literature proper, were cultivated in relation to numerous translations from the Latin. The result was that grammar, rhetoric and dialectic became ends of learning in themselves, quite apart from the subjects to which they were related.

It was in spite of the trend of education, therefore, rather than because of it, and then only in sporadic cases, that the university formed the background for literary and artistic inspiration in the fourteenth and fifteenth centuries. When we come to consider Rabelais, we shall see how his soul rose against the kind of education we have been describing. As late even as Descartes, medieval pedantry seems to have retained its hold on education.

CHAPTER III

THE CYCLIC DRAMA AND THE FARCE OF MAITRE PATHELIN

In the thirteenth and fourteenth centuries the drama had been largely a product of the literary guilds or *puys* (see Bk. I, Ch. III). During the fifteenth century it passed into the hands of special societies known as *confréries*, and it then attained its apogee in the medieval form. As a popular genre the drama now takes the place of the epic, which continues to be written, but in prose redactions, based on the earlier *chansons* and intended more and more for the " reading " public.

The *confréries* were not what we should today call professional troupes, but companies of artisans and trades-people devoting their Sundays and holidays to acting. Weekday performances were unknown until 1597. Serious plays were of course preferred. Thus in 1443 shoemakers played the *Mystère de Saint Crispin et Saint Crispian,* and in 1512 masons and carpenters performed the *Mystère de Saint Louis.* The best known of such societies was the famous Confrérie de la Passion, mentioned as early as 1380, to which Charles VI. in 1402, gave an exclusive privilege for Paris and its environs. Here it flourished until 1548, when Parliament, unwilling to tolerate the further profanation of Holy Writ, suppressed the *mystères sacrés.* But this date also marks the purchase — by the Confrérie — of the Hôtel de Bourgogne, the most important Parisian theater during the hundred years that followed, and thus the beginning of the modern secular stage.

As applied to a dramatic performance, the word *mystère* was first used at Rouen in 1374. Henceforth it supplants the older The terms *jeu* and *miracle.* Its derivation goes back to Mystères Greek through the Latin form *misterium* (indicating a religious origin), although Lat. *ministerium* [1] (" perform-

---

[1] Compare the Spanish *auto*

ance ") was contaminated with it. Except for the *moralité*, which is a dramatized allegory, the name *mystère* came to embrace all forms of serious drama, sacred as well as secular.

About sixty *mystères* are extant today. Of these only some twenty treat Biblical subjects; the remainder deal with the lives of saints or occasionally an important secular event, such as the siege of Orleans or the fall of Troy. Beyond the central event which they celebrate, the *mystères* have no particular unity; indeed, generally their parts hang together loosely like rings upon a string; for example, the *Passion* of 1431 is composed of several distinct plays. The majority are of inordinate length, a *mystère* by the brothers Greban having some sixty-two thousand lines. Like the epics, they fall into families or cycles, according as they treat the Old Testament, the New Testament, the Acts of the Apostles, and the like. Most of the *mystères* are in eight-syllable verse, although other measures are also found and short-stanza forms, like the *triolet*, occur in the lyric passages of the text. It is only natural that, with the tendency to be encyclopedic, the author of a *mystère* should vary the tone of his composition to suit the situation he is treating; not only do realistic details abound but the serious dialogue, consisting of scholastic and moralizing quips, is frequently interrupted with interludes of fun and satire (see the *farce*). Thus, in the main, it is the drama that epitomizes the real life of the time.

In order to visualize such a dramatic performance in the fifteenth century the reader should bear in mind the background of town and city life. A town has just escaped the scourge of the Black Death and its citizens in a burst of gratitude celebrate the event by giving a play. This was the case in 1508 at Romans (Dauphiné), where it required the efforts of all the citizens and an outlay equivalent to about fifteen thousand francs to have a *mystère* performed, and even then the preparations took some ten months. Or the visit of some prince or potentate is expected and the town welcomes him with a dramatic performance. In either case, the representation would be entrusted to the *confrérie* or directly to an *acteur* (author), who would get the play ready or, if need be, write it. It took Andrieu de la Vigne five weeks to write the twenty thousand lines of his *Vie de Saint Martin*. The intention of giving a play would be announced to the town by a popular appeal, called *cry;* and when the play was ready the festivities would begin with a grand parade or *monstre* through the city streets. As the performance usually lasted several days, the plays were divided into *journées* (in place of acts), each *journée* having a prologue and an epilogue, and the entire representation concluding with a Te Deum, in which the public joined. In this last respect, at least, the liturgical character was preserved.

In preparing such a show considerable attention was given to the scenery. Since the representation took place in the open air, in the square next to the church (see Bk. I, Ch. III), or, as at Autun and Bourges, in an amphitheater seating many people, it was possible to depict practically the whole of creation. The manuscripts show that the stage was surrounded by various booths or *mansions* representing the chief places of the action. Thus a miniature of the *Passion*, as given in Valenciennes in 1547, portrays an elaborate set of structures, which represented Paradise, Nazareth, the Temple, Jerusalem, the Palace of Pilate, the House of Bishops, the Golden Gate (with the sea in front of it), the Limbo of the Fathers, and Hell. A sign or *escritel* might be attached to each booth stating what it represented. Especially graphic, of course, was the *mansion* of Hell, since this appealed strongly to the popular imagination.

As to the actors, these were recruited from various classes, particularly the guilds. The female parts were generally taken by men, whereas the rôles that amused the public most were the " devils," the " beggars " and the *sot* or fool. An important *mystère* might have as many as five hundred participants.

It follows that the *mystère* is a much confused genre. Outwardly it was a kind of pageant, with as strong an appeal to the eye as to the mind. Unity of action, in our modern or the classical sense, is of course lacking. A similar freedom exists with respect to the unities of time and place. Since the genre was popular in its aim, it is inevitable that few *mystères* can be said to rank high as literature. In England the transcending genius of Shakespeare built his theater on medieval foundations. But in France, although the tragi-comedy of the sixteenth century is really an offspring of the *miracle* and the *mystère,* the Classical drama of the seventeenth century transforms tragi-comedy by conformity to Aristotelian rule and precept. With all this we shall deal presently. Meanwhile, several *mystères* deserve notice here.

Most noteworthy of them all is the *Mystère de la Passion* by Arnoul Greban, written before 1452. Greban was a native of Le Mans, studied in Paris and later held a post at the University, while also acting as master of the choir boys of Notre-Dame. His brother, Simon, was likewise a playwright. Indeed, Marot eulogizes the pair for their " bien resonnant stile," and as late as 1547 Du Bellay speaks of them as " divins esprits." In later life they collaborated on the *Actes des Apôtres*, performed at Bourges in 1536. What distinguishes the *Passion* is the framework in which the drama is set. The action itself contains nothing to stir the modern reader; Christ, the central figure of the plot, goes willingly to his fate, and although the forces that oppose him are vividly portrayed, there is no dramatic conflict in the accepted sense of the word. On the other hand, the setting is skillfully and poetically worked out. This consists of a familiar medieval *motif:* the dispute of four virtues, Justice, Truth, Peace and Mercy, before the throne of God, as to the fate of Man. Mercy makes a strong plea for human salvation; but as Wisdom points out, this can be effected only through the sacrifice of God Himself. At the close of the drama the virtues reassemble, this time in blissful concord; Truth embraces Mercy, and Peace makes friends with Justice. As Gaston Paris observes, Arnoul has at times " des vers bien frappés, des élans poétiques, un maniement heureux du rythme "; but more often he is stilted, merely rhetorical and affected. His best passages are undoubtedly those in which he forgets his lofty theme and speaks the simple every-day speech of the common folk — and such passages on the whole are rare. In its totality the work may be compared to a Flemish painting on the same subject; it is rich in color, grotesque and often somber in detail, heart-rending in some of its naïve pathos, but diffuse in concept and execution.

Greban's play was exceedingly popular — indeed, it was imitated four times. Of these reworkings, that by Jean Michel (about 1486) — physician to the city of Angers — is the most celebrated. Michel's text passed through fifteen editions and

" La Passion " by Greban

was officially adopted by the Confrérie de la Passion, thus supplanting its own more illustrious prototype.

Two well-known *mystères* based on the lives of saints are the *Vie de Saint Martin* and the *Mystère de Saint Louis*.
Other non-Biblical Mystères The author of the former, Andrieu de la Vigne (1457–1527), was the court poet Charles VIII, in whose honor he wrote the *Vergier d'honneur*. He is also known by his *ballades, rondeaux* and *complaintes*. He was a member of the Basoche (see below) and composed his play in 1496 for the citizens of Seurre, who wished thus to honor their patron saint. In Andrieu piety and cynicism mingle; as a curtain raiser to the *mystère* he produced his *farce* of *Le Meunier*, which is one of the most licentious works of the age. The *Mystère de Saint Louis* is a tour de force by the famous Gringoire or Gringore, whose perplexing figure Hugo has revived romantically in *Notre-Dame de Paris*. We shall hear more of him presently. It is enough to note now that in this play Gringoire did not do himself justice; not only is his account of Louis IX drawn from inferior sources but the play itself is dull and platitudinous, at least to modern ears.

Far superior to the preceding are two extant secular *mystères:* the *Siège d'Orléans* and the *Destruction de Troie la grant*. The first, begun before 1439, is of unknown authorship and celebrates in dignified, patriotic accents the tragedy of Joan of Arc; in addition, it is interesting because of its reference to John Falstaff, "the worthy knight," a character whom Shakespeare was at once to ridicule and to embellish. The second, by Jacques Millet, a law-student of Orleans, composed about 1450, was intended chiefly for reading. Millet's main source was Guido delle Colonne (see above), whose Troy legend he treats in true medieval fashion, exalting the bravery of the Trojans and underscoring the perfidy of the Greeks. The use of musical interludes in this play is probably an innovation. Curious, too, is the name of *transgredie* (tragedy) which Millet gives to his work.

Dealing directly with every-day life, comedy in France was less subject than tragedy to classical influences and therefore **Types of Comedy** presents a more continuous history from the Middle Ages down to the present. This is especially true of its dominant form, the *farce*. Moreover, like tragedy, comedy owes little as regards origin to the drama or antiquity. Medieval society possessed the means to develop the comic in all its satire and irony; for this the playwright found ample provision in the licence of the lower classes and their hatred of the powerful and great. Besides, the " comic spirit " — that readiness to contrast the exaggerated and unnatural with hard common sense — is one of the inborn and abiding traits of the Gallic race.

It is customary to divide medieval comedy into *farces, sotties* and *moralités,* although the last class is more often serious than truly comic. As its name implies, the *farce* (meaning " stuffing ") is a comic interlude placed between the parts of a *mystère* in order to vary the intellectual diet of the audience at the opportune moment. In spirit it is akin to the *fabliau,* the aim being to amuse at the expense of the characters shown. Ethics is thus the weakest side of the *farce,* which is " moral " only in the French sense that it may be psychologically true to life. The *sottie,* which takes its name from the fact that the performers were *sots* or fools, serves the more definite purpose of political satire. And the *moralité,* a dramatized allegory like the well-known English *Everyman,* could be either constructively moralizing or merely cynical; its purpose, like that of the *sottie,* was often political.

The two Parisian societies that played comedy were the Basoche and the Enfants sans Souci. In other cities there were similar groups, such as Cornards at Rouen, who continue until the time of Corneille. The members of the Basoche (from the Latin *basilica*) were clerks of the Parisian law court or Parliament. They were well organized, possessed such special privileges as that of coining a kind of money (tokens), and on Shrove Tuesday held a feigned lawsuit, called *cause-grasse.* Their repertory was limited to *moralités* and farces, although the *Cry de la Basoche* (1548) is the only extant play that can be attributed to them with certainty. The *sottie* was the specialty of the Enfants or Gallants sans Souci, who as fools or *sots* paraded about in parti-colored costume with cap and bells. At the head of this company stood the Prince des Sots, and about equal in importance was La Mère Sotte, a post worthily filled by Gringoire — in the words of a contemporary:

Robert Porcin devers Auxerre
Bien scet coucher sa rithme en serre;
Mere Sotte appelé Gringoire
Est dit docteur en cest affaire.[2]

This type of organization was popular also in the provinces; in Dijon it bore the motto: *Stultorum numerus est infinitus* (" The number of fools is unlimited "), of which the implication is clear.

An excellent idea of the scope of medieval comedy is obtained from Gringoire's *Jeu du prince des sots*, produced at

Gringoire   ¯the Halles in Paris in 1512. Pierre Gringoire or Gringore (about 1475–1539) was of Norman descent, and in spite of various attempts to regard him as the Villon of the French stage, he seems to have been a thoroughly respectable member of the bourgeoisie. Of his youth we know nothing, but about 1500 he appears as the poet of the *Château de Labour*, written in the allegorical style of his day; and he helps organize a performance in honor of an archduke of Austria. The brilliant period of his life is from 1505–1512; it is then that he shines as a pamphleteer, official mouthpiece of Louis XII, popular jester and entertainer — in a word, as La Mère Sotte. We have already mentioned the *Mystère de Saint Louis;* his minor works are *Les folles Entreprises* and *Les Abus du monde*. Gringoire's forte is satire; he can be simple and incisive, sparing neither morals nor personalities. He knew what the public wanted and supplied it. Thus, Louis XII, aware of the poet's power, took pains to befriend him; and Gringoire was not slow to appreciate the royal favor, as appears from his praise of Louis in the words:

Mais il est si humain tousjours
Quand on a devers luy recours,
Jamais il n'use de vengeance.

But Francis I preferred Italian players to this popular favorite, so that in 1518 Gringoire moved to Nancy and became tournament-herald to Antoine de Lorraine. Here he found shelter for his later years and without ceasing to write saw the dawn of a new epoch break over France.

[2] Robert Porcin from Auxerre
Is skillful in compressing his verse;
Mère Sotte called Gringoire
Is acknowledged master in such matters.

To revert to the *Jeu* of 1512, this play not only shows Gringoire at his best but also is typical of medieval comedy as a whole. It consists of four parts: a *cry* to summon the people, a *sottie* to provoke them against the Pope, a *moralité* to win them to the policy of Louis — whom Julius II had shamefully betrayed — and a *farce* to satisfy their thirst for ribaldry and fun.

The *sottie* constitutes a sort of *revue* or " follies " of the burning question of the day. Sotte Commune (the People) cares little about the merits of the quarrel; her cue is

Faulte d'argent, c'est douleur non pareille.

Prince and Church are equally acceptable to her provided she does not suffer; but she exaggerates rumor and easily believes the worst; thus Mère Sotte (the Church) by her very appearance evokes Sotte Commune's enmity, whereas the Sots that surround the Prince are at least joyful and generous, like Louis himself:

Toujours gay et joyeulx
En despit de voz ennemys.

Gringoire's *moralité* is the logical sequel of his *sottie*. The tone of this part is graver, and Sotte Commune is now the French People. Previously the Church had been blamed for leaving her pacific rôle and becoming warlike. Here the poet opposes the Italianate Frenchman to the French patriot, who thinks first of his own country. The conclusion is that both the Church and the People are reproved for their respective faults.

Totally different from the preceding is the *farce, Faire et Dire*. Gringoire is as licentious, as *gaulois*, as any of the writers of this genre. Raoullet, the hero, has deferred marriage too long, and Doublette, his wife, has a reason — if not a justification — for the contemptible part she plays.

In general, Gringoire's *Jeu* is to the point, its characters are life-like and real, and the psychology is keen — anticipating not a little that of seventeenth-century comedy.

As a type, the *moralité* throve especially during the second **Other** half of the fifteenth century. Some sixty *moralités* **Comedies** are extant. These vary in manner and theme, the oldest and best being *Bien-avisé, Mal-avisé,* written at Rennes in 1439. This play enforces a general lesson: Bien-avisé arrives through Reason and Faith to Good End, whereas Mal-avisé is led by Licence and other evil traits to Bad End.

On the other hand, but few *sotties* have been preserved and these few belong mostly to the sixteenth century. Perhaps the most popular was *Monde et Abuz*, composed about 1513. Here we are shown an old and weary World, whom Abuse has put to sleep. The latter then releases Sot-corrompu (a lawyer), Sot-trompeur (a merchant), Sot-ignorant (a peasant), and Sotte-folle (a woman); together they try to make a new world after fleecing the old one. The result of course is anarchy. In the end, the old world wakes up and warns the public against utopian ideals.

None of the types of drama we have mentioned produced a masterpiece. This distinction was reserved for the medieval *farce*. The great body of *farces* (some one hundred and fifty are extant) appeared between 1440 and 1560. According to Gaston Paris, the play called *Du garçon et de l'aveugle*, given in Tournai about 1277, is in reality a *farce*, though this word does not occur until later. Farcical in nature, but termed a *bergerie*, is *Mieulx que devant*, produced during the reign of Charles VII. The characters are: Flat-Country, Long-suffering People, a shepherdess and Better-than-before. The action consists of diatribes against the miseries and devastation of France, and the play concludes with Better-than-before offering protection under Roger Bontemps, a topical character. The folk-lore theme of a husband, wife and mother-in-law, furnishes the plot of *Le Cuvier*. Here, as also in the *Farce de la Cornette* by Jean d'Abondance, the husband is the prospective victim; but in the end the wife falls into the tub — the *cuvier* — and he refuses to rescue her unless she releases him from servility, a request which in the circumstances she is only too willing to grant. This brings us to the one masterpiece mentioned above, the *Farce de Maître Pathelin*.

Michelet has said that *Pathelin* is the "epic of an age of rogues." And roguery is indeed its key-note; but the handling of the theme, its marvelous characterization and its economy of detail place it in a class by itself.

Pathelin

The plot runs as follows: Pathelin, a village lawyer, with the aid of his scheming wife, Guillemette, cheats a Draper out of a piece of cloth. To the Draper's insistent calls, Pathelin pretends to lend a deaf ear by feigning illness. The Draper, who refuses to pay his shepherd, Thibaut Aignelet, is in turn cheated by him out of one of his sheep. The matter is brought to court, and Pathelin defends the shepherd, who wins his case by assuming stupidity and replying " ba-a " to all the court's questions. But when Pathelin asks for his pay the wily shepherd continues to say " ba-a "; thus one rogue outwits the other.

. The authorship of *Pathelin* is still unknown, though the play has been recently assigned to Guillaume Alexis, author of *Le Blason de faulses amours*. It must have been written about 1469; probably in the Seine-et-Marne district, not far from Paris. The play scored a great success; it was frequently reprinted, it had two sequels, and was often quoted. Fournier has revived the play for the modern French stage.

The characters of course are types, not one of which, says Professor Holbrook, has " any sense of right. Their morality . . . is to succeed; their greatest weakness, their only absurdity, is to be outdone. Philippe de Commines sums up their ethics in the maxim: 'Ceulx qui gaignent en ont toujours l'honneur!'" Yet each is also an individual: the lawyer who craves to be arrayed like his fellow barristers " in silks and satins " (*de camelos et de camocas*), the judge who sups with a criminal fresh from the stocks, the wife who knows and fears her husband's foibles, and the numskull of a shepherd " with his bump of villainy." The irony of the situation lies in its eternal verity. It is the function of this *farce* to set in a clear light the lead which French comedy was to take, as revealed by the unsparing representation — and caricature — of life in its familiar, domestic situations. From this point of view Molière was not to depart, and the best French comedy remains a genuine descendant of its medieval prototype, in theme and often in plot.

THREE INDIVIDUALS: ANTOINE DE LA SALE, VILLON, COMMINES

A STORY-TELLER, a poet, an historian; the common feature of these writers is their individualism. Belonging to the fifteenth century, all three draw their material from the traditional channels, yet each gives to his work the imprint of a thoroughly personal reaction: La Sale in his ability to characterize several points of view, Villon in the directness of his emotion, and Commines in his unfettered sense of political fact. With them the medieval period formally closes.

The life of Antoine de La Sale was unusually rich in experience. Born in Provence in 1388 as the son of a famous *condottiere*, at **Antoine de** the age of fourteen he became page to Louis II of **La Sale** Anjou. This prince took him to Italy and Sicily, where he visited Messina and attempted to ascend Stromboli (1407). He then made several short stays at the Burgundian court and wrote a summary of Louis II's Italian expedition. In 1415 he volunteered in the bombastic crusade of the Portuguese against Morocco and was present at the capture of Ceuta. On the death of Louis he accompanied the latter's successor again to Italy. In 1425 he reappears in the official records as *viguier* (provost) of Arles. Seven years later René of Anjou praises La Sale for the service he had rendered his son as a tutor. About this time La Sale seems to have married. In 1438 we find him again in Italy, where René made him commander of Castel Capuano (Naples), while he himself took the field. But the Angevin cause did not prosper, and in 1440 La Sale is back in Provence. He now devotes himself to literature, *La Salade*, his first extant work, being of this period.

In 1448 La Sale left the service of the Angevins, to whom he had been attached for nearly half a century, and entered that of Louis of Luxemburg, Comte de Saint-Pol, who appointed him to educate his three sons. In this function he spent the next ten years at Châtelet-sur-Oise and there wrote his remaining literary works: *La Sale* in 1451; *Petit Jean de Saintré* in 1456; *Le Réconfort,* completed during a casual visit to Vendeuil-sur-Oise in the same year; and *Des anciens tournois,* finished in 1459. It is probable that the last years of his life were spent with Philip the Good, Duke of Burgundy, in Flanders. At least, the *Cent Nouvelles nouvelles* (1462) speak of him as " premier maistre d'hostel de monseigneur le duc," and one of his own manuscripts is dated from Brussels in 1461. This is also the probable date of his death.

There was room in this variegated life for the most discordant elements. Sober fact, history, legend, superstition — all have **La Sale's** their place in it and are reflected in La Sale's works. **Works** He was well-read; he had seen the art of Italy and of Flanders; and he knew human nature on a broad scale. His first work, *La Salade,* a medley, is a symbol of the man's nature. It begins with a sober disquisition on governments and rulers; then comes a list of the authors La Sale would have had his pupil read: Livy, Orosius, Suetonius and Lucan; and these are followed by examples or models for the future politician and warrior. Suddenly, then, didacticism gives place to a realistic account of the author's visit to the mountain grotto of Queen Sybilla together with a description of the Lipari Islands and the ascent of Stromboli. Lastly, there is a chronicle of the Houses of Sicily and Aragon and a chapter on heraldry. Thus, in spite of its *longueurs,* the work predicts La Sale's most striking qualities: his ability to wed the serious with the fantastic, his sense of detail, his grasp of the art of the *nouvelle* — compressed, simple and psychological.

This modern love of a dramatic situation is especially evident in the *Réconfort de Madame de Fresne,* offered to this lady on the death of her only son. The theme is illustrated by two *exempla.* The first, in which La Sale ignores historical fact, tells of the Sire du Chastel, governor of Brest, which the English Black Prince is supposed to be besieging. Chastel, hoping for relief, has signed a truce with the Prince and has given his only son as a hostage. The relief arrives but the Prince, false to his word, threatens to put the youth to the sword unless the town is

surrendered. In his despair Chastel turns to his wife, who refuses
to take the responsibility of a decision but points out to her
husband what his decision must be:

> "Nous sommes assez jeunes pour avoir encore des enfants;
> mais si vous perdez votre honneur, vous ne le recouvrerez plus."

The second *exemplum* is taken from an event in the crusade
against Morocco in which La Sale was a participant. Here, also,
a mother seeks consolation in the heroic thought that her child
died in a patriotic cause. In both instances, but particularly
in the first, La Sale shows a power of communicating emotion
and an understanding of character that are rare at this time.

His greatest work, however, is the combined novel and short-
story, *Petit Jean de Saintré.* At the court of the French King
The "Petit there lives the beautiful young widow Madame des
Jean de
Saintré" Belles Cousines. Having vowed not to remarry,
she devotes herself to the education of one of the King's pages,
Jean, eldest son of the Lord of Saintré. Jokingly at first she
introduces him to the subject of " courtly love " and the deeds
of the great lovers of the past: Lancelot, Gawain and Tristan.
Thus she plays with fire, and as the youth grows up her relationship to him assumes the outward aspect of a liaison. But
Jean, she thinks, must win fame, and so she sends him forth
against the Saracens of " Pruyse." This enforced absence,
however, has one result; namely, that on Jean's return she
tries henceforth to hold him for herself. During fifteen months
she wages a losing battle. When the break comes, as it of
course must, the Dame des Belles Cousines is in the anguish
of despair. Here begins the second part of the story. This
consists of a *nouvelle* in which the formerly virtuous lady falls
a victim to her confessor, a pleasure-loving abbé. Gay and
amiable, but tricky, the latter is a type worthy of the eighteenth
century. Jean is soon forgotten by the lady in her new lover's
embraces. Then the unforeseen happens. Jean, who had left
the court on a military expedition, suddenly returns home and
broods vengeance on the faithless pair. At first he is no match
for the abbé's superior cunning and strength. But finally, during a dinner at which the lady is present, Jean proposes that
he and his rival joust in armor. In vain does the lady try to

dissuade him from this plan; Jean insists, and the result is that the abbé is defeated and his helpless mistress is held up to the scorn of the court.

The second part of this narrative — the *nouvelle* — is superior in workmanship to the first part. M. Söderhjelm speaks of it as:

> un morceau d'art du premier ordre, empreint des meilleures qualités que la prose française ait jamais possédées: clarté vivacité, vérité, grâce, et d'un esprit supérieurement railleur.

The first part — the *roman* — for all its poetry, suffers in comparison. But how reconcile these seemingly disparate parts, with their respective qualities of idealism and cynical reality? Some critics have thought that La Sale purposely wished to satirize under the same cover the first part of his story. But a second reading will show that the contradiction lies not in the story but in life itself, of which La Sale gives a genuine picture. From the start the Dame des Belles Cousines has the two sides to her character, and the art of La Sale consists precisely in making them appear successively, in accordance with the thwarting of her first love and the triumph of the second, for even her idealism is not lacking in a sensual background. Thus depth of observation is the quality of this work, "the first," says Saintsbury, "in point of date of the long series of realistic novels for which French literature is so famous."

Little literary value can be attached to the author's *La Sale* and his *Des anciens tournois et faictz d'armes*. They are both didactic and lack originality. A poem of his, *La Journée d'onneur et de prouesse* (1459), is a frigid and wearisome allegory.

On the other hand, a word is in place on the *Quinze joyes de mariage* (date uncertain) and the *Cent Nouvelles nouvelles* **The "Quinze joyes de mariage"** (1462), since several prominent scholars attribute them to La Sale and they are among the really notable works of the period.

The first of these belongs to the rich misogynic literature of the Middle Ages, of which we had an example in the second part of the *Roman de la Rose*. It is written in a terse, forceful style, and excels by its well-drawn and realistic pictures of marital infelicity. The victim of the marriage relation is, of course, the " husband," described as " debonnaire comme le boeuff à la charue "— a type so abject in his humility that the author is forced to exclaim: " je croy que c'est cy une des grans douleurs qui soit sur terre." Each chapter of the work — and there is one for each " joy " — ends on a variation of the victim's misery. The objection to assigning the *Quinze joyes* to the authorship of La Sale is partly their early date (about 1400) and partly the fact that his imitation of the *Quinze joyes* in his own *La Sale* is dull and awkward, indicating that the forceful style of the original was after all beyond his power.

As for the *Cent Nouvelles nouvelles,* they are a revival of the *fabliau* in the Italian garb of the *novella.* The "Cent Nouvelles nouvelles" The influence here of the *Decameron* is obvious, although the themes are taken from Poggio's *Facetiae.* Again, unlike Boccaccio, the author remains aloof from his material; he relates for the mere sake of the story and he has no sympathetic interest in his characters. Thus he is extravagantly indecent, and the point of his tales lies wholly in their wit. But he is dramatic and manages the technique of narrative ably. A distinct merit of his work is its use of every-day French —" la langue alors parlée." But most of these traits make it unlikely that the collection is by Antoine de La Sale.

François de Moncorbier (or des Loges), surnamed Villon, is so romantic a character that at times he has seemed legendary. For one thing, his weatherbeaten figure has François Villon wielded a strong fascination over poets and novelists, many of whom — from Victor Hugo to Stevenson — have overdrawn his traits. As a matter of fact, life dealt more sternly with him than with most of his race. He was born (1431) at the moment when the English Duke of Bedford reigned in the Louvre and the theological faculty of Paris had just decreed that Joan of Arc deserved to be burned:

> Jehanne la bonne Lorraine
> Qu'Englois brulerent à Rouan,

as Villon sang later. Although the Montcorbier family was poor, the poet had relatives among the well-to-do; from one of these, Guillaume de Villon, chaplain of a collegiate church near the Sorbonne, Villon derived help and took his name.

He was both a Bachelor (1449) and a Master (1452) of the University. But apparently he led in larks and brawls of the Latin Quarter rather than in the classroom. Pathetically he himself said:

> He! Dieu, se j'eusse estudié
> Ou temps de ma jeunesse folle
> Et à bonnes meurs dedié,
> J'eusse maison et couche molle.
> Mais quoi! je fuioie l'escolle,
> Comme fait le mauvais enfant —

lines which show both the sincerity and the weakness of his nature.

A burlesque *roman*, written by Villon but lost, clearly refers to the events of 1451–1453, when the University had to suspend its courses because of the licence of its students. But the poet knew also the Paris of the *rive droite* and its haunts, especially the Cemetery of the Innocents and its far-famed fresco of the Dance of Death or *danse Macabré*. Occasionally he mentions the great and powerful. But generally his companions were of a different sort: irresponsible creatures like Gui Tabarie, Colin des Cayeux (Villon's particular bad angel), and the edifying galaxy of fair ladies, from " la petite Macée d'Orléans " to " la grosse Margot," not to mention his " chère Rose," who preferred to the poet:

> Quoi? une grant bourse de soie
> Pleine d'escus, parfonde et large.

Of his actual life we have only meagre facts. In 1455 he was involved in a scrape that led to the murder of a parish priest, one Philippe Sermoise. Later he figures among a band of ruffians who broke into the Collège de Navarre. Then after writing his *Petit Testament*, more accurately termed *Les Lais*, he appears in Angers and was present in 1457 at the " court " of Blois, held by Charles d'Orléans. Soon after he was arrested at Meun-sur-Loire. Pardoned by the general amnesty of Louis XI when he ascended the throne, Villon returned for a brief visit to Paris and shortly after composed his [*Grand*] *Testament*, which contains the best part of himself. In 1462 he was again locked up, this time in the Châtelet, and, upon

being released, he soon after returned to prison under sentence
to be hanged. In the face of death he then wrote his admirable
Ballade des Pendus. But Parliament relented and changed the
decree to one of banishment from Paris during ten years. Subsequently Villon disappears completely from view; we know only
that the first dated edition of his works was published in 1489.

Villon is preëminently the poet of the unfortunate. Like
Heine, to whom critics have compared him, he knew the pathos
of life and also its ironies; and in an eternal union he welded
the tender note with the shrill. He says himself " Je ris
en pleurs." Thus he stands out from amidst chivalric convention and interminable allegorizing as the one profoundly lyric
figure, sinning and sinned against, sorrowful and gay, blas-
phemous and idealistic; above all, sincere. Of all French poets,
he is probably the least rhetorical.

The total of his verse is small. It consists mainly of the *Lais*
(Mod. Fr. *legs*), or *Petit Testament,* and the [*Grand*] *Testament.*
In both works, written in stanzas of eight-syllable verse, he
has followed a medieval convention of making imaginary legacies
to one's friends and foes. Such already were the *congés* of Jean
Bodel. But into this framework Villon has breathed all that
was most vital to him, and he relieves the monotony of the
form by the dexterous introduction of wonderful *ballades* and
rondeaux. Most lovers of poetry have read, if not in the original, then in the English rendering by Rossetti, the *Ballade
des Dames du temps jadis.* The theme is immemorial, but
the refrain:

> Mais où sont les neiges d'antan?

has an allusive quality equalled only by the telling adjectives
whereby Villon visualizes each of the heroines enumerated.
So, too, the picturesque horror and the deep pathos of the
following from the *Ballade des Pendus* will live as long as
poetry is read:

> La pluye nous a buëz et lavez
> Et le soleil dessechiez et noircis;
> Pies, corbeaulx, nous ont les yeux cavez,
> Et arrachié la barbe et les sourcis.
> Jamais nul temps nous ne sommes assis;

Puis ça, puis là, comme le vent varie,
A son plaisir sans cesser nous charie,
Plus becquetez d'oiseaulx que dez à couldre.
Ne soiez donc de nostre confrairie;
Mais priez Dieu que tous nous vueille absouldre!

We are all blanched and soddened of the rain,
And eke dried up and blackened of the sun:
Ravens and corbies have our eyes out-ta'en
And plucked our beard and hair out, one by one.
Whether by night or day, rest have we none:
Now here, now there, at the wind's lustihead,
We swing and creak and rattle overhead,
No thimble dinted like our bird-pecked face.
Folk, mock us not that are forspent and dead:
The rather pray, God grant us of His grace!

JOHN PAYNE [1]

The wonder is that Villon could be so expressive and so utterly simple in his means of expression. Or take his description of Christmas, so wintry and desolate:

morte saison,
Que les loups se vivent de vent
Et qu'on se tient en sa maison,
Pour le frimas, pres du tison.

But all this is the simplicity of a great imagination, which sees a situation as it is and renders it in eternal verity. As a final example, the reader should turn to the *Ballade pour prier Nostre Dame,* where Villon immortalizes his own mother, " povrette et ancienne," praying to the Virgin in her humble unlettered faith. And if a contrast be needed, there is the sensually satiric *Contreditz de Franc-Gontier,* an answer to Philippe de Vitry's poem on the joys of rural life. For all his wanderings, Villon remained the poet of Paris, indeed of the *quartier* in which he had tasted life to the dregs. One *ballade,* beginning " Je meurs de soif aupres de la fontaine," is purely conventional, in the antithetical style so much favored by the Petrarchists of the Renaissance.

[1] From the *Poems of Master Francis Villon,* London, 1878 — a masterful translation of the poet's works.

As an historian Philippe de Commines ranks with Villehardouin and Froissart, although his style lacks the precision
Philippe of the one and the opulence of the other. Like
de Com- Froissart, he was really a Fleming, the family
mines name being Van der Clyte. He was born about
1445 near Aire, not far from Ypres. His father, of wealthy
bourgeois extraction, had been *bailli* of Ghent and then of
Flanders, but died leaving a dubious financial reputation to
cloud his name. At twenty Philip went to the Burgundian
Court and soon became attached to the Comte du Charolais
— later Duke of Burgundy — whom he followed on various
warlike expeditions.

In 1471 he was in London, negotiating in behalf of the
Burgundian Court, of which he was now a counselor and
chamberlain. He also visited Brittany and Spain for the purpose of reviving the coalition against Louis XI. In fact, however, this *secretissimorum secretarius* deftly played into the
French King's hands, for he had never liked Charles of Burgundy. Won either by the wiles of Louis or more probably by
his gold, he went over completely to his side in August, 1472,
apparently without the slightest thought of his former bene-
factor.

Louis XI, always astute, at once employed Commines on
matters worthy of his talents. Besides a liberal pension, Louis
enriched his favorite with spoils which Commines helped him to
take from others. And, when in 1473 Commines married
Hélène de Chambes, the King enlarged this lady's dowry so that
her husband became one of the richest men of France. In 1475
Commines rose to be the head of the French diplomatic service;
he then won over the English to the French cause and went
to Italy to form a league against the Pope. As long as Louis
lived Commines continued to thrive; characteristically, it was
he who as *valet de chambre* faithfully attended Louis in his
last illness.

But Fortune, against whom Commines warns his readers
in the *Mémoires*, forsook her favorite with the advent of
Charles VIII. Accused of favoring the Orleans party (Louis
XII), Commines was compelled to make restitution of his ill-
won property and to suffer imprisonment. In 1492, however,

he returned for a brief period to the royal favor, employing his great talent in successful negotiations in Italy. But the accession of Louis XII, in 1498, robbed him of all further political power. He now lived in retirement, except for various lawsuits which further reduced his revenue, and tried to forget his sorrows by writing his *Mémoires*. He died on October 18, 1511.

This *grandeur et décadence* of the man is the background and much of the substance of his writing. The *Mémoires* fall into two parts: the period of 1464–1483, and that of 1484–1498 (the Italian campaign). A born politician, Commines is exact, clear, forceful and, above all, clever. He is the first French apostle of "success," and has frequently been compared, as to point of view, with Machiavelli. Personally he was cold and calculating, and of course lacks the extraordinary culture of the great Italian. But he was far-seeing, especially in regard to England, and his insight into human motive and character is remarkable.

He claims in his work to give instruction (*enseignements*): "non point aux bestes et simples gens mais aux princes et gens de court." Practically he claims to inculcate foresight and distrust, on the part of the ruler, as regards his fellow men. Trust no one but yourself, especially not Fortune, is the moral of all his writing. His attitude toward religion is essentially that of Louis XI, though he is probably less superstitious than the latter. At the same time, he lacked the moral courage to regard religion as other than a cult, and Commines was a scrupulous observer of religious rites.

Thus the effect of his work is depressing. We miss the enthusiasm of a great purpose, the belief in the worthiness of a cause, a glint of any spirit of sacrifice and honor. The world which Commines lays bare is ignoble and corrupt — like his own soul it is tainted with an underlying falsehood. As he said, "Ceux qui gaignent ont toujours raison." But Commines is no man's fool: he observes with penetrating clarity and often justly. On the whole, his style matches his thought. In an age of bombast, he manages to be lucid and direct even if he is often digressive and never eloquent. His main value lies in his grasp of politics and the record he gives of his own age.

PART II
THE RENAISSANCE

Raphael, "School of Athens"

BOOK I

HUMANISM AND THE REFORMATION

CHAPTER I

THE INFLUENCE OF ITALY AND THE RHETORIQUEUR POETS

THE great cultural movement called the Renaissance began in Italy and swept over Europe in the course of two centuries. **The Rebirth** It came to France in the sixteenth, following the **in Italy** campaigns of Charles VIII and Louis XII on Italian soil. Renaissance means " rebirth," and the rebirth was that of humanity itself aroused to a new sense of its own powers, new opportunities and new concepts of the physical universe. For Columbus discovered a New World (1492), and Copernicus laid the foundation of the modern system of astronomy (1517), both of which events made the medieval " fixity " a dead letter, quite aside from their influence on the development of commerce and the rise of a scientific spirit. The printing-press, a German contribution, stimulated the diffusion of knowledge and the interchange of ideas on all subjects. The Reformation — to some extent a reaction — represents a rebirth of the human conscience and a return to Christian origins. How conscious the awakening was is seen in the words Rabelais addressed to his friend Tiraqueau:

> Hors de cette épaisse nuit gothique, nos yeux se sont ouverts à l'insigne flambeau du soleil.

And light and sunshine are forever associated with the period upon which we are now entering.

But the Renaissance has also another side, no less important

than those we have mentioned, in the revival of the art and lit-
Greek and erature of the ancients. Being the seat of Roman
Latin Art civilization, Italy possessed not only a large share
of the relics of antiquity but also the facilities for turning them
to account when the enlightenment came. In Italy the awakening
occurred earlier than elsewhere owing to her contact with the
East and the early development of her city life. The forerunners
were Dante, Petrarch and Boccaccio: first, because they made
Italian as well as Latin a vehicle of artistic expression; and
second, in their intuition as to the truth of ancient thought and
the beauty of classical style. In Petrarch especially, aptly
called " the first modern man," the chief features of the revival
are essentially revealed. Poet, scholar, diplomatist and patriot,
he prized Greek and Latin literature in the spirit of a discoverer,
and in his own sonnets he perfected a poetic form which other
nations besides Italy were to regard as classical. So that when
after 1400 many Greek scholars came to Italy, that country
underwent a paganization of culture which is in sharp contrast to
medieval thought as we have described it. Greek and Latin
models now became supreme, a new style of architecture arose,
academies and libraries were founded, and the modern self-
sufficient political state came into being. Above all, human
life is considered an object in itself; the problem is to gain
mastery over it, by every means possible — wealth, statecraft
and scientific inquiry — and to enjoy it for its own sake by the
cultivation of art and literature. In short, the point of view is
worldly (*mondain*) and not theological. To this attitude, based
on antiquity, we give the generic name of " humanism."

The true humanist, then, was many-sided. The unity he
sought he found in himself: in the development of his various
Humanism faculties, physical as well as spiritual — for a healthy
soul can flourish only in a healthy body; and the
cult of the body is again a point in which the period is anti-
medieval. In the beginning the great men of the Renaissance were reconcilers of opposing ideals. This was their
" universality." Petrarch's position between St. Augustine and
Vergil is essentially that of Ficino (1433–1499), the harmonizer
of Plato and Christianity, as it remains that of Erasmus (1465–
1536), scholar and reformer, and of Montaigne. Naturally, the

highest product of humanism was aristocratic, since birth and
wealth alone could provide the education and leisure needed to
win distinction. Castiglione's *Il Cortegiano*, or "Book of the
Courtier" (1528), portrays this ideal. Here the "complete
man," the *uomo di virtù*, is set forth in detail, and on this model
are built the French *honnête homme* and the English *gentleman*.
The courtier is the embodiment of the world's culture. His
loftiest expression is the prince, the state his handiwork; the rest
of humanity being but the marble out of which he — the political
artist — "should hew the form that pleased his fancy best"
(J. A. Symonds). Thus it is significant that the Renaissance
type of man is primarily undemocratic, self-centered and mundane; yet he is gracious, well-bred and high-minded. His
greatest and characteristic virtue is magnanimity. In making
Prospero say, in the *Tempest:*

"The rarer action is in virtue,"

Shakespeare has his character speak as a Renaissance gentleman
should.

In Italy, then, the Renaissance signifies a conscious cult of
the beautiful. "Art," in the classic sense of harmony and order,
Poetic Art is the commanding word. Beauty is divine; but
its recovery by mankind demands cultivation, effort,
rational endeavor. For a short period, at least, the Italians
exploited the aesthetics of every subject. Confronted with the
marvelous literatures of Athens and Rome, they sought to discover and codify the rules whereby they were produced. Plato's
Dialogues, Quintilian's *Institutes of Oratory* and Horace's *Ars
poetica* were to them so many literal guides in the art of expression, of which the *Iliad*, the *Aeneid*, the tragedies of Euripides,
Sophocles and Seneca were the startling confirmation. Lastly,
Aristotle's *Poetics*, in innumerable Italian interpretations, came
to complete the list of critical works. If the Classic Age were
to return, the Italians thought, it behooved them to "imitate"
the ancients. The fact that it is never possible to prescribe,
much less to follow logically, the means by which great literature
and art are produced seems never to have occurred to them.
In so far only as the imitation of the ancients was not an

imitation but a recreation did the men of the Renaissance produce the great works for which they are known today.

At the same time, no age ever carried further the enthusiasm
for beautiful things. The papacy of Leo X. (1513–1521) in its
artists alone equalled the splendor of the age of Phidias; and,
as for literature, the *Orlando furioso* (1516) of Ariosto is the
best illustration of what aesthetic treatment could achieve. Moreover, henceforth literary criticism is itself a branch of literature,
and for France certainly the " restraining influence " of classical
form becomes an invaluable acquisition.

The Renaissance broke upon French shores in three distinct
waves, or rather, after the first impact the French reverted to
Italian inspiration on two different occasions.

The first period is roughly coincident with the reign of Francis
I (1515–1547). This is the age of scholarly inquiry, of humanism
The Revival in general as a counter-current to the " medievalism "
in France. of the church and the university (Sorbonne). Its
Periods characteristic trait is enthusiasm born of a fresh
and vivid experience. It saw the rise of great individuals, like
Budé, Rabelais, Calvin; and it culminated in the Reformation,
a movement which France shares with Germany and England.

The second period, extending from the accession of Henry II
and covering the second half of the century, is concerned more
particularly with literature. The aesthetic theories of the Italians
now take hold of *belles lettres;* a new school of poetry, the
Pléiade, arises and inaugurates the conscious " imitation " of
the classics, while, on the other hand, bourgeois " common
sense " reasserts itself and in the person of Montaigne establishes
the boundaries of the human reason.

Finally, the third influx of the Italian spirit occurs in the
second quarter (1620-1640) of the seventeenth century. This
phase of the movement is mainly social and based on the idea
of decorum. The French salons begin, with their tendency
toward preciosity of thought and speech, under the leadership
of the Marquise de Rambouillet, herself an Italian; the rules
of the drama are worked out according to Aristotelian treatises
imported from Italy; the French Academy is founded, under
Richelieu, for the purpose of regulating the language and literature of the realm — a dictatorship which is the forerunner of
absolutism of Louis XIV.

During all this time Italy is the inspirer and guide of France. Not that other tendencies were not manifest nor that reactions did not occur. The *Précellence du langage français* (1579) by Henri Estienne is directly aimed against the supposed superiority of Italian. But such protests were rare, for the reason that Italy after all was the road to the classics, and French Classicism was to be built on ideals and models furnished by Rome and Greece. In place of the scholastic "dogma," the Renaissance established a new principle of authority in Graeco-Roman tradition. In what respects the change represents a revival and yet a French creation this and the following chapters will show.

When Francis ascended the throne, literature was in the bondage of the *rhétoriqueur* school. The prevailing literary forms **The Age of** were those of Machaut and Deschamps, and in longer **Francis I** compositions that of the *Roman de la Rose.* Except for a reaction against the tendency to Latinize (*la muse latiale*) and to be florid, these forms persist until the Pléiade.

As for the King himself, although known as the *restaurateur des bonnes lettres* he merits this title less than one would at first suspect. Married to Claude, the eldest daughter of Louis XII, not only did he continue the Italian campaigns of his predecessors — until defeated and captured at Pavia in 1525 — but his love of glory and display made him an active promoter of the revival. He was the friend and patron of great artists and sculptors: Leonardo da Vinci, Andrea del Sarto, Benvenuto Cellini and Jean Goujon. He knew personally and encouraged Castiglione: it was his secretary, Colin d'Auxerre, who first translated (1537) the *Cortegiano* into French. The Louvre (1515) and the handsome Renaissance wing of the Château de Blois testify to the encouragement Francis gave to architecture. Above all, he inaugurated, even if he did not always uphold, vital educational reforms. Under him Budé established the *Trilingue et noble Académie* (the future Collège de France), which attracted the attention of scholars the world over and mitigated the influence of the reactionary Sorbonne. Francis signed a *concordat* with the Pope which gave the former control over the French clergy. He established a royal press for the publication of Greek texts. In 1539 the royal decree of Villers-Cotterets substituted French for Latin in all legal documents. "How happy is France under such a prince," says Erasmus in a letter of 1517. Nevertheless, Francis had neither the grasp nor the force of character to lead his age or give it direction.

The first impression we thus get of the new epoch in France is of intellectual confusion. Humanism is in the air. Paris, Rouen and especially Lyons, open their gates to Italian scholars and to the influx of the new culture. The chief figures, Rabelais, Calvin, Dolet, Marguerite d'Angoulême, seek the light of classical scholarship to guide them. Translations are eagerly made from Latin, Greek and Italian. Budé writes his *Commentarii linguae graecae* (1529), a pioneer work in the field of classical learning; and Ramus advocates the study of Plato (1543). Yet literature as such (poetry and the drama) shows little, if any, fundamental change. It took time for the new ideas to become clarified sufficiently to compel artistic expression; and, then, the medieval forms were not easily dislodged. Besides, the House of Burgundy, allied to Flanders during the second half of the fifteenth century, had given to poetry the tortured and complicated imprint of Flemish art. Gothic architecture became " flamboyant," and poetry *rhétoriqueur*. With the union of Burgundy to the French crown (1482) this influence spread. Marot, the one " modern " poet of the early sixteenth century, still uses the medieval forms. Thus the *grands rhétoriqueurs* represent the decadence of the later Middle Ages. To what lengths they carried their complicated measures is seen from the *Grand et vrai art de pleine rhétorique* (1522), by Pierre Fabri.

Written for the Puy de Rouen, Fabri's work is a guidepost for the poetaster bent on winning royal or princely favor. The genres
The Grands Rhétoriqueurs treated are all lyrico-didactic: the *rondeau*, the *ballade*, the *chant royal*, and so on, to which may be added the *épître* as the form in which Lemaire and Marot were to excel. Here, at least, we see the influence of Ovid's *Heroïdes*, rendered into French (1496) by Octovien de Saint-Gelais; and poetry assumes the trappings of classical imagery. Indeed, Fabri warns against tasteless Latinizing, a common fault of the time. But he has no inkling as to the real value of ancient and Italian models, and he never refers to the epic or the drama. What the versifier or *faiseur* would draw from this work were directions about rime, figures of speech, alliteration, sound-to-

sense effects, and the like. Fabri is perhaps the first to urge the alternation of masculine and feminine endings, and he opposes the so-called lyric and epic cesuras (a reform that Lemaire was to put into effect); otherwise he merely confirms established views.

Of the *grands rhétoriqueurs*, mentioned by Fabri as exemplars of their art, Meschinot and Crétin — " le bon Crétin au vers equivoqué "— hold a prominent place.

A Breton, Jean Meschinot (1420–1491) belonged to the en-
Meschinot tourage of Anne of Brittany, later the wife of Louis XII, and wrote much occasional verse and a political allegory, the *Lunettes des princes*. Like most of his associates, unable to see reason in life, Meschinot beholds the realm of reason through spectacles. He produced a *huitain* which made equally poor sense when read in thirty-two different ways. But he ably characterized Louis as an " innocent feint, tout fourré de malice," and he enjoyed great popularity.

More representative of the school, however, is Guillaume Crétin (before 1525), who forms also the connecting link be-
Crétin tween Burgundy and France proper. Crétin rose to be historiographer of Francis I, at whose behest he put the fabulous history of his country (beginning with Troy and including the *Pseudo-Turpin*) into verse, which still slumbers in manuscript form. Marot calls him " souverain poète français," which remained the verdict of contemporaries until it seems Rabelais ridiculed him as " Raminogrobis, vieux poète français " in his *Pantagruel*. The acme of Crétin's poetizing is seen in the elegiacal lines on Bissipat, with their absurd *rime léonine:*

> O Bissipat,
> Qui eust pensé que Mort anticipast.
> Ainsi ta vie et si tost dissipast.

Still, he was not incapable of a natural, incisive note, particularly when he satirizes the clergy or pleads with his patron for money.

With Jean Lemaire de Belges we reach a poet of a distinctly higher order than his contemporaries. *Rhétoriqueur* that he is,
Jean Lemaire de Belges he has both personality and distinction. He was born (about 1473) in the Low Countries at Bavai, the Latinized form of which is Belges. For some un-

known reason Fabri fails to record his name; some think because of Lemaire's early death, variously placed between 1514 and 1520. He grew up in the household of his uncle Molinet, the historiographer of Burgundy, to whom he also owed several positions he held. Lemaire himself attributes his attachment to the muses to the persuasion of Crétin, who honored him with a visit. In 1503 he entered the service of Margaret of Austria, and passed some time on her estates at Pont-d'Ain near Lyons, in which city Italian influences were then dominant. In fact, he later visited Italy and was the first to imitate the *terza rima* in French. In 1512 he became historiographer of Louis XII. Although his *Concorde des deux langages* (1511) advocates a harmonious cooperation of France and Italy, he had long been a supporter of Louis' nationalistic policy. Thus, while Lemaire is still a long way from being a real humanist, metrical ingenuity is not his first consideration and he gives evidence of a knowledge of classical culture, especially in his prose. Taken all in all, he begins the transition in poetry which leads through Marot to the Pléiade; and his technique was apparently carefully studied by both Du Bellay and Ronsard.

His verse compositions are: the *Temple d'honneur et de vertu*, the *Couronne margueritique*, the *Epistre de l'Amant vert* and the musical *Plainte du desiré*. Titles as well as concept of these are thoroughly *rhétoriqueur*. Yet with considerable variety and firmness of expression Lemaire unites occasional humor and a vivid sense of color. Brunetière justly lauds the verses beginning:

> Un grave accent, musique larmoyable
> Est bien seant à ce jour pitoyable
> Pour parfournir nos lamentations.

But his best poetic work remains the semi-humorous *Amant vert*. This consists of a letter supposedly sent by Margaret's dead parrot from the Netherworld. The poem is gracefully turned, reminiscent in substance and style of Vergil and particularly Ovid (the *Amores* II, vi), and appropriate in tone to the matter treated. Lemaire is not profound, but he is never commonplace.

His chief work, however, is in prose. This is the ambitious *Illustrations de Gaule et singularités de Troie* (1510–1513), a curious blending of erudition, pedantry and charming naïveté;

incidentally, a mine of patriotic inspiration for the century and the source of Ronsard's *Franciade*. Lemaire's idea was to revise the Troy story, that theme so dear to the Middle Ages, in accord with more reliable authorities. With this in mind, he followed during the first book the fabulations of Annius of Viterbo connecting in typical Renaissance fashion the mythical ancestors of the human race; thus Priam is related to Noah (*le bon père Noé*) and Jupiter is identified with Osiris. In the second book, which treats of Troy proper, the model is Lorenzo Valla's prose rendering of all the *Iliad* (1502), with the reservation always that Francus (a neglected son of Hector) is to become the ancestor of the French nobility — after the fall of Ilion — and thus the progenitor of the royal houses of France and Burgundy. Besides seeing in the work a sort of Almanach de Gotha, Lemaire's contemporaries (so Brunetière suggests) were won by the *style soutenu* with its *précieux* coloring. Thus the author speaks of the " detroits d'insatiable avarice," the " rochers de cupidité effrenées," the " plage d'outrage sanguinolent "; and he makes Athena say: " Sejourne les pupilles . . . au miroir de ma speciosité celeste." Yet, such allegorizations are nothing new in French and when the occasion arises, as in depicting the idyll of Paris and Oenone, Lemaire is both simple and poetic, with touches recalling Sannazzaro, resident in France in 1501–1504. A trait which Lemaire does not share with his epoch is his scrupulous decency of expression.

It may have been Lemaire's misfortune that he was ahead of his age. As it is, he gave impetus to both literature and art (he was also a musician), and we understand why Du Bellay acclaimed him as having " illustré et les Gaules et la langue, luy donnant beaucoup de mots et manieres de parler poëtiques " (*Défense et Illustration* II, Ch. 2).

CHAPTER II

MAROT AND HIS IMMEDIATE FOLLOWERS

ELUSIVENESS has long been recognized as one of the main traits of Clément Marot. This is half his charm. He characterized himself in the following lines:

> Sur le printemps de ma jeunesse folle,
> Je ressemblois l'arondelle qui vole
> Puis ça, puis là: l'aage me conduisoit
> Sans paour ne soing, où le cueur me disoit.

And it is not only in his youth that he eludes us, but throughout his life, up to the day of his death.

Of an apparently frivolous nature, more or less a temporizer as his position of *valet de chambre* to King Francis required, Marot has not a little courage, a wonderful command of the subtler shades of language, luminous clarity and the eternal quality of wit. La Bruyère, certainly not superficial, considered him more modern than Ronsard:

> Il n'y a guère entre ce premier et nous que la différence de quelques mots.

We must not look to Marot for lyric passion or depth of sentiment. His gifts are common sense, lightness of touch and a determination to say nothing that is not said well. In so far as he thus discards the fetters of medieval pedantry he represents the Gallic side of the Renaissance.

His father, Jean Marot, had married a lady of Cahors in Provence. Here Clément was born in 1496 or 1497. When the **Marot's** boy was ten, the elder Marot, anxious to have him **Life** succeed in the "rhetorical art," took him north to France proper.

> Que j'oubliay ma langue maternelle
> Et grossement apprins la paternelle
> Langue françoyse,

136

is the poet's significant comment on this step. Thus Marot, like Monluc and Montaigne, is virtually a child of the south.

Like Villon, he was not an industrious student, and humanly he blames his instructors. Even his knowledge of Latin was defective, as the inaccuracies of his translations show. But he was an extensive reader, and his library contained such works as the Spanish *Celestina*, Boccaccio's *Fiammetta*, various books condemned by the Sorbonne, the chief Latin writers, the works of Villon and of course the *Roman de la Rose*. In verse his master was Jean Lemaire de Belges, whom he ignorantly compares to Homer. Crétin was also a youthful admiration. Characteristically, however, he regarded court life as his most important teacher:

> La court du roy, ma maistresse d'escole.

And, in fact, after a short period as a law student, when he was a member of the Basoche, Marot became page to Nicholas de Neufville, seigneur de Villeroy (1513). Henceforth he trod the uncertain path of princely favor. In 1515 he greeted the youthful Francis in his *Temple de Cupido*, with its burst of allegory but revealing also the poet's innate charm. Three years later he became secretary of Marguerite d'Angoulême, under whose influence his spiritual sympathies were broadened so as to make him at least a doubtful Protestant. His translation of the Sixth Psalm appeared in the edition of Marguerite's *Miroir de l'âme pécheresse* (1533). The *Epistre du Despourveu*, addressed to her in 1517, however, still shows the poet as a typical *rhétoriqueur*:

> Ces motz finiz, demeure mon semblant
> Triste, transy, tout terny, tout tremblant,
> Sombre, songeant, sans seure soustenance,
> Dur d'esperit, desnué d'esperance,
> Melancolic, morne, marry, musant.

And *rhétoriqueur* he remains until after 1524.

In this year he accompanied the King to Italy and was present, if not actually wounded and made a prisoner, at Pavia (1525). On his return to Paris he was arrested and confined in the Châtelet, whence, however, influential friends (among them a certain Lion Jamet) had him transferred to more comfortable surround-

ings at Chartres, where he was soon set at liberty. The charge
was that Marot had broken the ecclesiastic rules as to fasting
during Lent. However this may be, the poet whom the King
finally liberated is the real Marot, the author of the Epistle to
Bouchart, in which he denies his heresy, the famous Epistle to
Jamet containing the Fable of the Lion and the Rat, and the
Enfer — a satirical poem on his treatment in the Châtelet. All
these show Marot's vigor, directness and dramatic power, in
full play.

In 1526 Francis appointed Marot to the post left vacant by
his father's death. According to M. Lefranc, the same year marks
also the beginning of the one serious love-affair of the poet's
life. But the date is uncertain, just as it is doubtful that Anne
d'Alençon, the niece of Marguerite, inspired Marot's love — as
Lefranc also maintains. The sincerity of the poet's emotion,
however, can hardly be doubted, fleeting as it may have been;
witness the lines:

> J'ayme le cueur de m'amye
> Sa bonté et sa doulceur,
> Je·l'ayme sans infamie
> Et comme un frere la sœur.

Such frankness is matched only by the more characteristic note
which Marot strikes in the Epigram satirizing the unjust execution
of Samblançay, superintendent of finances (1527), and the delicious *Epistre au Roy pour avoir esté derobé* with its vivid character sketch of the poet's rascally valet —

> Au demourant, le meilleur filz du monde.

Marot is now famous, and to guard against pirated copies of his
works he employs Geoffroy Tory to publish his poems under the
playful title of *Adolescence Clémentine* (1532). So, too, a feeling of piety for the poetic art prompts him to reëdit Villon in
1533 and to translate several of Petrarch's sonnets. Yet the times
are fraught with danger, and a person of Marot's liberal associations is none too secure. On October 17–18, 1534, the Protestants,
goaded to action, placard the King's door with an attack on the
Mass. Hesitating before, Francis now allows Parliament to act,
and the result is that our poet is forced to flee. He goes first to

Nérac, seeking the protection of Marguerite, but very soon moves to Italy, where he finds an asylum at the court of Francis' sister-in-law, the Duchess Renée of Ferrara. Here he meets the Petrarchist Tebaldeo and Serafino dall' Aquila — whose influence he shows in several *huitains* and particularly in his revival of the *blason* (a versified catalogue of physical traits) — and he celebrates his new protectress as the embodiment of *vertu*:

> De quoy Vertu perpetuoit sa vie:
> Dont il trouvoit sa perte et son soucy
> Moins ennuyeux.

But the ornate and affected Ferrarese were not suited to one of Marot's frolicsome temper. Besides, his heretical leanings were distasteful to the Duke, Ercole d'Este, who did not share his wife's generous spirit. Marot longs for France, and thither he goes in 1537, after making a public disavowal of his " errors " with an apparently light heart. He thanks Francis officially for his return to grace in the *Eglogue au Roy soubs les noms de Pan et de Robin*, a mingling of the medieval and classical forms of the pastoral and one of the most biographically rich of Marot's works. In 1539 Francis seals the compact by presenting the poet with a house in the suburb of Saint-Germain-des-Prés.

Meanwhile, however, Marot's enemies had not been idle. Profiting by the poet's equivocal attitude, a Norman priest, François de Sagon — whom Marot had offended personally — launched against the absentee a truculent *Coup d'essai*, in which amid much other abuse occur the lines:

> Maro sans t est excellent poëte
> Mais avec t il est tout corrompu.

The quarrel that ensued is not without its interest. It marshaled the literary men of the time into two opposing camps: *rhétoriqueurs* and Marotiques; and on the latter side were Despériers, Fontaine and Mellin de- Saint-Gelais. The broadsides put forth by the opposing parties were adorned with wood-cuts of the grossest sort; thus printing joined in one of its earliest battles, and invective followed invective. As for the documents, the most noteworthy for its satire is the witty but scurrilous *Valet de Marot contre Sagon,* in which the poet hides under the name

of his servant Frippelippes.   Finally, the matter was settled to
Marot's advantage when the Confrérie des Cornards declared that
even in Rouen Sagon was considered inferior to his opponent.

The year 1538 sees Marot busy with a new edition of his works
(including the *Enfer* and a *Dialogue de deux amoureux*), which
was finally printed by both his friend Dolet and the publisher
Gryphius of Lyons. ' With the encouragement of the King and
the help of Vatable — the Biblical scholar — Marot now works
on his translation of the Psalter.   This *Saint Cancionnaire* of
thirty Psalms, whose couplets were sung according to popular
tunes on the spinet, appeared in 1541 with a dedication to Francis.
But when the Sorbonne protests against such profanation of
the Bible, the King with characteristic weakness deserts his
favorite, and Marot flees to Geneva (1542), never to see France
again.   There his Psalms were incorporated into the Protestant
liturgy and republished in more than twenty-four editions before
1550.   They were thus the greatest poetic success of the time,
though their author was not to profit by this popularity. ' After
a year's sojourn in Geneva Marot left for Chambéry and died the
following year (1544) in Turin.

His Works   In an epistle, *A un sien amy*, written shortly before
his end, he takes leave of the world and propheti-
cally voices the judgment of posterity with regard to his work:

> Ne voy tu pas, encore qu'on me voye
> Privé des biens et estats que j'avoye
> Des vieulx amys, du pays, de leur chere,
> De ceste Royne et maistresse tant chere,
> Qui m'a nourry (et si, sans rien me rendre,
> On m'ayt tollu tout ce qui se peult prendre),
> Ce neantmoins, par mont et par campaigne
> Le mien esprit me suit et m'accompaigne?
>
> . . . .
> Abandonné jamais ne m'a la Muse
>
> . . . .
> Et tant qu'ouy et nenny se dira
> Par l'univers le monde me lira.

Thus, Marot is especially a writer of *occasional verse*.
This was his forte, and in this field he remains the master.   We
may regret his lack of direction, the absence in him of any one
lofty ideal, the inability to grasp and make his own the moral

strength of Protestantism; what we cannot deny is his captivating charm and his great virtuosity.

His Epistles are his best product. Mostly written in ten-syllable verse, which he handles with great skill, they are rapid in movement, picturesque and concrete in language, and humorous, pathetic, pleading or satiric, as the poet wishes them to be. Take the detail of a passage like the following from the Epistle to Jamet:

> Trouva moyen et maniere et matiere
> D'ongles et dens, de rompre la ratiere,
> Dont maistre rat eschappe vistement,
> Puis meit à terre un genouil _gentement,
> Et en ostant son bonnet de la teste,
> A mercié mille foys la grand beste,
> Jurant le Dieu des souris et des ratz
> Qu'il luy rendroit;

and contrast it with the distinguished grace of the three-syllabled Epistle *A une Damoyselle malade:*

> Ma mignonne,
> Je vous donne
> Le bon jour;
> Le sejour
> C'est prison.
> Guerison
> Recouvrez,
> Puis ouvrez
> Votre porte,
> Et qu'on sorte
> Vistement.

Or compare the familiar tone of one of Marot's *Coqs-a-l'asne* — thus the poet designates his helter-skelter discussion of contemporary topics in epistle form:

> Tu ne sçais pas? Thunis est prinse,
> Triboulet a freres et sœurs,
> Les Angloys s'en vont bons danseurs,
> Les Allemans tiennent mesure.
> On ne preste plus à usure,
> Mais tant qu'on veut à interest.
> A propos de Perceforest,
> Lit on plus Artus et Gauvain?

with the sustained utterance of one of his Elegies:

Ton gentil cueur si haultement assis,
Ton sens discret à merveille rassis,
Ton noble port, ton maintien asseuré,
Ton chant si doulx, ton parler mesuré,
Ton propre habit, qui tant bien se conforme
Au naturel de ta tres belle forme.

Again *esprit* is the note of his epigrams, where he imitates Martial. The *rondeau* with the refrain *Au bon vieux temps* is in most anthologies, while the *ballade, De frère Lubin*, is also well known.

As for the sonnet, he did little more than introduce the genre into French and lay the foundation for the standard French type (where the tercets rime ccd eed or ede) — yet this is not unimportant in view of the popularity of the sonnet with the Pléiade.

Marot was not a successful translator, though his range included Erasmus as well as Vergil and Ovid; nor was he a striking innovator in rhythm. In both respects, his Psalms perhaps are an exception. Obviously, he was not exactly at home in the lofty religious atmosphere of Hebraic inspiration; but his renderings are singularly close at times and his arrangement of rimes is original. The translation of the Thirty-third Psalm contains the ten-line strophe which we later find in the French *ode*:

Resveillez· vous, chascun fidele,
Menez en Dieu joye orendroit.
Louange est tresseante et belle
En la bouche de l'homme droict.
  Sur la doulce harpe,
  Pendue en escharpe,
  Le Seigneur louez.
  De luz, d'espinettes
  Sainctes chansonnettes
  A son Nom jouez.

In short, it was Marot's function to deliver French poetry from *rhétoriqueur* complexities and to guide it into the highroad of clear and sensible expression. On these grounds the contempt with which Ronsard and his followers treated him is unmerited. At the same time, he utterly lacks the afflatus of the Renaissance, its great enthusiasm and its towering thoughts.

It is interesting that in such an age a poet could display "the literary characteristics of the ordinary Frenchman" (Saintsbury). This is at once his achievement and his limitation.

Of Marot's immediate successors, the so-called *Ecole marotique,* little need be said. In general, they maintain the position The Maro- outlined above. Among them are Charles Fontaine, tiques La Borderie, Eustorg de Beaulieu, Charles de Sainte-Marthe and Mellin de Saint-Gelais.

Fontaine (1515–1570?), the honest defender of the "master," was also the champion of the rights of love. An ardent discussion divided the literary circles of the years 1541–1546. In some respects a revival of the dispute launched by Jean de Meun on the nature of woman, it assumed an entirely new aspect under the influence of Neo-Platonism, recently imported from Italy and cultivated by Marguerite d'Angoulême. With her and Rabelais' share in the quarrel we shall deal presently. Fontaine's part in it was to answer a cynical attack on the fair sex by La Borderie, who in his *Amye de Court* (1541) had represented the "court lady" as a materialist. To this slur Fontaine replied with his *Contr'Amye de Court,* which, rambling and prolix as it is, contains an interesting adaptation of Plato's conception of "universal love":

> Amour partout sa bonne graine seme,
> Et de là vient que toute chose s'ayme.

Eustorg de Beaulieu (1505–1552) continued Marot's *blasons,* which had become popular, together with other forms of the Marotic type; and having reformed, morally and religiously, he published at Geneva religious songs set to his own music. Charles de Sainte-Marthe (1512–1555) at least is frank enough to say:

> Que dira l'on de me veoir si hardy
> De composer apres toy, ô Clement?

His "rather weak attempts at Platonism" have the merit of forming one of the links between Marguerite's court at Nérac and the flourishing Renaissance city of Lyons, where his poems appeared in 1540.

Thus Mellin de Saint-Gelais (1481–1558) is the only notable standard-bearer of the group. A natural son of Octovien (see above), he was highly cultured, quite a student of Italian and a rival of Marot for the credit of having introduced the sonnet into French. He was aptly called *l'Homère des vers d'album.* Mellin was a favorite at the court of Henry II, who liked his Italianate manner. *Mignardises* is the name of the formal blossoms which he culled for the court circles of his time (1547). He prepared an edition of the French translation by Colin of the *Cortegiano,* and he himself translated into French the *Sophonisba* of Trissino, a play that is important in the development of the drama. In triumphing over Mellin, Ronsard triumphs over the Marotic muse in its Italianized form. An excellent sample of Mellin's style is found in his rendering of a sonnet by Sannazzaro, also translated by the English poet Wyatt. We cite the first quatrain:

> Voyant ces monts de veue ainsi lointaine,
> Je les compare à mon long desplaisir:
> Haut est leur chef, et haut est mon desir,
> Leur pied est ferme, et ma foy est certaine.

CHAPTER III

RABELAIS AND CALVIN — THE EPICUREAN AND THE STOIC

FRANÇOIS RABELAIS and Jean Calvin are respectively the positive and negative poles of the Renaissance. Drawing alike their inspiration from the newly discovered classics, with an equal opposition to medieval pedantry, they yet represent the parting of the ways in their conflicting ideals: Rabelais the exuberant apostle of freedom, and Calvin the rigid disciplinarian. To the one, human nature appeared essentially healthy and hence trustworthy; to the other it appeared totally depraved and therefore in pressing need of renewed contact with the Deity. Thus, if personal emphasis is characteristic of this period, they are its representatives. Moreover, the principles for which they stand continue in favor through the epoch of French Classicism. As regards point of view, Molière and Racine are their descendants.

Today we think of Rabelais primarily as a humorist. We are swept along by his laughter — the expression of his prodigious vitality — and we are apt to overlook his wisdom. Does he not say in his dedication to his readers:

François Rabelais

> Vray est qu'icy peu de perfection
> Vous apprendrez, si non en cas de rire;

and quote Aristotle to the effect that

> rire est le propre de l'homme?

His contemporaries, however, knew him as a great scholar and physician, whose mirth — gross and indecent as it is — is secondary to the profounder qualities of the man. In him, if anywhere, the asceticism of the Middle Ages finds a corrective in an exultant but thoughtful expression of life; and this side of him should not be overlooked. But his genius has also another

145

characteristic aspect — strange as it may seem — in his art as
a writer. Rabelais is one of the great moulders of French prose.
This shows itself in a tremendous rush of words, overflowing the
page or concentrated into telling phrases, as the case may be,
but always with an underlying rhythm, an indication of the truly
masterful nature of the man.

It is not known exactly when he was born. The traditional
date is 1483 — the year of the birth of Luther and Raphael. This
is certainly wrong, as is the tradition that Rabelais' father
was an inn-keeper of Chinon, a town in Touraine. It is now established that his father was Antoine de Rabelais, *seigneur de
Chavigny*, a barrister of Chinon, and owner of the farm and vine-
yard of La Devinière, where François was born at a date estimated as 1494 or 1495.   Little is known of his early education
except that it was pedantically medieval and that the Thubal
Holofernes satirized in the *Gargantua* was probably his first
preceptor. He doubtless went to the Franciscan convent of La
Baumette, near Angers. In 1519 he qualified as *frère mineur* at
Fontenay-le-Comte in Poitou, and here it was that he underwent
the humanistic influences that were to shape his career.

In general, these were Greek studies, pursued in conjunction
with his brother-monk Pierre Amy under the supervision of Budé.
The two friends also discussed problems with André Tiraqueau,
later a member of the Parisian Parliament, and with Geoffroy
d'Estissac, Bishop of Maillezais. But difficulties were soon to
disrupt this learned coterie. Tiraqueau had written a pamphlet
attacking the female sex, the *De legibus conubialibus et jure
maritali* (which Rabelais later quotes in his Third Book) ; and the
controversy to which the pamphlet gave rise, as well as the fact
that the young humanists were suspected of friendliness towards
the religious reformers, led to the flight of Amy and the transfer
of Rabelais to the more lenient Benedictine order at Maillezais
(1524).

The succeeding years were crowded with events. It is uncertain how long Rabelais tarried at Maillezais but it is probable
"Gargantua   that he soon began the study of medicine at Paris
et   and of law at Bourges. In 1530, we know, he re-
Pantagruel"   ceived his baccalaureate in medicine at Montpellier,
and he then gave lectures to large audiences on the *Aphorisms*

of Hippocrates and the *Ars Medica* of Galen. By 1532 he had migrated to Lyons, and here in the thriving Renaissance city he divided his time between his profession as a physician and the editing and publication of books.

Among the latter he either wrote or merely edited a chapbook called *Les grandes et inestimables Chroniques du grand et énorme géant Gargantua*, following the general lines of an Arthurian prose-romance. Published in 1532, this work was immensely popular, more copies of it being sold in two months " than there will be Bibles in nine years "— as Rabelais himself testifies. The account which he there gives of Grangousier, Galemelle and their son Gargantua, who, transported over the sea by Merlin, takes service with King Arthur, was followed in the same year by a far superior continuation, the *Pantagruel*, and a facetious almanac, the *Pantagrueline Prognostication*. The first of these is now the Second Book of Rabelais' immortal work.

In form of a romance, the *Pantagruel* relates the origin, birth, education and adventures of the hero, interspersed with copious **Book II** references to burning questions of the day and an account of Pantagruel's sojourn in Orleans and Paris [Chs. II–XXXIII], which doubtless reflects Rabelais' own experience. Rabelais' sources were practically everything he read: from classical authors to the Italian Folengo (from whose Cingar he took the attributes of Panurge), and books of travel and science. But the background of the work rests on the romances of chivalry, of which the *Pantagruel* is a burlesque interwoven with modern instances and classical illustrations.

Thus Pantagruel, originally a salt-water demon in the *mystères*, is in part Rabelais himself, who later [Book III] apostrophizes his hero as

> le meilleur petit et grand bon homet que oncques ceign. ᷅ée.
> Toutes choses prenoit en bonne partie, tout acte inteₗ.
> bien. Jamais ne se tourmentoit, jamais ne se scandalisoit.

Book II describes the pedantic collection of the Library of St. Victor, provides an antidote to this pedantry in the admirable Letter of Gargantua to his son, aptly called " the triumphal hymn of the Renaissance," and records Pantagruel's disputations

on the study and practice of law. It then relates his meeting
with Panurge, companion and counterpart to himself, whom
Rabelais describes in terms borrowed from the account of
Marot's "valet de Gascogne." The actual plot of this Book,
however, is chiefly an attack on the Dipsodes or Thirsty, to
which Gargantua summons his son and which includes an
account of a voyage around the Cape of Good Hope to Utopia
or Cathay in India.

Rabelais was now physician to the hospital of the Pont-du-
Rhône in Lyons. But his studies could not have been exacting,
for he maintained his connection with printers and writers,
addressing a remarkable letter to Erasmus in 1532, and accepting
early in 1534 an invitation to go to Rome in the suite of Jean du
Bellay, soon to be made a cardinal. All this time, however, he
was busy on an elaboration of his romance, and soon after his
return from Rome (the close of 1534) he brought out the *Vie
inestimable du grand Gargantua, père de Pantagruel* — now
reckoned as Book I. The year 1534 was the date of the Placards
(see Ch. II), and the sneering remarks in the book on the doctors
of the Sorbonne probably made Rabelais cautious of his own
safety; at any rate, by March, 1535, he had been so long absent
from his post at the hospital that another was elected to fill his
place. In July of that year he was once more in Rome, this
time as physician to the Cardinal.

The *Gargantua*, meant to replace the earlier chap-book of this
name, is a more elaborate performance than the *Pantagruel*,
whose general lines it follows in the manner of the
enfances of some epic hero. There is a prologue
burlesquing the medieval device of the literal and figurative
meanings or *sensus*, which has led many commentators astray
in the belief that the book veils a political or religious attack.
The book proper gives a description of the young giant's birth
and education; Gargantua steals the bells of Notre-Dame and
listens to the amusing protest of Janotus de Bragmardo, a
pedant of the Sorbonne; his tutor Ponacrates initiates him into
the new learning by first demonstrating the absurdities of the
old, and so on. But the central episode of the book is the war
between Grangousier and Picrochole, ending in the foundation
of the Abbaye de Thélème.

Book I

This war, beneath which lies a family squabble of the Rabelais and their neighbors in Touraine, the Sainte-Marthes, satirizes in the guise of an attack of the cake-bakers of Lerné on the shepherds of Grandgousier the frivolous causes that may lead nations to fight — an obvious echo of the pacifistic ideals of Erasmus. The Abbaye de Thélème, a monastery without "rule," open to both sexes with the right of free entrance and departure, symbolizes Rabelais' concept of humanism. A model of Renaissance architecture, this institution has but one precept, *Fay ce que vouldras* — considering that "men who are free, well-bred, well-educated, conversant with genteel folk, have by nature an instinct and spur which impels them to virtuous actions and restrains them from vice; and this they call honor." The attitude is aristocratic: the model of the *Cortegiano* doubtless hovered before the author's mind; but the important fact is that Rabelais invokes instinct and not dogma, freedom and not restriction, for the salvation of man. If we add hereto the observation that the Thelemites never have an idle moment we get activity, or work, as the other essential condition of human happiness. These, together with Pantagruel's trait of cheerfulness even in the face of adversity, are the leading features of *Pantagruelisme* or the Rabelaisian philosophy of life.

In March, 1536, we find Rabelais once more in Paris attending a dinner to Dolet, who speaks of him on this occasion as "the glory of the healing art." Indeed, the next few years are devoted to medicine. Rabelais takes his Master's and Doctor's degrees at Montpellier; there and at Lyons he dissects a human body — an event which Dolet has celebrated in Latin verse; and but for a Latin poem on the exploits of Guillaume du Bellay, and new editions of the *Gargantua* and *Pantagruel*, he is not active in literature. Not until 1546 was the Third Book so far written as to be ready for the printer. In the meantime, Francis I had taken stringent action against the Protestant heresy. Rabelais, whose courage was tempered by common sense or, as he states, extended "jusqu'au feu exclusivement," again took his precautions. The Third Book appeared with a thoroughly patriotic preface, doubtless inspired by the fact that France was having trouble with Spain, and with a ten-year privilege from Francis calculated to prove the author's orthodoxy. Nevertheless, Rabelais found it prudent to flee to Metz, where he remained as town physician until the summer of 1547.

Thus the Third Book, which is contemporaneous with the *Querelle des femmes* (see Ch. II), is in the opinion of M. Lefranc **Book III** a document in the quarrel. Certainly Rabelais' treatment of the sex is far from flattering. Panurge, now governor of Salmigondin, has gone heavily into his revenue (*mangé son blé en herbe*), and when taken to task by Pantagruel he enters upon a rollicking but eloquent eulogy of Debt as the unifying principle of the universe. He treats this theme first in the large, under the heading of the " macrocosm," and then in the small as the " microcosm " (here choosing the Fable of the Belly and the Members for his illustration) — a procedure employed later by Pascal, who draws on this passage. Then Panurge, who had pretended to be miserable, suddenly changes his tone and proposes to marry. This leads to a tirade against divination, extending from Cicero to Cornelius Agrippa, whom Rabelais humorously calls Her Trippa. Finally, the attack on women — strong throughout the Book — reaches its climax in the mouth of Rondibilis, the physician:

> Quand je dis femme, je dis un sexe tant fragile, tant variable, tant muable, tant inconstant et imparfaict, que Nature me semble (parlant en tout honneur et reverence) s'estre esgarée de ce bon sens par lequel elle avoit creé et formé toutes choses, quand elle a basti la femme.

As a piece of " learned drollery," much of this section is indebted to borrowing from Rabelais' friend Tiraqueau, as we noted above. The upshot of the discussion is that Pantagruel, Panurge and Frère Jean decide to visit the oracle of La Dive Bouteille in Cathay and consequently equip themselves for the long voyage thither.

Once more Rabelais returns to Rome, whence he writes a series of letters (*La Sciomachie*) on the festivities held by his patron; and he seeks friends and supporters in the Cardinal de Lorraine and others. About this time (1551) he was appointed by Jean du Bellay to the vacant cure of Meudon. In 1552 he published his Fourth Book, which despite his usual precautions was condemned by the Sorbonne and forbidden by Parliament to be sold. But before the printing was complete, he had resigned the positions he held — the reason for this step is unknown — and he utterly disappeared from view. He must have died before May, 1554, the approximate date of the epigram entitled *Rabelais trépassé*. An obscure ending for one of the keenest, wisest and most genial of writers; a man admired and loved by his contemporaries, who doubtless revelled in his romance though they hardly saw in it one of the greatest works of all French literature.

The voyage to Cathay or India via the Northwest passage, planned in the Third, is carried out in the Fourth Book. The Odyssey of Pantagruel and his companions takes the **Book IV** travelers to a series of islands, in each of which some human infirmity or abuse is held up to ridicule. Thus *Procuration* is infested with the Chicanoux or Lawyers; *Tapinois* is ruled by Lent, a revolting, misshapen creature; *Papefigues* belongs to people who scorn the Pope, just as *Papimanes* are those who adore him. As elsewhere in his writings, Rabelais here mingles the real and the fanciful: the episode of Panurge's sheep [Ch. VI] and the description of the great storm at sea [Ch. XVIII] are mosaics of fact and imagination. But he also knows and uses the literature of geographical discovery, and again he amazes us with his erudition. _

A Fifth and concluding Book appeared after Rabelais' death; first in sixteen chapters, the so-called *Isle sonnante* (1562); and then as *Le cinquième et dernier livre des faits et* **Book V** *dits héroïques du bon Pantagruel* (1564). Thus its authenticity is doubtful. There are evident interpolations, the allegorizing is overdone and the tone is severe, at times strident. On the other hand, countless passages show that an outline by Rabelais himself was used. Here, in addition to the Isle sonnante where the voyagers encounter such ecclesiastical " birds " as Clergaux, Cardingaux, and Papegaut, Pantagruel and his company visit the haunts of the Chats-fourrés or Furred Lawcats and the kingdom of Dame Quintessence or Abstraction, and finally reach the priestess Babuc, who leads them to La Dive Bouteille. It is significant that the answer to Panurge's elaborate questionings, as given by the oracle, is the simple word *Trinc*. " Car Trinc," says Rabelais, " est un mot celebré et entendu de toutes nations et nous signifie: Buvez." In other words, " experience " is the solvent of life, and on this note the romance ends.

The paradox of Rabelais is the contrast between his exuberance and his unshakable sanity. He addresses his work to
drinkers, and drinking is his recurrent symbol; he
affirms that he wrote his *livre seigneurial* while
Summary
beuvant et mangeant. This is far from being derision. It is
the affirmation of life itself: the resolve to live it and the
courage to see it through. For experience alone can keep us
sound and sane; whereas speculation, abstraction, monastic rule
and abnegation — when placed in control — wreck Nature and
are its negation. Among moderns, only Goethe has this philosophic vision. As scholars have been everlastingly pointing
out, the quotations in Rabelais, the borrowings, the references
and the allusions, if put together would constitute a small
encyclopedia. The vast erudition of the Renaissance is literally there on the printed page. The wonder is that it is so
well fused, so flowing, so much a part of the common purpose.
Titanic is the suitable word: characters, events, details —
whether it be the accoutrement of Gargantua riding to Paris on his
giant mare, or the description of the storm at sea, or Panurge's
excursus on debt — everything is tributary to one large, overflowing stream of thought and expression. And the reason for
this, as Bruntière says, is that the work is a prose poem. " Elle
en a l'apparence et l'allure; elle en a l'inspiration profonde; elle
en a le charme ou le séduction du style: on pourrait dire qu'elle
en respire encore et surtout l'enthousiasme."

But having made this assertion, we should observe some distinctions. The four or five books of the *Gargantua* and *Pantagruel* are in a sense coextensive with their author's life. Hence
the repetitions and changes in point of view. This many-sided-
ness is typical of the Renaissance itself. The first two books
stand for the earlier period of humanism, when the " new enthusiasm " and the Reformation are still indistinguishable:
Grandgousier's letter to his son refers to the " free will," which,
however, must be guided by " grace." In general, a spirit of
benevolence prevails, which is indeed the keynote of the program
outlined by Gargantua for Pantagruel's direction. But with
the Third Book the tone changes and becomes aggressive — just
as patriotism is underscored, and policies and discoveries that
are French are upheld (see Book IV). Not only does Rabelais

now poke fun at the medieval spirit, he strikes at its foundations and excoriates its specific and lasting abuses: Physis and Antiphysis are represented as rival progenitors, and the offspring of the latter are all "fools and senseless people," not excepting *les demoniacles Calvins, imposteurs de Geneve*. In addition, the work as a whole betrays its medieval basis, which it cannot entirely shake off. It is humorous and grotesque, but unaesthetic. In particular, the attitude towards women — *des femmes je n'ai cure* — is not only temperamental, it is directly medieval; for all his references to Plato (and there are many), Rabelais is out of sympathy with the the Neo-Platonists and especially with Marguerite d'Angoulême. But this again is in harmony with his conviction that all doctrine, all education must be an expansion, a development, not a suppression, of Nature's gifts. Egotism, if you will, but not "ambition and self-interest," for in Rabelais being and action, nature and life are one — a thoroughly French point of view (see Introduction). It is well to remember that Rabelais was a physician.

As we have seen, he came to literature through humanism; that is, via Budé, Erasmus, Politian, Sir Thomas More, and all the rest. He is the first to represent the afflatus of the Renaissance in French, and he does so preëminently as a realist. This explains his style, which again is of a piece with himself. He does not portray impressions, for he lacks our modern subjectivity. Rabelais is never sentimental. But Panurge, Pantagruel, Frère Jean, Gargantua are as real in his pages as if we saw them ourselves — the figures are on a large scale, like the Moses of Michelangelo; that is their characteristic feature. As for words and expressions, they flow from his pen in abundance but also with precision. How he sketches each detail of the great storm; how controlled in its eloquence is the praise of Debt; and, on the other hand, how riotous are the verbs designating the rolling of Diogenes' tub! A single phrase, *Je me pers en ceste contemplation*, is the model of Pascal's *Notre imagination se perd dans cette contemplation*. As for the sources of this vocabulary, it is drawn from every conceivable source: dialects, foreign tongues, classics, contemporaries like Geoffroy Tory and Marot, even the *rhétoriqueurs* and Villon. Modern French is indebted to Rabelais for more than six hundred words.

Thus Rabelais is a giant among men; an expression of French common sense wedded to elemental, earthborn strength and humor. Jonathan Swift and Sterne are among his English followers; whereas in France, in addition to Molière, Montaigne and Anatole France have understood him best. Without Rabelais, the *Ile des Pingouins* is unthinkable.

In a sermon of 1516 Luther speaks of " Our Picards and other schismatics." Such a one was Jean Calvin, or really Cauvin,
Calvin   born at Noyon, in 1509. Compared to Rabelais, the jovial and robust son of Touraine, Calvin the Picard was high-strung, dyspeptic, solitary and disputatious. There is little doubt that he waged a continual battle with himself, his prodigious productivity being the triumph of an imperious and indomitable will over a frail physique. But like all " heroes of the spirit," forced to struggle alone, he saw life intensely but narrowly, opposition was to him anathema, and once well started his mind went forward in a groove, carving out geometrical, rectilinear figures for the administration — and as he profoundly believed, the salvation — of man. Calvin was born to be a Protestant *à outrance*. However, the Renaissance needed him, and it is part of his glory that his influence in literature is second only to what it is in theology.

Mindful of the boy's fervid nature and with an eye to the practical, Gérard Calvin directed his son's education at first towards the church. The Cathedral loomed large in the little town of Noyon, and Gérard, who was a lawyer, served as its attorney. Thus he secured for his twelve-year-old son an ecclesiastical appointment, carrying a slight income, to which was added somewhat later another — this practice being common in France at the time and requiring of the boy little more than that he should undergo the tonsure. But in 1523 Jean was sent to Paris, first to the Collège de la Marche, where Cordier gave him systematic training in classical Latin, and then, somewhat against his will, to the Collège de Montaigu with its austere rule and strict discipline in dialectics. The story that Calvin bore the nickname at school of " the Accusative " is probably a legend. It is certain that he made influential friends and that he was mentally alert and interested.

Already the Reformation was in the air. Luther's Ninety-Five

Theses against indulgences had been posted on the church door at Wittenberg in 1517, and in 1521 the Faculty of Theology in Paris had formally denounced the Lutheran " heresy." Moreover, France had her own reformers though of a milder, less radical sort. Lefèvre d'Etaples, also a Picard, early translated the Psalms, upheld the doctrine of the Word of God and justification by the faith in a Commentary on the Pauline *Epistles*, and in 1523 translated the New Testament — an act which roused the watchfulness of the Sorbonne. But whatever interest the young Calvin took in these preliminary skirmishes, we have no reason to believe that his attitude was other than humanistic: a sympathy for the benignity rather than the heterodoxy of the enlightenment. And he maintained this attitude until 1533, which thus becomes the turning point in his career.

Meanwhile, Gérard started his son in a new direction by train-ing him for the law. At Orleans, whither Calvin was sent in 1528, he won a reputation as a rising jurist, and at Bourges, one year later, he continued his legal studies under the celebrated Alciat and began the study of Greek. Both influences were soon to bear fruit. After a serious falling out with the Cathedral chapter at Noyon, Gèrard died in 1531, and, left to his own choice, Calvin settled in Paris as a devotee of the new learning, to which he now added the study of Hebrew. The result is that in 1532 he pub-lishes a Commentary on Seneca's *De Clementia*, which enrolls him under the humanistic banner. Not unlike the *Gargàntua* in one point, this work breathes the hopefulness of the early Renaissance. Its learning is unquestionable — Calvin cites one hundred and fifty-five Latin and twenty-two Greek authors — its judgments are sound and scholarly, and if it discusses the duties of a king it does so without animus, in the same spirit in which it demonstrates the weakness of Stoicism and the superiority of Christianity, which appeals to the affections and " does not forbid tears." Obviously, it is primarily the work of a scholar and not of a theologian.

But the decisive event was close at hand. In November, 1533, Calvin's friend Cop was inaugurated as rector of the University of Paris. The speech on this occasion dealt with the Beatitudes, which are interpreted as proof of the good-will of God towards man and as opposed to the teaching of the Old Testament. The position, while characteristic of Calvin, was not in itself provocative, but it was stated in phrases obviously culled from Erasmus and Luther, and the address, which is partly in Calvin's own handwriting, sought to commit the Sorbonne to the Protestant doctrine. This was more than the reactionary University could tolerate, and after a futile defense Cop was forced to flee. Calvin also fled, unfortunately leaving the incriminating papers behind, and henceforth his life is that of a wanderer and finally of an exile.

The immediate reason for Calvin's declaration of attitude is unknown. Perhaps it was merely the indiscretion of youth. At any rate, a stand had been taken — and the die was cast. Calvin thereby became the champion of the non-German side of the Reformation, though only indirectly in France through the effect of his writings; his life work was to be performed beyond her borders. For a while he merely keeps moving; he goes to Noyon, then to Angoulême, next to Nérac, the seat of Marguerite's court, then back to Paris. Twice he undergoes a short imprisonment. At last, there comes the day of the Placards (October 18, 1534), and Calvin flees to Bâle, whither Cop had preceded him.

Here, in March, 1536, Calvin published the first Latin version of his *Institution de la religion chrétienne.* The first draft was The "Insti- a small octavo of some five hundred and twenty tution" pages, intended as a "brief manual" for those whose religion was defamed in France. For Calvin was of course unaware that in subsequent revisions his work was to grow into the apologia of Protestantism in general. At the moment it behooved him to point out that his French coreligionists were not the "anarchists," not the "enemies of peace and order," such as Francis I was representing them to their German brethren. And so in a letter, which is remarkable both for its elevation and its force, prefixed to the book, Calvin reminds the King that it is the duty of the monarch to acknowledge himself the minister of God; that no kingdom can prosper that is not ruled by God's word; that sinners as the Protestants are and having nothing to boast of but God's mercy, their doctrine is yet superior to the sovereignties of this world:

Car elle n'est nostre; mais de Dieu vivant et de son Christ;
lequel le Pere a constitué Roy, pour dominer d'une mer à l'autre,
et depuis les fleuves jusques aux fins de la terre.

Calvin then attacks the clergy, the instigators of the accusation,
and refutes the charges against the Protestants, point by point.
The early Christian fathers condemn the errors of the present
Church of Rome: the celibacy of the priests, the doctrines of fasting and the " real presence," and the withholding of the sacra-
ment from the people. Finally, the King is urged to read the
exposition of religion that follows.

The letter was a courageous appeal, couched in courteous yet
trenchant language, and impeccable in its logic — given the major
premise.

Soon after the publication of the *Institution* Calvin left for
Italy to visit Renée, Duchess of Ferrara, whom we already know
as a friend of the reformers. However, by June, 1536, he is back
in France, profiting by a momentary change in Francis' attitude
towards the reformers. Farel now appealed to him to assist in the
organization of the Church of Geneva, which had recently declared its political independence. Hesitating at first, Calvin
finally goes to Geneva and lays the foundation of the repressive
policy which he was later to carry into execution. But in 1538 the
Genevans turn on the reformers, Farel and Calvin are forced to
leave, and in September of that year Calvin becomes pastor of the
small French congregation of Strassburg. Here, in comparative
poverty, he develops the marvelous energy and stoicism of character which marked the remainder of his career. With his duties as
an evangelist we are not concerned. What interests us is the form
he now gave to his great intellectual and literary treatise. In 1539
he expanded the original six chapters of the *Institution* into
seventeen, and two years later (1541) he himself translated
these into French. This edition, while not the final or most
elaborate text, is yet the standard whereby Calvin's achievement
as a thinker and a stylist is to be judged. It is now recognized
as *the* edition of the *Institution de la religion chrétienne*.

We may pass quickly over the subsequent events of his life.
During the Strassburg period he married and also joined in the
famous Colloquies, which were the last attempt to reconcile the
two forms of Christianity. In 1541 the Genevans revoked their

decree of banishment and Calvin returned to Geneva an absolute
master, having previously stipulated that discipliné should be
enforced and the power of excommunication should lie in his
hands. A new Catechism was promulgated, the strictest *Ordonnances* were drawn up, and Geneva, in the words of John Knox,
became "the most perfect school of Christ that was on earth
since the days of the Apostles." As head of the Church of Geneva
Calvin was virtually commander of the Protestant world. His
correspondence, addressed alike to great and humble, was voluminous. Certainly he spared himself neither effort nor tribu-
lation. The one blot upon his career — the burning of Servetus
at the stake — has at least the extenuating feature that it had the
approval of many contemporaries, including the mild-mannered
Melancthon, and that it was consistent with the doctrines in which
Calvin believed. At last, in 1564, Calvin succumbed to the
frailties of a body no longer able to bear the enormous burdens
that were laid upon it. As his own *Ordonnances* provided, he was
buried simply and without ostentation, like his "humbler associates in death."

As a man of the Renaissance, Calvin's point of departure is
the reconciliation of the moral life of man with antiquity; the
His Re- Bible being to Calvin what Homer and Vergil were
naissance to others: a guarantee of truth. What is more, the
Attitude Bible was the highest form of truth, the truth of
the spirit; the living, undying Word of God. This the "medieval" Church had excluded from men's view by a mass of doctrine, commentaries and practices. Thus Calvin's method does
not differ from that of any other humanist, from that of Rabelais,
for example, in being a protest in the favor of reason and a
benignant Deity against the asceticism of Rome: *Celui grand
bon piteux Dieu, lequel ne crea oncques le Caresme* (Rabelais).
Wherein Calvin differs from his great contemporary and the
bulk of humanists is his appraisal of man. Here his own
physical infirmities, the corruption of the Roman clergy, his
study of Seneca and his knowledge of the Old and New Testa-
ments, not to mention St. Augustine, united to make him consider man a weak and miserable creature, incapable by his own
efforts of doing anything good and durable. Pessimistic as this
view is, Calvin is not only a moralist (in our restricted sense

of the word), he is also and primarily a psychologist, and he analyzes human nature with an insight, a directness and a vividness that are astonishing. Thus the reactionary and Romanist Bossuet, finds elements in him to praise (see *Les Varia-tions de l'église protestante*) and Pascal, author of *Les Pensées*, ideas and even passages to imitate.

To all of this the *Institution* of 1541 bears ample and convincing testimony. With unaffected simplicity Calvin says at the beginning:

> Toute la somme de nostre saigesse, laquelle merite d'estre appellée vraie et certaine saigesse, est quasi comprinse en deux parties, à scavoir la congnoissance de Dieu, et de nousmesmes.

The sources of this knowledge lie within ourselves and in the Bible. There is no nation so barbarous, no people so savage, that **His** has not implanted in its heart the conviction that **Theology** there is a God. Even Plato — and Calvin does not hesitate to use Plato — teaches that the sovereign good of the soul is the similitude with God. But the nexus has been broken, if not entirely, by Adam's fall, whence the utter depravity of human nature [Chs. I–II]. Therefore, salvation is to be won not merely through the Law or by the performance of Works but through Faith — Faith which moves mountains and also humbles the pride of man by making him realize his own worthlessness. To be sure, Christ is the redeemer, but only because God *willed* him to be, and in the inscrutable will of the Almighty lies the fate of each of us. From this abject state we are saved, not through any merit we may possess, but through God's grace, and to be receptive for election into the Divine grace we must aspire after piety and lead holy lives [Chs. I–II]. Thus, by the rigor of his logic, Calvin avoided the pitfall of antinomy; the suspicion that his doctrine is a theory of salvation rather than a system of ethics. As for the sacraments, they are a manifestation of our Faith, a confirmation and strengthening of our submission to the Divine order. Hence, the false ones, superimposed by the Roman Church, are to be shunned [Chs. X–XVII]. "Il faut procurer leur bien," said Calvin of the people, "maulgré qu'ils en ayent."

The dramatic quality of the *Institution* is beyond cavil.

In the confrontation of Man and God, stripped of all accessories, Calvin has stated the problem of the Renaissance in its simplest form. And in submerging the former in the latter he has anticipated the absolutism of the seventeenth century: *une loi, un roi, une foi*. His logic was ethical, that of the seventeenth century, social and political. Again, the appeal to the emotions in the redemption by Faith has a parallel in the quickening of the soul through Love and Beauty of the Neo-Platonists. In fact, in Marguerite d'Angoulême the two ideals, theirs and his, are merged. Thus Calvin's references to Plato are significant. That he actually operated the break between the Renaissance and the Reformation is here beside the question, nor was this probably his intention. What impresses us is his humanistic origins.

These again manifest themselves in the French he writes and in his wealth of apt and telling quotation. The *Institution* is not **Calvin's** only the first theological treatise in French, it is **Style** also a monument of French style. Brunetière, inimical as he is to Calvin's ideas, cannot withhold his praise from the *Institution* as a literary composition. Ungrudgingly he terms it: " Le premier livre que l'on puisse appeler classique." This is due above all to its Latinity. Calvin carried over into his translation the compactness, the clearness and the precision of the Latin original. Moreover, the work is by its nature argumentative and oratorical — another approach to Classicism. But it does lack the suavity and grace of the French of a century later. Calvin is still rude, he does not temper his expressions, he calls his opponents harsh names; and it is not strange that Bossuet gave his style the epithet of *triste*. In short, while the French were to reject their "reformer," his treatise passed into the heritage of their literature and served to carry a knowledge of the French language far beyond the boundaries of France. *Habent sua fata libelli.*

CHAPTER IV

PLATONISTS AND NEO–PLATONISTS

OUR study of the Renaissance has now reached the point where we can consider the dominant philosophical idea of the age: an idea that culminates in definite form about 1540. Opposed to the Pseudo-Aristotelianism of the Middle Ages, this philosophy is known by the generic name of Platonism, since it is in the name of Plato that it finds its justification. Two currents, however, are visible: the one, dialectic or metaphysical and based more or less directly on the Plato of antiquity; and the other, literary or emotional and derived especially from the Neo-Platonism of Marsilio Ficino (Ch. I), whose works began to appear in France in 1489 and whose translation of Plato — republished there in 1533 — calls him " the god of philosophers."

The advocate of the " original " Plato in the university group was Ramus or, to give him his French name, Pierre de la Ramée. **Pierre de** His *Dialectique* (1555), which employs the Socratic **la Ramée** method of the Platonic *Dialogues*, is the earliest philosophical treatise in the French tongue. The humanists Budé and Dolet had both attempted to extract from the ancients the wisdom of which their age stood in need. In his *De studio litterarum* the former had advocated a form of French *bon sens* under the guidance of the Greeks, and it was for an alleged mistranslation of Plato that the latter had been condemned to death. But it remained for Ramus to establish the Socratic rationalism on French soil and thus to inaugurate the free discussion of philosophic questions.

By birth (1515) a Picard, like Calvin, Ramus took the arts course at the Collège de Navarre in Paris. At that time Aristotle's *Organon* was still the apostle's creed of philosophy. Ramus' own words are instructive:

161

When I came to Paris I fell into the subtleties of the sophists, and was taught the liberal arts by questions and disputes . . . never did I hear a single word on the applications of logic. . . . Having devoted three years and six months to the scholastic philosophy according to the rules of our academy. . . . I wanted to learn how I should afterward apply the knowledge I had gained at the cost of so much labor and fatigue. At last I met with Galen's work on the opinions of Hippocrates and Plato. That . . . inspired me with an ardour still greater to read all the dialogues of Plato which treat of logic.

What I loved in Plato was the method by which Socrates refutes false opinions, attempting above everything to elevate his hearers above the senses, the prejudices, and the testimony of men, in order to lead them to their own Natural Sense of Right and Liberty of Judgment. For it appeared to him insane that a philosopher should let himself be led by the opinions of the vulgar, who for the most part are false and deceitful, instead of applying himself only to facts and their true causes. . . . Perhaps Aristotle has deceived us by his authority; if so, I need not be surprised at my having studied his books without deriving profit from them, since they contain none. . . . What if all that doctrine should be false! [1]

The conviction which Ramus here voices is of a piece with the famous burlesque which Rabelais [Bk. I] places in the mouth of Janotus de Bragmardo:

Apres avoir ergoté pro et contre, fut conclud en baralipton que l'on envoiroit le plus vieux et suffisant de la faculté theologale vers Gargantua, pour lui remonstrer l'horrible inconvenient de la perte d'icelles cloches (the Bells of Notre-Dame).

In Ramus' case the reaction was so strong that in 1536, at his examination for the Master's degree, he enunciated the extravagant thesis that all of Aristotle's writings were wrong. [2] This was followed in 1543 by the *Dialecticae partitiones* — which Ramus put into French in 1555 — and the *Aristotelicae animadversiones.*

The excitement produced by this attack spread to every university in Europe. But, in spite of various reproofs and condemnations, Ramus managed to gain the support of the powerful Cardinal de Lorraine, through whose influence he advanced

---

[1] Quoted from Owen, *Skeptics of the French Renaissance*, 1893.

[2] The title of Ramus's dissertation is *Quaecumque ab Aristotele dicta essent commentitia esse.*

to a professorship at the Royal College (Collège de France), in 1551. In this capacity he busied himself with other matters besides logic: he wrote on Cicero and Quintilian and on linguistic problems generally, he is the advocate of the consonantal *j* and *v* of the alphabet (*les lettres ramistes*), and he published a Latin (1559), a Greek (1560) and a French grammar (1562). Thus he contributed not a little to the improvement of French, a movement in which Louis Meigret (the advocate of nationalism in grammar), Peletier and others took part. Without being a political Huguenot, he later in life bécame a Protestant and met with a violent death during the Massacre of St. Bartholomew, in 1572.

It was Ramus' endeavor to place the French mind on an objective basis, with the ancients as a guide; to free it from the incubus of theology as to material and of the syllogism as to method. His opposition to Aristotle was due to the perversion of the Aristotelian method by the church, just as his espousal of Plato arose from the weighing of the pros and cons of which the Platonic *Dialogues* are the eternal model. In short, his importance lies not in his conclusions, many of which are clearly false, but in the new start he gave to dialectics. By appealing to the spirit of " reason," as Socrates does in the Platonic *Dialogues*, Ramus more than anyone except Montaigne prepared the way for the dogmatism of Descartes, by whom, as we shall see, " reason " and " truth " are made identical and even the ancients are accepted only in so far as they seem rational. In this way, humanism locks arms with " rationalism," and all that is needed to make the French Classical doctrine complete is the codification of artistic rules on the basis of Aristotle's *Poetics*. This, however, belongs to a later chapter of our book. Meantime, let us bear in mind that it is Plato whom Ramus helps to enthrone in the minds of his time; and that the Platonic *Dialogues*, interpreted in the light of Neo-Platonic feeling or mysticism, constitute the background from which the middle period of the sixteenth century draws its inspiration.

When in 1549 Du Bellay refers to " ces idées, que Platon constituoit en toutes choses, aux queles ainsi qu'à une certaine **Neo-** espece imaginative, se refere tout ce qu'on peut voir," **Platonism** not only has he in mind a well-known passage of the *Symposium* (212) but he is speaking in terms which all his contemporaries understood. Plato's *ideas* or "types," of which reality was thought to be only a dim copy, belonged to the familiar topics of discussion in the court circle that surrounded Marguerite d'Angoulême — as Héroët, the chief defender of the fair sex in the famous *querelle*, had sung:

> Il me souvient luy avoir ouy dire,
> Que la beauté que nous voyons reluyre
> Es corps humains n'estoit qu'une estincelle
> De ceste-là qu'il nommait immortelle;
> Que ceste-cy, bien qu'elle fust sortie
> De la celeste et d'elle une partie
> Si toutes foys entre nous perissoit,
> Si s'augmentoit, ou s'elle decroissoit,
> Que l'aultre estoit entiere et immobile.

Héroët's verse paraphrase in 1542 of the Androgynos myth (according to Ficino's translation of the *Symposium*) was accompanied by the three cantos of the *Parfaicte Amye*, where he took the position of the *Cortegiano* and upheld the court lady against La Borderie. Thus the ideal lover would find in his lady an embodiment of *vertù*, which in turn was a reflection of the celestial type; and the human soul retaining a remembrance of the latter would strive for it in a spiritual love far above the love springing from senses.

This central idea of the object of love in the " sovereign good " (*le souverain bien*), intuitively remembered and therefore passionately desired, is the crux of the entire Neo-Platonic system. During the Renaissance it occurs in innumerable forms, notable among which is Spenser's rendering in immortal English:

> The noble hart that harbours vertuous thought,
> And is with childe of glorious great intent,
> Can never rest, untill it forth have brought
> Th' eternal brood of glorie excellent.

Socially the idea falls in with the new aristocratic ideal of the times, with its fresh category of worldly virtues, such as *virtù*, glory, fame, magnanimity, foresight, and the like. But the system is also related to, and thus easily confused with, the *amour courtois* of the Middle Ages, the Petrarchism of the sonnets to Laura, and the Christian concept of charity found in the

Pauline *Epistles*. As we noted before (Ch. I), the Renaissance is rife with the spirit of identification. Its impulse is constantly towards unity of the works of the mind. Ficino's *De Triplici Vita* (1489) is one of the earliest examples of the identifying process, whereas Corneille's Christian drama *Polyeucte* (1642) is one of the latest. Both works are Neo-Platonic. That is, Neo-Platonism is characteristic of the Renaissance in general; its influence is found in such divergent writers as Rabelais and Calvin, and it is the inspiration of much of the poetry of the Pléiade. Its main difference from Platonism proper is that it is a "system," which true Platonism never is. In a much confused form it afforded solace to the agonized soul of Marguerite d'Angoulême.

Marguerite was born in 1492 and died in 1549. Neither of her marriages was happy: the first with Charles d'Alençon and the **Marguerite,** second with Henri d'Albret, King of Navarre, were **Sister of** due to a state policy in which Marguerite was **Francis I** guided by the interests of her brother Francis I. Indeed, it was upon him that she lavished the affection which was part of her ardent nature.

> Oh, qu'il sera le bien venu
> Celuy qui, frappant à ma porte
> Dira: Le roy est revenu
> En sa santé tres bonne et forte. . . .

she wrote when Francis lay seriously ill. Her chief works are: the evangelical verses known as the *Miroir de l'âme pécheresse* (1531) ; the *Marguerites de la Marguerite des Princesses* (1547), a collection of her lighter verse; the *Prisons*, a long composition in five thousand ten-syllable lines on the errors of mankind; and the *Heptaméron* (not published until 1558), an imitation of Boccaccio.

Opinions as to the value of this output vary. M. Lanson, on the whole Marguerite's apologist, thinks that in spite of many admirable traits she lacks "métier" and art. Critics are agreed however, that the *Heptaméron* is her best work.

The keynote of her poetry is disquietude. Amid the welter of conflicting ideals Marguerite finds none to which she can give undivided adherence, and so she yields to the sentiment of

the unattainable, towards which the Neo-Platonism of her neophytes directs her. Thought leads to madness, and faith alone
can save. Thus, the *Prisons* mingle the allegory of the *Rose*,
the gallantry of Alain Chartier, the somberness of Dante and the
aspirations of the Protestant. Marguerite's thought and style
are a mixture of the medieval and the modern, of the religious
and the mundane. She delves into mathematical formulae and
mystical symbols but with no definite purpose except to fortify
her own ungratified longing.

To all this the prose of the *Heptaméron* offers a partial corrective, for the tales of which it is composed have a practical
lesson to teach. In reality *exempla*, they exemplify — to repeat
Brunetière's jest —"les jeux de l'amour et du hasard." The
Decameron is perhaps too obviously their model, just as the dialogues which accompany the narrative are often severely Neo-
Platonic. Yet outspoken as the tales are, what dignifies them
is an element of real tragedy, and Marguerite affirms that they
were drawn from actual life.

The background is Notre-Dame de Servance in the Pyrenees,
whither the company of " bathers " has retired after a summer at
Cauterets. Some of the narrators are probably contemporaries
in disguise: Oisile may be Louise of Savoy; Parlamente, who
gives the definition of the *parfait amant*, Marguerite herself, and
Hircan her second husband; whereas Dagoucin represents the
ideal Platonist, and Saffredent and Simontault the ironical
esprit gaulois. Thus we obtain a vivid impression of a sixteenth-
century salon, so different from the *précieux* product of the
seventeenth century.

As for the tales themselves, one of the most typical is *Les Amans
en religion* (XIX). Here a knight and a lady being unable to
marry decide each to enter a monastic order. Thus they give each
other " le saint baiser de dilection " and realize their love in God.
" Si est-ce," says Geburon, " que Dieu a plusieurs moyens de nous
tirer à luy, dont les commencemens semblent estre maulvais,
mais la fin est bonne." And Parlamente subjoins the general
maxim that never did a man love God perfectly without first loving some creature in this world. Another tale (XXV) philosophizes on a gallant adventure in the life of Francis I. Again, in
Rolandine et le bastard (XXI) the sentiments of woman, " fondés

en Dieu," are opposed to those of man, "fondés sur le plaisir." Marguerite does not hesitate to mingle *exempla* of a lofty type with descriptions of every sort of infidelity, for the paradox of idealism and licentiousness is singularly hers.

Fortunately, her prose is more fluent than her verse. She can be serious or sprightly, sentimental or ironic, as the occasion requires. Doubtless the model of the *Decameron* here helped to clarify her style. Unlike Boccaccio's work, the *Heptaméron* is incomplete.

To the free-thinker Bonaventure Despériers (about 1510–1544), Marguerite entrusted the translation of Plato's *Lysis*. **Bonaventure** Despériers was her secretary and had published, **Despériers** as early as 1537, a *Cymbalum Mundi*, where in four dialogues he gently upbraids the "resveurs theologales." But Parliament understood the satiric vein of this composition and ordered the book to be burned. A better fate awaited the author's *Nouvelles recréations et joyeux devis*. Inspired by an easy-going sensualism, Despériers here refines on Rabelais and accepts the philosophy to enjoy life aesthetically. The book was very popular, going through seventeen editions before 1625. The tales, of which there are one hundred and twenty-nine, remind one of Sacchetti. But Despériers depicts admirably, often with a few strokes; and as a romantic ironist he has few equals, even in French. He is thus the most "modern" story-writer of the epoch. He died by his own hand, apparently in order to escape persecution.

It is rare in French history to find another city rivaling Paris as a center of culture. Such, however, was the rôle of Lyons **The Ecole** towards the middle of the sixteenth century. While **de Lyon** it was the tendency of Marguerite's group to enforce the desire for a chosen and lofty literary art, and although it transmitted this desire to the poets of the next generation — the Pléiade — it was especially through the influence of Lyons that the idea was to be brought to a head. The Ecole de Lyon being close to Italy emphasized the value of Italian models and especially the example of the Petrarchists in the treatment of love. Both of these traits are found in the Pléiade.

In Maurice Scève (exact dates unknown), the chief of the Lyonese school, the Neo-Platonist and the Petrarchist combine. In

1533 he won notoriety by his supposed discovery of the grave of
Laura.   In 1544 he published under the title *Délie, objet de plus*
Maurice   *haute vertu,* a collection of four hundred and forty-
Scève   nine *dixains* in honor of his lady, probably Pernette
de Guillet. The arrangement of the volume is symbolic. *Délie* is an
anagram for l'Idée, the prototype of the numerous Delias, Ideas,
and Diellas that occur later on in English.   The poems themselves
are printed in groups of nine, separated by various figures and em-
blems.   Scève follows closely the conceits of the Italian strambot-
tists, particularly Tebaldeo and Serafino dall'Aquila.   But like
the earlier Italian lyrists, he also likes to fill his works with
scientific arguments.   This last trait is characteristic of his
Microcosme, a long poem in Alexandrines, which was not printed
until 1562.

Scève's Platonizing appears in such a *dixain* as this (306):

> Ta beauté fut premier et doulx Tyran
> Qui m'arresta tres violentement;
> Ta grace apres, peu à peu m'attirant,
> M'endormit tout en son enchantement:
> Dont assoupi d'un tel contentement
> N'avois de toy, ni de moy connoissance.
> Mais ta vertu, par sa haute puissance,
> M'esveilla lors du sommeil paresseux,
> Auquel Amour, par aveugle ignorance,
> M'espouvantoit de maint songe angoisseux.

On the other hand, as Brunetière observes, the adaptation of
the Petrarchizing spirit to the circumstance of Scève's own life is
best seen in the following:

> Sur le printemps, que les aloses montent,
> Ma dame et moy sautons dans le bateau,
> Où les pescheurs entre eux leur prise comptent,
> Et une en prend: que sentant l'air nouveau,
> Tant se debat, qu'en fin se sauve en l'eau,
> Dont ma maistresse et pleure et se tourmente.
> — Cesse, luy dis-je, il faut que je lamente
> L'heur du poisson que n'as su attraper,
> Car il est hors de prison vehemente,
> Où de tes mains ne peux onc eschapper.

It is only natural that Du Bellay should have hailed the author
of these " alembicated " verses as one who

> Premier emporte le prix
> Auquel tous vont aspirant.

Louise Labé (1526-1566) and Pernette de Guillet (*Petites et louables jeunesses*, 1545) belong to the emancipated women of

Louise Labé

Lyons. While they were hardly types of the aristocratic *cortegiana, onesta* so much lauded in Italy, we need not go to the extreme of certain of their contemporaries who called them by a harsher name. Of Pernette we know little beyond the fact that Scève was in love with her and that Du Bellay, in the *Défense et Illustration*, deprecates her lyrics. Louise Labé, however, won lasting fame under the name of La Belle Cordière, a title due to her being the wife of Ennemond Perrin, the Rope-maker.

Her work consists of three elegies, twenty-four sonnets (one of which is in Italian) and the prose *Débat de folie et d'amour*, based on classical myth. In all these compositions Louise combines Italianate conceits with accents of real passion and poetic inspiration. The poet Olivier de Magny addressed her in no uncertain terms, and after passing in review the " unfortunate " heroines of antiquity she herself sums up the experience of life in the following melancholy reflection:

> Comme ce pale essaim de malheureuses Ombres,
> Du Styx au triple couvrant les rives sombres,
> Au penser doux-amer de son ancien martyre
> S'agite tristement et doucement soupire!
> Ainsi par un beau soir, au milieu de la pleine,
> La tige que le vent bat d'une tiede haleine.

Obviously the Ecole de Lyon had one of its most inspired singers in Louise Labé.

In conclusion let us note that one member of the Pléiade, Pontus de Tyard, was spiritually akin to the Lyons group. Translator of the far-famed *Dialoghi d'amore* of Leo Hebraeus and author of *Les Erreurs amoureuses* (1549) — a sonnet collection showing the influence of Scève — he defined the " poetic madness " as:

> l'unique escalier par lequel l'ame puisse trouver le chemin qui la conduise à la source de son souverain bien et felicité divine.

The last point is also brought out in the *Art poétique* of Thomas Sebillet published at Lyons in 1548. But of this more in the next chapter.

BOOK II

LITERARY THEORY AND THE RETURN OF THE BOURGEOIS IDEAL

CHAPTER I

THE DOCTRINE OF IMITATION
THE PLEIADE

THE idea of formal perfection or *virtù*, mentioned above, when applied to literature results towards 1550 in the doctrine of Imitation. Incidentally, literature is recognized as a branch of art. In both respects Du Bellay's *Défense et Illustration de la langue française* (1549) is important. It is not the originality of Du Bellay, nor his critical depth, nor indeed his style — for the work gives every evidence of being hastily written — but mainly the timeliness and the enthusiasm of the work that place it among the great critical documents of Europe. What Dante's *De Vulgari Eloquentia* is for Italy, that and even more the *Défense et Illustration* is for France.

The Greeks had no specific name for "creative literature." To them all art was primarily an " imitation." But they thought of imitation as itself experimental and creative. For while Art imitates Nature, it appeared to the Greeks to go a step further in seeking out and realizing Nature's " unfulfilled intentions " — to use Aristotle's phrase. That is, the Greek view was that Art employs the particulars furnished by Nature to arrive at the unity, the ideal or the universal truth that lies behind Nature. Thus Nature produces blindly, the artist consciously. Nature gropes, the artist discerns. In this way Art aims at a higher reality than that given by Nature, and the poet or genius is the person with the insight and control to set this higher reality before men's eyes. Fundamentally, then, the classicism of the ancients rests on the inner or psychological apperception of the universal in a world that presents itself to the senses as constantly changing; and the balance, the repose, the completion (all important elements) in Greek art are the outcome of this fact.

As far as the terms go, this was also the standpoint of the neoclassicism of the Renaissance. But between the world of Nature and themselves the men of the Renaissance saw the perfection of the finished products of antiquity, and this gave them a different point of departure. Thus their approach was through preëxisting literature, and they began by imitating the ancient "forms." Critically viewed, Renaissance literature has two marked features: matters of form outweigh matters of content, and for a long time there is considerable dualism of thought and expression. In the lyric this attention to external form served to curb an exuberant and often violent emotion, and hence did not fail to produce very happy and beautiful results, especially in the sonnet, which has been aptly called *le précieux condensateur de l'émotion lyrique.* Other genres — the epic and the drama — were not so fortunate, for the desire of Ronsard in his *Franciade* to be Vergilian and of Jodelle in his dramas to be Senecan accounts largely for the sterility of these works. Not before the second part of the seventeenth century did French critics understand that the ancients were great, not because they were *ancient,* but because they were true — as Boileau maintained, *rien n'est beau que le vrai.* Thus the dualism of form and matter is finally overcome in the works of the great French Classicists, and the seventeenth century is the Classical Age in France.

In 1549 Du Bellay ostensibly aimed his treatise at the *Art poétique* of Sebillet (see above), which despite references to classical models moves in the atmosphere of Marotic experimentation and lacks the force of a definite purpose. Du Bellay supplies this deficiency by his patriotic appeal throughout to the resources of French as capable of the best and loftiest expression. Mistaken are they who would consider the French as barbarians; it all depends on *la fantasie des hommes* and the conscious effort towards *quelque plus haut et meilleur stile* such as the ancients had evolved. As the Romans imitated the Greeks, so the French must imitate both Greeks and Romans.

The " Défense et Illustration "

se transformant en eux, les devorant; et apres les avoir bien
digerez, les convertissant en sang et nourriture (I, 6).

Thus it is not a question of translation but of innutrition; the
recovery of the methods of the ancients and their absorption
into French. The idea is not new, but Du Bellay expounds it
with freshness and vigor. Of Aristotle he seems as yet to know
only the name, but he quotes Horace, Quintilian and Vida
(1527), whose adoration of Vergil the neo-classicists shared as a
group, and he pilfers with liberal hands the ideas of Sperone
Speroni (1534) on language.

The two parts of the treatise are divided into twelve chapters each. The first part, or *Défense* proper, presents arguments
on behalf of the language; the neglect it has suffered artistically even from those who like Marot should have known better,
the folly of Frenchmen trying to write literary Latin, and the un-
tried possibilities of French itself. Here, then, Du Bellay vindicates his position and holds out promises for the future. In the
second part or *Illustration* he outlines his specific reforms. He
would not leave the two pillars of artistic speech, the poet and
the orator, to the guidance of Platonic ideals; definite instructions are necessary. Talent (*le naturel*) alone is not sufficient,
the artist needs also knowledge (*la doctrine*), and knowledge
can be won only through work. The charge of excessive erudition, later brought against the Pléiade, here finds its explanation. Thus Du Bellay summons the poet to " finger by day
and by night " his ancient authors and to renounce once for all
the literary genres of the Middle Ages. *Epiceries* they are,
unworthy of the temple of fame. The one exception he would
make is the *épître* — a Middle French genre — provided it is
elegiacal like the *Epistles* of Ovid or sententious like those of
Horace. His emphasis, however, is placed on the ode and the
sonnet for the expression of emotion, and on the epigram and
satire for the display of wit; and he hopes for the restitution
of ancient tragedy and comedy. The eclogue, already employed
by Marot, is to be modeled on the practice of Vergil, Theocritus
and Sannazzaro. An entire chapter (V) is devoted to the epic.
The models for the epic are of course the *Iliad* and the *Aeneid*,
but the French poet is to rework such Old French works as the
Tristan and the *Lancelot* over into these classical forms. or

else like Jean Lemaire to exploit chronicle sources for the purpose. The real spirit of the epic, its *raison d'être* in national feeling, utterly escapes Du Bellay (as well as most of his contemporaries), and he again appeals to the poet's quest of fame:

> la gloire, seule eschelle par les degrés de laquelle les mortels d'un pied leger montent au ciel et se font compagnons des dieux.

In all this we see Du Bellay's scorn of the *populaire ignorant*. The school which the manifesto inaugurates is aristocratic. Varied meters, classical reminiscences and metaphors, rich rime are to be the rule — though quantitative verse is not directly advised. Above all, poetic speech is to be representatively French, and the patriotism of the appeal is evident. Archaic terms, dialect words, expressions drawn from the trades and professions, are to be deliberately chosen, especially when justified by classical prototypes. The names of ancient heroes are to be Gallicized: thus Thésée, Achille, Horace. And the enriching process is to include the use of the epithet for the proper name (antonomasia), such as *Père foudroyant*, as well as neologisms, like *jour-apporte* and *aile-pied*, according to ancient models. Syntactically, Du Bellay recommends the use of the adjective and the infinitive as nouns, the extension of the definite article and the employment of gerundive constructions. Carried to excess, many of these changes were later to be attacked by Malherbe (see Ch. IV). For the most part, however, Du Bellay proceeded in accord with the genius of the language, and his reforms — especially at the hands of such a master as Ronsard — led to considerable gain in poetic expression. For the time being, French certainly acquired a richness and exuberance comparable to Elizabethan English.

Thus the *Défense et Illustration* brought a new and vitalizing spirit into French literature. It made the man of letters a leader and inspirer of his people. It put literature frankly on a foundation that is ultimately aesthetic. And while the treatise is shamefully weak in its estimate of the French literary past, it was the source of creative impulses that were long to survive the particular theory Du Bellay advocated.

An insignificant protest, the *Quintil-Horatian* by Barthélemy Aneau, on behalf of the old school, was unable to mar the rapid triumph of Du Bellay's ideas. The fact is, the position of the *Défense* was also that of his friends and collaborators, **Other Poetic Arts** Jacques Peletier and particularly Pierre de Ronsard. Peletier's *Art poétique* is in some respects more mature than the *Défense*, but it did not appear until 1555, and by that time the new school was in full blast. Peletier's idea that French poetry must be daring and aristocratic is again typical of the poets of the Pléiade, who differed from the later Classicists mainly by their "unsociable and scornful" attitude of mind. Yet Ronsard's chief critical document, the *Abrégé de l'art poétique* (1565), while it upholds the doctrine of inspiration elaborated in his earlier *Ode à Michel de l'Hospital*, dwells on the factor of "conscious invention" upon which the successful imitation of the ancients would depend. In this advocacy of a rational control of the imagination he voices the growing tendency in favor of poetic rules. Important, too, is his choice of the Alexandrine as the future heroic verse of the French, a dictum which makes one regret that he rejected this meter for the *Franciade*. The *Art poétique français* (1605) by Vauquelin de la Fresnaye represents the extreme of Pléiade theorizing and is important — if at all — because it gives expression to the late-comers of the school. The era of "rules" was now at hand; Vauquelin spoke of his own poem as "cet art de règles recherchées." He was a lavish borrower from the Italian critic Minturno (1564). His idea that the poet should choose scriptural themes:

> Si les Grecs, comme vous, Chrestiens eussent escrit,
> Ils eussent les hauts faits chantés de Iesus Christ,

was derived from Minturno[1] and found favor with the Protestants, who combined the two antiquities: the classics and the Bible.

The crux of Italian criticism during the sixteenth century, the doctrine of verisimilitude or *vraisemblance* as deduced from the study of Aristotle's *Poetics*, does not essentially affect the French until the seventeenth century. Aristotelianism is, so to speak, in the air. Jodelle (1552) has an allusion to the unity of time in his tragedy, *Cléopâtre;* Jean de la Taille's *Art de la*

---

[1] This is the beginning in art of *le merveilleux chrétien.*

tragédie formulates the three unities in imitation of Castelvetro (1570); Vauquelin voices Minturno's views on the subject; and Scaliger, whose Poetics were published at Lyons in 1561, calls Aristotle *imperator noster, omnium bonarum artium dictator perpetuus*, thus inaugurating the Stagirite's hold on criticism for centuries. But, as we shall see, Aristotle does not become a factor in French literary composition until the generation of 1630, when rationalism and taste together — *le bon sens et le bon goût* — force the French to turn to Aristotle for a practical theory of dramatic composition (see Bk. III, Ch. III). In general, the French sixteenth century worshiped Plato rather than Aristotle; as for literary precept, the influence of Horace and of Vida remained paramount.

The group of enthusiasts who put the new theories into practice — and the *Défense* shows how deliberate the attempt was — are today known as the Pléiade. The restrictive nature of this term, however, should not lead us to think that the new school was limited to seven stars in the poetic firmament. To be sure, Ronsard, by reason of his genius the leader of the movement, twice celebrates seven names: in 1553, when he mentions Baïf, Du Bellay, Jodelle, Tyard, and along with himself, Des Autels and La Péruse; and again in 1555, when Belleau and Peletier replace the last two. Only in 1556, when Belleau published the *Odes d'Anacréon*, does Ronsard welcome him as "the seventh of the Pléiade." His favorite term for the group of his associates and followers was *la brigade*. "Ce fut une belle guerre," said Pasquier, "que l'on entreprit lors contre l'ignorance." And to both Ronsard and Du Bellay the proselyting character of the enterprise stood uppermost. In reality, many besides those mentioned coöperated to further the cause. Among these were the humanists Daurat and Lazare de Baïf, who contributed towards the inception of the movement, Marc-Antoine de Muret, the commentator of Ronsard's works, Olivier de Magny, known for his skill as a Petrarchist, and so on. So that *brigade* was the general and appropriate name. On the other hand, Ronsard's enemies fixed derisively on the name Pléiade; it was further given currency through use by the poet's biographer, Binet; and from Binet it has passed into literary history as the name of the school.

La Pléiade

In this larger sense, then, the poets of the Pléiade may be considered in three successive groups: (1) The Pléiade proper or the intimate associates of Ronsard, altogether the nine he mentions. Of these Du Bellay alone merits a place by the side of the master, as his equal and counterpart. Jodelle, the only Parisian of the group, is also the only one who has left a name for himself in the drama, a genre which he cultivated in imitation of Seneca and the Romans (see Bk. III, Ch. III). Antoine de Baïf, an early friend of Ronsard's, devoted himself to reforms in prosody and meter. This is probably the reason why Du Bellay called him the " docte, doctieur et doctime Baïf." At all events, Baïf founded an Academy for poets and musicians under the aegis of Charles IX and strove to broaden the function of French verse by inventing a line of fifteen syllables, the so-called *vers baïfin;* but this, like his experiments in quantitative French meter, was doomed to failure. No less learned and certainly more philosophical was Pontus de Tyard (1521–1603), the author of *Les Erreurs amoureuses* (1549), in sonnet form. As we have seen (Bk. I, Ch. I), he is the link between the school of Scève and the Pléiade. A Burgundian, of noble origin, he strengthened the stream of Platonic inspiration by rendering into French the *Dialoghi d'amore* of the Spanish Jew Leo. Remy Belleau, called *le gentil*, was the " miniaturist " of the school, though to his contemporaries he was mainly the honored translator of Anacreon (1556). Peletier we mentioned above and shall refer to again. Des Autels and La Péruse have only an incidental interest.

(2) The so-called *seconde volée*, headed by the *précieux* and Italianate Desportes. They appear after the accession of Henry III in 1573 — the date which marks the retirement of Ronsard from court. As we shall see, it was against this group in particular that Malherbe was to aim the shafts of his common-sense mind.

(3) What is often regarded as an offshoot of this second class; namely, the Protestant school of Du Bartas and D'Aubigné. In reality, however, these gifted poets are akin to the Ronsard of the *Discours* and even of the *Franciade* (1572), and although they belong to the generation of Henry III, they stand outside of its control inasmuch as they represent the militant Protes-

tantism of Henry of Navarre, later the apostate Henry IV, into whose reign much of their work falls. Thus by a stroke of irony they most resemble Ronsard in technique, inimical as they are to him in religion. At the same time, they had little influence in France, where the cause they advocated met with disaster.

Such is a working outline of the Pléiade movement, with the prominent figures of which we shall deal presently. Meantime, it will be well to keep in mind certain general features. First, as a matter of background, the cultivated but corrupt court, which under Catherine de Médicis (wife of Henry II and mother of Charles IX and Henry III) was more Italian than French, ever ready in the unequal battle it waged with the Protestants on the one hand and reactionary Catholics on the other to resort to intrigue and double-dealing. Then, there is the cult of ephemeral and evanescent beauty — the *carpe diem* or *carpe rosam* theme of the classical poets — so persistent in the lyricism of the age. Imitative as this idea was, it drew impetus from the insecurity of fortune and it encouraged poets to seek permanence in artistic form. Thirdly, there is the romantic appeal of Nature, in her bucolic aspects, constantly renewing herself in a glorious rebirth. With his Vergil or Theocritus in mind, the poet finds a balm for his troubled spirits in effects, gentle and slight as they may be, that are reposeful and idyllic in character. And when he is a Ronsard or a Du Bellay his identifications are not only imitative but also rich in personal observation and originality of detail. Undoubtedly, the poetic product is uneven. For one thing, the frequent quips and conceits annoy the modern reader; for another, the repetition of theme and manner is considerable. A genuine defect is excessive erudition, which frequently cloys the verse and renders it unintelligible. But, on the whole, the verse is at once plastic and rich in color, varied in meters and genuinely musical, with a rhythm and stateliness — particularly in Ronsard — closer to the Greek than anything earlier or later in French. A realization of beauty was the Pléiade's preoccupation and main asset.

CHAPTER II

THE CHIEF POETS OF THE PLEIADE

PIERRE DE RONSARD was born in 1525 at the Château de la Poissonnière near Vendôme. His father was a lesser French noble, who had won distinction abroad and made himself useful to the household of Francis I. The poet would have us believe that the Ronsards descended from a Danubian baron domiciled in France at the time of Philip of Valois. It befits such traditions that Pierre was removed at the age of eleven from the Collège de Navarre in Paris and made a page at court. In this capacity he went twice to England and Scotland and was finally attached to Francis' third son, the Duke of Orleans. In 1540 he was sent to Germany with Lazare de Baïf on an official mission. Returning, Ronsard contracted an illness which left him partly deaf and ended his diplomatic career. In 1543 he received the tonsure.

Ronsard

He now joined Baïf's son, Antoine, in the study of classical literature under the direction of the Hellenist Daurat. This apprenticeship lasted five years (1544-1549), first at Baïf's house and then at the Collège de Coqueret, of which Daurat became the enthusiastic and successful principal. The legend is that the two students kept the candle burning throughout the long winter nights by alternating at the study table. Others who shared their zeal at Coqueret were Belleau and Jodelle; and in 1547 came Joachim Du Bellay, whose literary career, previously guided by Peletier, is henceforth allied with that of Ronsard.

Daurat's teaching bore rapid fruit. It is apparent in all of Ronsard's early work, and, among countless other examples, is seen in the enthusiastic sonnet beginning:

Je veux lire en trois jours l'Iliade d'Homere.

It is not surprising that Ronsard took to imitating the ancients with enthusiasm, while the care he lavished on his productions has become proverbial. His first odes date from 1547, but it was not until the year following the *Défense* (1549) that he could bring himself to publish his first collection. In the following we shall consider his works in three fairly distinct periods:

1550–1560 — or the period of the *Odes, Amours, Hymnes, Bocage Royal* and *Mélanges*. This is the innovating epoch of Hellenistic and Petrarchian imitation.

1560–1574 — the time when Ronsard is the official court poet and writes his *Elegies, Mascarades, Bergeries, Discours* and the *Franciade*. He is now the *poète oratoire,* in conscious possession of his own genius, with a distinct tendency towards nationalism.

1574–1584 — when retired from active life Ronsard meditates and seeks fresh inspiration in the tranquillity of field and forest. The works of this autumnal period are the *Sonnets pour Hélène,* the *Dernières Amours* and the last part of the *Bocage Royal.*

Ronsard's rise to fame is as significant as it was rapid. Following so soon on the *Défense,* the first four books of the *Odes* (1550) boldly announce the poet's break with the school of Marot and his imitation of Horace and Pindar. As "father of the French ode," he claims the title of first lyricist of France. This vainglory is typical of the epoch in which he lived; and in the *Ode à Michel de l'Hospital* — one of the successful imitations of Pindar — he sings with astonishing virtuosity of the victory of the Muses, triumphing in himself:

First Period

> C'est luy dont les graces infuses
> Ont ramené par l'univers
> Le chœur des Piërides Muses,
> Faites illustres par ses vers.

This ode is of 1552, the year that saw the publication of a fifth book of *Odes* and the *Amours de P. Ronsard,* a collection of one hundred and eighty-one sonnets. In the latter Ronsard sounds the gamut of mingled classical and Italian imitation in honor of Cassandre Salviati, a proud beauty of Blois. Both here and in his *Odes* he reveals artistic powers of the highest order. "Eloigné du vulgaire," as the *Défense* had said, he follows the new path of complicated Pindaric forms, plastic and picturesque imagery, and mythological allusions. Yet his natural sense of harmony and beauty is striking, as when in celebrating the muses he says:

> Et à qui vrayment aussi
> Les vers furent en souci,
> Les vers dont flattez nous sommes,
> Afin que leur doux chanter
> Peust doucement enchanter
> Le soin des Dieux et des hommes.

How completely the ancients had him in their thrall appears in the elegiacal *Election de son sépulcre*, written at the age of twenty-three and reminiscent of Propertius, Vergil, Ovid and Horace. Here romantic imagination, love of Nature and classical imitation are welded into a verse that reminds Sainte-Beuve of a " clocher funèbre":

> Antres, et vous fontaines
> De ces rochers hautaines
> Qui tombez contre-bas
>   D'un glissant pas.

All this is far removed from the triflings of the Marotiques. Mellin de Saint-Gelais, still in the ascendency at court, foresaw his own eclipse. But if Mellin lacked genius, he did not lack friends and he enlisted the envious against his rival. That Ronsard resented the opposition he shows clearly in his gratitude to Marguerite de Valois for taking his part:

> N'est-ce pas toy, Vierge tres-bonne,
> . . . qui tant me fus favorable
> Quand par l'envieux miserable
> Mon œuvre fut *Mellinisé?*

Outwardly, at least, the quarrel with Mellin is over by 1553, and there follow Ronsard's most fruitful years.

In 1553 the poet published forty new sonnets, an ode on his reconciliation with Saint-Gelais and the famous *Mignonne, allons voir si la rose:* the final expression of the *carpe rosam* theme, which Ronsard here borrows from the Fourteenth Idyll of Ausonius. Assured of success, he now makes concessions in behalf of clearness and simplicity, composing with that " ardeur et allegresse d'esprit " lauded by Du Bellay, and with all France at his feet. The *Bocage* and the *Mélanges* (both of 1554), the one predominantly serious, the other frolicsome and gay, reflect an interest in Anacreon — after Homer and Pindar, the third Greek poet to influence Ronsard. But the greatest compositions of this time are the *Hymnes* and the *Continuation des Amours*, both of 1555-1556. The former definitely establish Ronsard's position as a skillful panegyrist of his patrons, while the latter inaugurate his second manner.

Dedicated to Marie Dupin — a village beauty of Bourgueil **Second** in Anjou — the new *Amours* are arranged on the **Period** Petrarchian plan of celebrating first the living and then the dead Marie. The poet apostrophizes Marie as:

> Douce, belle, gentille et bien flairante Rose,
> Que tu es à bon droit à Venus consacrée

— a notable softening in tone from that in which he sang the lofty and haughty Cassandre. His models now are Theocritus, Vergil and the neo-classic Marullus. Further, the Alexandrine supplants the ten-syllable as the true *vers héroïque*. One poem in the collection, *La Quenouille* (" The Distaff "), is a splendid adaptation of an idyll by Theocritus — again illustrating the principles of the *Défense* as to language:

> Aime-laine, aime-fil, aime-estaim, maisonniere,
> Longue, Palladienne, enflée, chansonniere,
> Suy-moy, laisse Cousture, et allons à Bourgueil.

But most characteristic of the Renaissance spirit is the celebrated sonnet *Comme on voit sur la branche au mois de May la rose,* with its anapaestic movement, its rich rimes, its vivid imagery and its complete aesthetic appeal which death itself does not mar:

> Afin que, vif et mort, ton corps ne soit que roses.

Here the poet has seized the essence of classical antiquity — pagan, fatalistic, sensuous and beautiful.

In 1559 Ronsard received the post of royal almoner, the success of the *Amours* having long since won him the unofficial title of " Prince des poètes français." Fame had confirmed his self-esteem. We find him reminding Henry II that kings are responsible to their people and that

> apres votre mort, fussiez-vous empereur,
> Vous ne serez non plus qu'un simple laboureur

— this was still before the outbreak of the disastrous religious wars which were to lay France waste. With the accession of Charles IX his ties with the monarch are even closer, and he speaks out boldly in behalf of his native land. The *Discours des Misères de ce temps,* the *Continuation du Discours* and the *Remonstrance au peuple de France* were produced in 1562–1563, at the beginning of the First Civil War. While Ronsard is unequivocal in his support of the Romanists, he does not hesitate to score their faults. Only when the Protestants resort to abuse does he actually take up arms against them, showing as the Protestant d'Aubigné admiringly states that " Les vers n'avoient pas osté l'usage de l'espée." Again poetry profited by Ronsard's directness; discarding all mythology, he makes his Alexandrines speak the language of the hour — forceful, ironic and eloquent: the first example of the *poésie oratoire.* Note the dramatic visualization of Christ in Ronsard's confession of faith:

> Il arresta les vents, il marcha sur les ondes,
> Et de son corps divin, mortellement vestu,
> Les miracles sortoient, temoins de sa vertu;

and observe how regal is the imagery.

Meanwhile, Catherine ordered the " royal poet " to send Queen Elizabeth a collection of his " occasional verse " under the title of *Elegies, Mascarades, Bergeries* (1565). Ronsard's attachments had been wholly for Mary Queen of Scots, and the diamond which Elizabeth sent him in return could have warmed his heart but little. Yet the poems had his usual verve, reflecting the glamour of his surroundings, not a little humor and a wistful tenderness for the young Charles IX, of whom Ronsard was genuinely fond and whom he was sincerely to mourn.

St. Bartholomew's Day (1572) drew not a line from Ronsard, though many others stooped to laud its horrors. If Ronsard was discreet, his silence left no doubt as to his opinion. In 1560 he had published the first edition of his collected works, others followed at close intervals, and in 1572 there appeared four books of the *Franciade* — the longed-for French epic, the dream of the *Défense,* heralded twenty years earlier in the *Ode à Michel de l'Hospital.* Its failure was complete. Why? Ronsard seemingly never knew. No more did his continuators, the last of whom, a certain Viennet, rewrote the work in Alexandrines under the Bonapartes. Ronsard himself attributes the collapse to matters of detail: lack of rigid application of the " epic " rules, erroneous choice of ten-syllable verse, and so on. He explained himself in three prefaces, made revisions in 1572 and 1578, and then desisted. The subject of the *Franciade* was bookish (the Troy legend), the technique Vergilian and the mythology classical: three factitious elements in a poem which should have had an unquestioning feeling of human destiny to guide it — the *sine qua non* of any successful epic. As we shall see, Chapelain in the seventeenth century, and Voltaire in the eighteenth, fared no better in their attempts at epic verse, whereas d'Aubigné in the sixteenth and Victor Hugo in the nineteenth came closest to the coveted goal. On the other hand, the real epics of the Renaissance are Tasso's *Gerusalemme liberata* and Milton's *Paradise Lost.*

The last period of Ronsard's life was passed mostly in the country, either at Montoire and Croix Val or in his priory at Third Saint-Cosme near Tours. He was now quite gray, Period often ill, and bereft of his friends: Du Bellay, Jodelle and finally Belleau (1557). Yet his genius was to shine forth on two further occasions. The one was the publication of his last sonnets, the *Sonnets pour Hélène;* and the other, the completion of the *Bocage royal,* included in a celebrated folio edition of his works (1584). With Hélène de Surgères the poet held a position of equality; as a consequence the sonnets to her are more intimate and truer to reality than those he dedicated to Cassandre or Marie. Here Ronsard does not fail to give us " lesser details ":

> Seule, sans compagnie, dans une grande salle
> Tu logeais l'autre jour, pleine de majesté,

and the well-known *Quand vous serez bien vielle, au soir, à la chandelle* illustrates this trait without sacrificing the earlier, more literary features. Characteristic of this period is also an ode, *Magie ou délivrance d'amour,* where the verse itself is suggestive, as M. Jusserand points out, of evanescence and liberation:

> Vents qui soufflez par cette plaine,
> Et vous, Seine, qui promenez
> Vos flots par ces champs, emmenez
> En l'Ocean noyer ma peine.

Lastly, in one poem at least of the *Bocage royal* the poet's sympathy with Nature reaches a climax in an expression of universal melancholy, and the forest of Gâtine falling before the woodman's ax:

> Tu deviendras campagne et en lieu de tes bois,
> Dont l'ombrage incertain lentement se remue,

becomes the symbol of universal change:

> La matiere demeure et la forme se change.

Thus when Ronsard died in December, 1585 — regretted by the civilized world — he had rounded out his life and his experience. A lesser star, that of Desportes, was in the ascendency, and a new age was preparing. But Ronsard remains *the* poet by preference of the sixteenth century. Both in variety of genius and in wealth of performance he transcends the others. "C'est le premier poëte de ce siecle," said Du Verdier in the very year of Ronsard's death.

The princely Ronsard has a counterpart in the gentle Du Bellay. Contemporaries likened him to Ovid; another comparison would be to Lamartine. In any case, Du **Du Bellay** Bellay was by nature a romantic. More modern in this respect than Ronsard, he was at odds with the world, fell short of the program he had planned, and died prematurely and broken in spirit in 1560. Not to be compared to his fellow craftsman for poetic sweep and power of execution, he had a finer perception and a more delicate, less sensuous temperament. Hence his Petrarchizing seems more natural and his Neo-Platonism is more effective. Sainte-Beuve applies to him the lines written by Du Bellay himself to a friend:

> L'amour se nourrit de pleurs,
> Et les abeilles de fleurs;
> Les prés aiment la rosée,
> Phoebus aime les neuf sœurs,
> Et nous aimons les doulceurs
> Dont ta muse est arousée.

Joachim Du Bellay was born about 1525 at Lyré, upon the left bank of the Loire, not far from Angers. His father Jean Du Bellay was a Sieur de Gannor, governor of Brest, and belonged to a family made illustrious by Cardinal Du Bellay and M. de Langey, a notable general. Losing his parents during boyhood, Joachim fell to the care of an elder brother, who neglected his education and his health. Thus necessity rather than choice led him to seek in French the glory that was denied him in the field of the classics. This idea lies back of the *Défense*.

When Du Bellay joined Ronsard's circle in Paris his devotion to poetry was already established. He says pointedly in *L'Olive*, his first sheaf of poems (1549): " Ce fut pourquoi à la persuasion de Jacques Peletier, je choisi le sonnet et l'ode." Two thirds of the sonnets of this collection (2nd ed. 1550) are from the Italian, while the odes follow the model of Horace. But already Du Bellay shows great metrical skill and his particular spiritualizing trend, for his lady's name, Olive, is symbolic of Pallas Athena. The climax of this Platonizing mood is reached in Sonnet 113 (*Si notre vie est moins qu'une journée*), the theme of which can be traced back to Petrarch through Daniello, and forward into Lamartine's *Isolement*. Yet the inconstancy of his enthusiasm appears in his translating the Fourth Book of the *Aeneid* (1552) — he who had inveighed against translators in the *Défense*. A year later his *Recueil de poésie* goes so far as to ridicule in sprightly verse the excesses of the Petrarchian style. The fact is that Du Bellay's sensitiveness easily turned upon itself. This is seen in the ironic close he gave to many of his sonnets and, above all, in the capital *Poète courtisan* (not published until 1559), where he mockingly advises those whom a desire for success has lured into the servilities of the court circle. Possibly his " court poet " was Mellin de Saint-Gelais, though the satire also reflects Du Bellay's personal experience.

In 1553 his relative, the Cardinal, invited him to come to Rome. This trip marks the turning-point in Du Bellay's life and inspired his distinctive verse: the *Antiquités de Rome*, the *Regrets* and the *Jeux rustiques* — all published after his return to France in 1558. With what high expectation Du Bellay entered the Eternal City can be imagined. The enthusiastic *Descriptio Romae*, in Latin heroics, depicts the renascent city recovering

the treasures of antique sculpture and architecture. As a matter
of fact, Du Bellay promised himself the impossible:

> Je me feray sçavant en la philosophie,
> En la mathematique et medicine aussy:
> Je me feray legiste, et d'un plus hault soucy
> Apprendray les secrets de la theologie:
> Du lut et du pinceau j'esbatteray ma vie,
> De l'escrime et du bal. Je discouray ainsy
> Et me vantois en moy d'apprendre tout cecy
> Quand je changeay la France au sejour d'Italie.

The *Antiquités de Rome,* in sonnet-form, are the record of his
early impressions. For pathos of vanished grandeur and for
sentiment of ruins they have seldom been surpassed, certainly not
in French. On the Horatian theme of *Suis et ipsa Roma viribus
ruit* Du Bellay builds a vision of Rome's ancient splendor:

> Rome seule pouvoit Rome ressembler,
> Rome seule pouvoit Rome faire trembler:
> Ainsi n'avoit permis l'ordonnance fatale
> Qu'autre pouvoir humain, tant fust audacieux,
> Se vantast d'egaler celle qui fit egale
> Sa puissance à la terre et son courage aux cieux.

But only the memory of that power now remains, and in an
admirable sonnet the poet muses on what the shades of the old
Romans — *les ombres poudreuses* — would say if they could
behold their city under the rule of the popes, the ruined city which

> Chascun va pillant: comme on voit le glaneur
> Cheminant pas à pas recueillir les reliques
> De ce qui va tombant apres le moissonneur.

Du Bellay's post in the Cardinal's household was that of a
head steward. In this capacity he had to attend to the hundreds
of details which his Eminence imposed, and he accompanied
his master to the consistory. It was an interesting but on the
whole a wearisome life, especially for one of Du Bellay's ideals.
For a while the glamour of the official life held him. But soon
his heart sickens at the corruption in high places; an unfortunate
passion for the Faustina of his *Poemata* and a longing for his
native heath hasten the break, and in 1557 he sets out for home.
The stages of the return trip (via Venice, the Grisons and Switz-

erland) are recorded as a part of the *Regrets*, the most intimate of the poet's sonnets and those in which his mingled sentiment and satire are best expressed. Every Frenchman knows the sonnet beginning:

> France, mere des arts, des armes et des lois;

though few know that it is modeled on a Latin hymn by Petrarch. Unsurpassed, however, in all respects is the *Sonnet du petit Liré* with its ringing conclusion:

> Plus me plaist sejour qu'ont basti mes ayeulx
> . . . .
> Plus mon Loyre gaulois que le Tÿbre latin,
> Plus mon petit Lyré que le mont Palatin,
> Et plus que l'air marin la doulceur Angevine.

This same *douceur* is characteristic of the poem which more than all others is associated with Du Bellay's memory: the famous *Vanneur de Blé* imitated from the Neo-Latin poet Navagero. Here the silvery grace of Du Bellay's fancy comes into full play, and his love of the fields, typical of his later *Jeux rustiques*, finds an echo in the very texture of his versification. But Du Bellay did not long survive his return to Anjou. Weakened in health, grown entirely deaf, he also found himself deserted by the relatives from whom he had sought support. When he died he was barely thirty-seven. A complete edition of his works did not appear until after his death.

"Depuis . . . Ronsard et Du Bellay," said Montaigne, "je ne vois si petit apprenti qui n'enfle les mots et qui ne range les **Lesser** cadences à peu pres comme eux." This is unfortu- **Stars** nately true of almost all of their associates, not to mention the large band of purely servile imitators. Antoine de Baïf (1532–1589) wrote various *Amours*, the second collection of which, addressed to the lady Francine, consecrates the use of the Alexandrine in the sonnet (1555). Baïf tried to make up in learning what he lacked in genius; but his attempts at spelling-reform, *vers baïfins* (Ch. I) and quantitative blank verse, while laudable in themselves, met only with a passing success. Remy Belleau (1526–1577) had at least more talent, which he expended on his version of Anacreon and especially in adapting the medieval " lapidary " to Renaissance taste in the *Nouveaux échanges des pierres précieuses*. When at his best, he paints with a delicate brush, in miniature style. One of his songs, *Avril*, reveals the same delicate feeling for Nature and owing to its charm is still a favorite anthology piece. To mention a poet who stood outside the immediate circle of the Pléiade, Olivier de Magny (1529-1561) has a certain freshness of expression. He was in love with Louise Labé and won honor at the court of Henry II with his *Soupirs,* a collection of Italianate sonnets in *précieux* style; but although he also wrote odes imitating Anacreon his personal contribution is nowhere signficant.

With the rise of the *seconde volée,* represented by Desportes and Bertaut, the Hellenizing period in poetry is practically at an end. The well-known lines of Boileau on Ronsard,

> Ce poète orgueilleux, trebuché de si haut,
> Rendit plus retenus Desportes et Bertaut,

however, express only a half-truth. For if the generation of 1573 shows restraint with respect to Greek and Latin, its imitations of contemporary Italian can hardly be called *retenues.*

Philippe Desportes (1545-1606), remembered chiefly because of the criticism by Malherbe — the famous *Commentaire sur Desportes* (see below) — " made flattery into a fine art." Taken early to Italy, he became secretary to Nicolas de Neufville, minister of state, and in 1572, the Duke of Anjou — the future Henry III — gave him " dix mille écus " to publish a sumptuous volume containing his *Premières Poésies.* On Henry's accession to the throne Desportes became court poet. As such, he lived the life of a *grand seigneur,* celebrating in verse the supposed virtues of the royal favorites and receiving from his master benefices that annually amounted to some 30,000 livres. Says Sainte-Beuve: " Plus on regarde dans la vie de Desportes, plus on y trouve d'abbayes." Yet sycophant that he was, he remained a *grand seigneur,* and his munificence and liberality charmed friends and foes alike.

Desportes and Bertaut

In addition to elegance, Desportes' verse has a certain formal compactness wedded to an abiding gift of *esprit.* He is the Marot of the Pléiade school, and like Marot or the English poet Herrick he wrote both worldly and devotional poems.

How polished his verse could be can be seen from the sonnet
later translated into English by Daniel:

> ⁕ Sommeil, paisible fils de la nuit solitaire.

But his *Chansons*, set to music, were even more popular in
his day; and one in particular, imitated from Ariosto, is the
essence of graceful expression:

> O Nuit! jalouse Nuit! contre moi conjurée,
> Qui renflamme le ciel de nouvelle clarté,
> T'ai-je donc aujourd'hui tant de fois desirée
> Pour estre si contraire à ma felicité?

For the most part, however, Desportes is merely facile and
mundane — a slave to the worst type of Italianism. Here
his models were Tasso, Tebaldeo, Angelo di Costanzo; in imitation of whom he abounds in hyperbole, exaggerated conceits
and antitheses. His *Poésies chrétiennes* contain the strange
Italian device of uttering in the same breath the name of Christ
and that of the poet's " belle meurtrière."

Less talented than Desportes, Jean Bertaut — later bishop
of Séez — is at least free from the latter's exaggerations. Indeed,
Bertaut, whose productive period (1580–1602) falls within the
reign of Henry IV, is a transitional poet, having some of the
impersonality we later find in Malherbe. Certain of his lines
have the sonorous melancholy of Lamartine:

> Et vous, humbles costeaux où les pampres foisonnent
> Et vous, ombreux vallons, de sources arrosés,
>
> . . . .
>
> Chantez-la sur les vents qui vous servent de voix.

But such passages are rare; only occasionally and then in his
religious verse (such as paraphrases from the Psalms, funeral
panegyrics, and the like) does Bertaut attain this lofty tone;
more often he is prosaic and stilted. Less of a plagiarist than
Desportes, he nevertheless imitates the Italian Tansillo and —
in his most inspired moments — Tasso. Ronsard lauded his
sagesse. His works, however, were not published until 1601–1602.

The French, says M. Lanson, are often severe to minorities
and to the awkward genius who dresses out of fashion. This

remark does not apply to Du Bartas, whose imperfections did
Du Bartas not prevent him from winning a contemporary suc-
and cess second only to that of Ronsard; but it fits
D'Aubigné exactly that far more original genius D'Aubigné,
whose poetic works, appearing between 1616 and 1630, were
hardly noticed.

The Huguenot poet Guillaume de Salluste, Seigneur du Bartas
(1544-1590), was a Gascon by birth and by temperament. He
was faithful to Henry of Navarre, who sent him on various
missions, including one to England and Scotland. The last poem
Du Bartas wrote was a celebration of the victory of Ivry. Endowed with a picturesque imagination, he carried the principles of
Ronsard to the extreme. *Enjambement,* inversion, neologisms,
abound in his work. While his poetry has sweep and a certain
grandeur, it startles the reader with such grotesque effects as:

> Mais le cœur de Judith, qui sans cesse ba-bat

or

> Le ciel d'un fer rouillé sa face voilera.

But this love of the baroque would shock a foreigner less than a
Frenchman; and it is significant that Goethe admired Du Bartas
sufficiently to translate him.

Du Bartas began his poetic career by answering Du Bellay's
call for an epic. The subject,. given him by Jeanne d'Albret,
Queen of Navarre, was the liberation of Jerusalem from Holofernes by Judith. This *Judith*, written in 1565 but not published
until 1573, gains its interest mainly from the fact that Du
Bartas treats the Biblical subject according to the Vergilian
technique then in vogue. But at least Du Bartas had vindicated
poetry by the choice of a lofty theme and prepared the way for
the publication of *La Semaine,* a work on the Creation, in 1578.
A comparison of this work with the original *Genesis* shows at
once that he had overestimated his powers of thought and expression. The subject was epic — certainly for a Protestant — the
plot was well planned, but again Du Bartas had neither the depth
nor the restraint to achieve more than a contemporary success.
Yet *La Semaine* received twenty editions in five years; and in 1584
the poet began to publish *La Seconde Semaine,* which though
never completed was to reach to the Last Judgment. The expla-

nation is that not only Protestants but the entire world honored the seriousness of the attempt. Here was a Christian poet with vigor and imagination, and so Du Bartas was translated into Latin, Italian, Spanish, German and English (by Silvester in 1605–1606). *Notre Milton manqué* M. Morillot calls him, a verdict that sums up aptly Du Bartas' noble failure. In France the magnificent folio edition of his works in 1611 properly marks Du Bartas' tomb (Sainte-Beuve); for neither Malherbe nor Boileau mentions his name.

Theodore-Agrippa d'Aubigné (1550–1630) was by nature ardent, intolerant and pleasure-loving — quite a contrast to Du Bartas. Reared in a world of strife by the most Protestant of fathers, he studied in Paris and Geneva, and took up arms in the Protestant cause at eighteen (1568). But warfare was not his profession; in the intervals of peace he enjoyed life and cultivated the arts with the same whole-hearted passion that characterized the Huguenot. He boasts in his *Vie, à ses enfants* that at " seven and a half," he translated Plato's *Crito*. He was proficient in engineering and in magic. And between the two Civil Wars he shone at court sufficiently to compose the *Hécatombe à Diane*, one hundred Ronsardian sonnets addressed to Cassandre Salviati's niece, and he pleased Charles IX with a lyric tragedy called *Circé*. Ronsard himself could have done no better. It was D'Aubigné who helped the later Henry IV to escape from the Louvre during the Massacre of St. Bartholomew. Though the poet never forgave Henry his apostacy he continued to serve him as governor of Maillezais and vice-admiral of Guyenne and Brittany. In 1620 — under Louis XIII — he retired to Geneva, where he died. The great sorrow of his life was the betrayal of the Protestant cause at La Rochelle by his son Constant, whose daughter — strange to say — was no less a person than Madame de Maintenon.

Thus D'Aubigné sums up in his person the Renaissance and the Reformation. He mingles the enthusiasm — *la fougue* — of both movements in a last expression. With the Renaissance exuberance of life he combines the intensity of the Calvinistic point of view. Hence his really great work, the epico-lyric *Tragiques*, resembles an alloy of gold and iron, beaten out on an anvil. Divided into seven cantos, half historical and half satir-

ical, the work is the Jeremiad of the religious wars. D'Aubigné
is neither a Dante nor a Milton. His work, as a whole, is hastily
written and poorly revised; above all, it is not firmly conceived
from start to finish, the supernatural in it — *le merveilleux
chrétien* — lacks clearness, and the style, while forceful, is devoid
of harmony and cadence. In short, the poem is a torso rather
than a finished work of art. Nevertheless, the *Tragiques* contain
some of the finest and most inspired passages of which French
poetry can boast — passages that are comparable to the best we
find in the *Châtiments* of Victor Hugo. For concision, let us note
the following:

> Ici le sang n'est .feint, le meurtre n'y defaut,
> La mort joue elle-mesme en ce triste eschafaud;

for irony and satire, the whole section on *Agrippa d'Aubigné à
la Cour*, where the poet outstrips Du Bellay in excoriating the
king's favorites; for love of country, the section beginning:

> O France desolée, ô terre sanguinaire!

and lastly, for dramatic visualization, the description of Cain:

> Il estoit seul partout, hormis sa conscience,
> Et fut marqué au front, afin qu'en s'enfuyant
> Aucun n'osast tuer ses maux en le tuant.

As was said, D'Aubigné's *Tragiques* did not appear in print
until 1616. Between this date and 1630 his prose works were
published. Chief among these are the *Histoire universelle*, in
which he patiently strives to give a nonpartisan view of human
history, and the amusing, almost picaresque, *Aventures du Baron
de Fæneste*. This latter is an account, interspersed with delightful tales, of a parasitic nobleman, a sort of courtly Panurge
living on the toil of others; whereas the *Confession catholique
du Sieur de Sancy* is a mordant satire of a recalcitrant nobleman.
In all these works D'Aubigné shows his dominant traits: imagination, directness and color — coupled with unrestraint, lack
of taste and carelessness. The best in D'Aubigné is " personal ";
this we should not forget in considering that his works were
published at the beginning of the most impersonal age of French
literature, the age of *les idées générales*.

CHAPTER III

AMYOT, MONTAIGNE AND BRANTOME.

THE three writers treated in this chapter, the first a translator, the second an essayist and the third a compiler of memoirs, are embraced under what the French call by the generic name of *moralistes*. That is, they were all three interested in the problem of conduct, not that like Calvin they necessarily wished to reform it, but rather that they sought to extract from human affairs whatever practical philosophy they could. Ronsard and his school had revived, as we saw, the cult of ancient forms. In the manners and customs of the ancients they took little stock. What if antiquity had no practical lesson to teach? if the pagan world so long misunderstood had no vital force to transmit? It was such an estimate of the life and ideas of the ancients apprehended in their everyday aspect that Amyot and especially Montaigne were to give. Last in the procession comes Brantôme, disillusioned as to general principles, but vividly curious as to the doings of his contemporaries. But whatever the translator revives, or the essayist dissects, or the writer of memoirs records — the portrayal is striking, an image of mankind as in a mirror: graphic, detailed and very human.

Jacques Amyot's life practically covers the century (1513-1593). Born of plain folk in the little town of Melun, he rose by

Amyot dint of toil to be Master of Arts at nineteen and tutor to the nephews of Abbé Colin, translator of the *Cortegiano*. Won by his personality, Marguerite d'Angoulême appointed him to a professorship at Bourges. Here he remained until in 1547 Francis I made him abbot of Bellozane, the last foundation to which Francis chose the appointee. Some think Amyot owed this favor to his translation of the romance *Théagène et Chariclée*. Thanks to the studies of M. Sturel, however, we now know that as early as 1542 Amyot received the commission " par le commandement du grand roy François " to translate the

Parallel Lives of Plutarch. This translation, achieved nearly seventeen years later, when the magnificent in-folio containing the *Vies* appeared in Paris, is the monument of Amyot's life. To accomplish it he spent four years in Italy, searching through libraries and collating manuscripts, and incidentally discovering the works of Diodorus the Sicilian. In Rome he won the friendship of the Cardinal du Tournon, through whose influence he returned to France as the tutor of the Dukes of Orleans and of Anjou, the future Charles IX and Henry III. In 1559 he became " grand aumônier de France," and in 1570 bishop of Auxérre. His last years were darkened by tragedy. In December, 1588, the Duc de Guise was murdered at Blois. Amyot, who unfortunately was in Blois at the time, was indirectly accused of having been an accomplice in the crime. He wrote an *Apologie* and even obtained an absolution from the papal legate in 1590. But he died, more or less under the cloud of the tragic event, in February 1593. His charge of *aumônier* had been taken from him two years earlier.

Passing over Amyot's lesser works, which include a rendering of the Daphnis and Chloe story, we may center upon his *Vies des hommes illustres de Plutarque* and the *Œuvres morales* of the same author (published in 1572) as the works upon which his fame rests. We all know the importance of North's translation of Plutarch for the works of Shakespeare. The *Parallel Lives* are in themselves inspiring reading, and Amyot's *Vies* is one of the masterpieces of French prose. " Nous autres ignorants," says Montaigne, " étions perdus si ce livre ne nous eût relevés du bourbier: sa merci, nous osons à cette heure et parler et écrire . . . c'est notre bréviaire." And the book retained this function down through the seventeenth century, when Corneille took from it subjects for his dramas and Racine read it to Louis XIV, up to the very threshold of the Revolution, when it stirred Rousseau and still fascinated Madame Roland. In this tremendous vogue the *Œuvres morales* are a close second to the *Vies*.

First of all, Amyot was fortunate in choosing such an author. As a writer Plutarch suited the social genius of the French precisely. Through him they felt at one with the world of antiquity. If the ancients loved glory, here were examples of glory; if they were heroic, here were the illustrations of this heroism, *saisi sur le vif* — the expression occurs in Amyot. In other words, Plutarch enabled the French to see how the ancients lived, how they worked, thought, spoke, conducted themselves at home and abroad, with all their virtues, vices, foibles and idiosyncracies laid bare.

In the second place, Amyot did not attempt in any sense a literal translation. On the contrary, keenly alive to Du Bellay's warning that observing "la loy de traduyre, qui est n'espacier point hors des limites de l'aucteur, vostre diction sera contrainte, froide, et de mauvaise grace," he deliberately made Plutarch over into a French author by giving him a form which, while true to the original in idea, never slavishly followed the wording of the original Greek. And in so doing he made his Plutarch the best collection of the words and idioms of sixteenth-century speech. Coming after Rabelais and Calvin, he is thus the third to reveal the capacities of French literary prose. Not that he has not faults both of style and of interpretation. His sentences are often involved and loose in structure, just as he mistakenly calls the vestals *religieuses* and the favorites of Alexander *des gentilshommes de chambre*. But this is all a part of his larger purpose; namely, to give his author contemporaneousness. Thus it is that he made Plutarch the most accessible of the ancients to his and to future generations: to mention Plutarch to a Frenchman is to name Amyot.

If Amyot was the mentor, Etienne de la Boétie (1530–63) was the friend of the great Frenchman whom we are now to con-

Montaigne sider. La Boétie is the author of the *Discours de la Servitude volontaire* or *Contr'un* (not published until 1574), a violent but youthful invective against tyranny, but he is probably remembered with better reason for his relationship with Montaigne — a relationship which the latter has immortalized in the words: "Parce que c'était lui, parce que c'était moi."

Michel Eyquem, Seigneur de Montaigne, was born near Bergerac at Périgord in 1533. His father, whom Montaigne always remembered with affectionate reverence, was an original figure: a public-spirited citizen of Bordeaux, who after leading for a while the life of an Italian campaigner, was pleased to forget that the family fortune rested on the sale of wine and of fish.

His mother came from a family of Portuguese Jews named Louppes or Lopez — a fact that may account for the intellectual curiosity which our author valued so highly in himself. The Eyquems were a sturdy lot; *une race fameuse en prud'hommie.* Of Pierre's eleven children, eight grew up, the oldest being Michel.

The father gave his eldest the full benefit of his originality. Michel's first two years were spent in a peasant village; thus was he to absorb a sympathy for the poor and lowly; the father's idea, says the poet, " succeeded not ill." The boy's next tutor was a German physician who spoke Latin to him. With Greek, attempted next, the experiment was not very successful. As an instance of parental care, Montaigne records that he was waked in the morning to the sound of music. From the age of six to thirteen he was at the Collège de Guyenne, where he took leading parts in Latin tragedies by Muret and Buchanan. In the essay called *De l'institution des enfants* Montaigne regrets that this education did not profit him more.

Little is known of Montaigne's life from 1547 to 1554 — the supposition is that he studied law at Toulouse. In the latter year he succeeds his father as a member of the Cour des aides at Périgueux, and, upon its suppression (1557), he replaces him in the Parliament of Bordeaux. Here he meets and makes friends with La Boétie, whose untimely death in 1563 he mourns with all the poignancy of youth. But nature did not fit him for the magistracy; he is often absent from his post: at Paris or at Rouen, where in 1562 he sees in the suite of Charles IX the Brazilian natives whom he mentions in *Des cannibales.* Three years later he married Françoise de la Chassaigne, who was eleven years his junior, and whom he esteemed but did not love. With his father's death (1568) Montaigne lost the one person after La Boétie for whom he seriously cared. A year later he published a translation of the *Theologia naturalis* of Raymond de Sebond, a piece of work undertaken at his father's request and the publication of which marks his appearance as a writer.

Choosing, as Professor Dowden has said, " rather to fail in justice than humanity," Montaigne now retires from his post and devotes himself to private affairs and to study. For this the Château de Montaigne was beautifully adapted. In its tower Montaigne arranged a study with long galleries leading from it (like Aristotle he was a peripatetic), and collected a rich library. Of his one thousand books eighty have survived to this day, and on the margin thereof we can still read his observations on his favorite authors. These commentaries jotted down on the inspiration of the moment are the groundwork of his famous *Essais*, of which the first two books appeared in 1580.

Meantime, however, Montaigne discovered that along with many admirable traits his father had left him a tendency toward gravel. In order to correct this malady he travels in foreign lands. For the advice of physicians — *la mer trouble et vaste des erreurs médicinales* — he has little use. But he trusts nature, and after a journey of a year and a half through Switzerland, Germany and Italy he settles in Rome. The *Journal de voyage*, first published in 1774, is a record of his observations as a traveler. These are mainly about human nature, as we should expect of one who says " I have an apish and imitating character " and " I like a Pole as well as a Frenchman." He is, however, impressed with the vanished grandeur of Rome; and the gift of Roman citizenship conferred upon him greatly flatters his pride.

It is during a sojourn at the Baths of Lucca that Montaigne receives news of his election as mayor of Bordeaux. Reluctantly he wends his way home (1581) to acquit himself of a duty but not a pleasure. He tells his constituents that he will take the affairs of the city in hand — *non pas au poumon et au foie, de m'en charger et non de les incorporer.* Montaigne's casualness, the unprofessional attitude of the Renaissance gentleman, is nowhere more evident than in this remark. In 1583 his fellow-citizens reëlect him; yet when the city is swept by the plague he takes excellent care to avoid the danger-zone and, at the expiration of his term of office in July, 1585, he gladly lays down the reins of government. At the same time, his contemporaries never whispered a reproach, and Montaigne assures us that he shunned " no action which duty rightly demanded of him."

His final retirement into private seclusion now took place. Such worldly honors as a knighthood in the Order of St. Michael and membership in the King's Chamber were long since his. Henceforth he lived for his thoughts, shared often with his newly won friend Charron, whose *Sagesse* is a codification of Montaigne's ideas. The *Essais* had appeared in new editions

(with additions) in 1582 and 1587. In 1588 Montaigne published a so-called " fifth edition," which contained a third book,
with "*six cents additions aux deux premiers.*" Having gone to
Paris to supervise the publication, he there met Marie de
Gournay, whose idealistic devotion to him won for her the title
of *sa fille d'alliance.* She it was who directed the editing of
the posthumous edition of Montaigne's works in 1595. He was
now growing old, *mais à reculons.* The library of Bordeaux
still has his copy of the 1588 edition into which he wrote his
last corrections and additions. It shows how he constantly
sought to improve his text, cancelling repetitions, modernizing
or shortening sentences, and so on. Montaigne died on September 13, 1595 — of quinsy or grippe — surrounded by his
family and friends, and having received the last rites of the
church according to his own wish.

It would be a mistake to look in Montaigne's writings for any
consistent philosophy. His point of view is more nearly prag-
The matic than anything else, provided always we remem-
" Essais " ber that Montaigne the epicurean, the lover of peace
and tranquillity, furnishes the background. This granted, the
Essais give the general impression of a kaleidoscope: the ground
seems constantly to shift, the thesis is never maintained, at least
not for long. The letter-writer Balzac said: " Montaigne commence et finit pour ainsi dire à chaque phrase." And Etienne
Pasquier thought that more than one of the essays might be called
a *coq-à-l'âne.* The position to which Montaigne constantly returns is found in the words: " Certes, c'est un sujet merveilleuse-
ment vain, divers et ondoyant, que l'homme: il est malaisé d'y
fonder jugement constant et uniforme." [1] Consequently: " Je
n'ai rien à dire de moi entièrement, simplement et solidement,
sans confusion et sans mélange, ni en un mot. *Distinguo* est le
plus universel membre de ma logique."

To understand Montaigne, then, there is but one correct
method; namely, to follow the evolution of his thought, to gather
as it were the mosaic of his differentiations, piece by piece, and
see what conclusion can be drawn from the completed picture.

The bulk of Book I and the beginning of Book II, composed
before 1573, show the influence of Seneca and Plutarch. The

---

[1] The spelling is modernized according to the edition of Jeanroy.

first problem attacked is that of our passions, which Montaigne considers in the light of the Stoics. Essay I contrasts pity with resolution: it is right to alleviate suffering but not to grow soft with it. Alexander was stern but he was magnanimous. In Essay III the theme is that our passions destroy our sense of reality: "la crainte, le désir, l'espérance, nous élancent vers l'avenir et nous dérobent le sentiment et la considération de ce qui est, pour nous amuser à ce qui sera." Essay VII, on the question of intention, concludes: "qu'il n'y a rien en bon escient en notre puissance que la volonté, en celle-là se fondent par nécessité et s'établissent toutes les règles du devoir de l'homme." Finally, the culmination is reached in Essays XIX and XX, which deal with death and reproduce the maxim of Cicero, deduced from Plato's *Phaedo*, that "le but de notre carrière, c'est la mort." In all this there is little that is personal except the method; that is, the constant comparison of ideals with facts in dealing with human life, the subject of Montaigne's inquiry. But Book I contains also three extremely original contributions: Essay XXVII, *De l'amitié*, which, according to Montaigne, (cf. his friendship with La Boétie), is the highest and noblest of our affections; Essay XXX, *Des cannibales*, where the idea of the "noble savage" — so important for the later Rousseau — is first exploited, and Montaigne ironically concludes that *l'homme simple et grossier* may be a better witness of the eternal truth than *les fines gens*, just as what really distinguishes the savage from the Frenchman of the period, accustomed to war and pillage, is that he is morally better and does not wear trousers; and Essay XXXVIII, *De la solitude*, in which the author inveighs against public life with its ambitions and servilities and points out that "la plus grande chose du monde, c'est de savoir être à soi." This is probably the most Socratic of his ideas, that which has found most favor outside of France, and certainly the least French.

We now reach the second period in the evolution of Montaigne's thought. In 1576 he became acquainted with the late Greek skeptic, Sextus Empiricus, a Latin translation of whose *Pyrrhoniae Hypotyposes* was published by Henri Estienne in 1562. There were ten quotations from Sextus on the walls of Montaigne's library. Book II, Essay XII, the so-called *Apologie de Raimond*

Sebond, has as its subtitle *Ou la vanité de la raison humaine,* and amounts really to an attack on the human mind — especially on the proud Reason which the Renaissance had exalted.   Essay II, *De l'ivrognerie,* had shown how easily the mind is carried away.   Essay VIII had dealt with the treatment of children: our affection for them should be neither animalistic nor artificial; parents must be the companions of their children, who should not be beaten into obedience or they will not love honor and liberty.   This essay, dedicated to Mme d'Estissac, should be compared to XXV, Book I, *De l'institution des enfants,* dedicated to Diane de Foix but not composed until 1579.   Here Montaigne advocates an unstoical *sévère douceur*: the object of education is to train the judgment, not to amass facts; children must be made to like learning, not to fear and abhor it; above all, the world is the school in which the great minds are trained. Finally, Essay X, *Des livres,* corroborates these ideas: Montaigne admires the moral works of Cicero but he abominates his style; to Vergil and Lucretius he gives undivided admiration.

Thus, when we reach the *Apologie* — aptly termed *le recueil de toutes nos ignorances, incohérences et contradictions* — the current of skepticism has grown into a mighty river threatening the solvency of man himself.   "La présomption," says Montaigne, "est notre maladie naturelle et originelle.   La plus calamiteuse et fragile de toutes les créatures, c'est l'homme et . . . la plus orgueilleuse."   Here Montaigne is at one with Calvin, though his attack is against the intellect and not the will.   And in another passage he all but writes a page of Pascal:

> Considérons donc pour cette heure l'homme seul, sans secours étranger, armé seulement de ses armes, et dépourvu de la grâce et connaissance divine, qui est tout son honneur, sa force et le fondement de son être. . . . Qui lui a persuadé que ce branle admirable de la voûte céleste, la lumière éternelle de ces flambeaux roulant si fièrement sur sa tête, les mouvements épouvantables de cette mer infinie, soient établis et se continuent tant de siècles pour sa commodité et pour son service?   Est-il possible de rien imaginer si ridicule que cette misérable et chétive créature, qui n'est pas seulement maîtresse de soi, exposée aux offenses de toutes choses, se die maîtresse et empière de l'univers, duquel il n'est pas en sa puissance de connaître la moindre partie, tant s'en faut de la commander?

And there follows a long disquisition on the life of animals, all to the disadvantage of man, who is blamed for deserting Nature:

> Le soin de s'augmenter en sagesse et en science, ce fut la première ruine du genre humain; c'est la voie par où il s'est précipité à la damnation éternelle. . . . Comme la vie se rend par la simplicité plus plaisante, elle se rend aussi plus innocente et meilleure.

— again an approach to Rousseau.

Finally, with Book III — written in 1586-88 — he takes himself as the object of study, as exemplifying the genus Man. Pascal once said: " ce n'est pas dans Montaigne, mais dans moi que je trouve tout ce que j'y vois." A remark that justifies Montaigne's superb avowal as to mankind in general and himself in particular which we have had occasion to admire before (see Introduction).

> On attache aussi bien toute la philosophie morale à une vie populaire et privée qu'à une vie de plus riche étoffe. Chaque homme porte la forme entière de l'humaine condition. Les auteurs se communiquent au peuple par quelque marque spéciale et étrangère; moi le premier par mon être universel, comme M. de Montaigne, non comme grammairien, ou poète, ou juris-consulte. Si le monde se plaint que je parle trop de moi, je me plains de quoi il ne pense seulement à soi. (Essay I.)

This concept of the " universal being " — inherent in all of us — now furnishes the counterpart to the "relativity " in which our limited life as individuals has placed us. The obstacles of time, space, ignorance, the differences of religion, nationality, manners and morals, vividly set forth in the *Apologie,* are thus overcome in the experience of mankind as a whole. Insular and circumscribed we remain; our institutions which have grown up with us we cannot shake off. But we can become circumspect and open-minded in proportion to our self-knowledge and our acquaintance with other human beings. " Le pris de l'âme," Montaigne now maintains, " ne consiste pas à aller hautement, mais ordonnéement." There is no " plus utile science " than wisdom (III); moderation is the best maxim. Socrates was right: " le mourir lui semble accident naturel et indifférent (IV)." In the essay *Sur les vers de Virgile (V)*, and there is no essay less Vergilian, Montaigne advocates measure in temperance: even

" la sagesse a ses excès." Here the worldly, epicurean note rings clear and confronts us with the antithesis to stoicism in the words: " A mon avis, c'est le vivre heureusement non comme dit Antisthènes le mourir heureusement qui fait l'humaine félicité."

Concerning Montaigne there may be as many opinions as there are minds. His very popularity has been prodigious. In English alone the Florio (1603) and the Cotton (1685) translations of the *Essais* have been frequently reprinted, whereas Shakespeare and Bacon are among his most notable debtors. Our own Emerson never wearies of paying him tribute. Besides, as Montaigne himself said, *un abrégé sur un bon livre est sot abrégé.* Montaigne is no logician; " carried along on the wings of his subject from one mountain top to another " (Miss Norton), he is reckless in argument, digressing, interpolating, giving us opinions for fact, and the like. Thus, even the single essays lack unity and cogency. The famous *Apologie,* when closely studied, shows signs of being hastily made up of several originally distinct essays. All of this a summary necessarily misses. Nevertheless, on one thing his critics may agree, and that is his representative character. He portrays mankind in its characteristic and conflicting moods as possibly no other writer ever has. And this remains his greatest quality.

In the *Essais* we see the " man " Montaigne in every detail: vain, alert, peace-loving, inquisitive and tolerant. Despite a tendency to startle — *épater* — no writer is intellectually more honest. He is, it seems, precisely what he claims to be, neither more nor less. Such probity is not only interesting, it is enticing. It leads the reader — for once at least — to be himself, to imitate his author and look narrowly into his own soul, no matter how shallow it may be, for profundity was not the long suit of this gentleman of Périgord. Important in this connection are the charm and vividness of Montaigne's style. *Sans coûture* is the epithet that has been applied to it. But this is equivalent to saying that it is conversational and sprightly. On the other hand, Montaigne can be elevated in tone and even eloquent: witness the passage quoted above on *l'homme seul.* Few writers, however, have had a juster sense of the value of words. " Cut these words," said Emerson, " they are vascular and alive "— an opinion that rather belies Montaigne's own conviction that the French language lacked vigor:

> Il succombe ordinairement à une puissante conception; si vous allez tendu, vous sentez souvent qu'il languit sous vous et fléchit.

Montaigne, then, is preëminent in at least two respects. First, with reference to his negations. This aspect is Montaigne the

Importance of Montaigne   skeptic: the Pyrrhonist whom Pascal both admired and feared, feared because of his lighthearted acceptance of our human limitations; the ancestor of the Voltaires, the Sainte-Beuves, the Renans and the Anatole Frances of French literature. The Montaigne, in short, of the sentence: *Que sais-je?*

> Skepticism — says Emerson — is the attitude assumed by the student in relation to the particulars which society adores, but which he sees to be reverenced only in their tendency and spirit. The ground occupied by the skeptic is the vestibule of the temple . . . it turns out that he is not the champion of the operative, the pauper, the prisoner, the slave. It stands in his mind that our life in this world is not quite so easy of interpretation as churches and school-books say. He does not wish to take ground against these benevolences, to play the part of the devil's attorney, and blazon every doubt and sneer that darkens the sun for him. But he says, there are doubts.

This is the Montaigne who belongs to world-literature. In many respects he represents the best the French spirit has to give. It is true he is a constant interrogation. But he leads us through doubt to take pleasure in thinking and to admit views that are not necessarily ours. For, as Emerson concludes:

> The lesson of life is practically to generalize; to believe what the years and the centuries say against the hours; to resist the usurpation of particulars, to penetrate to their catholic sense.

This brings us to Montaigne's second or positive side; namely, Montaigne the generalizer. In this respect he stands in close relation to his own time as the solvent of its conflicting forces. Rabelais, Calvin and Ronsard, to mention only the greatest, were enthusiasts. Each pressed and exaggerated his particular view. Each saw in antiquity an image of himself and forced the note as all enthusiasts will. By the seventies the world was disrupted into hostile camps on the basis of the *libre examen*. Montaigne the pacifier came; he compared, he leveled. In his haphazard way he objectified human experience. The result was that he humbled the pride of man, very much like Calvin; but, unlike Calvin, he himself submitted to the conclusion he had reached. If, therefore, from his bourgeois and worldly standpoint, he recognized the value of human tradition and bent his head before the authority of Rome, it was not as a believer but as a forerunner of the seventeenth century, as one convinced of the validity of the *opinion générale*. And this *opinion générale* he created, on the basis of the common traits of mankind. " The proper study of mankind is man "; this would express the essence of his humanism, for the realization of which he indicated both the direction and the method that the seventeenth century was to pursue.

If Montaigne is the moralizer of this period, Brantôme has been correctly called its Suetonius. What Suetonius did for **Brantôme** the lives of the Caesars, that Brantôme has done for the Valois, especially Charles IX and Henry III. Like Montaigne, he was intensely curious as to life and persons, and he was well-bred and fond of travel, but whereas Montaigne reacted against his age, Brantôme takes an almost childish joy in his surroundings, which were anything but elevating. The end of the sixteenth century produced a flood of memoir writers, who like Monluc, Margaret of Valois and La Noue all have an interest for the historian of social customs and manners. But while some of these are Brantôme's superiors in style and most of them his betters in decency, none excel him in vividness or in the peculiar flavor with which he reproduces the nonchalance of the dying sixteenth century. As in a brightly colored picture-book he marshals before our eyes the pageantry, the bigotry, the corruption and also the charm of that troubled period. Of all this he himself was part and parcel.

Pierre de Bourdeille, *révérend père de Dieu,* as this lay-holder of the Abbey of Brantôme called himself, was born about 1540 and lived until 1614. Originally from Périgord, he spent his early youth at the court of Marguerite d'Angoulême, and after studying in Paris he went to Italy, where he served as a soldier. He sailed with Mary Stuart to Scotland, joined the Spanish forces in Africa, was present at the relief of Malta against the Turks, and in general led the life of a *condottiere*. Returning to France during the wars of religion, he finally became gentleman of the King's Chamber and aspired to be made governor of Périgord. But Henry III refused; whereupon Brantôme planned to desert his ungrateful sovereign and enter the service of Spain. From this seditious step he was saved by a fall from his horse (1584), which, besides incapacitating him physically, turned him into a writer. During the next twenty years he recorded in his anecdotal way the occurrences of the preceding thirteen.

Brantôme's works fall into two parts, treating respectively of the lives of men and of women. The *Hommes* consists, in M. Lalanne's edition, of the *Grands capitaines*, French and Spanish, the *Couronnels*, the *Discours sur les duels* — an institution which Brantôme exalts — and the *Rodomontades espagnoles*. The original draft of the *Hommes* was completed as early as 1599. The *Premier et second livre des Dames* is better known today as the separate treatises of *Dames illustres* and *Dames galantes*. A circumstance to be remembered is that Brantôme left an elaborate will directing that his works be published *en belle et grande lettre et grand volume, pour mieux paroistre*. That this wish was not carried out was due to his niece, who feared the scandal that the publication might cause. Indeed, the works were not published until 1665-1666, just in time it is said to inspire Bussy-Rabutin.

Brantôme is too inaccurate to be a good biographer. His works abound in expressions like *j'ai ouy parler* and *j'ai veu*, which often not only conceal his source but permit him to have no source at all. Some of his more detailed " lives," like that of the Duc de Guise, are too rambling and discursive to give an adequate idea of the personage concerned. On the whole, the figures of Catherine de Médicis, Anne of Brittany, Charles IX and Michel de l'Hospital come off best. But if Brantôme fails as a historian, his portraits are life-like and striking. His art consists in nailing a trait and then making us see its significance. For example, he records of Catherine:

> Quand elle appelloit quelqu'un *mon amy*, c'est qu'elle l'estimoit sot, ou qu'elle estoit en colere;

or, in depicting Anne of Brittany, he slyly remarks:

> Au reste elle estoit tres bonne, fort misericordieuse et fort chari-
> table, ainsy que j'ay ouy dire aux miens. Vray est qu'elle estoit
> fort prompte à la vengeance;

and there follows a startling example of how cruel she could be.

It is such vivid snatches as these that explain Brantôme's vogue with later generations. Monluc's *Commentaires* (1592) are better planned than anything of Brantôme's, but they are concerned with military history and despite their excellent struc-ture contain far less of real life. So, too, the *Discours politiques et militaires* (1585) of La Noue — of whom we have a sketch from Brantôme's pen — are remarkable for their impartiality and tolerance, a valuable asset in a historian, but again La Noue's refinement, which was considerable, does not make up for the solemn dullness of his style. Thus, licentious as he is — and this trait is confined largely to the *Dames galantes* — Brantôme remains the most gifted chronicler of his epoch: his range is large, his sparkle delightful, and his sense of detail as keen as it is frank. In many ways he is comparable to Froissart.

THE AGE OF HENRY IV AND THE COMMON SENSE OF MALHERBE

THE accession of Henry IV in 1594 heralds the restoration of peace and order on French soil. The Gascon King united in himself high political wisdom, a love of *panache* and a forgiving and tolerant nature. The famous *Satire Ménippée* — the first successful journalistic satire in France — amid considerable jocularity and buffoonery made short shift of the opposing Leaguers and vigorously welcomed Henry as " Notre vrai roy légitime, naturel et souverain." From now on, politics were to converge more and more towards the absolutism of Louis XIV.

It is characteristic, however, that the reign of Henry IV and the beginning of Louis XIII's stand for a transition; certainly in things artistic and literary. Side by side, we find literary rule and literary freedom. The epicurean common sense (*bon sens*) set free by the *Essais* of Montaigne culminates on the one hand in the stoical and religious reactions of Du Vair and François de Sales, and on the other in the brilliant but erratic satire of Mathurin Régnier — to which, however, the final answer is the triumphant, impersonal muse of Malherbe. Freedom again there is in the new-born tragi-comedy, made popularly successful by Hardy, and in the heroic pastoral, D'Urfé's *Astrée,* of which so sensible a person as La Fontaine could say:

> Etant petit garçon je lisais son roman
> Et je le lis encore ayant la barbe grise.

But in these genres also (see Book III) the effort is nevertheless toward uniformity of the spirit, which accompanies the great socialization that French literature is to undergo before becoming " Classical."

Thus, on the whole, the sixteenth century ends and the seventeenth begins with a confident look into the future. This vision

includes: peace; a stable and unified government; a surcease of
the turbulent individualism of the Renaissance proper; above all,
a growing recognition of the social function of man; and finally,
a gradual nationalization of language and culture and a closer
welding of thought and expression — that is, a sense of style.

In Etienne Pasquier, whose *Recherches de la France* began
to appear in 1560, we already find a judicious spirit as regards
life and letters. Pasquier was a magistrate; his turn
Pasquier of mind was not original, but he belongs to that large
group of French jurists whose breadth and solidity have done
honor to the legal profession. His *Recherches* consist of a
desultory but thoroughly interesting collection of remarks on
the history, politics, culture and literature of France. In all this
there is much keen appreciation, not a little humor and, among
other matters, an excellent account of the Pléiade movement.
Pasquier does not hesitate to combat Ronsard's excessive imitations, throughout he upholds common sense and a certain innate
taste, and while honoring the ancients he also defends French
against Latin. He has the charm of an engaging and sensible
causeur. Though he belonged strictly to the age of Ronsard, he
lived until 1615 and took an active part in the royalist polemics
against the Leaguers.

With Henri Estienne (1528–1598), also of the earlier generation, we reach a writer whose nationalistic views on language
Henri did much to prepare the field for Malherbe. Author
Estienne of a *Thesaurus* of Greek, with which language he advocated the "conformity" of French, Estienne was a Huguenot,
a Hellenist and a bourgeois to the core. Belonging to a family
distinguished for its scholarship, he published (1554) a manuscript of *Anacreon* which deeply interested the Pléiade, and he
wrote an *Apologie pour Hérodote*, in which he aired his Protestant and scholarly ideals. His main importance, however,
is that he fought the Italianate influence at court. In his
Dialogues du nouveau langage français italianisé (1578) Estienne speaks through the mouth of Celtophile — admirer of
French — and upbraids the courtiers who, like Philausone, would
corrupt the native stock of rich and pure words. The same
theme is treated in his better written but incomplete *Précellence*

du langage français (1579): not only is Italian foreign to France, it is actually inferior to French in grace, force and excellence.

In 1567 Jean Bodin published the six books of his *République*, where in words devoid of passion — but also of charm — he laid **The** down the theory of the French monarchical state. **"Satire** With singularly clear vision Bodin saw in absolute **Ménippée"** monarchy the extension of the tribal or family idea, and in the monarch the patriarch of the French people. The *Satire Ménippée* (1594) confirms this idea at the very moment when the efforts of patriotic Protestants and Catholics triumphed in the victory of Henry IV. Thus the pamphlet lacks the political influence often attributed to it. As a matter of fact, it is a literary parody of the Estates of the League that had been unsuccessfully called to choose a king.

In its original form (the present title is taken from the *Saturae Menippeae* of Varro and did not appear until the sixth edition) the satire was the work of Jean Leroy, whose collaborators were Gillot, clerk-advocate of the Parliament, the poets Passerat and Rapin, and Chrestien and Pithou, converted Protestants. The *Ménippée* opens with a harangue in Rabelaisian style on the panacea Catholicon — *quintessence catholique-jesuite-espagnole* — whereby the Leaguers would achieve their own fortune and the enslavement of France. Then follows an account of the opening of the Estates; a description of the tapestries with which the hall is hung, each portraying some betrayal of the French cause; a catalogue of the leaders of the League, with pointed remarks on their unsavory private and public lives; and finally, in mock-heroic style, the speeches of the Leaguers themselves. These display unusual variety and skill of treatment. Partly burlesque, partly true to reality, always witty, they culminate in the speech of Claude d'Aubray, which is wholly serious and eloquent. It covers about half the book and is a happy combination of historical retrospect, analysis of politics and arraignment of the Leaguers. D'Aubray was the leader of the *Politiques* or enemies of the League; and it is likely that his speech was actually delivered before the Estates.

While the *Ménippée* is too disproportionate and uneven to rank as a classic, it yet shows a great advance in the scope and art of French satire. It analyzes political corruption with a minuteness worthy of Rabelais, and it drives its lessons home by a series of thrusts that are in the best vein of Gallic irony.

But the ethical force of the time is found in Charron and Du Vair, both of whom followed in the footsteps of Montaigne. In **Charron and** fact, Pierre Charron (1541–1603), who had been **Du Vair** Montaigne's pupil, was the chief organizer of his master's thought. Like Du Vair, Charron was a legist and a theo. logian, who began his literary career with a treatise on the *Trois Vérités* (1593), in which the existence of God, the truth of Chris. tianity and the orthodoxy of the Roman Church are defended as unassailable. This work was followed by his philosophical *Traité de la sagesse* (1601), where he systematized Montaigne's ideas in orthodox form. Taking the *Apologie* seriously, Charron turned the *Que sais-je?* into a positive *Je ne sais*, and set up this maxim as a rational basis of the Christian religion. Thus he antici. pates Pascal, but he does so without genius, heavily and dully. How closely he builds on Montaigne is evident from the state. ment:

> La nation, le pays, le lieu donnent la religion — l'homme sans son seu est fait Juif ou Chrestien, à cause qu'il est né dedans la Juiverie ou Chrestienté.

But Charron would use tolerance to uphold tradition. Mindful of the " three truths," he would reintegrate his nation in Roman Catholicism, which makes *citoyens du monde* and avoids the dangers of the *opinion triée et particulière*. This is an important step toward the French Classical point of view. Charron's book had great success, although the Sorbonne found it reprehensible.

As a personality Guillaume du Vair (1556–1621) is far superior to Charron. Councilor of the Parliament of Paris, envoy to England, and finally bishop of Lisieux, Du Vair was one of the leading *Politiques*, defending this cause with steadfastness and eloquence. To him the stoicism of the early Montaigne was the rule of life. Accordingly, his *De la philosophie des stoïques* and *De la constance* show him as a practical moralist to whom philoso- phy is a guide to conduct. Direct and even poetic in style, Du Vair discards all show of erudition and comes out strongly for Reason in its two-fold function: first, as the liberator from passion, and second, as the guide to faith by its demonstration of our human limitations. In all this there is nothing new except the force and cogency of statement. But Du Vair's sense of conviction, shown again in his *De l'éloquence française,* won him readers and explains his hold on the next generation, especially on Malherbe.

Although the stoicism of Du Vair gave strength it did not console; and the times were now ripe for a conciliation of religion
Saint François de Sales with the emotions of the heart. To have achieved this was the beatitude of Saint François de Sales. The path he mapped out was, like that of his teachers, the Jesuits, a *chemin de velours*: a path festooned with roses, where religious devotion became attractive and moral regeneration was opened to the " worldly " by an appeal to their sense of delicacy and refinement. De Sales' psychology is essentially a casuistry of love, with the gradations and nuances carefully drawn. But beneath his docile exterior this reformer concealed an austere and unshakable will. He knew that the Christian life demanded humility, and humility before God on the part of his aristocratic flock became the goal of his unsparing efforts.

He was born in Savoy, whose prince he served in trying to redeem the district of Chablais from the Protestant heresy. This attempt met with little success, and being sent to Paris in 1602 on a mission, he associated himself with a group of mystics, the chief of whom was Mme Acarie. He now gave up the plan of converting Protestants, and although he resisted the allurements offered by Henry IV and returned to Savoy as titular bishop of Geneva, he never loosened his hold on his French followers. His influence was great with women; through Mme de Chantal, grandmother of Mme de Sévigné, he established the order of the Visitation, and it is to her that his best *Epîtres spirituelles* are addressed.

But his great work, second in popularity only to the *Imitation* of Thomas à Kempis, is the *Introduction à la vie dévote.* This and the complementary *Traité de l'amour de Dieu* (1606) contain all that is most distinctive in de Sales' teaching and theology. Starting with the premise that the Christian life is essentially a life of love — an idea already exploited by Luther — de Sales evolves the thesis that the redemption of man proceeds, not from sudden abnegation and sacrifice, but from the gradual diffusion of love into every act, even the smaller ones, of this earthly life. Thus he mollifies the externals of religion, without, however, giving up its main doctrines, and by beginning with the social virtues — such as good breeding and consideration of others — he seeks to insinuate into the social complex the sterner, unworldly qualities of Christianity. François de Sales' style — *langage de la paix* he calls it — is in the main winsome, however flowery it may seem at present. Many of his images are far-fetched, though it is part of his general purpose to draw them with abundance from Nature and literature. On the other hand, with an eye to *le commun usage*, he writes excellent, singularly modern French, and in this respect as in so many others he leads up to Bossuet and Bourdaloue.

In short, the *Introduction à la vie dévote*, begun as a formal course of instruction for Philothée — in real life, Mme de Charmoisy — anticipates the courtly, religious literature of the era of Louis XIV. Its special significance is that for the first time de Sales bridges the gulf between theology and worldly society. Its author was canonized by the Roman Church in 1665.

While the new movement towards socialization was thus claiming the support of the church, its influence was also manifest in the domain of pure literature, in poetry. And in this transformation Malherbe is the outstanding and significant factor.

François de Malherbe is best known by the title of *docteur en négative*, which relates him to the Pléiade as the antithesis of

Malherbe

Ronsard and as the orderer and purifier of poetic style. A curious mixture of pedant and artist, Malherbe is one of the pillars of Classicism because of an instinct for harmony and his unswerving common sense:

> Le sens commun, contre lequel, la religion à part, vous savez il n'y a orateur au monde qui me pût rien persuader.

No man was surer of himself than he. We can picture him to ourselves, in his room at the Hôtel de Bellegrade in Paris, delivering orders on the distinction between *pas* and *point*, the gerundive and the present participle — as if, says Balzac, it were a matter of two neighboring peoples, jealous of their frontiers. But it was this meticulous care that gave to the French language the clarity, purity and cadence which it has in Corneille and

Racine. Thus what Malherbe took away in variety, exuberance, and emotionalism, he restored in firmness, structure and restraint. In his treatment of the Alexandrine he fashioned the vehicle in which the generation of 1660 was to find glorious expression. Hence the aptness of Boileau's appraisal:

> Enfin Malherbe vint; et le premier en France
> Fit sentir dans les vers une juste cadence.
>
> . . . .
> Marchez donc sur ses pas, aimez la pureté,
> Et de son tour heureux imitez la clarté.

Malherbe's ascent to Parnassus was slow and painstaking. He was born at Caen, Normandy, in 1555. Having been trained for the bar at Bâle and Heidelberg, he went with the Duke of Angoulême to Provence, and there he married a widow from whom he had two children, both of whom he survived. It is significant that Malherbe, whose best remembered poem is the *Consolation de Monsieur du Périer sur la mort de sa fille,* never gave expression in verse to his own grief. He believed that a poet should be the objective purveyor of rationalized emotions, and he could never bring himself to regard the death of his own children in this stern light. His first published poem, *Les Larmes de Saint-Pierre,* is an imitation of Tansillo and still in the Italianate manner of Desportes. But with the famous *Consolation* (1598) and an Ode to Marie de Médicis (1600) Malherbe comes into his own. Henceforth he follows unerringly the path of simplicity and versified prose.

In 1605 Malherbe took steps to be appointed poet laureate of the Bourbon dynasty. Besought by the poet's friends, Henry IV, who hesitated at first, was charmed by Malherbe's *Prière pour le Roi allant en Limousin* and finally gave orders to M. de Bellegarde to provide for the poet in Paris. Under Louis XIII Malherbe's prestige suffered no relapse; on the contrary, Marie de Médicis clung to the person who had celebrated her charms, and in spite of opposition from without, his position as arbiter of French letters was unshaken until his death (1628).

The amount of his published verse is small — some four thousand lines. In these, as has often been said, Malherbe follows the lead of Ronsard — but of the Ronsard of the *odelette* and the *élégie.* And these genres he emasculates and rationalizes.

" Malherbe," says Brunetière, "conçoit un sonnet ou une élégie comme une unité logique qui démontre, discute, tout au moins expose quelque chose de bien déterminé." Poetry to him is a *métier* like any other; it is not a matter for the learned, and least of all for the " divinely inspired." Therefore his remark that the porters of the Port au Foin were his guides in speech, by which he meant that even they would understand his verse, so clear and unmistakable it was. Negatively, then, he opposed the Pléiade, accepting the classical genres, but restricting their scope, omitting everything that seemed obscure or learned or imaginative. Positively, he developed *la poésie oratoire* — so peculiarly French — with its sumptuous commonplaces, its instinct for the right word in the right place, its succession of harmonious Alexandrines. This type of verse lacks color; it is architectonic, not picturesque; it does not move the reader, it persuades him; it appeals to the universal reason and not to the individual imagination. Malherbe's most famous verse:

> Et, rose, elle a vécu ce que vivent les roses,
> L'espace d'un matin,

is a case in point. Embodied in a long argument on the inevitability of death — and what could be more commonplace? — this line is the expression of the Pléiade's favorite theme in as simple, as clear, as grammatical and as universal a form as possible. And yet the line carries a sense of conviction, a stoical peace and tranquillity, which are perhaps unique. It need hardly be added that Malherbe achieved such impeccable effects rarely. An Ode on the victory of Louis at La Rochelle, written at the ripe age of seventy-two, is probably Malherbe's most " artistic " success.

But if Malherbe's muse was oratory rather than poetry, this quality stood him in good stead as a critic of language and versification. His *Commentaire sur Desportes*, although merely a marginal comment on a copy of Desportes' works, embodies the principles of his reforms.

Here the leading idea is " usage," controlled by the trinity of purity, clearness and precision. Desportes seemed to him " padded " and " redundant," and his first desire was to put French vocabulary into a strait-jacket. In this he followed the tendency of his period against improvisation. Besides, many of the Pléiade's archaisms were out of date; quite a number of their foreign borrowings and dialect words had remained un-French; Desportes and even Ronsard had made too free a use of diminutives. In these directions Malherbe's pruning was wise. On the other hand, he went too far in his objection to certain adjectives like *soucieux*, to all gerundives, to the use of technical terms in literature, above all to the word *idéal* — " un mot d'école et qui ne se doit point dire en choses d'amour." With much better reason he tried to fix the exact meaning of words; he practically established the modern word-order; and he correctly considered rime as the important feature of French versification, thus his opposition to " overflow " (*enjambement*) and his advocacy of " rich rime." As Brunetière observes, Malherbe is in many respects the ancestor of the Parnassian poets of the nineteenth century. Chapelain affirmed that " il a ignoré la poésie." But certainly Malherbe understood the instrument of poetry better than Chapelain. This we should not forget when we have in mind the sum total of his negations.

It must not be thought, however, that the reforms of Malherbe won easy or immediate acceptance. Those followers who did **Malherbe's** him most honor were of the generation of Boileau. **Disciples** Among his immediate disciples were François Maynard (1582-1646) and Honorat de Bueil, Marquis de Racan (1589-1670). It has been justly said that these two, if combined, would have made one excellent poet. Malherbe himself thought that Maynard lacked force and that Racan was careless in style; probably the reverse is closer to the truth. In any case, despite much repetition and monotony, Maynard has left us two noteworthy selections: the one a charming *Dédicace* to his own book —

> Petit livre que j'ai poli;[1]

and the other, an ode entitled *La belle Vieille*, where for a brief moment he soars on the wings of sentiment:

> Ce n'est pas d'aujourd'hui que je suis ta conquête,
> Huit lustres ont suivi le jour que tu me pris,
> Et j'ai fidèlement aimé ta belle tête
> Sous des cheveux châtains et sous des cheveux gris.

[1] See Catullus, Liber I, 1.

Yet Racan, who had a distinguished career in the army and at court, excelled both Maynard and Malherbe in the musical quality of his verse and in a truly poetic grasp of simple and natural situations. His *Arthénice ou les Bergeries*, a pastoral drama, is charmingly written; while his celebrated *Stances à Tircis* is a melodious development of a poetic commonplace and elicited the admiration of La Fontaine.

Foremost in the opposition to Malherbe were Mathurin Régnier, Mlle de Gournay, and the *libertin* but truly lyrical Théophile de **Malherbe's** Viau. In general, they represent the last outburst of **Opponents** the Renaissance *furor poeticus* before it was smothered under the weight of Classical rule and decorum.

Mathurin Régnier (1573-1613) was the nephew of Desportes and Malherbe's junior by eighteen years. He spent part of his youth in Italy and later enjoyed the protection of the Marquis de Cœuvres, who wished to present him at court. But Régnier refused, quite content to bask in the glory reflected by his uncle, whose excellent dinners, however, he did not fail to attend. It was at one of these that Desportes invited Malherbe to listen to one of his compositions, whereupon the latter replied: " Let us dine first, your soup is better than your psalms." Whether this tale is literally true or not, Régnier took his uncle's side; and every word he wrote breathes opposition to Malherbe. His fame rests on his Satires, the best of which is *Macette*, and, as regards Malherbe, the well-known Ninth Satire, addressed to Rapin.

The key note of Régnier is gayety; it is characteristic of his satire that it is never ill-humored. Thus he unites the Gallic wit of Marot with the enthusiasm of the Pléiade, and he owes not a little to Ovid and the Italians, especially Ariosto. But he has also the defect of his quality. However sprightly, he lacks moral indignation; the only exception to this being *Macette*, which is also his best written work. As his satire is social and not political, Régnier has given it a note of universality; and Boileau, who condemned his platitudes and lack of order, yet saw that for knowledge of human nature Régnier is comparable to Molière.

Régnier excels in bold strokes and brilliant flashes rather than in sustained utterance. Already in the Second Satire, on poets, he hits off the telling line:

Méditant un sonnet, médite un évêché —

which might apply to Desportes. Nowhere does his insight appear better than in describing the pedantry of Malherbe. It is the old problem of art versus nature, and Régnier is of course for nature. The Ninth Satire is a brilliant excursus on this theme, negatively presented:

> Ils rampent bassement, faibles d'inventions,
> Et n'osent, peu hardis, tenter les fictions,
> Froids à l'imaginer; car s'ils font quelque chose
> C'est proser de la rime, et rimer de la prose.

And so in *Macette*, Régnier combines nature with wit in order to give us one of the best portraits in French literature. Macette is the pandering woman: a kind of female-Tartuffe, a descendant of the Faux-Semblant of the *Roman de la Rose*, but admirably individualized by Régnier, who detested hypocrisy:

> Sans art elle s'habille, et simple en contenance
> Son teint mortifié prêche la pénitence.
>
> . . . .
> Loin du monde elle fait sa demeure et son gîte,
> Son œil tout pénitent ne pleure qu'eau bénite,
> Enfin c'est un exemple, en ce siècle tortu,
> D'amour, de charité, d'honneur et de vertu.

Such portraiture as this redeems Régnier's faults of style — and of person. He is, if we make due allowances, the Villon of his time; and because of his spontaneity he has never lacked readers.

Mlle Le Jars de Gournay (1556–1645) had no such good fortune. She who called herself the *fille d'alliance* of Montaigne, whose works she edited, was old-maidish in appearance and character. On the other hand, she was not lacking in *esprit*, and her prose work *L'Ombre* (1687) defends Ronsard and banters Malherbe in an engaging and picturesque style. It appeared to her that Malherbe's entire contribution consisted in *polissure*, and she regretted, but in vain, that

> ils tondent la poésie de liberté, de dignité, de richesse, et pour le dire en un mot, de fleur, de fruit et d'espoir.

The third figure of the opposition, Théophile de Viau (1596–1626), is described better as a free-lance than as an ally of Régnier and Mlle de Gournay. Indeed, he was not above combining

> La douceur de Malherbe et l'ardeur de Ronsard.

But life made him a profligate, and he squandered his powers on unworthy objects and in defying — *par bel air* — the pedantry of Malherbe. He is generally remembered by his irregular tragedy *Pyrame et Thisbé* (1617), where with true Elizabethan freedom he produced the hyperbole:

> Le voilà, le poignard qui du sang de son maître
> S'est souillé lâchement; il en rougit, le traître;

and thus merited the censure of Boileau. But *libertin*[1] that he was, he possessed an inborn sense of form and a feeling for Nature. Note the harmony of the lines that he attributes to Apollo:

> C'est moi qui pénétrant la dureté des arbres
>
> . . . .
> Qui fais taire les vents, qui fais parler les marbres,
> Et qui trace au destin la conduite des rois;

and compare the soft, caressing mood of his *Solitude:*

> Un froid et ténébreux silence
> Dort à l'ombre de ces ormeaux,
> Et les vents battent les rameaux
> D'une amoureuse violence.

If Théophile was a late-comer, a survival of the age of Ronsard, his verse shows that after Malherbe lyrism was not dead in France but only slumbering. Twenty-two editions of his works appeared in fifty years, and the youthful Academy picked him as one of the authors on whose vocabulary its Dictionary should be based. It was the satire of Boileau that killed his vogue; but some of his quality passed into Voiture and Racine, until finally Romanticism gave it a glorious rebirth.

[1] On the *libertins* or epicureans, see Bk. III, Ch. V.

BOOK III

PRE-CLASSICISM

CHAPTER I

SOCIAL FORM AND THE SALON WRITERS

THE seventeenth century is the *grand siècle* of the French. It is for them what the age of Elizabeth is for the English, the Cinquecento for the Italians. It is then that France has her most representative writers, those who reflect the national qualities at their best. It is then that the Renaissance ideal of absolute monarchy, realized in Louis XIV, places France at the political head of Europe. Not only does the much abused phrase *l'Etat c'est moi* express the degree of unity to which French culture was to attain, but the court at Versailles is the symbol of this resplendent time. Here politics and art and literature, centering about the person of the King, achieve a harmonious coöperation that is the keynote of Classicism.

This "point of perfection in art," which La Bruyère later compares to "ripeness in Nature," was however not reached **Different** at once. The Classical Period itself does not begin **Periods** until 1653, with the triumphal entry of Mazarin into Paris after the Wars of the Fronde, and it ends before the century is over, with the Quarrel of the Ancients and the Moderns in 1687. The preceding age, from 1624 — when Richelieu came into power — until 1653, is one of struggle and preparation. We give it the name of Pre-Classicism, as showing at once its direction and its formative character.

In politics this period stands for the destruction of the enemies of the crown, both within and without the kingdom. With great singleness of purpose Richelieu shattered the last stronghold of the Protestants (La Rochelle, 1628), combatted the supremacy of Spain, crushed the conspiracy of the nobles led by Cinq-Mars, and in every way strove for national unity. His own interest in letters, and Richelieu's literary gifts were not conspicuous, was made contributory to this purpose. He worked for the principle of national authority in literature with the same zeal with which he discouraged the French admiration for Spain (see below, his attitude on the *Cid*). The hand he took in the establishment of the French Academy in 1629 is another proof of his policy; namely, to give the country a standard of speech which though national should be universally clear and precise. Mazarin, who succeeded Richelieu as prime-minister — a post that he held during the minority of Louis XIV — was the indirect cause and central figure of the Wars of the Fronde. These were the last attempts of the feudal aristocracy to throw off the usurpations of the crown. Serious as the revolt was, it had in it the elements of opera-bouffe. The Frondeurs, including such illustrious persons as the Grand Condé, Cardinal de Retz and the Duchess of Longueville, were divided among themselves; personal vanity and bombast influenced greatly their actions; and when peace and order were finally restored in Paris, the effect on the youthful Louis XIV was to discourage in him any attempt to govern the country by constitutional means.

It was principally in the development of social form or etiquette that the Pre-Classical period was fruitful. Under the impact, first of Italy, but also of Spain, social intercourse is cultivated on a new scale; good manners and deportment are encouraged for the distinction they give; and this movement furnishes the background for most of the art and literature of the century.

The courtiers of Henry IV deserve that name only by tolerance. Fresh from the battle-field, they carried into social relations the swagger, the rudeness, the license of their honest but boisterous natures. .s true that Henry's own attitude was offset by his marriage in 1600 to Marie de Médicis, who invited the Italian Marino to Paris in 1615. Marino was a representative of the euphuistic or affected style, and he undoubtedly had an influence on the refinement of manners and speech in France. At the same time, the birth of social form occurred not at the French court but in the house oɪ a private citizen: the famous Catherine de Vivonne, Marquise de Rambouillet.

Catherine was the daughter of Jean de Vivonne, French ambassador to Rome, and Julia Savelli, a Roman lady of **The Hôtel de** distinction. She had married Charles d'Angennes, **Rambouillet** who in 1611 became the Marquis de Rambouillet. Of her social and intellectual charms Mlle de Scudéry writes as follows in one of her well-known " literary portraits ":

> L'esprit de Cléomire [one of the anagrams applied to Catherine, Arthénice is another] n'est pas un de ces esprits qui n'ont de lumière que celle que la nature leur donne, car elle l'a cultivé soigneusement. Elle sait diverses langues, et n'ignore presque rien qui mérite d'être su; mais elle le sait sans faire semblant de le savoir, et on dirait, à l'entendre parler, tant elle est modeste, qu'elle ne parle de toutes choses admirablement que par le simple sens commun et par le seul usage du monde.

But distinguished as Catherine was, her delicacy was overdone. Her sensibilities were offended by such a word as *teigneux* (" scurvy "), and, as Tallemant des Réaux records, she and her husband " vivaient un peu trop en cérémonie."

Yet it was precisely through ceremony that she aimed to give her countrymen that much needed refinement. Withdrawing in 1613 from a court which seemed to her barbarous, Catherine opened her house near the Louvre to her own circle of admirers and friends. The house had been previously remodeled, according to plans made by the Marquise herself, to receive a larger company than did most dwellings of the period. The drawing-room, which was also the Marquise's bed-room, had been tinted in blue — hence the *Chambre bleue* — and had been divided by a railing, behind which stood the bed. On each side of the bed were spaces known respectively as the *devant* and the *ruelle*. It was the habit of Catherine, seated on the bed, to receive the evening's guests first in one passage and then in the other; so that *ruelle* soon became synonymous with a reception itself — just as later on, when with advancing years the Marquise moved her bed into an alcove, an *alcoviste* is one who frequents such receptions.

The company who were invited to share this official intimacy were not only people of rank but also men of letters. Among the former were Richelieu, the Duc de la Tremoïlle, Mme de Longueville, the Marquis de Montausier,[1] and later, Mme de La Fayette and Mme de Sévigné. The men of letters included most of the illustrious; notably, Malherbe, Chapelain, Voiture, Scudéry, Rotrou and Corneille. Conversation, of course, was the great attraction of this feast of reason; although actual parlor games — imported from Italy — dancing, music and impromptus of various kinds, were part of the entertainment. Yet conversation claimed the foreground with these adepts of culture, and their discourse sparkled with conceits after the manner of Marino and hyperboles in the style of the Spaniard Góngora.

Affected purism or "preciosity" has a bad name. At the beginning of the seventeenth century, forms of affectation, partly independent of each other, spread through Europe like a disease. Lyly's *Euphues* appeared in England as early as 1579; considerably later in Spain came the *culteranismo* of Góngora. But in France the *précieux* movement was probably the most productive of good results. The Marquise lived until 1665, and the Hôtel de Rambouillet had several periods of influence.

La Préciosité

Its greatest brilliancy was from 1630 to 1648. Between these years it served the useful purpose of listening eagerly to a letter from Balzac, a criticism by Chapelain, a play by Corneille — even if it pronounced Chapelain's epic[2] "beautiful but excessively tiresome" and went into raptures over the *Guirlande de Julie*, a chaplet of poems presented by Montausier to the Marquise's daughter on her birthday. The effect of such feminine control was bound to be two-sided. On the one hand, conversational and epistolary style flourished; both language and literature shook off the last vestiges of pedantry and gained measurably in precision and sparkle; never was wit more brilliant or more trenchant. On the other hand, the cleavage between "society" and the "people" is increased; literature becomes mainly the expression of a super-refined class; the quip or *pointe* is cultivated for its own sake, and the

---

[1] Montausier was the suitor of Julie d'Angennes, the Marquise's daughter. It is characteristic that he was kept waiting fifteen years before Julie married him.

[2] *La Pucelle*

commonplace shunned. It is enough, in order to understand the loss to language, to note that a useful word like *poitrine* was tabooed because the butcher said *poitrine de veau* or that Somaize in his *Dictionnaire des Prétieuses* records *soustien de la vie* for " bread." Most of all, the romances of the age were to suffer from this restriction: their characters do not eat or drink, nor breathe any other atmosphere than that of their own sublimated sentiments.

For many of these characteristics the Hôtel de Rambouillet was not to blame. The word *précieuse,* meaning an " affected woman " gains currency about 1655, while a " mannered style " is a recurrent phenomenon in French from the Middle Ages forward. But what a distinguished woman might permit herself, in an imitator would seem distorted and out of place, and Catherine had many imitators. Among them were Mme de Sablé — the friend of Pascal — and Mlle Paulet, called *la belle lionne* because of her tawny hair. Most noteworthy of all is Mlle de Scudéry, whose *samedis,* over which she presided under the name of Sappho, gave the entrée to people quite as literary as the frequenters of the Marquise, but less distinguished in social rank and thus visibly more affected in their attitude. Finally, when we add to these great ladies those numerous provincial dames who easily fell a victim to the refining habit, we understand the reason in 1659 for Molière's *Précieuses ridicules,* where not only the imitation but preciosity itself is satirized. From this date on, *précieuse* could have no other than an unfavorable meaning, while the movement itself lapsed of its own ineptitude. As Ménage remarked, when after the performance of Molière's comedy he took Chapelain aside:

> Monsieur . . . nous approuvions, vous et moi, toutes les sottises qui viennent d'être critiquées si finement et avec tant de bon sens. Il nous faudra brûler ce que nous avons adoré et adorer ce que nous avons brûlé.

Moreover, at that moment the eyes of the cultivated world were fixed on another spectacle: the rising glory of the court of Louis XIV. With this arbiter of elegance no other could compete, though the literary and artistic salon is henceforth a French institution.

Associated intimately with the Hôtel de Rambouillet are two letter-writers of note. The first is Jean-Louis Guez, Sieur **Louis Guez de Balzac** de Balzac (1597–1654), whose grandiloquence laid the foundation for French oratory and the rise of a Classical style.

Educated by the Jesuits, Balzac traveled and then entered the service of a French grandee, the later Cardinal de la Valette, with whom he passed two years in Rome. But the greater part of Balzac's life was spent on his estates in Angoulême, whence he kept in contact with the refined world by his writings, especially his Letters. In addition to these and various *discours* addressed to Mme de Rambouillet, Balzac also wrote a *Prince*, the *Socrate chrétien* and *Aristippe ou de la cour*. But it was his Letters, the first of which appeared in 1624 and which were an event at the Hôtel de Rambouillet, that made him famous.

In Balzac's ideas there was nothing very original; little that cannot be found in Amyot or Montaigne or the ancients. Moreover, no writer is less intimate; Balzac has no abandon, no moment when he is not consciously building a phrase. As Lanson remarks, it is the author and not the man who speaks to us in him. Balzac wraps in a cloak of rhetoric even the little things of life. Thanking a friend for a gift of peacocks, he writes:

> Je connais mes richesses et en suis connu, et après avoir lu jusqu'à ne voir goutte, je viens délasser ma vue travaillée dans cet admirable vert, qui m'est tout ensemble un divertissement et un remède.

But he accomplished two notable things. He made French prose eloquent by giving it cadence, and he incorporated into it the Renaissance concept of the Roman patriot and of the *honnête homme*. It is easy to imagine with what effect his high-sounding phrases fell on the ears of Mme de Rambouillet's circle, especially when they contained such grandiose commonplaces as:

> Un peu d'esprit et beaucoup d'autorité, voilà ce qui a toujours gouverné le monde.

Thus Balzac did for prose what Malherbe had done for verse. His type of Roman lives again in the plays of Corneille; note the following from the Letter on *Cinna,* addressed to Corneille himself:

> L'empereur le fit consul, et vous l'avez fait honnête homme: mais vous l'avez pu faire par les lois d'un art, *qui polit et orne la vérité.*

That is, the French Cinna is a Roman plus the rules of decorum, and it is the function of art to embellish nature.

The significance of Balzac, then, lies in the impetus he gave to writing as such. He lacked the genius to create ideas or to invent new forms. He spent his life in making phrases, but of these he was a master-builder. He understood the harmonies of French to an eminent degree, and he taught his generation the value of paragraphs, transitions and the *mot propre.* His sentences, unlike those of his predecessors, are balanced and well-proportioned. Thus he fashioned the instrument of rhetorical French prose for future writers; the style of Bossuet is built upon that of Balzac.

On the other hand, the so-called *Œuvres* of Vincent Voiture (1598–1648) remain landlocked in Mme de Rambouillet's **Vincent** salon. They are in every way its expression; and **Voiture** therefore the elegant badinage with which they are filled has long since lost its flavor. However, Voiture was not a professional writer, and his poems and letters were not published until after his death.

Son of a wine merchant of Amiens, Voiture was another of Cardinal de la Valette's protégés. He was presented early in life to the Marquise, whose unofficial master-of-ceremonies he became. Grace and wit fitted him well for this rôle; and he organized dances and excursions, played practical jokes on the Marquise and bantered his associates in trifling verse and prose. These gifts and an undercurrent of sound judgment won him the favor of Richelieu, who sent him on diplomatic missions and permitted him to round out his career as an *honnête homme.*

In his *Letters* Voiture displays *finesse* and an innate delicacy of phrasing, which are in sharp contrast with the Spanish bombast then in fashion. How effective his mockery was appears from the Letter to Mme de Rambouillet on the word *car,* which it was rumored the Academy would banish from the language. He writes:

> Je ne sais pour quel intérêt ils tâchent d'ôter à *car* ce qui lui appartient pour le donner à *pour ce que,* ni pourquoi ils veulent dire avec trois mots ce qu'ils pouvaient dire avec trois lettres. On ne fera point de difficulté d'attaquer *mais,* et je ne sais si *si* demeurera en sûreté.

But his greatest merit is as a writer of *vers de société* —a genre of which he really established the vogue. He revived what was best in the lighter lyric vein — for example, the *rondeau* — and he made these shorter forms the perfect vehicle of grace and distinction. His charming *Sonnet à Uranie,* with its time-old hyperbole —

> Je bénis mon martyre, et content de mourir,
> Je n'ose murmurer contre sa tyrannie,

had the honor of rallying a group of partisans, the Uranists, during the Fronde; while Mme de Rambouillet's praises, but hardly her traits, survive in the following madrigal from his pen:

> Jamais l'œil du soleil
> Ne vit rien de pareil,
> Ni si plein de délice,
> Rien si digne d'amour,
> Si ce ne fut le jour
> Que naquit Arthénice.

Among Voiture's rivals and followers were Benserade, whose sonnet on Job was preferred to that on Uranie; Boisrobert, the favorite of Richelieu; Maleville, another sonneteer; and Sarrasin, a clever writer of *ballades* and of prose. Yet none of these could surpass the exquisite gallantry of Voiture.

While polite society was thus cultivating manners, a smaller group, known officially as *les doctes,* was busy at codifying the **The Academy Group** rules of art. At first the meetings were secret. They began in 1626 when various literary men formed the habit of dropping in on Valentin Conrart, a wealthy Parisian, for the exchange of ideas. The group included Gombault, a minor dramatist, Godeau, bishop of Vence and known to the *précieux* world as the *Mage de Sidon,* and the critic Chapelain. In 1629 Richelieu proposed the formation of a formal body for the pursuit of literature. This plan was finally accepted, and the new society took the simple and effective name of *l'Académie française* — in imitation, more or less, of the various Academies then flourishing in Italy.

The first meeting of the Academy was in March, 1634, although Parliament, jealous of its own prerogatives, waited until 1637 before granting a charter. From the very start the membership of the organization was limited to forty, and in 1640 Patru introduced the custom of receiving a new member with a *discours*. The members themselves also propounded various topics; thus Chapelain spoke against "love," Gombault discussed the still more elusive matter of the *Je ne sais quoi*, and, lastly, Chapelain proposed the excellent idea of making a Dictionary and of compiling a Grammar, a Rhetoric and a Poetic Art.

The Dictionary alone saw the light, though not until 1694, the date of the first edition. The work had been entrusted to Claude Favre de Vaugelas (1585–1650), a native of Savoy and the author in 1647 of the excellent *Remarques sur la langue française*. Vaugelas followed Malherbe in declaring for a purified form of French, based on "usage." But unlike Malherbe, he meant by usage the speech of the court and of "the best authors of the time." So that again the tendency was toward aristocratic norms and a neglect of the every-day French of the people. In fact, the Dictionary urged the elimination of "les vieux mots," "mots nouvellement inventés," "les termes d'emportement et qui blessent la pudeur," as well as the technical words once dear to Ronsard. This severity, however, did not pass unnoticed. As early as 1650 Ménage — the grammarian — launched a witty satire, which began:

> A nos seigneurs académiques,
> Nos seigneurs les hypercritiques,
> Souverains arbitres des mots,
> Doctes faiseurs d'avant-propos,
> Cardinal-historiographes.

And Furetière, driven from the Academy because of his independence, found in Holland an asylum for a Dictionary of his own, published after his death in 1690. Moreover, Vaugelas

himself — with all his prestige — did not live to complete his
own work: he died insolvent, and his unfinished manuscript
was among the papers seized by his creditors. Nevertheless,
when the Dictionary was restored to the Academy it was
completed along the lines Vaugelas had laid down. Only in the
fourth edition is the " language of the people " considered, to_
gether with various words taken from the " arts and sciences."

In general, then, the rôle of the Academy has been reactionary
from the beginning. Even in the seventeenth century such
illustrious names as Descartes, Pascal and Molière are lacking on
its roster. Preserver of tradition, the Academy has often been
fifty years behind the times. But this conservatism has lent
weight to its pronouncements. Time and again its definitions
have been invoked to solve knotty questions, even in diplomacy,
and amid the changing policies and politics of France the
Academy has been the guardian of the best French culture.
The oft-cited witticism on the Academicians:

> Ils sont quarante, mais ils ont de l'esprit comme quatre

is brilliant but unjust.

Academic in criticism, Jean Chapelain (1595–1674) was
thoroughly so in poetry. An eclectic as to culture, he lacked
the inspiration and the talent to be creative. His
long-heralded epic, *La Pucelle* — on the theme of
Joan of Arc — appeared in 1656, and although it met with a
succès d'estime among people like Mme de Longueville, even she
admitted that it was a bore. But while we may admit with
Boileau that Chapelain is a mediocre poet, as a critic he had an
important share in formulating the Classical doctrine. He wrote
an ode on Richelieu which ingratiated him in the latter's favor.
In 1632 he even became secretary to Louis XIII. It was by virtue
of the esteem he enjoyed that he wielded his influence on the
Academy and that he moulded the *Sentiments sur le Cid* in a
way not to be unfavorable to Corneille. His Letters, though
without literary merit, are valuable in reconstructing the details
of his time. Finally, his library, rich in Italian works, contained
the treatise of Castelvetro on Aristotle's *Poetics* from which the
" rules " of the drama were to be derived; but of this, more in
a subsequent chapter. Between Malherbe and Boileau the
notable name in criticism is that of Chapelain.

CHAPTER II

HONORE D'URFE AND THE ROMANESQUE

THE devotees of " society," however, craved other outlets of expression than the quips and conceits of Mme de Rambouillet's circle. They had youth and imagination, and they sought a larger canvas for the portrayal of their ideals than the framework of the salon permitted. This they found in a revival of prose fiction, which leads us back momentarily to the sixteenth century.

The barber in Cervantes' immortal work proclaims the *Amadís de Gaula* — the Spanish version of which appeared in 1508 — "the best of its kind in the chivalric line," and so it remains until long after the time we are considering. In 1540 d'Herberay des Essarts translated the *Amadís* into French. Although the supernatural agencies of the story did not appeal to its Gallic admirers, the purely chivalric adventures, the love-making and the tone of courtesy it breathed struck upon sympathetic ears. Another work that stimulated the portrayal of adventure in the service of love was the Greek tale of *Theagenes and Chariclea*, translated in 1549 by the able hand of Amyot. But again it was Italian influence, coming this time through Spain, that gave the real start to a revival of French fiction. Throughout the sixteenth century the pastoral romance had flourished in Italy, notably in forms modeled upon Sannazzaro's *Arcadia*. So that when in 1607 Honoré d'Urfé undertook to adapt to French surroundings the *Diana Enamorada* of Montemayor, itself an adaptation of Sannazzaro's work, the ground was prepared and the times were ready for such an attempt. Since love is " the desire for immortality in beauty," [1] it follows (so argued d'Urfé) that loving is to seek the person worthy of this ideal. This quest, minutely pursued, is the theme of the thirty and more episodes, with their seven pairs of lovers, of d'Urfé's *Astrée.*

[1] See Plato's *Symposium*, § 207.

Chance placed the birth of Honoré d'Urfé (1568–1625) in the busy port of Marseilles, whither his mother had gone on a visit. **D'Urfé's** His real home and the Arcadian scene of his story **Life** was the county of Forez, near Lyons. Here the d'Urfés had lived for centuries and here Honoré, fresh from the Collège de Tournon in 1585, spent the most peaceful and enjoyable years of his life. Thirty years later he sentimentally reflects on these haunts of his boyhood:

> Belle et agréable rivière de Lignon, sur les bords de laquelle j'ai passé si heureusement mon enfance et la plus tendre partie de ma première jeunesse . . . à l'ombre de tes arbres feuillus et à la fraîcheur de tes belles eaux, quand l'innocence de mon âge me laissait jouir de moi-même, et me permettait de goûter en repos les bonheurs et les félicités que le ciel . . . répandait sur le bienheureux pays que tu arroses de tes claires et vives ondes.

From this peaceful retreat Honoré was torn by the civil wars in France. He joined the party of the Leaguers, was twice thrown into prison by his adversaries, and finally retired to Annecy in Savoy and devoted himself to literature. A notable fact is that he is thus a contemporary and compatriot of Saint François de Sales. Besides his great romance, he wrote a pastoral poem named, after its hero, *Sereine* (1600–1604), and an unfinished heroic on the House of Savoy, *La Savoysiade*. Of the *Astrée*, Honoré actually wrote three volumes, the first of which appeared in 1607, with a dedication to Henry IV.[2] But so great was their success that he planned at least a fourth, which was published a year before Honoré's death through the efforts of his niece and his secretary, Baro. This was followed in 1626 by two additional spurious volumes, appearing over the name of Borstel, Sieur de Gaubertin.

The charm of the *Astrée* lies in the reality of its setting and the nobility of its sentiment. Its characters are the virtuosi **The "Astrée"** of the pastoral, won to a life of peace and frankly in disguise. All are courtly, adepts in conversation, if need be, poets. The events are staged in Merovingian times, on the banks of the Lignon. Celadon has been in love for three years with Astrée; but Alcippe, father of Celadon, is a Capulet, and the lovers arrange that Celadon shall feign devotion

---

2 The third volume, dedicated to Louis XIII, appeared in 1619.

to another shepherdess. Misunderstanding ensues: Astrée scornfully banishes Celadon from her presence, and the unhappy youth seeks death in the waters of the Lignon. Rescued by nymphs, he escapes the amorous pursuit of Galatée, their princess, and finds refuge in a cave, near which he raises bowers to his beloved, also a temple of leaves, where are inscribed the Twelve Laws of Love. Celadon then places in the hand of the sleeping Silvandre a letter to Astrée, who infers that it is Celadon's wraith who is writing. At last, the Druid Ademas brings together Astrée and her lover, now disguised as the fair Alexis, daughter of Ademas. The consequence is that Astrée loves the supposed Alexis. A second banishment ensues. Celadon in despair offers his body to the lions of the Fountain of Love, but they refuse to prey on so true a lover, and the work closes with a grand reunion, in which Celadon and Astrée, Silvandre and Diane, the light-hearted Hylas who refuses to believe in the constancy of love, all take part.

Into this framework are woven the " affairs " of many other lovers, each with his particular *traverse*, as well as considerable warlike adventure and much edifying discussion of *l'honneste amitié* or gallantry. Thus, Ademas explains to Celadon the genesis of love in Neo-Platonic terms:

> Toute beauté procède de cette souveraine bonté que nous appelons Dieu, et c'est un rayon qui s'élance de lui sur toutes choses créées.

We learn that lovers attract one another like magnets, and that thus joined, their souls mount to the pure essence of all loving. But the real expositor of this theme is Silvandre, the model of fidelity, just as Hylas, the inconstant shepherd, is the foil to the extravagances of others. Indeed, there is a peculiar irony in the fact that d'Urfé has made Hylas, a Provençal, the voice of Gallic common sense. Hylas, to whom inconstancy was an article of faith, seems the master-creation of this idyll; and one can picture the delight with which some of Mme de Rambouillet's frequenters read the passages in which Hylas' raillery brings back to earth his nympholept companions. If the heroic romance of the century derives from the *Astrée*, its counterpart — the *roman comique* — may well have taken hints from d'Urfé's mocking shepherd.

But it would be easy to exaggerate the merits of d'Urfé's work. The Italian pastoral is a poetic fiction consistently maintained. D'Urfé's attempt to make it a lesson-book in which the crude would learn good manners, and above all, the mixture of the heroic with the idyllic, jar on the modern reader as infractions of good taste. Granted that the period rather than d'Urfé is responsible for the blemishes in the *Astrée,* it is yet true that d'Urfé's tendency to treat the sentimentalizings of his characters as important moral truths needs but the confrontation with a Montaigne or a Du Vair to show how vaporous his idea is. D'Urfé has the suavity of Saint François de Sales, but he lacks the latter's underlying strength, and successful as the *Astrée* was, it should not be forgotten that the author and his public were both enamored of *panache* — that quality which Rostand wittily defined as " a delicate refusal to take life seriously."

On the other hand, d'Urfé has considerable descriptive power (the *Astrée* still was a favorite with Rousseau), a marked sense of distinction, charm of style, and the ability to render courtly traits effectively. All this made for the vogue of his romance during the first half of the century. The *Astrée* supplied endless themes of conversation to the salons. It was a veritable mine for plots and characters of the drama; a year before the *Cid* a troupe of actors still advertised plays by Du Ryer, Scudéry and Mairet, as containing " subjects borrowed from the *Astrée.*" Particularly, it committed the novel in France to an analysis of sentiment, and in its union of a pastoral with a pseudo-historical setting, it laid the foundation for numerous romances that were to follow in its wake.

The first of these is *La Carithée* (1621) by Marin le Roy, Sieur de Gomberville (1600–1674). This is a pale reflection of the **Historical** *Astrée,* with scarcely more history than the Roman **Romances** name of Germanicus, its hero. But the same author's *Polexandre* (5 vols., 1629–1637) replaces the pastoral by the full-blown heroic, developed amid exotic surroundings, which gave the work an immense success. The principal scene of this romance is the Canary Islands, where the heroine Alcidiane is protected by a shore that disappears from view as the mariner approaches it. To win this inaccessible bride Polexandre goes through inextricable adventures with Turks, Moroccans, Portuguese and

Spaniards; he patiently listens to a whole course on Mexican history by Zelmatide, heir to the Empire of the Incas; and he himself becomes Prince of the Isle of the Sun, to which gorgeous ships bear gifts. Wild and extravagant as Gomberville is, he has an eye for color, and his fantasies on America found favor with a generation to whom the New World was the land of marvels and of gold.

If *Polexandre* is French in background, Desmarets' *Ariane* (2 vols., 1632), which excels through its brevity, transports us to the Rome of Nero. It contains the usual love intrigue, interwoven with the burning of the city and a number of unlikely adventures, until the hero Mélinte weds the sumptuous Ariane. But Desmarets, known also by his successful comedy, *Les Visionnaires*, has a direct style, which graces particularly the numerous letters and oracles with which his tale abounds.

The historical subject was now to the fore; Corneille was exploiting it in the drama, when the Gascon, Gautier Coste de
La Calpre- la Calprenède (1609–1663), began staging it mag-
nède   nificently in his romance *Cassandre* (10 vols., 1642–1645). This work was soon followed by the still more elaborate *Cléopâtre* and *Faramond ou l'Histoire de France*, each in twelve volumes.[3] La Calprenède also wrote tragedies, but he owed his reputation to his romances, which continued to be read in England until Richardson's *Pamela* destroyed their hold in the eighteenth century. What distinguishes La Calprenède is the adroit handling of long narrative. His works abound in " oracles," "letters," descriptions of tournaments and disguises. The author plunges *in medias res* and develops his characters through narrative which is given either by themselves or by subordinate personages. One feature, the " literary portrait," found in previous romances, is elaborated. But the main trait is that the plot moves rapidly on, uncloyed by long-spun disquisitions on love; also the Oriental setting is deftly unfolded, and the separate episodes have point and direction. All this was a great gain, aside from the fact that the names of La Calprenède's heroines were soon on all lips and that " fier comme Artaban " — one of his heroes — has become proverbial in French.

[3] The last five volumes of *Faramond* are by a continuator, Vaumorière.

Still Oriental and Roman, though contemporary in their reference to actual figures and events of the day, are the works of
The Scudérys Madeleine de Scudéry (1608–1701), with whom her brother George collaborated, at least in name. With these authors, the sentimental romance reached its greatest popularity, which was destroyed only by the combined satire of Molière and Boileau.

The Scudérys, brother and sister, were from Normandy. George early entered the army, but resigned in 1630 and began cultivating the dramatic muse. As we shall see, he took a leading part in the Quarrel of the *Cid*, and like many contemporaries he tried his hand on an epic, *Alaric*, which had the honor of making Boileau very angry. His position in the world gave him the entrée to the Hôtel de Rambouillet. Hither he led his sister (about 1639), and two years later they published their first romance, *Ibrahim ou l'Illustre Bassa*, the scene of which is laid in Constantinople under Soliman II. In 1649–1653 their joint labors resulted in the ten parts of the celebrated *Artamène ou le Grand Cyrus*. Here, beneath the thin veil of the Persian war, the entire aristocratic world — from the Grand Condé (Cyrus) to Voiture (Aristhée) and Chapelain (Callicrate) — found itself reflected in detailed " portraits." The stir that this work produced can be imagined. Tallemant des Réaux affirms that a key to the romance was in circulation; and we may be sure that more than one key was used. Meanwhile, however, Madeleine de Scudéry had begun her own *samedis*, where *précieux* gallantry rose to melodramatic proportions in the form of maps and indices of sentiment, like the well-known *Carte de Tendre* in *Clélie* and the so-called *Conversations galantes*. Once more, it is a question of whether it is sweeter to be loved than to love, of love via friendship, of absence as a cure to love, and so on.

The Scudérys' third romance, *Clélie, histoire romaine* (10 vols., 1654–1660), plants these flowers of preciosity on Roman soil and surrounds them with the noisy atmosphere of the Fronde. Clélie is the daughter of a noble Roman, Clelius, whose family Tarquin has compelled to fly from Rome to Carthage. On the voyage thither Clelius' own son is lost and in his place Aronce, son of Porsenna, is rescued and later brought up with Clélie, who of course becomes the lady of his choice. Then follow various adventures and rivalries. Clélie has other suitors for her hand — among them the tyrant Tarquin himself, a conspiracy is formed against Tarquin by Brutus, and this patriot's history is narrated in detail. Finally, Porsenna, in obedience to an oracle, deserts Tarquin and allows his son, Aronce, to marry Clélie, while Tarquin retreats to Cumae. But the interest of the work lies in the " conversations " and the twenty-seven or more " portraits," including such notabilities as Louis XIV, Fouquet, Mlle de Scudéry herself, the Duchess of Longueville, Ninon de Lenclos and Scarron — in short, most of the social set of the age. In *Clélie* the long-winded heroic romance attains its summit, and fortunately its term.

Thus, differing from La Calprenède mainly in the systematic use of the disguised character, Mlle de Scudéry supplies the sociology with which to judge the *grand siècle* in its making. Her works offer an opportunity to the historian which Victor Cousin (*La Société française*) has not failed to seize. Outside of the idealized " portrait," however, they contain little that common sense and art could approve, and the ridicule that they evoked came near destroying the genre they represent. Luckily, Mme de La Fayette rescued the novel for Classicism by substituting psychology for heroics in her *Princesse de Clèves*, but Mme de La Fayette was a follower not of the Scudérys but of Corneille (Ch. IV). As for the sentimental novel, Molière derided it in his *Précieuses ridicules*, and Boileau sounded its death-knell when in *Les Héros de roman* (1664), a Lucianic dialogue, he marched the heroes of the romances down to Hades, to be cast into Lethe.

Such reaction and satire, however, were not new. As early as 1622, Charles Sorel (1602–1674), obviously inspired by Spanish **The Realistic** works, began his *Histoire comique de Francion,* **Types** a tale of picaresque character, in which such writers as Malherbe, Racan and Balzac appear in disguise. Five years later he published *Le Berger extravagant,* where in the manner of Cervantes he recounts the mishaps of a young Parisian whose mind has been upset by reading the *Astrée*. Amid the latter's pastoral ravings is placed an attack on all fiction, both prose and verse. The work, which was extremely popular, is also directed against the pompous and *précieux* style. But the weak

side of Sorel is his pedantry. His wit is too obvious, his arraignment too sweeping, and he lacks the realistic and sympathetic insight for which the *Don Quixote* is immortal. A similar
fault, that of pettiness, attaches to the *Roman bourgeois* (1666)
of Antoine Furetière (1620–1688), the friend of Molière and
Racine. Here the types are Parisian bourgeois; Sorel himself
figures among them, and *précieux* society comes in for its due,
Mlle de Scudéry (Polymathie) being extolled for her wit but
derided for her ugliness. A telling stroke of Furetière's is the
tariff of prices he gives for the insertion of a character in a
romance. As satire, the *Roman bourgeois* is the most graphic
account the century produced of the foibles of the middle class,
however inferior it may be as art to Molière's *Bourgeois gentilhomme*.

The novelist of the period in whom realism does approach art
is Paul Scarron (1610–1660). Hopelessly deformed and bent
by disease, Scarron, in spite of his loose morals, had an inflexible
spirit which evidently won him the affection of the remarkable
lady he married: Françoise d'Aubigné, granddaughter of the
Protestant poet, and later, as Mme de Maintenon, the most
influential woman in France. Scarron had a turn for the
burlesque, which he manifests in his plays and also in his
Virgile travesti, a vulgar satire on the epics of his day that he
should have allowed to die by their own dead weight. His one
noteworthy feat was *Le Roman comique* (1651), the history of a
strolling troup of comedians, thought by some critics to be
Molière's. Here we have not only types but genuine characters,
individualized in their proper setting and possessing the imprint
of actuality. The narrative is short and sprightly, and its vigor
contrasts sharply with the sugary tone of La Calprenède and
the Scudérys.

It must be apparent from the foregoing survey that the French
novel of the seventeenth century does not stand for that
The observance of rule and order toward which French
Romanesque, literature as a whole was moving. The reasons for
in General this are clear. In the first place, the romance was
not an Aristotelian or Horatian form. Thus there were no
classical rules to follow; and as for the influence of the late
Greek romances, their tendency was entirely in favor of the dif-

fuseness and complicated intrigue that one observes in the *Amadis*
and the *Astrée*. In the second place, those Italian critics who
treated the romance were careful to note its distinctive, modern
character, as not bound by form but as open to the imagination
in search of the new and adventurous. Lastly, feudalism itself,
the survival of Arthurian themes in Ariosto, Tasso and the
Amadis, as well as the printing in the sixteenth century of many
Old French romances, are factors that served, each in its way,
to further the revival of prose fiction.

However, the Age of Louis XIII was romantic, if not emo-
tionally in the modern sense, at least, intellectually or rationally. The salons with their extravagances, their cult of Spanish
and Italian mannerisms, their dabbling with the *je ne sais quoi,*
their naïve desire to see themselves " portrayed " ideally, illustrate this fact. In the field of politics the Wars of the Fronde
exemplify it again: it was the toying with politics rather than
any systematic attempt at revolution that made the Frondeurs
such easy victims to the astuteness of a Richelieu or a Mazarin.
It was these intellectual vagaries, impelled by a laudable desire
to excel and be brilliant, that inspired seventeenth-century
romance. Rostand has revived the spirit of the time in his
Cyrano de Bergerac, which brings back not only the relatively
obscure author of the *Etats et empire de la lune* but also the
whole epoch of his life (1619–1655), with its buoyancy, its af-
fectations, its humor and its heroism.

> " Moi, c'est moralement que j'ai mes élégances,"

says Cyrano in the play. This is not yet the *grandeur d'âme*
of a Cornelian hero, but an approach to it. The truth is that
with all its faults the *romanesque* always possesses a moral
element of generosity and distinction. As a literary form,
however, the sentimental novel of the period failed because it
lacked the necessary curbs, both from within and from without.
These it was finally to acquire from the drama, and thus
seventeenth-century fiction excels only in the single instance
of *La Princesse de Clèves* (see Book IV, Ch. I).

CHAPTER III

THE DRAMA PREVIOUS TO CORNEILLE

THE Edict of 1548, by which Parliament established the Confrérie de la Passion in control of the Parisian stage (Bk. I), had relegated the *mystères sacrés* to the provinces. Such plays of medieval inspiration as survived in the capital assumed a secular, classical form, which — as we shall see — was often more apparent than real. In 1578 the Confrérie itself, unable to change with the changing world, took professional actors into its pay; and finally it rented the Hôtel de Bourgogne to outside troupes of actors. In 1583 its boards were occupied by Italian players, the *Gelosi*, famous for their portrayal of the so-called Improvised Comedy or *Commedia dell' arte;* and these were followed in 1599 by the *Comédiens français ordinaires du roi,* a strolling troupe which under the leadership of Valleran Lecomte had won favor at court. It was to compete with this troupe that the actor Mondory opened a second Parisian theater, in the quarter of the Marais, in 1628. But the Confrérie was not easily dispossessed; clinging to the proprietorship of the Hôtel de Bourgogne, it interfered in theatrical affairs until in 1676 Louis XIV, annoyed at its meddling, dissolved the corporation.

Within these dates (1548-1676) came the rise and development of French Classical drama.

In considering its origins it is important to keep two facts in mind. First, in the sixteenth century the French shared with the rest of Europe the view that the drama is " an exposition of emotion, of misery or joy " rather than " a conflict of wills in the form of action." Secondly, it is less from tragedy or comedy thus conceived that the Classical drama descends, than from a hybrid form, called tragi-comedy, as developed by Garnier and Hardy, and as perfected by Corneille. Tragi-comedy is the real link between the medieval theater, with its multiplex stage-

238

setting, and the plays of Molière and Racine. Thus we can distinguish two preliminary periods: (1) 1548–1600 — the period when France, together with other countries, is striving to produce a type of expository lyrical drama; and (2) 1600–1636 — the period when the more popular tragi-comedy is definitely established and then (1628), through the influence of the unities, is transformed into the Classical forms of tragedy and comedy.

The Renaissance had inherited the name " tragedy " from the medieval grammarians. A tragedy was any plot, whether **The Renais-** drama or not, that ended in bloodshed and horror: **sance Type** " Injustices que l'on raconte ès tragedies," said **of Tragedy** Nicolas Oresme. But the concept that tragedy is a dramatic representation of human misery is Senecan. In this respect the Italians again anticipated their northern neighbors, the first vernacular drama on a Senecan model being the *Sophonisba* of Trissino in 1515. Italian actors and stage-settings were popular at the court of Francis I; and in 1548 Sebillet (see Bk. II, Ch. I) said in his *Art poétique*:

> La moralité françoise represente en quelquechose la tragedie grecque ou latine, singulierement en ce qu'elle traite sujets graves et principaux. Et si le François s'estoit rangé à ce, que la fin de la moralité fust toujours triste et douloureuse, la moralité seroit tragedie.

Greek influence was added to Senecan by the translations of Lazare de Baïf from Euripides and Sophocles, and with the same insistence on the tragic ending, for Baïf defines as follows:

> Tragedie est une moralité composée des grandes calamitez, meurtres et adversitez survenus aux nobles et excellents personnages comme . . . Œdipus qui se creva les yeux apres qu'il lui fust declaré comme il avoit eu des enfants de sa propre mere, apres avoir tué son pere.

Thus, it is clear that when, after 1548, the French began writing tragedies of their own the underlying concept was lyric rather than dramatic; the chief element of the plot was the dénouement; and the subject invariably was the misfortune which befalls several souls or the misfortunes which befall one soul. A typical model was the *Hecuba* of Euripides, of which there were four

translations besides innumerable editions. Here the audience
delighted in the spectacle of a queen who has become a slave, a
wife who witnesses her husband's death, a mother who sees her
son and daughter perish; three calamities overwhelming a noble
and virtuous character. And the best example in all literature of
this lyrical form of tragedy is Shakespeare's *King Lear*, where,
with characteristic lack of poetic justice, the destruction of Lear
carries with it the just and the unjust to a terrible end. It is
needless to say that no lyrical tragedy written in France is comparable to this masterpiece.

The main difference between Renaissance tragedy and the
old *moralité* therefore was one of form — granting the adoption
also of the Greek or Latin subject. The plot was now divided
into acts instead of *journées,* to agree with Horace; the occasions
for lyrical verse were increased through the use of monologues,
descriptions and choruses, modeled on the ancients; above all,
attention was given to stylistic expression, and when a tragedy
was acted — though few sixteenth-century tragedies were — an
elaborate Renaissance setting was the rule. Obviously, such
plays had but little action, since the victim, and not the agent
of the drama, was the main character in the plot.

Most of the above traits appear in the first French tragedy,
Cléopâtre captive, by Etienne Jodelle (1552). Here the action
begins only after the death of Antony. In the first act the
ghost of the murdered Roman recounts the story of his tragic
love, Cleopatra discusses with her attendants a dream she has
had, and the chorus dilates upon the inconstancy of fortune.
In the second act Octavius deliberates on the fate reserved for
the Egyptian queen. The agony of Cleopatra is then the subject of the third and fourth acts, which are followed by a recital of her death. In the entire play there is but one real episode (that of Seleucus), the work being an endless elegy on an
inevitable death. Unfortunately, Jodelle for all his association
with the Pléiade was an inferior poet, and rare are the lines in
which beauty of expression redeems paucity of incident and
action. Yet there is imagination in the words in which Cleopatra
envisages Antony's love:

> Ha! l'orgueil et les ris, la perle detrempée,
> La delicate vie effeminant ses forces,
> Estoient de nos malheurs les subtiles amorces.

Jodelle's tragedy was played before the court at the Hôtel de Reims. In 1560 Jacques Grévin's *La Mort de César* was performed at the Collège de Beauvais. Republican Rome was a favorite subject with the Renaissance, and Grévin followed the general outlines of a Latin tragedy on Caesar by Muret. Being a superior poet, he infused the well-ordered original with warmth and idealism. Mark Antony, with the toga of the dead Caesar in his hands, is not yet the Shakespearean spellbinder, but his plea for the rights of conquest over against the rights of the people, as set forth by Cassius, is dramatic in concept and expression. There is, in fact, in the clash of Grévin's lines an occasional approach to the rhetoric of Corneille:

César
C'est peu d'avoir vaincu puisqu'il faut vivre en doute.
Antoine
Mais s'en peut-il trouver un qui ne vous redoute?

Better than either of the plays mentioned is *Saül le furieux* by Jean de la Taille, in 1562. Like Grévin, La Taille was a Protestant with a classical education; but he had greater knowledge of dramatic technique. When his tragedy appeared in print (1572), it was preceded by a treatise on the *Art de la tragédie* in which the dramatic unities are borrowed from the Italian work of Castelvetro (see below). The theme of *Saül* is the man crushed by fate. Saul, who had been the instrument of the Divine will, now becomes its victim. But his spirit, struggling with doubt, open revolt and heroic despair, remains unconquered in the face of death. Meeting destruction at the head of his troops, he says:

Je ne veux, abaissant ma haute majesté,
Eviter le trepas qui predit m'a esté;
Je veux donc vaillamment mourir pour ma patrie;
Je veux acquerir gloire en vendant cher ma vie.

The play closes on this note of moral grandeur, which is the more firmly conceived inasmuch as the opposing fate is God Himself.

Thus Biblical and Graeco-Roman themes alternate as the subjects of tragedy. A trilogy by Louis Desmasures — a friend of the Pléiade — covers the life of King David: *David combat-*

tant, David triomphant and *David fugitif* (1566). By the early age of eighteen Jacques de la Taille (a brother of Jean) had composed a *Daïre* and an *Alexandre*. But the most prolific, and in general the most original, dramatist of the age was Robert Garnier (1535–1601).

Of Garnier's six classical tragedies, the *Hippolyte* (1573) is the most interesting because it continues the tradition of Seneca. **Robert** Far from anticipating Racine, Garnier makes **Garnier** Phaedra die of love, not remorse, and lets her find in death the union with Hippolytus. Thus the lyrical strain is strong in Garnier, and death crowns Phaedra's passion with a halo of glory:

> Mes pensers ne sont plus d'amoureuse detresse,
> Je n'ai rien de lascif qui votre ame reblesse —

is the final reflection of this chastened heroine. On the other hand, as Faguet has shown, Garnier's *Les Juives* (1580) is the *Athalie* of the sixteenth century. Elegiacal by nature and hence slow in action, this Biblical tragedy is yet powerful in dramatic suspense. The plot is the story of Zedekiah, King of Judea, overwhelmed by the cruelty of Nebuchadnezzar. The first act reveals the situation: the life of the King and his city are threatened; the chorus of Jews bewails the oncoming doom. In the second, an appeal to the conqueror's wife gives new hope. In the third, Nebuchadnezzar veils his grim purpose in obscure language. The fourth shows the family of Zedekiah, imprisoned, but trustful as to their final release. In the fifth, the blow falls as from a clear sky: Zedekiah's children are murdered, his high-priest is beheaded, and he himself is blinded.

Garnier's style lacks richness, but his motivation is well-knit and his characters stand out as individuals. With his tragi-comedy *Bradamante* — his most original work — we shall deal in another place. As for his verse, it often has the harmony of the Pléiade. How Ronsardian he can be appears in such lines as these, from the chorus of *Hippolyte:*

> Faisons, ô mes compagnes,
> Retentir les montagnes
> Et les rochers secrets
> De nos regrets!

In Garnier, lyrical tragedy had reached its apogee; with Antoine de Montchrétien (1575–1621) it had a final
Montchrétien flare before its extinction in the seventeenth century.
Montchrétien's life was full of incident, with which the sententious rhetoric of his writings is in sharp contrast. Son of an
apothecary of Falaise, left an orphan and robbed of his patrimony in youth, he made his way as a servant, won back his
estate and became embroiled in duels. In 1605 he was in England. There his tragedy, *L'Ecossaise*, on the subject of Mary
Stuart, won the approbation of James I, who effected his return
to France. He then engaged in the manufacture of steel. But
he agitated against Louis XIII, joined the recalcitrant Protestants and was shot down with several of his followers. He left
considerable lyric and some epic poetry, six tragedies and a
bergerie.

Of the dramas the Biblical tragedy, *Aman ou la vanité*, and the
aforenamed *L'Ecossaise ou le désastre* are the best. But they are
good only in their lyrical qualities: a smooth and elegant diction and an abundant imagery which is all too harmonious.
" What is man? " asks Montchrétien:

> Une fleur p̄assagere
> Que la chaleur flestrit ou que le vent fait choir,
> Une vaine fumée, ou une ombre legere,
> Que l'on voit au matin, qu'on ne voit plus au soir.

His *Aman* has five acts; Racine, a far greater poet, found in
the same subject material for only three. The first two acts of
L'Ecossaise are composed of rhetorical speeches, ending in the
death-sentence pronounced by Queen Elizabeth; the next two
contain the expostulations and prayers of the victim; and the
last act is the recital of Mary's execution. Thus, Montchrétien
closes a type of tragedy which lacked the vigor and originality
to make it blossom into life. It was not, as a type, suited to the
French sense of clarity and poetic justice. Moreover, those
Frenchmen who essayed it were not of the first rank.

As regards comedy, the failure of the sixteenth century was
even greater than in tragedy. " Comedy," said the best comic
Renaissance writer of the time, " shows dexterity of the mind,"
Comedy and a comedy writer who is merely dexterous is not

apt to be true to life. This misconception, however, was not due to inadequate models. By 1539 the plays of Terence had almost all been translated into French. In 1567 Baïf gave a clever rendering of the *Miles gloriosus* of Plautus. The types of Italian comedy of intrigue, the *commedia dell'arte*, were gaining rapid and lasting recognition: we shall see how Molière learned from them. That curious medley of genres, the Spanish *Celestina*, went through five translations. Nevertheless, the French were neither first-class imitators of foreign wares nor wielders of a successful comedy of their own.

Thus Jodelle's *Eugène* (1552) is a *farce* dressed up in classical costume. It is divided into regular acts and scenes, and some of the characters have a gravity of tone that is not unlike the later bourgeois drama or *drame*. But the pointed satire of the wealthy and dissolute priest, Eugène, is farcical in concept without achieving the light and frolicsome spirit of the medieval genre. A similar wavering spoils the effect of Jacques Grévin's *La Trésorière*, although the same author's *Les Ebahis* (1561) has the merit of ridiculing Italian affectation in the character of Pantalone — himself a favorite comedy type — and of realistically portraying the dotard in love. In imitation of the Italians, Jean de la Taille's *Les Corrivaux* (about 1563) and Odet de Turnèbe's *Les Contents* (1584) employ prose instead of eight-syllable verse. The latter play is also noted for its sprightly dialogue and its clever delineation of the "nurse," another popular Renaissance type. Lastly, the best sixteenth-century comedy in French is a direct adaptation from the Italian; namely, Larivey's "Ghosts" or *Les Esprits*.

A descendant of the Florentine publishers Giunti, whose name he Gallicized, Larivey was a cleric of Troyes who mingled re-

Larivey

ligion with a bent for the burlesque and licentious. Although his *Six premières comédies facétieuses* in prose (1549) were never performed, Larivey had an eye for the dramatic and knew the French equivalents for Italian roguery and picaresque phrase. *Les Esprits*, based on Lorenzino's *Aridosio*, has fewer characters than its original, but these are well drawn, and in particular the third act — with the conjuring of the "ghosts" by M. Josse, sorcerer, and the deluding of Ruffin, the importunate creditor — develops excellent farce. As late as 1611 Larivey published other comedies, none of which reach the high level of the earlier group. It should be noted that Molière read Larivey with profit.

A position between tragedy and comedy was given by the Renaissance to the dramatized *bergerie* or *pastorale*. As the last
The Pastorale name indicates, the chief features of this genre are the disguise of the characters as shepherds and the idyllic, Arcadian setting made fashionable by Sannazzaro. The traits in question appear first in a comedy called *Les Ombres* (1566), by Filleul. The translation of Tasso's *Aminta* and Guarini's *Pastor Fido* thereupon increased the vogue of such idealized portraiture, especially among the aristocratic. But it was not until after 1600 that Hardy made the *pastorale* a distinct genre by separating it from the leading dramatic form of his time, tragi-comedy.

The striking thing about Hardy is his timeliness. He came at a moment when the theater needed a practical person to guide
Alexandre Hardy and Tragi-comedy it: one who was not primarily a poet or a theorist but a playwright trained to the stage and the romanesque taste of the theater-going public. This rôle Alexandre Hardy (1570–1632) was eminently qualified to fill. Employed by the comedians of Valleran Lecomte as a sort of *poète à gages*, Hardy slaved to supply them with a repertory, at first in the provinces and then in Paris at the Hôtel de Bourgogne. That his output does not rank high as literature is not surprising — particularly when we consider that he produced hundreds of plays, of which only eleven tragedies, twenty-five tragi-comedies and five *pastorales* were ever published. Lanson thinks he scented the importance, without being able to realize it, of psychological action, and queries whether Hardy had not read Montaigne. Certainly he knew, besides much miscellaneous literature, the *Astrée* with its elaborate love analyses.

In the main, Hardy followed the lead of Garnier and pushed the drama toward a freer and yet firmer issue. The tragedies, with which he apparently began, retain the Renaissance feature of a long dénouement: in *La mort d'Alexandre*, Alexander drinks poison early in the play, thus leaving two full acts for a display of his suffering. But Hardy innovated even in tragedy, from a practical point of view: he eventually gives up the chorus, increases the number of characters and strives in every way to set the action before the eyes of the spectator. The result is a fortified unity of action. In *Coriolan* the question is, Shall Rome or Coriolanus be the victim of ingratitude? But this strengthening is coupled with a disregard for the unities of place and time. Thus Hardy's tendency was toward a form of the *drame libre*, and in view of the stage setting of the Hôtel de Bourgogne, which represented several localities at once, he next turned to tragi-comedy.

This genre had arisen out of the detritus of the medieval stage. The name " tragi-comedy " alone is classic, Plautus having used it to designate a comic plot containing characters of high rank (gods and kings). In 1545, however, the Italian critic Giraldi applied the term to a tragic plot with a happy ending, and with this usage the sixteenth century fell in. Indeed, after 1552 the name was employed for any play of medieval origin which possessed " a happy dénouement and at least a partly classical form " (Lancaster) — so that not only the *miracle* but also the *mystère* and the *farce* came thus to be disguised. When, therefore, the generation of 1600 became enamored of the romanesque (Ch. II), it was the non-historic, romanesque plot for which tragi-comedy was used. In Hardy the genre is virtually a dramatized novel.

Here again Hardy takes his departure from Garnier, whose *Bradamante* (1850) was the best model to follow. Borrowed from the *Orlando Furioso* — and it is noteworthy that Garnier drew directly on a " romance " — the subject of this play is the marriage of Roger and Bradamante. Charlemagne had decreed that the latter should marry the man who could conquer her in combat. Roger wins the contest but in behalf of Leon, who had previously saved Roger's life; an appeal is then made to the Emperor, who declares that the matter shall be decided by a duel between the rivals. Leon now discovers Roger's identity and, rather than oppose him, magnanimously gives up Bradamante. The double marriage of Roger and Bradamante and Leon with Charlemagne's own daughter then brings the play to an end.

How closely Hardy adopted Garnier's technique can be seen

from his *Gésippe ou les deux amis* and his *Elmire ou l'heureuse bigamie*. Both plays are novelistic in origin, *Gésippe* being a tale of Boccaccio's, and *Elmire* the well-known Legend of the Count of Gleichen. Both deal with a love-affair; both disregard the unities; and both end happily. Thus Hardy brought the stage into active coöperation with contemporary taste, and won for the drama what it had previously lacked; namely, popular support. His style is undistinguished, his attempts to imitate Ronsard often absurd, and his lack of probability startling; but his drama has action and he enormously enriched its sources of material. From Amyot's *Théagène et Chariclée* he drew eight plays of five acts each; *La Force du sang* and *La belle Egyptienne* are dramatized *novelas* of Cervantes; *Phraate* is taken from Giraldi Cinthio, and so forth. Finally, Hardy made the *pastorale* a distinct genre by giving it a completely bucolic atmosphere (no chivalry, no royal personages) and a light, bantering tone, in ten-syllable verse.

In short, it was Hardy's achievement to reconcile stage-craft and dramatic art, and to set up tragi-comedy as a point of departure for future experimentation. It is significant that Schélandre's *Tyr et Sidon*, a tragedy in 1608, is transformed into a tragi-comedy in 1628 and is preceded by the words of Ogier:

> That to separate the comic and tragic elements in the same play is to ignore the condition of men's lives, of whom the days and hours are often intermingled with laughter and tears, with contentment and affliction, according as they are moved by good or evil fortune.

This sounds like the practical creed of Shakespeare. More especially it voices the opinions of De Laudun, whose *Art poétique* (1598) had argued against the unities, and of Lope de Vega, whose *Arte nuevo de hacer comedias* (1609) was having its effect in France by the side of Spanish subjects and models.

The period from 1628 to the appearance of the *Cid* (1636) is marked by unusual productivity, considerable quibbling as to **Irregulars** dramatic principles and the final establishment of the unities. In this struggle the court and the public were on one side; on the other were the theorists led by Chapelain and Richelieu, and known as *les doctes.*

At first Hardy's irregularity was all the rage. The leading dramatists, Rotrou, Du Ryer and Scudéry, all wrote tragi-comedies; and the more romanesque the subject the better. As late as 1639 it was by means of a tragi-comedy [1] that Scudéry tried to silence the *Cid;* whereas Rotrou's *Occasions perdues* (1633) added the direct imitation of the Spanish *comedia* to that of the novel. There was, in fact, scarcely a dramatic freedom (blank verse, prose, murders on the stage) that did not find some defender in France.

Nevertheless, the generation of Malherbe was now in the saddle. The Hôtel de Bourgogne might favor the romanesque drama; the friends of rule and order had the offi-**Regulars** cial world on their side, and when the Théâtre du Mairais opened its doors (1628) it did so for a presentation of their wares. The spokesman of this movement, Jean de Mairet (1604–1686), lacked genius but he heeded the critics, who, together with the followers of the Marquise de Rambouillet, pushed him to the front.

As early as his *Chryséide èt Arimant* (1625), a tragi-comedy, Mairet had shown a tendency toward unity of plot. In 1631 he published *Silvanire*, another tragi-comedy, with a preface on the unities which emphasized two points: (1) the subject of a tragedy must be known and hence grounded in history, and (2) the law of verisimilitude must be observed — and he adduced the example of the Italians and the ancients. Finally, in 1635 he put forth the first concrete example of such a tragedy in his *Sophonisbe*. The expense lavished on the performance, marked by the use of special scenery and " crystal chandeliers " was equalled only by the enthusiasm with which the Hôtel de Rambouillet welcomed the play. Dramatically speaking, however, there was little to recommend it — except that it was superior to *Mirame*, a " regular " tragedy by Richelieu and one of his favorites, Desmarets de Saint-Sorlin.

The Three Unities   Meantime, the main critical factor in the struggle for " regularity " was Castelvetro's version of Aristotle's *Poetics* (1570), a copy of which was in Chapelain's library.

---

[1] *L'Amour tirannique*, praised highly by Balzac. Scudéry was constantly passing from one dramatic camp to the other.

Castelvetro supplied the technique, for which Scaliger (*Poetics*, 1561) had outlined the theory, that led to the triumph of the dramatic unities.

From Aristotle, Scaliger deduced the fundamental ideas that each literary genre has its discoverable norm and that the drama in particular should approach as closely as possible to the portrayal of actual truth. The spectator, he thought, should be moved by the actions of the play exactly as if they were those of historical reality. This interpretation of verisimilitude or *vraisemblance* — which is quite opposed to Aristotle's own idea of " poetic truth " — is fundamental in French Classicism. What made it so is that Castelvetro based the technique of the drama entirely upon stage representation. Since the stage is a circumscribed space, he argued, it follows that the action must be limited in time to the period spent by the spectators in the theater. Thus, out of Aristotle's unity of action and his observation that " tragedy endeavors, so far as possible, to confine itself to a single revolution of the sun," there arose the fixed unities of time, place and action. It is evident why after a lapse of some fifty years Chapelain should have advocated them anew, about 1630. The stage area of the Hôtel de Bourgogne was restricted, yet the multiplex stage-setting forced the actor into that part of the background in which the action was located. Not only verisimilitude but common sense demanded a simplification: this the unities gave.

But the drama suffered thereby in picturesqueness; and despite Chapelain many authors refused to sacrifice *le beau sujet* to the rules. How Corneille found a solution of this difficulty by making the drama psychological — through the substitution of the external action by an inner one, often in defiance of verisimilitude — the ensuing chapter will show.

In the main, Chapelain won the day: the Abbé d'Aubignac's *Pratique du théâtre* (1640–1657) proclaimed the sacred nature of the rules; they became part of the " decorum " of the drama at the very moment when kings and lovers alike were condemned to observe the forms of polite society. The unities did not suppress the emotions; on the contrary, they made their expression intense. Thus the French drama attained that concentration which it alone has. This last step is the achievement of Racine.

As to criticism, the final attitude of Classicism is found in the words of Boileau:

> Un rimeur, sans péril, delà les Pyrénées,
> Sur la scène en un jour rassemble des années.
>
> . . . .
>
> Mais nous, que la raison à ses règles engage,
> Nous voulons qu'avec art l'action se ménage;
> *Qu'en un lieu, qu'en un jour, un seul fait accompli*
> *Tienne jusqu'à la fin le théâtre rempli.*

CHAPTER IV

PIERRE CORNEILLE

PIERRE CORNEILLE, surnamed the Great, " non-seulement," said Voltaire, " pour le distinguer de son frère mais du reste des hommes," was by origin and disposition a Norman· The poet rejoices at the fact in one of his early plays. He was born in Rouen, in 1606, as son of a barrister who by dint of long and faithful service came to be made a noble; indeed, in the very year that his son produced the *Cid*. The eldest of six children, Pierre was first educated at a Jesuit school, where he twice won prizes for excellence in Latin verse, and then he studied law. But he made little use of his legal training until, in 1628, he purchased the offices of attorney-general in the " department of waters and forests " and " of harbors." This double duty he fulfilled conscientiously for over twenty years, returning from Paris to Rouen as occasion required. Public documents show him as " investigating " an illegal sale of wood made by the Duke of Orleans and as " defending " the ship-builders of Havre against the pilots of Rouen. Thus in reality the law was Corneille's profession; the theater his avocation. In addition, Corneille was a church-warden in 1652 and kept the accounts of his parish. Another singular post for a great dramatic poet.

But poetry, especially the drama, was the ruling interest of his long and fruitful life. Tradition affirms that his first play, *Mélite* (1629), embodies a love affair of his youth: an attachment he had formed for a certain Catherine Hue who in 1637 became Mme du Pont. Certain it is that *Mélite*, performed in Paris by Mondory at the opening of the Théâtre du Marais, was a success, and that Corneille had found a public for his productions. At a stroke, he had won all hearts by the simplicity and grace with which he had presented the rather commonplace theme of the girl who prefers charm to riches in her suitors. From now on, Corneille was a constant visitor to the capital and a regular producer of plays. So well had he succeeded that in 1633 he ventured to boast: " few are my equals in the drama and none surpass me." This he states in a Latin poem declining an invitation to welcome in verse the visit of Louis XIII and Richelieu to Forges-les-eaux near Rouen. But apparently the Cardinal did not resent the refusal, for in 1635 we find Corneille among the five collaborators on Richelieu's *Comédie des Tuileries*. A year later he rose to fame with the tragi-comedy of the *Cid*.

But the *Cid* also provoked opposition. Corneille's rivals in the drama were Mairet and Scudéry; the fact that Mondory's troupe had won such a triumph aroused their irritation, which broke loose against our poet when in some verses entitled *Excuse à Ariste* he flagrantly said: " I owe to myself alone all my renown." Such vainglory could not be brooked, and after some preliminary skirmishes Scudéry published his *Observations sur le Cid*, the main points of which were that the play violates the " dramatic rules " and that the subject is worthless and stolen from the Spanish. At length the matter was submitted to the newly formed Academy for a decision; this body demurred, presented an opinion largely the work of Chapelain, and then in 1637 issued the well-known *Sentiments* upholding Scudéry on the ground of verisimilitude but lauding Corneille for

> la force et la délicatesse de plusieurs de ses pensées et cet agrément inexplicable qui se mêle dans tous ses défauts.

For the nonce the rivals seemed to have scored. Corneille's pride was hurt; how deeply it is impossible to say. It is known that in 1639 he paid Chapelain a visit. At all events, after three years, spent partly in Rouen, whither business and family cares had called him, Corneille produced *Horace*. Here was a tragedy according to the " rules," on a historical Roman subject, glorifying patriotism — a combination sure to please Richelieu. Corneille had found the type of " moral " tragedy in which not only he but also his successors were to excel.

Shortly after the appearance of *Cinna* in 1640 Corneille married Marie de Lamperière, a lady belonging to the same *noblesse de robe* or legal gentry as himself. He was now in the plenitude of his powers as a dramatic poet. With that mixture of self-assurance and bourgeois timidity which was peculiarly his, he alternately mingled with the gay life of the capital and kept a watchful eye on his interests in Rouen — writing verses for the *Guirlande de Julie*, exchanging visits with men of letters, or exercising the sedate and exacting duties of a provincial magistrate. In 1647 he was elected to the Academy, five years after Richelieu's death, and after twice having seen others preferred to himself. Then came the failure of his tragedy *Pertharite* (1652) and his retirement to Rouen, where he remained seven years, devoting himself mainly to a verse translation of the *Imitation of Christ*.

His return to the theater followed a performance of Molière's troupe in Rouen toward Easter, 1658. The irresistible charm of one of the actresses, Mlle du Parc — then in her prime — doubtless rekindled Corneille's enthusiasm for the stage. This and the fact that at the instance of Pellisson his pension had recently been renewed led Corneille to reappear on the boards with *Œdipe*. Other plays followed, but his hold on the public was only for a time. A second failure awaited him in *Attila*, 1667.

Meantime Corneille had published his plays in a three-volume edition (1660) together with explanatory prefaces, the *Examens*, and three essays on dramatic art — the latter in reply to the critical *Pratique du théâtre* of the Abbé d'Aubignac (Ch. III). Moreover, he had the courage, in the admirable prologue of his *Toison d'or*, to warn Louis XIV against the dangers of his imperialistic policy:

> Ah! Victoire, pour fils n'ai-je que des soldats?
> . . . .
> A vaincre tant de fois mes forces s'affaiblissent;
> L'Etat est florissant, mais les peuples gémissent;
> Leurs membres décharnés courbent sous mes hauts faits,
> Et la gloire du trône accable les sujets.

But later on this critical note disappears entirely from Corneille's works and the Roi-Soleil is lauded to the skies.

The chief embitterment of this later period was the rising fame of Racine. Boursault, who to be sure was no friend of Racine's, depicts Corneille for us, alone in his box, gloomy and sulking, at the first performance of *Britannicus* (1669). A year later the two poets are brought into active competition on the stage with the subject of Berenice, which Fontenelle — Corneille's biographer — avers was given them independently by Henrietta of England, the sister-in-law of Louis XIV. However that may be, Corneille's *Tite et Bérénice*, performed exactly eight days after Racine's great tragedy, was a distinct failure. Corneille still had his partisans; Mme de Sévigné was one of them; but it is abundantly clear that neither his gifts nor his method were able to vie with the genius of Racine in treating such a subject. Obviously he had outlived his day. The world-empire of Louis XIV was not romanesque but real; its dramas were externally unheroic in order to be internally the more intense — just as the spirit of comedy had ceased to be sentimental and had become actual and mordant, striking at the foundations of the society which Corneille had so gloriously idealized. Valiantly, it must be said, the old poet struggled on. He had long since moved to Paris and was sharing his home with his less gifted but suaver younger brother, Thomas Corneille, who was also writing for the stage. He even tried the Racinian manner — he who in his prime had essayed every dramatic expression—but in vain; the collapse of *Suréna* in 1674 forced him into definite retirement. The last years of his life were clouded by sorrows, personal and domestic. An occasional poem addressed to the King alone reminds us that he was still among the living. At last the end came; in 1682 he finished the labor of half a century with a final revision of his works, and two years later his proud but shattered spirit was at rest. He was buried at Paris in the church of Saint-Roch. His brother Thomas succeeded him in the Academy, and Racine — now living in retirement himself — pronounced a eulogy which for critical insight and beauty of diction is one of the noteworthy documents of that august body.

Corneille's career as a dramatist thus falls into three distinct periods.

The first, the period of preparation, begins with *Mélite*. This comedy, written practically without rules or models, was **Corneille's** followed by a trial of tragi-comedy in *Clitandre*. **Dramas** Then came four additional comedies, interrupted by the Senecan tragedy *Médée* and eclipsed by the *Cid*. These early comedies, however, are far from being second-rate. It was something to have swept away the conventional comedy types of Rome and Italy, with their intrigues, disguises, concealments of sex and the like, and to have gone directly after "life." It was even more to the poet's credit that the figures with which he replaced them are true to the courtly world of Louis XIII. In the *Place Royale* and the *Galérie du Palais* he shows the places this society frequented: the shops and bookstalls where they made their purchases and waged the warfare of youth and love. If their speech is *précieux*, it represents that part of Paris brought up on the *Astrée*. A creation of Corneille's is the *suivante* or soubrette who replaces the nurse of earlier comedy. Thus the first plays of Corneille approach the sentimental comedy of the later dramatist Marivaux: in *La Veuve* — the best of them — a trickster is caught in his own trap and the situation is deftly and delicately handled. On the other hand, *L'Illusion comique* is a boisterous fantasy on a Spanish model, a type of comedy that the poet was to perfect in *Le Menteur* (1643).

The *Cid* (1636) begins for Corneille, as well as for France, the period of dramatic masterpieces. Now indeed "the sun had arisen and the stars might retire," as Scudéry had said on an earlier occasion. Everyone knows that Corneille's play is indebted to the *Mocedades del Cid*, by the Spanish dramatist Guillén de Castro. But Corneille shifted the interest from the outer world of incident to the inner world of psychology — the truly French world — and thereby created a new type of action. Formally the *Cid* may be a tragi-comedy with a romanesque subject and a happy ending, yet intrinsically it is the first French tragedy. The youthful Chimène loves the youthful Rodrigue, not for himself, but because of his heroism; and to merit his heroism she herself becomes heroic.

> "Tu n'as fait le devoir que d'un homme de bien,
> Mais aussi, le faisant, tu m'as appris le mien,"

says Chimène to the lover whom fate has made the slayer of her father. If love triumphs in this play, it is yet true that in the intellectualized atmosphere which these characters breathe individual impulse must always submit to public duty. The *Cid* is a tragedy inasmuch as it involves this renunciation, over and over again. Contrary to the Spanish, Corneille's characters are contending forces of will, impulse, pride and duty — and the greatest of these is duty. Compare *Romeo and Juliet* and you will note in the treatment of a similar situation the gulf that divides not only two poets but two civilizations.

With his next two plays, *Horace* and *Cinna* (both 1640), Corneille chose subjects better suited to illustrate his theme. Both plays deal with Roman history, both are termed "tragedies" and observe the unities. The combat between the Horatii and the Curiatii is turned into a mental conflict because the two families are bound by marriage and love: Horace, more patriot than lover, wins out, whereas Curiace, less heroic but more human, dies in battle — leaving his beloved to be slain by her own brother, Horace, for cursing his patriotism. In *Cinna* the main struggle occurs in the mind of Augustus, swaying between magnanimity and vengeance as regards the conspirators against his life, and choosing magnanimity, as Prospero does in the *Tempest* — but with more rhetorical emphasis:

> Je suis maître de moi comme de l'univers,
> Je le suis, je veux l'être.

In *Polyeucte* (1642 or 1643) Corneille carries the theme of duty into the field of religion. The Christian martyr, Polyeucte, has a Roman wife whom duty teaches to love her husband, and finally as a Christian convert to win others to his cause. In all this there is an overstrain, a tendency to carry the victory of the human will to an extreme, to produce "admiration" rather than pity and fear, as is generally the case in tragedy. Yet in the four plays mentioned we see the genius of Corneille at its best. Enamored of spiritual strength in the service of society, he had portrayed it under the guise of family, country, monarchy and religion, in original and enduring dramatic form.

The winter of 1643 brought another tragedy, *La Mort de Pompée*, in which the stoicism of the dead Pompey is the energizing force of the characters in the play, and then follows *Le Menteur* — Corneille's most distinguished comedy. Again the subject is borrowed from the Spanish; this time a more or less free adaptation of Alarcón's *La Verdad Sospechosa*. Dorante, the victim of the comedy, is not so much a liar as a prey to his inborn bent for romancing. His lies are thus a continuous extravaganza — lightly and gayly expressed, yet in a style remarkable for its fitness and measure. Corneille could not resist writing a *Suite du Menteur*, which besides having the defects of a sequel shows that his return to comedy was only a digression. The extraordinary or exceptional was henceforth his field, but seriously and even solemnly conceived, and tending more and more to melodrama as time went on.

Rodogune (1645) was Corneille's own favorite and over a century later called forth the special criticism of Lessing. Only the strictest attention, it is true, will enable the spectator to follow the complicated motivation of the first four acts of this tragedy — never did Corneille " invent " more — but the fifth act in which the Medea-like heroine, Cléopâtre, stands revealed has some of the majestic terror of ancient tragedy. And like an idyll, in the midst of so much horror, Corneille has set the fraternal love of Cléopâtre's two sons, both in love with Rodogune, their mother's rival, yet each longing to sacrifice himself for the other. Once more only, in *Nicomède*, is Corneille able to attain the grandiose; but this play is properly a tragi-comedy and adds little to Corneille's previous achievements. *Andromède*, a spectacle-play set to music, and *Don Sanche d'Aragon*, in some respects the prototype of the romantic drama of 1830, are evidence of his undiminished versatility as a playwright. However, his inspiration is waning, and as we enter upon his third and last period this fact is all too apparent.

Œdipe, brought out in 1659 at the request of Fouquet, Louis XIV's notorious Chancellor of the Exchequer, is a strange misconception of this epic character coupled with a protest — placed in the mouth of Theseus — in behalf of free-will. Stranger still is the fact that the love affair with which Corneille tried to embellish it gave the play great popularity during the second part of the seventeenth century. Politics — the *raison d'Etat* — becomes the obsession in these last plays. As early as *Horace*, Camille, when speaking of the gods, had said:

> Ils descendent bien moins dans de si bas étages
> Que dans l'âme des rois, leurs vivantes images,
> De qui l'indépendente et sainte autorité
> Est un rayon secret de leur divinité.

The Maréchal de Grammont is supposed to have called *Othon* (1664) "the breviary of kings." Certainly the exaltation of the monarchy, in the Machiavellian sense, never rose higher than in the maxim of this play that:

> Tous les crimes d'Etat qu'on fait pour la couronne,
> Le ciel nous en absout, alors qu'il nous la donne.

Thus *Othon, Pulchérie, Sertorius,* are rhetorical, financially perhaps profitable to Corneille, but evoking the opprobrium of Boileau and Bossuet. "God," said the latter, "sends kings to His Law to learn their duties." Such, as we said, is the fate of a genius who has outlived his time, although personally the poet never compels our admiration more than when he haughtily admits the truth in the lines, addressed to Louis himself:

> C'est le dernier éclat d'un feu prêt à s'éteindre;
> Sur le point d'expirer il tâche d'éblouir
> Et ne frappe les yeux que pour s'évanouir.

As Brunetière makes clear, Corneille's sense of style remained unimpaired to the end.

Corneille, therefore, belongs definitely to the Pre-Classical Period: the age of the romanesque. His dramas, which

Point of view and summary bristle with the word *vertu,* are like a long-drawn-out page of Balzac's *Discours sur le Romain.*

> Il estime [says Balzac] plus un jour employé à la Vertu, qu'une longue vie délicieuse; un moment de gloire qu'un siècle de Volupté . . . Rome était la boutique, où les dons du ciel étaient mis en œuvre. . . . Elle a su mêler, comme il faut, l'art avec l'aventure; la conduite avec la fureur; la qualité divine de l'intelligence dans les actions brutales de la partie irascible.

Three propositions that fit Corneille to the dot. It has been claimed that his characters are modeled on real life: 'Richelieu, Retz, Turenne, being heroic in the Cornelian sense. But this is merely to say that in his quest of life he sought the exceptional. His was an age of action, of strength, of rapid and simple decisions; when men were struggling to realize an ideal, and intelligence and will-power were in the ascendency. Of such a view of humanity the dramas of Corneille are the quintessence: in their constant appeal to the reason, in their over-emphasis on the will, in their complex yet swift-moving plots, and in the crashing rhetoric of their style; nay even in the vanities, the preciosity and the pettifogging they contain.

Having said this, there remains that inexplicable thing called "genius," which no amount of background can even partially explain. Corneille took the irregular drama of the age of Hardy and gave it content and form. In comedy, which he made presentable to a cultured audience, he shows, in a joyous rather than a critical mood, the extravagances to which human nature is liable and the foibles to which it succumbs. *Le Menteur* has none of the trenchant ridicule of the later Molière, but it also lacks the cruel pessimism of that observer of men. In lyrical tragedy Corneille could emulate Seneca, but his *Médée* remains an emulation, little else. What made tragi-comedy his medium is that his genius was romantic, but romantic in an unusual and very definite sense. His muse was the Reason, not my reason or yours, but the "socialized reason" which was the peculiarly French contribution to the Renaissance. Imaginative as he was, Corneille saw its possibilities, and lawyer-like he states them as only a lawyer could: bereft of their accessories but with "an intensity of intellectual precision that burns and blazes." Of all this the four great dramas, the *Cid*, *Horace*, *Cinna* and *Polyeucte*, are a continuous illustration. Each has a great subject, timely and yet universal — honor, patriotism, absolutism and martyrdom — and each problem Corneille solves by a victory of the deliberative will, before which all other considerations, no matter how human they may be, give way. Indeed, his failures may be explained by the fact that one cannot multiply such victories indefinitely and write successful plays.

As a consequence, Corneille's characters are Neo-Platonic types, actuated by a superimposed rational self. They do not Characters succumb to Fate, they make Fate subserve their particular ends. The poet's interest in them may be psychological; they themselves are generally poor psychologists. They understand but one thing and strive for it in a straight line. Horace, exasperated by his sister, justifies his fury with the strange words:

> "C'est trop, ma patience à la *raison* fait place;
> Va dedans les enfers plaindre ton Curiace."

And the villains of Corneille's plays are similarly motivated; rarely, as in the case of Félix in *Polyeucte,* do they show any criminal subtlety or political astuteness. This masculine simplicity is of course unfavorable to the portrayal of women types; and, but for such notable exceptions as Camille (*Horace*) and Emilie (*Cinna*), Corneille's heroines are not womanly in the usual sense of the word. Either, like Pauline in *Polyeucte,* they are " obedient " to the point of mysticism, or they are furies with scarce a vestige of humanity, like Cléopâtre in *Rodogune.*

As for plot and action, Corneille's dramas stand midway between the loosely constructed tragi-comedies of Hardy and the finished Classical product of Racine. (Although

Structure

he accepted the unities in *Horace,* he was never more than a nominal Aristotelian. Again and again, but especially in his *Discours,* he used the Italian critics to justify himself against Aristotle. His whole conception of drama — as of life — was *invraisemblable.* In the preface of *Héraclius* he has the boldness to say that " le sujet d'une belle tragédie doit ne pas être vraisemblable." Corneille understood as little as his critics the real purport of Aristotle's distinction between the truth of history and the truth of poetry, and so, like Mairet before him, he tried to conform to the critics by treating a historical subject. While his plots culminate in a " crisis "— as all French Classical tragedy does — he constantly confuses the spectator by multiplying the obstacles which his heroes have to overcome, and he never quite succeeds in obtaining more than a conventional observance of the unities. The stage direction for *Horace* reads:

La scène est à Rome, dans une *salle* de la maison d'Horace

— this arrangement whereby the characters all meet in the same room being, to a large extent, casuistical. Thus, master-playwright that he was, Corneille is not yet formally a Classic.

Of the last fact, his style — that truly Cornelian style — is probably the best evidence. His lofty and grandiose ideas

Style

have a fitting garment in his high-sounding and brilliant diction. Certain of his lines rise to a climax like a storm, and then break on the ear with a crash of sound unique in French poetry. Occasionally he attains a simple grace that is all too rare in his work, as when he writes:

Souvent un je ne sais qu'on ne peut exprimer
Nous surprend, nous emporte, et nous force d'aimer.

On the other hand, Corneille often lacks taste: some of his lines are sublime; others are banal or unconsciously grotesque. Too often he is over-emphatic, merely sententious as when he answers one maxim with another (the well-known *coupe cornélienne*), and unnecessarily *précieux* — in short, a rhetorician. Further, he repeats rime-words and even entire verses. But let us not forget that Malherbe had placed poetry on stilts; in Corneille it was learning once more to soar, not in images of sense but in unadorned flashes of thought. The genius of Corneille must be sought in his best verse as well as in his best plays.

Out of the oblivion into which the greatness of Corneille has cast his contemporaries in the drama, two names survive as **Du Ryer** possessing some of the glamour of their illustrious **and Rotrou** comrade. They are Pierre Du Ryer (1605–1658) and Jean Rotrou (1610–1650).

Du Ryer began to write earlier than Corneille in the manner of Hardy. Indeed, his *Cléomédon* (1633) is still taken from the *Astrée*, although it contains such Cornelian lines as:

> Qui conservë un sceptre est digne de l'avoir,

and

> Qui vante ses aïeux ne vante rien de soi

— another proof that rhetoric was what people liked. After the *Cid*, Du Ryer took to writing tragedies. The best of these is *Scévole* (1644), in many ways a counterpart and to some extent a copy of *Cinna*. While Du Ryer knew his audiences, whose emotions he echoes — especially in *Alcionée*, a tragedy with a romanesque subject — his verse lacks distinction and his talent was not original.

On the other hand, Rotrou fills a niche of his own, although he was a great admirer and a friend of Corneille. His gifts are a vivid imagination — shown particularly in the range of his subjects — and a real sense of pathos. Thirty-five of his plays have come down to us, consisting of comedies, tragi-comedies and tragedies. He began to write young, presumably as a successor of Hardy, for the Hôtel de Bourgogne. His first play was *L'Hypocondriaque* (about 1628), containing the motive of letters that are intercepted and the ensuing madness of one of the characters. It is possible that Corneille borrowed this motive for his own *Mélite*, although it was a commonplace at the time. Besides borrowing from the Romans and Spaniards, Rotrou preceded Racine as a student of Sophocles, and while his version of the *Antigone* is not remarkable, Racine mentions it in one of his *Examens*. But his leaning was nevertheless in the direction of the Cornelian type of drama.

His best tragi-comedy is *Laure persécutée*, where we find the vigorous line:

> Je veux ce que je veux, parce que je le veux;

and his masterpiece in tragedy, *Le véritable Saint-Genest* (1645), while partly drawn from Lope de Vega's *Lo Fingido verdadero*, recalls *Polyeucte*. Rotrou's tragedy represents an actor who in performing the martyrdom of Adrian is so carried away by the heroism of his rôle that he openly professes his faith and receives a martyr's crown. The play within a play — as in *Hamlet* — was a favorite device of the time; Corneille had used it in his *Illusion comique*, but Rotrou's tragedy is the best example of it in French.

Rotrou wrote two other noteworthy tragedies: *Venceslas* (1647) and *Cosroès* (1648). The latter, which goes back to the same source as *Héraclius*, is close in situation to *Nicomède*. The former, taken from a Spanish play by Francisco de Rojas, exhibits Rotrou's emotional genius in a plot that would have pleased Corneille. Venceslas is king of Poland; his sons are both in love with the same woman; the one kills the other rashly and through an error; Venceslas, placed in the dilemma of passing judgment on his own son, abdicates in his favor. In the main the situation is that of Rojas, the title of whose drama is: *No hay ser padre siendo rey;* but the motivation, as well as the compassionate language of the characters involved, is Rotrou's — an indication that with more care and less haste he might have produced a really great drama. But Rotrou, in addition to being a playwright, was a public-spirited citizen of the little town of Dreux, whose inhabitants honored him with an official post. His death has a halo of glory: he died during an epidemic at Dreux, a victim to his sense of public duty.

CHAPTER V

DESCARTES

The rational spirit of the Renaissance has its purest expression in Cartesianism or the philosophy of Descartes. As we have seen, Calvin defined the province of knowledge as limited to God and ourselves. Similarly, Ramus had appealed from scholastic philosophy to human reason, although the reason he had in mind was that revealed by the ancients. Finally, Montaigne set his own reason by the side of that of the ancients and, skeptical as he was in regard to both, he thereby demonstrated the necessity of a method of thought. It remained for Descartes (1) to discover the method; and (2) to show by it that the moderns are equal, if not superior, to the ancients.

Thus Descartes is the founder of modern philosophic thought: he began where the ancients stopped, with the problem of cognition ("By what means do we know?"); he defined the reason scientifically (*Cogito ergo sum* — "I think, therefore I am"); and he opened the door to the idea of progress, so essential to the eighteenth and nineteenth centuries.

In temperament Descartes was a survival of the sixteenth-century type of Frenchman. Apparently, no man was less social. Yet no man, certainly no philosopher, traveled about the world more in order to acquaint himself with the subjects he was to treat. He was born at La Haye, between Tours and Poitiers, in 1596. His family belonged to the nobility, and as a matter of fact Descartes was never compelled to make a living or do anything he did not like. Educated at the Jesuit college of La Flèche, he left it in 1612 thoroughly convinced of the futility of book learning but with a strong aptitude for mathematics. After a short stay in Paris, where like Pascal he developed an interest in gambling, Descartes took his law degree at Poitiers (1516) and then enlisted in the army of Maurice of Nassau in Holland, in order to gain experience of life. Here he wrote his first treatise, a *Compendium musicae*, which applies to music the principles of geometry. The Thirty Years War then led him to take service with the Bavarian army, and it was in 1619 that — being in winter quarters, " alone in a room with his stove" — the idea came to him of making mathematics the foundation of a universal theory of knowledge.

With characteristic caution, Descartes was willing to abide his time. His first concern was with Nature, not with metaphysics. Accordingly, we find him at Prague, seeking traces of Tycho Brahe and of Kepler; he visits Rome and Florence in search of Galileo, whose astronomical views are in accord with his own; in the Alps he makes observations as to avalanches and lightning. From 1626 to 1628 he is again in Paris, meeting with the men of his time and active in their discussions. At one of these gatherings Descartes sets forth the error of reasoning by syllogisms and thus wins the plaudits of the Cardinal de Berulle, who urges him to publish his own philosophy. Accordingly, Descartes definitely left France for Holland on the maxim that *bene qui latuit, bene vixit* (" he who has been well hid has lived well ") in order to procure the necessary philosophical repose.

His first residence in Holland was at Franeker, where it is said he wrote the *Meditationes de prima philosophia* in 1629. All the while he is also busy with experiments in physics. Yet his chief scientific work, the *Traité du monde*, was never published as such. Hearing of the condemnation of Galileo, Descartes destroyed his treatise and vowed never to publish any of his writings. From this resolve he was fortunately shaken by his affection for his illegitimate child Francine. For her, the only human being that he really loved, he planned to issue at least a summary of his ideas. To this wish, more than to anything else, we owe the *Discours de la méthode*, printed anonymously at Leyden (1637) and the first of his works to be published. But Francine died soon after and thus never read her father's " autobiography of a thought," as M. Lanson has cleverly named the *Discours*.

Emboldened by this first adventure in print, Descartes brought out his *Meditationes* (1641), and there followed a period of controversy in which he was as ardently defended as he was bitterly attacked. But among his adherents was one amiable and powerful person: the Princess Elizabeth, daughter of Frederick V, Elector Palatine. She had long been Descartes' favorite pupil. In 1649 he completed for her the *Traité des passions de l'âme* — next to the *Discours* the most important French work that he wrote. Through Elizabeth, Descartes now became acquainted with Catherine, Queen of Sweden. Finding Holland no longer safe, he accepted Catherine's invitation to visit Stockholm and be her tutor. But the northern climate and the early hour of five in the morning, set by the Queen for their interviews, were too severe a drain on a constitution that had never been robust. Soon after his arrival Descartes fell ill of pneumonia and died in February, 1650. His body together with his unpublished manuscripts was returned to France in 1667. But the oration prepared for Descartes' funeral was never pronounced; a royal order forbade it just as the Congregation of the Index in 1663 had forbidden the circulation of his works. As early as 1641, however, a Jansenist, the Duc de Luynes, had translated the *Meditationes* into French.

While Descartes' works constitute an entity in that all are applications of the same mathematical ideal, yet the *Discours* **Works and** *de la méthode* and the *Traité des passions* have **Significance** particular significance for the student of literature. Written designedly in French for the purpose of bringing philosophy — or the problem of being — within the ken of *les honnêtes gens*, they respectively establish the two pivots upon which this problem turns: (1) the truth with regard to our existence; and (2) the truth with regard to our conduct. Learn to see things rationally, says Descartes, and you will realize that two plus two makes four not only in theory but in fact; act on this principle, and error will disappear from the world.

Of the two works in question, the *Traité des passions*, though posterior to the *Discours* in date, belongs essentially to the **The "Traité** Pre-Classical age. It contains the mechanics of **des** Corneille's conception of character. Not that the **Passions"** treatise accounts for Corneille's conception, but it elucidates it — rationally. Descartes explains our passions on the basis of what he terms the "animal spirits." Being particles of blood, to which the heart communicates its heat, the " animal spirits," according to Descartes, are the channels through which the brain receives impressions of the external world. When excited by a stimulus from either the external world or the brain, they produce passion and thus influence our actions. It was not Descartes' fault that his knowledge of physiology was defective; he could not go beyond the discovery of Harvey on the circulation of the blood; " qu'on me donne l'étendu et le mouvement," he said, " et je vais faire le monde "; — more important is the fact that he views the passions un- sentimentally as part of this "movement," and that he views them as originating with the body.

Morally, then, a passion is to be judged by its action or result, with which it is inextricably bound up. A passion is good or bad only in so far as the ensuing action is beneficial or harmful to mankind; and the latter question can be decided only by the *reason*. For the reason supplies the judgment with which to approve or condemn a passion. Thus love is good when it leads us to choose good things:

> pour ce que, joignant à nous de vrais biens, elle nous perfectionne d'autant.

The love of Rodrigue and Chimène, Descartes would have said, is good inasmuch as it makes them sacrifice self to duty; Horace was justified in killing Camille because his passion had the approval of his reason. It is clear that Descartes considers the reason as autonomous: no passion can sway it, and therefore no passion is in itself interesting or worthy of detailed description. To the Cartesian there are no mysteries, no obscurities, no shades of feeling — such as we shall find in Racine. What is important to him is the mind, with its faculty of judgment, a vicious act being invariably attributed to a false or bad judgment.

But if reason, argues Descartes, is the absolute judge of good and evil, it yet has no power to enforce its choice between them. This depends on the *will*, which.is the faculty whereby we set one passion against another or with the help of the imagination evokē a good passion which is lying dormant. There is no stronger advocate of the free-will than Descartes. He summarizes:

La volonté est tellement libre de sa nature qu'elle ne peut jamais être contrainte . . . les actions sont absolument en son pouvoir (de l'âme) et ne peuvent qu' indirectement être changées par le corps.

Such an extreme attitude is, as we noted above (Ch. IV), romantic. In this respect Descartes is the child of his age, the *Traité des passions* being a complete (though probably unconscious) vindication of its ideals.

The *Discours de la méthode,* while maintaining the dualism — essential to Descartes' philosophy — of thought and matter, is The " Discours de la méthode " a far more sober piece of reasoning. Its object is no other than to show how Descartes arrived at a criterion for scientific truth, and it records the experience step by step for the benefit of the reader, the subtitle being *Pour bien conduire sa raison et chercher la vérité dans les sciences.* Thus it is the method that matters in philosophy or science, not the conclusions, which will vary according to the material at hand. Herein lies the progressiveness of Cartesianism as a whole.

Descartes begins *ab ovo,* by rejecting the acquired learning of the ages. In a memorable sentence he states that:

le bon sens est la chose du monde la mieux partagée.

Why not use it? since it constitutes the greatness of man. Let us therefore accept nothing that after examination our bon sens does not inevitably sanction. Under the ban of this analysis would fall most of the things that Descartes had learned at La Flèche, more especially of course scholastic philosophy. An apparent exception is made of mathematics and theology; of the first because Descartes is convinced *a priori* of its value, and of the second because he would remain orthodox and is not concerned with the immortality of the soul.

Assuming, he says, that we can doubt everything — the authority of the senses, the truthfulness of God, the accuracy of mathematics — there remains one thing that we who doubt cannot question; namely, that we think. And if we think, we exist; hence *cogito ergo sum.* Upon this, the most logical of all propositions, the certainty of all our knowledge depends. That is, whatever the mind perceives clearly and distinctly must be true. The later objection of Gassendi, that thinking does not prove existence, that we might as well say " I walk, therefore I am," Descartes answered with the statement that of all our actions we can be certain only of the one; namely, that we think.

On this simple foundation Descartes proceeds to construct the existence of God and of the universe.

The existence of God is capable of three proofs. The first is that we find the idea of God within us, and that there must be a primal substance behind the idea. Again, the reality of God may be inferred from our own imperfection, the consciousness of which shows our dependence on a being that is perfect. And thirdly, the strongest proof of God is gained from our clear and entire conception of Him. Just as the mind knows that in every triangle the three angles are equal to two right angles because the fact is involved in the idea of a triangle, so, says Descartes, existence is a necessary predicate of a perfect being. This proof, the so-called ontological one, of a Supreme Being, had already been used by Saint Anselm of Canterbury. Wherein Descartes' argument differs from Anselm's is the fact that *actuality* to Descartes is contained in perfection: you cannot conceive that a being is perfect who does not exist.

Upon this perfect and eternal Being, Descartes then throws the responsibility for the external world. He is, so to speak, the *Deus ex machina* who establishes the union between our thinking selves and the natural world about us. God is the only complete substance, containing within Himself the attributes of the other two incomplete substances, mind and matter. Mind has as its attribute thought, and matter has as its attribute extension. God possesses both qualities; and therefore it is from Him that our knowledge of matter is derived. It is inconsistent with God's perfection to deceive us, and thus our notions of matter, in proportion as we think them clearly and distinctly, must be true.

The style in which Descartes has propounded these ideas is not always of the best. His aloofness from society had kept him in ignorance of the contemporary worship of form. He has neither the delicacy of Voiture nor the eloquence of Balzac. Too often his sentences are involved and his thought burdens and chokes his phrase. Yet his expression has order and sequence, his definitions are clear and accurate, and his similes are simple and well chosen. His two treatises are addressed to the general reader; it was an achievement to have done this with so difficult and abstruse a subject. With Descartes, philosophy ceases to occupy exclusively the learned, and supplies reading-matter also for the average educated person in France. He himself has defined such reading in the famous words:

> Une conversation avec les plus honnêtes gens des siècles passés . .. et même une conversation étudiée en laquelle ils ne nous découvrent que les meilleures de leurs pensées.

It must not be thought that Cartesianism won immediate or complete acceptance. First of all, Descartes' ideas were too bold, his conclusions too far-reaching, not to produce **Influence of Descartes** opposition even among those who were his partisans. His mechanical theory of nature, dependent only on extension and movement, penetrated the salons and provoked at least the discussion that such a novelty would. In the *Femmes savantes* Molière ridicules the blue-stockings who revel in such Cartesian terms as *tourbillons* and *mondes tombants*. Mme de Sablé and Mme de Grignan were themselves confirmed Cartesians; whereas Mme de Sévigné, fond of animals, objected to a philosopher who would deny her pets a soul, just as did La Fontaine, who in his *Discours à Mme de la Sablière* expostulated:

> Qu'est-ce donc? une montre. Et nous? c'est autre chose.
> Voici de la façon que Descartes l'expose,
> Descartes, ce mortel dont on eût fait un dieu
>   Chez les paiens. . . .

In the second place, there was tradition: that of antiquity and that of the church. The current of the times was strongly set for a triumphal union of the two in the absolutism of Louis XIV. Against this current the scientific method of Cartesianism struggled in vain; it could at best move with it, not against it, and add its power to the general stream. And this it accomplished by giving clarity and precision to the ideas which Classicism was to treat; and also by insisting — more effectively than would otherwise have been possible — on the subordination of beauty to truth: the type of rational truth which Descartes had defined. Even to Pascal, who regarded Descartes as *inutile et incertain,* the dignity of man consists nevertheless in reason-

ing. It was the dogmatism of the reason — the tendency of
Cartesianism to deny the soul all other qualities but this, to make
the existence of God Himself depend on the thinking ego — that
brought forth the greatest opposition.

In the field of philosophy the enemies of Descartes were the
so-called *libertins*. We have met with a similar group among the
Opponents of poets of the first quarter of the century (Bk. III,
Descartes   Ch. IV). They now combatted the dogmatism of
Descartes with the skepticism of Montaigne; while not denying
the "reason," they questioned its unerring validity. Specifically
they objected to the Cartesian theory of innate ideas, and
temperamentally they had an aversion for the severity of
Descartes' ethics, they themselves being epicureans. Bayle and
Fontenelle continue this line of attack in the eighteenth century
(see Part III, Bk. II). Meantime, the *libertins* were all those to
whom nature — in the Rabelaisian sense of Mother Nature —
is the safest guide in life. Guy Patin, the physician, and especially Molière belong to this group; whereas Pierre Gassendi
(1592–1622), the chief philosopher of the *libertins*, was Molière's
teacher.[1]

Gassendi, who claimed to be an orthodox Christian, was a
frank epicurean. He wrote in Latin and applied the philosophy
of Lucretius (the atomic theory) to the domain of physics.
This was in direct opposition to Descartes, for whose "innate
ideas" Gassendi substituted an empiricism which made the mind
an emanation of the body. Like the Jesuits, he held to the
view — handed down from the Middle Ages — that "there is
nothing in the mind which was not first in the senses." But he
coupled this view with a rather broad eclecticism or tolerance,
and the force of his arguments won him a large following, despite
his unoriginality. Thus Gassendi represents the liberal current
of the century, running counter to its idealism and dogmatism.

But Cartesianism was to have a recrudescence during the
Malebranche   second part of the century. This was due mainly
to Nicholas Malebranche. Born at Paris in 1638,
Malebranche at the age of twenty-two became a member of the

---

[1] Other *libertins* were Cyrano de Bergerac, La Mothe le Vayer, Saint-Evremond, and the notorious Ninon de Lenclos of whom Mme de Sévigné said
'Qu'elle est dangereuse, cette Ninon!"

Congrégation de l'Oratoire, and, being won over to the philosophy of Descartes, he enlarged its scope in the *Recherche de la vérité* [2] and then applied his theory to controversial questions in his *Traité de la Nature et de la Grâce* — a book that Bossuet criticized tersely in the words " pulchra, nova, falsa." Malebranche died in the heat of controversy in 1715.

Malebranche's point of departure was Descartes' separation of mind and matter, and their coalescence in God. The problem had already disturbed his predecessor, Arnold Geulincx (1625–1669), a Dutch Cartesian. Geulincx had sought the principle of union in what he called " occasionalism." My will is the *occasion* — he argued — whereby my body moves. It is not that my will moves my body, but that God who has imparted motion to matter has so arranged the world that my body moves *when* my will acts. This type of casuistry Malebranche expands by a return to Neo-Platonism.

In this way, God not only becomes the author and cause of all things but it is in Him that all things have their being and perfection. The Deity comprises, says Malebranche, the world of matter as well as the archetypes (the Platonic Ideas) to which it is related. As to *reason*, God is its supreme form; and according as man grows intelligent he beholds the operation of reason in everything — in Nature, in himself and in religion. Reason is the *logos*, made visible in Christ.

Malebranche was a mystic and a theologian. Hence, he took the step from which Descartes held back; namely, that of identifying theology with philosophy. His system, as such, based on the confusion of reason with God, was to lead straight to the monism of Spinoza, to whom all individual being seemed accidental and God alone the exclusive reality.

On the other hand, the appeal to reason [3] as authority is the logical and extreme position of Cartesianism. Applied to the world of phenomena, *reason* is made the driving force of the eighteenth century. It destroys tradition, places the moderns — in their self-consciousness — above the ancients, suggests the

---

[2] Thus in 1674 Malebranche did for Descartes what Charron had done for Montaigne at the close of the sixteenth century.

[3] On reason as *bons sens* — the practical, as distinguished from abstract, reason — see below, under Classicism.

idea of progress and perfectibility, and in its attention to the sciences undermines the rule of art as incorporated in the ancients. On the last question, the pages of Malebranche's *La vérité* dealing with Aristotle are significant.

The seventeenth century, however, was more literary than scientific, in spite of Descartes. As Voltaire said, it was a century "de grands talents bien plus que de lumières." Although the philosophy of Descartes stands at the apex of the Renaissance, of which it is *the* philosophy, we should bear in mind that in the seventeenth century it was merged with the current of Graeco-Roman tradition, as pointed out above. From this happy fusion came the underlying restraint of the Classical Spirit.

Rigaud, "Louis XIV"

BOOK IV

CLASSICISM

CHAPTER I

LOUIS XIV AND THE CLASSICAL SPIRIT

THE reign of Louis XIV, the longest in French history, extended from 1643 to 1715. Louis was but a child of five when he came to the throne, and the Queen-mother, Anne of Austria, continued the policy of Richelieu with the help of the astute but unscrupulous Mazarin. Thus the young King was bred in the school of the most uncompromising absolutism under the direction of an Italian. A "realist" in politics, Mazarin had but one aim: to serve himself by serving his king. In this he was aided by a sentimental attachment for the Queen-mother herself. Mazarin's greatest achievement, the Peace of Westphalia (1648), had made France a self-sufficient modern state. By the annexation of Metz and Alsace, it had indicated her present boundaries, and by reducing the Holy Roman Empire to an empty shadow it left France the leading continental power. Through this peace, says Lavisse, "la France a pratiqué la première avec éclat la politique de l'égoisme national." Other nations could but follow in her wake. So that when Mazarin died in 1661, the framework of absolute monarchy was complete: the Roi-Soleil had only to step into it and supply the picture of his own commanding personality. Louis was not a genius. He was, in the common opinion of historians, more of an actor than a creator — in the political sense. But until the fatal Revocation of the Edict of Nantes in 1685 he strove wisely, on an ever ascending scale, for the development of those qualities for which France and French culture are justly famed. In the words of Voltaire: "l'Etat devint un tout régulier, dont chaque ligne aboutit au centre." This center was the king — in art and literature as well as politics. Louis is the embodiment of the

273

cultural ideal inherent in the Renaissance. He is the *uomo di virtù* made real. But being a realization, he is also an end. The year 1685 marks the pinnacle of his career. With the Quarrel of the Ancients and the Moderns in 1686 a new period of French history begins.

Personally, Louis blended admirably the qualities of mind and body required for such a difficult rôle. He was twenty-two when **Personal** Mazarin died, and besides the charm and grace **Traits of** of youth he had a majesty of bearing which **Louis** reflected a self-possessed but generous attitude of mind. "Le métier de Roi," he tells us in his Memoirs, "est grand, noble, délicieux." If fortune had honored him, he at least meant to prove worthy. Never was a king more industrious nor, with few exceptions, more circumspect. In his work of organization, it is true, he was assisted by the cool-headed Colbert — him whom Mme de Sévigné had fitly termed "le Nord." Colbert was a Cartesian and an indefatigable worker; he prepared for his royal master a *dossier* on every conceivable matter: law, commerce, politics, war, and even literature and painting. It behooved Louis, he thought, to "divide up" the affairs of state and set them in their "natural order." Owing to Colbert the fiscal and the legal system were modernized, the French colonies were developed through the establishment of a merchant-marine, and the *Canal du midi*, connecting the Mediterranean and the Atlantic, was planned and in part carried out. But if Colbert proposed, it was Louis who "disposed" and where it was feasible executed his own orders. Doubtless Louis should have followed Colbert's advice and given his country peace; whereas, glorious as they were, his wars exhausted his people's strength. When Louis realized his mistake, Colbert was dead and the damage irreparable. On the other hand, Louis did not generally lack prudence. Not being a quick thinker, he improvised nothing. His speeches — one might add, his every act — were prepared with care. Passionate by nature, as his successive "affairs" with Marie Mancini, La Vallière, Madame de Montespan and Madame de Maintenon show, he was in no sense a profligate and rarely allowed emotion to control his mind. When his own brother, the weak Duke of Anjou, asked him for a sinecure, he slyly replied: "the best sinecure is the heart of your King." Thus, in the main, Louis was hard-working, intelligent, moderate and extraordinarily regular. " With a calendar and a watch in hand," wrote Saint-Simon, " one could at a distance of three hundred leagues predict what he was doing."

But it should be observed that the chief function of this monarch was to " act a part." Where pomp and ceremony are The Court of the rule, pride and vanity become a second nature. Louis XIV And mindful of the disruptive forces that produced the Fronde, the monarchy bent every energy to organize its " glory " in a concrete form. Says Lavisse:

> Louis voulut, dans cette concupiscence de gloire . . . être glorieux comme Auguste, le protecteur des lettres, comme Constantin et Théodose, les protecteurs de l'Eglise, comme Justinien, le législateur. " Il faut," pensait-il, " de la variété dans la gloire."

But however varied the manifestations of glory, they were clearly to center upon the King. Colbert, who in 1664 bought the office of superintendent of buildings, virtually became a minister of fine arts. He awarded pensions to scholars and writers, he acted as vice-protector of the Academy, he gave employment to artists and architects — in short, he directed the intellectual life of the country with the same masterful design as he did the finances and the laws. But it was Louis himself who created Versailles — the focus of all this activity, the vast stage of French grandeur, the symbol at once of his absolutism and his universality.

It is unnecessary to dwell on the magnificence and cost of the court of Versailles. The palace, which, with its galleries, courtyard, park, fountains, embodied the art of Le Vau, Mansart, Le Nôtre, Le Brun and Perrault, was planned to admit a multitude — not as guests but as spectators and workers. Taine estimates that the official household of the King involved some fifteen thousand individuals with an outlay of forty to fifty million francs or one tenth of the public revenue. What concerns us here is the symbolic aspect of the place, the fact that human life could be organized on so formal a plane, that it was in effect possible to compress the activities of a nation into the dimensions of a well-ordered salon. For the Court of Versailles was not

an inner circle — closed to the eyes of the world — but a continuous public function, in which every act of the monarch, from
his getting out of bed (*le lever*) to his evening prayer and retirement (*le coucher*) was elaborately staged and observed. When,
for example, the youthful Louis wished to proclaim his attachment for La Vallière, he gave at Versailles the " Plaisirs de
l'Ile enchantée " — a fête that lasted nine days, and in which
Molière was the chief entertainer. Riding on a chariot, the
great dramatist impersonated Pan, the most pagan of the
gods; and he celebrated in verse the justification for Louis'
passion:

> Dans l'âge où l'on est aimable
> Rien n'est si beau que d'aimer.

Thus the court of Louis XIV appealed to the sociability and
the histrionic sense of the French. It was exclusive only in the
respect that training and genius made it so. It is noteworthy
that the main talents of Louis' reign were of bourgeois extraction: Racine, Boileau, Molière and La Fontaine. Only La
Rochefoucauld, Madame de La Fayette and Saint-Simon were of
the hereditary noble class. Yet noble or cleric or bourgeois,
it was part of Louis' deliberate plan to make them all contribute
to his fame: Racine and Boileau as historiographers, Bossuet
as chaplain to the court and as tutor to the Dauphin,[1] Molière
as chief entertainer and *comédien du roi.* To ignore such a
king was practically to forego worldly success. " Sachez,"
says one of Molière's characters, " que les courtisans ont d'aussi
bons yeux que d'autres; qu'on peut être habile avec un point
de Venise et des plumes, aussi bien qu'avec une perruque courte
et un petit rabat uni," and finally, " que la grande épreuve · · ·
c'est le jugement de la cour." Even the vagabond La Fontaine
— as free a spirit as France has ever produced — was to recognize
the fact.

It would have been impossible, however, for Louis to concentrate upon Versailles unless he had had the resources of Paris
to draw from. By the seventeenth century Paris
had become what it has remained since: the metropolis with a character and temper of its own; " the
torch-bearer of France," as Victor Hugo has called it, but not

Paris; The Urban Aspect of Culture

---

[1] Known as Monseigneur.

the whole of France nor the expression of a single faith, religious, political or artistic. Yet if French literature has a metropolitan aspect, this was never more the case than during Louis' reign. The ancients had seen in their cities — Athens and Rome — the opportunity for a definite and well-rounded life of culture; and the French succeeded to this idea, again through the medium of Italy. Ronsard and Du Bellay had been proud of the fact that they hailed from the provinces; but the Classical Boileau is first and foremost a Parisian. Nicolas Poussin, the court painter, admits without hesitation:

> J'ai choisi la demeure de la ville, et non pas celle des champs où je vivrais déconsolé.

Thus Classical culture has the two phases, summed up in the expression *la cour et la ville,* and between them it would be hard to choose. For if the court gave form and polish, it was the city that furnished matter and ideas to literature and art. Vaugelas, that *arbiter elegantiarum* in respect to language, is forced to grant that:

> Le consentement des bons auteurs (most of them Parisians) est comme le sceau, ou une vérification, qui authorise le langage de la cour, et qui marque le bon usage.

And so it happens that Racine, a Jansenist at heart, produces the most courtly form of tragedy; that Molière, a radical in almost any other age, lifts his voice in behalf of the social virtues; and that Pascal, a dissenter if there ever was one, clothes his thought in the most aristocratic of styles. Variety in unity is therefore the hall-mark of French Classicism. It is without doubt a literature of form, but it is also a literature of great individuals, whose personal qualities are none the less marked for being artistically on much the same plane.

In the alignment of Classical traits, *reason* would come first, then *art,* then *social form,* and finally *nature.* With all of these The Classical except the last we have dealt in preceding chapters. Traits As we have seen, the idea of reason permeates the Renaissance as that of faith does the Middle Ages and as the idea of personality characterizes modern times. In regard to art, its influence dates from the Pléiade and the introduction of critical theories from Italy. In both respects there was — as we have observed — a return to Graeco-Roman antiquity; thus the authority of the ancients became in a measure sacrosanct. Yet there could be no organization without social form, which would harmonize conflicting ideals under the banner of decorum and give to the social body ease and grace of expression. This was the work of the Hôtel de Rambouillet and the various salons arising therefrom. Lastly, as a culmination of these traits, came a better understanding of man's intrinsic qualities, a psychological grasp of his actual being — in a word, *nature,* which thus is the crowning feature of the Classical edifice.

It cannot be too strongly stated that to the seventeenth century nature was primarily " human nature." The generation of 1660, thinks Brunetière, was quite capable of enjoying landscape; but it enjoyed it objectively, *sans phrases.* It was far from conceiving landscape, in its primitive majesty and beauty, as an inspiration for poetry and art. That revelation was to be reserved for Rousseau and the eighteenth century to make. Meantime, this was the age of the formalism of Le Nôtre, when the regularity of the drawing-room was the model for gardening, when trees and shrubbery were arranged like furniture, and lawns were currently called *des tapis verts.* In general, then, the fundamental idea was *la belle nature;* that is, " civilized nature," a world thought of as conforming to the universal laws of the human mind. The more the opposing factors of mind and matter could be harmonized, the better — provided always that reason or mind remained in the ascendency. On this basis Boileau laid down the rule:

> Jamais de la nature il ne faut s'écarter;

and, in England, Pope repeats this thought in the dictum:

> True wit is Nature to advantage dressed,
> What oft was thought but ne'er so well expressed.

On the other hand, a departure from nature was now the *précieux,* the bizarre, the grotesque and the *invraisemblable* — like the lawless and savage aspects of a universe untouched by the civilizing hand of man. " Let there be no mistake," says that later-day Classicist Brunetière, " if the heroes of Shakespeare are more passionate than others, they are not on that account more true to life but only more brutal " —

ils sont plus proches de la nature dans la mesure où le sont aussi les sauvages et les barbares.

Classicism would admit of no such imperfection.

But if Classicism is at once natural, artistic and rational — it is by its very definition opposed to an exaggeration of any one feature. The real Classicists (Pascal, Boileau, Racine, La Fontaine, Bossuet and Molière) held not only to reason but also to intuition as the two essential qualities of man. They did so with Pascal, who maintained — and this is the most extreme statement of his position:

> Le cœur a ses raisons que la raison ne connaît point;

and again with Boileau, who said:

> Mais la nature est vraie, et d'abord on la *sent*.

There has been much discussion of the famous passage in which Pascal sets in opposition these two functions of man as the *esprit de géométrie* and the *esprit de finesse*. By the one, he affirms, we reason abstractly, and by the other we apprehend immediately and concretely. Other terms are: *la raison* (the pure reason) and *le bons sens* (the practical reason). And it is the second quality, so frequently emphasized by both Molière and Boileau, that is invoked for the guidance of mankind. Certainly, the trait is typical of the French *honnête homme*, who by antecedent training has acquired the aptitude to judge delicately and therefore correctly.[2] Cléante in *Tartuffe* holds this point of view when he says:

> Les hommes la plupart sont étrangement faits!
> Dans la juste nature on ne les voit jamais.

— whereas the man of good breeding is considerate and balanced in his conduct. But names are deceptive, and the *esprit de finesse* ranges all the way from *le bon sens* to the most delicate intuition. Similarly, in the field of art it appears as *le bon goût* or taste; and, again, to some critics taste is based on inflexible rational laws, whereas to others it is mainly delicacy of perception

---

[2] "Measure" as characteristic of the *honnête homme* — a reflection of the Italian *sprezzatura* — is seen in La Rochefoucauld's maxim that "l'honnête homme est celui qui ne se pique de rien."

or feeling. La Bruyère, who believed that there is " un bon et un mauvais goût," nevertheless made the criterion of taste a matter of cultivated instinct.[3] The important point, however, is that Classicism conceives of man's nature as " complete." The gestation of centuries is achieved: man has become conscious of himself, of his position in the universe, of his functions, of what he can and cannot do in life. If he is sensible like the Chrysaldes and Aristes of Molière's Comedy, he will know that the " middle course " (le juste milieu) is the best, that it is folly to fly to extremes,[4] that only he is happy who can bring his life into accord with the lives of his fellow-men. But even when he is not sensible, when like the Phaedra or Orestes of Racine he is mad with passion, or like Pascal he is at odds with the universe, his reason mirrors his weakness and justifies the position that:

Toute notre dignité consiste . . . en la pensée. Travaillons donc à bien penser: voilà le principe de la morale.

In other words, Classicism clings to reason as the foundation of intuition, and its " nature " is the harmony between idea and fact.

In this essential position, Classicism is the realism of seventeenth-century literature. Racine and Molière are related to Corneille as Honoré de Balzac is to Victor Hugo. The difference is that neither Balzac nor Hugo regards man as a finality, and least of all as a rational finality, such as he is to both Corneille and Racine. The Classical world, we repeat, is a closed universe. Its tendency is constantly to identify the city and the world (in urbe et orbe). Classicism gravitates towards a center, not away from it. Humanity is not asked in Nietzsche's phrase, " to surpass itself," but to be itself. The breadth of Classicism lies in the supreme fact that it considers nothing human as alien to it — though this is true only as an ideal. In fact, having decided what is normal for man or a special group of men, the Classicist sets up this norm as his model and imitates it. And how is this norm determined? The simplest answer to this ques-

[3] "Celui qui le sent et qui l'aime a le goût parfait: celui qui le sent et qui l'aime en deçà ou au delà a le goût défectueux." — Des ouvrages de l'esprit.

[4] Compare Pascal, Pensées, 378: "C'est sortir de l'humanité que de sortir du milieu."

tion is to say: by a comparison of civilized men throughout the ages; and to the seventeenth century such a comparison necessarily embraced the ancients. Thus French Classicism is not merely a revival of ancient classicism, but an attempt to define the *genus* Man by eliminating from him all that seemed local and ephemeral. Racine's tragedies are not Greek, Roman or French; they are — within the limits we have stated — universal.

Having said this, we must grant that there is little or no room in such a program for the imagination. " The fairyland of fancy," where genius " may wander wild," is in itself contrary to the Classical creed. The Classical vocabulary is restricted to words that were socially approved as universally expressive. [5] Even the rational imagination, considered as " quickness," or " wit," or " conceit " — qualities so much lauded in Pre-Classical days — had become abhorrent to the age of Boileau and La Bruyère, who regarded false wit as lacking in common sense and judgment. The amiable and sensible Bouhours defines *le bel esprit* as *le bon sens qui brille.*[6] In all this, Classicism again represents a reaction, and correctness or " decorum " easily became a tyranny. Above all, and here is the objector's best argument, Classicism would leave no illusions, no mysteries, no undiscovered bourns, in man's spiritual makeup. Where the momentum is towards clearness and precision it is away from lyricism or metaphysics.

On the other hand, genius is always an exception and no system can fully explain the great work of art. Racine has a lyrical side just as Pascal is metaphysical, if any Frenchman ever was. If Classicism means anything it signifies control and not suppression. Indeed, the French spirit is so nearly Classical that it would be hazardous to attempt a distinction. What makes it so is the sense of balance: the ability of the cultivated Frenchman, illustrated again and again in history, though never better than in the generation of 1660, to strike a middle course. The Classical traits of reason, art, social form, and nature were then held, so to speak, in suspension — not in fixed proportions, but in deference to the value of each. Beneath the veneer of art, there were the social problems, rationally

---

[5] Racine's vocabulary is much less than one-half that of Shakespeare.

[6] See Wright, *French Classicism*, page 104.

considered, with great wealth of observation.   Or the emphasis
might be reversed: a social or scientific problem is to the fore
and art is accessory; yet the form being artistic the problem
treated carries delight and conviction to its public.   It may be
doubted whether, as " truth," the character types of Racine and
Molière have ever been equalled.   They have their limitations,
of course.   They may lack individual freedom, power — some
may say — beauty.   But that they are " real " is beyond cavil.

Thus the Age of Louis XIV is the representative French age.
Classicism is the harmonious inter-working of life and art./
It is the time when the individual and the type are most evenly
matched; when men look beyond the individual for the actual
traits of the type, and when, at the same time, " à mesure qu'on
a plus d'esprit, on trouve qu'il y a plus d'hommes originaux.
Les gens du commun ne trouvent pas de différence entre les
hommes."   Into these words Pascal has distilled the essence of
French seventeenth-century culture.

CHAPTER II

THE WRITERS OF MEMOIRS AND MAXIMS
WOMEN WRITERS

THE first Classicist, in his attitude towards human nature, was La Rochefoucauld. There is an exquisite page by Sainte-Beuve **La Roche-** in which the great critic recalls that Mme de Sévigné **foucauld** once suggested papering a bedroom with the backs of playing-cards. Thus the trumps of the evening before would appear to us in the morning in a wholly different light: we had retired believing in Chimène, Polyeucte, Auguste or some other queen or king of romance; we would awaken to behold the other side of the picture. This other side of life, *le revers de la médaille*, is La Rochefoucauld. He, too, has his interest, the interest of a fresh discovery. And as we proceed to drain his bitterness and wax enthusiastic over it, we ourselves grow calm and collected, aware of the fact, which La Rochefoucauld never allows us to forget, that life has the two sides, ideal and real, separated by an attitude.

François VI, Duc de la Rochefoucauld, Prince de Marsillac, was born at Paris in 1613. He had an adventurous and noisy **His Career** youth, taking a very active part in the Fronde. " Il y eut," said Cardinal de Retz, " toujours du je ne sais quoi en tout M. de La Rochefoucauld." This irresolution, seen chiefly in a sentimental attachment for women — Mme de Chevreuse, the Duchess of Longueville, Mme de Sablé and Mme de La Fayette — led him to turn his back on fortune. Wounded at the combat of the Porte Saint-Antoine, and disappointed at the triumph of Mazarin, he retired in 1653, first abroad, and then to his estate at Verteuil. In 1656 he returned to Paris to enjoy a disillusioned but peaceful old age in the distinguished circles which he helped to create. He died in 1680, in the arms of Bossuet. His *Mémoires* were first published in 1662, and his *Maximes* in 1664–1665.

Unlike Montaigne, La Rochefoucauld prizes his personal observation as on a par with general truth; he distinguishes the two, does justice to each, and hence is aware of the bearing of each on the other. His truest observation is probably that " Nobody deserves to be praised for doing good unless he possesses the power of doing evil." Goodness to him is an exceptional act — this is the keynote of his aristocratic code. The fact that humanity is mostly a failure is no reason why it should always be one. Thus La Rochefoucauld's " truths " are the reflections of a spirit essentially idealistic.

His Works

The *Mémoires* are the record of his own failures, objectively told. With intentional coldness the work recounts the fiasco of the Fronde and the futile attempt of La Rochefoucauld to free the Queen from the tyranny of Richelieu. The *Maximes* crystallize the poignancy of human experience in a phrase. In itself, the maxim was a product of the salon of Mme de Sablé. This great lady, daughter of the Maréchal de Souvré, united good breeding with a keen intelligence and an interest in the Jansenists of Port-Royal. Under her direction it became a social game not only to draw portraits in words but also to summarize discussions in a sentence. For this there were Italian models,[1] and Mme de Sablé's own " maxims " were not without merit, while those by a certain Esprit — the *Faussetés des vertus humaines* — attained considerable vogue. Those of La Rochefoucauld were offered at the lady's shrine as incense: years were given to polishing and improving each maxim; and when the slender volume at last appeared it was to undergo both excision and expansion and, thanks to the later influence of Mme de La Fayette, considerable softening in tone. The success of the *Maximes* rests as much on the happy turn of the thought — the trimness and ingenuity of expression — as upon the observations expressed. La Rochefoucauld has an instinct, improved by practice, for the *mot propre*. " Quand les vices nous quittent," he says, " nous nous flattons de la créance que c'est nous qui les *quittons*." And again, " Les vices entrent dans la composition des vertus, comme les poisons entrent dans la composition des *remèdes*." For the most part, however, the exaggeration is slight and the observa-

---

[1] See especially Guazzo, *La civil Conversazione*, 1574.

tion is not only telling but also profound. Thus poetry unites with truth in such maxims as " With true love it is as with apparitions — every one talks of them but few persons have seen them," and " Virtues lose themselves in self-interest as rivers lose themselves in the sea." Like Molière, La Rochefoucauld is a remorseless critic of life. He is not without pity, but he is as relentless to himself as to society in regard to the motives which we constantly misrepresent, for " Society rewards more often the appearance of merit than merit itself."

Finally, there is his Parnassian style — a style that has the quality of an inscription: lapidary, concise, completely adequate. But it is a style without relief, having no transitions, and hence wearisome in the long run. La Rochefoucauld is not a great writer: he harps too much on one string, but the vibrations from that string are true to human nature the world over.

Without a scintilla of La Rochefoucauld's nobility but possessing far more dash and brilliancy was his contemporary, Paul de The Cardinal Gondi, Cardinal de Retz (1614–1679). Never a de Retz   sentimentalist, Retz was an Italian by birth and tradition, and he sought to play a rôle as a worldly and profligate churchman. At seventeen he wrote the *Histoire de la conjuration de Fiesque*, a work that opened Richelieu's eyes to the potential dangers of this fledgling. In 1652 he was made a cardinal through intrigue. Imprisoned because of his part in the Fronde, he escaped, passed eight years in Spain, Holland and Rome, and in 1662 returned to France after having resigned his bishopric with a *grandeur d'âme* which was truly Cornelian (Lanson). His *Mémoires*, written about 1671 though not published until 1717, are an attempt to rehabilitate himself in the eyes of posterity — another trait of the Frondeur. In an admirable portrait of him La Rochefoucauld emphasizes these qualities: " beaucoup d'élévation, d'étendue d'esprit, et plus d'ostentation que de vraie grandeur de courage."

There is something demoniac in Retz's audacity (Dowden), of which the *Mémoires* are the expression. This work relates what Retz desired to be believed. He changes dates, falsifies facts and motives, but is always vivid and intensely real. In particular, his account of the " Journée des Barricades " pulsates with the vigor of an actual occurrence and reveals his power as a descriptive artist of the first rank. The same trait appears in the extended correspondence he exchanged with the notables of his time. Retz is particularly strong in his discussion of politics and in his portraits. In both directions he shows astuteness and a sense of color, although brilliancy of idea and of style remains his chief asset. Thus in every regard he is a survival of the age of Corneille.

Another Frondeur, but this time an ardent defender of the royal faction, was Charles de Marguetel de Saint-Denis, Seigneur
Saint- de Saint-Evremond (1613–1703). Yet in his writ-
Evremond ings he maintains a detached point of view. Having publicly criticized the Peace of the Pyrenees, he had to leave France (1661) in order to escape the Bastille. He retired to England and there spent forty-two years of his life, dying on the threshold of the eighteenth century and being the only Frenchman buried in Westminster Abbey. Thus Saint-Evremond spans the century, touching only its extremes and uninfluenced by Classicism itself. He is one of the really "free" spirits. *Précieux* and *libertin* by origin, he holds to Corneille against the rising fame of Racine, and he concludes by admiring Bayle and by breaking a lance for the Moderns (see below) in his treatise *Sur les Poèmes anciens* (1685). Less of a writer than a cosmopolite of liberal ideas, he was not keen to publish, and in fact his *Véritables Œuvres* did not appear until after his death in 1705. These works consist of reflections on diverse topics, generally more interesting than sound, but always expressed with ease and simplicity. Sainte-Beuve regarded him as the most distinguished example of the courtiers of 1660.

Others there were of a similar but less worthy type, such as the vainglorious Chevalier de Méré (1609–1684) and the captious but
Women very able and witty Bussy-Rabutin (1618–1693).
Writers Méré gave one of the earliest and most elaborate definitions of the *honnête homme*, besides suggesting to Pascal various fruitful reflections; whereas Bussy excelled by the perfect trimness of his epistolary style, seen above all in his correspondence with distinguished women. But it is these latter who illustrate best the mundane spirit and the background of social brilliancy and intrigue upon which Classicism was nurtured.

This background is still covered with a veil of romance in the works of Mme de La Fayette, the "truest" woman whom La Rochefoucauld had ever known. Her maiden name **Mme de** was Marie-Madeleine Pioche de la Vergne, and she **La Fayette** was born in Havre (1634), of which city her father was governor. She received an excellent education, partly at the hands of Ménage and of Rapin, and was early introduced to the *précieux* circles of the capital. Married at twenty-one to the Comte de La Fayette, she became the intimate of Mme de Sévigné and of the gracious but unhappy Henrietta of England, whose Memoirs she wrote. During the later years of his life La Rochefoucauld found in her a devoted friend, and she in him doubtless a helpful literary mentor. She survived him by thirteen years, dying in 1693.

Her greatest work is *La Princesse de Clèves* (1678), one of the classic novels of French literature. This was preceded by several works [2] published under the name of Segrais, the most interesting of which is *Zayde, histoire espagnole*, in which Mme de La Fayette attempts to reduce to reasonable proportions the complicated intrigue of the heroic romances (see Bk. III, Ch. II). But success along this line was reserved for the first-mentioned work; borrowing the technique of the Cornelian drama and applying it for the first time to the domain of the novel, the author here presents a simple situation in terms that are psychologically true to life.

The subject of *La Princesse de Clèves* is, according to Lanson, that of "Polyeucte moins la religion." A married woman loves a courtier who is not her husband, and becoming aware of the growth of her affection appeals to her husband to protect her against herself. Thinking himself deceived, M. de Clèves falls ill and dies, though not without being told of his error; whereupon his wife, free to choose her lover, chooses a life of seclusion instead. The plot and personages were borrowed in part from Peréfixe,[3] who recounts an event at the court of Henry II. But the motivation, the characterization and, above all, the charm of the novel belong to Mme de La Fayette. There is about the story an air of the medieval *roman d'aventure*; and although

---

[2] She began with a short-story, *Mlle de Montpensier*, 1662.
[3] *Histoire de Henri le Grand*, 1662.

realism is not its strongest side, its pathos and its beauty are alike impressive — and its psychology is that of an aristocratic soul. As regards form, *La Princesse de Clèves* is a landmark in the history of its genre. With it the historical romance acquires not only depth but proportion as well.

On the whole, Mme de La Fayette writes simply and without affectation; her style is luminous rather than passionate, nor does it lack ironic touches and an occasional bit of malice.

A letter-writer only, but probably the greatest one the world has ever had, is Mme de Sévigné. Her correspondence is the Mme de Sévigné "tableau-vivant" of the seventeenth century, and for social portraiture it equals the works of Saint-Simon, while written with much more fairness though less scope.

Marie de Rabutin-Chantal, who at eighteen married the Marquis of Sévigné — a Breton nobleman — was born at Paris in 1626 and died at Grignan in 1696. A granddaughter of that Mme de Chantal whom François de Sales knew, and a cousin of Bussy-Rabutin, she belonged to one of the best families in France. Left an orphan in childhood, she fell to the care of an uncle, the Abbé de Coulanges, who gave her an excellent education, to which both Chapelain and Ménage contributed instruction in foreign languages. Personally, she had beauty despite the square nose and the *yeux bigarrés* with which she reproached herself. In addition, she possessed a sparkling wit and, what is more remarkable for her time, an outright and sincere manner of speech. Thus she was fitted to become a social leader without falling a prey to preciosity or to worldly intrigue.

Her husband, another light-hearted Frondeur, was killed in a duel (1651), leaving his young wife with two children, a daughter Françoise, and a son Charles. She married her daughter (1668) to the Comte de Grignan, a lieutenant-general of Provence, and supported her son in the army. Meanwhile, she consoled herself for her solitude by leading an active social life. In 1677 she bought the Hôtel Carnavalet, where she kept open house until her death. But she also visited other parts of France, passing the summer at Les Rochers, the family estate in Brittany, or going to Provence for a sojourn with her daughter. Mme de Sévigné was fond of bucolic Nature, while the great passion of her life — the only passion that ever blinded her — was her affection for her daughter.

The great bulk of her Letters, and they fill many volumes, are addressed to Mme de Grignan. Others were written to **The Letters** Bussy-Rabutin, Mme de La Fayette, and a few friends — in short, a rather intimate circle. But in a day when the means of communication were slow and journalism was in its infancy,[4] the arrival of a letter was an event and the composition thereof a matter of consequence. Thus, writing from the center of the world to her daughter in the provinces, Mme de Sévigné was not merely a purveyor of information on all important subjects, but also a sympathetic and imaginative critic. Indeed, her greatest gift is a vivid imagination, one which permitted her to gauge at a distance the effect that her messages would make upon the recipient. As M. Lanson has observed, her Letters have light, color and movement. They are not over-emotional: the execution of the Marquise de La Brinvilliers (convicted of poisoning) becomes under her pen a masterpiece of piquant description. Or take her Letter on the Death of Turenne, written a full month after this general died; nothing that is significant is omitted, the details are presented vividly, with extraordinary freshness — but what is more, they are intelligently presented, the particular passes over into the general, and such facts as escaped her eye her fancy supplies. Having no theory to uphold, she thus becomes the mirror of her age. In a style that is at once brilliant and rational, she touches upon all aspects of her time: the court, the city, the country-side, her own domestic life and, lastly, her extensive and solid reading. The Letters are not only an invaluable social and literary document but also the expression of a spirited and sensible woman of the world. They include also the doings of her many friends, for she was amiable and widely esteemed.

Masculine perseverance, rather than feminine charm and wit, accounts for the remarkable rôle which Mme de Maintenon **Mme de Maintenon** was to play in the destinies of France. Noteworthy, too, is the paradox between her common-sense mind and the startling romance of her career. " C'est une fortune d'aventurière, avec l'esprit le moins aventurier du monde," says M. Lanson.

[4] *La Gazette de France* published four pages weekly, from 1631 on, and *Le Mercure Galant* began as a quarterly in 1672.

Granddaughter of the great Protestant poet, Françoise d'Aubigné (1635–1719) [5] was born in a prison. Taken to the West Indies by her father, whom she lost in childhood, placed in a convent in order to be converted to Catholicism, dependent on her own efforts for an education, she married early the talented but broken-down Scarron. On the latter's death, her steadfastness won her the position of governess to the children of Mme de Montespan and Louis XIV. This was her " stroke of fortune." Painstaking, regular, faithful to the point of self-effacement, she gradually became the confidant and friend of the King — and soon after the death of Marie-Thérèse she was secretly married to him (1684). As her correspondence makes clear, she had not the genius to intrigue for this post; on the contrary, it came to her by force of circumstance: among all those close to Louis she alone had the power to heal and reform, at least to attenuate, the ills of Louis' declining years. Thus she made it her calling to bring him back to the church.

It is possible to exaggerate this influence. At the same time, the Revocation of the Edict of Nantes (1685), following so quickly upon her marriage, had her approval, just as it was due to her that Louis henceforth surrounded himself with followers and not with leaders. In one respect Mme de Maintenon showed genius; namely, in the foundation of Saint-Cyr, a school for the daughters of poor but well-born people. Here she, a Romanist, carried into execution the principles of the Jansenists of Port-Royal. It was for Saint-Cyr that Racine wrote his last two plays: *Esther*, with which he justly triumphed, and *Athalie*, with which he unjustly failed.

As for literature, Mme de Maintenon is known by various *Lettres, Avis, Conversations* and *Proverbes*. Of all these it is the *Lettres* that reflect her character best. They are not, like Mme de Sévigné's, the creation of genius. But they reveal a knowledge of human nature, a sense of justice and balance, and a passion for Reason — a name by which Mme de Maintenon was currently known. Again the masculine note is dominant; accordingly, Mme de Maintenon is just to others, direct and natural, and her business letters in particular are products of a practical and efficient mind.

[5] In 1675 Louis XIV gave her the title of Marquise de Maintenon.

MOLIERE AND LA FONTAINE

By giving rise to the writing of Memoirs and Letters the Fronde had distilled the pungency of realism. In the two geniuses before us realism is a gift of the gods; hence it is creative rather than merely critical and ironic. Molière and La Fontaine are linked with the tradition of Rabelais: both belong to the *libertin* or epicurean current of the century; both affirm life on a rational, common-sense basis; in both dwells the spirit of comedy. "What great writer has most honored my reign?" Louis XIV once asked of Boileau. "Molière, Sire," replied the great critic. La Fontaine, being more lyrical, is less universal; but he is a great French poet, possessed of a sensitive and highly artistic temperament.

Jean-Baptiste Poquelin, who took the stage-name of Molière, was born in the Rue Saint-Honoré (Paris) about the middle of January, 1622. His mother, Marie Cressé, who was well-to-do in her own right, died when her eldest was ten. Jean Poquelin, his father, bought in 1631 the post of *tapissier ordinaire de la maison du roi*, to which was later added the title of *valet de chambre*. There were but eight such "royal upholsterers," and it is clear that the Poquelin family enjoyed some distinction among the bourgeoisie. In 1637 the reversion of the father's office was settled on the poet, who was, however, to have an excellent education. The Collège de Clermont, today the Collège Louis-le-Grand, had been founded in Paris by the Jesuits and was attracting the scions of the better-class citizens. Thither Molière was sent. He there followed the regular courses in science and grammar, which included a careful study of Plautus and Terence, and he became attached to his schoolmate, Chapelle, who was already somewhat of a wit and society dandy. When young Chapelle and Cyrano de Bergerac were placed under the tutelage of the philosopher Gassendi, Molière probably joined them. Certain it is that Molière tried his hand at a translation of Lucretius' *De natura rerum,* the influence of which is reflected in *Le Misanthrope* (Act II, Sc. V). The result of such an education was two-fold: it grounded the poet in a knowledge of Roman Comedy, and it initiated him into the philosophy of epicureanism.

It is also said — this time by an enemy of the poet — that Molière studied law at Orleans. But this is doubtful, as is also the claim that the poet accompanied Louis XJII as an apprentice " upholsterer " to Narbonne in 1642. Whatever may have been his previous intention, at the age of twenty-one he renounced his father's succession and became an actor — and an impresario.

His associates in this career were a family of vagabond players, the Béjarts, one of whom, Madeleine Béjart, figures cruelly in his private and professional life. With them Molière founded the so-called *Illustre Théâtre.* But the difficulty of finding a stage for their performances and the choice of heavy tragedy parts, for which Molière in particular was unsuited, spelled disaster, and by 1645 the elder Poquelin was obliged to rescue his son from a debtors' prison.

For a period of thirteen years, the company then toured the provinces as " barn-stormers." The ox-cart of Madeleine became the chariot of Thespis; Scarron in his *Roman comique* has described the vicissitudes of a strolling troupe which cannot be unlike those that proved Molière's metal. Hard as these years were, they had their compensation. The company won the services of Mlle Du Parc, then in her prime; it displayed its wares before princely patrons; and finally, it discovered Molière's genius as a writer of comedy — *L'Etourdi* (" The Blunderer "), the first of his undoubted plays, being performed at Lyons in 1655. We learn this from La Grange, who joined the troupe in 1658, and whose *Registre* is the most authentic account of the poet's subsequent activity. In the interval Molière had produced his *Dépit amoureux* (" Lovers' Quarrel "), like his first play, composed in the manner of the Italian Comedy of Masks.

But real success awaited him in Paris. His troupe had returned to the capital in 1658 and on the invitation of Monsieur (the Duke of Anjou) had given a performance before the court.

A week later the company was given permission to use the stage of the Petit Bourbon, a theater adjoining the Louvre. Here it was, on November eighteenth, 1659, that all Paris laughed at *Les Précieuses ridicules*. Apt and timely, this trim little satire was a page from real life. And it was in Molière's true vein, bubbling over with hilarious humor. But if it pleased the multitude, it angered the blue-stockings and the petty marquises who resented the fidelity of Mascarille's impersonation. Obviously, Molière had sown dragon's teeth. On the other hand, he had won the support of the Grand Monarque, who rejoiced when Molière returned to the charge with *Les Fâcheux* ("The Bores"), a dramatic skit which was composed overnight for the royal visit to Vaux-le-Vicomte, and which elicited the following praise from La Fontaine:

> jamais il ne fit si bon
> Se trouver à la comédie . . .
> Nous avons changé de méthode;
> Jodelet n'est plus à la mode,
> Et maintenant il ne faut pas
> Quitter la nature d'un pas.

Meanwhile, our dramatist was busy with more serious questions. *L'Ecole des maris* (1661) broaches the eternal question of the education and marriage of women. The theme was a favorite one during the Renaissance: Terence's *Adelphi* had shown how futile harsh methods are with the young male; the Spanish Mendoza had shifted the interest to the treatment of wives in his *Marido hace mujer* ("The Husband makes the Wife"). On this double basis Molière constructed his play. Sganarelle, who treats his charge severely, is outwitted by her; whereas Ariste, who consents to Léonor's "young wishes," captures her affection. As pure comedy, based on an obvious but easily ignored truth, the *Ecole des maris* is admirable; Voltaire thought it "the best that Molière ever contrived," but Voltaire was writing in the eighteenth century. A goodly portion of Molière's spectators might well be nettled at his liberalism. They manifestly were when in December, 1662, the dramatist brought out his far more emphatic *Ecole des femmes*, with its immortal contrast of old age and youth as revealed in the characters of Arnolphe and Agnès.

One need not see in an author's work mainly the revelation of his own life in order to realize that *L'Ecole des femmes* treats the incompatibility problem unsparingly. On Shrove Monday, 1662, Molière had married Armande Béjart, the daughter of Madeleine and many years his junior. Frenchman that he was, he could have had no illusions on such a relationship. Be that as it may, his play vindicates the right of youth and woman to choose a mate. Agnès is no Miranda, but it is nature that guides her and no evil instinct of her own; whereas Arnolphe, the comic character of the plot, is a victim of his personal machinations. Here, then, we see Molière's genius for treating a serious situation comically. Herein lies the germ of his greatness: his passion for truth-telling, his sense of contrasts, his clear-sighted vision of inevitable fact — and also his heroism, which compels him to speak when speaking is contrary to his interest, to rail when the subject of his raillery is his personal misery and suffering. Quite aside from his plays, the character of Molière has endeared him to the world.

Among his contemporaries, however, there were those whom his frankness scandalized. And these, together with his former victims, now gathered for an attack. De Visé said he lacked literary principles; the Prince de Conti, a former friend, accused him of indecency; the Jansenists quoted against him Nicole's *Traité de la comédie*, a vehement piece of polemic literature. To this uproar Molière replied with the charming *Critique de l'Ecole des femmes* and the clever *Impromptu de Versailles*. The first, in the form of a salon conversation, contains excellent dramatic criticism, and the second, portraying the rehearsal of a play to be given before the King, exploits Molière's ideas on acting, and burlesques the rival players of the Hôtel de Bourgogne. The result was that all the reactionary forces of the capital launched a cabal that was to pursue the poet to his grave.

For the nonce the King encouraged the poet with a pension, of one thousand francs; and others who sided with him were Colbert and especially Boileau, henceforth a reliable friend. The next six years were to see the masterpieces *Tartuffe, Don Juan, Le Misanthrope* and *L'Avare*. Undoubtedly Molière had the material ready to hand, but would he have written these works without the stimulus of opposition?

In May, 1664, Louis XIV gave at Versailles the festival known as " The Pleasures of the Enchanted Isle," in honor of Mlle de la Vallière. Here seemed a chance to strike a blow at the upholders of cant and reaction. Accordingly, Molière came forward with the first three acts of *Tartuffe.* To his astonishment, the play was immediately forbidden after its first performance. Evidently Molière had undervalued the power of his opponents. It might do for a Bossuet to excoriate hypocrites in his sermon on *Le Jugement dernier;* for the stage to attempt it was an unheard-of insult. Besides, excepting the momentary defection of Louis, the stakes were set in France for a religious revival on a large scale. To distinguish hypocrisy from religious zeal is always a delicate task; in 1664 it was an impossible one. But Molière was not to be suppressed. Unable to play *Tartuffe,* he produced *Don Juan ou le Festin de Pierre* (1665), in which hypocrisy becomes the crowning vice of the " grand seigneur mauvais homme." A vast improvement on its Spanish and Italian sources, the French *Don Juan* is a character study on a Shakespearean scale — doubtless, one of the greatest of Molière's creations. But again the censor interfered, though not until the play had been performed some fifteen times to crowded houses. In fact, the very year of its appearance Molière's company received the title of "Troupe royale " and an allowance of six thousand livres. Then came *L'Amour médecin* (" Love as a Doctor "), ultimately derived from the Old French fabliau of the *Vilain mire,* and, after a considerable interval, *Le Misanthrope* and *Le Médecin malgré lui.* Two of these plays are again militant: this time the poet lashes the medical Tartuffes; whereas *Le Misanthrope,* often called " the French Hamlet," states the problem of the Individual versus Society — two forces irreconcilable, unless, like Philinte in the play, men can be made to compromise:

> La parfaite raison fuit toute extrémité,
> Et veut que l'on soit sage avec sobriété.

Thus, in a nutshell, Molière sums up the Classical doctrine in all its implications.

He himself now attempted a compromise. *Tartuffe* is tried on the stage in the guise of *L'Imposteur* (1667), the hero being no longer a cleric but a man of the world, and the action being lengthened so that he may scheme to marry his victim's daughter. This ruse of Molière's did not succeed. But it did benefit his play, for when Pope Clement proclaimed a *Paix de l'Eglise* and the ban against Molière was finally lifted, the drama appeared as *Tartuffe* (1669), but in its expanded five-act form.

The rest of Molière's story is quickly told. In the four or five years that remained to him of life he was content to please his King and go his own way, heedless of what his enemies might contrive. His health was now impaired by a serious illness; his father, whose solvency he had twice rescued by a loan, died in 1669; but his success as a producer was reasonably secure. *L'Amphitryon* and *L'Avare* had appeared in 1668 — the one in a lighter, the other in a heavier vein, though both are modeled on comedies of Plautus. In the first, Molière toys delightfully with the amorous proclivities of Jupiter (Louis XIV) " emprisonné dans sa grandeur," while in *L'Avare* he improves on Plautus by representing the miser as rich, and avarice as a fixed trait of character. *Georges Dandin, Monsieur de Pourceaugnac, Le Bourgeois gentilhomme, La Comtesse d'Escarbagnas* are four social portraits drawn largely from real life; all on the general theme that man must not aspire in the wrong direction, or Nature (this time, " society ") takes vengeance. The social or intellectual climber is foredoomed. This philosophy shines forth most clearly in *Les Femmes savantes*, the next to the last play from Molière's pen. Here, in inimitable verse, the poet gives us a picture of a typical " woman's club " of the seventeenth century. Trissotin (a caricature of the Abbé Cotin) is the exploiter of these ambitious women; Vadius (possibly Ménage) is a self-centered pedant. One may sympathize with the intellectual aims of the strong-minded Philaminte; but shall her daughters' happiness be sacrificed to these ideals? There can be but one answer, and the charming Henriette gives it:

> Et qu'est-ce qu'à mon âge on a de mieux à faire
> Que d'attacher à soi, par le titre d'époux,
> Un homme qui vous aime et soit aimé de vous?

And, finally, we come to the heroic *Malade imaginaire*, Molière's last gibe at physicians and their victims. Argan, the " imaginary invalid," would sacrifice his family to his paranoia. Thus the poet never tired of puncturing the egoisms of life. What justifies the epithet of heroic, applied to this play, is that Molière, a real not an imaginary invalid, acted the part of Argan in it and during the third performance, on February 17, 1673, had a hemorrhage from which he died. Three days later, at nine in the evening, his fellow-actors buried him in the cemetery of Saint-Joseph.

"C'est une étrange entreprise que celle de faire rire les honnêtes gens," says Molière. True comedy requires experience **Molière's** on the part of poet and audience; both must be **Art** cultured, sophisticated, and to a certain extent dis-! illusioned. To laugh at our ills demands a fortitude of spirit, greater than that necessary for tragedy. Further, it implies a ready passage of wit from actor to spectator; the apperceptions must be quick, discriminating, and, above all, sincere. It is no exaggeration to say that in Molière comedy achieves all this; and he is therefore the greatest comic genius among the moderns.

In the first place, Molière is profound. His friend Boileau called him "le grand contemplateur," which is another way of saying that he looked human nature through and through. Consequently the sources of his laughter are genuine. With a flash, he penetrates the absurdity and presents it to us in a phrase, an attitude, a gesture. "Nous avons changé tout cela," is the reply of the physician whose ignorance is so abysmal that he places the heart on the right side of the body; Orgon, convinced of Tartuffe's humility, lulls his own mind to sleep with the phrase, "Le pauvre homme"; "Tant de choses en deux mots," says the simple-minded M. Jourdain,—"Oui," replies his betrayer, "la langue turque est comme cela." Molière rarely strikes a false note — which is the more remarkable when we consider how rapidly he wrote. The reason is that his comedy is a comedy of character rather than one of situation. To be sure, his point of departure is the *farce* and the romantic Spanish *comedia*, to say nothing of the Italian Comedy of Masks, from which he borrowed not only situations and plots but also comic types, such as Mascarille and Sganarelle. In many respects, he remained essentially a *farceur*, as M. Lanson contends. At the

same time, given the time and opportunity, his imagination always transcended the type and reached the individual. Thus
in *Le Bourgeois gentilhomme* we forget " the farce " and remember the innocent, kindly but beguiled figure of M. Jourdain;
and in *L'Avare* the screamingly amusing incidents of the plot
sink into oblivion beside the hard, old and cringing form of
Harpagon, the miser. In all this Molière's touchstone was nature.
Realist that he was, he knew that for the most part human
character cannot be changed. Reason and ridicule are good
weapons, but only for protection — they do not win souls. The
Alceste of *Le Misanthrope* remains atrabilious to the end. Don
Juan is " an alarming image of intellectual power and pride ";
we rejoice at his doom but we cannot hope for his salvation.
Even Tartuffe, the seducer and swindler, has a stately grandeur
that came to him with birth.

The second great trait of Molière is his unalterable
common sense. On occasion Molière could be gay: *Les Précieuses ridicules* and *Le Médecin malgré lui* are continuous ripples
of laughter. More often, however, his comedies verge on tragedy.
— a notable example being *Le Misanthrope* which varies with
one's point of view: Rousseau regarded its action as tragic.
But Molière never fails us in common sense. Thus his point of
view has balance, measure, universality of application. Unlike
Bernard Shaw, he has confidence in the wisdom of the world at
large. To Shaw, illusion is part of the universe's structure;
not so with Molière. The self-deceptions of his characters are
individualistic; they can be dealt with competently by society,
taken generally. This, as we have noted, is the Classical creed.
Hence the comic in Molière is what flies in the face of the sense
of mankind: Alceste is ridiculous because he wants to have
things his own way. So, too, we may allow that Philaminte —
in *Les Femmes savantes* — is admirable in her devotion to grammar and astronomy; she becomes comic when this trait destroys
her common sense.

Finally, there is Molière the artist. " Encore une fois, je le
trouve grand," said Fénelon, " mais ne puis-je parler en toute
liberté sur ses défauts?" To the " decorous " seventeenth century
Molière's faults were obvious. His style seemed careless, inorganic, slapdash. It was as a matter of fact the style of every-

day Parisian speech, conversational, yet fitting his personages
like a garb.

> Et fort dévotement il mangea deux perdrix
> Avec une moitié de gigot en hachis

is the verbal nutshell in which Dorine encases Tartuffe. *Tartuffe*,
notably, is an artistic masterpiece. The first two acts, with
their description of a French bourgeois household, the exposition
they contain of the hypocrite's character as revealed by its effect
on others, the coup de théâtre produced by Tartuffe's opening
words in Act III:

> Laurent, serrez ma haire avec ma discipline
> Et priez que toujours le Ciel vous illumine

— aroused the admiration not only of Goethe but also of dramatic critics the world over. Or take *Le Misanthrope* — nowhere
is there a more harmonious blending of social wit and psychological observation. The scene is a salon of the age of Louis
XIV: Célimène, who presides over it, will not give up her rôle in
order to marry Alceste; the latter, whose sensitiveness embroils
him with others, will marry her on this-condition only. The
situation is an impasse — yet it is Molière who makes us realize
the fact, once for all. *Amphitryon*, one of the most charmingly
written of the plays, is a poetic treatment of a distinctly shady
affair. The comedy of Plautus adhered to the tenets of a myth;
these Molière had to discard. Never did a dramatist set himself a more delicate task. Yet how excellent is the treatment
and how modern in its psychology! If Jupiter would win
Alcmene he of course could; but Molière stresses the fact that
he wins her only as Amphitryon and never as Jupiter — is this
a lover's triumph?

To conclude — we may admit that being a playwright and
an actor Molière worked against odds, hastily. Many a scene
in his works is pure farce, thrown in as a filler, in order to
produce a laugh or relieve a tenuous situation. His dénouements,
in particular, are weak, though Molière's emphasis on character
necessarily made a happy ending difficult. In any case, he was
not a strenuous Aristotelian. But French comedy — with the
notable exception of Corneille's *Menteur* — was in low estate in

his day. /It was Molière who raised it to the highest plane, as a criticism of life. /To compare his contemporaries, Quinault, Baron, Montfleury, shows how true this is. What a gallery of portraits he has left us! How vivid is his presentation, how brilliant his wit! Above all, how well he knew the human race!

Contrasted with Molière, La Fontaine is not at first impressive. A writer of fables and short-stories (the latter of a dubious char-**La Fontaine** acter), his preëminence in these lighter genres is due to lightness and delicacy of touch, to an instinct for the *nuance*, to a desire for finish and perfection — all of which qualities endear him to the French but render him less accessible than Molière to foreigners.

By nature a vagabond and a dreamer, Jean de La Fontaine was born at Château-Thierry in 1621. The profligacy of this son of Champagne showed itself early. Lacking in self-control, he was sent to the religious seminary of the Oratoire; then like Molière he studied law. Returning to his native heath, he planned to succeed his father as *maître des eaux et forêts* and allowed himself to be married at twenty-six, to Marie Héricart, a romantic child of fifteen; with the inevitable result of a disagreement, which sent La Fontaine back to Paris to try his fortune in literature.

In his reading, La Fontaine had adored the *Astrée* and delved into the mimic world of Ovid, " in which every plant and flower has a story, and nearly always a love story." His own writing began with an adaptation of the *Eunuchus* of Terence (1654) — notable, if at all, because it is his longest work. Already, however, his epicurean attitude declares itself and his gift of phrase is apparent. In 1657 he became a hanger-on of Fouquet, still the wealthy and powerful minister of Louis XIV; in this capacity he wrote various short poems, the best of which is *Adonis*, showing a remarkable feeling for bucolic nature; and in 1661 he became acquainted with Molière. Parasite that he was, he yet had the courage to stand by Fouquet, after the latter's fall from grace, in the *Elegie aux nymphs de Vaux,* one of the most eloquent of his compositions. Henceforth his protectors were women.

From 1667 to 1672 his patroness was the gay and pleasure-loving Duchesse de Bouillon, niece of Mazarin. In his paraphrase of *Psyché,* belonging to this period, he records his converse with Boileau, Racine and probably Molière, in the gardens of Versailles, and in the rôle of Polyphile celebrates his joy in all creation, natural and artificial:

> Volupté, volupté, qui fut jadis maîtresse
> Du plus bel esprit de la Grèce,
>
> . . . .
> J'aime le jeu, l'amour, les livres, la musique,
> La ville et la campagne, enfin tout . . .
>
> . . . .
> Jusqu' au sombre plaisir d'un cœur mélancholique.

Could a soul born for pleasure speak more plainly? It was probably Boileau who induced him to publish a first volume of *Nouvelles en vers* (1665), containing a translation of Ariosto's *La Gioconda* and a tale from Boccaccio. This was soon followed by a collection of *Contes et Nouvelles,* to which other collections were added in the course of La Fontaine's life. The spontaneity, grace and vivacity of the verse were admired, but the defenders of morality protested rightly against the success of a book which made licentiousness attractive. La Fontaine replied in the name of art; and among the notables on his side was not only his patroness but also Mme de Sévigné.

When the Duchesse de Bouillon became involved in the " affaire des poisons," La Fontaine transferred his allegiance to the Marquise de la Sablière. Her hospitable and cultured spirit consoled him for the loss of other friends; just as it is said that on her retirement from the world she took three things with her: her cat, her dog and La Fontaine. Never was a spiritual relationship described better than in the famous *Discours* (see Bk. III, Ch. V) which La Fontaine addressed to her — hers is a world of

> Propos, agréables commerces,
> Où le hasard fournit cent matières diverses;
> Jusque-là qu'en votre entretien
> La bagatelle a part: le monde n'en croit rien.
> Laissons le monde et sa croyance.

Mme de la Sablière also inspired La Fontaine's inaugural speech before the French Academy. He had been elected in 1683, but Louis XIV withheld his confirmation until that body

had installed Boileau — to whom our poet had been preferred
— and La Fontaine had given some assurance of reform.   The
last years of his life were passed under the roof of Hervart,
maître de requêtes; here he died in 1695.   Three days before
his end he wrote in perfect candor to his friend Maucroix:

> Mourir n'est rien, mais songes-tu que je vais comparaître devant
> Dieu? Tu sais comme j'ai vécu.

One can view such a character only sympathetically.   La Fontaine was what the French call *un bonhomme;* unfit for the
sterner duties of life, he was childlike, outspoken and likeable.
He treated life, as he treated himself, " without a disguise."
The only discipline he admitted was his art, and to it he
paid unremitting homage.

It was Mme de Bouillon who first called her favorite a *fablier.*
By this epithet she recognized the born story-teller.   La

His Fables Fontaine's canvases are not large; his imagination
worked best in a small compass.   In an earlier age
he might have been a *jongleur,* regaling his Gallic listeners by the
fireside of a tavern, during some wintry night.   As it is, he polishes
the *esprit gaulois* for the devotees of a salon.   His *Contes,* as we
have said, are strikingly indecent.   But they were not written for
prudes, and the skill with which the tales are handled is their
most conspicuous element.   On the other hand, they have
neither the range nor the poetry of the *Fables,* in which genre
La Fontaine is the greatest master since Aesop.

The first six books of Fables appeared when La Fontaine
was forty-seven (1668), and succeeding books, to the number of
twelve, followed at intervals until 1680.   As the poet says in
his dedication to the Dauphin:

> Je chante les héros dont Esope est le père.

But to Nevelet's *Mythologica Aesopica* (1610 and 1660), on
which he drew, he added Sanskrit apologues from Bidpai and
Latin fables by Phaedrus and others.   Besides, as we have
seen in previous chapters, the " beast-epic " was no novelty
to the French; although it is improbable that La Fontaine's
memory of his French predecessors went back beyond Marot.
Marot uses the Fable of the Lion and the Rat admirably in

order to make a special plea; La Fontaine draws a more general lesson and, in this particular case, contents himself with a few bold strokes of the brush. Otherwise, the method of the two poets is similar: a remarkable observation of detail, the ability to convey swiftly the humor of the situation, a vivid merging of the human and the animalistic.

But it remained for La Fontaine to extract from the genre its full poetic value. His first step is to establish a *balance* between the subjective and the objective worlds, that of men and that of the animals. La Fontaine is careful to anthropomorphize Nature only to the extent of maintaining his particular fiction.

> Tout parle dans mon ouvrage, et même les poissons,

he remarks, with a twinkle in his eye. Again, in *Le Chêne et le Roseau* the Reed answers the condescending Oak with the assurance of one who is humanly conscious of his position:

> Votre compassion . . .
> Part d'un bon naturel; mais quittez ce souci;

then La Fontaine resumes the objective attitude; a storm sweeps in from the north; the Reed bends before it, but the Oak is uprooted; and this final scene assumes epic proportions:

> si bien qu'il déracine
> Celui de qui la tête au ciel était voisine,
> Et dont les pieds touchaient à l'empire des morts.

In this way, the individual fables are miniature dramas of which one would not change a particle. *La Cigale et la Fourmi* tells the fate of the improvident; they need expect no pity: "Eh bien! dansez maintenant" is the Ant's merciless reply to the Grasshopper who chirred all summer. The Wolf, being stronger than the Lamb (*Le Loup et l'Agneau*), needs no further justification than just this for his rapacity, since "la raison du plus fort est toujours la meilleure." On occasion La Fontaine could strike off as good maxims as La Rochefoucauld, to whom he more than once pays tribute. "The Frogs desiring a King" represent the stupidity of the masses; they ultimately get what they deserve: an oppressor. But La Fontaine is not always in this cynical mood; he can be playful, joyous, reflective and even tender. The Cat teased by the Mice is judiciously taken as a " sage et discrète personne "; the Mice themselves are playfully termed " la gent trotte-menu "; the Wood-Cutter weighed down by life's cares evokes sympathy:

> Quèl plaisir a-t-il eu depuis qu'il est au monde?

Thus the method is to shift the interest from one point of the situation to another; to give us glimpses rather than full-tone pictures; to vary the metre with the mood; to strike off in a phrase or even a word the essence of the matter. All this shows Classical balance and control.

Another feature of the Fables is " style." La Fontaine had at his command immense technical resources. He knew French as few of his contemporaries did; his language is the French of the soil, rich and colorful, like that of the sixteenth century. Much of his vocabulary doubtless came to him from his extensive reading: thus he calls the Cat, Raminogrobis, Grippeminaud or Rodilard; the Stomach is Messer Gaster; the Lion — a certain one, at least — is a " parent de Caligula." Yet concision is La Fontaine's watchword, and the *mot propre* his goal. Why should the Crow eat a " cheese " and the Fox covet it? Did La Fontaine know nothing about natural history? Manifestly, he was no literalist but a poet, and to the poet the symbol is everything and the word only what it suggests according to the context. Thus his verse is a continuous creation, not only in rich and suggestive detail but also in rhythmical variety and beauty. It is *vers libre* in the sense merely that each Fable has its particular verse, each idea or mood its particular line — adapted, in all cases, to the thought to be expressed. But La Fontaine does not violate traditional metres, he invents no new ones, and his very freedom is the product of painstaking art and care. The fact is that he makes verse do what he intends — now it is gay and swift, now solemn and grave, but it is always poetic.

Lastly, the philosophy of the Fables is that of Classicism in general, and of the *libertins* in particular. An epicurean by instinct, La Fontaine became a " realist " through experience. The " morals " of his Fables count for little. Far be it from

La Fontaine, with his bent for pleasure, to dogmatize on life. Much more important are the pictures he etches, the love of truth he reveals. Least of all were his books intended for little children. Again, Taine's idea that the Fables consciously satirize the monarchy of Louis XIV goes too far and would be one-sided, if it were true. Such a Fable as *Les Animaux malades de la peste* is a typical picture of the miscarriage of justice; the blame falls on the Ass because he is an " ass," and the concluding moral:

> Selon que vous serez puissant ou misérable,
> Les jugements de cour vous rendront blanc ou noir,

applies as well to the police-courts as to the tribunal presided over by a king. Thus La Fontaine is an observer. He has few illusions; but he glorifies common sense. Happy are they who have tolerance and measure, who know that a " rat is no elephant," and who have learned that:

> Patience et longueur de temps
> Font plus que force ni que rage.

As for himself, he wrote in the *Discours à Mme de la Sablière*:

> La bagatelle, la science,
> Les chimères, le rien, tout est bon; je soutiens
> Qu'il faut de tout aux entretiens.

He extracted from life, as its essence, the joy and the humor of a spectacle, and these he incorporated in his perfect verse. Few poets, even among the French, have been better craftsmen.

CHAPTER IV

PASCAL AND RACINE

Up to this point Classicism has offered us a finite universe in which " common sense " operates as the measure of all things. What cannot be reconciled with " common sense " is discarded. This is but an application of the Aristotelian Golden Rule, worked out in a rational, social milieu. With Pascal and Racine we enter a field of enlarged vision and perception. The torturing claims of " conscience " now make themselves heard; and humanity is turned aside from its worldliness to be confronted, in the case of Pascal, with the problem of the Infinite; and, in the case of Racine, with the problem of Evil. Such deepening of the spirit is due primarily to Jansenism, which we shall now consider briefly in its bearing on the century.

Cornelius Jansen, bishop of Ypres, had died in 1638. Three years after his death appeared his treatise, entitled *Augustinus,* **Jansenism** which advocated a return to the Christianity of St. Augustine, presented under the following captions: (1) that " free-will " ceased with the fall of Adam; (2) that human nature is thus thoroughly-depraved and can be redeemed through no effort of its own; and (3) that redemption can come only through " grace." The position of Jansen is essentially that of Calvin, with the important difference that the authority of Rome is never questioned and that the mystery of the sacraments is reaffirmed. Thus Jansenism is not opposed to Catholicism but only to those Catholics who had made salvation a path of roses, a *chemin de velours.* Such were, above all, the Jesuits. Following in the footsteps of Molina (1588), they had taken the stand that God renounces his omnipotence in so far as he allows humanity the power and privilege of saving itself. In short, the Jesuits maintained that man has the " free-will " necessary for salvation.

The person who gave the ideas of Jansen the impetus of his

personality was his friend, Jean de Hauranne, Abbé de Saint-Cyran. In 1636 he became *directeur spirituel* of Port-Royal-de-Paris, an institution with which the fortunes of Jansenism are intimately bound up. The older foundation was Port-Royal-des-Champs in the valley of the Chevreuse. Through the efforts of a member of the Arnauld family — called Mère Angélique — early in the century this convent underwent a religious reform, which not only affected the Arnaulds as a group but also attracted other people of station and influence. In 1626 the transfer was made to Paris, the original convent becoming a retreat to which men of distinction, known as *solitaires*, retired in order to lead a life of study and meditation. The intellectual activity of Port-Royal was considerable. It busied itself with the question of education, was receptive to the ideas of Descartes (at least, as regards "method"), and particularly fostered the study of Latin and Greek classics with the view of enriching "human nature" and redeeming it from itself. Thus Jansenism gave its followers a cultural and scientific training which, aside from the moral discipline involved, is its greatest contribution to the age. If Descartes still inveighs against the "medieval" instruction he received at La Flèche, a Jesuit school, Racine can have only words of gratitude for his Jansenist teachers. Among the educators of Port-Royal, three are especially noteworthy — Claude Lancelot, the main author of the well-known *Grammaire générale et raisonnée* (1660); Pierre Nicole, to whom more than to anyone else is due the Port-Royal *Logique ou l'art de penser* (1662); and, most important of all, Antoine Arnauld, the author in 1643 of *La fréquente communion*.

This treatise fanned the controversy between Jesuits and Jansenists into a bright flame. A great lady, the Princesse de Guéméné, had been invited by Mme de Sablé to a ball; she refused on the ground that having "communed" it behooved her, according to Saint-Cyran, to abstain from worldly pleasures. Mme de Sablé consulted the Jesuits, who replied that the Communion is not an extraordinary event in our life but an aid or succor for the sinful; the more freely it is taken, the better. The matter was not settled by Arnauld's treatise; nor were things improved when Innocent X condemned the *Augustinus* of

Jansen, and Arnauld took up its defence. Finally, in 1656, the quarrel reached a climax. Unable to uphold the Jansenist cause alone, and being rebuked also by the Sorbonne, Arnauld looked about him for a champion. So it happened that Pascal came to his rescue with the first *Lettre à un provincial*, on January 23 of that year.

Nature gave Blaise Pascal a frail body and a singularly active and brilliant mind. He was born in Clermont-Ferrand (1623)

Pascal   as the youngest son of a distinguished *famille de robe*. In 1631 the family moved to Paris, where Pascal's father continued to instruct his son in languages and mathematics. For the latter science Blaise showed great aptitude and while still a child wrote a book on Conic Sections. This was followed by experiments in atmospheric weight, conducted with much skill, and a treatise containing *Nouvelles expériences touchant le vide* (published in 1647). But overstudy had the inevitable result of undermining his already weak physique; and becoming acquainted with the works of Jansen, Saint-Cyran and Arnauld, he had what is generally called his " first conversion," in which his entire family shared.

In the case of Blaise, however, there was a brief respite in which he tasted the pleasures of the world. This occurred in 1649, when the rest of the family went on a visit to Auvergne and Blaise remained in Paris. At that time the master of his thoughts was Montaigne, the skeptic — and his actual companions were such worldlings as the Duc de Roannez, the Chevalier de Méré and the *libertin* Miton. From them it is assumed that Pascal derived his sense of literary style, besides various of his philosophical ideas and the attitude which underlies the short essay *Sur les Passions de l'amour,* if the work is really by Pascal's pen. Meanwhile, he appears to have kept alive his interest in science. He invented a counting-machine, worked out a hydraulic press, studied the question of probability in games of chance (a contact with Descartes), and anticipated to a certain extent the higher mathematics of calculus. Then came his final " conversion."

Such events are always open to speculation. But whether we explain it by the accident in which his life was saved as by a miracle or account for it on a Freudian basis, the fact is that on

November 23, 1654, Pascal suffered the change of heart which made him definitely renounce the world and drove him into the arms of Port-Royal. Thus it was that he came to place his great talent at the service of Arnauld in 1656. Besides the *Provinciales,* published at first anonymously and then under the pseudonym of Montalte, Pascal planned an Apology of the Christian Religion, of which *Pensées* are presumably the stray fragments. They were found after his death, among his papers; but for various reasons, among which was the fear that they might be unorthodox, a complete edition of them did not appear until 1844. In addition to their many excellences, the *Pensées* confirm the view as to their author's intense but keenly intellectual nature. His character was tried but not shaken by the experiences through which he had passed. We shall never know, of course, the part that physical illness played in his renunciation of science. But that Pascal considered it as complete is apparent from the written words discovered on his dead body: " renonciation totale et douce " — " joie, joie, joie, pleurs de joie." He was only thirty-nine when he died in 1662.

" Silence," said Pascal, " is the worst of persecutions; the saints never held their peace." The *Lettres· Provinciales* show how " **Les Lettres** knowingly he made this assertion. They are eight- **Provinciales** " een in number. The first three and the last three treat of Arnauld's affair with the Sorbonne; the intervening twelve openly assail the moral philosophy of the Jesuits. Taken as a whole, they show us Pascal the ironist at his best; logic, subtlety and a sense of comedy are here placed at the service of a cause which, in spite of its emotional appeal, Pascal was compelled to defend with purely intellectual arms. In doing so, he created, so to speak, French controversial style. The subject of the Letters may have lost its interest today. But their reasoning is like the play of sunlight on a mountain brook; the effect is scintillating, vibrating and enchanting. Never was a theological question presented with greater charm. Having in the First Letter subtly confounded those who, without examination of the text, assert that the *Augustinus* contains the propositions which the Pope and the Sorbonne considered heretical, Montalte (Pascal) — in his rôle of an amiably inquisitive layman — probes in the Second Letter into the question of grace. The Jesuits affirm that divine grace is *sufficient* but they deny that it is *efficacious.*

> " To come to business, Father," says Montalte to his inter-
> locutor, " this grace given to all men is sufficient?" " Certainly,"
> said he. " And yet it has no effect without efficacious grace?"
> " None whatever," he replied. " Then," returned I, " all have
> enough grace, and all do not have enough — the grace is sufficient
> in name, and insufficient in reality. On my word, Father, that
> is a very subtle doctrine."

This shows the temper of Pascal's method. Obviously he is not fair. The one hope of safety for the Jansenists lay in rousing public indignation against the persecutors. Pascal was too astute to misquote his enemies, in fact, he is scrupulous in giving chapter and line of his victim's text. But he is sensational, and he does keep his reader's eye fixed on the most noto-rious casuist that the Jesuits possessed, the Spaniard Escobar. Many a biographer of Pascal has been disturbed by his hero's flat denial of any close connection with Port-Royal. Again, Pascal is technically correct inasmuch as he was not himself a *solitaire.* Yet most of these objections vanish when we con-sider the nobility of the Jansenist creed, the necessity of defend-ing that creed against an overwhelming group of powerful en-emies, and lastly Pascal's zealous nature. He was not only a thinker but also a stylist and a lyricist. Once started on a subject, he could not refrain from penetrating to its marrow. Several of his Letters cost him weeks of continuous labor; all were rewritten at least six times. When pressed for his Six-teenth Letter owing to the fact that the police were on the heels of his printer, he remarked: " This letter is long because I did not have time to make it shorter."

Thus it was the *Provinciales* (named thus because ostensibly addressed to a reader in the provinces) that gave Pascal liter-ary renown during his lifetime. Here was a work combining the logic of Descartes with the insight and charm of a man of the world. Most men, Pascal thought, could be classified according to whether they had the one or the other quality — the *esprit de géométrie* or the *esprit de finesse.* It was characteristic of his own genius that he had both traits; and therefore the Letters won immediate recognition as a land-

" Les Pensées "

mark in French prose. But while their subject is ephemeral, that of the *Pensées* has never-ending interest.

Here again the approach to the problem — the defence of Christianity — is through the gateway of skepticism. Pascal the Pyrrhonist is little more than a seventeenth-century Montaigne, made perfect as to style. Man is irretrievably caught between the two Infinities — the macrocosm and the microcosm, the infinitely large and the infinitely small.

> Qu'est-ce que l'homme dans la nature? Un néant à l'égard de l'infini, un tout à l'égard du néant, un milieu entre rien et tout.
>
> Que fera-t-il donc, sinon d'apercevoir quelque apparence du milieu des choses, dans un désespoir éternel de connaître ni leur principe ni leur fin?

Furthermore, man is vain, hopelessly vain:

> Le nez de Cléopâtre: s'il eût été plus court, toute la face de la terre aurait été changée. [1]
>
> Notre propre intérêt est encore un merveilleux instrument pour nous crever les yeux agréablement.

If these reflections betray the ideas of others, Pascal reassures us: " Do not say that I have said nothing new: the disposition of the matter is new. In playing tennis both use the same ball, but the one places it better." Certainly the metaphysical attitude, the torture and pathos of speculation — *le frisson métaphysique* — is new, at all events in French; and so is the inference that despite all his weakness man is yet a superior being:

> L'homme n'est qu'un roseau, le plus faible de la nature, mais c'est un roseau pensant.

Moreover, there is intuition, the highest of our qualities:

> Nous connaissons la vérité, non seulement par la raison, mais encore par le cœur.
>
> C'est le cœur qui sent Dieu, et non la raison.

How then is truth to be attained? Only in one way — through union with God. The dissonance of human nature, our moral

---

[1] This is more obviously a reflection on the rôle of Chance in history.

depravity, the inability to see beyond the circuit of our own experience — all this is overcome in Jesus Christ. In Him we are made whole and perfect.

Like most seekers of finality, Pascal can solve the problem of truth only by self-immolation. But he annihilates the ego — *le moi haïssable*, as he called it — in so far merely as it is egocentric, as its foibles and sophisms block the road to truth. He never gave up his confidence in man as a thinker nor in our superiority to the brute world of Nature. The acquisitions of culture he would not surrender — far from it. Saint-Evremond said that Jansenism is the preciosity of religion; an opinion to which we can in the main subscribe.

Thus Pascal's *Pensées* are the expression of a great intelligence. Many of them have the austerity of a Hebrew prophecy; most of them have also a bewitching beauty of thought and expression. They seem most modern when they are most abrupt and simple, as in flashes like:

> Condition de l'homme: inconstance, ennui, inquiétude.

No style could be more direct, no feeling more intense than Pascal's. The agony of his soul often gives to his phrase the force of an interjection. Yet the longer passages in the *Pensées* have a placid depth, a scientific objectivity, a rigor of logical structure, which show that the poet in Pascal was always subordinate to the scientist. It is probable that Pascal saw deeper into the recesses of the human soul than any other Frenchman. It is certain that no Frenchman ever united feeling and intelligence into a greater expression of beauty.

There is in Pascal a quality that reminds us of Milton; but Racine, the greatest dramatist in France after Molière, has **Racine** been difficult for Anglo-Saxons to understand. Bred in the Shakespearean tradition, they find him stilted and artificial, "with an incapacity for the finest original strokes of poetry," and "an almost unlimited capacity for writing from models" (Saintsbury). It is needless to point out that such a view is thoroughly superficial. To be sure, Racine was eminently a court poet; without the background of Versailles and Louis XIV his tragedies are unthinkable; his characters move across the stage in full-bottomed wigs and with peerless external manners; of his own Andromache, Racine remarked:

J'ai cru me conformer . . . *à l'idée que nous avons main-*
tenant de cette princesse.

He was not interested in " local color," nor in that more modern
fetish, " archeological detail." His was the task of interesting
a court to which decorum was a necessity. But let the reader
penetrate the shell of Racine's dramas, and he will behold an
unmasking of characters, a penetration of hidden motives —
in short, a truth to human nature, that is startling in its psychology. Thus, at the outset, it becomes clear why Racine realized
the Classical ideal of *art* and *nature* united. Racine is in practice what Boileau is in theory. To him truth and beauty are one;
and as a consequence his dramas are swift, concentrated in
action, taking life at a " crisis "— as Napoleon said — discarding whatever seems unessential, and thus achieving as complete
a realization of a literary genre as seems possible. Shakespeare's
plays, superior as they are in scope, are today difficult to perform. On the other hand, Racine's conception of tragedy is still
the model of what an acting-play should be.

Jean Racine was a child of the Ile-de-France. He was born
at La Ferté-Milon about the twenty-first of December, 1639.
Racine's Losing both parents in childhood, he was placed
Life at ten in the Jansenist college at Beauvais and at
fifteen in the *maison des Granges* at Port-Royal, where Pierre
Nicole taught him Latin and Lancelot taught him Greek. His
early reading included the romance of *Theagenes and Chariclea*
by Heliodorus, in which occurs the theme of adulterous love,
and he delighted also in the " nature poetry " of the lovelorn
Théophile de Viau and Tristan l'Ermite. If he was introspective by nature, such contacts fostered his introspection.

In 1658 he attended the Collège d'Harcourt in Paris and dwelt
for a while with his cousin Nicolas Vitart at the house of the Duc
de Luynes. Vitart, who was both a Jansenist and an *honnête*
homme, had an interest in literature and was liberal with his
purse. Here Racine met La Fontaine and the Abbé Le Vasseur,
the latter of whom introduced him to two of the popular actresses of the day. Then his relatives became concerned and
sent him to Uzès, in the south of France, to study theology under
an uncle's supervision. The hope was that he would thus obtain a church benefice. From Uzès, Racine wrote letters full

of charm and grace to his friends in Paris. Already his style
is singularly pure and precise, and as appears from other evidence, his reflections on Pindar, Homer, the Bible (especially
the *Book of Job*) are interesting and original. The result,
therefore, of Racine's education was three-fold: it developed
his sensitive, artistic nature; it gave him a knowledge of Greek
classics, including Euripides and Sophocles; and it led him
to identify the Greek sense of fate with the Jansenist doctrine
of original sin.

In the autumn of 1662 Racine reappeared in Paris, having
given up hope of an ecclesiastical preferment and determined
to succeed as a writer. He began with a display of official verse,
Sur la convalescence du Roi and *La Renommée aux Muses*, the
latter of which, admirably expressed, won him the esteem of
Boileau and, finally, the entrée to the court. In 1664 Molière
played *La Thébaïde*, Racine's first tragedy, at the Palais-Royal.
The circle of the poet's friends was now complete; besides La
Fontaine, Boileau, Molière, it included Chapelle and Furetière,
their meetings occurring at such cabarets as the *Mouton blanc*,
where the repasts served were not merely literary.

The *Thébaïde* is not a great play, though it had a momentary
success. For its sources Racine drew on Euripides (*The Phoe-
nician Women*), Seneca and the *Antigone* of Rotrou. But where
these were involved, Racine was simple, and his tendency towards unity of plot is quite apparent. Necessarily, at twenty-
three, he showed the influence of the elder Corneille, which was
again a factor in Racine's second play in 1665. But although
the *Alexandre* is a heroic-comedy and contains such Cornelian
rhetoric as:

> Je suis venu chercher la gloire et le danger,

an evident reference to Louis XIV, it is clear that Racine is
addressing a different public from that of his great predecessor.
In the serious drama of the time heroics had been supplanted
by love. This was due partly to the influence of the novel;
more so, however, to the success of Thomas Corneille's *Timocrate*
(1656), the most popular stage play of the century, and of the
works of Philippe Quinault. Mediocre as *Timocrate* was artistically, it dramatized La Calprenède's *Cléopâtre*, and its languor-

ous hero soothed an audience grown weary of Cornelian grandeur. Similarly, Quinault's *Stratonice* (1660) approached opera in harmonious lyrism and in mere elegance of expression. From such works as these Racine was now to take his cue. Meanwhile he had broken with Molière, in a rather discreditable manner, by taking away from Molière's troupe the *Alexandre* and giving it to the rival company of the Hôtel de Bourgogne.

The triumph of *Andromaque* (1667) is a parallel to that of the *Cid*. Love is the theme, but unlike his contemporaries "Andromaque" Racine treats this subject dramatically and with the utmost simplicity. The plot turns on the maternal love of Andromache for her son: as Andromache causes Pyrrhus, jailor of her son and victim of her charms, to hope or despair, so Pyrrhus approaches or leaves Hermione, who in turn calls or repels Orestes. Orestes kills Pyrrhus, and Hermione, unable to live without him, hurls at his slayer the reproach:

> Ah! fallait-il en croire une amante insensée?

whereupon Orestes goes mad on learning of her death. Racine took his material from the poets of antiquity (Homer, Euripides, Vergil) ; in the balancing of characters there is some similarity with the *Cid;* otherwise the drama is a stroke of genius — swift, powerful and beautifully expressed. " Pas un vers," says Lemaitre, " qui n'exprime, en mots rapides et forts comme des coups d'épée, les illusions, les souffrances, l'égoïsme, la folie et la méchanceté de l'amour."

Contemporary critics, however, were not all on Racine's side. Many of them still preferred the great Corneille and were not so indulgent even as Mme de Sévigné, who yielded " six reluctant tears " when she saw the play. Racine, always irritable, replied with sarcasm and invective. Then he turned aside to produce his one comedy, *Les Plaideurs* (1668). In part an imitation of *The Wasps* of Aristophanes but especially a rollicking satire of the antiquated Paris law-courts, this comedy was coldly received until Louis XIV saw it and laughed, when suddenly all Paris discovered its wit and charm. Racine's next tragedy, *Britannicus* (1669), was a direct challenge to the admirers of Corneille.

As he himself as said (see the *préfaces* to the play), Racine here offers us a historical play, bereft of unnecessary incidents, conforming absolutely to the unities, and concentrated into one powerful action: the unchaining of the brute in the character of Nero. The situation, drawn from the *Annals* of Tacitus, is political, and it is domestic; Versailles might well take heed. Nero, still young enough to fear his mother Agrippina (who has committed every crime for his sake) and his "tutor" Burrhus, is tempted by the innocence of Junia, betrothed to Britannicus. He knows the evil of such a passion and confesses it to himself:

"Britannicus"

> Et cette vertu, si nouvelle à la cour,
> Dont la persévérance irrite mon amour.

During three acts he hesitates. In the fourth, Agrippina makes a last attempt to bend him to her maternal will. Narcissus, Nero's depraved counselor, shatters all opposition: Britannicus is poisoned, Narcissus is slain by Junia, who dies by her own hand, while Agrippina foretells the burning of Rome.

It is quite clear that the success of *Britannicus* fell below Racine's expectations. Louis XIV might be charmed and thus again show his insight and magnanimity; Saint-Evremond reports that the public considered the idea of the play *noire et horrible*. In any case, the poet's next production, *Bérénice* (1670), is so devoid of physical action or violence as to be a tragedy only by implication. It is, indeed, the extreme of what Racine thought a tragedy might be; namely, a dramatic elegy.

"Bérénice"

It is said that Henrietta of England, Duchess of Orleans, suggested the subject of Berenice independently to Corneille and to Racine (see above, Bk. III, Ch. IV). She may even, as Voltaire affirms, have hinted to Racine that Louis XIV would be pleased with a situation which would recall his youthful affection for Marie Mancini. However that may be, this time Racine turned six words of the historian Suetonius — *Titus reginam Berenicen dimisit invitus invitam* — into a five-act drama. As regards form it was Racine's greatest triumph; the Abbé d'Aubignac's rules were amply vindicated. Yet beneath the surface of its external beauty, *Bérénice* contains a tremendous struggle: the renunciation of each other by two royal lovers for reasons of state. Titus gives up Berenice because the inexorable laws of Rome forbid an emperor to marry a foreigner. Thus in the little room of the palace, where the scene is laid, the destinies of empires are decided and the tragedy of royalty — the greatest tragedy, that of the spirit — is laid bare. Can there be any doubt of the realism of this drama in such an age as Racine's?

If *Bérénice* is Roman, *Bajazet* (1672) is Oriental not only in subject but also in its display of violence. This drama has been called the French *Othello;* and it may be that its heroine, Roxane, was as inscrutable to the French seventeenth century as the Moor of Venice was to the age of Shakespeare (Wright). At all events, a drama of the seraglio had its interest after Molière's *Bourgeois gentilhomme* (where the *Grand Turc* was burlesqued), while Racine's treatment of the Vizier Acomat shows that he could depict a thoroughly virile character. Then followed *Mithridate* (1673) and *Iphigénie,* the latter of which was presented at Versailles in 1674.

Mithridate is again characterized by the submergence of the political side of the drama — the purely external part — to the love affair of the hero with Monime, the incorporation of feminine chastity, fidelity and courage. With *Iphigénie* Racine returns to the Greeks. No play of Racine's is more regal. Yet the French Iphigenia is a pale reflex of Euripides' national heroine: she loves Achilles, and death means to her the sacrifice of that love; just as Eriphile, Racine's own creation, is the voice of sensual passion, leaving ruin in her path, destined to be Iphigenia's substitute in death and uttering phrases of haunting beauty:

> Je sentis le reproche expirer dans ma bouche.
>
> . . . .
>
> J'oubliai ma colère et ne sus que pleurer.

This brings us to a culmination in Racine's career. *Phèdre* (1677), his masterpiece, led to his retirement as a writer for the stage at the age of thirty-nine. Could anything **"Phèdre"** be more dramatic? Unless it be the conflict of the tragic motives that form the basis of the play itself. *Phèdre* is a complete recast of the Euripidean *Hippolytos.*

Racine's first and most significant change is the emphasis he
places upon the heroine. The chaste Hippolytos becomes, so
to speak, a sighing marquis of Louis' court, whereas Phaedra,
the most powerful woman's rôle in all French drama—and
destined by Racine for the actress La Champmeslé—is a
female Nero; but with one important difference: she has a
searching, Jansenist conscience. In other words, *Phèdre* is
not only a tragedy of jealousy but also one of remorse; it is
a picture of sinning and suffering humanity driven by fate to
its doom. And yet this Christian Phaedra, the victim of

> Vénus toute entière à sa proie attachée,

remains intrinsically Greek. Never does Racine allow us to
forget her origin. She is the daughter of Minos and Pasiphae
and the granddaughter of the Sun. Driven to bay, she cries out:

> Misérable! et je vis! et je soutiens la vue
> De ce sacré soleil dont je suis descendue!
> J'ai pour aïeul le père et le maître des dieux;
> Le ciel, tout l'univers est plein de mes aïeux.

This harmonizing of civilizations, Greek, Christian and French,
is the pinnacle of Classicism. As a play, *Phèdre* may lack the
fine proportion of *Andromaque*, but as an expression of passion
on a grand scale it is probably unsurpassed in literature.

Whatever may have been the actual cause, the poet's retirement was opportune. His sensitive nature, together with his
vanity as a successful playwright, had made him scores of enemies. The Duchess of Bourbon, learning that he was busy on
Phèdre, had induced Pradon—a second-rater—to oppose Racine
with a play on the same subject. Determined to have her favorite
succeed and Racine fail, she bought up the seats in two theaters
(see Boileau's Seventh Epistle), and during six successive eve-
nings packed the one with applauding spectators and left the
other empty except for a handful of hissers. Such an intrigue
had its undoubted effect. In addition, Racine's own play
might make him consider. Was he not, in the theme of
Phèdre, lending a hand to acts of violence? Mme. de Brinvilliers had recently been executed for poisoning; other crimes
no less sinister were gossiped about; Racine's own name was

unfavorably associated with the sudden death of the actress Mlle Du Parc.

Yet the Jansenists saw in *Phèdre* signs of contrition on Racine's part. At least the play did not mince Phaedra's guilt; she could be considered only as a pagan woman lacking in God's grace. Thus the Jansenists welcomed Racine's return to their fold. On their advice he married a woman who knew nothing of the stage, and devoted himself to bringing up a family. He had long since become a member of the Academy. This relationship led him to maintain an external interest in literature. Moreover, he did not break with the court, and we find him, as historiographer to the King, journeying in the trail of Louis' armies.

Finally, after twelve years of dramatic silence, he composed at the behest of Mme de Maintenon his Biblical tragedy of "Esther" and *Esther* (1688–1689). Intended for the schoolgirls "Athalie" of Saint-Cyr, it was there performed by the daughters of the nobility themselves before the brilliant and admiring guests of Louis. The beauty of *Esther* lies in the melody of its verse and its power as a spectacle. Mme de Maintenon doubtless saw in the portrayal of the Jewish queen a reference to her own fortunes. Then came *Athalie* (1691) — the last of Racine's plays and as regards form (choruses, *récits*, and the like) one of his masterpieces. Here the protagonist is God; the plot relates how the child Joash triumphs over his enemies — the enemies of church and state — including the frenzied and heretical Athaliah. But Mme de Maintenon feared the excitement such a play might cause at Saint-Cyr, and she had the performance given privately, without scenery and without costumes; so that no one except Boileau recognized its greatness during Racine's lifetime. The first presentation of *Athalie* to a Parisian public was in 1716.

The dramatic situation is not so intense in *Athalie* as in Racine's secular tragedies. The action is lyrical, much as in the Old French *mystère*. Yet nowhere in Racine's works is his power as an artist more apparent. His choruses, modeled on the Greek drama, heighten and relieve the action. His verse was never so expressive, so well suited to the solemnity of his theme, so freely and exquisitely managed. Moreover, the setting, laid in the temple at Jerusalem, enters into the verse and gives to the drama an impressive grandeur which it would be hard to match. If *Phèdre* is Racine's greatest tragedy, *Athalie* is his most perfect dramatic poem.

With the " failure " of *Athalie* Racine's poetic career ends. A slight rebuff from the King may have hastened his death. His Jansenism was not eyed with favor, and when he appealed to Louis to relieve France of the burden of war (we remember that Corneille had made a similar request) the King was visibly displeased. Before Mme de Maintenon could dispel the misunderstanding, Racine had died in April, 1699, in his sixtieth year.

As we have observed, Racine's works are important in two respects: as drama and as poetry. As a writer of stage-plays **Racine's Art** Racine aims primarily at one thing; namely, at **and Style** dramatic effect. What is not essential to the dramatic conflict he discards, and what is lacking to it he adds. Thus he is not historical in the Cornelian sense; for he alters history in behalf of simplicity, and he will add a non-historical character in order to strengthen the plot. *Peu d'incidents et peu de matière* is his own statement of his aim. Thus his plays have verisimilitude: they are true to life even when they are not true to fact. It is extraordinary, as in the case of *Bérénice,* how he discerns the drama that lurks in a few words of some ancient poet or historian. The power to visualize this into an acting play of universal application is the greatest element in his genius. Lemaître, who has written the best book on Racine, calls this quality *invention,* and it is safe to say that no poet ever had more of it.

Consequently, striving as he does for concentration, it is not difficult for Racine to observe the unities. Having chosen the " crisis " which he wishes to present, Racine leads up to it in his first two and solves it in his last two acts, thus determining his plot. This settled, the unity of place is of no great importance: either the place is an apartment in a palace (which might just as well be in Versailles as in Greece), or it may be shifted about somewhat, as Racine suggests in the *préface* to *Esther,* for the amusement of the spectators. As for the unity of time, this is coincident with the " crisis " and the events which immediately precede and follow it. In all respects, Racine's plays had the added advantage of obeying the Classical rules as outlined by d'Aubignac and Boileau.

As a poet Racine has two preëminent qualities: a strongly lyrical vein and an imaginative and harmonious style. Racine is a great psychologist. But his idea of character is of something dark and subtle. He turns our gaze on the mysteries of the heart, not like Corneille on the triumphs of the reason and the will. The result is that the larger part in his dramas is played by women. In *Andromaque, Bérénice, Bajazet, Iphigénie* and *Phèdre* it is always a woman who dominates the action. The protagonist of *Britannicus* is Nero, but he is swayed by love and not primarily by the desire of power, like the more masculine Shakespearean heroes. While, therefore, Racine's field is restricted, he treats love in all of its varieties, from passion to devotion, including jealousy, coquetry, tenderness and rapture. It is Racine's knowledge of Greek, in which respect he is unique among *les grands classiques,* that accounts for the creative quality of his style. Paraphrasing Sainte-Beuve, Lemaitre says: " il rase la prose, mais avec des ailes." Racine's similes and metaphors are simple, direct, inevitable; he does not seek the out-of-the-way or the unexpected. Orestes, hounded by fate, sums up his misery in the phrase:

J'ai *mendié* la mort chez des peuples cruels;

Berenice expresses her scorn of flatterers in the words:

Je fuis de leurs respects *l'inutile* longueur.

To suggest the silence of the night by the sea-shore, there is the line:

Mais tout dort, et l'armée, et les vents, et Neptune;

and the omnipotence of God crashes upon the ear in the alliteration of:

Et du haut de son trône interroge les rois.

In spite of a rather small vocabulary, Racine understood the range of French verse to perfection. He can pass from sustained utterance to pure familiarity; he can be ironic and sublime. In short, his style matches his thought and gives to French verse a precise beauty and an undying splendor.

Compared to his contemporaries Racine is like an oasis in a desert. Pradon imitated Racine but is remembered only by his opposition to Racine in the matter of *Phèdre*. Quinault and Thomas Corneille had of course been entirely outdistanced. Thus on Racine's retirement the theater was left without a great leader. Minor dramatists there were: Chancel, Longpierre, La Fosse. Campistron, in particular, singled out Racine's weaker qualities for imitation. The *Comédie française* had been founded in 1680, but its repertory consisted mainly of the plays of Corneille, Rotrou and Racine. Thus the curtain falls on the theater of the century without producing another great name.

CHAPTER V

BOILEAU AND BOSSUET

BOILEAU is the Nestor of French Classicism. His sterling character reveals itself in two respects: first, as a judicial rather than an imaginative critic, and, secondly, as a sympathetic friend of the great writers of the age.

Common sense is again the guiding principle of all his work. It lies at the root of the *Art poétique* (1674), of the doctrine that grounded his criticism in " la haine d'un sot livre " and caused him to make literature consist in " true thoughts and just expressions." Common sense, in its most intellectual aspects, inspired the attacks of his Satires and all his protests against extravagances. It divides his minor works into so many excoriations of the varieties of human folly. It made Boileau, in his eyes of extremists, " reason incarnate." Common sense is the distinctive mark of the man in his private life and his relations with other men.

Nicolas Boileau, known to his contemporaries as Despréaux, was born at Paris in 1636 — the year of the *Cid* — and lived **Boileau's** there, until his death in 1711, the prudent career of **Life** a confirmed bachelor. He was " bourgeois " by descent, breeding and disposition. His two brothers, like himself, had strongly marked leanings toward satire. Nicolas had a rather narrow youth and his views of country life amounted to no more than glimpses: two facts which help to explain the lack of feeling in his poetry. His education must have given him a knowledge of Latin and Greek and an esteem for polite literature; he shows early some taste for theology and considerable distaste for the law, the profession from which so many French writers have reacted into letters.

When Boileau reacted, at the age of twenty-one, he displayed his balance in refusing to alter forthwith his moderate manner

323

of life. It was the death of his father that had left him free for
poetry, and we shortly find him cultivating the muses with an
illustrious body of friends.

Chief among these was the celebrated trio — Racine, Molière,
La Fontaine — whose early work Boileau did so much to form,
and whose fame he greatly helped to establish. If he represents
the " defense " of Classicism, they are its " illustration." But
this early association was marked less by dogma than by enthusiasm. We have previously mentioned (Ch. IV) their meetings at the *Mouton blanc* and similar cabarets. To Racine
especially Boileau's friendship was helpful. He acted as a
damper to the dramatist's temperamental outbursts, and he
recognized the merit of *Phèdre* in the striking appraisal:

la douleur vertueuse
De Phèdre malgré soi perfide, incestueuse.

On the whole, Boileau's tastes ran more to the society of men
than to that of women, though we see him consorting with La
Champmeslé, Racine's actress-friend, and with the beautiful
and brilliant Ninon de Lenclos.

He began publication with *Les Satires* in 1666. Already the
way to success had been paved by their circulation in manuscript and by readings before distinguished auditors. But he
was not an assiduous frequenter of " salons "; as a courtier, when
his fame had spread, he paid the usual compliments to Louis XIV,
without losing his self-respect and independence. Boileau and
Racine were both historiographers to the King, and in this capacity they went campaigning — as we have seen — doubtless
to the amusement of the military men. Neither was at home on
horseback or in the field; yet Louis XIV was satisfied with
Boileau's efforts and insisted on his being made an Academician
(Ch. III). The *Art poétique* had preceded Boileau's election,
but the enlightened authority of Louis was of more immediate
effect on the Academy than was the celebrated poem.

About 1677 Boileau was taken up by a "grand seigneur," De
Lamoignon, who appears in the mock-epic called *Le Lutrin*, and
who gathered at his mansion the more thoughtful society of
that time. In this setting the critic felt at ease, though he was
never a brilliant conversationalist. The latter part of his life

was spent more and more in retirement, clouded by two serious quarrels: the one with the Jesuits in behalf of Arnauld, Pascal's friend; the other with Charles Perrault in behalf of the Ancients (see Part III, Bk. I, Ch. I). As an old man, Boileau lost the use of his voice, and this together with other infirmities soured his disposition. He lived well into the new century, but his work is indissolubly connected with the Age of Louis XIV.

Thus Boileau was a French *bourgeois* to the core. His idea of human nature —

Etudiez la cour et connaissez la ville —

is that of his period in general; it looks neither back of Versailles and Paris nor beyond them. He was a Parisian as Dickens was a Cockney, each the product and the expression of *his* universe. But Boileau was a prudent and sensible citizen. He had plain habits, lived in a simple and straightforward way, and was constant to his friends and principles. His respect for letters prevented him from being a hack or accepting any galling patronage. "Reason" even made him speak the truth to Louis about the latter's verses and tastes. He was not expansive or emotional. But he warms to the attack, and his best work is that in which his common-sense aesthetics are at stake. If literature is a criticism of life, Boileau's life was a criticism of literature.

We may follow Sainte-Beuve in dividing Boileau's work into three periods: that of the early *Satires*, during the sixties, a **Boileau's** vigorous and youthful phase; the next decade, **Works** when the critic assumes the part of a "legislator of Parnassus," writing the *Art poétique*, the mellower *Satires* and most of the *Lutrin*; and, finally, the period of his weakest efforts in satire and epistle, when his inspiration is disturbed by the defense of Jansenism and the quarrel with Perrault.

Of the two elements, satire and criticism, it is hard to say which predominates in Boileau's work. Frequently they are coördinated. But certainly much of his writing, besides that labelled "satire," is satiric in idea and execution. Several of the *Epîtres* — modeled on those of Horace — contain impatient indictments of human folly. The best of these are the Seventh Epistle (to Racine) and the Ninth, which mirrors Boileau's view of his own calling. The mock-heroic called *Le Lutrin*, in the style of Tassoni's *Secchia rapita* and Pope's *Rape of the Lock*, narrates a theological dispute about a reading desk in the Sainte-Chapelle. Here the satire rallies the clergy for their sloth and ease, while mimicking in burlesque the artifices of various ancient and modern epics. The poem is notable for its grace and wit, qualities which find an even more amusing expression in Boileau's *Les Héros de roman*. This is a prose dialogue, in the manner of Lucian, where the personages in the romances of La Calprenède and Mlle de Scudéry file before the judges of Hades, to give themselves away by their stilted and ridiculous conversation. Ridicule, then, is the acid test which Boileau constantly applies. This quality appears to the best advantage in the *Satires* proper. Here Boileau, imitating Horace and Juvenal, transmutes into Parisian terms the perennial violations of *le bon sens*. To quote his own words:

> Des sottises du temps je compose mon fiel.

The *Satires* are of two classes, general and literary. Boileau expresses the folly of gluttony in the Third Satire; of certain types (the pedant, the miser, the gallant, and so on) in the Fourth; of false nobility in the Fifth; of unreasonable desires and ambitions in the Eighth; of women in the Tenth. In the Seventh and the famous Ninth he states his views concerning the social value of satire; and the Second, addressed to Molière, discusses the discord between " la rime et la raison " which it was Boileau's endeavor to solve.

But the *Satires* also constitute a polemic. Many of their shafts are aimed at the extreme fashions then in repute, which Boileau did much to mitigate if not banish. Thus he excoriates the epic-writing school of Chapelain; the feminizing romancers and the *précieuses;* the writers of " conceits " and *pointes*, and, finally, those who burlesque great works of art, like Scarron and his *Virgile travesti*. All these faults and foibles of the time are scored by Boileau in dozens of passages. Thereupon, having accomplished the work of destruction, the theorist in Boileau turns to erect the working code of Classicism.

The manner in which Boileau crystallizes the Classical dogma (see Ch. I) will best appear from an analysis of the *Art poétique*.

The first canto deals with the poet's vocation and the qualities of literary composition. The vocation must be founded in *nature*, since the poet is born rather than made, and nature also disposes him to the kind of poetry that he should undertake. This conventional tribute to Pegasus having been paid, *reason* steps in and directs the remainder of the canto:

The "Art poétique"

> Aimez donc la raison: que toujours vos écrits
> Empruntent d'elle seule et leur lustre et leur prix.

Let there be no "mad inspiration," because to the Classicist imagination is inferior to reason. The latter principle is now made to control, in detail, such necessary poetic qualities as inevitability in expression, variety, noble rather than burlesque language, clearness and purity, polish and order, the rules of versification and harmony.

Thus good sense becomes the arbiter of art, and it is primarily with the *art* of versification that Boileau is concerned. He interposes a biased sketch of French poetry that emphasizes this attitude. There was nothing of significance before Malherbe:

> Enfin Malherbe vint, et, le premier en France,
> Fit sentir dans les vers une juste cadence,
> D'un mot mis en sa place enseigna le pouvoir,
> *Et réduisit la muse aux règles du devoir.*

The last line states the chief defect, not only of Malherbe, but of Boileau himself and of the whole trend of the Classical theory. Malherbe is praised, not as the first poet, but as the first harmonious versifier.

The second canto takes up the minor Classic genres: the idyll or eclogue, the elegy, the ode, the sonnet and the epigram. These are considered, principally on the authority of *the ancients*, as the most acceptable forms, and each is treated with reference to its special style and aptitudes. The Old French forms are condemned in the name of "good sense and art," while satire, both ancient and modern, is recommended as a weapon of *truth*. The third canto, in its treatment of tragedy, epic and comedy, instances Boileau's general indebtedness to the theories springing from Horace and Aristotle. The tragic writer must strive for a "gentle terror" and a "charming pity," by force of passion rather than of reasoning. But the external rules of *reason* must nevertheless be observed; especially —

> Qu'en un lieu, qu'en un jour, un seul fait accompli
> Tienne jusqu'à la fin le théâtre rempli.

Boileau admits that

> Le vrai peut quelquefois n'être pas vraisemblable;

in which case, however, the probable rather than the actual truth must be told. As we have seen, the Renaissance had placed a momentous stress on verisimilitude, of which the theater is the stronghold — and this idea Boileau repeats. He then gives due importance to other elements of tragedy, such as the recital of events, the climactic rise and the sudden catastrophe — in short, "crisis action." Love, he says, is now the main interest, but it must be truly depicted and should seem an amiable weakness; above all — and here we hear the voice of *decorum* — each age and each person must keep the "proper character" in action and in language; for

> La scène demande une exacte *raison*.

The section on the epic is interesting mainly as showing that the hope for a great modern French epic poem was not yet dead. Boileau holds by the *Iliad* and the *Aeneid* as standards. In ruling out the use of Christian mythology he condemns Tasso and, quite unawares, Milton, as well as his more usual butts, the small fry of epic-writers of the time.

Comedy, for the Classical generalizer, again tends to portraits and types. In order to paint them,

> Que la *nature* donc soit votre étude unique.

She is the great portrait-painter. Study of nature — in town and court — is what makes the excellence of Molière, whenever he does not dip, unworthily, into farce. There should be no mixture of tragedy and comedy: the Classicist abhors any *mélange des genres*. Let reason guide the comic action and refrain from jests at the expense of *le bon sens*.

The fourth canto consists mainly of thrusts at Claude Perrault and of general advice to poets as representative men.

The *Art poétique* is, in its very limitations, a most important document. It sums up, for the seventeenth century, the literary ideals which it helps to promulgate throughout the eighteenth. Its narrowness of range was broad for that time, and what it lacks in range it has in thoroughness and polish. If we add a few points from the Ninth Epistle and mention one general underlying inspiration, we have practically the whole of Boileau's doctrine.

The Epistle in question lays down categorically that

> Rien n'est beau que le vrai . . .

This is intended to rule out disordered fancy, but it operates also as an argument against sovereign imagination. It tends to make logical *truth* the sole foundation of art. The Epistle continues:

> Mais la nature est vraie . . .

The material for imitation then is *nature,* and properly human nature, according to types. But nature should be followed in a broad way, not specialized or localized, adapted rather for universal appeal. The guide in this matter of just imitation is again *reason.*

Such are the outlines of Boileau's "civilized" program. In it he again and again pays homage to the *ancients,* not because they are the ancients but rather as the models in the imitation of universal nature. Thus he unfurls the Classical banner, under which, championing the geniuses of his age, he fought against the lesser writers — who were mostly hostile to his applications of truth, nature and reason. As a critic, he is the successor of Malherbe, whose precepts he elevates and broadens. He is the first great author to insist upon the importance of "taste" (*le goût*), which in the eighteenth century becomes a point of frequent discussion. Underlying his thought is the conviction that the great work of art is always simple, truthful and intelligible. Thus he has an understanding of the eternal human values, lifted above time and place. Accordingly, his main critical judgments have been strikingly in agreement with those of posterity.

At the same time, Boileau is not a creative critic. In his

Satires aione does he sound an individual note — that of the concrete and picturesque detail:

J'appelle un chat un chat et Rolet un fripon.

He is not a profound psychological observer, a *moraliste*, like Pascal or La Rochefoucauld; he lacked the temperament for such profundity. Save in the *Art poétique*, he shuns the abstract style, which he frequently satirizes. He cannot depict the inner world of sentiment, or of subjective ideas and impressions.

At his best, then, he is the lawgiver of Classicism. He knew and formulated its technique. The balanced Alexandrines of the *Art poétique*, its fixed divisions, its terse epigrammatic lines, recalling those of Pope — who was Boileau's greatest imitator — its clear and smooth finish, are evidence of his sense of Classical harmony. But again like Malherbe, he achieved these results only through effort. His early *Satires*, in particular, show want of ease and suggest the difficulties with rime of which he complains in addressing Molière. But he overcame this handicap, and his middle period proves that he was as thoroughly Classical in his style as in his doctrine. Thus the Parisian bourgeois vindicated his position as the guardian of Classical culture.

If Boileau was the defender of authority in literature, Bossuet was its evangelist in religion. No one has ever preached a re-
Bossuet   actionary program more eloquently than he, nor, be it said in his honor, with greater sincerity. A devout Catholic, he was not what we should call an original thinker; he defined a heretic as " *celui qui a une opinion.*" For this reason alone it is difficult to agree with Nisard and Brunetière, who regard Bossuet as entirely representative of Louis XIV's time. But he had a seductive personality, a great intelligence — placed in the service of a high moral idea — and he treated vital questions with the simple seriousness of a really great soul.

Jacques-Bénigne Bossuet, born at Dijon (Burgundy) in 1627, came of a family of sturdy magistrates. Educated by the Jesuits in the two antiquities, Hebrew and Graeco-Roman, he was sent to Paris to complete his studies at the Collège de Navarre, his subjects being philosophy and theology. At twenty-four he became a Doctor of the Sorbonne and was soon made archdeacon of Metz, having previously declined the social allurements which

Paris offered to his talents. He remained at Metz until 1659, combatting Protestants and Jews and fortifying himself generally in his vocation. But the influence of Saint Vincent de Paul, whose natural Christian charity Bossuet admired, brought him back to the capital, where during ten years his fame as an orator grew until it reached the purlieus of the court. A funeral oration, now lost, on Anne of Austria is of this period in his career.

In 1669 he was appointed bishop of Condom, a small town of southern France. But his nomination as tutor to the Dauphin made him resign his bishopric and devote himself, with characteristic zeal, to forming the mind of a pupil which, however dull and unappreciative, might some day rule the world. To this endeavor we owe several of Bossuet's greatest works, such as: the *Traité de la connaissance de Dieu*, the *Politique tirée de l'Ecriture sainte* and the famous *Discours sur l'histoire universelle* (begun in 1678). While these works failed of their immediate purpose — the Dauphin having no brain to instruct — they are the basis of Bossuet's philosophy and they serve as an index to both the epoch and the man. Absolute monarchy could have no other historian than a theologian: one who would see in the established order a foreordainment of God. At the same time, Bossuet is no flatterer — he lauded the monarchy, but he lauded it as an obligation and a trust, and he spared no pains to make clear the terrific duties that weigh down a king. Bossuet's appeal is neither overbearing nor servile; it is psychologically true and to the point; it shows his good sense and his *justesse d'esprit*. Finally, it reveals his courage.

He was then elected to the Academy and, in 1681, to the bishopric of Meaux. Meantime he had preached funeral sermons on the deaths of Henrietta of France and Henrietta of England — to be followed later by orations on Marie-Thérèse, the Grand Condé and Mlle de la Vallière. When the clergy of France met in 1682 it was Bossuet who opened the assembly with an exhortation on the unity of the church, and who by force of argument won for the Gallican Church the liberty to manage its own affairs and to pronounce itself on the question of infallibility.

His last years were crowded by disputes with the Protestants — the *Histoire des variations des églises protestantes* appearing

in 1688 — by a controversy with Fénelon over the heresy of
Quietism, by a famous pronouncement against the subjects
treáted on the stage, and by a crushing indictment of the views
of Richard Simon, a higher critic of the Bible. He died in 1704
after a life of continuous toil and combat.

The major qualities of Bossuet are his probity and his sense
of reality. He had little vanity and almost no personal ambition.
He did not seek literary glory, and if he has splendor and perfection of form he used them as instruments to win to his cause
a world that no other method could reach. But if poets are born,
so are orators; and the youthful Bossuet addressing the Hôtel
de Rambouillet close to midnight elicited from Voiture the
remark: " I have never heard anyone preach so early or so late."
He had a mind that was serene and self-possessed, which in the
course of time he stored with information on philosophy, physiology, history, archeology and even drama; but again his mind
was intense rather than far-seeing, fixed on one point — the grandeur and glory of God as reflected by the grandeur and glory
of Louis XIV.

Bossuet's works fall into three groups: the Sermons, especially
the funeral orations; the works intended for the instruction
Bossuet's of the Dauphin; and the controversial writings. It
Works must not be forgotten that preaching was in low
estate when Bossuet began. The pulpit style of the Jesuits was
traditionally florid and stilted. Saint François de Sales had
socialized the " sermon " and given it charm. But his imitators
exaggerated these qualities; their effects were sugary and soft,
and preaching lost its dignity. This trait Bossuet restored. He
did not write out his sermons, he was too much of an orator to
forego the advantages of improvision — thus the text of many
of his sermons only approximates his actual words, and it is
known that his editor, Déforis, took liberties with that text.
Nevertheless, Bossuet preached from a sketch that was carefully
and logically organized, with all the devices of Classical rhetoric.
In the *Sermon sur la mort*, delivered at the Louvre in 1662,
the exordium states that man

> est infiniment méprisable en tant qu'il passe, et infiniment esti-
> mable en tant qu'il aboutit à l'éternité,

This is followed by the *premier point*, stating that earthly life is brief, and by the *second point*, which stresses our control over Nature, our sense of duty, our idea of God — so many proofs of immortality. Death, the great leveler, is the central figure of Bossuet's thought. It alone gives significance to life. In praising the illustrious dead he strives to instruct the living, pointing out to them obvious truths, giving them portraits — for their emulation or avoidance, such as that of Cromwell in the *Oraison de Henriette de France* — and rising at times to great eloquence, as in the famous passage on the death of Henrietta of England:

> O nuit désastreuse! ô nuit effroyable, où retentit tout à coup comme un éclat de tonnerre cette étonnante nouvelle: Madame se meurt! Madame est morte!

Contrast the simple majesty of this with the more worldly panegyrics of the epoch, and the genius of Bossuet is at once apparent.

As for the instructional works, the *Discours sur l'histoire universelle* remains the outstanding one. Its importance as a serious philosophy of history may be questioned. Yet there is no doubt that it served as such for Classicism. Bossuet aims at nothing less than a "theology of human progress," from Adam to Charlemagne. The *Discours* is divided into three parts: (1) On Epochs, which gives a chronological outline; (2) On Religions, which establishes the idea of Providence ruling the world through his chosen peoples; and (3) On Empires, which confirms the succession of Rome. Thus historical unity is found in religion: Judea, Christianity and Rome. Having determined this fact — *de parti pris* — Bossuet is free to deal with secondary causes, and here he is at his best. He would make his royal pupil see the true character of kings and peoples; why they succeed, why they fail. Events mean little to him; it is the man behind the event whom he would make the Dauphin understand. Lacking modern erudition, Bossuet is yet a master of his material; he seeks to be impartial and is led — as far as his thesis permits — by psychological and rational considerations. Above all, he has the ability to survey a movement, and he points the way to, even if he does not attain, the position of

Montesquieu. On the other hand, the effect of his theory is
static. He reënforces the old absolutes of *une loi, un roi,
une foi;* and he does so with the optimism of his vigorous
personality.

Bossuet's works of controversy have the same unified purpose
as the *Discours.* The *Histoire des variations des églises protestantes,* in fifteen volumes, is a clever piece of argumentation.
Moreover, it is thoroughgoing. On the side of the Protestants
he finds discord, on the side of the Catholics, unity; thus Bossuet
would confound those who had deserted Rome. Why they
deserted, Bossuet does not explain. But he has no doubt as to
their eventual repentance; he feels sure that the enlightened
policy of Rome will reintegrate the Protestants in the Universal
Church. For the moment Bossuet wished to strike them in their
most vulnerable spot; and so he sets them against one another,
Lutherans, Calvinists, Anglicans and the rest, in ruinous
opposition.

His controversy with Fénelon we must leave for a later chapter
(Pt. III, Bk. I, Ch. II). Suffice it to remark here that the *Réla-
tion sur le quiétisme* is inspired by the general attitude found
in Bossuet's other works. Quietism, encouraged by Mme Guyon,
was a form of mysticism which seemed to leave religion to the
impulse of personal emotion, and any such type of individualism
was abhorrent to the rationally minded bishop.

As for Bossuet's style, it places him in the front rank of
seventeenth-century prose writers. Its great quality is cadence.
Bossuet's His periods roll forth like great waves of emotion.
Style He not only cites the Scripture, he incorporates
it into himself, so that its imagery, its sententiousness, its gravity
appear to spring from the speaker's own mind. But in his
periodic style he commands many variations. " Tout lui sert,"
says Joubert, " le langage des rois, des politiques et des guerriers;
celui du peuple et du savant, du village et de l'école, du sanctu-
aire et du barreau." Picturesque and poetic as his images are,
and taken for the most part from Latin writers and the Church
Fathers, he can also wield the plainer *style coupé:* rapid, logical
and always to the point. He says in a *discours:*

> On me blâme, on me méprise, on m'oublie: quel est le plus rude
> à la nature, ou plutôt à l'amour-propre? Je ne sais.

Could language be more direct and forcible? It was this mastery over French, coupled with Bossuet's soaring vision of mankind and of history, which more than any other quality gave him the epithet of the " Eagle of Meaux."

A contemporary of Bossuet's in the pulpit was Bourdaloue (1632–1704), whose Sermons, commonplace as they often were, **His Con-** pleased the court. In the words of his biographer **temporaries** Vinet: " Il prêcha, il confessa, il consola." Although a Jesuit, Bourdaloue had the moral intensity of a Jansenist; and the pictures he gives of corruption in high places elicited the admiration of Boileau. His style has none of the lyrical splendor of Bossuet; it is clear and telling, but it tends toward logical precision and abstraction. Bourdaloue is the Descartes of oratory, and in the controversy about *Tartuffe* he ably discerned the difficulty of distinguishing religious observance from hypocrisy.

But a spirit of decadence pervaded the close of Louis XIV's reign. Massillon (1663-1742), another churchman, comments on the " enervating atmosphere " as one enters Versailles. A charitable Christian, Massillon strove against it valiantly and then succumbed. His Sermons have grace and elegance of form and a certain philosophic breadth which made them appeal, later on, to Voltaire. But they lack the force of a strong personality and readily go off into hyperbole and the worst type of Ciceronian imitation.

Lastly, Fléchier (1632–1710), a writer of charming Latin verse and a frequenter of *ruelles*, is more of a society wit than a cleric. He preached conventionally on the sins of the world — the little sins, those of pride, unpaid debts, money-marriages, and so on. At the same time, his words seem to have been spoken with an exquisite ironic smile, and his funeral Orations, in particular, swayed his hearers by the musical rhythm of their rhetoric.

Thus the Age of the *Grand Monarque* closes on a note of plaintive eloquence. It was eloquent as to the glory and grandeur of its achievements — in politics, literature and religion. It was plaintive — and ironic — at the thought that no form of human culture, however well planned, can last, and that the forces which were undermining the body politic were too powerful to be stopped. Moreover, a new movement in ideas was claiming recognition, and this brings us to the Quarrel of the Ancients and Moderns, with which Classicism definitely ends.

As a final word on this great period, let us note that the humanism of the Renaissance finds an enduring expression in Bossuet's formulation of the " objective " judgment:

> La vraie perfection de l'entendement est de bien juger. Juger, c'est prononcer au-dedans de soi sur le vrai et sur le faux; et bien juger, c'est y prononcer avec raison et connaissance.

PART III
MODERN TIMES

BOOK I

THE TRANSITION FROM CLASSICISM

CHAPTER I

THE QUARREL OF ANCIENTS AND MODERNS: RESULTS

THE drive against absolute Classicism dates its success from the " Quarrel " between Boileau and Charles Perrault. This dispute, as to whether the ancients or the mod-

Importance erns are the best writers, is, in its larger aspects, neither academic nor futile. The quarrel as to mere pre-eminence may have been vain, but its importance in literary history is due less to the ostensible matter of debate than to the new criticism which it awakened and to certain significant forces which it released. These center, it will appear, around the idea of Progress.

It has been shown that the ancients themselves were not without glimmerings of this idea. It is implicit in the Renaissance, if not an " organic phenomenon " of French Classicism.

Antecedents For what does the Pléiade, especially Du Bellay, maintain, if not that the ancients may be equalled in many ways? Pride of progress is visible in Rabelais and in Etienne Dolet; and the early liberalism of Corneille tends in the same direction. Yet none of these believe that the moderns are superior *en bloc* and none wish to overthrow the authority of antiquity. That is rather the intention of Descartes, who is the direct ancestor of modernism. Descartes' impatience with scholasticism extended to ancient literature and in making reason the guide in all worldly matters, he threw out many suggestions for later philosophers. For instance, it is Descartes who, building apparently on St. Augustine's notion that humanity may be viewed as developing like a single man, upholds that *we* are truly the ancients, since we represent the maturity of the world. This thought is more or less repeated by Pascal, Bacon and Fontenelle, and it underlies certain phases of the Quarrel. Descartes' general principle of rationalism (see Pt. II, Bk. III, Ch. V) results, through the widening skepticism of the Moderns and of the *libertins*, in eighteenth-century philosophy.

But in seventeenth-century literature, ancient authority was not so easily overcome. A return to scholasticism, the establishment of the Academy, the pedantry of the University, and chiefly the triumphant example of the great Classicists submerged for a time the worldly and revolutionary currents. There were irregular independents; there was always a majority in favor of the light salon taste; the " honnête homme " usually considered ancient culture pedantic and inelegant. But the great triumvirate, Boileau, Racine, Molière, succeeded for a generation in subduing the *précieux*, in linking hands with ancient tradition, in combining that tradition harmoniously with a wise modernity, reason and a fine taste, and especially in securing royal and influential favor. It was part of their nemesis that in succeeding as Ancients,[1] they also succeeded as moderns [1] and left their own productions as the best arguments for the clever propaganda of Perrault.

Reactions

The actual story of the Quarrel still has its human interest. It is divided into two epochs, that of the Boileau-Perrault controversy (1687–1700), and that in which Lamotte maintains against Madame Dacier the small worth of poetry in general and of Homer in particular (1714–16). The former epoch is decidedly the more important and alone need concern us.

The first resounding note was struck, about 1670, by Desmarets de Saint-Sorlin, in his defense of the Christian *merveilleux* in the epic. Naturally, as poet and as Christian, he is disposed, to quote Brunetière, to " mingle his pleasures and beliefs," and doubly to slur the ancients: their mythology on the one hand, and their literature on the other, are represented, in spite of Boileau, as inferior to the modern

Saint-Sorlin on the Epic

[1] These words, when written with a capital, will indicate the partisans of the ancients and moderns respectively. The Ancients included: Boileau, Racine, La Fontaine, the learned bishop Huet, La Bruyère, Ménage, Rapin (the model for the President in the *Parallèles*) — and Mme Dacier. More cautious and moderate Ancients were Fénelon and Bouhours. The Moderns included: Saint-Sorlin, P. Perrault, Ch. Perrault, Fontenelle, Th. Corneille, Pradon, Bussy-Rabutin — and Lamotte and the Abbé de Pons. Moderate Moderns were Segrais and Saint-Evremond, "le plus classique des modernes."

possibilities. Before Chateaubriand, Saint-Sorlin pleads for the "genius of Christianity" and especially for the religious epic. He views poetry as consisting in the truth of its ideas — hence Christian subjects are preferable — added to the processes of mere mechanical composition; he praises the moderns indiscriminately, and finally he appeals to Charles Perrault to carry on the war.

The four Perrault brothers demand some personal attention. They were all clever, versatile, advanced and rather original. Claude, the doctor-architect, who erected the façade **Claude,** to the Louvre, is credited by Sainte-Beuve with a "genius for comparative anatomy and . . . noble artistic conceptions." But he was satirized by Boileau in the fourth canto of the *Art poétique* and was later stigmatized as a "very great enemy of health and good sense." Pierre Perrault translated the *Secchia rapita* of Tassoni (who was one of the first Italian **Pierre and** Moderns), attacked Boileau and the Ancients in **Charles** a preface thereto (1678), and had previously been **Perrault** convicted of ignorance (*in re* Euripides) by Racine, in the smiling and stinging preface to *Iphigénie*. Charles, the Baron Haussmann of his day, was in-general control of the royal architectural projects. He is better known to fame as the popularizer of the Mother Goose rimes — *Contes de ma mère l'oye* (1697). And he was well suited by his restless enterprising nature to stand out as the head and front of the Quarrel. He was fertile, ingenious, forward-looking; he respected the ancients little and knew them even less; but he could argue with a dangerous amiability and, as regards science and religion, with a sincere faith. As a self-taught man of action, he had a wide if superficial curiosity, considerable energy and a talent for organization.

He began hostilities, on January 27, 1687, at a meeting of the Academy held to celebrate the convalescence of Louis XIV. Perrault read aloud his poem entitled *Le Siècle de Louis le Grand*. This poem deftly flatters the King, his "century," and certain **Ch. Perrault's** of its luminaries, to the detriment of the ancients. **"Siècle."** These are men like ourselves, the author declares, and deserve no greater reverence —

I view the ancients with unbending knee.

The age of Louis may be favorably compared with the age of Augustus, which it surpasses in scientific knowledge and in various inventions. As to literature, ancient eloquence may yet be equalled, Aristotle should no longer dominate, and the *Iliad*, tiresome and brutal poem, would be much better done today. This part of the attack disgusted Huet, who was wont to groan, " Les dieux s'en vont," and it particularly offended Boileau, who, seated by the learned bishop, could scarcely control himself and soon left the *séance*, declaring that such a reading was a disgrace to thé Academy.

Perrault gave an incomplete and biased list of moderns, excluding on that occasion Boileau and Racine, mentioning Malherbe, Voiture, Molière, on a par with a dozen names forgotten today. But he clearly sets forth two main ideas, which are henceforth part of the world's patrimony. First, there is a stability and perpetuity in the forces of nature, on which man may safely build. The roses, the stars and the birds are as fine as they ever were. Therefore, as regards Nature,

Its Argument

> The ceaseless might of that abiding hand,
> Produces Genius for each age and land.

The companion thought is that with this support in nature — and with the further support of a great king — the materials of knowledge are always piling up and are now honored by " many inventions." It speaks significantly for the increasing attention paid to science that Perrault is among the first to particularize, in periphrastic verse, the telescope, the microscope, and the study of physiology. The defect of his reasoning, and that of his coterie, is that he considers art also mainly a matter of increasing knowledge, the evolution of rules and precepts. But the " Ancients " themselves, from the Italian Renaissance through Boileau, had done much to encourage that attitude.

Some very bad verses together with very advanced ideas are contained in this poem. Racine answered it by a bitter-sweet compliment which sought to destroy its importance. La Fontaine wrote a temperate Epistle to Huet, in which he insists upon the need of a choice among moderns as well as ancients, and stoutly upholds the latter as the only safe

Counter-attacks

guides for worthy imitation and lasting excellence. But already La Fontaine hints that the Modern cause is the more popular. Boileau launches various epigrams, as much against the Academy as against Perrault. To think that this disgraceful thing should occur in Paris instead of among the Hurons and the Topinamboux!

Supporters now rally to the side of Perrault. Chief among these is the earlier Fontenelle, the wit and the ladies' man, **Fontenelle's "Digression"** whose *Digression sur les anciens et les modernes* follows and develops Perrault in several directions. For instance, if trees formerly grew larger than today, then Homer and others cannot be equalled. But if not, there is hope. Our fibers and vital spirits have not changed, and the laws of physics protest against the assertion that after producing the ancients, Nature broke her mould. Fontenelle's interest in science is already dawning. He continues to the effect that much of the advantage attributed to the ancients lies in their mere priority; to which it might be answered that several of the arguments of the Moderns rest on their mere posteriority. Antiquity, says Fontenelle, carried eloquence and poetry to a " point of perfection " (a favorite phrase in both camps), because the slight number of truths demanded by these subjects could soon be amassed and the necessary vivacity of imagination needs no amassing. But the sciences, composed of an infinite number of " views," have no end, and the latest scientists are always the best. Fontenelle also perceives that the moderns have the superiority in (Cartesian) reasoning. Humanity — again considered as one man — had its unsurpassed youth of poetry and eloquence; it has now its virility of science and reasoning; but it will have no decrepit old age; it will be ever capable of repeating the achievements of its youth and its prime. Fontenelle, somewhat inconsistently, declares that even poetry may be indefinitely perfected. Anticipating Lamotte and the other radicals, Fontenelle's appreciations of poetry as a sort of versified gallantry are significant. So is his **His Strength and Weakness** development of Perrault's suggestion concerning the perpetuity of natural forces and his emphasis on the sciences. But he does not thoroughly distinguish these from the arts, ultimately viewing both as capable of accumulations. He thinks the ancients should be surpassed by virtue of the great modern dramatists, the novel and the improved technique of poetry. He concludes that " nothing so hampers the progress of things, nothing so limits intelligence as an excessive admiration for the ancients."

Fontenelle's reception into the Academy (1691) and La Bruyère's admission (1693) were both made occasions for literary battles, in which the sturdy moralist tries to hold the traditional ground against the dexterous undermining of " Cydias " (see next chapter).

The main document in the Quarrel is Perrault's *Parallèles des anciens et des modernes* (1688-97). These sprightly The dialogues — they are appropriately staged at Ver-" Parallèles " sailles — present a Chevalier and an Abbé who uphold the moderns against a Président, to whom is assigned the bad end of the argument. The first interlocutors seem in the right more frequently than they really are, because the Président has little to plead save respect for authority. Perrault's taste and judgment are superficial, with little appreciation of the magnificent or the delicate. He tries to make a universal survey through all the ages and arts, but practically his knowledge limits him to modern France. His arguments, though often tricky and partial, are varied and plausible, and they proved effective enough. He adopts an agreeable *dégagé* tone, and he allows for differences of opinion, which Boileau does not. Among the reasons which Perrault advocates for the superiority of the moderns are: the fact that they are the last-comers and can best carry forward the " mind of the race "; an improvement in psychological handling — of love affairs, for example — and in the method of reasoning; the perfecting of inventions, especially the invention of printing; the fact that we may now get all the meat of the ancients in translation (this was also Lamotte's contention) ; the protection of the King; the advantages of Christianity, particularly in eloquence and epic. All these superiorities are applicable as much to the arts as to the sciences. There is an insistence everywhere on a measurable and calculable progress. And Perrault, like Fontenelle, uses the creative productions of the Ancients to vitiate their own cause; by his praise he forces them into the paradoxical position

of attacking themselves and their friends. Much of this brings
to mind the familiar and perennial debate between humanists
and scientists, in the matter of education. Building on Descartes,
Perrault, in fact, attacks pedantic education, under which heading he would include —like others —a good deal of true culture
and knowledge. It has been pointed out that most of the
Moderns were ignorant alike of the ancients and of the essential
principles of poetry. They propose translations as giving the
root of the matter and they have little art-sense; they confuse
genius with the mechanics of the *métier* and they do not savor
the historical aroma of masterpieces; they reduce art to the
intelligible element, expressing a pure Cartesian reason, embracing scientific rather than sensible symbols. The chief con-
tentions of the Moderns are thus summed up by M. Gillot, the
latest historian of the Quarrel:

Summary

> La poésie moderne est supérieure à la poésie antique parce
> qu' inspirée d'une religion plus pure et plus vraie. Art ou poésie,
> les productions modernes l'emportent sur les modèles antiques
> parce que plus achevées de forme et plus conformes aux exigences
> d'un goût délicat. Science ou philosophie, les modernes savent
> mieux et plus que les anciens. Armé d'une méthode nouvelle et
> formé par la discipline cartésienne, le génie moderne laisse bien
> loin derrière lui la science rudimentaire des savants anciens. . . .
> Industrie ou arts appliqués, il n'est aucune des inventions, qui
> facilitent et embellissent la vie, dont ne se soit avisé un siècle de
> découvertes et de merveilles ingénieuses.

It is mainly with regard to the supposed advance in beauty
and taste that we need to question this claim. Perrault himself is breaking down the barriers of taste in his lightness of
treatment, in his constant appeal to the standpoint of society
women and the world; he is willing to do without imaginative
style and metre, the specific marks of poetry; he has a poor
sense of beauty, which he considers a very mobile and fashionable thing, since all that concerns style, proportion, elegance,
is relative; he insists on the perpetual relativity of taste, whose
Perrault's boundaries he widens by cross-references to archi-
Doctrine of tecture, statuary and painting. Nor does he stop
Taste there. He is constantly dealing with and drawing
analogies from natural history, medicine, music and the indus-

trial arts. Small wonder, then, that with these fresh interests, aided by the social revolt against the severe .régime of the Ancients, Perrault's novelty and urbanity won the day.

For his cause triumphed, as a matter of general opinion and results. Neither the surly indirect retorts of Boileau and his **Results** *Réflexions sur Longin,* nor his intelligent concessions in the *Lettre à M. Perrault,* after Arnauld had patched up a reconciliation between the leaders, could gainsay or withstand the strength of the current. The wise and judicial compromises of Fénelon and of Saint-Evremond were alike un-availing. Emancipation was in the air, the respect for authority was seriously shaken, and the Quarrel spread with reverberations to England and other Northern shores. In France, the force of the Renaissance was spent. The neo-classicism of the following century, reacting and striving to return to Boileau and a modi-fied ancestor-worship, proved only that the real power of the modern world lay in developing those relations and widening those spheres of knowledge which Perrault and Fontenelle had first indicated. Classicism, poetry and taste deteriorated as science, philosophy and the industrial arts advanced.

In fact, two main tendencies may be seen as helping to dif-ferentiate the thought and literature of the eighteenth century **Relativity** from those of the seventeenth: the tendency toward *relativity* and the tendency toward *expansionism.* Relativity, or Relativism, may be defined as a philosophic atti-tude which views creeds and standards as not absolutely true but as dependent on certain conditions of time and place. For instance, the nineteenth century has made a great deal of his-torical relativity in matters of climate and race, political insti-tutions and religious truth. But the way had already been pointed out by Bayle and Voltaire, by Montesquieu and Diderot. The modern mind — beginning in the eighteenth century — is then relative in that it is frequently skeptical concerning abso-lutes and also in that (see Perrault above) it seeks to relate or associate the various fields of knowledge and art.

Likewise the modern mind, beginning with the eighteenth **and** century, seems more expansive as regards literary **Expansionism** forms; it has enlarged their number and broken down the barriers between them; it has made more and more domains of knowledge susceptible of literary treatment. So the term Expansionism may be used to indicate the inclusion in literary history of subjects hitherto considered outside of that field. For instance, Fontenelle brings popular astronomy into literature and Montesquieu adds the study of laws. In each case it is the excellence of the treatment that admits and promotes the new subject; and there are, as we shall see, many such cases in the eighteenth century.

Now French Classicism, dealing more with permanent and universal human values, had striven everywhere after unity and **Vs.** concentration. Largely owing to the influence of **Classicism** the ancients, Expansionism is much limited in the Classic production viewed as a whole. With the addition of certain polemical and moralistic writings, the genres are much the same in the age of Boileau as in the age of Horace. In fact, to adopt De Quincey's distinction, the seventeenth century represents the more imaginative literature of *power*, while the eighteenth puts the emphasis on the literature of *knowledge* and lets down the bars to admit its many varieties. The former concentrates, as already said, on art and the inner nature of man; the latter stresses society and science, which ever " grows from more to more."

The wide divergence between Classical and modern aims is still more conspicuous on philosophic grounds. The attitude of the seventeenth century towards its Absolutes, the great traditional beliefs in king, church and literary law may be summed up in the phrase, " une loi, un roi, une foi " (See Pt. II, Bk. IV). Belief in this triad is orthodox and almost universal. The dogmatism of Boileau was thus paralleled by the dogmatism of Bossuet and by the despotism of Louis XIV. In every field the absolute was supreme and there was allowed little discussion of fundamentals. " Les grands sujets sont défendus," complained La Bruyère in 1688, and it is from La Bruyère that issue the first mutterings of social revolt (see next chapter).

The significance of the Quarrel is that it helped make way for the new forces. The literary skepticism of the Moderns **Significance of** liberates the conception of possible progress, or evo-**the Quarrel** lution, which in one form or another has dominated thought ever since. And the idea of progress may itself contain the corollaries of a skeptical relativity — hence tolerance — a thickening solidarity of knowledge, a growing expansionism, a tendency to welcome new notions, new forms, new relations. Progressivism thus amplified is a characteristic mark of the eighteenth century, to which the nineteenth is so much indebted. Modern thought dates from the twilight of Louis XVI (see p. 274), and it starts invading literature with Perrault's revolt against the ancients. The Quarrel then is extremely important on both philosophic and literary grounds.

CHAPTER II

WRITERS OF THE TRANSITION:
LA BRUYERE, SAINT–SIMON, FENELON

POLITICALLY, the most conservative of these three men is Saint-Simon, but the most Classical in taste is La Bruyère (1645-1696).

La Bruyère Coming at the end of the great century, recognizing that the age had reached its "point of perfection," this writer rounds off the Classical doctrine and completes the courtly picture. Clinging to the past, he disliked the present and distrusted the future.

Little is known of Jean de la Bruyère's life, until, in his fortieth year, he entered the household of the great Condé, to publish,

Life shortly afterwards, his one masterpiece — *Les Caractères* (1688). These are the two main events in an existence which remains for the most part silent and mysterious. Without knowing why, we know only that he had accepted various offices merely to give them up, that he lived unmarried, in an obscure tutorial position. The most plausible explanation seems to be that La Bruyère was emphatically the man of one book, which became his fixed idea. To serve *Les Caractères*, he renounced a good deal of living, while subordinating himself to the study of society.

His later years were packed with enough events and publicity to atone for his early obscurity. There were many outbreaks of feeling and opinion in connection with the thinly disguised portraits in *Les Caractères* and with the consequent rejection of La Bruyère by the Academy. He was finally elected (1693) in the face of stormy opposition, and his uncompromising *discours* on that occasion was a notable expression of dogged independence.

That is the chief mark of his character throughout. Independence and originality are the qualities that he constantly recom-

Character mends and practices in his writings, and it must have been a bitter pill for him to subdue his individuality in the service of the grandees. The results are visible in a somewhat soured disposition. La Bruyère, like Boileau, is a crusty bourgeois bachelor, sardonic and downright. He was also sensitive and not at ease in company; he preferred quiet, a few good friends and a library. Withdrawing into himself, he devoted his studious leisure, as a contemporary put it, to the task of " distilling " his immortal book.

The author's material is indicated by the subtitle; *les Mœurs de ce siècle.* [1] His declared intention is psychological, generalizing, instructive. He portrays society's divisions

The Book and occupations, of which his chapter-headings give a fairly complete survey. As regards composition, the volume was first issued as a collection of " remarks "; it presents in fact a series of observations, covering a number of years and suggesting an expanded and polished diary. Neither chapters nor portraits are composed all of one piece; we have rather a mosaic of maxims, a gallery of paintings. This comparative freedom of composition adds to the effect of naturalness and life.

In another direction of form, the author shows the most constant care. Style was his main delight and preoccupation. Here

Style he is really a creative artist. His diction is picturesque and incisive. He has his own strong phrasings and metaphors, his " mots aventuriers," as he termed them, together with a considerable play of fancy. All this tends towards a vividness of expression, conspicuous in his portraits. His sentences are often long and analytical, his figures realistic and precise, but he remains Classical in his addiction to epigram and balance. On the whole it is an elaborate laborious style, hard and bold rather than smooth or flowing. A lapidary is at work, an assorter and refiner, whose main desire is to be distinct and individual.

The chief literary types used are maxims and portraits, which correspond, it has been well said, like text and illustra-

Maxims and Portraits tions. The maxims suggest at once La Rochefoucauld and Pascal, though they lack the concise perfection of these masters. They are more freely expressed and more like Montaigne in style, in the personal truth, and in the view of human mobility. Many fine and subtle thoughts are given

---

[1] His model was the Greek work of Theophrastus, also called *Characters*, which La Bruyère himself translated.

adequate wording, but the great achievement of La Bruyère is rather in the portrait. To this genre he gives final consummate form. He gives it indeed many forms, since all varieties of portraits are to be found: moral or psychological, physical, full-length, sketches, pendants, pastels. The characters may bear *précieux* or ancient names, but their physiognomies are living and moving likenesses, usually drawn from celebrities of the time. Thus Cydias, the wit, represents Fontenelle; Emile, the great general, is Condé or Turenne; Roscius is Baron, the comedian; Ménalque amusingly depicts a certain absent-minded Comte de Brancas. Other striking portraits are those of Arrias, the conceited dogmatist; Emire, the heartless woman; Giton and Phédon, respectively the rich and the poor man. The effect of vividness is attained not only through the lively style, but also through the use of physical and characteristic details. The author poses his subject in many ways, walks all around him, exhausts him, and will not leave the main trait of the victim alone; he twists and wrings it to the last drop; or, sometimes, there is a dramatic reservation of the real point until the very close. In certain directions La Bruyère appears as fuller and more subtle than Molière, but he is less universal; his portraits, for all their variety, bear more the mark of his own age.

His thought is Classical and conservative, in that he insists on the old qualities of reason and truth, measure and sobriety.

Ideas He holds by the rules and stands firmly on the side of the Ancients in the Quarrel. As regards the monarchy, La Bruyère praises Louis for his real qualities — the rest are " forbidden subjects." But he slips in theories concerning an ideal government that makes for the happiness of the people. In religion, he favors the extinction of heresy; the idea of tolerance has scarcely reached the Parisians. He has no doubts concerning dogma and is pronounced in his condemnation and ridicule of freethinkers.

Yet throughout the work, one is conscious, as La Bruyère himself was conscious, that he comes during the twilight of the Classical gods. A certain weariness in their support, a **Social Criticism** feeling of surfeit and decadence, is noticeable. That critical spirit which he would not direct against the major powers, he turns against the lesser orders. There are savage cuts at nearly every kind of wealth and aristocracy. The fortune-hunters, the *nouveaux riches*, the farmers-general, patrons, misers and gamblers, are all cursed with the money taint. Especially does La Bruyère excoriate the court. It is ruled by self-interest, it displays only vanity and waste, it leads only to unhappiness. Some of the best portraits, of great satiric strength, are those depicting the courtiers. The grandees themselves find little favor in La Bruyère's eyes. They have left their opportunities to do good unimproved. They are ignorant and neglectful and are already being ousted from government by the rise of more intelligent classes. We do not need to wait for the eighteenth century to find out what was the matter with the seventeenth, and there is no heavier indictment of the age of Louis XIV than this prepared by his humble servant.

With the people La Bruyère is more preoccupied than any other writer of his time. There is a famous and dreadful passage in which he describes the peasants, those " beasts bound to the ground," who are yet articulate and human and who deserve a share in the bread they have so mournfully sown. La Bruyère, hating the aristocrats, declares, " je veux être peuple." But he has no conviction of a new order and little sense of progress. He enforces neither the rights of man nor the wrongs of woman — whom he considers a poor creature. The fact is that La Bruyère, like La Rochefoucauld, is mainly pessimistic and destructive in spirit. All his wit and art cannot disguise his misanthropy. He is not a cynic, for he has standards. He is a sensitive critic, disappointed of perfection, an idealist gone morose. He shows a touch of heart in several passages, but almost no gaiety nor cheer.

A Pessimist

Thus he lacks the broadness of the profounder moralists, whose level he also misses by having no deep and original system. He rarely penetrates to the obscure reason which is at the core of human sentiments, as La Rochefoucauld, rightly or wrongly, seeks to penetrate. La Bruyère is more occupied with modes of thought and passion; he is not universal nor philosophic. Yet in his thorough description of his own day and time, he is without a peer and shows a relative profundity. He is not greatly constructive; but he follows faithfully the receding tide of a remarkable era.

Comparative Position

The French have long been unequalled in the writing of Memoirs, and those of Saint-Simon are the greatest in the language. What the Cardinal de Retz did for Louis

Saint-Simon XIII, Saint-Simon accomplished for the age of Louis XIV and the Regency, with still more remarkable merits of extent, interest and literary power. He gives full accounts of the inner workings of the most brilliant period in French history. He makes the picture galleries of Versailles and the Louvre step down from their frames and live and move before our eyes.

Louis de Saint-Simon (1675–1755) was born of a noble house. He was a " duke and peer " like his father. Both men believed in the divine right of nobles as well as in their responsibilities (*noblesse oblige*), and both showed a conservative tendency to prefer the " good old days." With these feudal ideas and with a fondness for reading history, Saint-Simon left home a rebel against the actual order. In person he was rather small and ill-made, but he had much vital force. He married a worthy lady for whom he had due affection and respect. Entering the army, he went through a campaign or two without distinction, and displeased Louis XIV by resigning his commission.

The greater part of Saint-Simon's active life was passed at Versailles, where he was an assiduous observer and critic. He

Court Life, 1702–1724 was too punctilious about small matters, too little of a courtier and statesman to please the powers; and the Great Monarch once told the free-spoken nobleman that he must learn to " hold his tongue." Twice he approached a position of influence, with the Dauphin and under the regency of the Duc d'Orléans, of whom Saint-Simon was a staunch friend. But though instrumental in forming the Regent's " councils " (see next chapter) and in forcing the degradation of the illegitimate sons of Louis XIV, he avoided positions of trust and wavered in large matters. He withdrew to his estates on the death of the Regent.

His rôle at court was in accordance with his character, which was that of a very fussy person. He was always occupied with

Character, questions of etiquette, precedence and trappings; when the Great Monarch died, Saint-Simon was above all concerned about what sort of a " bonnet " a certain Président should wear. He considered these things as symbols of the waning aristocratic power which it was his chief desire to restore. He had a fiery disposition, with much capacity both for hating and loving — their " nerve and principle is the same," he significantly says. His friends were few but well chosen, and his abundant curiosity kept him many channels of information among high and low. Ministers, valets and women of the court unconsciously supplied the materials for his Memoirs.

These were written during his retirement, a period of thirty years which he spent partly on his country estate, partly in his Paris library. Without occupation, disheartened by family afflictions, Saint-Simon once chanced to read Dangeau's *Journal de la Régence*. The old courtier amused himself by jotting down " additions " which vivified Dangeau's facts and personages. Gradually he was possessed with the idea of completing his own Memoirs, which he had started as a youth. From this beginning and from a mass of notes accumulated during his court life, the actual *Mémoires* had their birth. For fifteen years Saint-Simon spent many feverish midnights remembering and recording the great days which he knew so well. He had time to recopy the whole text before his death (1755), and for two generations the dangerous manuscript lay in the Foreign Office. A fairly complete edition was published only in the days of Romanticism.

The "Mémoires"

As a writer of history proper, of which he had rather a personal and imaginative conception, Saint-Simon is far from perfect. He makes numerous errors of date, of fact and of judgment. Furthermore, his prejudices stood tremendously in the way. He could see no good in any class but the hereditary nobility, and he particularly disdained the crowd of court " lackeys," *i. e.* the parasites, as well as the royal favorites and ministers. This makes him unjust to the Cardinal Dubois and to Mme de Maintenon. Differing from Montesquieu, he had no esteem for the *noblesse de robe* or the parliamentary and judicial families. He was impatient if not ignorant of financial matters, as appears in his accounts of the famous banking system introduced by John Law. He was no soldier and so he cannot understand the professional merits of such marshals as Villeroy and Villars, whom he condemns simply as courtiers and individuals. Even the higher ranges of diplomacy and international

The Historian

politics are seen mainly from the angle of precedence and
ceremony. Finally, his frank opinion of Louis XIV, though
well warranted in some respects, is unjust as a whole and
diminishes too greatly that princely figure. Saint-Simon
admits that he is " lacking in charity." Another disappointed
courtier, like La Rochefoucauld, he finds fault with the life
which found no great place for him. His pessimistic picture
is thus the reverse and the complement of Voltaire's *Siècle
de Louis XIV*.

On that very account the Memoirs have their historical value.
They are thoroughly sincere. Despite some errors of fact, they
are crammed with a wide general knowledge and
Chief Values with keen observation. They are realistic and
personal above all. They excel in two things: in vivid portraiture
and in striking accounts of impressive scenes. Saint-Simon is a
psychological and picturesque historian, and the Memoirs are
greater than many histories because they are closer both to life
and to literature.

Unlike La Bruyère, he rarely deals with abstract types. He
depicts an actual pageant crowded with innumerable distinct
figures. These are often characterized in powerful
Portraits and disdainful language. " Monseigneur," the son
of the king, is " sunk in fat and apathy," the Duc de Maine is
" like a demon in malignity and perversity of soul," another ·
man is called a " court rat," and Voltaire is haughtily dismissed
as a scalawag son of a notary, influential " in a certain set."
For the ladies, Saint-Simon wields a more graceful brush and
gives usually a living physical portrait. So the Duchess of Burgundy is described in her habitual gestures and manners. For
her and for her husband, the lamented Dauphin, the writer shows
much admiration and tenderness. But toward his enemies he is
implacable and excessive. The Duc de Noailles, who had shown
himself a perfidious friend, is the " serpent who tempted Eve and
ruined the human race." Apparently Saint-Simon could shrivel
the Duke with a glance, and his whole account of their relationship gives a deep impression of thoroughly savored vengeance.
In all these portraits the effect is gained by accumulation of
details, by vivid depiction and a biting force of language.

The same is true of the famous scenes, in which the narrator

shows also his dramatic ability. Of these, the most celebrated
is the long description, from council-chamber to Bed
"Tableaux" of Justice, of how the Duke of Maine and the Count
of Toulouse were degraded from their ranks. This was the chief
event of Saint-Simon's life, for he was the senior among the peers
from whose number the King's natural sons were expelled. The
historian frankly makes himself the center of all eyes, depicts
his exuberant physical joy, and carefully notes the successive
steps in the proceedings. As the " spy of his century," he made
it a point to be present on all memorable occasions; he is supreme
in reporting them and in reading the faces of the participants.
Death-beds, royal levees, hunting and gaming, fêtes and meetings
of the councils, are described over and over again, with an effect
of absorbing interest. Throughout, people conduct themselves
most naturally. Doors open and shut, real faces flash forth,
grandees blow noses and box ears, there is much particularity
about all doings, great and small, anecdotes and incidents,
ceremonies and usages, — a sort of court gazette palpitating with
life, and displaying the imposing figure of the monarch behind all.

Saint-Simon's language is very individual. Incoherent in
syntax, sometimes obscure and faulty, it rises in high moments
to a torrent of vehement eloquence. Lacking Clas-
Style sical measure and repose, it is a style peculiarly
adapted to his " tableaux vivants " and to passionate invective.
It is the natural reflection of the man himself, careless of academic perfection, hurried, lordly, involved. Saint-Simon uses
the strongest adjectives, vivid figures and expressions; his diction
is chosen with startling accuracy or imaginative appeal and he
reproduces dialogue to the life. His violent sensibility, says
Taine, was too acute for sober action, but constituted the very
marrow of an ardent and eager literary genius.

In his thought and position, Saint-Simon was a lonely Moses
without a Promised Land. He faces backwards, not forwards.
Both his high-seriousness and his conservatism are
Conclusion of the seventeenth century; he was scarcely aware of
the eighteenth. Though he discerned many of the faults in
Louis XIV and his age, Saint-Simon clings to the royal and
aristocratic prerogatives, disdaining the *philosophes*, a devout
churchman, little concerned with the people. And his indi-

vidualism repelled his own order, which he served better in literature than in politics. He holds his unique place through the majestic sweep and the finished detail of his great historical frescoes.

" Une magnifique créature et infiniment séduisante " — this is Saint-Simon's tribute to François de Salignac de la Mothe-Fénelon (1651–1715), archbishop of Cambrai and **Fénelon** author of *Télémaque*. A writer distinctly of the second order, Fénelon lives chiefly through the charm of his personality and the weight of his influence. The whole purpose of his life and work was to give sound moral instruction: this is seen in his tutoring of the Dauphin, in the tone and content of his various writings, and in his power as spiritual " director " of many congregations and people. As a studious and well-nurtured youth, he was early marked for the church, sent through Saint-Sulpice, and designated, in two communities, to lead Protestants back to the fold; a delicate task, in which he showed both tolerance and tact. His complex nature was able to combine worldly knowledge and ambition with a sincere piety, tending towards mysticism. Appointed preceptor to the Duke of Burgundy, favored by Mme de Maintenon and a choice circle at court, he was at the height of his career when made archbishop in 1695. But already certain clouds were forming; Fénelon had become the friend of Mme Guyon, a semi-hysterical mystic; according to Saint-Simon, " leur sublime s'amalgama." The two friends were partial to the doctrine called Quietism, which included absorption in the divine spirit through prayer and the " pure love " of God, independently of future reward. This doctrine was condemned as unorthodox and a long controversy raged between Fénelon and Bossuet. The former was finally disapproved by the Pope, exiled from court and restricted for the rest of his life to his diocese of Cambrai, which he administered admirably.

Fénelon's best writings are associated with his brief court career or with the controversy about Quietism. As for the **Miscellaneous** latter we need notice only the plaintive and seduc-**Writings** tive eloquence which Fénelon opposes to Bossuet's dogmatism. A similar winning tone characterizes the *Lettres spirituelles*, containing a liberal and persuasive theology. For the young prince Fénelon wrote some Fables, the *Dialogues des Morts* — anticipating Fontenelle, though not so good — and particularly the *Télémaque*. This and two other important works may be considered more at length.

At first reading, the famous *Télémaque* (1699) is likely to prove a disappointment. It seems too juvenile and shows too The plainly its purpose of moral and Christian instruc-"Télémaque" tion, insinuated through antique disguises. But as in other works of this period, the Classicism of *Télémaque* needs to be pondered and assimilated. It is throughout an imitation, mainly of the *Odyssey*, partly of the *Aeneid* and other ancient masterpieces. The adventures of Telemachus are like those of Ulysses, the nymph Calypso corresponds to Circe, there are many voyages, even to the lower regions, and the style, in descriptions, episodes and long Homeric similes, is a medley of classical phrases and allusions. To one nourished on antiquity, as Fénelon himself was nourished, the book should have an agreeable reminiscential flavor. Written with much charm and grace, it is now a standard volume for youth and for foreigners learning French; but its initial success was due to its political criticism. Everybody saw that Louis XIV was indirectly reprimanded, and Fénelon's central thought was to form the Dauphin on a very different model. He was taught the dangers of " les conquêtes, le faste et le luxe . . . et le pouvoir absolu,' and he was warned against flattering ministers and women Fénelon preaches gospel morality as opposed to the politics the current. He is capable of fine psychological portrayal and with all his clericalism, he depicts love as one who knows. Hi imagination is not grandiose, but lively and colorful. Hi simplified style is harmonious and flowing. At his best, he ha a rapid narrative gift, and his dialogue is superior to his rathe conventional descriptions. Of its kind, as a neo-classical imi tative work, *Télémaque* contains a good deal of placid beauty

The little treatise, *De l'Education des Filles* (1687) has bee called the point of departure for modern French pedagogy As Educator Fénelon points out how feminine education (in th widest sense) has not been commensurate with the importance of woman in family and social life. Her dignit must be maintained, her faults, such as vanity and ignorance must be corrected in girlhood, and especially must she be strengthened by reason. and self-government, rather than by imposed authority. Then there are sensible precepts, suggesting Rousseau, as to the education of very young children, whose brain is " always wavering, as a lighted candle in a windy place." Returning to young girls, Fénelon seems to restrict their cultural education, in that music, art and poetry are considered dangerous. The great object is to gain the heart of Mademoiselle for Christian virtue. None of these principles seem very startling now, but they represented some distinct novelties for that time.

Fénelon as literary critic is seen to considerable advantage in his *Lettre à l'Académie* (1714). Here as in the correspondence with Lamotte (a radical Modern), the Quarrel

As Critic reappears. The polite Fénelon refuses to commit himself and shows an evident desire to please everybody, but on the whole he is a liberal Ancient. His taste, his heart and his education place him on the side of antiquity, but he is not blind to certain modern excellences. In criticizing genres, he deplores the reforms of Malherbe, as limiting the French vocabulary and regulating poetry too narrowly. Ancient eloquence is certainly superior to the modern. In tragedy, Racine's merits are recognized, but Corneille is considered bombastic and there is too much love-making in French plays. A great poet will always tend toward virtue and religion, and Molière's greatness is impaired by his easy morals. Fénelon is sound on history and foresees such modern developments as the history of institutions and careful revivifications of past epochs. Such points may exemplify his approach to many questions agitated during the eighteenth century, and Fénelon clearly possesses a critical and appreciative mind. His preference for simplicity above everything appears in his own prose, which is easy and natural, like that of Voltaire.

Of the three writers dealt with in this chapter, Fénelon, the least remarkable for individual literary talent, is the most liberal

His Liberalism and forward-reaching in his ideas. His " tolerance " is almost a legend and was respected by the earlier generation of *philosophes*. In politics, all three men were dissatisfied with the court régime. Fénelon alone dares point out how a monarch should govern in connection with the people. His essential aristocracy of temper, his delicate nature and his almost feminine charm interfered neither with his courage nor with his clear-sightedness.

CHAPTER III

THE EIGHTEENTH CENTURY: HISTORY AND SOCIETY

SOME knowledge of the historical and social features of the *ancien régime* is essential to an understanding of its literature.

The Regency Louis XIV had ended in unpopularity and gloom, and a period of formality was followed by a period of license. The regency of Philip, Duke of Orleans, lasted only eight years (1715–1723) and except for a small war with Spain contains little external history. But it is a significant epoch on account of the experiments in administration, the restlessness of thought and especially the degree of license that has imparted a peculiar flavor to the word *Régence*. Philip himself seems a replica of Charles II of England: immoral, indolent, good-natured, a connoisseur rather than a statesman. It was the Duc de Noailles who wrestled with the finances and repressed certain expenditures. The financial salvation of the country was entrusted to John Law, who established the modern system of paper credit, founded the Banque de France and the Mississippi Company. But France was deluged with paper and a crash was inevitable. In the meantime an attempt to govern by six administrative councils had yielded to a ministry along the old lines; the Abbé Dubois, as premier, seemed another Mazarin in craft and shrewdness. Dubois' main title to respect is that he negotiated the Triple Alliance of England, France and Holland.

The ministry of the Duke of Bourbon, who succeeded Orleans as Regent, lasted only three years. It is distinguished by a

Reign of Louis XV bitter persecution of the Protestants in the Cévennes and by the marriage of the young King to Maria Leczinska of Poland. The reign of Louis XV was a period of general and cumulative disaster. At home, there was political stagnation and growing discontent. Abroad, little of distinction marked the deeds of France and she gradually lost her place in the estimation of Europe. Louis XV was a useless and unworthy king; the temper of the nation sank towards his level; the influence of favorites, mistresses and incompetents became pronounced; and the national finances went from bad to worse.

This general decadence was not so conspicuous until after the middle of the century. Cardinal Fleury took charge of affairs in 1726. His policy was cautious and dull. He **First Half** enforced the bull Unigenitus, imprisoned and removed Jansenists, did something for commerce, and won Lorraine for France by a treaty of 1738. In the war of the Austrian Succession (1741–48) the French did not play a creditable part save in the matter of isolated victories. France had recognized the right of Maria Theresa to the Austrian throne and yet joined Frederick the Great in attacking her. The battle of Fontenoy was won from the English by the genius of Marshal Saxe. The war, carried into India and America, assumed worldwide proportions. But France, left in the lurch by Frederick, signed the peace of Aix-la-Chapelle without gaining any substantial advantages. " Bête comme la paix " became a Parisian byword. The governors of the country had proved themselves a weak lot. The national prestige was tarnished, and the result was a torrent of popular criticism. Louis was no longer " le Bien-Aimé." Immorality and even oppression the French could stand, but not the loss of glory.

Frederick's bad faith started the famous Seven Years War, but the deeper cause was that opposition of English and French **Second Half** interests which now extended from the Mississippi **(1750–74)** to the Ganges. This war meant for France the loss of America and India. Montcalm and Dupleix were not steadily supported in their brilliant efforts abroad; in Europe incapable ' generals and ministers, " tumbling one after the other like magic lantern pictures " (Voltaire), were responsible for signal defeats in diplomacy and in the field. The Duc de Choiseul was appointed too late to save the situation. Another most unsatis-. factory peace for France was concluded, and Choiseul could turn his attentions homewards, where there was much to call for healing measures. But this minister, like his greater successors under Louis XVI, could not wrestle with the enormous national debt nor with the whole rotten system of taxation. The Jesuits were expelled from France, the Parisian Parliament was curbed once more, and the well-meaning sluggish Dauphin was married to Marie Antoinette of Austria. The Beaumarchais incident (see Book III, Ch. II) discredited the law-courts. In the meantime, the corrupt *far niente* of the dying monarchy was revealed once again by the French inactivity before the first shameless partition of Poland. Louis XV ended his reign in 1774 amid the ignominies of smallpox, a fleeing court, a jesting populace, and an extreme unction indefinitely postponed to accommodate an unworthy favorite.

Taine's analysis of the old régime shows that the feudal domination of the upper orders was no longer warranted. The Social privileged classes included the king, the nobles and Structure the higher clergy; they still retained their great privileges; but they had lost all ability to rule and all desire to serve the nation. The nobles, laity and clergy, numbered over two hundred thousand. They were powerful and rich, owning two-fifths of the land in France and to a considerable extent exempt from the taxes which oppressed the people so heavily.

The nobles were supposed to represent the public at the capital and to serve as magistrates in the country. But they were largely absentee-landlords. Those who re-The Nobility mained on their estates were generally too poor and inadequate to help the peasantry, who frequently surrendered four-fifths of their income to their various overlords. The tithes, the poll-tax, the salt-tax, other impositions and burdens, particularly in connection with the lordly diversion of hunting, crushed the hearts of the people. Some of the resident nobles were mildly inclined, but their debts placed them simply in the position of creditors and oppressors of their tenantry. The absentees were still worse, having no knowledge of the people, and enforcing their demands through heartless overseers. The funds required for the extravagance of court life made them pitiless. Not only did they abandon their home responsibilities, but they served no useful function at court. A thousand of the oldest and highest aristocracy set the pace and drew everything towards Paris and Versailles. France has never recovered from the excessive centralization of the old régime. Much of the country-side was then deserted, exhausted agriculturally, stag-

and the nant politically, without good roads, and in the
Provinces direst poverty. But between Paris and Versailles a double row of carriages thronged the highway all day long. The provinces were actually ruled by thirty "intendants" responsible only to the king; the taxes were farmed out to the *traitants* (farmers-general), who paid a lump sum for the privi- lege of grinding the poor; such offices, as well as the sinecures about court, were bought and sold with no thought save for the loot involved. The great nobles, like the lesser courtiers (con- temptuously called *laquais* by Saint-Simon and Montesquieu), were for the most part selfish and rapacious. Gambling and extravagance gave rise to colossal debts; the Duke of Bourbon owed six millions at the time of his death, and the first Regent paid two millions for the celebrated diamond which bears his name. The higher clergy were equally extravagant, as the pomp of the Rohans demonstrates, and ecclesiastical sinecures were also preëmpted by the nobility. The whole class had little feudal leadership, little taste for farming or politics. They were interested mainly in gambling, gallantry and court life. The nobles did not rule; they took. They were no longer instruments, but merely ornaments.

Many of these abuses began under Louis XIV, and it has been seen (Pt. II, Book IV, Ch. I) how in his time the court was the

King and center of pomp and magnificence. But it was also
Court then the center of real power in every field. Now the personal centralization of the Great Monarch is no longer possible. "The nation has no longer a head, history no longer a focus; together with a master of the higher order, great servants also fail the French monarchy" (Guizot). Yet the king's authority in important matters remains absolute and despotic. The "intermediary bodies" (see Montesquieu), such as the judicial Parliament of Paris or the provincial States-General, have only a limited and occasional interference in affairs. The king is a pasha attended by lesser pashas. He is considered the commander, the owner of France, the perpetual representative of the people, the delegate of God. The nobles flocked to Paris, hailing the youth of Louis XV with affection and veneration, as

Watteau, "L'Embarquement pour Cythère"

did the entire body of the people. They clung pathetically to a trust in the monarchy, their barrier and hope, even when the person of the king had palled, as it did towards the middle of the century. Beginning with the freedom of the Regency, the *petits soupers* of the Regent, and the scandalous vices of his daughters, France enters on an era of gambling, debauchery, extravagance, wit and license. Louis XV participated, somewhat coldly, in all this, but for one Louis as for another, the life of parade and " representation " is of the first importance. This life has a splendid setting, especially at Versailles, where everything is arranged for the pleasure of the eyes. The park is an open-air salon and everywhere the panorama of court life unfolds in gorgeous extravagance. Louis XV plays the actor all day long; his dressing is a drama in five acts, and Frederick the Great said that he would have appointed a dummy monarch for these functions. Neither king nor courtier has any time for business; everybody is careless or stupid about politics and expenditures. The grandees also " represent " and entertain enormously, in the capital and in the country. Their main duty is hospitality, as their châteaux still witness. " Leur grand talent est le savoir-vivre," and their real business is society.

For those fortunately placed, the social life of the epoch must have been delightful. " Qui n'a pas vécu avant 1789," said Talleyrand, " ne connaît pas la doceur de vivre." **Social Charm** Never was life conducted with more amenity, never were its details and processes managed with such attention to the agreeable and the artistic. From childhood on, the convent-bred women were educated chiefly to be attractive and beautiful, the men to be gallant and pleasing. Private life was nothing, public pleasure and display were everything. " We are," sighed Voltaire, " the whipped cream of Europe "; and the whole age was marked by a careless levity. Pastimes and pageants, *fêtes galantes* and theatricals, prodigality and gaiety rang the chimes of a universal and continuous carnival. From a faded pastel, a page of Marivaux, a picture by Watteau, comes a delicious perfume, as of lingering violets. Many gossiping records, hundreds of engravings, and particularly the stately or voluptuous paintings of the period show us lords and ladies perpetually embarking for the Cytherean Islands or enacting the set comedies of their lives. That is why private theatricals were the rage; the aristocracy performed and posed in life itself, and at least they carried the pose through to the very scaffold.

In all this the rôle of woman is supreme. In politics, the succession of royal mistresses forms almost a dynasty, just as in Power of literature the dynasty of salon-leaders is all-impor-Women tant. In this age of art and artifice, woman is considered the chief artistic product, the embodiment of the pleasure-. ideal. As an *ingénue*, she is handed over to her husband and the world, and the latter quickly supplants the former in her interest. Every day a dozen pleasures solicit the senses, refine the taste, agitate the mind. The day of a Marquise, from her reception on rising to her masked ball in the evening, reads like some impossible " romance of high life." Yet her power is real enough and often her capacity. She rules the fashions, the king, the court, writers and artists. Devoid of moral sense as these women mostly were, the more intelligent among them (Mme de Tencin, Mme du Pompadour) had a real knowledge of men and affairs, and the others had at least charming tongues and faces. Some show a fundamental common sense, a critical sense that goes to the core of questions; and always they possess the prime social art, the art of conversation, free, gay, delightful, influential, whose charm still reverberates in their letters and memoirs.

It was an age of great talk, and nowhere does this appear more conspicuously than in the salons which dominated the minds and habits of many writers. " All this literature," says The Salons Taine, " was spoken before it was written." The socialization of French thought and art was never more evident. Even in non-literary circles, there are traditions of witty cultivated conversation, under the " laws " of good taste and good company. The dynasty of literary salons began with the Marquise de Lambert (c. 1710–33), who yielded her scepter and subjects to Mme de Tencin (c. 1730–49), who in turn was succeeded by Mme de Geoffrin (1749–77). A rival dynasty was that of the Marquise du Deffand (c. 1740–80), part of whose power was usurped by Mlle de Lespinasse in 1763. The dates are those of the actual social sway of each lady. The great feature of the eighteenth-century salon, as distinguished from that of the previous period, is that it actually amalgamates, often on an equal footing, the writers and the cultured public. From now on, the salon really helps writers, financially and socially, launches them, gives them desirable contacts, initiates the success of the play or poem, influences the distribution of prizes and makes academicians.

This tendency started with Mme de Lambert. Her house was called the "antechamber of the Academy," half of whose members she was at one time credited with creating. **Mme de Lambert** She is described as an "honnête femme, moraliste sans pédantisme," highly considered in every way. She was a woman of sense, cultivated without affectation, who checked gallantry and promoted some fusion between good society and writers. It is to be noted, however, that she had two distinct days, one for the élite and one for the rank and file of literary men.

The four chief figures whom one was likely to find in any or all of the salons were Fontenelle and Voltaire, whose long lives covered both dynasties; Montesquieu, whose correspondence shows that he had to do some delicate **Mme de Tencin** balancing between the rival reception-days of the great ladies; and the Président Hénault, a scholar and wit, who occupied an intermediate ground between society and the young Republic of Letters. Fontenelle and Montesquieu were welcome at the house of Mme de Tencin, whose chief pet, however, was Marivaux. This indicates that she was more interested in the sparkle of wit than in social guarantees, and in fact Mme de Tencin holds a much freer salon than that of Mme de Lambert. She had been the mistress of the Regent and of others; then, reforming, she decided to found a *bureau d'esprit*, which was the main resource of unreligious elderly women at the time. In character, she was an audacious and ambitious woman, adroit, fond of intrigue, strongly intelligent and imaginative. Intelligence and wit were what she demanded of her guests, and her salon was the first where the writer counted for his own merits, on a par with the aristocrats. His hostess gave him full liberty and encouragement. She was a good listener, looked out for the comfort and entertainment of her "menagerie," enjoyed their social comedies and sallies, and helped them fill the salon with intellectual fire.

Fontenelle's "poetized astronomy," the subtlety of Marivaux, Montesquieu's thoughtful arguments were applauded and fostered here. Already there were cosmopolitan visitors, like Chesterfield and Grimm, while Mme de Tencin, with little dignity and much eagerness, gave and took freely from all. The other salons of the century carry on the tradition of these brilliant gatherings.

Quite different in character was Mme de Geoffrin, who stands witness to the growing force of the bourgeoisie. Without birth **Mme de** or conspicuous charm, she held her circle together **Geoffrin.** through her steady sense. She helped to bring plain truth and sincerity, of sentiment and language, back into repute. She was a severe woman, something of a prude, putting the damper on any show of license as well as any political free-thinking. Her home was the great resort of the *philosophes;* their discussions and personalities she really liked and encouraged. The positive and practical tendencies of this group chimed in well with her own personality, intellectual, forthright, somewhat cynical. Horace Walpole speaks of her excellent powers of observation, her common sense, her cleverness in securing desirable guests and in making them play up. She took over the survivors of Mme de Tencin, added such figures as Marmontel and Galiani, the witty Neapolitan, and she brought forward artists, like Greuze and Van Loo, who were hardly received elsewhere. But it was the *philosophes* who gave the tone at Mme de Geoffrin's.

Her rival, Mme du Deffand, was extremely aristocratic, not fond of the philosophers (save Voltaire), preferring the stately **Mme du** Classic tradition. She was haughty, despotic, and **Deffand** for twenty-five years quite blind. She sought refuge from the darkness of her mind and life in the company of distinguished writers and visitors from abroad. Hers was essentially the aristocratic and cosmopolitan salon. Her suppers brought together the cream of the court and church, as well as writers and intermediate people like the Président Hénault and Lord Chesterfield. If writers were in the minority, her salon was at least given over to theatrical and literary novelties. One day the actress Clairon would recite *Phèdre*, another day the latest philosophical pamphlet would be discussed. It is strange to see this rather arid and bitter nature turn to an impulsive romanticism in her old age. She became devoted to Horace Walpole and sustained with him a correspondence, which, together with her letters to Voltaire and others, constitutes one of the most interesting monuments of the time. She had a strong vital personality, much insight into character and a brilliant wounding wit; these qualities appear fully in her correspondence.

In 1763, the Marquise du Deffand's companion and helper, a certain Julie de Lespinasse, found that she could no longer **Mlle de** bear with the old lady's caprices and withdrew to **Lespinasse** set up housekeeping for herself. This she did in a modest way, but the unforgivable thing was that she carried with her many of Mme du Deffand's brightest parlor ornaments. The élite of intellectual Paris climbed the humble stairs of Mlle de Lespinasse, for she had probably the most winning personal charm and the most responsive mind of any of these ladies. An intense passionate soul, imaginative and romantic, she became the great friend of Dalembert and threw herself with zeal into everything that concerned the *Encyclopédie*, for which she provided an " intimate boudoir and laboratory." Courtiers and soldiers also came to her, distinguished churchmen and foreigners. She exhibited no trace of Mme de Geoffrin's prudery or timidity; she and her set were afraid of no powers in earth or heaven. Diderot's writings give the tone, absolutely emancipated in every ' field. Julie de Lespinasse was wonderfully endowed, she had more real knowledge than the other women, she was an omnivorous reader and a genuine inspirer of literature, an authentic genius herself, keen at reflection and rejoinder, clever in assorting people. She lives in literature as the writer of the most remarkable personal letters of the century, letters to an unworthy lover, which " still burn the paper on which they are written," so tense they are, so passionate, so simply and powerfully appealing, in their frank exaltation and tenderness, their delicate perception and understanding. It is evident that her great charm consisted in her ability to appreciate and listen to others. Small wonder that a woman like this received the homage of the extraordinary men who surrounded her.

Enough has been said to indicate the overweening influence

of the salons upon literature. Most of the works of the period are written under this influence and many writers, from Fonte-

Salon Influence on Literature

nelle and Voltaire through the minor poets, are " pro- tected " or inspired by ladies of fashion. The re- sults were not always fortunate. The salon taste required writers to be " popular," witty and above all agreeable. That is why natural directness, concrete imagination and per- sonal feeling are long excluded from literature, and with their exclusion *belles lettres* became infected with a " colorless ele- gance." But Rousseau and Diderot largely escaped the con- tagion; and for another kind of literature, the earlier *bureau d'esprit* or the later *salon philosophique* was no bad foster- mother. It is the literature of exposition and discussion that ` the salon refines and clarifies. It encouraged the play of intel- ligence and wit, the polished expression of ideas in clear attrac- tive untechnical speech. The habit of genteel conversation and gossip permeates not only the numerous *Discours, Lettres, En- tretiens,* but the various fields of knowledge. " Spirituelle, lumi- neuse, instructive, mais sèche et impersonnelle, telle est notre littérature du XVIIIe siècle, et c'est ce que signifie littérature des salons." The salons helped, at any rate, to give a being and a hearing to the New Liberalism.

Two other important influences of the period were the vogue of the sciences and that of English authors. The incentive toward the first issued in part from England, since the methods of Locke and Newton became popular during the first half of the century.

Science

Montesquieu indulges in physical experiments, the Regent has a chemical laboratory, Voltaire espec- ially promotes Locke's sensationalism and Newton's physics. In this he was encouraged by Mme du Châtelet, who herself was more addicted to mathematics. The latter science tends to become supreme, as Dalembert warns us, about 1750. Great ladies take up the various sciences, study physics, chemistry, natural history, even anatomy, follow pet courses at the Sor- bonne and have their portraits painted in laboratories. The Academies of Science become important not only at Paris, but in the provinces and even at Berlin, where Maupertuis, the discoverer of biological evolution, is perpetual secretary. The name of Buffon and the main interests of the Encyclopedia bear witness to the inspiration and value of the natural sciences throughout the century.

The vogue of English literature and philosophy is almost unlimited. It may be summarized by saying that nearly every The English English author of note, from Shakespeare down, at-Influence tracted attention in France during this period, and that almost every French author is indebted to some Englishman. In fact, just as France had previously gone to Italy and Spain for method and material, she now goes to England. The mention of certain salient facts and personages will make this clear.

Voltaire successfully launches the English vogue in the four main directions of philosophy, science, politics and *belles lettres*. Chief The general literary impulsion was three-fold: Manifesta- towards an interest in Shakespeare; towards English tions rationalism and Deism (Locke, Bolingbroke, Collins, Toland, and others); and later towards a sentimental reaction. Thus the two main French movements, skeptical philosophy and Rousseauistic Romanticism, were in considerable part based on an English background. Of the four great names of the century — Voltaire, Montesquieu, Rousseau and Diderot — the first three visited England with significant results, and all four were considerably affected by English influences: Voltaire, by Locke and the Deists, by Pope, Shakespeare and others; Montesquieu, by the liberal English constitution, whose fame he spread throughout Europe; Rousseau, especially by Richardson; and Diderot, by Richardson, Sterne and Shaftesbury. The *Grande Encyclopédie* was modelled on the original of Chambers (see Bk. IV, Ch. I). Translations of English authors are numerous and popular; a mere list of them covers twenty pages in Lanson's Bibliography. Every author of consequence is translated, some of them several times, by such men as Prévost and Letourneur. " Bibliothèques anglaises " or " Bibliothèques brittaniques " appear as anthologies or compendiums. The Queen Anne writers, as was natural, are the most favored before 1750, and after that date the contemporary sentimental school. The latter would include, as dominant names: James Thomson, for the return to outdoor nature; Young's *Night Thoughts* for melancholy combined with religiosity; Sterne, who brought in " l'humour " together with a rather sickly sentiment; Richardson, for bourgeois sentiment and morality; and the misty, melancholy or pseudo-epic features of Macpherson's *Ossian*. All these authors were eagerly read, and even today a whole scholarly literature circles around the reputation and influences of such English writers in France. The cosmopolitanism of the age inclines towards the literature of the "North," thus preparing the way for Mme de Staël and for many currents of Romanticism proper.

The eighteenth century exercises a wide fascination, because it offers enough to attract the most varied types of mind. The **Conclusion** aristocrat, the epicurean and the artist find there a certain ideal of elegance, wit and beauty. The liberal skeptic and the democrat observe how from the ruins of the old order emerge most of the principles of modern progressivism and humanitarianism. These opposing tendencies are reflected in the literature of the period. The traditional genres, especially poetry and drama, still partly preserve the courtly ideal; the New Philosophy urges other ideals, chiefly of the liberal kind. It will be our task, in the next two Books, to trace these conflicts and developments, first in philosophy, then in *belles lettres*.

BOOK II

THE NEW PHILOSOPHY

CHAPTER I

THE POPULARIZERS:
BAYLE AND FONTENELLE

In a preceding chapter we discussed those writers of the transition who on the whole belong to the age of Louis XIV. In that age there appeared two men who really belong to the eighteenth century. By their views, methods and knowledge, Bayle and Fontenelle are true precursors of Voltaire and the Encyclopedists.

Pierre Bayle (1647–1706) was primarily a Protestant, in the full sense of the word, both as regards religious upbringing and the inquiring tendency of his mind. Born near the Pyrenees, of a persecuted Huguenot family, he was banished from France and taught successively at Coppet and Rotterdam. In Holland, he settled among the refugees, of whom Jurieu was chief. Bayle's liberal and skeptical spirit caused him to protest against the excesses of Protestantism itself, and, driven out of his professorship, he spent the remainder of his life in theological disputes and a varied literary activity. Yet he was a mild passionless scholar, caring little for practical affairs or for pleasure. As one biographer says: " All the life of Bayle was absorbed in his thought, in the search for human truth and the devotion to reason."

Besides his great Dictionary, Bayle published anonymously several pamphlets, of which two have real importance. His **Minor Works** *Pensées sur la comète* (1682) were ostensibly written to relieve superstitious minds of the fear that comets presaged disaster. But in attacking superstition, Bayle also launches several ideas that assail the current orthodoxy: it is unlikely that Providence interferes, by prodigies or miracles, with the course of nature; there is a wide difference between the principles and the practice of believers; the atheist may be a well-behaved person; and tolerance is always to be recommended. The last tenet is also the key-note of another pamphlet, the *Commentaire philosophique sur le " Compelle Intrare "* (1686), a protest against the Papal bull " compelling " everybody into the church.

Bayle's fame and influence, however, derive mainly from the *Dictionnaire historique et critique* (1697), which has been paradoxically styled the " Bible of the eighteenth century." This work was ostensibly compiled to correct the mistakes of a dictionary already issued by a certain Moréri. As a matter of fact, it is an encyclopedia, almost the first of its kind, containing in its great folios all the learning, thought and critical power of the chief *savant* of his time. The extended footnotes, where Bayle feels at his ease to gossip and digress, are the most interesting part of the work. Its salient features are, first, the use of modern scientific and critical methods; a very great erudition, including much Latin and far-fetched knowledge; the insertion of allusions and anecdotes of doubtful taste; and a peculiar confusion of subjects and arguments, used to insinuate skepticism and to throw the reader, particularly the censor, off the track. Faguet calls the work less a dictionary of knowledge than of what Bayle knew. The extent of his knowledge is thus stated by the same critic:

The "Diction- naire "

> Ce qu'il savait c'était la mythologie, l'histoire et la géographie ancienne, l'histoire des religions . . . la théologie proprement dite, la philosophie, l'histoire européenne du XVIme et du XVIIme siècle.

Add to this list such subjects as jurisprudence, philology, and far-ranging biographies, and it will be seen that, as regards Expansionism, the author outstrips his own age and announces the eighteenth century.

Bayle's general method shows a " véritable esprit scientifique." He is not strong on the natural sciences, but in other fields he evinces the spirit of objective research, curiosity, impartiality and exactness. His two main ideas are relativity and tolerance. Since in every direction he finds

Method

only " des vérités particulières," it behooves us to tolerate and not to persecute the views of our neighbors. So Bayle, in an indirect and insinuating way, is a tranquil skeptic of the most thorough sort. In the thick of the old régime, he gave intellectual credence to no authority, no tradition and no dogma. The significance of his philosophy, far more destructive than systematic, is best realized by following the workings of his skepticism in the domains of metaphysics, morality, religion and history.

Except where he uses it as a weapon against theology, Bayle is skeptical about metaphysics. He warns us of the dangers **General** of the old philosophic spirit with its sterile dialectics, **Philosophy** and he thinks metaphysical speculation vain, because there are no absolutes. His own philosophy, like his religion, underwent vicissitudes. He leans to Descartes and to *la raison* as the criterion of truth, but he recognizes that reason is often obscured and prejudiced. All philosophers are "inventors of conjectures," who entertain us sometimes, but cannot prove anything. Truth, that " belle inconnue," is forever to be sought but never to be reached by speculation. Such a negative creed is neither high nor deep, but it is a good instrument for analysing other creeds. Starting with a thorough knowledge of ancient philosophy, the skeptic passes in review many modern theories, especially those of Descartes and of Leibnitz. Bayle records various controversies concerning the notions of substance, soul and movement. His own tendency is to hold to the world of sensible fact and reject metaphysical explanations.

Bayle is more interested in problems of practical morality, though here we are confronted with some contradictions in his **Ethics** thought. On the one hand he suggests a relative standpoint: morals and manners vary with latitude, and Sparta and China have rightfully their own conceptions of behavior; this view is considerably developed by the eighteenth century. But on the other hand there is a universal law, applicable everywhere, and making its appeal directly to the conscience and the reason of man. Reason, however, is generally conquered by the passions, which rule men and manners and found societies. Hence average morals are likely to be based on the essential passions. But the true guide is an innate and individual moral conscience, together with the light of reason; for while " la puissance de la raison s'est perdue, sa lumière s'est néanmoins conservée "; and Bayle supports the Protestant doctrine of the "errant" or free individual conscience, which is the voice of God speaking in man. The majority are, nevertheless, always making mistakes, for only a few sages sufficiently control their passions to submit to reason and to "natural" morality. The latter is based on the usages of civilization, and Bayle has little regard either for primitivism or for perfectibility. He believes only in a limited progress, chiefly in the spheres of knowledge. His is a morality of experience.

Bayle's early misadventures, his establishment among the refugees and his cast of mind, all contributed to make theology **Theology** his main preoccupation. But here again he investigates only to attack. The orthodox outworks, as built up by church-fathers, rabbis or commentators, he demolishes to his own satisfaction. As regards central dogmas, he suggests certain contradictions in Biblical texts and a certain laxness in Old Testament morals (" Les plus grands saints ont besoin qu'on leur pardonne quelque chose "), and again he holds that miracles are contrary to natural laws. Otherwise he leaves matters of faith and revelation almost intact. Into that domain he throws insoluble mysteries, such as the problem of free-will and the existence of evil, and his chief contention is that faith and reason should be absolutely divorced — the dogmatists are to be shorn of rational support. The best argument for the existence of God is to be found in the *Credo quia absurdum* attitude — " I believe because it is beyond belief." The attributes of Divinity are very doubtful, and in this connection Bayle revives the startling theory of Manicheism. According to reason merely, the universe is best explained as ruled by the rival deities of good and evil — God and Satan. This hypothesis was suggested by Bayle with his customary doublings and reserves. If we then add an atomic theory, according to which each particle of matter is bound up with and animated by spirit (modern monism), we have the two most positive doctrines of Bayle.

Historical researches constitute the greater part of the Dictionary. Bayle anticipates modern carefulness about sources and gives the spirit of contradiction free play. Finding errors everywhere, he really respects and desires the truth. Historical

History truth for him consists in a series of small verified facts, dissociated from legend and the partisan passions of man. He shows a lack of hero-worship, an effort to rationalize and lower the great figures and patriarchs of the past. He indulges in pleasantries, uses comparative treatment and suggests the " higher criticism." All this Voltairianism is best illustrated by the famous article on David, which created a furor, was suppressed, reintroduced, and circulated in thousands of pamphlets. In general history, the method is the same, though employed with a freer hand. By depreciating the value, as evidence, of such ancient writers as Plutarch and Livy, Bayle lines up with the Moderns in the Quarrel. By contemptuously dismissing the legends of heroic Greece and of early Rome, he rejects the artistic view and helps inaugurate historical positivism. In dealing with French history, he is a genuine road-breaker, doubtful of accepted authorities. Trying to keep his neutrality in all quarrels, he disliked but made fair statements about the Turks, the Papacy, and even the Jesuits. He makes, then, a general crusade against tradition, whether historical, theological or philosophical.

The tone of the Dictionary is sprightly, especially in the foot-notes. Like the later *philosophes*, Bayle was careful to serve

Manner his heavy diet with the sauce required. Yet his style, in spite of verbal felicity, is without grace or suppleness —" diffuse, lâche, incorrect," as Voltaire calls it. Bayle was less of a stylist than a supreme dialectician and a laborious man of letters; he helps to found literary journalism by his *Nouvelles de la République des lettres* (1684–87), the first important clearing-house for new publications and ideas. Sainte-Beuve calls him the genius of criticism, in the widest sense, on account of his versatility, curiosity, equilibrium and independ-ence. But he had small appreciation of literary beauties.

Bayle is the chief skeptic between Montaigne and Voltaire, with each of whom he has much in common. Yet he is not wholly

Conclusion a *philosophe*, because he is moderate and systemless. His chief legacy was his method: he thought it pos-sible to reach sure facts in all positive fields of knowledge, in history and ethics, as well as in physics; the negative application of

and this is seen in his attack on revelation and philosophic dogma. Doubting the watchwords of the coming century — humanity, progress and nature — he would have

Influence found the propagandists too violent, as they found him too mild. But the *philosophes*, often without giving Bayle the credit, use the Dictionary as their " arsenal," whether for information or for arguments. Eleven editions were published within forty years. Voltaire, Montesquieu, Diderot, private citizens and memoir writers, public figures like Frederick the Great, all bear witness to the extraordinary influence of Bayle. It was largely exercised in negative directions; he cleared the ground for the steam-roller of the Encyclopedists.

The life of Bernard de Fontenelle (1657–1757) is richer and more varied than that of Bayle. It lasted exactly a century,

Fontenelle less one month. Fontenelle could speak of the contemporaries of Richelieu to the contemporaries of Rousseau, and the annals of literature record fewer lives of fuller extent and interest. Born at Rouen, he was educated mainly by the Jesuits, and he always kept some friends among that body. Visiting Paris, Fontenelle came early under the influence of his uncles, Pierre and Thomas Corneille. The great Corneille was then in his gloomy last days; the more alert and sociable Thomas was really the companion of Fontenelle. He introduced his nephew to the editors of the *Mercure galant,* and this journal published the youth's early poetic endeavors.

The scientific studies of Fontenelle were of more consequence than any of the dramas and operas by which he hoped

Chief to win fame. It was after the failure of one of these

Writings that he decided to retreat to his province and make more sure of his ground in physics and geometry. From Normandy he brought out the *Dialogues des morts* (1683). These dialogues, deriving from Lucian and cast in the same mold as Landor's *Imaginary Conversations,* had a considerable success. The Parisians enjoyed hearing historical celebrities talk down to their level in the matter of philosophy and up to their level in the matter of wit. Next came the *Entretiens sur la pluralité des mondes* (1686), which were the first fruits of Fontenelle's popu-

larizing genius. He could now talk science to the "belles marquises" and remain interesting. That same year saw the publication of the *Histoire des oracles*, the last of the trio of masterpieces that made Fontenelle's fame. His mind was now set on
winning a place in the Academy, which he obtained, after four
attempts, more on his reputation as a wit than as a scientist. His
reception there was an event; his uncle Thomas delivered the
address of welcome, and Fontenelle, in his reply, praised the
other Corneille to the detriment of Racine and the Ancients
generally.

Having, as he thought, attained in literature, he could henceforth turn his attention wholly to science. The earlier youthful
The Scientist Fontenelle is mainly *esprit;* the latter is mainly scientific popularizing. His universal curiosity sought
satisfaction alike in laboratories and in personal relations with
men of science. He was no specialist, but he knew enough of
geometry, astronomy or physics to associate with specialists and
learn from them. He had a born aptitude for acquiring and dis-
seminating knowledge; and the members of the Academy of
Sciences recognized this when in 1697 they crowned his ambition
by making him perpetual secretary of that body. This office
Fontenelle filled with genuine ability. His labors here hardly
belong to the province of literature, but tended much to the diffusion of knowledge. He wrote a large readable History of the
Academy, which appeared with annual regularity, and he instituted the composition of *Eloges* on his fellow-academicians, which
were admirable specimens of eloquent propaganda.

Another way in which Fontenelle represented science was
through the rôle that he played in society. During nearly sixty
The Social years he was the king of such gatherings as the salons
Lion of Mme de Lambert and of Mme de Geoffrin. He
was a "delicious" talker, an excellent listener, a promoter of
amiable conversation, in which he displayed the prime qualities
of subtlety and skill. The recollections of his youth came to
enhance the triumphs of his age. At ninety-five he was almost
venerated — a monument to be visited, an oracle to be consulted.
He was able to prolong his life, because he cared for his health and
eluded material responsibilities. The decline of vitality in him
was almost imperceptible and he died in the odor of serenity.

Poetic and other tributes were showered upon his memory to a fantastic extent.

Yet the character of the man is not sympathetic. La Bruyère's " portrait " of him, under the name of Cydias, has been mentioned:

Character

> Prose, vers, que voulez-vous? il réussit également en l'un et en l'autre. . . . Il a un ami qui n'a point d'autre fonction que de le présenter dans les maisons comme homme rare et d'une exquise conversation. . . . Cydias évite uniquement d'être de l'avis de quelqu'un. . . . C'est un composé du pédant et du précieux, en qui néanmoins on n'aperçoit rien de grand que l'opinion qu'il a de lui-même.

Another satirical portrait is to be found in Voltaire's *Micromégas* — where the scientist appears as the Perpetual Secretary of the Academy of Saturn. Fontenelle's best friends, particularly the women, admitted that he had very little heart or soul. His social mildness and amiability adequately veiled his fundamental egotism. The most important work of his life was not the History of Oracles or of the Academy — it was the happiness of M. de Fontenelle. He made no sacrifices either for his friends or for his ideas. He was gallant with women, but as Mme de Lambert complained, he never loved them. An intellectual epicurean, he remained always moderate and cool.

His three chief books have already been mentioned and will shortly be discussed. Besides these, there are such critical essays as the *Réflexions sur la poétique*, also his views on the eclogue and on the Quarrel.[1] He was too much of a *bel esprit* to have the true feeling for antiquity. His notions about the pastoral are that Vergil is too coarse and that country life must be vaguely indicated and conventionalized. The Reflections on Poetry are decidedly prosaic; and Fontenelle's whole attitude towards literature is neo-classical.

Minor Works

The *Dialogues des morts* were composed when Fontenelle was only twenty-six. They are partly " philosophic," with strains of preciousness and gallantry. Sappho and Petrarch's Laura argue about the tender passion in a discursive manner which would have pleased Mlle de Scudéry more

" Dialogues des morts "

[1] See above, Bk. I, Ch. I.

than Petrarch. In fact, few of these historical personages really speak for themselves or their age; they are modernized mouthpieces and they are much too witty. Subtle always and occasionally profound, the book swarms with ideas thrown out with youthful abandon. The dialogue is often quite engaging, and Fontenelle cleverly pairs off striking contrasts: Anacreon converses with Aristotle, Scarron with Seneca, Phryne with Alexander. They all argue indefinitely because — and here is the philosophical importance of the book — the method employed is still the Cartesian analysis as regards intellectual matters.

The *Histoire des oracles* went through five editions by 1707. After Bayle, this book is the first indirect attack of the new **"Histoire des** spirit on Catholic orthodoxy. Its arrangement and **oracles"** composition are done with skill. It is mainly a **(1686)** translation and digest of a learned Latin work by a certain Van Dale. Fontenelle accepts the latter's view that the common opinions about pagan oracles, first that they were inspired by demons and second that they ceased with the coming of Christ, are false. But the bulky arguments of the original are condensed, illustrated, linked together and written up with clearness and charm. Nowhere did Fontenelle's intelligence find a happier field. He formally recognizes the truth of Christianity and even the probable existence of demons, but such statements of conviction could barely deceive his contemporaries. He begins very soon to bring forward arguments against the behavior of the early Christians and the authority of the church fathers. The authority of the ancients, of course, is exposed to frequent sarcasms. What does hold for Fontenelle is the scientific method, and that is a question of facts and deductions. The ancients were blind enough to believe in the oracles, though fraud was written on the face of them; and the moderns still believe the pseudo-historical things about the oracles that he, Fontenelle, set out to overthrow. In overthrowing them he suggests what he would like to overthrow next; and the hidden moral of the book is, If oracles are contrary to fact, why not miracles?

The *Pluralité des mondes* is still more scientific in content. Its high importance is that it practically begins the popularization of science, which has gone on uninterruptedly ever since. It is the most celebrated and well-timed of Fontenelle's "Pluralité works, and it shows his usual ingenuity in recon- des mondes" ciling learned matters with the requirements of a polite audience, particularly women. The combination is made with an apparent ease and joyousness of execution. His masterly hand smoothes out for the "Marquise" the difficulties of the Copernican universe, passes lightly over details, and dexterously spins into her view the elaborate solar systems. The language is always easily clear and shows at times an amplitude rising to the heights of the subject. Its vigor of vision at the close makes the Marquise implore mercy: "La terre est si effroyable- ment petite." But Fontenelle's constant point is that man is smaller still.

Some of his scientific ideas may be indicated. He believed, as did Bayle, in the fixity of the laws of nature, their necessary Fontenelle's continuity. He was one of the first to promulgate, Ideas before the Academy, that conception of the soli- darity of the sciences, the interdependence of knowledge, which has helped the cause so much. He believed in the progress of this knowledge. Yet there were serious gaps in Fontenelle's literary equipment. He had neither much imagination nor wide observation. His fondness for wit and "ornaments" frequently operated against the best taste and against enthusiasm. His intellectual keenness was sometimes attained at the expense of sentiment and conviction. Finally, he was hampered by pru- dential considerations in the search for and the His Value defense of truth. But he adds to the domain of literature the popularization of scientific facts, and he insists upon their *rapports*. His influence is not easy to estimate, for it is largely diffused; Voltaire, for one, profited by the lessons of Fontenelle. In his line he ranks among the pathfinders of the new century.

CHAPTER II

VOLTAIRE: LITERATURE AND LIFE

THE life of Voltaire (1694–1778) is an epitome of the eighteenth century. Versatility, longevity, great activity — these are the salient characteristics of his career. His incessant energy displays itself no less in literature than in living; in his case the two things are inseparable. No more interesting and representative life was ever lived by a man of letters. To narrate only the chief events and contacts, five periods, of differing length, may be considered. First, his fashionable and tumultuous youth.

Life

He was born in Paris of respectable bourgeois stock on both sides. His father, François Arouet, was an intelligent notary. Arouet *le jeune*, known to the world as Voltaire, was put to school with the Jesuits and then entered a law office. He was also introduced into the brilliant "Société du Temple," a group of free-thinkers founded by Saint-Evremond. The young Arouet began boldly as a poet. He competed for Academy rewards, satirized that body, and won the attention of the Café Procope and the liberal wits. But soon the Regent quietly imprisoned him, in May, 1717. It is with this date that Voltaire's public career really commences. *Œdipe* was already on the boards, and after many intrigues the author was freed from prison in order to get this tragedy acted. Its success was complete and widespread.

Youth

Voltaire took naturally to "la bonne compagnie," which he considered the source of literary reputation. Therefore he usually conciliated this inner circle, and it is to his credit that, by a mixture of cleverness and perseverance, he improved the rank of the *littérateur* during his century. For himself, he saw clearly that social independence needed to be guaranteed practically, and he set about making a large fortune by adroit speculation. We may pass over the details of his

Worldly Success

courtly and theatrical intrigues. Other plays had not duplicated the success of *Œdipe*, but the *Henriade* was soon to appear and attain a vogue astonishing for an epic. So far, Voltaire stood almost entirely for *belles lettres*, being rated at the time of his flight to England as an excellent dramatist and an amusing poet. That flight was caused by a break in the social edifice which he had so carefully built up. He ventured to gibe at a stupid noble, the Chevalier de Rohan. Voltaire was seized and beaten by the lackeys of this lord, who then refused the writer's challenge to a duel and had him shut up in the Bastille. Raging at this second imprisonment and its cause, Voltaire was shortly released. But in order to spare the Chevalier de Rohan, the authorities decided to exile the poet. He embarked for England, with mingled feelings of bitterness and eagerness, ready for the strongest intellectual influence of his life. This was probably in May, 1726, when Voltaire was in his thirty-second year.

The sojourn in England constitutes the second important phase in his life, and its significance is out of proportion to its brevity. The dates are still subject to dispute, but it is prob-

England   able that he remained in the country rather more than two years. His contacts were various and fruitful. He had already known Bolingbroke, who counted for so much in his philosophy, and with whom he now spent some time. Among other writers who entertained and influenced him were Pope and Swift. His interest in Locke and Newton shaped his practical philosophy, the leaders among the Deists made him a partisan of natural religion, association with men of affairs gave him his exaggerated conception of English liberty — free government, free thought and free writing — and his attendance at the theaters resulted in his introduction of Shakespeare into France. He learned the English language and literature fairly well.

His new experiences and ideas were embodied in the *Lettres philosophiques* (1734), which inaugurated the English vogue. He also published, with the aid of clever advertising, the widely popular *Henriade* (1728-30). On the whole, his stay in England sobered his thought and directed more definitely his purpose in the domains of skeptical philosophy, cosmopolitan criticism and dramatic enterprise.

There was an interlude in Paris before fresh exile. We now

find Voltaire producing semi-Shakespearean plays. *Zaïre,* in 1732, swept its author's name, as he said, into the " smoke of vainglory." He had not waited for this tribute to spur him on to the unceasing labor which was the chief merit of his next decade. The *Histoire de Charles XII* appeared. The *Temple du Goût,* a satire in the vein of Pope's *Dunciad,* raised a storm among the critics of the capital.

This opposition may have helped to banish him, but the efficient cause was the publication of the *Lettres philosophiques.*

At Cirey   In 1734, Voltaire, anticipating arrest, had fled to take up his residence at Cirey, a château on the edge of Lorraine. The hostess, Mme du Châtelet, was among the first women of her time in intellect. The connection lasted fourteen years, until her death. It was characterized from the first by comradeship in hard mental labor. The Marquise stood for mathematics and a Leibnizian universe; she also shared Voltaire's interests in Newton and history. Together, they indulged in the fashionable physics, and they had time left over for practical cares and for entertaining. Amateur theatricals were frequently in order, also brilliant suppers and conversation, after the day's work. In spite of his ailing body, Voltaire seems to have had the energy for everything. He called himself " l'éternel malade," but he was also an eternal traveler and busybody. Flying visits to Paris and to provincial courts were slight distractions to his ceaseless productive activity. History, · physics and metaphysics do not destroy his abiding interest in the drama. Several more plays, together with the scandalous *Pucelle,* belong to the early part of this period. Cantos of this mock-epic circulated through Europe long before actual publication.

In 1736 he began the correspondence with Frederick the Great, who took at first the attitude of a humble young Telemachus towards his Mentor. The publication of the flippant *Mondain* sent Voltaire flying from the police into Holland. From his cordial reception there he stole the leisure to print his *Eléments de la Philosophie de Newton* (1738) — and soon he was back at Cirey, entertaining visitors and attacking his enemies. He had a succession of literary quarrels that lasted half a century. The journalist Fréron, later ridiculed as *Frelon,* the hornet, was soon to ply his sting, and the two Rousseaus occupied in turn the post of enemy extraordinary. The skirmishing with J.-B. Rousseau belongs to these days, as also the bout with the despicable Desfontaines. The latter's *Voltairomanie* was an outbreak of scurrility against more deadly epigram. Shortly afterward, in 1739, the "divine Emilie" (Mme du Châtelet) dragged her friend from the *Siècle de Louis XIV* to a round of festivities in Brussels and then in Paris.

The correspondence with Frederick had gone on, with extravagant compliment and mutual adoration. The Monarch had written a refutation of Machiavelli and then refuted himself and disappointed Voltaire by invading Silesia. But before this the two most remarkable men of their age had arranged a meeting which passed delightfully. *Mahomet* was produced in Paris (1741) and met with great applause, until its attacks on fanaticism were twisted by enemies into the semblance of "infamous blasphemy." The authorities once more intervened, and Voltaire left the city in disgust. But he soon tried again with *Mérope*, which gave him one of the most dazzling *premières* on record.

It is about this time that Voltaire's fourth phase, combining his Parisian with his Prussian celebrity, may be considered as inaugurated. With his dramatic success and **Paris** with deft religious prostrations and protestations, he made a second bid for the Academy and again failed. He fell back on diplomatic missions to Frederick, sanctioned by the French court, but at that game the King proved himself far cleverer than Voltaire. In 1745, he was again in Paris with a playlet, won some court favor, superintended festivities and was appointed Historiographer Royal. This wedge once driven in, it was not so hard to win the smiles of the Pompadour and even the benedictions of the Pope, who actually accepted the dedication to *Mahomet*. Finally, Voltaire was elected to the Academy (1746). But falling into disgrace at court, he and the Marquise had to flee overnight. They went into hiding, first at Sceaux, and were later received by the good-natured Stanislaus, King of Lorraine and protector of a handsome guardsman and minor poet called Saint-Lambert. We need not dwell on Mme du Châtelet's infatuation for this lover, her abandonment of Voltaire, his rage and grief, and her death, which was the greatest affliction of his life. He found himself back in Paris, where he set up an establishment with his niece, Mme Denis. He sought distraction in a theater of his own, playing tragedies in opposition to the gloomy Crébillon, discovering the great actor Le Kain. Voltaire's tales were also running through delighted Paris at this period. But Frederick the Great had renewed his invitation, and this time the guest was ready. He obtained an ungracious leave of absence from Louis XV and arrived at Potsdam in July, 1750.

The first months in Prussia were a genuine delight to the two men in Europe who were wholly capable of appreciating each other. Not only was Voltaire lavishly provided for; he was publicly honored and fêted in a way certain to stimulate his vanity and pride. Whole theaters rose at his entrance; royal apartments were given him to work in; royal consorts smilingly excused him from their heavy dinners; and he was the chief light of the royal suppers in that little octagonal room which contained night after night the concentrated wit of Europe. Officially he was Court Chamberlain and the arbiter and polisher of the King's literary endeavors. These varied joys the exile paraded in letters to his niece, but he already doubted if the glory could last.

Prussia

The rift came when the visitor began illegally speculating through the medium of a usurer, whom Voltaire dragged through a rather disgraceful lawsuit. Frederick stood coldly aloof. The quarrel with Maupertuis followed. This eminent if socially stupid mathematician could not get along with Voltaire. He was President of the Berlin Academy and could bear no rival near the throne. Voltaire found his opportunity, satirized Maupertuis in the *Diatribe du docteur Akakia*, and convulsed the court with laughter. Frederick, however, was estranged, and it became necessary for Voltaire to leave. The two parted with the semblance of amity. But at Frankfort Voltaire was arrested by the royal orders and detained several weeks. Possibly through Frederick's influence the return of the native was balked by the French government on the frontier; also a pirated edition of the *Essai sur les mœurs* rendered official opinion in France intractable.

Where was Voltaire to turn? He was now sixty years old. Neither king nor priest in any of the Catholic countries would

Switzerland tolerate him. During the three years that he had spent with Frederick, his literary accomplishment had been slight. The same may be said of his previous courtier-life in Paris. He now wanted leisure, peace and health. He sought them first just outside of Protestant Geneva on the property he called Les Délices; and then at his famous estate of Ferney, which was really in Burgundy, but next to the Swiss frontier. Thither Madame Denis came as his housekeeper, and he rolled up his sleeves for the literary fray.

The *Siècle de Louis XIV* came out in 1751. The pirated version of the *Essai sur les mœurs* called for his own definitive edition, which he delivered in 1756. The same year saw his most earnest philosophical poem — that on the disaster of Lisbon. Two years later the masterpiece of *Candide* appeared. In the meantime, Voltaire's first home had become a rendezvous for the gayer life of Geneva, and he had, as usual, established a private theater. The stricter Calvinists objected, notably J.-J. Rousseau, and Voltaire, after several skirmishes with the Genevans, thought himself happier out of Switzerland. Just across the border, at Ferney, he was henceforth absolutely his own master.

At this point we may pause to consider his strictly belletristic activities, including, where necessary, some few productions of the Ferney period. In the first place, it is evident that such a life will leave its mark on composition, whether in the direction of facility and haste, or of actuality and vitality. The divisions to be dealt with here are poetry, fiction and history. Voltaire's theater, as well as his pamphleteering and *philosophie*, will be treated separately (see Bk. III, Ch. I and Bk. IV, Ch. II).

His poetic, as well as his dramatic performance, follows in the main his theories and corresponds to his nature. In the more serious forms of verse — the epic and the ode — a

Verse constant sense of the rules, combined with a natural lack of elevation, makes for dulness and an absence of warmth. In the lighter genres — epistles, tales or impromptus — Voltaire's gaiety, grace and talent appear unrestrained. Even his correspondence is interlarded with verses. He wrote a great many and of almost every kind: dramatic, epic, mock-epic, narrative, didactic; odes, satires, epistles, critiques, and especially *vers d'occasion*. Some idea of the content and character of his chief works may be given.

La Henriade or *La Ligue,* as it was first called, portrays the period of the religious wars and glorifies the name of Henry IV. Voltaire evidently hoped in this poem to write the great national epic that had been vainly awaited since the time of Ronsard. But it was too late for the indigenous kind of epic, and despite many admirable verses and descriptions, *La Henriade* remains decidedly artificial. Voltaire's odes, for the most part, are cold and restrained; they evince rhetorical preoccupations and that fondness for capitalized abstractions so characteristic of the century. His didactic poems are more important for philosophy than for art. This is seen in *Le Pour et le Contre (Epître à Uranie)*, the *Discours en vers sur l'homme,* the *Poème sur la loi naturelle,* and the famous *Poème sur le désastre de Lisbonne.* Of these, the first and the last show the most fire and finish; the other two, longer, stiffer in style, and perhaps more profound, consist mainly of moralizings in the vein of Pope. The latter's *Dunciad* may also have furnished the idea for Voltaire's *Temple du Goût,* a critique and satire on contemporary letters, written in mingled prose and verse. Addison's *Campaign* probably inspired Voltaire's retort in the *Poème de Fontenoy,* where his muse for once is clearly patriotic. Among his satires may be mentioned *Le Mondain,* or " Apology for Luxury," a subject germane to the spirit of the times.

But it is rather in the hundreds of light verses, loose leaves from his portfolio, that Voltaire's deft hand and ready wit appear. The stanzas and epistles, arising from all sorts of occasions, are addressed to most of the celebrities of the time. Frederick is apostrophized as the " Solomon of the North " and Mme du Châtelet is thus adjured:

> Si vous voulez que j'aime encore,
> Rendez-moi l'âge des amours.

On the bewildered head of Lefranc de Pompignan is heaped a succession of stanzas, beginning respectively with *Pour, Qui,*

Quand, etc. — a rapid fire of impudent and stinging wit. The manner is usually the *genre badin,* the light verse of rather free stanzaic form, often epigrammatic and always of a graceful easy flow. The stories in verse are scarcely to be distinguished from the stories in prose, save that in the former the Voltairian qualities are likely to appear with more emphasis on decoration and a frequent suggestion of La Fontaine. Among the most amusing are *Ce qui plaît aux dames* and *La Bégueule.*

The philosophic *contes* in prose are probably, in modern eyes, the best known and best liked portion of Voltaire's work. Ten or twelve of these would constitute the most artistic volume of all his contributions to literature. They are novelized pamphlets — but they are also delightful apologues. The rapidity of action, the brilliancy and potency of style, the shrewd doses of milder philosophy, and the constant play of a laughing intelligence rank these tales among the world's little masterpieces. Objection has been made to the intrusive personality of the author — but his personality is worth intruding. Another reproach is the lack of character-drawing, and it is true that the people are silhouettes, though sharply defined. Judging from several standards of today, particularly that of dramatic concentration, we can see how the tales might have been bettered; but the Oriental apologue of the eighteenth century was a special genre, with rules and practices of its own.

Stories

The usual form, briefly, is this: personages of queer and sometimes symbolic names (Candide, Micromégas) are set to traveling in strange countries; the East is the favorite field, though we may have a Huron in Paris (*L'Ingénu*) or terrestrials in other worlds. Either their experiences are designed to illustrate some one principle dear to the *philosophes* (*Candide*), or there is a succession of skirmishes along philosophic, economic or sociological lines. The eighteenth-century " veil " is thus applied, not only to the (alien) setting, but also to the personages, often disguised acquaintances of Voltaire's, and to the ideas, which are both stated and symbolized. The idea of relativity is constantly present, because of the comparisons involved.

For instance, in the first of the series, *Le Monde comme il va — Vision de Babouc,* Persepolis represents Paris, and the question of destroying the city is posited through a series of tableaux. *Zadig*, drawn from many sources, intimates many morals. Episodes and adventures of the wandering prince, cosmopolitan conversations, a hermit, and detective methods that anticipate Sherlock Holmes — such are the elements that diversify a rambling narrative, whose chief message seems to be that there is much uncertainty in human affairs. *Micromégas* ("The Little-Great One") deals with interstellar visitations and satirizes Fontenelle as the secretary of the Academy of Saturn. It preaches relativity in insisting that size and other apparent advantages are matters of comparison (cf. *Gulliver's Travels*). *Candide* (1758), the most famous exemplar of the *conte philosophique*, is also the most artistically told and unified. The burning earnestness that animated the *Poème sur le désastre de Lisbonne* is still present in *Candide* as a deep, partly hidden ground-tone. The surface of the story reveals the familiar Voltaire — the controlled mockery of an optimism blind in the face of senseless and endless misfortunes, the dazzling wit evidenced in sustained caricature, the spontaneity of handling and the rapidity of movement. The chain of adventures simply shows the travelers as constantly falling from the frying-pan into the fire. The characters stand on their feet here better than elsewhere, particularly Pangloss the Leibnizian, who gives the ironic key to the story by declaring that all is for the best in the best of possible worlds.

The merits of Voltaire's style are conspicuous in these and other *contes*. He mixes the conversational with the dignified Oriental manner, but he stamps all with his own image. The main features of this style are its swiftness, its smoothness and graceful wit. The sentences fly to the mark like poisoned arrows. Voltaire is the ablest manipulator of that *style coupé* which has succeeded to the long sentences and elaborate rhetoric of the previous age.

As historian also, Voltaire still has his interest and value. He added much to historical conception and he relativized much in historical treatment. Before him history had **History** been largely a matter of dry compilations or of rhetorical generalities. Voltaire and Montesquieu show critical care and some modern sense of values. To these qualities they add literary talent and a general appeal, turning history into a notable example of the better side of the salon influence. Voltaire's special achievement was to rationalize the subject and to consider as its chief content the march of human civilization.

With his usual universality, he wrote every kind of history: the annalistic, the biographical, the political and the philosophical. The biographical is brilliantly exhibited in the *Histoire de Charles* XII of Sweden (1731), where Voltaire's mind undergoes and communicates the fascination of the individual leader — a capital illustration of Carlyle's " great man " theory. The narrative and dramatic interest of this kind continues to a considerable extent in Voltaire's masterpiece — the *Siècle de Louis XIV* (1751), where the writer still sees the " enlightened despot " as the main figure of his age. Louis and the able men around him are viewed, however, less as conquerors than as civilizers. It is above all " l'esprit humain," as developed in a great period, that interests Voltaire. Hence his treatment of the epoch, while allowing for biographical data and even court gossip, presents first a large tableau of the political history of the reign, then includes chapters on commerce, sciences, arts, letters and religion. This treatment has been criticized as too analytical and too piecemeal; but it is still largely the procedure of scientific historians today. Voltaire was particularly qualified to undertake such a survey, and the result is that the *Siècle de Louis XIV*, though in certain ways too panegyrical, is the best work of its peculiar kind in the century. The author here shows tendencies to regard any great age as primarily marked by its successes in literature and the arts; to make reason rather than religion the light of civilization; to view periods not so distinguished as benighted and worthless; and, curiously enough, to exalt the empire of chance, of the small apparently unrelated fact, in human affairs. Such tendencies appear still more conspicuously in the wider scope of the *Essai sur les mœurs et l'esprit des nations* (first ed., 1745–46; more fully, 1756).

This work is a universal history and practically the first history of civilization. Purporting to begin where Bossuet left off, Voltaire yet has much to say, by way of introduction, concerning the ancients and the nations of the Orient. In many respects this book shows its modernity, not only in such ideas as humanitarianism and its estimates of social service, but also in the novelty of its method. For instance, the chance-theory seems here a part of Voltaire's "pyrrhonism" (compare *Le Pyrrhonisme de l'histoire*, 1768), or of the skepticism that makes him doubt the facile explanations of priests and populace, as well as the unsupported testimony of such writers as Tacitus, Bossuet and of course Herodotus. The skeptic is opposed to the inclusion in serious history of various legends and stories, particularly such as seem to debase human nature. Voltaire everywhere recommends the test of natural probability and of sound, sufficient evidence, without party prejudice.

In the *Essai*, the " spirit that denied " sometimes dimmed the author's philosophic view of causes and led him into various forms of injustice toward certain influences. Modern progress for him starts definitely with the Renaissance. He can appreciate the rôle neither of the early Christians, nor of the perennial Jews, nor of the Middle Ages, with their feudalism, their " horrors and miracles," their greedy Popes, their religious wars and schisms, their crusades, ill-conducted and ill-starred. He simply removes the romance from the Middle Ages and considers them as almost wholly " barbarous." Voltaire is often occupied with wilfully smashing windows. Otherwise, the treatise gives a fairly spaced view of the past; it has been called a monument to the spirit of humanity, which Voltaire deems " greater than the Pyramids "; and its influence and utility are alike indisputable. It subordinates, of course, Bossuet's Providence as a manipulator of history, it shows the preponderant importance of *les mœurs*, of industrial and cultural manifestations, it often gives a panorama rather than a profound explanation of the course of empire, and it offers interesting pictures of the world outside of Europe. Voltaire's hatred of war is pronounced; usefulness to the race is considered the final test for movements and for men.

Voltaire's rationalizing of the Middle Ages, of the miracles and crusades, is akin to the method of modern research, which, however, rises above his prejudices. For in spite of all his cautions about judging each age relatively, by its own purpose rather than by that of another period, he frequently falls into the latter blunder. In virtues and vices he remains intensely *dix-huitième;* and he is too often inaccurate in detail. Yet he gave his century its record of civilization; he thereby stands at the threshold of modern history, and his two main works are still highly considered, though corrected, by the historians of today.

CHAPTER III

MONTESQUIEU

INTO the restless world of the Regency came the old Roman profile and allegiance, the aristocratic temper, the inquiring omnivorous mind of Charles-Louis de Secondat, who **His Career** took the name of Montesquieu (1689–1755). Born near Bordeaux, of a family belonging to the *noblesse de robe*, he underwent the influences of this Gascon heredity and habitat throughout his well-ordered life. He was educated, with emphasis on the Latin classics, by the Jesuits; he was trained in legal procedure, though his interest was rather in the " spirit " of legislation; he entered Parisian circles equipped with those powers of observation and irony which produced the brilliant and iconoclastic *Lettres persanes* (1721). His preoccupation with wit and social satire was further strengthened by his association with the leaders of the salons. All four of these were at various periods of his career among his helpful friends: the Marquise de Lambert pushed him for the Academy, Mme de Tencin addressed him in a tone of intimate raillery, the others placed him among their pet lions. Already at Bordeaux, Montesquieu had indulged in that cultivation of the physical sciences which is at once a sign of the times and of his own positive bent. Now in Paris he attends the Club de l'Entresol (see below, p. 409), an organization for political discussion. These two interests, especially the political, were newly and vitally stirred by Montesquieu's travels, which began in 1728, after his election to the Academy, and ended three years later in England.

This sojourn in England represents a turning-point in his thought. As in the case of Voltaire, what had been held in solution was now precipitated, and the result in each case is a fresh and significant conception of liberty. Returning to France, Montesquieu divides his time between Paris and his

estate of La Brède, shows his practical sense in the administration of the latter, disposes of his " charge " as President of the
Bordeaux Parliament, and concentrates more and more on his
masterpieces. The *Grandeur et décadence des Romains* (1734)
was probably largely conceived before his trip to England.
The *Esprit des lois* (1748) was the result of two laborious decades, varied only by occasional journeys or visits .and the
usual cares of life.

The Latin characteristics of Montesquieu are amply evidenced
by contemporary testimony and his own aptitudes. But he is
His an " old Roman " crossed with a Gascon magis-
Personality trate. The first appears in the stoicism which
makes him reserved in emotion, which leads him to justify
suicide, and stamps his correspondence as less expansive than
that of his friends. The Gascon appears in a more natural,
though frequently checked, disposition toward liveliness and
exaggeration in expression. The magistrate appears in his
domestic masterfulness and sense of leadership; the aristocrat,
in his emphasis on heredity and the Parliaments. In fact, he
goes back to the Classic ideal of *l'honnête homme*, ripened by
many contacts and tastes, holding to standards of moderation
and virtue, not without his point of pride. More in the spirit
of his own time are his humanitarian qualities and his tendency
to view things from a sociological and philosophic standpoint.

His mind is primarily legal, in that he is accustomed to the
weighing, sifting, and coördinating of evidence. But he is also a
philosophe and a relativist in his concern with the
His Mind new interests, his distrust of the old absolutes of
metaphysics, church and state. More than this — he is the foremost generalizer of his century. No such grasp of principles, no
such display of synthetic ability had yet been known, and Montesquieu is only surpassed by Bayle for wealth and catholicity of
knowledge. History, law, ancient lore, contemporary travels,
physical sciences — the President learned and linked them all
into his system. The search for moral and physical causes impels
all his work. He is an investigator and a spectator first; and then
he is a *philosophe*. Like the leaders of the Renaissance he is
infinitely curious — " that noble curiosity " for more and more
knowledge — and the *Esprit des lois* is once interrupted by a

startling yet characteristic invocation to the Pierian Muses. He has no other sentiment for art than that. He names as " great poets " four philosophic thinkers — Plato, Malebranche, Shaftesbury and Montaigne; his taste is of the colorless neo-classic variety; and positivistic science has now replaced the sweep of the imagination. Yet he is not distracted from " the proper study of mankind." His impressive dominance in half-a-dozen fields of thought will appear from a survey of his works.

The *Lettres persanes* came out anonymously, and as a contemporary prophesied, the book " sold like bread." Better than "**Lettres** any other product of the time, this satire holds the **Persanes**" mirror up to the Regency, faithfully reflecting its (1721) mocking spirit, its license and its ferment. Nothing so daring, so amusing and brilliant, had yet been allowed in print, though many such ideas must have floated among the free-thinkers and the coffee-houses. To such an extent do the *Lettres persanes* crystallize this *frondeur* criticism and revolt that Montesquieu never formally acknowledged the work and in later life seemed ashamed of it.

The sources, in form, are negligible; much of the matter comes from Chardin's *Voyages en Perse*. Montesquieu's plan is that two Persians, Rica and Usbek, visiting Paris, shall write home their apparently naïve and unprejudiced account of French customs. The frame-work is then a veil, similar to that used by Swift and Voltaire, behind which a great many indirect blows can be delivered. Dealing with actualities, the book is partly journalistic; it is partly fiction, in that we have the story of the women whom the Persian travelers left behind them. The harem atmosphere thus introduced is heavy and unwholesome. The illusion of the Oriental viewpoint is, however, skilfully maintained through most of the book. There are also " portraits," in the manner of La Bruyère, of such public figures as the busy inventor, the reporter, the speculators and the dandies. There are certain other Classical and conservative features, seen in the balanced style, the frequent appeal to " reason " and " good sense," the aristocratic contempt for writers, pedants and sycophants, somewhat indiscriminately mingled.

The *Lettres persanes* has its serious as well as its frivolous side. Towards the end, the tone changes and the real importance of the pamphlet appears: it announces not only the *Esprit des lois* but the *esprit* of the century. The book is nearly always forward-looking and often revolutionary.

As regards government, Montesquieu adopts categorically the standpoint of the relativist. "The best government is that which attains its end with the least expenditure of energy."

Ideas   The kinds of governments and their principles are sketched very much as we shall see them in the *Esprit des lois*. Only here it is significant that Montesquieu can imagine all these principles as obtaining in a Republic, which on the whole is the kind of government that he now prefers. He satirizes, not without regret, the failure of the monarchical and aristocratic régime. He sees the French monarchy as degenerate and pleasure-seeking, criticizes Louis XIV, and admits the decline of the aristocracy with impatience and shame.

As regards philosophy, Montesquieu states the ideas of the relativist and the semi-materialist in connection with the varying testimony of the senses and with the persistent intrusion of the ego. The divine order of the universe appears less as a matter of sublime mysteries than as a manifestation of a few immutable — and simple — physical laws. In moral precepts, there is again no absolute. Materialism also shows its head in the emphasis on the bodily " machine " and in several passages concerning the influences of climate and soil, which foreshadow the famous doctrines of the *Esprit des lois*.

Believing apparently in natural religion, Montesquieu, in the *Lettres persanes*, openly assails the foundations of Catholicism, declaring that it can scarcely last five hundred years, that the Pope is an idol worshipped only from habit, that he and the king are simply " two magicians." The writer gibes at nearly all the standard doctrines, berates the theologians, those super-subtle " dervishes," laughs at the Capucin missionaries, takes a fling at the temporal power of the church and anticipates Voltaire's indictment of the terrible religious wars. We have a defense of free-will, as not really discordant with God's power — it is better to follow his precepts than to analyze his cloudy attributes. We have a distinct approach to the method of comparative religion in the passage where a Mohammedan believer condones the Christians. Irony still appears in the treatment of these questions, but there is no flaw in the sincerity with which the author here and elsewhere stands up for the principles of tolerance. In fact, he finds nothing more offensive to the gods than the absence of humanity and equity. Justice tempered with mercy is both divine and human. So a diatribe against the Inquisition is paralleled by one against the cruelty of the Spaniards in the Indies, and Usbek, the author's mouthpiece, regrets the revocation of the Edict of Nantes. The Protestants are defended as useful merchants and artisans, and it is also on grounds of utility that Montesquieu suggests what he later partially retracts — the establishment of several religions in a state.

His whole approach to the religious-question is, indeed, not only from the standpoint of the rationalist, but also from that of the tolerant humanitarian and statesman. It is noticeable that he allows the Troglodytes their own religion, in order to soften manners and to aid virtue. This idea of the creed as serviceable to the state is in accordance with his conception of social solidarity, which lies at the base of the Troglodyte republic. Here all labor for the common interest. It is emphasized that the general aim is not separable, in a " virtuous " state, from the individual good, and such solidarity even reaches the point of communism in Montesquieu's doctrine. However, in answering objections as to the pernicious effect of the " arts " (industries) and inventions, Usbek associates them with the advance of civilization, and maintains that they are desirable chiefly as creating a state of " luxury," needed for the general welfare. This is one of Montesquieu's most idiosyncratic theories.

Such are the main ideas of this remarkably fertile book. Its form has doubtless interfered with a full appreciation of it, especially in our own times. Its fragmentary character, its hop-skip-and-jump manner, its apparently haphazard construction are disconcerting; but it was always Montesquieu's ideal to " provoke thought rather than (mere) reading," to stimulate by alternate piquancy and depth. His lax construction matters less in letters than elsewhere. When the Persian veil is nearly dropped towards the end, we are certainly reading the direct utterances of a very competent thinker. Contemporaries, we are told, pardoned the book's temerities for the sake of its gaieties; today one is disposed to do exactly the contrary.

In 1734 appeared the *Considérations sur les causes de la grandeur des Romains et de leur décadence* — to give the volume "Grandeur et décadence des Romains" its full and exactly appropriate title. Like all of Montesquieu's works, it was issued anonymously, but here, as with the *Esprit des lois*, the authorship was soon apparent and was not denied. The book is a classical masterpiece: classical not only because it is saturated with the spirit of Latin antiquity, but French Classical in that it mirrors the abiding qualities of harmony, proportion, universal truth and dignified style; it is a masterpiece because of these qualities and the correspondingly elevated thought, because for once Montesquieu reaches artistic unity and balance of parts. The history unfolds, indeed, like a Classical tragedy, rising through "grandeur" to fall through "décadence," with Pompey as the climax of the plot. The dramatic value is enhanced by the spectacular, by those visions of men and races which Montesquieu draws with so large a sweep. The Roman side of him is now thoroughly at home, and you feel the spirit that has long known comradeship with Tacitus and Livy, with the imposing austere virtues of the Republic, as well as with the graces of the later orators. In these respects the book looks backward; but it is emphatically of its own century by its method of "considering" history.

Montesquieu is primarily philosophic. He seeks historic truth in the "esprit général," in the movement of profound moral and physical causes. "The general march drags with it all particular incidents." Before him Bossuet almost alone in France had represented a concept of philosophic history. The two men have similar interpretations of many facts, a like admiration for antiquity, a like instinct for historical observation and induction. But they soar as rival eagles. The idea of Providence, the operation of the First Cause dominates the panorama of Bossuet, as God the protagonist dominates the Biblical dramas of Racine. Montesquieu deals only with directly human and natural causes. The power even of the Roman religion is scanted in his survey, which analyses mainly politics, war, the moral status. The reasons for Roman greatness are founded on the wisdom of the citizens and their "virtuous" institutions. The decay of these principles spelled the decay of Rome, which also suffered from the unwieldy extension of the Empire.

The treatment is suitably elevated, somewhat aphoristic, reminiscential of Latin masters, adapting strikingly their figures and vocabulary, eloquent, yet not merely rhetorical. This famous passage will show us Montesquieu on the heights:

> C'est ici qu'il faut se donner le spectacle des choses humaines. Qu'on voie dans l'histoire de Rome, tant de guerres entreprises, tant de sang répandu, tant de peuples détruits, tant de grandes actions, tant de triomphes, tant de politique, de sagesse, de prudence, de constance, de courage; ce projet d'envahir tout, si bien formé, si bien soutenu, si bien fini, à quoi aboutit-il, qu'à assouvir le bonheur de cinq ou six monstres? Quoi! ce sénat n'avait fait évanouir tant de rois que pour tomber lui-même dans le plus bas esclavage de quelques-uns de ses plus indignes citoyens, et s'exterminer par ses propres arrêts! On n'élève donc sa puissance, que pour la voir mieux renversée! Les hommes ne travaillent à augmenter leur pouvoir, que pour le voir tomber contre eux-mêmes, dans de plus heureuses mains!

In handling his sources, Montesquieu is usually careful, stating nothing without authority; he sometimes exaggerates dramatically, but he never simply perverts; yet he is not wholly critical, in the modern sense; he is too respectful of the ancients to question their credibility. Also, he naturally knows little or nothing of epigraphy and archeology. These deficiencies, while rendering the book old-fashioned, do not deprive it of its principal values. Its philosophic method, as concerned with eternal verities, and its consummate literary form remain. The method inspired Gibbon and Buckle, and that modern study of the ancient city by Fustel de Coulanges (see Bk. VIII, Ch. III). Stylistic merits have given this history its place as part of the regular education of French youth.

The *Esprit des lois*, often considered the greatest work of the century, is a book of many facets. Purporting to reveal "L'Esprit des lois" (1748) the relations of laws to natural and social institutions, it really touches upon nearly every department of civilization, nearly every land and time. It originated from a nexus of contemporary discussion and therefore is not " created without a mother," as its author proudly declares. But he gives here the fullest expression of his own mind and doctrine, though much of the latter has been anticipated in the *Lettres persanes*. It is a pity that the *Esprit des lois* is the least well-written among Montesquieu's works, the most poorly composed and directed.

The main intention and divisions are none the less manifest. It expresses essentially the conception of a relativist. Laws may represent a struggle towards the type of " eternal justice," but more apparently they are and should be the reflection of special conditions; or, as Montesquieu's subtitle expresses it, the " spirit " of laws consists in " the *rapport* which they ought to have with the constitution of each government, with its customs, climate, religion, commerce, etc." To these relations he shortly adds other physiographical points, the kind of life led in each country, the degree of liberty allowed, and the interaction of laws among themselves. They are even hazardously defined as *rapports* — " the necessary connections deriving from the nature of things." This idea of a " consensus," of a complex which hangs together in a given civilization, constitutes the chief merit of the book in modern eyes. Rejecting the theory of caprice and relegating that of Providence, Montesquieu, still historical in approach, perceives that behind the code of each country stands its *mœurs* and behind them, " certain moral and physical causes." That is his first great generalization. His second is that the laws appropriate to each country reflect its morale particularly as crystallized in its form of government. The third, especially associated with his name, concerns the theory of climate and other physical forces as variously dominating races and their legislations. All of these are *relative* considerations.

For years, as he tells us, Montesquieu struggled towards these " principles." When the light came, his material fell readily — perhaps too readily — into place; first, along the lines of the division and nature of governments. These he divides into despotic, monarchical and republican, animated respectively by the *principes* of fear, honor and civic virtue. He then proceeds, in the first ten books, to analyze his definitions, in the Cartesian manner, by recording their applications in the fields of education, of civil, formal and penal legislation, sumptuary laws and luxury. A book on the corruption of the principles is followed by a discussion of the connection of laws with militarism.

Two criticisms may at once be made. The fields in which operates the spirit of laws succeed one another, as is evident from the last two sentences, in a disjointed and scrappy manner, without satisfactory exhaustion and coördination. When Montesquieu thought of a fresh *rapport*, he added a new book. This was the method of the works on jurisprudence preceding and partly influencing him. The other objection concerns his division of governments. The traditional and logical division of Aristotle, into governments ruled by one, several or many, is displaced by associating the aristocratic with the democratic kind and by enlarging the one-man government into the two types of monarchy and despotism. The latter is of course a derogation from the former, but Montesquieu here proceeds on historical and spatial rather than on logical grounds. Broadly, by despotic government he always means the Orient, by democratic he means ancient republics, by monarchical he means modern western Europe. The specific modern applications are usually left to the reader. As regards the three *principes* — fear, honor and *vertu*, — they seem in part acceptable, though with limitations which Montesquieu did not seek to impose. In fact, his insistence throughout a good part of the work on returning inappositely to the kinds of government and their principles, results in some distortion and an excess of simplification.

With the eleventh book we have a change of basis, and the influence of Montesquieu's visit to England is readily seen. He is now preaching the English conception of liberty, as embodied in the English constitution, with particular stress on the balance and division of powers. This part of the work is probably the most famous and the most far-reaching in effect. Following Locke with some modifications, Montesquieu urges the conservation of the monarchy by balancing and separating the powers in the three forms with which we are acquainted — legislative, executive and judicial. Two lesser books intervene before we reach his next great contribution. The potency of physical causes appears át its height in the treatment accorded to climate and the nature of the land, as they affect the bodily machine, character, institutions, and hence laws. Certain generalizations here are too hasty, but the main division by zones of climate is notable as influencing Mme de Staël, Buckle and much of modern thought. Yet it is significant that just as Montesquieu sets manners and customs above laws, so he sets moral above physical causes and conceives it to be the legislator's duty frequently to contravene the latter. Polygamy and slavery may have their *raison d'être* in despotism and climate, but they are not therefore desirable.

With Book XIX on the "general spirit" of the nations, the truly vital part of the *Esprit des lois* closes. The rest is more and more rambling, though there are interesting considerations as to evolution, cautious safeguards as to religion, and learned disquisitions on Roman and feudal laws. But the chief points have been made, a sociological method has been inaugurated, and we may group together some of its more forward-looking elements.

First, an attempt has been made to study the psychology of races. Without accepting all of Montesquieu's gleanings from

Results

books of travel, discounting such flights as those to China or Paraguay, allowing for his ignorance of natural history and the great modern democracies, one may yet see the impulsion, in method and in fact, toward a main nineteenth-century preoccupation. Secondly, ideals of tolerance and humanitarianism are conspicuous. Along with despotism, torture and slavery, religious persecution and unnatural usages are accounted for, but ultimately reproved. A faith in progress and a belief in some ordering of the universe are occasionally expressed. Thirdly, jurisprudence is lifted from its dry and dusty tomes to the rank of a human force of the first order. A control of legal forms and influences, making for amelioration, is suggested. If Montesquieu's growing conservatism, manifest also in his attitude towards the monarchy and religion, makes him in the large more static than evolutionary, he yet recognizes development in each legal field or what he calls *révolution*. Finally, a theory of government is combined which will have far-reaching results. Holding to the ideal liberty of a constitutional monarchy, he devises for that a system which has been partially conveyed into the American Constitution. In France, theorists and legislators have made abundant use of this system, which rests essentially on the checking, balancing and separating of the three main powers. Montesquieu thus expanded French literature to include jurisprudence, the science of government and something of political economy. Add to these the treatment of philosophical history initiated by the *Grandeur et décadence des Romains*. Voltaire, in spite of the fact that he and Montesquieu were antipathetic, declared that the latter had " restored to humanity its lost titles." This should mean that the President gave to a skeptical age a rational and casual account of itself, as well as of other periods and their laws.

The handling of these matters is, however, not uniformly successful. The salon taste demanded a certain lightness, wit and spice. Hence the inappropriate insertions, the false starts and the literary caviar which made the *Esprit des lois* more palatable for its contemporaries than for us. Moreover, the work seems rather a collection of notes, shot through with fine speculations, than an organic whole. Montesquieu's style generally is *coupé*, moving by short jerks, dispensing with connectives and transitions, lacking Voltaire's grace. But it is often forceful and brilliant, and in the *Grandeur et décadence des Romains* it can rise to heights of noble declamation.

CHAPTER IV

MISCELLANEOUS WRITERS

UNDER this heading will be treated certain moralists, theorists and memoir-writers, whose work, for the most part, falls within the first half of the century. Few of them are professionally *philosophes*, though the majority are tinctured with the new spirit. They are secondary figures who yet have their importance historically, as well as through their contacts with better-known men. Two *moralistes* who have won an assured place in the records, rather as a matter of personal character than by strictly literary excellence, are Luc de Vauvenargues (1715–47) and the Chancellor d'Aguesseau (1668–1751).

The career of Vauvenargues was almost constantly unfortunate. As a lad he had poor health and received no regular education. He entered the army, and after a brief
Thwarted Career of Vauvenargues brilliant campaign in Italy he was relegated to the dulness of provincial garrisons. He was sent on the ill-fated expedition to Prague (1742), from which he returned with frozen limbs and ruined health. The old Marquis de Mirabeau (Carlyle's " Friend of Man ") and Voltaire were among his protectors and admirers, and the latter tried, unsuccessfully, to launch him in diplomacy. It was through Voltaire's advice that Vauvenargues settled in Paris, but he lived there as a retiring invalid barely two years. He had time to publish a single rather imperfect volume before his death.

Much less than this would have broken a man of average caliber; but it is Vauvenargues' strong mark that he remains always captain of his soul. Serious and religiously minded, his personal force and charm could yet attract a Voltaire and a Marmontel. Successive disillusions, in military life, in diplomatic hopes and in literary output — which he considered as a last resort — only served to temper the well-forged steel of this character. In poverty and agony, his Spartan endurance impressed a lighter age, and he gained from his trials that spirit of elevation, of integrity and serenity, which shines through his writings. These are few in number and mostly unfinished.

His Writings The *Introduction à la connaissance de l'esprit humain* (1746) is not the work of a thoroughly formed philosopher, and though it shows individual penetration and fineness of feeling, it is not a masterpiece. Its chief interest is that it reveals the humanity of Vauvenargues' nature. Coming midway between Pascal and Rousseau, he reacts from the Jansenism of the former in that he maintains the worth of man's endowment in mind, sentiment and passions; he anticipates Rousseau in the predominant rôle given to the feelings and passions, if virtuously directed. " On ne peut être dupe de la vertu " — and the virtue that Vauvenargues most esteemed was magnanimity. His personal ideal was for a career of glory attained through action: " d'employer toutes les activités de son âme dans une carrière sans bornes." This desire is visible in all his work and gives a personal note of endeavor and of disappointment nobly borne to his *Réflexions et Maximes*, where the best of Vauvenargues appears. These contain many excellent judgments both on deeds and books. The writer is more concerned with moral self-perfection than with general *perfectibilité* or progress. Thereby he belongs to the previous century, whose Classic qualities he exemplifies both in spirit and in form. Believing in the harmony of man and nature, his eclectic philosophy tends towards simplicity, moderation and the golden mean. His best pages (and he should be read in selections) are orderly, harmonious, and psychologically penetrating. But too often his maxims are either obscure or obvious and his thought is not wholly reconciled — defects due perhaps to the shortness of his life. As a whole, the work of Vauvenargues presents rather a fine promise than a thorough finish. His philosophical system may be illustrated by his central much-quoted maxim: " Les grandes pensées viennent du cœur." To this a recent writer (Morley) has added the proviso: " Yes, but they must go around by the head."

The Chancellor d'Aguesseau was also a man of excellent virtue, though without Vauvenargues' personal power. Unlike the latter, d'Aguesseau was extremely well educated, long-lived and favored by every advantage of position and circumstance. He came of a good legal stock and was much dominated by the stronger character of his father. His originality was further overlaid by considerable erudition; the Jansenists were his moral masters. He had essentially the judicial mind, excellent on the bench or in directing assemblies, but inapt for closer action. As *procureur-général*, as Chancellor and finally as minister under the Regent, he instituted various wise laws and

D'Aguesseau showed at first a capacity for mediating between the throne and the Parliament. But later he vacillated and lost his power. He was a " good man and magistrate," but not supreme as a writer. His *Mercuriales*, or addresses before the *Parlement* (courts of justice), exhibit a respect for tradition, a mild persuasiveness and a dignified moral tone and style. The style, in fact, is often heavy and slow, an eloquence that resembles a diluted Bossuet or Bourdaloue in its elaborate solemnity. Like Montesquieu, d'Aguesseau had a thorough belief in and respect for Justice, which was his ruling idea both in theory and administration. His *Méditations sur les vraies et les fausses idées de la Justice* are praised by good critics. He shows circumspection rather than vehemence in his manner of writing as in his career. A " chrétien philosophe," he was conservative and Classical both in taste and in morality. As Chancellor, he applied the power of censorship rather severely. Saint-Simon comments on his studious intelligence, his piety and amiability, together with a certain " paresse "; all of these qualities are evidenced in the writings of d'Aguesseau, who was a worthy but not highly interesting figure.

As regards the theory of literature, the final charge of the Moderns was led by Lamotte, whose idea was to rationalize

The Abbé **Du Bos** poetry into prose (see below, Bk. III, Ch. IV). A weightier name is that of the Abbé Du Bos, the friend of Bayle, whom he resembles in the boldness of his criticism and the diversity of his interests. Du Bos touches upon almost every field; history, archeology, political economy, theology, literature and art. His two important works are; *Réflexions critiques sur la poésie et la peinture* (1719) and *L'Histoire de l'Establissement de la Monarchie française dans les Gaules* (1734). As a historian, he is careful in controlling and indicating his sources, and though he was taken to task by Montesquieu for his theories concerning the origin of the French monarchy, the author of *L'Esprit des lois* owes much to his predecessor. As an aesthetic critic, Du Bos follows the Moderns in basing genius on a favorable material environment; but he is opposed to the rationalistic and mathematical conception of beauty which Lamotte and others were propagating; he considers that the aesthetic sense has less to do with the mind than with the body and that it is almost a sixth sense in itself. It is an "immediate and direct perception of the beautiful," which is viewed as a physical emotion. Hence the relativity of aesthetic judgments, dependent (1) on the individual eyes, nerves, etc., of the observer and (2) on variations in climate and atmosphere. The emphasis on climate has long been considered Du Bos' chief contribution, because of its influence on Montesquieu and others. Almost equally valuable is his division of the fields of art and their functions, which leads up to Lessing. And finally, one should stress a sort of experimental attitude towards artistic appreciation. Instead of dogmatizing, Du Bos watches himself and other people "react" in a picture-gallery or at the theater. He amasses significant data from all sources, ancient and modern. He was ahead of his time in his sense of the concrete, and the immediate influence of his *Réflexions* was further limited on account of its badly mixed composition and its poor style. Today he seems a very advanced and realistic thinker.

Equally advanced was the Abbé de Saint-Pierre (not to be confused with the later Bernardin), who had the honor of trying to establish a League to Enforce Peace two hundred years ago. His was the chief voice lifted in behalf of peace between Fénelon and Kant. His own age considered him a kindly harmless Utopian. He was, however, banished from the Academy because of his attacks on the monarchy of Louis XIV. Later he became one of the founders of the Club de l'Entresol (1724), The Club de which has been mentioned in connection with Monl'Entresol tesquieu. This was an informal club for the presentation of papers and for liberal discussion. As a sort of "academy of political and moral sciences," it anticipated, in a milder way, the Jacobin clubs of the Revolution. It met in the house of the Président Hénault, in the apartment (*entresol*) of the Abbé Alary, and among its most important adherents were d'Argenson, who describes it in his memoirs, and for a time Montesquieu and Bolingbroke — about twenty members in all. The reunions lasted seven years and then attracted the attention of the prudent Fleury, who caused the club to be dissolved.

The writings of the "philanthropic Abbé" antedate that period. Among his chief "projects" were the *Discours sur la polysynodie* (1718) and the *Projet de Paix universelle* (1713). There was also a much-needed *Projet de rendre les ducs et pairs utiles*. Whatever the Utopianism of these theories, the first and the last were actually tried out under the Regency (see above, Bk. I, Ch. III). The "polysynodie" was simply the government by councils, in which Saint-Simon participated from a similar desire to make the dukes "useful." Saint-Pierre's various ideas on reform mostly sprang from his tolerance and his humanity. He is credited with creating the word *bienfaisance,* and his whole tendency was toward practical morality and the improvement of society. As regards universal peace, his schemes have a striking similarity with the plans current at present. He pleads for a League of Nations which shall be primarily juridical, extending to governments the civil status and morality of individuals. It should be a permanent association and tribunal, in which the sovereigns figure as perpetual allies, making proportionate contributions to the expenses of maintenance, submitting themselves to the arbitrament of their peers. Where this fails, the force of the League is to be called in for purposes of repression. Armaments should be greatly reduced, and Saint-Pierre tried to make the rulers understand the calamities of war as opposed to the prosperities of peace. The sovereigns are still the leaders and spokesmen, because scarcely any writer could then conceive of popular representation. Esteemed a visionary by his contemporaries, Saint-Pierre should come into his own when his views are realized.

Passing to the memoir-writers, the one who most worthily succeeds Saint-Simon, in individual talent and general interest, is another member of the Entresol group — the Marquis René-Louis Voyer d'Argenson (1694-

[side note: Writings of Saint-Pierre *]*

[side note: On Peace *]*

[side note: The Memoirs of d'Argenson *]*

1757). He is to be distinguished from his father of the same name, a minister of police under the Regency. This d'Argenson, nicknamed " la bête " because of his heavy integrity and lack of suppleness around court, flourished during the best years of Louis XV and was Foreign Secretary about the time of the battle of Fontenoy. His *Mémoires* begin with the death of the Regent and come down to Rousseau. They give a thorough picture of the period, its political and social intrigues, its chief figures, its manners and literature. D'Argenson is not really " bête " at all. He had a bold rich intelligence, if occasionally heavy in manner and style, and he does not lack for wit. His mind goes deep enough to penetrate the people and circumstances around him and it also reaches out to an elevation and an idealism beyond his time. The double value of his memoirs, then, is that they give both political narratives and political views; the worth of his own mind is added to that of his observations on his age. In ideas, he represents the liberals and the *philosophes*, but he had the power and position of a great noble. His program is often prophetic of future reforms, gathering around the idea of philanthropy which he shared with Saint-Pierre. Among the changes that he urged, the substitution of departments for provinces, of prefects for royal intendants, the uniformity of weights and measures, the wider establishment of provincial courts of justice, have all been realized. His main political scheme was to unite the monarchy with popular liberty, especially as represented by the municipalities. He really cared for *le peuple;* he portrays excellently the change in popular sentiment about 1750, and he suggests how the growing inadequacy and despotism of Louis finally turned the people against him. " L'opinion républicaine," according to d'Argenson, was born at that time. He comments on the increase of luxury and license, the advance of materialistic philosophy, the significant hatred of priests. And he foresees and foretells the Revolution. D'Argenson, like Saint-Pierre, was a man of vision. His style is too often cumbersome and incorrect, but it is personal, full of provincial and proverbial expressions, and it is acute in thought if not in form. It shows a blunt honesty like the man himself, without the characteristics that enliven the pages of de Retz or of Saint-Simon.

As a whole, the collected memoirs of the century are imposing in their mass, their interest and their variety. They occupy
Memoirs in General altogether several hundred volumes and no preceding age was so prolific. The greater part of our
knowledge concerning history, society and literature derives
from this source, to which one should add the familiar letters
of the period. The memoirs themselves are divisible into three
interlocking groups: (1) the formal or impersonal correspondences, such as the *Correspondance littéraire* (1753–90) of
Grimm, Diderot and others, which usually circulated in manuscript long before publication; (2) the diary or journal form,
illustrated by that of the lawyer Marais (1715–37); and (3)
memoirs proper, sometimes based on the preceding form. Few
of these productions show real literary excellence, but their value
as furnishing an intimate picture of the times is unrivaled. The
more one studies the eighteenth century, the more one is impressed by the saliency of a few score of names, which recur,
like the reappearing characters of Balzac, in every variety
of writing; in the memoirs, these historic figures are displayed
in undress. Another characteristic is the amount of gossip about
court and capital, which is in evidence everywhere, but particularly in the *correspondances*. This is due to the dearth of
newspapers, which made readers clamor for news from other
sources. Certain illustrations may be given of the three types
of memoirs.

The literary gazette flourished from the time of Bayle to that of
Grimm and Diderot. A lesser but perhaps a more representative
Bachaumont, Marais and Marmontel name is that of Bachaumont, whose *Mémoires secrets
de la République des lettres* cover the period 1762–71.
They were rewritten from the " register " or recorded
conversation (which circulated as *Nouvelles à la main*) of Mme
Doublet's salon, and they are most interesting concerning the influence and apotheosis of Voltaire, the beginnings of Rousseau
and the importance of the Encyclopedia. Their tone is very free:
anecdotes, witticisms and irreverent *chansons*, on the most serious occasions, make us realize the brutality which underlay the
veneer of the century. In his criticism, literary and general,
Bachaumont allies good sense with a taste for progress; he gives
a swift actual view of a literature and a society in the making.

He uses the chronicle form, but for our purpose that class is best represented by the *Journal* of Marais, the " avocat des dames." This is the best reflection of enlightened public opinion under the Regency. A disciple of Bayle, an admirer of Voltaire, Marais had a wide knowledge, frequented the best company, and was strongly Classical in taste. He shows the limited beginnings of liberalism, and, in a style marked by simplicity and irony, he indulges in the usual court gossip, which he informs with the color and movement of life. The third class (memoirs proper) may be illustrated by two names: Duclos and Marmontel. The former, who became royal historiographer, plans to set forth the " history of men and manners " in the first part of the century. He is especially at home in discussing the Regency, the early literary *cafés* and the later salons. Duclos was a penetrating observer and a rude writer, caustic, piquant, " droit et adroit." Marmontel, as we shall see later (Bk. IV, Ch. I), was a milder person, who thought more of his own writings than posterity has been able to do; but in his time he was a very considerable literary figure and his *Mémoires d'un père pour servir à l'instruction de ses enfants* are important as depicting the life of a typical man of letters, his early struggles, his necessary prostrations, especially before the shrine of Mme Geoffrin, and the final savor of success. He gives an agreeable and apparently a faithful picture of the middle years of the century, and a certain complacency in narrating his love-adventures — even to his children — is perhaps as typical as anything else.

Finally, no account of miscellaneous writings would be complete without mentioning the beginnings of journalism (see p. 289). If **Journalism** the work of the *nouvellistes* or news-mongers antedates the modern newspaper, the modern review was initiated by Bayle and was continued, as a summary and criticism of fresh publications by various periodicals. The *Pour et contre* of the Abbé Prévost, the *Journal Etranger* and the *Gazette littéraire de l'Europe* were cosmopolitan reviews. More of a magazine was the (old) *Mercure de France*. Two of the most important journals were the *Journal des Savants* and the *Journal de Trévoux*. But the former was scientific in its interests and the latter strongly clerical in its tendencies. Probably the most representative if not the best of all the literary reviews was

L'Année littéraire, which flourished from 1754 to 1790, largely under the direction of Voltaire's enemy Fréron. . It presents a unity of subject-matter, doctrine and tone, and has been called the most interesting and equitable journal of its time. But Fréron is scarcely more than a fifth-rate critic and his impartiality is injured by his insistence on praising whatever Voltaire dislikes and vice versa. However, he follows the march of ideas to a certain extent, admitting the English influence, showing the pre-romanticism of the public, though ill-disposed toward the *philosophes* and preferring still the absolutism of Classical taste and rules. The many volumes of this review are interesting chiefly as reflecting contemporary tastes, opinions and quarrels.

BOOK III

THE OLD AND THE NEW GENRES

CHAPTER I

TRAGEDY: VOLTAIRE, CREBILLON, DUCIS

THE most important art form of the eighteenth century, the greatest in contemporary opinion, was still tragedy. But in **Voltaire as** original excellence tragedy was on the decline and **Critic** was becoming more a matter of critical discussion. In dramatic practice as in theory, Voltaire was the leader, and it will be well to state here his general position as a critic. First it is to be remarked that Voltaire was certainly a devotee of good literature. Among his few passions, this was the most lasting; among his few ideals, this was the most conservative. His taste, his belief in Boileau, his worship of Racine, all served to keep him in the beaten track as regards poetic and dramatic principles. Yet his restless curiosity, his devotion to the stage, and particularly his interest in English literature, made him the advocate of certain novelties pronounced for their time.

The *Lettres philosophiques* remains the document which most significantly combines these opposing tendencies. Voltaire's admiration for the English principle of liberty extends in part to English literature. But he prefers the dramatists of the Restoration and the classicists of the Age of Queen Anne — the two currents which were conspicuously French. His attitude toward Shakespeare is characteristic. This author, "barbarous" and "Gothic" as he is, typifies the irregular poetry of the English, by flashes of genius no less than by deserts of darkness. His "monstrous farces called tragedies" have yet their forceful effect. But Voltaire's opinion of Shakespeare became more bitter in his later years. Then he complained regretfully to the

Academy that this " clown " whom he had introduced to the French stage was likely to degrade and denationalize tragedy.

As regards poetry, Voltaire defends that cause against Lamotte, Fontenelle and Montesquieu; and reacting against their Philistinism, he actually swings the pendulum **Poetry** back towards a respect for the Classical tradition of form. The Age of Louis XIV was already endowed for him with that immutable and crystallized excellence which it possesses in the eyes of every " Classical " critic down to our own times. Therefore Voltaire can see little or nothing before that period; the Middle Ages are indeed the Dark Ages, and the word " Gothic," until Chateaubriand, was held a term of reproach. The Voltarian defense of poetry, then, is virtually a defense of Racine. Poetry is compact music. It requires rime and rules, and in the constraint of these the true artist reveals his force. Necessary elements of poetry are harmony, proportion and especially simplicity, which in the great genres should dispense with ornaments and wit. This self-denial Voltaire practices usually in his dramatic work.

Tragedy is the chief subject of his criticism, as it was the most serious field of his imaginative efforts. To consider first his Classical precepts, he urges Racinian technique **Tragedy** as regards the principal dramatic rules, the use of language and versification, the supremacy of the heart-interest. Love, fully depicted and not incidental to the subject, is the tragic passion *par excellence*. Yet love should still be presented as a weakness; and other natural affections — witness *Andromaque* and *Mérope* — can also cause strong emotions. A distinction is made between the rules and the *bienséances*, the mere dramatic proprieties. The latter may vary, but the former are according to " good sense " and are fundamental. Voltaire is neo-classical in the narrow logic with which he upholds and intensifies the unities, as also in his theory of the " difficulté vaincue " — a sort of acrobatic idea that the harder the rime, the better the poet — and in his recommendation of a mannered artistry of language. This last he considers the principal method of outdoing, while elaborating, Racine and Corneille. It is " style " that leads to posterity, and verse, necessary for tragedy, constitutes its chief artistic beauty.

As an innovator, Voltaire derives his ideas mainly from his observation of the English stage and from his personal liking for action. So he discusses and experiments with the use of crowds, with drawing blood on the stage, with ghosts, and generally with more apparatus and "business." The scene should be vast and even picturesque — though only in order better to display the beauty of sentiments and passions. A certain amount of terror may be admitted, the range of subjects should be extended — which he amply did — tragedy should still inspire the love of virtue and public good, to which he characteristically adds, " and the horror of fanaticism."

This body of literary theory scarcely shows Voltaire as an original or systematic critic. His doctrine is puristic and piecemeal, concerned more with details than with the total structure of creative ideas. And it is frequently vitiated by temporary conditions, by journalism or by jealousy of great names. These handicaps appear in the *Commentaire sur Corneille,* which " comments " almost to the exclusion of any broad criticism of that author. Yet Voltaire's judgments, often penetrating in detail and correct in taste, operated through his admirers to make him what he desired to be: the chief literary authority of the century. His criticism remains historically important as typical of that century, as forcing the reaction towards traditional poetry, as establishing a curiosity· about English literature, and particularly as prefacing the new· elements in his own tragedies.

When it comes to the actual writing of plays, Voltaire is divided between his Classical allegiance and his desire to present stirring novelties. Through Shakespeare he **His Dramas** steps forward towards Romanticism, but he is ever looking over his shoulder at Racine. He is essentially a dramatist of neo-classicism, more interesting historically than absolutely. Barring *Zaïre* and one or two others, his plays have little intrinsic appeal today. But they remain the chief tragedies of the eighteenth century. The theater was certainly Voltaire's main ambition, as well as his great pride and passion. He was always ready for amateur theatricals, he discovered and promoted professional talent and he wrote inordinately. He is credited with fifty-three plays, over half of which are tragedies, offering much variety of subjects and scenery. He uses nearly twenty different countries and periods — Greece and her dependencies, Biblical lands, Rome of course, Africa and America, several phases of the Orient and of France. In this respect and in the details of his subjects rather than in their general themes, he broadened the limits of tragedy, which he also romanticized in the directions of intrigue and action. These features will appear from a consideration of his chief plays.

Œdipe (1718) made Voltaire's reputation. The subject is that of the Greek tragedians — the son who has unwittingly slain his father and wedded his mother. The play **" Œdipe "** is neo-classical in two respects: the taste for horrors, for parricide and fratricide particularly, was just being fostered anew by Crébillon; and the heart-interest, overdone by the sentimental Campistron, demanded the introduction, in *Œdipe*, of some love-affair. So Voltaire provided the middle-aged Jocaste with a middle-aged lover and spoiled what is otherwise a well-written and moving drama. A few other, inferior tragedies preceded the visit to England. Returning, Voltaire soon shows the effects of this new interest, possibly in his *Brutus* (1730), and certainly in his imitations of Shakespeare (*La Mort de César* and *Zaïre*, 1732). It is a question of transposing English heroics according to French taste. The first two plays are political tragedies, in which an effort is made to deal greatly with the interests of state. But Voltaire never quite succeeded in this effort and his two dramas, as usual, are important mainly for their minor novelties: shifts of scene, senators in their robes of state, Caesar's blood-besprinkled corpse, many-voiced conspiracies and crowds.

The one unquestionable masterpiece, the happiest combination of old and new tendencies, is *Zaïre*. It is the only play by **" Zaïre "** Voltaire still acted, and it shows an unusual depth and tenderness. For once the author has really steeped himself in his story and characters. The latter are living and sympathetic figures; the former, romantic intrigue though it be, still stirs and seizes with permanent appeal. In fact, the universal qualities of Classic tragedy here make their final sincere appearance, while the depiction of the chivalry and Christianity of the crusaders is a distinct innovation. The subject of the play is sacred and profane love. Zaïre must choose between the claims of patriotic religion, as personified in her father, and her love for the sultan Orosmane, in whose palace she has long been held captive. Becoming jealous of Zaïre's fondness for her brother (a typical *méprise*), Orosmane imitates Othello by slaying his lady-love and himself. But our interest is less in mistakes and recognition-scenes than in the humanity of the emotions and the characters. Zaïre is a charming heroine, and her father, the aged Lusignan, though episodic in his appearance, makes an extraordinary effect of virility and idealism.

Alzire (1736) carries the scene to Peru and depicts the struggle between the cruel Spaniards and the unfortunate chil-

" Alzire " dren of the Incas. The author exhibits his usual brilliancy in the treatment of this attractive novelty, but the action is more clever than probable. Also the Peruvians talk too much like the *philosophes*. In his maneuvres concern-

and ing *Mahomet ou le Fanatisme* (1742), Voltaire
" Mahomet " flattered the Pope into accepting the dedication of a work which contains several veiled attacks on Christianity. *Le Fanatisme* is the truer title, for the personage of Mahomet is traduced historically, whereas his fanaticism and that of his proselytes is much to the fore. This is Voltaire's first big manifesto against intolerance. He seeks to demonstrate that the vice is horrible and that it takes a kind of Tartuffe to be a religious leader.

> Mon triomphe en tout temps est fondé sur l'erreur.

Among Mahomet's own errors may be counted his improbable self-revelation to an enemy; it is also unlikely that all the virtuous people should, without knowing it, be members of one family, for their ultimate disaster. *Mahomet* is not a perfect play, but it is interesting because of its *philosophe* leanings.

Mérope (produced 1743) closes the series of Voltaire's relatively first-class tragedies. He now returns to the classics,

" Mérope " mingling the Greek influence with that of the Italian Maffei, to whom he owes his best strokes. A mother, trying to avenge her son, almost slays him by mistake; and then, to rescue him, she almost marries his would-be assassin. Voltaire portrays maternal love with fair success, but not with the power and penetration shown in *Andromaque*. In comparison, *Mérope* seems cold and not sufficiently stirring, whereas, since maternal love is the only passion depicted, it should be all the more vehement. But simplicity and concentration are for once attained, the language is more carefully chosen, and the construction more satisfactory than usual. Of all Voltaire's tragedies this play suggests best the feeling of ancient doom. *Sémiramis* is significant chiefly as reviving the ghost of *Hamlet*. Of later tragedies, we need mention only the poignant sacrifice of *L'Orphelin de la Chine* (patriotism *versus* parental love) ; and the resuscitation of chivalry again in *Tancrède*, Voltaire's last success. All his principal tragedies belong to the period before the visit to Frederick. After his establishment at Ferney, Voltaire shows less regard for straight drama and more for philosophic propaganda. This element widely affects and usually damages his theater; for the *tragédie philosophique* generalizes its thought, even to the degree of becoming cold and lifeless.

Voltaire's dramatic deficiencies are due partly to the spirit of the age — neo-classicism and " philosophic livery " — partly **Defects** to the nature of the man and the way he wrote. The majority of the tragedies are hastily and feverishly composed. External events hindered concentration and meditation. The failure to attain unified force and excellence is revealed in plot, characterization and style. The first is often a matter of ingenious invention, rather than true creation. Voltaire is fond of painful family situations. He deals with such themes as parricides and dreadful loves, equally dreadful hates, unhappy wives and unfortunate daughters. Voltaire reminds us of Crébillon in the incessant use made of recognition — unlikely incognitos, followed by family reunions, " la voix du sang " suddenly calling out; and of " méprise," the suspension of events through somebody's improbable blindness. These devices are not according to Racine, yet otherwise the form adheres closely to the old Classical lines, and the plots are much hampered by the conventional rules. Voltaire's personal limitations are seen especially in his depiction of characters, who are seldom strongly conceived and individualized. They are remembered, if at all, rather as generalizations than as people. A few of the women escape this censure, but the majority of the characters lack depth and psychological truth, as their actions lack inevitability. They are not objective enough; they are all more or less Voltaire, talking as he talks, thinking as he thinks. They have distinction, but they lack life. The same tendency exists in his style. He aimed at the *style noble* under all circumstances. The care for expression was, in theory, the main thing with Voltaire. He is apt to build a play around its purple passages, and he lacks sustained force. Also, in copying his predecessors, Voltaire tries to weave the embroidery that he recommends, and the product is patchwork. A hemistich of Racine is completed by a banality, a metaphor from Corneille jars with a neo-classic abstraction. At best, Voltaire sought to fuse these elements into a monotonous elegance, a pale poetry that is seldom natural, falling into rhetoric and vagueness.

His more positive merits are that generally he keeps up the dignity, as he strove to keep up the artistry of tragedy; that his
Merits language can sometimes charm our tastes by its reminiscent and suggestive brilliance; that he has written certain fine scenes of tenderness and passion; that he can impart a vivacious color to exotic subjects; above all, that he is rich in dramatic constructions, surprises, sudden *coups de théâtre* and reversals, imbroglios, trenchant solutions of the Gordian knot. He provided more for the eye, more movement and "spectacle," than any one before him. He lacked not so much tragic skill as the tragic soul, the quality of high seriousness.

Much of the romantic side of Voltaire is akin to the work of his predecessor, Prosper Jolyot de Crébillon, whose lurid and
Crébillon unsubstantial melodramas were in great favor during the first part of the century. He represents, however, but a special point in the development of which Voltaire has exhibited the final leisurely curve. The work of Crébillon includes eleven titles, the most significant being *Atrée et Thyeste* (1707) and *Rhadamiste et Zénobie* (1711). He keeps thoroughly to the conventional form of tragedy, but within that form his talent displays itself in several directions. Mistaken identity, recognitions, and tangled family relations constitute nearly the whole of

Crébillon's dramatic system. He was credited, above all things, with stimulating terror, as in his strongest, most "atrocious" play, *Atrée et Thyeste*. This tragedy treats the old subject of the inimical brothers. Thyeste had carried off the wife of Atrée, and Atrée henceforth lives only for vengeance, endeavoring to use for that purpose the (unknown) son of Thyeste. When Crébillon adds the element of Thyeste's daughter, who is unwittingly in love with the son, he furnishes all the data for a typical drama of his school. An extra horror was the cup of filial blood which was too much for neo-classical taste. But the play is written with power and concentration. *Rhadamiste et Zénobie* is even more illustrative. The subject has close analogies with Racine's *Mithridate*. The heroine (disguised, of course) is loved by a whole family, who have been chiefly occupied with murdering her own. There are swelling speeches and occasional inspiration, but the drama is merely melodrama, with practically no truth or life. Crébillon has little depth; he appeals mainly to our curiosity or our shocked sensibilities.

The effort to combine new thrills with old traditions was continued by Jean-François Ducis, who worshiped Shakespeare by the side of Voltaire. An excellent family man and a man of feeling, Ducis thought of himself as a "wild bird" and a rugged oak. His true character and the compulsions of his period appear strikingly in his adaptations of Shakespeare — the first, after Voltaire, that were offered on the French stage, which they held successfully for two generations. Proceeding from partial translations of Shakespeare, Ducis binds and compresses him into the Classical strait-jacket. The results are ludicrous for English readers, but they give a most informing idea of eighteenth-century requirements. In general, since the unity of time is for the most part preserved, the action is much foreshortened, the list of characters is reduced by half, neo-classic verbiage replaces Shakespeare's lines, and his great personages become shadowy and abstract. As novelties, Ducis freely shifts the scene, shows early gropings after setting and stage-directions, and reflects two tendencies peculiar to the progress of the century: long "philosophic" moralizings and a mild-mannered *sensibilité* which prefers happy endings. Of his half-dozen versions, we may mention *Hamlet* (1769), *Le Roi Léar*

(1783), and *Othello* (1792). In this *Othello* there is talk about liberty and equality, a tendency conspicuous in the plays — also contemporary with the Revolution — of M. J. Chénier and of Sébastien Mercier. These two writers represent the last stage of declamatory tragedy. But the Revolution, which changed so much, hardly affected dramatic form. The old Classic tragedy was still played before the red-capped Terrorists and even before the grenadiers of the Empire. That is why the vogue of the three men treated in this chapter lasted well into the nineteenth century and was superseded only by the full advent of Romanticism.

CHAPTER II

COMEDY AND *DRAME*

THE importance of the theater in eighteenth-century life can scarcely be exaggerated.[1] Amateur theatricals were the rage among the upper bourgeois and aristocratic classes. The " Théâtre de la Foire " was the folk-theater for popular entertainments. The two regular establish-ments, the Théâtre-Français and the Théâtre-Italien (as re-vived by the Regent) rivaled each other in exhibiting the works of the chief playwrights. Comedy is a living form, echoing the manners, ideas and conflicts of the time. It is usually satiric, whether in the lighter vein of Regnard and Piron or in the deeper, more universal satire of Lesage and Beaumarchais. The last two writers are the greatest of their age in this field. The plays of other men, bounded by the conventionalities of the form and of the epoch, yet depict that epoch with more super-ficial variety than can be found in any other genre. The socio-historical value of comedy is then to be added to its fluctuating literary merit.

On the threshold of the century are found several transition writers who continue Molière as regards the comedy of manners, of characters, or simply of plot. Regnard (1656–1709) stands for gay intrigue, partly derivable from the old *gaulois* comedy in its free farcical wit. Regnard carries the *comédie-farce* to a high degree of classical finish. He is essentially a fun-maker, and his two main qualities are verve and gaiety. His *Folies amoureuses* and his *Joueur* show that he took neither love nor gambling very seriously. His master-piece is *Le Légataire universel* (1708), which resembles *Le Malade imaginaire*. A hypochondriac seems to be dead and his would-be heirs combine to seize his property, when he astonishes them by coming out of his lethargy. As in so many plays of

Social Significance of Comedy

Regnard

---

[1] See above, Bk. I, Ch. III.

the period, the impudent rapacity of master and valet seemed natural enough to author and audience. Regnard is merely amusing, not original, and not a master either of the *comédie de mœurs* or the *comédie de caractères*.

These two chief kinds of Molièresque comedy were con- tinued by others. There had been some suggestions of them in the work of Dancourt (1661–1725). His titles — **Dancourt** *Les Agioteurs, Les Bourgeoises de qualité*, as well as those which deal with mills and fairs and harvests — show his concern with the middle and lower classes, which he describes in good realistic prose. His sketches have little variety or invention in plot, but they exhibit well the decadence of manners toward the end of Louis XIV's reign; actual figures and events of the time lend some interest to Dancourt's second- rate art. His best play is the *Chevalier à la mode* (1687); it deals with the scrapes of an unprincipled gallant who mingles audaciously two kinds of " affairs " — financial and amorous.

The greatest writer of this transition period is Lesage,[2] whose *Turcaret* really equals Molière's creations. It was pre- ceded (1707) by *Crispin rival de son maître*, which **Lesage** combines a good plot with a new presentation of the perennial valet of comedy. Crispin, instead of supporting his master, rivals him in courtship, less for the sake of the girl than for her dowry and his consequent prestige. Lesage also wrote a great deal for the Théâtre de la Foire, an unliterary exercise which at least taught him easy manipulation of intrigue.

Turcaret (1709) is not, however, primarily a plot-comedy, but a serious satire on manners and an original treatment of a new and lasting type. This is the *traitant*, the **" Turcaret "** unscrupulous financier of the period, who lives by extortion and tries to shine as a spender and a lover. Like Tartuffe, this hypocrite is in the end humiliated by various revelations. His character and environment are built up by a series of firm sure touches, from the excellent exposition through the rounded *dénouement*. Turcaret appears as self-important, grasping, short-sighted and foolish in his love-making, shrewd and cruel in business and family matters. Lesage was offered a large bribe to suppress this portrait of a very actual type,

[2] For biographies of Lesage and Marivaux, see following chapter.

the kind of financier, who, like the Jew of the Middle Ages, seems to have been used and scorned in almost equal proportions.

The picture of society which Lesage presents is not flattering. There is a mixture of classes and ambitions, a feverish desire Social for luxury and money, and a callous lack of any Depiction idealism, particularly in affairs of the heart. There is not a single attractive character in the play, because the women who fool Turcaret are little better than himself, and the servants, as usual, cynically pull the strings. But this masterpiece produces no such impression of conventionality as we find in Regnard and even in Marivaux. It is a genuine expression of life in the domain of high comedy, sustained by a bold realism of colorful language, an authentic crisp wit and a definite air of modernity. The last quality is probably due to the fact that *Turcaret* is the first of the famous money-plays which later figure so notably in dramatic history. Balzac, Augier and Dumas *fils* are the true successors of Lesage in this respect.

Néricault Destouches (1680–1754), the last of the transitional group, brought from England a certain gift for portraying eccentric characters. He stands, indeed, for an Destouches attempt to resuscitate the comedy of character in a serious style; but he also possesses traits which foreshadow the sentimental *comédie larmoyante* and the moralistic *drame*.[3] His characters thus tend to become lay-figures, and his plots, though not badly conducted, contain a good deal of false romanticism, depending on recognition, virtue in danger, virtue rewarded, and so on. The play which marks the advent of the *drame* is *Le Philosophe marié* (1727); but the best comedy of Destouches is rather *Le Glorieux* (1732), where the haughty nobleman is brought low through a series of blows to his pride. " Mon fils est glorieux," says the forgiving father, " mais il a le cœur bon." Intermarriages between classes are again featured here, with much moralizing thereupon.

As the century wears on, the forms of comedy become more Kinds of diverse and numerous. To the staple kinds — the Comedy comedy of character, of manners and of intrigue — are added not only the hybrid *comédie larmoyante,* but such

---

[3] See end of the chapter.

forms as the satirical comedy of personalities (Voltaire's *L'Ecossaise*), the *philosophe* comedy of propaganda (Marivaux' *L'Ile des Esclaves*), finally the political comedy of social revolt (Beaumarchais' *Mariage de Figaro*). On the fringe of the regular drama are to be found marionette plays, coarse burlesques and especially light opera, which in the works of Favart grew as to importance and influence. As to content, *esprit* held the first place in drama, then came philosophic and social discussion, with the note of pathos as a poor third. Several single comedies, of individual merit and of illustrative value, may now be mentioned.

The satirical and personal kind is well illustrated by Palissot's *Les Philosophes* (1760), a group which is directly attacked and **Various Plays** even misrepresented in the play. Sedaine's *Philo-* **and Playlets** *sophe sans le savoir* (1765), which some consider a *drame*, seeks rather to combine two ideals of "philosophy" and good sense in a pleasant and moderate fashion. The sage here is M. Vanderk, a modest and mercantile nobleman who can make his points — for instance, that personal worth is superior to rank — without sermonizing. The thought is embodied in the action, the scenes are climatic, and the characters are true to themselves and to their respective conditions in life. The play is indeed a new and true creation, a model of artistic simplicity and measure, though on a small scale. Piron's sophomoric *La Métromanie* (1738) appeals to young writers rather than to the general public. It is a question of a poet's mania for verse and of the misfortunes which befall his sympathetic personality. But the play has a fine natural style and the wit which was always Piron's gift. Gresset's *Le Méchant* (1745) is equally well written and with a more vigorous touch; it is a genuinely Classical *comédie de caractères* in art and tradition. The "méchant," a type who cannot bear to see other people happy, is duly punished in the end. Molière is Gresset's master, but his playlet, like *Le Glorieux* and *Le Joueur*, is a delicate rather than a deep portrait.

The comedy of eighteenth-century society, together with the century's conception of art, is represented in a new way by Mari- **Marivaux** vaux, who definitely leaves the tradition of Molière and is nearer Racine in his treatment of love. The figures of Marivaux are well matched with the landscapes of Watteau. Delicate ladies and submissive gallants promenade through a " Carte du Tendre," occupying themselves with a subtle form of love-making often expressed in *précieux* language. The servants echo the demeanor and the style of their masters. There is something thin and unsubstantial about these " spiderweb " comedies, as Voltaire called them, in which ghosts of the old régime seem to be treading an eternal minuet. Marivaux gives the illusion of movement without much moving. His plots are slight, consisting of a sort of hurdle race, an accumulation of obstacles to the course of true love. The chief plays all repeat the same theme — " l'éternelle surprise de l'amour " — and it is their weakness that the difficulties would disappear at any moment, if the right word were spoken by the right person. This comedy of cross-purposes is exemplified by *Le Jeu de l'amour et du hasard* (1730), where servants are disguised as masters and vice versa; but each person falls in love according to his or her proper rank, and the deferred revelation of the true status of each constitutes the only suspense in the plot. *Le Legs* (1736) shows a more plausible strife between the pocket-book and the heart; but its action is maintained simply because the timid marquis can scarcely believe that the countess loves him. A similar situation appears in *Les fausses Confidences* (1737). These three are the best-known plays of Marivaux and are still kept in the repertory. They incorporate the tradition of the new Théâtre-Italien, where most of Marivaux was gracefully represented. They are all, in form, conventional prose comedies, with Classical balance of characters and interests. But they have certain conspicuous merits of their own.

" Quand l'amour parle," says one character, " il est le maître; et il parlera." He speaks at length, with a good deal of refined "marivaudage," containing both singularity and sensibility, which the author partly distilled from his

Sentiment

associations with Fontenelle, Lamotte and the salon of Mme de Tencin. It is nearly always a nascent timid love that Marivaux portrays. Its language is respectful and gallant, without passion, and with considerable delicacy.

and Distinction

The women, like Racine's heroines, are well analyzed and differentiated. These Sylvias and Aramintes, as well as the lesser coquettes, are possessed of undeniable charm, and charm in the long run is the master quality of Marivaux. He thereby rises superior to his failings and seems to reflect the fragile graces of his century with a peculiar manner and distinction. And he is a capable artist within his formal range. He really founds the modern drawing-room comedy, as it is later carried on in the work of Musset and of Pailleron.

Pierre Caron de Beaumarchais (1732–1799) was not only the most talented dramatist of his age, but he led a life closely **Life of** associated with his brilliant comedies. Like his **Beaumarchais** own Figaro, Beaumarchais was a veritable jack-of-all-trades. Of humble birth, he appears in turn as a watch-maker, a harpist, a successful candidate for court favor, the husband of wealthy widows, and always a master of intrigue. He was sent on a private mission to Spain. He aided the French Government by adventurous plotting in Holland and Austria. He furnished arms to the American colonists and found difficulty in getting payment. He established a society of dramatic authors and published the first complete edition of Voltaire. He was famous for his law-suits, which he turned, in his eagerly devoured *Mémoires,* to the confusion of the new courts of justice. Always in hot water as regards the authorities and his own finances, he was about to find a secure position when the Revolution over-threw everything. Unscrupulous, ambitious, energetic, gay and kind-hearted, Beaumarchais is one of the most fascinating and representative of eighteenth-century celebrities.

Literature with him, as with his counterpart Sheridan, is quite incidental to the adventure of life. But he had a natural gift for the drama of action, and his two great plays are alive with the personality of their author. These are the *Barbier de Séville* (1775) and the *Mariage de Figaro* (1784). The *Barbier,* which originated from the comic-opera plots of its own time, finds today its natural complement in the music **"Le Barbier** of Rossini. Its plot and most of its characters are **de Séville"** conventional in outline but are vivified by the dex-terity, wit and style of Beaumarchais. It is simply a question of conspiracies and disguises, of a jealous guardian, a pretty ward, a romantic lover and a helpful barber. The characters, however, are cleverly matched, and the scenes — for instance, the famous lesson scene — are conducted with dash and daring.

Beaumarchais' style is original, diversified and witty in the extreme. Above all, he created a new and immortal character in Figaro, who has been called the "*légataire universel* of all the valets of comedy" — Mascarille, Crispin and the rest. He is also, in his unabashed gaiety and his quick resourcefulness, the incarnation of Beaumarchais himself. A self-reliant individual, he is already heard murmuring against various social abuses.

This last feature is much more pronounced in the *Mariage de Figaro,* which though written (1778) shortly after the *Barbier,* **Le Mariage** was long withheld from the stage. It is here that **de Figaro** Beaumarchais turns comedy into "universal satire," into diatribes and insinuations against the lawyers, the courtiers and the privileged classes generally, who, says Figaro, are often inferior to their servants. The characters in the former play reappear, after the passage of time, and the reason for the barber's bitter spirit is that the Count, already weary of his wife, now wishes to seduce Figaro's *fiancée.* The main plot concerns the outwitting of the libertine by Figaro and the women; they use "double-crossing," double disguises and hiding-places, since Beaumarchais could not be content with simplicity. This play is highly elaborated and constructed on a very large scale as regards the number both of personages and of incidents. For example, there is the figure of Chérubin, another new type on the stage, a precocious youth who is in love with every woman and embroils everything. There is the plaintive Marceline, a lady really belonging to the *comédie larmoyante.* There is the act which takes off the courts of justice, as in Rabelais. There is the final garden scene, containing various incognitos and *coups de théâtre,* a bewildering accumulation of incidents and people. All this is far from the reduced size of the regular Classical comedy. In action, the play lives up to its subtitle of "*la folle journée.*" In characterization, the rather cynical development of the persons whom we already know is well marked, and the new figures are equally living. The language is swift and brilliant, even more elliptical, taking more for granted than in the *Barbier.* The *Mariage* "sounds the tocsin of the Revolution," and when one reads Figaro's great monologue in the last act, the wonder is that the play could have been represented at all. For the old order here seems dissolving in immorality, and the new order has insolently announced itself in this comedy, which is on the whole the most remarkable dramatic production of the century. It stands at the confluence of all genres, great and small, and is a résumé of the period, on both the dramatic and the political sides.

The two remaining dramatic forms, of little artistic worth, but of considerable historical importance, are the *comédie larmoyante* and its successor the *drame bourgeois*. The former is thus defined by M. Lanson:

> La comédie larmoyante est un genre intermédiaire entre la comédie et la tragédie, qui introduit les personnages de condition privée, vertueux ou tout près de l'être, dans une action sérieuse, grave, parfois pathétique, et qui nous excite à la vertu en nous attendrissant sur ses infortunes et en nous faisant applaudir à son triomphe. La Chaussée en fut l'inventeur.

Two plays of La Chaussée may be taken as typical of this kind. In *La fausse Antipathie* (1733), two married people who barely knew and heartily disliked each other at first, meet again after a long separation. They do not recognize each other until the " voice of nature " speaks. They are finally reunited after various obstacles and much weeping. The romantic sentimentality of this play pleased the women, and the same quality won a much greater success for the *Préjugé à la mode* of 1735. The aristocratic " prejudice " is that a husband must not admit any fondness for his wife. La Chaussée's husband is not really indifferent; he simply does not wish to seem ridiculous about his wife until jealousy conquers his pose. The wife is " vertueuse et sensible " and naturally loves her husband. The interest of the play is that it reflects a social condition which it helped ameliorate. La Chaussée " turned the woman of the world into a mere woman," capable of serious love. Among his other plays, of less consequence, are *Mélanide* and *L'Ecole des mères*. His chief imitator, curiously enough, was Voltaire, who though he officially scorned the genre, admitted the mixture of tragic and comic, and tried to affect the public in *L'Enfant prodigue* and *Nanine* — the latter a sort of Pamela. These works are scarcely successful, and what is more extraordinary is

La Chaussée

Voltaire

that Voltaire, in pure comedy, is not successful at all. Too
much propaganda and egotism impede his portrayal of character, and his natural wit seems to benefit him little as a
dramatist.

Other characteristics of the *comédie larmoyante* may be mentioned. Even with private domestic life is mingled a shoddy
romanticism of mistakes, disguises, recognitions and misfortunes.

There are practically no villains, since everybody must be virtuous — hence the need for the above devices. The action is
slowly and awkwardly conducted. The characters are seldom set
on their feet, since moral maxims replace analyses of real people.
The depiction of manners is slight and secondary. The real
importance of these plays is in their subjects; they show the
vogue of discussions about morality and virtue; the pleasures
of sensibility; the power, in love and life, attributed to sentimental
goodness; much talk about " nature " and the famous " voix du
sang " which causes recognition between long-lost relatives. In
the drama as a form of art, La Chaussée has scarcely a place;
but he partly expresses contemporary ideas and he paves the way
for Diderot's bolder theories.

Diderot stands for realism on the stage, as in most of his other
work.[4] His various *Entretiens* on the drama (1757 f.) make an
important addition to criticism. His chief prin-
Theories of
Diderot   ciples are: (1) that Classical tragedy is dead and
should be replaced by an intermediate form, serious in tone; (2)
that subjects should be drawn from everyday bourgeois life; (3)
that this life is best represented as a matter of social status or
" condition "; (4) that prose is better than poetry for domestic
drama; (5) that pantomime, tableaux and other aids to action
should be freely used. The last three points represent some
advance on La Chaussée. The result will be the *drame bourgeois*
in its various gradations and with its various nomenclature
(*comédie sérieuse*, etc.). The importance of this theory is that
it came fully into its own through the work of nineteenth-century
Realists.

But the *drame bourgeois* itself, whether handled by Diderot
or Beaumarchais, whether due to the English influence (translations of Edward Moore and of Lillo) or changing under the in-

‹ See Bk. IV, Ch. III.

fluence of Revolutionary propaganda, is of little artistic significance. As a social and historical fact, however, since several
The Drame hundred of these *drames* were produced, the form
Bourgeois has its importance: it shows the growth of bourgeois
class-consciousness and it becomes a vehicle for *philosophes* and
reformers. Fresh feelings and ideas are there, but they are
poorly expressed. Sensibility, morality, and pseudo-romantic
intrigue still dominate and thwart artistic composition. Persistent twaddle, feeble action, deficient observation and characterization deprive the *drame bourgeois* of the necessary dramatic
elements.

CHAPTER III

FICTION: LESAGE, MARIVAUX, PREVOST [1]

It has been said [2] that the whole history of fiction shows the evolution from the impossible, through the improbable and the probable, to the inevitable. If this be true, the transition in France from the improbable to the probable is nearly connected with the transition from the seventeenth to the eighteenth century. The former age barely laid the foundation for the modern " psychological " novel and the novel of manners; the latter saw a very considerable development in these and other kinds. The seventeenth century had rather frowned upon fiction as a light feminine genre not practiced by the ancients; in the eighteenth, we first find professional novelists of repute, and most of the important writers produced fiction of one sort or another.

Progress in this Period appears in left margin beside the above paragraph.

The first great writer of the realistic *roman de mœurs* was Alain-René Lesage (1668–1747), the author of *Gil Blas*. Lesage bridges the two epochs, passing his formative years and producing his early masterpieces under Louis XIV. His Breton birth and rearing have been held responsible for the vein of sturdy independence which marks his character. He stands on his own as a man of letters, seeking no patronage from the aristocracy, whom he freely criticizes. Educated in a Jesuit college at Vannes, he acquired there a wide knowledge of the ancients, whose cause he espoused in the Quarrel. Like so many others he came to Paris to study law, a profession which he soon abandoned for literature. It is worth noting that he married a girl of Spanish descent. He led a modest bourgeois life, not mingling in society nor seeking admission to the Academy; but he came in contact with actors, authors and apparently

Lesage appears in left margin beside the above paragraph.

[1] On seventeenth-century fiction, see Part II, Bk. III, Ch. I and Bk. IV, Ch I; on other eighteenth-century novels, see Part III, Bk. II, Ch. II (Voltaire), Bk.IV, Ch. III and Bk. V, Ch. I (Diderot, Rousseau); for the plays of Lesage and Marivaux, see preceding chapter.

[2] By Professor Brander Matthews

434

financiers, and his most pungent satire is directed against these classes. He cut something of a figure in the *cafés*, where free discussion was allowed. In his old age he retired to Boulogne, where he died.

The best works of Lesage are surrounded by a mass of hack-writing. He translated Spanish novels before writing his own, and even after *Gil Blas* he wrote three inferior romances, largely imitated from the Spanish. Thus it is no wonder that Spanish originals have been found for *Le Diable Boiteux* (1707) and for a part of *Gil Blas*. The former story uses the framework of Guevara's *El Diablo cojuelo:* in each book the devil obliges the hero by unroofing houses and by displaying the lives of the inmates. But the roofs removed by Lesage are Mansard roofs, his **"Le Diable** revelations are essentially Parisian, and this consti-**Boiteux"** tutes the main interest of the story. People were already getting a taste for actuality through the drama, through Dufresny (who anticipates the *Lettres persanes*) and particularly through the increasing editions of La Bruyère's *Caractères*. So the contemporary portraits and events, the scarcely veiled scandals and anecdotes of *Le Diable Boiteux*, as well as its crisp style and wit, immediately ranked Lesage as a successful author.

The same characteristics, as well as a similar looseness of composition, appear in *Gil Blas,* which is a far greater book. **"Gil Blas"** It is in fact a world-book, through the weight of its influence and the variety of its readers, and it has found even more favor abroad than in France. To illustrate, the history of the English novel, from Fielding to Dickens, could hardly be written without some reference to *Gil Blas*. Its own origins are clear: it is in the tradition of the Spanish picaresque romance or rogue-novel; it is also a road-novel, in that it often narrates perambulations and adventures in the open; and it underlies the modern novel of manners, using a Spanish veil to describe and satirize French people and conditions. The work was issued in three sections at widely separated dates (Parts I and II, in 1715; III, in 1724; IV, in 1735), and thus covers the social history of a whole epoch — the decay of Louis XIV, the Regency, and the ministry of Fleury. The first two parts deal more with private life, the last two with political matters and the world at large.

The "question de *Gil Blas*" concerns the extent of its in_debtedness to Spanish sources. Briefly, one-fifth of the book, Sources and especially in its first part, is freely imitated from Composition the *Vida del Escudero Marcos de Obregón* by Vicente Espinel. There are also borrowings from other picaresque novels and still other sources. These partial plagiarisms do not seriously impair the original force and attractiveness of Lesage's treatment. A more serious blot is his lax method of composition. Using the autobiographical form, then almost universal, he narrates the life and adven_tures of his hero, and since this is a road-novel he permits a "good deal of wandering about" in the plot. The author is little concerned with dramatic sequence: events are but loosely strung together by characters who happen to stroll in again, and too much use is made of chance and coincidence. There are two conclusions, very similar in circumstances and effect, at the ends of Parts III and IV respectively. Moreover, Lesage insists on introducing unrelated episodes and inset stories to an extent which reminds one of the *Arabian Nights*, recently (1708 f.) translated into French. Let us relate, suggests the captain in the robbers' cave, "par quel enchainement d'aventures nous avons embrassé notre profession." Thus the reader is off on the trail of Sinbad and easily loses the thread of the main story.

But it may be urged that the story is not the thing with Lesage. He announces his intention to give a succession of Portraits and portraits, a picture of true manners, and to Characters moralize therefrom. These three things he faithfully carries out. The picture is vast and varied. French society, bearing Spanish names, appears in all degrees. Many professions and "humours" are displayed in the portraits of great ladies and ministers of state, of rogues and adventuresses, of doctors, financiers, comedians and authors. Against the last four types the satire of Lesage is particularly directed. The "keys" indicate that Voltaire and Crébillon *fils*, Mme de Lambert and the actor Baron appear in suitable disguises. As a rule the author portrays low and middle-class life rather than the aristocracy; and rather than ideal or elevated characters he sets forth the "average sensual man." Such is the character of the unheroic hero himself. For Gil Blas is essentially an adaptable person, a chameleon who changes with his setting. Like the hero of *Manon Lescaut,* he begins his exploits at the age of seventeen, when moral instability is most excusable. He falls in with and reflects many *milieux* — from that of robbers and lackeys, bohemians and comedians, up to church and court circles. He adopts the vices and devices peculiar to each set, but it has been observed that he is gradually formed by the world and ends as a cautious steward of property. Among the other salient personages are such rascals as Don Rafaél; the vain Archbishop of Granada; Laure, the pretty and piquante adventuress; and the immortal Doctor Sangrado, who bleeds and purges people to death.

If the adventures are unusual — and adventures mostly are — the chief characters are probable and life-like, and the same is true of their environment. Lesage's realism anti-
Realism cipates the modern kind in that he makes much of external things. . " Il voit et il fait voir." Local color appears picturesquely in the use of Spanish words and customs, and Lesage's descriptions generally are picturesque. Furthermore, he seeks the characteristic detail of each person, gives his appropriate physiognomy, gestures and costume. Gil Blas complacently dons and describes his fine clothes. Money is frequently handled and in specific sums. People are seen walking, dressing, traveling and eating; they eat almost as much and as circumstantially as in Dickens; the motto of Lesage, says one critic, might be: " Je mange, donc je suis." There is little description of nature, but interiors, such as the robbers' cave or employers' houses, are given with moderate detail. Catalogues of concrete things are sometimes used, as well as other realistic devices.

Lesage's style is realistic in its simplicity and naturalness. He expresses himself easily, sometimes negligently, in everyday language. Though he was an " Ancient " and strews his book with classical allusions, as well as with abstract moral maxims, he is more like Voltaire in his short sentences, his light ironic touch and his general vivacity, especially in dialogue. Wit he has at command, not in excess, and he condemns the *précieux*. His survey of human weaknesses is abundantly satirical, but seldom bitter and always clean. Like Molière, he has only the average and practical morality of experience. He lacks sentiment, elevation, enthusiasm, which qualities hardly belong to the realistic manner. Lesage is one of the most French of French authors, and *Gil Blas,* thoroughly established as a world classic, remains a most attractive and readable book.

Pierre de Marivaux (1688–1763), as may be judged from his graceful plays, shone as one of the chief lights of the salons.

Marivaux His scintillating wit and preciosity were welcomed by Mme de Lambert and Mme de Tencin. His character was amiable, and in spite of serious financial reverses, he had a reputation for charity. He was successful first through his comedies, particularly at the Théâtre-Italien, less so at the Français, where cabals were formed against him. He also had difficulties with Voltaire and the philosophic party. He belonged to the school of the Moderns, while Fontenelle was among his best friends.

His two important novels are the *Vie de Marianne* (1731–41) and *Le Paysan parvenu* (1735–36). They are both unfinished,

His Fiction autobiographical in form, and, like *Gil Blas,* they relate the rise in fortune of the main character. Marivaux also represents the novel of manners, but he sticks more closely than Lesage to average folk and to every-day happenings rather than adventures. He uses episodes freely and cares little for the action, which he impedes by abundant analyses, moralizings and subtleties. Thus to the *roman de mœurs* he adds features of the modern " psychological " novel. His picture of life is intensive rather than extensive. He lacks the broad grasp of Lesage.

Marianne, at fifty, chatters freely to a friend about her early life — how she was left an orphan in Paris, pursued by an old hypocrite and loved by a young lord, whom she manages finally to marry. This thin substance is filled out by interesting feminine revelations. Marianne frankly confesses and

" Marianne " stages her wiles, coquetries and vanities. Retrospectively, she appears as an " honest " girl, though candidly reckoning on her beauty and vivacity to improve her fortunes. She displays her charms, hand and foot, and her lover, hand and foot, is bound to her chariot. She is a creature of address and finesse, but her conversational style is allowed to include certain subtleties of which Marivaux was more capable than Marianne. The author's main purpose is to study characters and passions, which he analyses both in their motives and consequences.

The counterpart to this work is *Le Paysan parvenu*. Here the *arriviste* is a handsome footman, who rises through the good **"Le Paysan** graces of ladies. Marriage is only one stage in his **parvenu"** career, which is attended by some very shady transactions; these are supposed to be offset by courage and generosity, as well as by an occasional scrupulousness. But this Jacob, as a person, is less acceptable than Marianne; and the novel, in spite of showing more action and alertness, is an inferior composition. Marivaux, like Richardson, was at his best when sympathetically penetrating feminine psychology. There he could distinguish and differentiate; accordingly, the two bourgeoises who fall in love with Jacob are among his cleverest successes. It has been said that Marianne herself personifies an epoch, typifying the reign of woman in society.

Marivaux's fiction has a good deal, though rather less than his drama, of the highly mannered style, to which the term **Marivaux's** "marivaudage" has been applied. This term may **Qualities** now be defined as a subtle preciosity of language and thought, the latter usually necessitating the former. But even where he has the choice, Marivaux prefers the deliberately elaborate to any simple expression. Wit and conceits and a "systematic refinement" of vocabulary make him the embodiment of the new *précieux* spirit for which the salons were responsible. Also he insists on drawing the last drop out of his analyses and putting down what everybody might have thought and said — a habit which makes him the Henry James of his day. The *précieux* effect is particularly visible in the love-making of his plays, which was in accordance with the tradition. With an over-abundance of subtlety and wit, he must be granted a scintillating quality, an amiable irony and a gentle gaiety which help to relieve the strain. But "marivaudage" is best read in small doses. Merely as language, his style, if *recherché* and highly distilled, is elegant, pure and apparently facile. His prose is everywhere most characteristic of eighteenth-century refinement. As a moralist, he shows a " sensibility " which Lesage has not, and a deeper understanding of what then passed as " virtue," as well as of the kind of .gallantry that flourished in the hot-house atmosphere to which he was accustomed. But he has by no means the creative power of Lesage or of Prévost at his best.

Like Lesage, the Abbé Prévost (1697–1763) was a hardworking man of letters, honorably making his way by the varied products **Prévost** of his pen. His youth was stormy and irregular. Destined early for the church, he escaped into the army for a time, probably experienced a deep love-affair, then for seven years sought rest and sanctuary in the order of the Benedictines. Wearying of their strictness, he again escaped, this time to England; there he found his true vocation as a novelist and started his journal *Le Pour et Contre* (see Bk. II, Ch. IV). After more adventures in Holland, he finally (1734) settled in Paris, where he regularized his position with the church and became an unattached abbé. Modest, laborious, endowed with a lively sensibility, he won his place in Parisian society, being respected by Voltaire and received by Mme de Tencin.

Before coming to his fiction, a word should be said about Prévost's miscellaneous writings. He helped the English **Miscellaneous** vogue not only by his journal, but by his excellent **Works** translations of Richardson's novels. These were much admired by the French and started the new currents of sentiment which culminate in Rousseau. Prévost goes farther afield in the compilation called the *Histoire générale des voyages*. Here eighteenth-century exoticism is well displayed as a liking for remote scenes and primitive social conditions. Something of the same trend, combined with a distinct taste for adventure, appears in Prévost's long romances.

The romances have lived chiefly by their names: *Les Mémoires d'un homme de qualité, Le Doyen de Killerine, Cleveland*. They **His** seem now, in spite of some enthusiasts, hopelessly **Secondary** old-fashioned, long-winded and " highly improb- **Romances** able." It is the kind of improbability that especially hurts a novel, because it takes away from the effect of life and adds the effect of ridicule. The plots are full of wild events: murders, shipwrecks, dark deeds, sudden plunges and changes of fortune. The composition is inferior and the psychology quite cloudy; but the romances have their importance as reflecting one taste of the times and as forming the matrix in which is embedded the gem, *Manon Lescaut*. Many characteristics of the latter appear in Prévost's other works: the " dark coloring " of perpetual tragedy, the great place given to passion and feeling, the autobiographical method, the exotic wanderings and particularly that romantic sense of fatality, of the mystery in life which the *philosophes* wholly lacked. " Les philosophes savaient tout sauf le je ne sais quoi " —and Prévost knew that.

Manon Lescaut is, in several respects, the masterpiece of the eighteenth century in fiction and is the first great modern novel " Manon of passion. It is among the most artistically comLescaut " posed, the most harmonized and unified of French novels, comparable in this respect to Flaubert's *Madame Bovary*. It first appeared (1731) as a sort of appendix to the *Mémoires d'un homme de qualité*, but the usual elements of Prévost's fiction are here compounded according to a very different recipe. In the first place, *Manon* is quite short, written concisely and without episodes. In the second place, the action is not mere melodrama, but is dominated by the thoroughly conceived, the living and appealing characters of hero and heroine. Finally, the constant note of pathos is inherent in the story, and the treatment of the heart-interest is superb and inevitable. These varied excellences are probably due to the fact that Prévost himself had lived through a similar experience.

The story, though widely known, may be briefly set forth. The Chevalier des Grieux, a youth of seventeen, falls in love " at first sight " with the adorable Manon. The lovers escape to Paris and for a few weeks live together in ideal bliss. But Manon, though she is fond of the Chevalier, is still fonder of luxury. To keep their establishment going, she yields to the advances of an old nobleman, who causes Des Grieux to be recovered and taken home by his father. The agony of the young lover presently yields to a resigned despair, whereupon he indifferently accepts a theological career. In the course of time, he appears at a public ceremony at Saint-Sulpice. Manon is among the audience and seeks an interview. " Perfide Manon! Perfide! " cries the young man, who is only too soon persuaded that her perfidy is skin-deep and that she really cared for him all the time. Again they elude their elders and find a cottage in the suburbs of Paris. Expenses accumulate, and under the tuition of Lescaut, Manon's rascally brother, Des Grieux becomes a card-sharper. In contrast to this character is Tiberge, the faithful friend to whom Des Grieux often has recourse. Through theft and fire, misfortunes overtake the lovers — and Manon is again ready to deceive the Chevalier with the old nobleman, her first "protector." But it seems better after all that the lovers and Lescaut should deceive and rob the old *roué*. He pursues them and has them shut up in different prisons, from which, employing the usual romantic devices, they presently escape. For a brief time they are again together and happy. Manon even discourages the suit of an Italian prince, but when the son of her first protector makes advances, she once more bids Des Grieux farewell. This would be the third betrayal, but now the Chevalier takes the upper hand and in a tremendous scene reproaches and persuades Manon to leave the young nobleman. They attempt to deceive this youth, dally too long, and are once more arrested. Des Grieux is finally released, but Manon is sent as a convict to America. There her lover accompanies her, both of them in great distress and poverty, and there at last he wins her whole heart for himself. But complications arise, the lovers must flee from New Orleans, and the story closes with their flight into the wilds, Manon's death, and her burial by her devoted and distracted Chevalier.

It is apparent from the above that Prévost has purposely contrasted Des Grieux, who is ever faithful, with Manon, who becomes so only at the end of the story. This "rehabilitation" is due less to the inflaming power of love than to the Chevalier's long devotion and to the shared sorrows in which even Manon has lost her taste for joys. Thus the plot unfolds a tragic accumulation of events, through which rides, even more tragically, the dominant master passion. The chief characters, with all their weaknesses — they are so very young — are exceedingly sympathetic. Manon says little and is scarcely described. But her living figure is placed among the Helens and the Guineveres of immortal legend. Absorbing as the book is in its endless pathos and strong in its delineation of love, the tone is Classically restrained, and uncontrollable passion is still viewed as a frailty rather than a virtue.

Thus the novel as a genre grew decidedly in favor and power during the eighteenth century. It assumed various forms, conforming to changing circles and periods, rather **Summary** than entering on a straightforward development. Realistic with Lesage, realistic and analytical with Marivaux, it becomes almost romantic in the sweet intensity of Prévost's masterpiece. Elsewhere, we shall see the latter strain continued and individualized in Rousseau's *Nouvelle Héloïse*. In the meantime, such *philosophes* as Voltaire had been using the short story for their own purposes. Finally, the scattered and formless fiction of Diderot expresses mainly the exuberant naturalism of his temperament. Propaganda, passion and reality, the eighteenth century had known them all, and the nineteenth will prolong and partially straighten out the twisted skein.

CHAPTER IV

POETRY

For the most part the eighteenth century does not shine in poetry, whether lyric or narrative. Voltaire can be credited with art and talent, and Chénier with a genuine **Two Features** Muse [1]; but apart from these we find throughout the century only third-rate writers. The chief interest in studying them is to observe how their artificial and graceful verse (*vers de société*) reflects the manners of the time; and how the English influence and the growth of the *élégie* led in the second half of the century toward some depiction of nature and emotion. But even in these attempts, mere elegance is the rule, lack of color and inspiration leaves us cold, and not until Chénier do we find any great poetry.

It is in light verse that the age is at its poetic best, and Voltaire is the main representative of this kind. We have **Lamotte** seen that, reacting against Lamotte and Fontenelle, Voltaire at least endeavored to put the writing of verse on an honorable and artistic plane. Lamotte's views about poetry were peculiar and bold; he simply tried to rationalize it into prose. His *Discours* and prefaces show an ingenious and critical mind, which happens to be wrong in most of its decisions. Rationalism and a factual standpoint characterize his combative attitude during the last phase of the Quarrel (1714–16). A modern of the Moderns, Lamotte rejects authority, despises Homer, and declares that reason alone is the judge of " truth." So the " true " language of poetry is prose: rime and rhythm are unessential, the thought-content is the real issue, though some vivacity in images and style is not out of place. Consistent with his paradoxes, Lamotte held that all verse of his contemporaries — and of Racine as well — would lose nothing by being turned into prose. He was

---

[1] For Voltaire, see above, Bk. II, Ch. II.

right as to the majority of his contemporaries, but wrong as to
Racine. And his attempts to bear out his theories resulted in
a translation of the *Iliad*, which is certainly prosaic enough.

Lamotte did not win his main contention, but his and Fontenelle's objections to the " coarseness " of Homer and Theocritus
are significant of the trend of the times. None of
Light Verse the minor poets to be mentioned had any vital contact with nature or with antiquity. " Genius was rare and
affectation common." It was a highly mannered age, and artificial gallantry and veneer stamp its verse as well as its fashions.
The *grand goût* and the controlled emotion of the seventeenth
century are lacking, while a dwindling neo-classicism is even
more conspicuous here than in tragedy. Mythological allusions
appear with a wholly conventional effect, the language is colorless
and much reduced in range, enthusiasm and passion are dis-
countenanced. On the other hand, there is an abundance of
esprit, of irony and piquancy coming suddenly to the fore—trick-
ling, for example, through the verse which Voltaire and Bertin
mingled with their correspondence and condensed in the epigrams
of Piron —

> Ci-gît Piron, qui ne fut rien,
> Pas même Académicien.

The epigram was, in fact, the one form to which the century
could do justice, and its hard glitter, its diamond-like brilliance,
are well represented by Piron, Voltaire and Lebrun. Much
clever satire is found in verse as well as in prose. But satire alone
will not support lyrical flights, of which there were very few. There
was too little inner life and too much social form. Conventional
epistles and odes, faded graces and facile rimes for albums are
found in this boudoir poetry, which amiably pretends to wander
among imaginary islands and temples, and presents ancient figures making modern love.

The elegy, for instance, is not a poem of grief but of gallant
love, inspired mainly by Ovid and Tibullus. The note of epicurean libertinism appears very early, with Chaulieu, who belonged to the Société du Temple and encouraged the young Voltaire. The *Epîtres* and the *Baisers* of Dorat continue this sensualism with a sort of frivolous effervescence. These masters of

gallantry — La Fare, Dorat, Gentil Bernard — show no idealism or faithfulness in their love-affairs. They frankly declare for inconstancy, on either side, as lending an added piquancy to amorous adventures. They mingle wit with their sensuality, as the later elegists try to mingle sentiment. Léonard and Colardeau give rimed versions of the *Temple de Gnide*, that youthful extravagance of Montesquieu. Gresset, who had a graceful talent,

Examples writes a mock-epic on a parrot (*Vert-Vert*). The vindictive Lebrun shows some power and boldness in his would-be Pindaric odes. There are also the pretty fables of Florian, almost the last fabulist, and the odes and hymns of Lefranc de Pompignan, that solemn bore, whom Voltaire unmercifully derided. A swarm of poetasters compose mythological *tableaux* or amorous trifles and describe their excursions to the country.

This last kind of subject has its interest, because it presently becomes associated with the so-called " genre descriptif," which

Thomson and Nature aimed at depicting country life. The English influence largely caused this change of base.[2] Thomson's *Seasons* were first translated in 1759 and were later freely adapted by Saint-Lambert, who induced a considerable vogue in the depiction of nature. Other *Saisons* followed, a series of *Mois* by Roucher, a poem on *Les Jardins* by Delille, who also wrote certain " Georgics " which put him in the front rank of wits. None of these men had any real nature-sense, such as was to be found in England. Saint-Lambert writes amateurishly of the country, as regards either its beauties or its labors, and keeps his eye on Paris most of the time. Roucher shows more personal feeling, and Delille, relatively speaking, had the best descriptive power and charm. But as a rule these writers are superficial and quite neo-classical in their verbiage, since it was still indecent to call a spade a spade, and since rhetoric was still more esteemed than truth. The importance of the movement is that it did to some extent combine with Rousseauism to forward the later Romantic interest in external nature.

Another popular English writer was Young, whose *Night Thoughts* (translated 1769) promoted a certain taste for the pleasures of melancholy; while Macpherson's *Ossian* (tr. 1776 f.)

---

[2] See above, Bk. I, Ch. III.

began to awaken a sympathy for ancient laments and misty land-scapes. It is rather startling to find the old régime, in its last

Young and Melancholy

days, addicted to meditations on solitude, death and tombs. This tendency should not be over-empha-sized, but several poets undoubtedly express a rather poignant and meditative melancholy. In this they pave the way for Lamartine, while in their unfortunate lives and early deaths they offer parallels with Chatterton. Gilbert, who killed himself at thirty-two, is the best case of the poet-martyr. He had a somber enthusiasm, a kind of genius, a strong proud troubled soul. He was a rebel, inveighing against the tastes and abuses of the age. His talent was not wholly formed, showing awkward-ness in the midst of real power. The verses written just before his suicide —

Au banquet de la vie, infortuné convive —

have been called the finest lyric of the century before Chénier. Malfilâtre, who also died young and unformed, had lyric feeling and aimed for true poetic beauties. He shows grace in the ele-giac manner and some descriptive force in his *Narcisse dans l'Ile de Vénus*. Finally, the unfortunate De Bonnard and Léo-nard sound at times the melancholy note in idyll and elegy.

The elegy, indeed, which ran through most of the century, found its culmination and made its greatest impression in the

Parny

work of Parny. It seems significant that the three men who figured best in poetry on the eve of the Revolution were all of exotic birth — Parny and Bertin being natives of the Ile-de-Bourbon and Chénier of Constantinople. Evariste Parny (1753–1814) brought from his Créole birth and breeding a considerable capacity for feeling and expressing pas-sion. He was of lively but sensuous character, leading with his friend Bertin a gay military and social life, studded with various intrigues. The artistic results of these appear in the *Poésies erotiques* of 1778, of which the best are " elegies " in form. In spite of his exotic birth, Parny had little feeling for nature and a frankly material view of love. But though a voluptuary he showed at any rate a certain freshness and eloquence in his ama-tory verses. He is neo-classical, without Chénier's great sense of pagan beauty; but he has facility and an apparent sincerity, and when abandoned by his mistress he writes with an almost passionate despair. Parny is the most harmonious of poets between Racine and Lamartine. He suggested certain moods and measures to the latter poet, but the Créole's Eléonore is far from foreshadowing the Elvire of Lamartine, so greatly does Romantic and idealistic love differ from the eighteenth-century variety. Eléonore is desired simply for herself or rather for the satisfaction she can give her lover; she has no spiritual aura, she is associated neither with religion nor with nature. Parny's best verses are these, *Sur la Mort d'une Jeune Fille:*

> Son âge échappait à l'enfance.
> Riante comme l'innocence,
> Elle avait les traits de l'Amour.
> Quelques mois, quelques jours encore,
> Dans ce cœur pur et sans détour
> Le sentiment allait éclore.
> Mais le ciel avait au trépas
> Condamné ses jeunes appas.
> Au ciel elle a rendu sa vie,
> Et doucement s'est endormie,
> Sans murmurer contre ses lois.
> Ainsi le sourire s'efface;
> Ainsi meurt sans laisser de trace,
> Le chant d'un oiseau dans les bois.

The short life of Bertin was spent mostly in the company of Parny, whom he also followed in imitating ancient elegists. His *Amours* are more elaborate, less natural, and more artistically arranged than Parny's experiences. Sainte-Beuve says

Bertin

with truth that Parny was original and Bertin a talented imitator. But the latter surpasses his friend in depicting both sweethearts and scenery more clearly, giving some fascinating descriptions of the Ile-de-Bourbon, which Parny had neglected. His art is rich and resourceful for his time, but now seems rather too deliberate. Bertin has been called less of a lover than Parny and less of a poet than Chénier.

André Chénier (1762–94), the only great poet of his century, was born of a Greek mother at Constantinople. His brother, Marie-Joseph,[3] was well-known as a dramatist (see Bk. III,

---

[3] Author of the *Chant du Départ;* the other great hymn of the Revolution, *La Marseillaise* (1792), is usually attributed to Rouget de l'Isle.

Pils, "Rouget de l'Isle chantant la Marseillaise"

Ch. I) and went further in his Revolutionary sympathies than did André. The latter knew Greek from his cradle, and his fruit-
André ful studies made of him a genuine representative of
Chénier the antique. As a boy he lived in Languedoc and then tried garrison life, for which he had no taste. About 1783 we find him in Paris, where he knew the sculptor David and others interested in the revival of antiquity. Chénier lived in London for a time, was unhappy there, undertook various travels and finally settled in Paris in 1790. His talent was now fully ma-tured, but his career was soon to be cut short. Enthusiastic at the " dawn " of the Revolution, he later revolted against the excesses of the Jacobins, attacked Robespierre and was con-demned to the guillotine. Before losing his head, he is said to have remarked: " Pourtant j'avais quelque chose là." The " something " was a fresh inspiration for poetry.

Chénier belongs to the stream of truly Classical French poets, which extends from Ronsard through Racine, down to Leconte
His de Lisle. He is not, however, a neo-classicist, but
Classicism goes directly to the Greek. His early work is thoroughly saturated with the spirit of antiquity, as regards both thought and form; he forges for himself a Grecian soul and apprehends nature and humanity from the ancient stand-point. As he matures, modern thoughts and feelings take hold of him and it is chiefly the form that remains Classical. This ideal is crystallized in Chénier's formula:

> Sur des pensers nouveaux faisons des vers antiques.

But always the grave and sober beauty of his verses stamp them like an ancient medallion, and in his interpretation of the Grecian spirit he is of the brotherhood of Keats.

Only a few of Chénier's verses were published during his lifetime, the first collected edition not appearing until 1819.
Poetry: Also much of his work remains in fragmentary
Four Kinds form. What we have may be divided into four sec-tions: the purely antique; the modern antique, including ele-gies; the political; and the philosophical. The first class, simple eclogues and idylls, would be represented by such poems as *La Jeune Tarentine* and *Le Malade*. The elegies, especially those to " Fanny," have a more modern passion and charm.

The political poems, consisting of strong invective and satire, are found in certain *Iambes* and in the well-known verses on the *Jeu de Paume*, which give the early program of the Revolution. The philosophic poetry was to represent the " pensers nouveaux," particularly modern history, science and discoveries. But death intervened, and we have only *L'Invention* and the incomplete *Hermès*. The latter, which is reminiscent of Lucretius, has been called the most promising effort toward a great philosophical poem in French. But most readers will prefer the finished productions, the idylls which exhibit best Chénier's harmonious beauty and his subdued feeling. These qualities may be illustrated from *La Jeune Tarentine:*

> Elle a vécu, ·Myrto, la jeune Tarentine!
> Un vaisseau la portait aux bords de Camarine:
> Là, l'hymen, les chansons, les flûtes, lentement
> Devaient la reconduire au seuil de son amant.
> Une clef vigilante a, pour cette journée,
> Dans le cèdre enfermé sa robe d'hyménée,
> Et l'or dont au festin ses bras seraient parés,
> Et pour ses blonds cheveux les parfums préparés.
> Mais, seule sur la proue, invoquant les étoiles,
> Le vent impétueux qui soufflait dans ses voiles
> L'enveloppe: étonnée et loin des matelots,
> Elle crie, elle tombe, elle est au sein des flots.   .

BOOK IV

THE WAR OF LIBERATION

CHAPTER I

THE ENCYCLOPEDISTS AND THE LATER *PHILOSOPHES*

IF the first half of the century collected much material for the battle of free thought, the second half actually fought the battle. "La Grande Therefore " philosophy " becomes more decidedly Encyclopédie "polemic after 1750. This is apparent both in the (1752–1772) changed tactics of Voltaire (see next chapter) and in the massed formation of the Encyclopedia. The latter has been called the true " center for the history of ideas " during this period. Its two chief tendencies were toward science and liberalism; it was an arsenal of positive knowledge and a rallying-point for skeptical criticism and reform. Appearing at the crucial moment, when all the old loyalties were decidedly shaken, it was from the beginning viewed suspiciously by those in power. To forward its insinuative propaganda, it assembled various writers of note, and it ranks as the first great modern Encyclopedia.

Denis Diderot (see Ch. III, below) was its chief editor. About 1748 a bookseller had proposed to Diderot that Chambers' English *Cyclopedia* be made the basis of a much larger Its History French work. The permission and coöperation of d'Aguesseau were secured. With the support of Mme de Pompadour and in spite of the opposition of the orthodox, seven volumes had appeared by 1757. Then there were various storms, led by the Parliament, abetted by Jansenists and Jesuits, and partly clustering around Dalembert's iconoclastic article on " Genève." Publication was suspended, Voltaire weakened in his adherence, and Dalembert withdrew altogether. But Diderot, with the

451

connivance of the government, carried on the task alone and finished in 1765 the main body of the Encyclopedia, which con_ sisted of seventeen volumes. Later eleven volumes of illustra_ tions were published, and still later a Supplement.

The title-page of the *Encyclopédie* declares that it was under_ taken by "une société de gens de lettres." The contributors
Chief represented every variety of occupation and taste.
Contributors Diderot and Dalembert were, as Voltaire said, the Atlas and the Hercules who carried the weight of this world. Di_ derot's efforts were immense and untiring. Not only was he main editor, but he wrote about five (octavo) volumes as a contributor. These articles are on the most diverse subjects and are not numbered among the best of his writings. Dalem_ bert, the natural son of Mme de Tencin and the great friend of Mlle de Lespinasse, was a geometer by profession, rather more of a precisian and less genial than Diderot. But the two agreed in their main tenets: skepticism as to theology, curiosity con_ cerning knowledge, and propagation of the scientific faith. Da_ lembert was more cautious than Diderot and served as a useful medium of communication with Voltaire and the Academicians. His main contributions were along mathematical lines, and he also wrote the celebrated *Discours préliminaire*, to which we shall return. The Chevalier de Jaucourt, the "jackal of the Encyclopedia," was an indefatigable editor as regards hack- work and also wrote many articles. Voltaire added the luster of his name, wrote several literary articles — for example, "Es- prit" — but became less enthusiastic after the crisis of 1757. The chief critic was Marmontel, *bel esprit* and society man, who had a great reputation in his time, partly from his adroitness in pleasing all parties. His contributions, which are informative and appreciative of novelties, have been mostly collected in his *Eléments de littérature* (1787). Rousseau was used for music; Montesquieu was much quoted on political matters, and his unre- markable *Essai sur le goût* appeared here; Turgot was repre- sented by five excellent articles and also tried to put into prac- tical effect some features of the Encyclopedists, social program. Incidental use was made of Buffon, Duclos and many minor specialists, such as the grammarian Du Marsais, the scientist Formey, and such abbés as Morellet and Mallet for theological

matters. The majority of the contributors, however, were of mediocre caliber.

Certain facts about the Encyclopedia are well stated by Morley. Both Diderot and Dalembert proceeded from Bacon's General classification of knowledge, thus giving a positive Features coherence to the eighteenth-century Enlightenment, which was largely based on Locke's philosophy of sensation. Also the writers constituted a fraternal group, and the work made a popular impression of "universality, of collective and organic doctrine." The attack against the church is conducted cautiously; the writers still use the theological "veil" (in the manner of Bayle and Voltaire) and speak as believers. The fact is that the Encyclopedia stood less against religion than *for* science, especially in its applications to human life. That is why even the court could become interested in the article on "Powder," and according to the anecdote, Louis XV "could not understand why they spoke so ill of this book." The wide popularity and influence of the Encyclopedia are unquestioned. Objective interests tended more and more to possess the mind of man, as mystery and theology were relegated to the background. Morley concludes that "energetic faith in possibilities of social progress has been first reached through the philosophy of sensation and experience," of which, after Voltaire, the Encyclopedists were the widest distributors.

These features can be best exhibited by considering in detail the *Discours préliminaire* and then by discussing the principles The "Discours of the *Encyclopédie* as operative in half-a-dozen fields Préliminaire "of human effort. There are two parts to Dalembert's (1751) *Discours*: a logical distribution followed by an actual history of knowledge. His first step is to examine the "genealogy" and then the filiation of the sciences and arts. Adopting Locke's sensationalism, he gives a rather fanciful picture of the order in which (primitive) mankind arrived at its perceptions. We hear much of the physical and mathematical sciences, to which the later, more humanistic sciences are made relative or subordinate. In fact, Dalembert urges the principle of relativity, especially as regards the interdependence of knowledge (*rapports*), and he believes that all knowledge, including that of the fine arts, is utilitarian at bottom. "Tout s'y rapporte à nos besoins."

With apologies to Bacon, he then draws up his genealogical tree on an *a priori* basis. There is a three-fold division of knowledge according to our faculties: memory produces history; reason, philosophy; and imagination, the fine arts. The subdivisions are according to the degree of spirit and matter in the various fields; so, for instance, history may be subdivided into spiritual (sacred and church), human (civil and literary), and natural history. The three main divisions may also be applied to people, who will then be " érudits, philosophes and beaux esprits." Foreseeing the objections to this systematizing, Dalembert hastens to add that it will not wholly work out in practice; and the stress in the Encyclopedia itself is less on systems than on facts and things.

.Passing to the historical sketch of the growth of knowledge, Dalembert also admits that this will not follow the logical **Historical** *a priori* scheme outlined for primitive man. He **Divisions** gives a "gradation" showing the progress of the human mind, mainly revealed in its geniuses, from the Renaissance down. His main thesis is thus asserted: " On a commencé par l'érudition, continué par les belles lettres et fini par la philosophie." Applied chiefly to modern France, from the sixteenth through the eighteenth centuries, this view has met with general acceptance (by Voltaire, Brunetière, and others). Dalembert is typically *philosophe* in his contempt for the " barbarous " Middle Ages and in his belief that the erudite Renaissance imitation of the ancients was so much loss for the " advancement of reason." He briefly expresses appreciation of the great writers and artists under Louis XIV and then passes to what really interests him, the birth of modern experimental philosophy. Here Bacon, by his method of inquiry, was the immortal founder — though Bacon was scarcely known in France until the Encyclopedists allowed him credit. Locke and Newton gave tangible form to philosophy, which has since invaded literature, not wholly, as Dalembert sees, to the benefit of the latter. He concludes that this process towards a liberalizing philosophy has been a necessary evolution. He agrees with Locke as to the limited extent of our knowledge, and he holds that mathematics offers a higher degree of certitude than any other field.

The *Discours* remains an imposing vestibule to the Encyclopedia, and it represents extremely well the philosophic attitude of the century. Dalembert's geometrical nature impels him towards a cautious balance in thought, as well as a poor and dry appreciation of literature proper. His " arbre encyclopédique," in spite of the fact that it proceeded from Bacon and was finally adopted by Comte, is open to objection. To classify sciences according to our often confused sensations is less satisfactory than to classify them according to their own fields and materials. The latter is real, the former is somewhat arbitrary and anthropomorphic; it was still the tendency of the century — witness Buffon — to relate everything to man. Again, in his devotion to utilitarian knowledge, Dalembert does not see man as poetizing and hence, contrary to Bacon, represents imagination, rather improbably, as the last-born of the faculties. He steadily advocates the treatment of the thing-in-itself, the fact; and often he is able to combine this with a natural and perhaps laudable tendency towards viewing the universe as one great fact; " la nature entière unifiée par la raison humaine " is the supreme object of all *savants* and thinkers.

Criticism of the Discourse

Diderot's Prospectus stresses scientific specialism, Progress, the chain of knowledge. He declares that the articles in the Encyclopedia will be linked by definitions, by manner of treatment and cross-references. He emphasizes the industrial and mechanical arts; he has visited the workshops and acquired much technical information as well as the *planches* or illustrations, which were certainly a notable feature of the Encyclopedia. It will serve, he hopes, as a true library, for consultation rather than reading. All this gives a fair idea, though a somewhat flattering one, of the work itself. The Encyclopedia is by no means exempt from faults. The " tree " of knowledge, which is supposed to help, often hinders the reader by the artificiality of the scheme and its confusions. It serves best when not too closely followed. Also the writing is at times poor and hasty, veritable hack-work; it is often " faked " bodily, copied from various sources of information. Finally, a declamatory tone, a fondness for abstractions and a theoretical primitivism sometimes hurt the sense of the real world which was, on the whole, the chief merit of the Encyclopedists. Diderot's own material is illustrative of these diverse tendencies; it is confused in its standpoints, rambling and without proportion. He copies

Faults of the Encyclopedia

and plagiarizes shamelessly. The work as a whole is badly composed, sometimes incoherent and chaotic. There are many grave errors and contradictions. Simply as scientific matter, not much of the Encyclopedia survives today; but that very fact speaks in favor of the scientific *spirit,* of the actual advancement of learning for which these writers strove. They would have been quite content that their edifice should crumble into ruins on which the masons of the future could rebuild.

The chief currents of the Encyclopedia flowed in these five directions: Science, social questions, politics, religion, literature.

Science, whether pure or applied, was the main pre-**Science** occupation of the contributors. They wished to summarize and popularize useful knowledge. The natural sciences are more to the fore than the humanistic, which were considered derivative. Metaphysics and psychology — the latter term was not yet invented — are poorly treated. But practical subjects, physics and physiology, agriculture, industry and political economy, are dwelt upon at length. Physiology, for instance, is viewed as most important; the doctrine of relativity is applied to the modifications of man through climate and travel. The physics of Newton are used as a basis for the whole work, and the English school generally, coupled with the skeptical method of Bayle and Voltaire, is responsible for the essentially scientific spirit of the Encyclopedists; this is manifest in the search for natural and secondary causes, the use of reason and experiment, the subjection of nature to human ends, the insistence on the solidarity of knowledge and on social progress through Enlightenment.

As regards social investigation and reform, the ideal of the Encyclopedia is practical beneficence. Hence the conception of **Social** " art " as largely industry, the respect demanded for **Reform** artisans, also Diderot's visits to the ateliers and his zeal for the *planches.* Hence the attention paid to the land; the full and clear treatment of agriculture; the exposure of old abuses and privileges, such as the *corvées,* the salt-tax, the hunting reservations; and Turgot's articles on " Fondations " and " Foires." The Encyclopedists demand both material and moral reforms; but they are timid in their insinuations against social and political institutions, and they have a vague and "rudimentary social science." But Quesnay, at least, here lays the foundation of the political economy which was later developed by him and other "Physiocrats." In criminal legislation, the principles of Montesquieu are followed and urged. The aim is not so much punishment of the criminal as prevention of like crimes and the attainment of the "greatest good" socially. This latter principle really obtained in France before it took root in England and is associated with the general humaneness of the Encyclopedists, seen in their opposition to torture and war.

The Encyclopedia devotes some space to political science, and again Montesquieu is the chief source for what concerns the mechanism of government. But in politics proper these writers, like Voltaire, are far from revolutionary. The social reforms mentioned above are simply "recommended" to the powers. The Encyclopedists cleave to the monarchy, to the *philosophe* idea of a beneficent and "enlightened" king. They demand certain liberties for commerce and industry, also civil liberty, that is, equality before the law. It is mainly in their attitude towards the nobility that they anticipate the Revolution. They insist that privileges should be abated and that the *noblesse* should either serve worthily or yield their position.

Politics

The hand of the censor, civil or religious, still weighed heavily at the time of the *Encyclopédie*. Its writers were officially orthodox and hence apparently insincere. One of their main purposes was to "sabrer la théologie," which could be attacked only with elaborate precautions. Their method, then, is indirect and much like that of Bayle. They apparently defend Catholic orthodoxy by granting the truth of all dogmas, of revelation, of sacred history and of miracles. These things belong to the domain of faith (compare Pascal, Bossuet, Voltaire) and not to that of reason. Hence the unreasonableness of dogma is already insinuated. Also the Encyclopedists indulge in violent praise of extreme dogmas, such as that of eternal damnation, thus "refuting by excess of admiration." These specious defenses of religion are little better than falsehoods, especially when displayed in Jesuitical articles, full of faith and unction. In the manner of Voltaire and Montes-

Theology

quieu, the Encyclopedists use foreign creeds to suggest comparative criticism; in the manner of Bayle, they thrust skeptical
arguments into out-of-the-way places and *renvois;* they quote
the feeblest of orthodox proofs, and list, through " impartiality,"
the various objections to Catholicism. These fall under two
main heads, as regards the real purpose of these skeptics: an
opposition to miracles and various dogmas as contrary to immutable nature; an opposition to intolerance and persecution,
as contrary to the principles of humanity. The best and the
sincerest writing of the Encyclopedists is found in the latter connection.

Their literary criticism, though not first-class, is very symptomatic. Here the chief names are Diderot (though his literary
articles are neither numerous nor excellent), de
Literature   Jaucourt, Voltaire, Mallet, Sulzer, a learned German, and especially Marmontel. The minds of these men are
more open to novelties than might be expected. As regards the
ancients, they are opposed to close or superstitious imitation.
As regards aesthetics, they partly follow the *beau idéal* of the
previous century, though with expansion through the use of more
modern *rapports* and material (Diderot and Marmontel). In
discussing genius and taste, they favor some emancipation from
the rules and they demand a larger rôle for imagination and
sensibility; they promote an interest in foreign languages and
literatures; on the whole, however, they chiefly urge the claims
of a useful and moralizing art. In criticizing contemporary
poetry, they protest against its lack of sensibility and its insignificant subject-matter. But they accept the confusion between
poetry and painting, as well as the century's views concerning
pastoral and didactic verse. In the drama, the Encyclopedists,
led by Marmontel, are clearly modern, supporting the reforms
of Voltaire and of Diderot. The *drame bourgeois* is accepted
in its main features — the use of prose, of contemporary average
characters, the rejection of neo-classical artificialities. Generally, more movement is recommended, together with the reform
of stage-setting and of declamation. The Encyclopedists are
partly progressive, because they recognize the decline in *belles
lettres* as due to the decay of the old genres and the rise of
philosophy. They accept the literature of knowledge but wish

at the same time to stimulate the artistic side of literature by the introduction of more spirit and of fresh forms.

The " conquests " of the Encyclopedia, according to its latest historian (Ducros), may be summed up along the three lines of
Three Main " nature, reason, humanity." These principles
Principles obtain in the conflict with the church, in the constructive endeavor to forward the arts and industries, in the approach to science and in the general effort to benefit humanity and knowledge. A reasoned humanitarianism is perhaps the greatest contribution of the Encyclopedists.

The connection of Georges-Louis Leclerc, Comte de Buffon (1707–88), with the Encyclopedia was incidental and rather
Buffon hostile; but his own monumental work is in itself a scientific encyclopedia, with literary aspects, and it may well be considered at this point. Buffon spent much of his life on his country estate in Burgundy; he also traveled abroad and formed relations with English and other scientists; from 1739 to his death he was the director of the Jardin des Plantes (Jardin du Roi), which he made the most valuable collection in Europe. In all of its phases, his life was given over to scientific observation and investigation, although his interest in natural history did not develop until his maturity. His career was laborious and highly honored, his character elevated, his mind a happy blend of the experimenter's zeal and the generalizer's ability.

His *Histoire naturelle* (1749–88) appeared as an official publication based upon the royal collection, owing something to
His Works collaborators and much to correspondents. It consisted of thirty-one volumes, dealing with the earth, man, animals and minerals. The vegetable kingdom was not treated, nor were certain of the smaller animals. Seven supplementary volumes (from 1774) contained the famous *Epoques de la nature*. The *Histoire naturelle* established the fortune and prestige of its chief author and had a wide popularity, five editions being published in Buffon's lifetime. The excellence of the treatment causes the work to rank as another great monument of literary Expansionism. Buffon added to the field of letters a complete natural history of birds and quadrupeds, as well as a fascinating cosmogony in his *Théorie de la terre* and *Les*

Epoques. He thus provided lasting foundations for zoölogy and materials for comparative anatomy; and he drafted that union of paleontology and cosmogony which made the fame of Cuvier. Parts of Buffon's scientific edifice have fallen, but his successors (Cuvier, Lamarck, Geoffroy de Sainte-Hilaire) have built from the débris. The literary features of this vast undertaking consist first in the author's general ideas and then in his style.

His view of the animal kingdom is hampered by anthropomorphism ("Buffon ramène tout à l'homme") and also by a certain indifference to classifications, as regards genus; he establishes the species by the test of self-reproduction and he upholds, on the whole, the immutability of species, though not of "varieties." Thus he both fostered and opposed the doctrine of biological evolution. The major part of the *Histoire* consists of monographs, dealing separately with each animal or substance, to which are added descriptions of experiments and more general *discours*. The monographs are mainly historical and descriptive; beginning with domestic animals, Buffon individualizes the species by the principle of generation and colors the picture by emphasizing human resemblances and moral traits (such as "nobility"); this kind of thing is less valuable than the more distinctive characteristics or habits which Buffon established for each bird or beast. Most valuable are the generalizing passages, and these appear at their height in the *Théorie de la terre* and the later *Epoques de la nature*. Buffon is not concerned with the origin of matter or of life. But continuing the work of various predecessors, especially Leibnitz, he was the first to give a history of the successive stages of the globe. Underlying this are two main theories, scientifically based: that the earth was originally covered with water; and that its interior was composed of fire or molten material. The "Seven Epochs" are then marked by incandescence, cooling off, the deluge, drying off, the great animals, the separation of continents, the appearance of man. The reconstruction of these epochs, the impressive vistas disclosed, the entrance of the great mammals and of man on the pre-historic scene, have remained a part of our cosmic vision.

It is in the broad sweep of such passages, rather than in the decorative tributes to the lion and the horse, that Buffon's style (*le style noble*) attains its full power. He had on this subject convictions which are found in his Academic *Discours sur le style* (1753). The best expression, he held, proceeds from cumulative action, from the forward march of facts **His Style** and ideas; therefore an orderly plan of one's knowledge (cf. Horace) is an understructure essential for good writing. One should aim at warmth rather than wit, and "truth" in style is to be found when it conforms with the subject and with the writer. Hence the celebrated dictum: "Le style c'est l'homme même" — that is, it takes on the coloring of his mind. Finally, Buffon knew that "les ouvrages bien écrits seront les seuls qui passeront à la postérité." His own writings have survived no less for his originative thought than for their excellent presentation, which is vivid in description, pointed and clear in diction, and majestic in panoramic effect.

A few of the later thinkers, who belong rather to the history of philosophy than to that of literature, may be mentioned. **The** Condillac is best known for his *Traité des sensa-* **Idéologues** *tions* (1754), which is fathered by Locke but gives no independent place to reflection. For Condillac derives immediately from the sensations all our experience and thought. He typifies the growth of consciousness by the allegory of a statue endued successively with the various senses and thus awakening into life. The followers of Condillac at the turn of the century — Destutt de Tracy, Volney, Garat, Laplace — were known as "les Idéologues." An earlier writer, C. Helvétius (*De l'esprit,* 1758), also derives all powers of the mind from the senses. The extreme phase of this movement, ending in a materialistic atheism, is found in the *Système de la nature* (1770) and other works by the Baron d'Holbach, who was a considerable figure, both intellectually and socially, in his time. This "gray and ghost-like book," in which the Deity is viewed as an oppressor, was repulsive even to Voltaire. It was more in line with the ideas of Diderot, an intimate of d'Holbach's circle, and it exemplifies one logical extreme of the *philosophe* movement. A more optimistic extreme, the highest loop attained by the theory of Progress, is represented in the theme of the "indefinite perfectibility" of man. This is best expressed by the Marquis de Condorcet, in his *Esquisse d'un Tableau historique des Progrès de l'esprit humain* (1794). It took both courage and conviction for a victim of the Terror, on the verge of suicide, to declare an immutable faith in the possibilities of human progress.

CHAPTER II

VOLTAIRE AT FERNEY:
POLEMICS AND PHILOSOPHY

WE left Voltaire established at Ferney near Geneva. It was on this estate that he passed the fifth and most important phase of **The** his career. His activities became more and more **Patriarch of** varied, his fame was resounding and his influence **Ferney** enormous. Ferney was practically a seigniorial domain, and Voltaire willingly plays the *seigneur*. He promotes agriculture and manufactures, he exempts his subjects from oppressive taxes, he stands firmly for social justice, and he even erects a church. The domain of Ferney still shows many traces of Voltaire's occupancy, and it must have delighted him to maintain and exhibit the beautiful château and grounds. He entertained on a vast scale, for he had now a princely fortune. Ferney was a great resort for literary pilgrims, such as Abbotsford became later. Private theatricals, aided brilliantly by Le Kain and Mlle Clairon, are again a main resource, despite the objections of Rousseau and other Genevans. But the real importance of this period is that Voltaire's skeptical philosophy becomes militant, and all his entertaining, his correspondence and literary activity are directed to one end: to fight the intolerance and superstitions of the Church, to *écraser l'infâme*. This watchword, repeated throughout his correspondence, became the war-cry of the Encyclopedic and philosophic army which King Voltaire directed from his stronghold on the border.

The leader was still in condition to order his hosts. Aging, sickly and emaciated, he complains a great deal of his ailments. **Generous** But they hardly hamper the power of his mind, **Activities** while his productiveness is unabated. It is as an old man, a " patriarch " of seventy or eighty, that Voltaire becomes the intellectual leader of Europe. His acerbity of temper increases; he quarrels with Rousseau and with Haller the naturalist; he cannot let Montesquieu and Crébillon rest in their graves; he is rabid against the crowd of pamphleteers, Fréron and Lefranc de Pompignan, and he descends to a sort of pamphleteering almost on their level. On the other hand, he reaches far and wide as the protector of the unjustly persecuted. He clears the name and memory of the unfortunate Calas family, wrongly accused of murder, and in this connection he writes the celebrated *Traité sur la tolérance* (1763). He awakens civilization to the cruelty shown towards young La Barre, who was executed for free-thinking. In the Sirven affair and in that of Lally-Tolendal, to whom the dying Voltaire wrote almost his last letter, he is still protesting against unjust sentences. The majority of these protests are aimed at the persecutions of the Church, and the majority are successful. More and more Voltaire wins public opinion to his side; he manages now to keep on good terms with sovereigns and ministers, and he acquires the friendship and following of such men as Diderot, Dalembert, Morellet, Marmontel and La Harpe. Certain of these and many others of the philosophic army are frequent visitors at Ferney.

For nearly a generation Voltaire agitated Europe, while steadily keeping away from Paris. But there too his name had come

His Death to be honored. A few years before his death a statue was erected to him, while, later, his bust was crowned by Mlle Clairon. In 1778, the patriarch took his last journey to the city, which now rose up to welcome him. He was fêted like a king at the Academy, at the theater, in public and private gatherings. He literally died of his glory, exhausted by his honors. That was his first " apotheosis "; his second occurred when his ashes were deposited in the Pantheon by the Revolutionists in 1791.

In reckoning with Voltaire's long labors as a *philosophe,* in foreshortening his many repetitions and contradictions, it will often be necessary to distinguish between the works that preceded and those that followed his establishment on the Swiss border. One must bear in mind the concentrated and aggressive spirit that animated his last phase. The form, too, of his Ferney writings indicates their militant character. He keeps up a small fire of pamphlets, of personal attacks, special pleadings and flying leaflets of all sorts. These are usually anonymous, they are unintermittent, they were distributed by thousands, they are vehement and frequently scurrilous in style. Their polemic doctrine is enforced by the enormous mass of his correspondence, running to more than twelve thousand letters, addressed to hundreds of notables and others, and constituting a vivid private history of the times.

The chief works which may be consulted for an understanding of his general ideas are, before 1755: the *Lettres philosophiques,* **Chief** already characterized; the *Traité de Métaphysique,* **Documents** which is the most thorough-going presentation of his earlier creed; such poems as the *Epitre à Uranie* and the *Discours en vers sur l'homme,* which imitates Pope's Deism; and the Introduction to the *Essai sur les mœurs.* The transition period, more serious or pessimistic, may be placed about 1755 and is represented by the *Poème sur le désastre de Lisbonne,* by the *Poème sur la loi naturelle,* and most brilliantly by *Candide.* Belonging to the Ferney period, the important *Traité sur la tolérance* must be emphasized and especially the *Dictionnaire philosophique portatif.* This work, published in numerous editions after 1764, became the handbook of revolutionary skepticism, attracting all classes by the wit and variety of its encyclopedic articles. Further confessions of faith are the *Sermon des cinquante* and *Le philosophe ignorant.* Voltaire's versions of theological and Biblical matters may be illustrated by *Un Chrétien contre six juifs,* the *Examen important de Milord Bolingbroke* and the *Bible enfin expliquée.*

The two fountain-heads for Voltaire's " philosophy " are the Dictionary of Bayle and the work of the English scientists and **Sources of** Deists. Both Bayle and Locke stimulated Voltaire **his** **Philoso-** in the expression of his great principle of tolerance. **phie** The critical method of Bayle, as we have examined it, is transferred freely to the pages of the *Dictionnaire philosophique.* Voltaire, though bolder in polemics, borrows from this predecessor the skeptical use of the interrogation-point in Biblical and historical matters, the rationalization and derogatory treatment of ancient patriarchs and heroes, the art of malicious insinuation, the ironic prostration before faith. From English freethinkers and Deists, such as Bolingbroke, Pope, and Shaftesbury, Voltaire derives most of his " natural religion." From Newton and Locke he gets his taste for the physical sciences, thus strengthening his own tendency towards the experimental method, towards dealing only with demonstrable fact and clear explanations. Locke, the best and " wisest " of philosophers in Voltaire's view, imposed upon the Frenchman his conception of the limitations of knowledge. Voltaire's general Anglomania, quite influential in the France of the earlier eighteenth century, became modified in the course of time, and his zeal for physical experiments dwindled together with his zeal for Shakespeare. But the profound influence of English thought remained with him to the end.

Le vrai philosophe, according to Voltaire, stands for reason, progress, industry and charity; *la philosophie*, in its widest sense, included for him physics and metaphysics, religion and ethics, politics and social reform. We shall consider his doctrine according to these divisions.

His physical experiments had no great value then and can have none today. They are simply important as indicative of the trend of his mind and of his times — a trend well ex-
Physics   emplified by such useful pieces of popularization as his *Eléments de la philosophie de Newton* (1738).

His views on metaphysics, taking form at the same epoch, continue Voltaire's practical and positive bent. It has been argued that his persistent dealing with metaphysical
Metaphysics   inquiries shows that he understood their importance; but this is contradicted in many passages, both by his directly expressed scorn of metaphysics and by the slight aptitude which he exhibited for such problems. No better example can be found than the *Remarques sur Pascal* (1734); here we are offered the most salient contrast between Pascal, the tormented thinker who quivers over the metaphysical " abyss," showing us his soul by lightning flashes, and the clear everyday sense — which is often lack of deeper sense — displayed by Voltaire. This is particularly true of his earlier or optimistic period.

Indeed, Voltaire's great contention is that metaphysical thought leads nowhere. He occasionally admits, though he never feels, that it may have a certain value as a mental gymnastic and even as a means to spiritual elevation. But he scorns the great philosophers, those " romancers of the soul," from Plato to Descartes, and he insists that we can never know the truth about the chief metaphysical problems. Why is this? Because all our knowledge comes from sensation, which can inform us only about the practical world of conduct. Voltaire's sensational philosophy, with regard to which he is very firm, is based on Locke; and he even goes farther than Locke in refusing to put reflection on a par with sensation and in allowing us no ultimate knowledge concerning the processes of the mind itself. He thoroughly rejects the Cartesian doctrine of "innate ideas," as regards any immediate appre-

Skepticism hension of the Deity, the soul, duty, truth. *Le Philosophe ignorant* (1766) is ignorant about the powers of the body and the nature of matter, about free-will, about the attributes of divinity, about the real essence and destiny of man.

We can best understand Voltaire's views on these subjects by bearing in mind that his basic standpoint is practical and social. Only those things are valuable and credible which tend towards the good of society at large. He objects to any "system" of philosophy as unpractical and probably false; and opposite the great interrogations he generally writes the verdict "not proven."

Voltaire defends the existence of the Deity, and therefore he is ranked as a Deist. His arguments are both Cartesian and cosmological. Some God there must be, because my existence presupposes the existence of some intelligence beyond mine (Descartes); and also because the universe demands an architect, as a clock demonstrates a clock-maker. These mechanical figures are frequent on Voltaire's lips. He also holds by the doctrine of final causes, if taken in a common-sense way. The only necessary attributes of Deity are omnipotence (within reason and nature) and absolute justice. This is a distant or "absentee" God, claiming our adoration but not concerned with individual human affairs. There is a general, but no private Providence, and therefore prayers for intercession are useless. The laws of nature are fixed. Morality proceeds less from the Deity than from social necessities. If a "dieu rémunérateur et vengeur" is often mentioned in Voltaire's later writings, it is because he appreciates the social force rather than the ultimate truth of such sanctions. "Il faut une religion pour le peuple." He feels the vastness of Godhead only under the stars, and his Theism at its loftiest is a cosmic Pantheism.

This is a much attenuated Jehovah, and Voltaire's religion — for he had one — is an attenuated religion. He called it "la religion naturelle," after Pope and other Englishmen. He maintains that though " all religions are false, *la religion* is true." But Voltaire had little religious sense, as that term is usually understood. His Theism is stripped bare of the elements commonly constitutive of religions: specific creed, ceremonial, mysticism, the supernatural, revelation, and reckoning with a future life. The soul may be immortal, but Voltaire scarcely holds this belief, admitting it mainly for retributive ends; furthermore, he is disposed to associate a possible immortality with the duration of matter, and thus he also allows animals their share of "la matière pensante." The problem of the existence of evil is, for him, an abyss. In his later writings he inclines towards determinism rather than free-will and towards a pessimism, which, however, admits of betterment. It is also true that in such writings as *Le Philosophe ignorant* he shows a deeper feeling with relation to the mystery of life and the helpless plight of humanity. This feeling involves something of a religious attitude.

Apart from the existence of God, Voltaire acknowledges his waverings and uncertainties. Often he is driving less at the absolute truth than towards some practical end, to attain which he will temporarily admit first one tenet and then another. No philosophic belief can be thoroughly grounded in that manner. Voltaire's real religion, as a whole, is virtually the modern Positivism, the service of humanity, and as such it will presently be considered. But first we must indicate the negative and scornful side of Voltairianism — his attitude towards the Bible and the Catholic Church.

Bayle's Dictionary is the fulcrum, but Voltaire's pen is the lever that shook most mightily the rock of St. Peter's. The **Attacks on the Church** Patriarch of Ferney uses any means, and often ignoble means, against the church. He exhibits the naïvetés of the Old Testament, the discrepancies of the New; he attacks the Christian emperors, ridicules the martyrologies, and treats church history as a contradictory and extravagant record.

One-fourth of the articles in the *Dictionnaire Philosophique* are directed against Catholicism, and everywhere it is Catholic dogma that Voltaire particularly reprehends. Christianity for his time meant primarily theology and the priesthood. As Morley says, neither Voltaire nor his adversaries argued holiness or any appeal to the heart of man, nor did either side deal with the loftiest and most general ideas of the Christian religion. For both, it was a question of ritual, details, tithes, sects, Papal bulls and the like. Voltaire's point was that on the formal side the church had fallen away from Apostolic Christianity. The dogmas were added by Church Fathers and Popes to the primitive and purer belief. Many of these dogmas, he holds, are contrary to reason; they are absurd as well as obscure; they are often immoral, in setting up wrong examples — for instance, the Biblical Patriarchs. Catholicism is inhuman in its asceticism, as in its persecutions and superstitions. Of specific dogmas, original sin is unjust to God and to humanity; the doctrines of divine grace, of penance and pardon through the church, do away with personal responsibility; transubstantiation and the Trinity are inconceivable or revolting. Any divine revelation of truth is improbable. Voltaire is then opposed to all dogmas.

The second great point of his campaign is that it was directed against the supernatural. The miracles that were frauds in his own day — visions provoked by flagellations and convulsions, and staged by " sorcerer-priests "— were, he believed, equally frauds in New Testament times. These manifestations Voltaire considers beneath divine and human dignity. Contradicting what he has said elsewhere in praise of the person and message of Jesus, Voltaire now attacks and rationalizes Christ whenever it is a question of miracles, viewing him often either as an impostor or an unenlightened peasant. Voltaire is always declaiming against what he thought impossible and absurd Biblical legends, and it is true that he declaims in a coarse, savage, and startling manner. His excuse was that men would not cease to be persecutors until they ceased to be credulous.

The third plank, then, in Voltaire's platform, was his hatred of intolerance, issuing directly from his relative point of view. As early as *Zaïre*, he contended that our beliefs usually spring from our environment, that there are many " tolerable " religions, partial reflections of the truth. Almost indifferently he would take up the cause of Mahometan, Huguenot, or Quaker — but rarely of Catholic. He argues the universality of common beliefs in the best religions and he would discard the more uncommon tenets of each creed. So his constant aim is to thin out the believable portion of Scripture. His religion, lacking reverence and stripped of mysticism, comes down to earth and consists largely in practical morality.

His ethics are based simply on the needs of society; goodness means the exercise of justice and of a wide charity. It is not a question of an inner individual perfection. Vol-
Ethics taire has often been called an epicurean in morals, and the pleasure-seeking side of that creed is especially marked in his earlier life. He always thought that the search for happiness is " our being's end and aim," and as a youth he naturally confused happiness and pleasure. But his later morality is more nearly that of an altruist and a social meliorist.

It is not primarily a Christian morality, it can dispense with grace and prayer, and even with divine sanctions. It is rather, thinks Voltaire, the morality which lies at the base of all religions, of Confucianism, as of Mahometanism. " Les principes de morale communs au genre humain " make the kernel of natural religion; but theology, he holds, is characterized by disunion and quarrels. Religions may be immoral, whereas ethical principles are clear and serve to unify humanity. In spite of local and national divergences which Voltaire maliciously notes when it suits his relativism, he claims to believe in one universal ethic: its major premise is that all men consider as good those things which are useful to society. (But all men do not esteem this the *summum bonum*). Therefore, concludes Voltaire, the only necessary attribute of God is justice, which is also the first of human virtues; it comes nearer being an inherent idea than any other. Its corollary is charity, not as pauperizing almsgiving, but almost in the New Testament sense. This virtue is equivalent to the term *bienveillance,* of which Voltaire makes so much. He makes very little of the other theological and cardinal virtues, of faith and hope, of force, prudence and temperance. These are mostly individual matters, and true morality, for him, applies only to social man. The great rule is the Golden

Rule, whether expressed by Christ or by Confucius. A spirit of moderation in pleasure, a spirit of service in labor — this seems the gist of Voltaire's creed.

The positive side of Voltairianism, which has been too much neglected, concerns the social reforms which this creed de-**Progress and** manded. It would be too long to list here all the **Reform** changes required and often enforced by the *philosophe*. He contends for liberty, though a limited and non-seditious liberty, of various kinds: free-speech and free-writing, the abolition of slavery, civil liberty of the person (*habeas corpus*), civil marriage overbearing the church form, some separation of Church and State, with dominance of the latter. So many of these reforms have been successfully carried out that we hardly realize the part of Voltaire and of the eighteenth century in inaugurating them. The same is true of more specific recommendations, such as proportional taxation and punishment, abolition of the *octroi*, of certain feudal rights and of the farming out of taxes; doing away with the venality of offices, with Star Chambers and tortures; the fostering of the rights of property, of agriculture and commerce. Civil and criminal legislation, he held, was conducted on an antique and cruel model, which should be thoroughly reshaped· and unified. In social legislation Voltaire is Progressive; but in politics proper he is rather conservative, favoring the *ancien régime* through natural sympathy as well as opportunism.

His political ideal is an enlightened monarchy, which is perhaps nearer to despotism than to liberalism. His ideal monarch is **Politics** *le roi philosophe*, such as he hoped for in Louis XV and Frederick the Great, a ruler so intelligent, able and altruistic that he might be allowed almost absolute power. He would hate war and conquest as did Voltaire; he would bend all his efforts towards improving living conditions at home and promoting culture. This monarch of a dream is a modified Louis XIV plus philosophic enlightenment. He should rule as a " benevolent despot," deciding all matters referring to the establishment of religions, directing education — which should not be extended to the lowest class — controlling priests and all other servants.

Voltaire is not enthusiastic concerning the Rights of Man or republicanism.   He is also less of a patriot than a cosmopolitan.

On Civilization He has no communizing tendencies as regards property, which is viewed as a sacred right, and he is no advocate of equality.   His theory of luxury (*Le Mondain*) resembles that of Montesquieu: inequality means circulation of wealth and consequently the better condition of the poor.   Wealth makes civilization, and civilization is, after all, the great object of his zeal and care.   Voltaire derides Rousseau for his primitivism and wants us to conserve, improve and embellish what we have. Truly " natural law " is followed by those who civilize humanity, carry on the arts, create efficient legislation and make life wiser and easier.   Rousseauism, he believes, bars progress and enlightenment, because it is anti-human.   Voltaire is strongly humanitarian, not socialistic, an intellectual Progressive, not a revolutionary.   He apprehends truth relatively and sometimes evasively. His theories of reform are pragmatic, practical, *terre-à-terre*.   His religion and morality refuse to leave the earth, they concentrate hope by denying its prolongation.   In his rather desiccated soul, in his adroitness, wit, finish and everyday wisdom, he typifies the age which he adorns and which he strove on the whole to ameliorate.   His influence counted upon the Revolution, while the Revolution was still Royalist, and has continued, in dispersed and varied forms, throughout the nineteenth century.

CHAPTER III

DIDEROT

DENIS DIDEROT, known to his contemporaries as "*the* philosopher," was the leader and the most original thinker of the Encyclopedic group. He circulated more modern ideas than any other man of his generation. A naturalist in his philosophic and literary creed, he was able to combine the boldest speculation with a close sense of fact and with a warm human sympathy.

He admitted the mobility of his temperament and styled himself "the weathercock of Langres," at which town he had been born (1713). He was educated partly by the **His Life** Jesuits, who seem to have taught him a mixture of shrewdness and Latinity. Quite early he showed his taste for science and philosophy. Thrown on his own resources, he led for ten years the typical life of the Parisian hack-writer and bohemian. An imprudent marriage was followed by some laxness in subsequent affairs of the heart. Diderot was imprisoned as a result of the *Lettre sur les aveugles* (1749), and then settled down for nearly twenty years to his great labor of directing the Encyclopedia. [1]

After a visit to Catherine of Russia, who pensioned him handsomely, he returned to Paris with broken health, but still worked industriously until the end (1784). His chief friends and collaborators were Dalembert, Grimm and d'Holbach; also Rousseau, until the unfortunate break in their relations. Diderot was never a haunter of the salons, though welcomed by Mme de Geoffrin and Mlle de Lespinasse.

By disposition he was expansive, exuberant and endowed with **The two** much "sensibility. He was a good friend and father, **Diderots** an ardent lover, as his correspondence with Mlle Volland reveals, and a great helper of needy writers and others.

---

[1] See above, Bk. IV, Ch.I; and Bk. III, Ch. II, for his connection with the drama.

He was prone to enthusiasm, and a friendly literary discussion or a new idea would excite him tremendously; his naturally fine features would then take on a noble and exalted air, and listeners to his incomparable talk would feel that they were indeed in the presence of a genius. In conduct he was often the " average sensual man," democratic, sanguine, with a large dispersive carelessness, " like Nature herself," abounding in effervescent vitality. As a lover and observer of humanity, he is constantly appealing from artificial to realistic standards. His more familiar writings strangely mingle these personal characteristics with those of the scientist and the philosopher. His formula was " faire le bien, connaître le vrai." He divided scientific workers into " those who have instruments and those who have ideas." Diderot had both and employed the combination very originally. His mind was like a powerful lens, reflecting both light and heat. But the true light is often obscured by sophistry and declamation, his " virtue " is scarcely to be distinguished from vice, low and elevated sentiments jostle each other, and there is a Rabelaisian mixture of flesh and spirit in his temperament. We find, indeed, a frequent opposition between his temperament and his principles: the man *versus* the philosopher. Furthermore, he left two main classes of writings, the official and the intimate. The Encyclopedia represents the former; of the latter, the majority were published at long intervals after his death, and they usually express the bolder and more speculative side of his genius.

It is as a *philosophe* that Diderot must stand or fall. His most vital writing and thinking develop from his practical "philosophy," mobile and confused as this may seem to be. But there exists a nebular center to his thought, denoted by the frequency with which the word "Nature" is on his lips. With Diderot, philosophy could properly be termed a "system of nature." The word is often used by him in the widest cosmic sense — "the scheme of things entire" — with a considerable amount of primitivism *à la* Rousseau. Diderot's knowledge of natural sciences led him finally to the full acceptance of a materialistic universe, and his evolution towards this standpoint may be observed in his chief works.

Idea of Nature

His formal philosophizing begins with the *Essai sur le mérite et la vertu* (1745), freely translated from the English philosopher Shaftesbury. Diderot writes here as an orthodox Deist, believing in God, revelation, immortality and morality, although a " reasonable " foundation for ethics already begins to allure him. From Shaftesbury, Diderot drew certain of his more lasting principles, such as the prominence of common sense and the conception of aesthetic morals; the two men were also alike in their enthusiasm and optimism.

In the *Pensées philosophiques* of the following year, the author begins his career of free thought; these *Pensées* are intended as an answer to those of Pascal, whom the First *philosophes* recognized as their greatest adversary. "Pensées" We have here a defense of the passions on a " natural " basis and a diatribe against priestly asceticism (cf. *La Religieuse*); also objections to miracles and to final causes. Through the light of physical experimentation Diderot still sees God as imprinted in nature; the next step is to see nature as her own God, hence the famous formula: " Elargissez Dieu." Abandoning the temple, the divine spirit now roves through a pantheistic universe. The principle of relativity again appears as deriving from the multiplicity of religions; ask the adherent of any creed what would be his second choice, and he will answer: " Natural religion." Thus dogma and revelation are questioned and Deism already inclines towards atheism in Diderot's widening thought.

The *Lettre sur les aveugles à l'usage de ceux qui voient* (1749) is a turning-point in the writer's philosophy as well as in his Sensation- career. The two main doctrines of this letter are alism relativity and sensationalism. Knowledge is made entirely relative to our senses; a blind man disputes the existence of God, because the evidence is unseen by him. The limitation of philosophic proof to any one sense, however, is extravagant, and the *Lettre* is too individualistic because it tends to deny credible testimony based on the senses of others. Its interest lies rather in (1) the idea of obtaining psychological data from abnormal cases; (2) the fact that the Deity is now considered an unnecessary hypothesis; (3) the corollary that the world can be self-explanatory, granted eternal movement; (4) definite transformism or evolution, in that the world is supposed to evolve, from a primal welter of formless creatures, by means of variability and adaptation, towards the survival of the fittest. Diderot manifests again his zeal for investigation, radically criticizes Deism and advances far towards a completely naturalistic conception of the universe.

This idea appears more distinctly in the *Pensées sur l'interprétation de la nature* (1754), which is Diderot's chief scientific
Second   testament. Somewhat obscure and fragmentary in
"Pensées"   form, the thought owes much to Bacon, whose influence was then dominating the Encyclopedists. The "interpretation of nature" is in a sense Diderot's life-work, and here he emphasizes the ideas of the continuity of knowledge, the distrust of metaphysics and the predominance of the nattural sciences, in the two directions of careful laboratory accumulations and the generalizations and intuitions of the scientific genius. The world of fact is throughout opposed to metaphysics, even mathematics being now viewed as too abstract. But Diderot passes on through evolution to the philosophy of the flux, in declaring that known species and the present natural sciences are also transitory, and that both mankind and knowledge are forever in the making. In these passages and in his concluding prayer, his style rises to a height of poetic power.

The same observation applies to the *Entretien* with Dalembert, followed by the remarkable *Rêve de Dalembert*, which
Dialogues   were too daring to be published in the author's life-
of 1769,   time. "Il n'est pas possible," as Diderot himself
printed 1830   said of these brilliant dialogues, " d'être plus profond et plus fou." For instance, the author maintains to his friend that a statue may change into a man by natural gradations; he hints at a Lucretian — and Nietzschean — Eternal Return of phenomena; he deliberately prefers an animalistic conception of life. Then Dalembert goes home and has a strange dream. His mutterings are recorded as partly spoken, partly reported by Mlle de Lespinasse to the Doctor Bordeu. These interlocutors consider such points as the unification of cell-life, figured as a swarm of bees; a new fermentation of being, which may result in the superman; the relative nature of our passions and capacities, as due to the *rapports* between the nerve centers

and their extremities; in short a definite, if partly erroneous, system of psycho-physics. A bold deterministic amoralism concludes this extraordinary document, which is not merely, as one critic warns us, "the wild dream of a poet drunk on the wine of the new sciences," but shows Diderot's usual method of combining what seems giddy speculation — so often prophetic — with a basis of close observation.

It will now appear that Diderot, who began as a cautious Deist, ended as a frank materialist, of atheistic and even amoral tendencies. As regards his ethical system, indeed, he can **Morality** hardly be said to have had one. Although constantly interested in problems of conduct, he had a distinct taste for lawless primitivism (*Supplément au voyage de Bougainville*), which left him with little belief in absolute vice or virtue; and he shared the besetting sin of the eighteenth-century relativists, whose concept of the relative inclined them more towards anarchy than towards making the comparatively civilized at least a cornerstone in progress. But Diderot's practice was better than his doctrine; his own nature disposed him to make a great virtue of charity (*la bienfaisance*), and he thereby posits a "natural" penchant towards one's neighbor. For him morality is essentially social and individual ethics scarcely exist. Revolting from the Church, he believes in the natural goodness of humanity, and he shows a certain enthusiasm for "virtue" and fine fictions. But since he declares that civilizations have on the whole repressed the natural kindly man, it is difficult to see how he would build humanitarian progress on any eighteenth-century basis. Personal happiness seems to him our main duty, while his various views of social morality are surely discordant. His main tendency is more and more to consider the moral world as a mere prolongation of the physical. That is why it seems paradoxical to hear Diderot as a preacher of morality. But if his ethical surrender to nature is anarchistic, he is saved from intellectual Bolshevism by some belief in progress and a scientific adherence to the Leibnizian law of continuity. In ethics, then, Diderot is critical and destructive, whereas the constructive side of him appears rather in the scientific field, both as regards popularizing knowledge and in fertile original generalizations.

His philosophy of nature is, in fact, a sort of " superior physics."
Here he is a phenomenist dealing with actual forms and facts,
trying to extend the domain of the knowable. In
his uttermost speculations, he remains concrete, un-
metaphysical, scarcely leaving the earth. Final causes do not
interest him; he declares that he is concerned rather with the
comment than the *pourquoi*. He believes in the essential unity
of forces and sees life largely as action and reaction, often auto-
matic and molecular. But he does not scorn tentative hypotheses,
nor discount the scientific imagination. This double tendency
towards facts and speculation reflects his own two-fold temperament. There is the Diderot who is a healthy jovial materialist,
and the Diderot who leaves the temple to promenade through the
cosmos.

Science

It has been well said that for this philosopher the famous
" état de nature " was really an " état d'âme." His evolutionary
ideas were implicit in the Lucretian school and had
been openly sustained by Maupertuis; other ad-
vanced *philosophes*, such as La Mettrie and d'Holbach, anticipated
him in complete materialism. But none of them had Diderot's
genius and crystallizing power, none of them finds such expressive
delight in the " vertigo of thought," none of them experiences
such happiness and enthusiasm, such poetic and creative fire from
communion with the goddess Nature. She lends herself to perpetually fresh creations; matter invested with motion not only
begot the universe, but can forever change it; so all things are
relative, unstable, and the place of man in this welter is most
precarious. Diderot has definitely reacted from the Classical
habit of referring everything to human standards (anthropomorphism).

Conclusion as to Philosophy

As a critic, Diderot ranks high, first because he everywhere
recommends realism, and also because of his capacity for enthusiastic appreciation. He brought life into criticism. If he lacks balance and judgment, he has wide
views and acute senses; he frequently shows penetration and a
marked preference for democratic realities. This broad underlying naturalism is consistent with what we know of the man, the
philosopher and the dramatic theorist. He distinguishes genius
from art in that the former is linked with creative enthusiasm,

Criticism

the latter with taste. Poetry " demands something enormous, barbaric and savage." Diderot prefers a rude simplicity to his own artificial epoch, and it is still the " return to nature " that he advocates. But the word keeps its wide inclusiveness, as instanced in the declamatory *Eloge de Richardson,* whose characters and deeds are praised as " in nature " — that is, in the domain of fact and probability; Richardson's detailed realism is as various and convincing as that of the natural world; and his morality is of the highest. Here and in the *Salons* Diderot seems to recur to the idea of aesthetic morality; but his own morality and taste are seldom above suspicion.

His *Salons* (1759 f.) have been variously judged. Severe censors object to their literary flavor, their insistence on the "anecdote," their subordination of technical art-criticism, and the introduction of rather spicy passages. It is true that Diderot and his age emphasize the idea behind the product. He wants a painting to say something, in the way of story or history; at the least, he wants a " speaking " likeness and insists on expression as opposed to coldness or monotony. He practically invented the *causerie* as an informal discussion of art, and this style has had a considerable influence. The form is capable of much variety. Diderot will fuse a rather vivid description of a picture with the impression, often enthusiastic, which it produces on him, and with any digression that he chooses to make. But he introduces as much technical discussion as, presumably, his audience would stand; especially in the three directions of color, line, composition, for all of which he had a keen eye. His sympathies are with those painters who observe and depict naturally; Chardin and Vernet rather than Boucher. His idol is Greuze, who combines naturalness of detail with scenes of domesticity, anecdotes and moralizings. In all this Diderot runs true to type. He boldly recommends the painter to leave the studio and go outdoors where he can get away from the " mannered " poses and the academic taint. He admits that he views painting partly as an amateurish connoisseur, partly as a pleasure-seeker of sensuous and sumptuous values. But theoretically he contends that art must have its morals and that the corruption of the one (Boucher) brings on the corruption of the other. He defines taste as an " acquired faculty for seizing the true or

As Critic of Art

good," circumstantially depicted. The *Salons* are written for the most part admirably and eloquently, if somewhat hastily.

The more significant of Diderot's miscellaneous writings can be best handled if we view them likewise as prolonged *causeries*, **Not a** — rather than under the more usual heading of fiction. **Novelist** It is difficult to see how *Jacques le fataliste*, for instance, can be considered a novel. Here and elsewhere Diderot shows little interest in fictional form and he rarely creates a character; his tales are all fact or closely founded on fact. He is a *raconteur*, relating the "small memoirs of his century." The form in which he excels, then, is dialogue, tending towards monologue; he is primarily a conversationalist and an improviser. This appears in the charming *Entretien d'un père avec ses enfants*, in various other dialogues, and conspicuously in his one indubitable masterpiece, *Le Neveu de Rameau* (c. 1726).

Goethe was the first to discover and make famous this amazing dialogue, which presents as interlocutors Diderot himself **"Le Neveu** (as a *philosophe*) and the cynical bohemian rela- **de Rameau,"** tive of Rameau — who is really another side of Did- **publ. 1823** erot. The debate thus shows a doubly personal vigor and penetration. The philosopher appears as reasonable, cautious, charitable, accepting the established order, fond of pleasures, but preferring those of the heart, interested in his friends, his work, his family. The bohemian is an individualist, displaying his "natural" vices and frank perversities, relishing the struggle for life, utterly materialistic; even animal in his desires and ideas. The two speakers are opposed as regards the value of morality, philosophy, genius and education; and each gives the best possible presentation of his case. Rameau's language is astonishingly vivid, an effect aided by his use of pantomime, the detailed account of his gestures, together with a style of breathless enumerations. All this is in the best realistic manner of Diderot and is done with brilliant precision and great speed. The dialogue has " cet air vif, ardent et fou " which Diderot claims for his own physiognomy.

Equally mad, though less interesting, is *Jacques le fataliste* **His Fiction** (1773, publ. 1796), which is a frank and free imitation of Sterne in its wilful neglect of plot, its sly sensuality, and the impertinent intrusions of the author. It is a

"Sentimental Journey" which never gets anywhere, and its humor is often labored. Diderot himself declares that he is not writing a novel and that he is simply telling the truth about various episodes. The nominal subject concerns the loves of Jacques as he relates them to his rather dull master on the king's highway and in hostelries. We have then a kind of road-novel, with echoes of *Gil Blas* and the like; but nothing much ever happens. Apart from the variegated pattern, the interest lies, as usual, in Diderot's talk, with its occasional wit and sprightliness, and in the several short stories interspersed. Of these the *Histoire de Madame de la Pommeraye et du Marquis des Arcis* has achieved deserved fame. It is a passionate tale concerning the vengeance of a deserted mistress who throws her quondam lover into the arms of a courtesan; the latter then attains virtue through marriage. This romantic rehabilitation, as well as the unnaturalness of the revenge, is cleverly criticized by Jacques and his hostess; but no one can criticize the absorbing thrill of the story, especially if read in an abbreviated text.

La Religieuse (1760, publ. 1796) is the best composed, in fact, the only novel proper that Diderot wrote. Even this story falls The English away towards the end and is unfinished. It is a Influence powerful and painful autobiography of a rebellious nun in several convents, a *conte philosophique* through moral intention; and Diderot demonstrates his theme as to the horrors of conventual life. There are certain gaps in the motivation and the characters are rudely sketched, with the exception of the heroine, who is a more innocent Diderot. Yet the work is a serious social and pathological study. The style is as usual vigorous, sometimes too choppy, detailed in its representation of scenes and people. The influence of Richardson probably appears in this sort of realism, as well as in the idea of a suffering heroine. Diderot's "fiction" frequently shows a sentimental morality and bourgeois preoccupations quite in the vein of Richardson. In fact, most of the Frenchman's important works, whether philosophic or imaginative, reflect some form of the English influence, so pervasive at this time.

Enough has been said to indicate that in the main phases of his activity Diderot ranks among the naturalists, and like those

of the nineteenth century, he links literary realism with the scientific approach. He has the eye, the hand, the spirit of the born
Realism Realist. Whether he is preaching natural philoso-
and Style phy and religion or demanding concreteness and
actuality in drama and painting or depicting the real democratic world in his own vivid sketches, he is the chief representative of this spirit · between Rabelais and Balzac. His
style and processes are also much like theirs; a manner compact of color and thought and freshness; a· circumstantial
method of narration, including enumerations and catalogue sentences; the emphasis on gestures, pantomine, physiognomies;
the observation, the crude force, the sense of variable life, the
animalism, the materialistic imagination and memory. Closer
to Diderot's own age are his taste for " tableaux," the rhetorical
effusions, and the peculiar habit of mixing licentiousness and
sentiment. But he is above all individual, thereby repugnant to
the traditionalists, and his strongest individual quality is undoubtedly *verve*, the mixture of liveliness, vividness and rapidity
in a suite of cascading sentences. Scherer says that Diderot
pours himself out in a facile, turbid stream, sometimes muddy
and all-carrying as a river at flood-tide, sometimes playfully rioting over clear rocks at the bottom. At his best he welds perfectly
form and matter, in a burst of creative energy; but his best is
contained in picked pages and in no single volume of his works;
he is too unequal, too hurried. His sentiment is often rhetorical
or vulgar, he has force rather than- taste, but through sheer
power and geniality, in spite of anarchy and confusions, he
manages to lift and impose his materialistic burden.

BOOK V

PRE–ROMANTICISM

CHAPTER I

ROUSSEAU. BERNARDIN DE SAINT–PIERRE

JEAN-JACQUES ROUSSEAU (1712–78), the most remarkable and unfortunate genius of the century, was by birth and preference a " citizen of Geneva." His Swiss origin helps to **Life** explain his independence, as well as his more persistent views on politics and religion and his moralizing vein. Thus he reaches and touches France as an alien force, and his impact is all the greater. We see him first at the age of seven, devouring sentimental fiction with his unstable father. His feelings and his imagination were awakened far too early — likewise his senses. Good-hearted, but quite uncontrolled as a boy, he soon becomes a rascally apprentice and at sixteen leaves Geneva in consequence of an escapade. He is taken under the wing of Mme de Warens, a charming, free and easy lady, who sends him to Turin, where he is converted (temporarily) to Catholicism. He becomes a lackey and falls in love with the daughter of the house. Again he follows the open road, passing through various journeys and adventures. From Paris, at the age of twenty-one, he takes his last long tramp and is installed at Chambéry as the companion of Mme de Warens, under degrading conditions. His partial self-education dates from this period, as does the beginning of his misanthropy. His establishment at Paris (1741 f.) soon involved him in a lasting *liaison* with Thérèse Levasseur. She was a kind-hearted but illiterate servant-girl who brought down her relatives upon Rousseau's head and decidedly hampered his career. She gave him five children, whom he turned over to the foundling hospital. Presently Jean-Jacques began to please writers and ladies, and in 1750, his first *Discours* won the prize of the Dijon Academy.

Professing a moral transformation, he then started to pose as a " bear," refusing to dress the part of a fashionable success. Yet he was honored in Paris and acclaimed in Geneva, where he was restored to his rights as citizen and Protestant. In 1756 he was established at his " Hermitage " in the forest of Montmorency, near Paris. There during the next six years he wrote his principal books — *La Nouvelle Héloïse, Emile, Le Contrat social* — and became the victim of his infatuation for Mme d'Houdetot. Rousseau's suspicions of his friends, especially of Grimm, Diderot and Mme d'Epinay, center around this epoch. Serious altercations followed. Rousseau left his retreat and found other protectors, while his literary reputation was growing. Exiled from France on account of *Emile*, he lived for a time at Motiers in Switzerland, where he experienced fresh dissensions and " persecutions." He finally renounced Geneva and Calvinism. In 1766–67 we find him in England, where he quarrelled with Hume and again fled onward. From place to place he carried his uneasy soul, more sinned against than sinning. At last he settled in Paris (1770), and his old age, if still eccentric, was calmer and kinder. He died in 1778; his ashes were carried to the Pantheon in 1791.

On the face of it, this is not a normal life, and Rousseau was evidently an unbalanced person. He has been accused of megalomania and of the mania of persecution; **Character** nevertheless, he was entitled to think himself a great man, and it now seems clear that there were actual plots against his happiness and reputation. He had too rare a nature to be readily understood. Where others reasoned, he felt and suffered. He was romantic, sensitive, self-centered, intoxicated alternately by passion and by " virtue." He was unstable in love and friendship, often anti-social in his independence, at war with himself and with his Parisian environment. These personal traits, as well as the new literary currents which he released, will appear best from a consideration of his *Confessions*.

This book ranks as one of the greatest of autobiographies, **" Les Confessions," publ. 1781–88** comparable to the writings of St. Augustine and Montaigne. Lemaître calls the work the most " candid, singular and passionate " confessions ever written. The story covers Rousseau's life down to the flight to England, and it was composed during the troubled years that followed. Its purpose was to defend his character against the libels of the Grimm faction, to prove his sincerity and to show the world that no better man than Jean-Jacques could be found. Yet he frankly admits many grievous faults and stains; he also pleads guilty to lapses of memory and certain embellishments in the presentation. The first six books are heightened in color and retrospect, just as the last six are deliberately darkened. But in the main the work does bear the stamp of sincerity, faithfully rendering Rousseau's emotions and memories. The vagabond charm of the earlier portions, the "portraits" and anecdotes and pictures of domestic life, the natural vivid style of these *morceaux*, alternating with the impassioned eloquence of the sentimental passages — all of these qualities give the *Confessions* their double value as a personal document and as one of the first monuments of Romanticism. These values may be traced under three headings: individualism, the love of nature, and the passionate expression of sentiment.

Rousseau's own characteristics, detailed with self-complacency, often amount to an individualistic doctrine. He appears as ardent, weak, vibrating between good and evil, between exaltation and despair. He constantly speaks of his *sottises, folies, délires, engouements*. For a time he would be captivated by friend or by mistress and then abandon them through indolence or, as his enemies claimed, ingratitude. Nervousness and poor health were responsible for various weaknesses; and at times his "case" seems pathological. He holds that virtue became his main passion about 1750; the facts show rather that passion became his main virtue a few years later. His individualism develops into a peculiar type of megalomania. Jean-Jacques declares that there was never anything like his *Confessions* or anybody like him. He was a prodigy as a child. Later he felt that "en me montrant j'allais occuper de moi l'univers." He claims that he is unique, if not superior, whether as regards his passions, his indolence, or the various circumstances of his life. His temperament is made to explain and excuse his many errors. Other forms in which the personal note appears are: a proud independence, a kind of wilful impressionism, imaginative exalta-

tion, vagabondage, and a taste for simple pleasures curiously
mingled with romantic sensations. These feelings were much
stimulated by his long tramps, during which he learned to love
and celebrate the charms of Nature.

Rousseau thus indicates the kind of nature that he prefers:

> Jamais pays de plaine. . . . Il me faut des torrents, des ro-
> chers, des sapins, des bois noirs, des montagnes, des chemins rabo-
> teux à monter et à descendre, des précipices à mes pieds qui me
> fassent bien peur.

Such a landscape, when encountered in youth and health, brings
life to a pinnacle. And through the " pathetic fallacy " one's
mood then colors nature; it also associates particular
scenes with the image of the loved one· In the

Nature

most powerful revery that Rousseau ever experienced, he was
chiefly occupied with transposing scenic elements into a future
life with Mme de Warens. Any occurrence in nature is likely
to arouse ethereal joys or floods of meditation. He thinks out
his books while walking, and it is in the forest that he attains to
the vision of primitive times. Nature is then depicted in the
Confessions, though not so frequently as in the *Nouvelle Héloïse*,
yet with the same sincerity and broad sweep, and even more
poignantly and personally.

The third modern note which Rousseau sounds is that of
sentiment. He declares that sensibility was the main gift of his
parents, that it has brought him both bliss and

Sensibility

despair. Even as a child all the sentiments were
known to him; he wanted to be loved by everybody. In old age
he still wept over the songs of his childhood. His intelligence is
slow as compared with his emotions, and he sets the value of
right feeling far above the value of ideas. " La froide raison n'a
jamais rien fait d'illustre." Jean-Jacques himself has essentially
l'âme aimante; and such expressions, together with " expansions
and ecstasies," tears and embraces and beating pulses, constantly
recur. He finds the Parisians shallow in sentiment; he affirms that love and friendship are the guiding stars of his own
life. His love affairs are in fact the most extraordinary thing
about Rousseau. They are of all varieties and moods, idyllic or
sensual. Generally imagination plays the greater part, Plato-

nism and idealism are much dwelt upon, but lasting serviceable affection is not conspicuous. In his affair with Mme d'Houdetot he insists that the delights of *l'amitié amoureuse* drew him more than the·senses, that women both consoled and educated him. With Rousseau love was rarely complete. The following passage, concerning the " idyll " with Mme de Warens, probably represents him at his best:

> S'il y a dans la vie un sentiment délicieux, c'est celui que nous éprouvâmes d'être rendus l'un à l'autre. Notre attachement mutuel n'en augmenta pas, cela n'était pas possible; mais il prit je ne sais quoi de plus intime, de plus touchant dans sa grande simplicité. . . . Nous nous accoutumâmes à ne plus penser à rien d'étranger à nous, à borner absolument notre bonheur et tous nos désirs à cette possession mutuelle, et peut-être unique parmi les humains, qui n'était point, comme je l'ai dit, celle de l'amour, mais une possession plus essentielle, qui, sans tenir aux sens, au sexe, à l'âge, à la figure, tenait à tout ce par quoi l'on est soi, et qu'on ne peut perdre qu'en cessant d'être.

The Romantic characteristics just enumerated made their first striking appearance in French literature in the long sentimental "La Nouvelle novel called *Julie ou la Nouvelle Héloïse* (1761). Héloïse " In this novel, the " new Héloïse " loves and yields to her tutor as her namesake loved Abelard; but Julie is finally rescued by domestic guidance and marriage. After being dutiful for six years she is again shaken by the reappearance of her lover, Saint-Preux, and the impossible triangle is resolved by her death. The sources of the book are two-fold: Richardson's *Clarissa Harlowe* and the personal adventures of Rousseau. Richardson probably furnished the epistolary form, the conception of the unfortunate heroine who is carried through ruin to death, and the tendency towards much analysis of sentiment. But Rousseau's experiences are what gave the book life in his own eyes and in those of his contemporaries. The scenes of his wanderings, especially around Lake Geneva, are portrayed with mingled precision and magnificence. Julie and Claire (her lively confidante) were orginally sketched from two young ladies of Rousseau's acquaintance, while the early love passages were in memory of Mme de Warens. But the book was intended to be more edifying than passionate, when Mme d'Houdetot suddenly

became Rousseau's main inspiration. There is thus a discrepancy between the various parts of the novel: passion and individualism as opposed to moralizing and didacticism; a discrepancy which again thoroughly reflects Rousseau. These personal
origins explain the main currents of the *Nouvelle Héloïse,* which
we may consider from the three aspects already chosen for the
Confessions.

Saint-Preux clearly resembles the author in that he is rash,
passionate, weak, easily exalted, loving above his station. Like
Rousseau, he talks much about virtue and fine sen-
Individualism timents and leaves us uncertain as to his capacity
for living up to what he feels. In fact, the novelist talks through
all his personages and shows little objectivity. The characters
insist that they are " unique " in their situations and sentiments.
Self-development is pleaded for in hundreds of passages. It appears that the individual (Julie) is sacrificed to ideals of family
and duty, but the sacrifice is rather made to artificial social distinctions which impede the course of true love. Thus the single
person is conquered in his or her strife with artificial society —
the favorite thesis of Rousseau. Society is more to blame than
either Julie or her lover. So the novel in its chief tendencies
remains individualistic.

The " voice of nature," in several senses, is constantly heard.
First we have the picturesque landscape, for which *La Nouvelle
Héloïse,* aided by English poetry, restored the vogue
Nature in France. There was born a fresh appreciation for
the long and loving delineation of nature, often associated with
man's sufferings and joys. The most invigorating passages are
those which depict the scenes preferred by Rousseau. It is nearly
always the lower Alps that he describes, the varying perspective
of the Valais mountains, the contrast between the cultivated fields
and the rougher hillsides, the shifting of color, the serenity of the
heights. Nature is combined with the individual in two principal
ways. It is of course associated with the loved one. The grove
which witnessed the first kiss of the lovers is forever made a
shrine. Saint-Preux thinks of Julie as definitely placed on this
sward or on that rock, and Julie sees him as suggested by all
the objects which he has left. Again, the pathetic fallacy is
frequent, and this is the second way of fusing nature with the
individual:

Je trouve partout dans les objets la même horreur qui règne au dedans de moi. On n'aperçoit plus de verdure, l'herbe est jaune et flétrie, les arbres sont dépouillés, le séchard [1] et la froide bise entassent la neige et les glaces; et toute la nature est morte à mes yeux, comme l'espérance au fond de mon cœur.

Rousseau also demands the simple life, simple pleasures, and prefers the country to Paris, " ce vaste désert du monde." He **Natural** praises the natural emotions, such as family affec- **Emotions** tions, friendship and love — " la solitude à deux." In love, nature seeks full possession, both of heart and body. Nature also rules the choice of lovers and should rule their marriages, in an ideal society. Nature, rather than civilization, makes the moral differences between the sexes, the aggressive man, the protective woman. Ethically, " la bonté naturelle " is Rousseau's ideal.

Streams of sentimental tears abound throughout the volume. Today we find the showers of Julie and the torrents of Saint- **Sentiment** Preux rather too *larmoyants*. But the old régime needed just this irrigation. It is difficult to free oneself from a suspicion of overdone feeling and rhetorical style; but such expression is largely a matter of varying taste, and what seems false now was true in its time. Some instances of Rousseauistic sentiment may be given. Julie attracts her lover primarily by her *sensibilité;* she speaks of affinities, of a " secret conformity of affections " proceeding from Nature. The best love should be unique and purifying. Saint-Preux, though less of a Platonist, agrees that love must be linked with morality, must have elevation and aim at perfection. Taken rightly, love is the whole thing in life, and the absolute view of this sentiment is one of the great novelties introduced by Rousseau. In the midst of their gallantries and frivolities, he made the worldlings " feel." Again, expansive virtue for Jean-Jacques is less a matter of practical ethics than an impulse from the bottom of the soul. His is a sentimental morality, and he declares significantly that sentiment is his conscience. It is also the judge of art, it makes the true power of music and the interest of fiction for him. Compared with feeling, reason is nothing, and he exalts, beyond reason and beyond sustained morality, the theory of the exquisite moment

---

[1] The north-east wind.

made immortal by recollection and revery. Certainly in the moral world Rousseau confuses kinds and values; but the *Nouvelle Héloïse* opened powerful fresh channels for literature. It still attracts readers through its appreciation of love and nature, as well as through its finely eloquent style, Romantic in its essence and influence.

To go back in time, Rousseau's first printed work was the *Discours sur les Sciences et les Arts* (1750). Probably under the influence of Diderot and in a state of imaginative **The Two "Discours"** exaltation, he decided to maintain, in the Dijon Academy debate, that the arts[2] and sciences are connected with the corruption of humanity. Much of the essay is declamatory and paradoxical and shows little historical knowledge. Yet in his praise of the old Roman *vertu*, the author indicates the main principle of all his subsequent work: the opposition of artificial society to a simpler life, to which, as far as practicable, man should make his civilization conform. This principle, in another aspect, also underlies the second essay, *Discours sur l'origine et les fondements de l'inégalité parmi les hommes* (1755). Rousseau here has a vision of primitive man as a happy amoral animal, equal in all respects to his neighbor. But he lives separated from this neighbor, and the " state of nature " is a state of isolation. With the organization of society, man becomes gradually less free and equal. Interdependence, strife, ambition are developed, particularly through the possession of property, which Rousseau views as the root of all evil, The foundation of the political State came about in order to protect property, to uphold the rich and oppress the poor. Inequality led to slavery, and Rousseau sees no escape save through a general uprising. The power and daring of this *Discours*, in spite of its many mistakes, made it figure along with the *Contrat social* in the propaganda of the Revolution.

The first chapters of the *Contrat social* (1762) **"Le Contrat social": Summary** are individualistic, but as a whole the work stands for a constructive organization of democratic society and for the recognition of moral principles in politics. Neither

---

[2] This thesis is developed with regard to literature in the *Lettre à Dalembert sur les spectacles* (1758), in which the drama and Molière particularly are condemned as immoral.

the right of the strongest, nor divine right, nor the family, is the true source of human society. In the (hypothetical) primitive " contract " which should today be reinforced, it was a question of mutual consent and obligation between members of a self-governing community. The forfeiture of "inalienable rights " in favor of an oppressive monarch is a void contract; but Rousseau then urges the alienation of many individual claims in favor of the community, the popular State. Each person is at once subject and citizen-ruler in this collective body politic. Such is the famous doctrine of popular sovereignty. The law is / the expression of the " infallible " general will. Its agent is the governing or executive body, which may be of several kinds. A sort of aristo-democracy is preferred, a cabinet ministry which shall be controlled by the sovereign people through referendums and the like. The general will implies both a collective consciousness and a public spirit, and Rousseau holds that under modern conditions " neither reason nor the moral law is to be realized by man except in and through the civil state." The author now modifies these abstract ideals by considerations of circumstance and expediency. He concedes that some of the rights which have been taken from the individual subject may be guardedly handed back to him. A small State should be democratic, but a large one rather monarchical (cf. Montesquieu). Having small democracies in mind, Rousseau held that representative government was not truly popular. Sometimes unanimity of the popular vote is demanded, sometimes merely a plurality. But such attenuations and uncertainties do little to modify the effect of the *Contrat social* in its main features: equality before the law; the rights of the individual as merging in the interests of the State; hence State sovereignty and what might be called democratic despotism.

Disregarding other errors and confusions, we may emphasize the last idea as containing the germs of much subsequent evil.

Criticism Fundamental personal rights — the right of free association, of choosing one's religion and of using one's property — are made subordinate to those of the sovereign State. The despotism of the Terror derived very considerably from Rousseau, and the modern German State owes something to his conception of absolute sovereignty. On the other hand,

Rousseau did a great deal to forward the general democratic idea; his theory of the Contract may be stripped of its hazy primitivism and taken more justly to mean that government must depend on the " consent of the governed." The *Contrat social* is the one work in which Rousseau leaves individualism; he goes indeed to the other extreme of collectivism. His errors are due both to a lack of the historical sense — any sense of development or of a complex of conditions — and to unbalanced or confused thinking. His " temperament," which had its great value in his imaginative or personal works, often leads him astray in matters of sound knowledge and reasoning.

The opposition between nature and society, particularly as regards education, is again enforced in *Emile* (1762). This "Emile" " educational romance " is partly fictional, partly autobiographical; as a treatise, it has links with the simplifying and realistic ideas of Rabelais and of Fénelon. The boy Emile progresses from the education of the senses to that of the intelligence and the emotions. The child should be brought up without constraint, knowing first a mother's care, then passing to a governor or father, whose primary object should be to " faire un homme." Between the ages of five and twelve, the boy remains in a " state of nature," receiving no regular lessons, learning rather from experience and example, talking with common folk and persistently asking questions. Emphasis is laid on physical exercises and only after the age of twelve does the youth actually study; even then he studies things (object-lessons) rather than books. During adolescence he will read a few " historians of the soul," such as Plutarch, and gradually his sentiments will be awakened. Finally, the youth will subdue his passions, travel a little, meet and marry his Sophie, who has 'been trained mainly to please Emile. And the author celebrates the wedding in a lyrical manner, not without absurdities.

The chief objection to this general theory is that it does not fit a man for social life. Emile is brought up in an improbable Criticism state of isolation, and his education is neither thoroughly human nor humanistic. The study of languages and literature is not encouraged, the memory is not trained, and the boy's mind and soul are long kept inactive. He is reared as a solitary Rousseauist rather than as a future citizen. But in many things concerning child-welfare the author's views are sound. In this respect he inaugurated an educational revolution. Mothers began to nurse their children, people began to study handicrafts, and physical exercises were made more prominent in France; in Germany, Rousseau's " Gospel of childhood," coming down through Pestalozzi and Froebel, forms the basis of the modern kindergarten. Rousseau's influence was due to the novelty and sincerity of his revolt against artificial systems and to the persuasiveness of his appeals to sentiments and passions. The natural education which he recommends stands for simplicity *versus* apparatus, for real objects *versus* forms, and for first-hand experiences *versus* authority.

The fourth book of *Emile* contains the gist of Rousseau's religion in the *Profession de foi du Vicaire Savoyard*. We have **Religion** seen how in practice he changed from Protestantism to Catholicism and back again, usually under personal influences. His religion is also a highly individual and sentimental affair. It does not need logical proofs, but only emotions, a swelling sense of virtue and contact with the infinite. It has been best defined as a " sentimental Deism," with strong Pantheistic leanings; Rousseau sees the divine spirit in all nature. This emotional religiosity finds many echoes in the nineteenth century, beginning with Chateaubriand.

Rousseau appears then as a man of unfortunate life and of very mobile character. His strivings towards virtue were in the end **Conclusion** sincere, but his ethical message is blurred by his egotism and by his tendency to exalt sentiment above knowledge and reason. The same objections apply to his dealings with politics and education, where the mind rather than the heart and imagination should be in control; yet in neither of these fields can his great contributions be ignored. Rousseau, more than any other writer of his century, counted powerfully upon the Revolution, through both the people and their leaders (Mme Roland, Robespierre), in both its idealistic and its excessive phases. Indeed, some hold that it is chiefly the excessive side of Rousseau that has prevailed, in matters of con-

duct as well as in politics and literature. In the last domain, however, in the *Confessions* and the *Nouvelle Héloïse,* his very defects become in some sort virtues. The exaltation of the ego and
the heart, the freeing of the imagination, the passionate expression of man's affiliations with Nature and with the vast unknown
not only give immortality to Rousseau's own Romanticism, but
make him the father of the subsequent Romantic movement.[3]
His eloquent prose is refashioned in the lyrics of Lamartine
and of Musset. Thus he exerts an expansive influence in several
fields, and with all his faults he appeals to something abiding
in human nature.

Bernardin de Sainte-Pierre (1737–1814),the immediate disciple
of Rousseau, resembled him in leading an eccentric, vagrant and
Bernardin dreamy life. He was subject to melancholy, mad
de Saint-
Pierre at times, but successful in both worldly and literary
ways, towards the end of his career. He first met Rousseau in
1772, and yielded at once to the spell which led him to produce
books and to preach the worship of Nature. Bernardin's
Etudes de la Nature (1784) is characteristic of the author in its
mingled exoticism and pseudo-science. Nature is viewed as
the source of all good, of all utility and beauty; she should be
observed less by *savants* than by sentimental believers. In the
latter rôle, Saint-Pierre undertook to show that the whole aim of
creation was the happiness of man, and he makes an excessive
use of the doctrine of final causes. (For instance, cantaloupes
are divided by kindly nature into sections for family eating.)
Better than his logic is Bernardin's analysis of sentiment. He also
forestalls Romantic melancholy in his fusion of man and nature;
when it rains the landscape seems to him " une belle femme qui
pleure." The ardor of his feeling imparts a communicative fire
to his descriptions, which are full of color and movement, and
he has a keen sense of the picturesque. The specific element
which he adds to Rousseau is exoticism. He describes not only
Europe but also tropical scenes, and this knowledge and feeling
for exotic nature is continued in *Paul et Virginie* (1788). Here
the setting is the Ile-de-France (Mauritius), which the author
knew quite well. The subject of the story is the development of a
young pair according to natural education and sentiment. The

[3] See below, Bk. V, Ch. II and Bk. VI, Chs. II and IV.

effects of landscape, as mingled with intimate human life, and the growth of adolescent love are well depicted, less so is the shipwreck and tragic climax. *Paul et Virginie* is a Rousseauistic idyll; it is not a great book, but it still retains a certain charm for the sentimentally minded.

CHAPTER II
MADAME DE STAEL. CONSTANT.

THE reader is doubtless acquainted with the series of dynamic changes that took place in France from the death of Louis

History XV to the battle of Waterloo. The succession of events, briefly, is as follows: the reign of the well-meaning but inadequate Louis XVI (1774–89); the vain endeavor of several excellent ministers, notably Turgot and Necker, to stem the rising tide; and during this period the participation of France in the American cause; the convocation of the States-General, the formation of the Constituent Assembly and the fall of the Bastille (1789); the defeat of the milder Revolutionaries (*les Girondins*) and the Reign of Terror (from 1793); the inauguration of European wars on a large scale; the National Convention superseded by the Directory (1795–99); Napoleon Bonaparte as First Consul (to 1804) and as Emperor (to 1815); his victories, his domination of Europe, the efforts of the Allies and the final abdication of Napoleon.

The effect of the Revolution on pure literature could hardly be immediately beneficial. As in the Great War, people's

Literature and the Revolution thoughts were running in other channels, and passions were too inflamed to allow the necessary detachment. The Revolution practically destroyed the old society, together with the tradition of the salons and the predominant influence of women — except that of Mme de Staël. Modern journalism took strong root in this epoch; at one time several hundred periodicals were in circulation, and Napoleon found it expedient to reduce this number materially. Usually journalism, in its virulence and prejudice, is the typical expression of Revolutionary literature. Better than the other periodicals were the *Décade philosophique,* the organ of the " idéologues," and the liberal *Journal des Débats.* Camille Desmoulins is probably the most noted journalist of the age;

his letters written from prison show a fevered sensitive soul, which the Revolution pushed almost to the verge of madness. The great orator of the time was the Marquis de Mirabeau, a man of strong passions and intellect; this double strength still vibrates in his speeches, whose eloquence now seems old-fashioned in some particulars but was based upon fact and logic as well as emotional appeal. The condition of the theater and of poetry under the Revolution has already been stated.[1] In short, no great books were produced until Napoleon had restored order. At the very beginning of the nineteenth century two great writers come to the fore: Mme de Staël and Chateaubriand.

Germaine Necker de Staël (1766–1817) was of Swiss parentage but French upbringing. The ministry of her father, the finan-
Her Life cier Necker, was virtually the last hope of the old régime. Her mother founded the brilliant " salon Necker." Germaine's happy home, its social spirit and the influence of her father counted for much in her life and ideals. She was a precocious child, listening eagerly to such talkers as Marmontel and Buffon. Her ardent sensibility appears in her early writings on Rousseau. She was led into a foolish *mariage de raison* with the Baron de Staël-Holstein, the Swedish ambassador, who gave her an eminent position, but who seemed uncongenial and unlovable. She immediately started a salon of her own and became a young queen among the most intelligent groups of the dying monarchy. Her influence was not political, and the Revolution soon submerged her power. She joined the party of victims and *émigrés*, whom she generously helped. In 1792, she began her series of flights to Coppet, an estate near Geneva, and after that date she appeared only intermittently at Paris. The crisis of her life was her affair with Benjamin Constant, who owed much of his success to Mme de Staël, but who finally wearied of her. In 1795 she was allowed to return to France, where she consorted with the liberals and the Republicans. But she was soon accused of political intriguing and was persecuted by several French governments. In 1802, however, she reached the height of her power in Paris, conducting a famous salon, frequented by Mme Récamier, Constant, Fauriel

[1] See above, Bk. III, Chs. I and IV.

and others. Her early hopes of Napoleon had ended in disappointment, and he became her enemy. The lady, as usual, was too free-spoken. Police decrees closed her salon and practically banished Mme de Staël. She traveled in Germany and Italy, but made her headquarters at Coppet, holding a court which rivaled that of Voltaire a generation before. The death of her husband did not lead to a marriage with Constant. Sorrow and bereavement deepened her mind, while her foreign experiences bore fruit in her masterpieces. As a middle-aged woman she married a young man named De Rocca, who seems to have really cared for her. She traveled in Russia and visited England for the second time. Soon after the triumph of the Allies, which did not realize her political ideals, she died, exhausted by her stormy career.

It was a pathetic great life, largely because Mme de Staël's enthusiasm and exceptional talents were frustrated by circumstances and therefore she never attained happiness. **Character** Impatient, frank and not very tactful, she dismayed men as different as Schiller, Scott, Byron, Napoleon and Joubert. Wherever she went, says Sainte-Beuve, she was " destinée à porter du mouvement et de l'imprévu." She had an eager need for fresh knowledge and fresh contacts, an almost universal intelligence and much capacity for affection. She loved her father and adored his memory, which is enshrined in *Corinne.* She was an excellent mother; and she said truly that friendship was the " religion of her life." When disappointed in the love of men — Narbonne, Talleyrand, Constant — she turned to the love of mankind. She had a good heart, benevolent and generous. Enthusiasm and sensibility were the salient traits of her youth; later she believed in a sterner stoicism and finally in the necessity of Christian duty and morality. She represented in her experience and work all the phases of France, from the epoch of the later *philosophes,* through the Revolution, down to the Empire and the Restoration.

Mme de Staël had a virile and energetic mind, but her heart was quite feminine, while her sociability was a marked characteristic. " La vie " is her favorite word, and she **Salon Spirit** tends to see life in terms of " society." Consequently she writes with clearness, swiftness and an appeal to general cultured interest. Again, she was the most charming and absorbing talker of her time. Her written thought would often spring from her conversation and is clothed in conversational form. Even in *Corinne*, the most artistic of her works, much is made of formal dialogue and of society. Thus her style shows a certain improvisation, a tendency to run on carelessly, but it has the qualities of impetuosity and naturalness. She is not a professional writer; books are simply the overflow from her very full life; literature with her is a way of keeping in touch with the world — " c'est de la conversation indirecte."

Her early works show particularly the reveries, passions and ideals of her youth. The *Lettres sur les écrits et le caractère de Jean-Jacques Rousseau* (1788) are a tribute to **Early Works** the writer who attracted her most. The book, *De l'Influence des passions* (1796), constitutes at once an indictment and a eulogy of such " dark influences " as love and ambition. The steadier lights of morality and usefulness are recommended, but Mme de Staël is not yet purged of the spirit of Romanticism; while declaring that one should flee from the passions, she still perceives their fascination and their absorbing power upon life. The *Réflexions sur la paix* (1794) show a singularly moderate tone and a political sagacity in the midst of turmoil. Sympathizing with the republican idea, she is yet opposed to fanaticism and wishes an even-handed justice. Finally, her *Essai sur les fictions* may be viewed as the stepping-stone to her greater productions both in fiction and criticism. She holds that the novel as a genre should be more esteemed and better done; it will be the form of the future, especially when it displays all sides of life and not merely the sentiment of love. She prefers truly psychological fiction, which turns into drama the changes and subtleties of the human heart; and she still believes in the consoling effect of romances, in their power to remove us to an ideal world. She said that the carrying off of Clarissa Harlowe seemed an " event " in her own youth, and on her death-bed she was found reading Walter Scott.

Mme de Staël's novels renovate the form of fiction and closely reflect her personality. " *Corinne* est l'idéal de **" Delphine "** Mme de Staël; *Delphine* est la réalité pendant sa jeunesse " (Sainte-Beuve). In other words, the former novel shows more of the writer's intelligence and the latter more of her sensibility. Both partake of the nature of " confessions." Both dwell on the idea that a superior woman is destined to misfortune, if she opposes the fixed views of man; but while Corinne has the superiority of talent, the heroine of *Delphine* (1802) surpasses through her character and heart. The latter story is a story of self-sacrifice in favor of a poor sort of lover, a copy of the one who made Mlle de Lespinasse so unhappy. *Delphine* has something of the passionate style of Mlle de Lespinasse, though it is more directly modeled on Rousseau. The form is that of the epistolary novel, and the book suffers from the artifices demanded by this method of narration. It is also a " lyrical novel," like the *Nouvelle Héloïse*, giving the greatest place to love, its transports and problems. It is modern in that it poses the question of a woman's right to struggle for her place in the sun and to keep her individual conscience. It states the ideal which permeates much of Mme de Staël's work — " the desire for happiness in marriage." The style is sometimes incorrect and hasty, whereas the plot is improbable and romanesque. But *Delphine* remains a stimulating and disturbing book, on account of its individualism, its subtlety and its fine conception of feminine character.

Corinne (1807) is a greater novel and the writer's masterpiece from an artistic standpoint. Here there is a closer sense of style and a better sustained eloquence. The novel not only revealed the beauties of Italy to France, but it showed the authoress at the apogee of her powers. For Europe henceforth she was known as the writer of *Corinne*, taken as the symbol of the independence of genius. The heroine, like her creator, is a talented improviser, who converses to a select circle on literature, love and death. She also resembles Mme de Staël in feeling the rivalry between fame and love, in experiencing much hostile criticism, and above all in her need for an understanding husband. She has apparently found him in Lord Nelvil, a rather stiff Englishman, but there are family vetoes against their union, and Corinne finally yields her sweetheart to a " truly English " maiden. Much of the action is laid amid Italian scenes and there are long digressions concerning Italian art, literature and manners, which remind one rather too much of a guide-book. This feature, together with certain improbabilities and conventions in the plot, give the story an old-fashioned air. But the intermingling of sight-seeing with heart-affairs is well done, and in sentiment and thought, *Corinne* is absolutely a first-class novel. It has spiritual unity and it is a cultural landmark. Its penetration, its melancholy, the sweet frank charm of the heroine, her nobility of character, and a deeply moving note which comes from personal experience are still most effective and give the story its high place in the finer literature of love. And, as Brunetière observes, the psychological excellence of Mme de Staël is only equaled by her historical importance. That is, *Delphine* and *Corinne* are the first modern novels to give an inside view of French society at a crucial epoch. Mme de Staël, then, succeeded in her effort to raise fiction to a higher dignity of intrinsic worth and of general consideration. Her wide powers of sympathy and her thorough feminism make her the ancestress of George Sand and the individualistic school. But it is notable that Mme de Staël does not allow passion to triumph and that she maintains the usual moral standards.

In literary criticism, her work emphasizes a new point of departure. She is the first wholly to break away from the abso-**"De la** luteness of Classical standards [2] and to emphasize **Littérature"** that cosmopolitan spirit which recognizes the relativity of taste and freely admires the beauties of foreign countries. Also she changes the direction of criticism from the study of detail (rhetorics, treatises on taste, commentaries) to the study of literature in its relation to other social currents — the modern idea of "Kulturgeschichte." In the introduction to *De la Littérature* (1801), she says :

> Je me suis proposé d'examiner quelle est l'influence de la religion, des mœurs et des lois sur la littérature, et quelle est l'influence de la littérature sur la religion, les mœurs et les lois. . . . On n'a pas suffisamment analysé les causes morales et politiques qui modifient l'esprit de la littérature.

These *rapports* and others, such as historical circumstances, the structure of society and especially the genius of each race, she connects with her special subject, quite in the manner of Montes-

---

[2] See above, pp. 346–47; Voltaire had not dared to go so far.

quieu, and she uses many of the divisions that appear in the
Esprit des lois. *De la Littérature* is, in fact, an eighteenth-
century book in that it revives the question of progress, aims
at human perfectibility and sets liberal philosophy above all
else. Its argument along these lines is hampered by the old
confusion between an advance in the arts and in the other
fields of human endeavor. Mme de Staël admits, indeed, this
"principe des beaux arts: l'imagination ne permet pas la perfectibilité indéfinie." But in practice she is so ardent in upholding the cause of intellectual progress that she diminishes
the rôle of creative genius and sets the thought of the
eighteenth century above the more artistic literature of the
seventeenth. Thus she is a "Modern." As regards other countries, she is disposed to set Rome above Greece, since the former
civilization came later in time; and she was not yet well
acquainted with Italy and Germany. In these connections, the
reader must allow for misconceptions and inaccuracies. But
Mme de Staël becomes a critical prophet in making her great
and lasting distinction between the "Literatures of the North"
and those of the South: Great Britain and Germany as opposed
to the Mediterranean countries, or the Teutonic *versus* the
Classical and Romance languages. The qualities of the
North are courage, a melancholy imagination, metaphysical
brooding and mysticism. These qualities are well displayed in
Ossian, who is erroneously called the "Homer of the North."
More plausibly, poetic genius is associated with the misty
English skies and comes to an admirable culmination in Shakespeare and Milton. For the Northern imagination loves the
sea, the wind and wild heather, and thoughts of the other world
are blown across these cloudy horizons. Thus Montesquieu's
theory of climate is renovated. Mme de Staël's liberal spirit
also attempts to reconcile the newly born political ideals with the
progress of literature. Intellectual progress must be "consecrated by liberty, guaranteed by democratic institutions and
manners, and reinvigorated by cosmopolitanism." But literature, together with other things, is an "expression of society,"
aristocratically viewed. This book was the first of the writer's
works to create a commotion. It was severely judged by the
semi-official and dogmatic critics of the Empire. It also in-

stituted the rivalry between Mme de Staël and Chateaubriand, who aptly said: " Vous n'ignorez pas que ma folie à moi est de voir Jésus-Christ partout, comme Mme de Staël la perfectibilité."

The bold distinctions between North and South are reinforced in *De l'Allemagne*, which was suppressed by Napoleon's orders in 1810 and finally published in 1813. This is cer-"De l'Alle- tainly the masterpiece of Mme de Staël as a thinker.
magne" It is the book which first disclosed Germany to France and which gave a worthy image of the outburst of genius associated with the age of Goethe. Apart from any theories, the basic qualities of the work are the unusual breadth, penetration and sympathy, which still make *De l'Allemagne* such satisfactory critical reading. It consists of four parts: (1) a general view of Germany; (2) its literature; (3) its philosophy; (4) a treatise on religion and " l'enthousiasme." Of these, the second part is of chief importance for us, since the writer's knowledge of the country itself was not very wide. Outside of court and literary circles, she had seen little of general manners or of middle-class life, which she idyllizes.

She begins her critical treatment by regretting that the French will not do justice to German literature, because of linguistic barriers and inherent national prejudices. Among these are the French faith in rules, the power of tradition, of public opinion, and especially the social standpoint which French writers too constantly bear in mind. Here and elsewhere, she holds — rather against the grain, one supposes — that solitary thought and feeling constitute the strongest basis for literary creation. The Germans now are independent and individual in their books, as they long were in their political units. It is true that they often tend to obscurity, " se plaisent dans les ténèbres," and their prose is negligent as compared with the cult of style in France. In the drama, all that concerns plot and action is better handled by the French; but a German play will go deeper in psychology, in heart-interest and in the study of strong passions. From this point on the writer pleads for international tolerance in letters and for the benefits which the French particularly would derive from admitting the best of German ideas and emotions.

All this illustrates the candor and personality which made the charm of Mme de Staël and which she most admired in the Germans. She revolted against the Classical rules and models, she preferred subjectivity, sentiment, imagination and revery. Therefore she is plainly for the North against the South (including in the latter division the Classic age of France). She now definitely connects the North with the word " Romanticism." In Germany, she says, the term " Romantic " has recently been introduced and applies to the kind of poetry that mingles chivalry and Christianity. The English have surpassed in this kind. The South is more clear-sighted and pagan; so classic poetry is that of the ancients and their imitators. Either kind is admissible, for a natural and national diversity of tastes springs " des sources primitives de l'imagination et de la pensée." But on the whole she contends for the inspiration of indigenous Romanticism rather than the imitation of transplanted Classicism. She chiefly admires Goethe, Schiller and Lessing. She is not thorough on philosophy, which she knew mostly through Schlegel, but she sees the importance of Kantian idealism — " the starry heavens above and the sense of duty within." She stresses morality in the third as well as in the fourth part of the book, where " enthusiasm " now takes on a deeper and sterner note. Genius for her should finally serve to manifest " la bonté suprême de l'âme." As a critic, her contact with art is not immediate and spontaneous, but rather intellectualized and ethical.

By selection and idealizing, Mme de Staël gave a rather rose-colored picture of Germany, as Heine showed in his *Deutschland*. But her impulse toward Teutonic studies was **Her Influence** felt by such men as Cousin in France, by Ticknor and Prescott in America. It was largely through her initiation that the movement towards German universities began. More widely, the critical and cosmopolitan spirit of Mme de Staël, together with her fine Romanticism of feeling, counted upon diverse groups. In poetry, her theory of enthusiasm influenced especially Lamartine. In criticism, the cosmopolitan tone of the *Globe*, Hugo's *Préface de Cromwell* and the exotic gleanings of Nodier owe a good deal to her guidance.[3]

---

[3] For these and other names, see next Book.

In politics and history, the liberal doctrinaires were certainly affected by the latest and most mature of her books, the *Considérations sur la Révolution française* (published posthumously, 1818). The "trio of the Sorbonne" — Villemain, Guizot, Cousin — are her disciples. The first-named more completely makes literature the expression of society and also studies international literary influences. Guizot figures among the group of translators and propagandists, who mainly through Mme de Staël's impulsion, promote the vogue of Shakespeare and of Schiller. In general, as Sainte-Beuve says, she helped restore the sense of the infinite, which is the spirit of the North. A ripe mind, a deep heart and a keen enthusiasm are the personal qualities which she impresses upon her work. She enlarged the borders of her country, she helped to Europeanize modern thought.

By the side of Mme de Staël, her lover cuts rather a poor figure. A native of Lausanne, Constant was early naturalized as a French citizen and played a considerable political rôle. His character forms a singular mixture of intellectual strength and moral weakness. He was a liberal skeptic, an acute logical thinker and a psychological analyst of the first order. But "Constant l'inconstant" had a feeble will, an excitable, over-active temperament, an arid egotistical nature. He was a perpetual diner-out, talker, duellist, Don Juan and sensation-seeker. On account of his two-fold nature, he has been called "un homme qui regardait un enfant," and like Chauteaubriand's René and Lord Byron, he was one of the great *blasés* of the Romantic period.

Benjamin Constant, 1767–1830

His character appears nakedly in *Adolphe* (1816), as a mixture of egotism, passion and irony. Adolphe falls out of love with his mistress and makes her suffer cruelly; he too suffers because of his very impotence in feeling. The successive steps in this affair are treated with rare profundity and give the impression of close living truth. Indeed, the chief scenes and sentiments were actually lived, since the heroine, Ellénore, is a compound of Constant's two loves, Mme de Charrière and Mme de Staël. The gentle devotion of the one and the impetuous and exigent temper of the other do not make a unified character. Otherwise, Constant shows much insight in

"Adolphe"

portraying human weaknesses. The decadence of love; the intervention of *amour-propre,* that great stumbling-block of
French lovers; the effect of Ellénore's mature age and of her
too clinging disposition; the self-torture of Adolphe and his
subjection to public opinion; the painful and false side of such
liaisons: all these phases are considered with penetration and
restraint. The style is sober, clearly fitting the thought, not
rhetorical. Constant did not have a creative imagination, and
his characters are real people, somewhat changed. But he had
the two gifts of clairvoyance and of precision. Consequently
Adolphe, an intensely psychological novel, is the first of **the**
ultra-modern variety and leads on to Stendhal.

CHAPTER III

CHATEAUBRIAND

OF THE THREE great forerunners of Romanticism, Chateaubriand exercised the most immediate and imposing influence.
Chief Qualities Cosmopolitan and eloquent like Mme de Staël, he has a less disciplined brain and a colder heart. Sensitive, imaginative and self-centered like Rousseau, he is more aristocratic, less primitive, and absorbed in more exotic landscapes. Where Rousseau pleads for a generous sprinkling of nature, Chateaubriand believes in total immersion. Where Mme de Staël is humanitarian and forward-looking, Chateaubriand is pessimistic concerning man, rejects every liberal belief of the eighteenth century, and stands for the " Catholic and monarchical reaction." Naturally, then, he turns to the Gothic and medieval. Yearning for remoteness, he also chooses his subjects and scenes from the farthest Occident and Orient. He thus leads the Romantic movement in these important novelties: medievalism; the revival of aesthetic Christianity; the impassioned description of exotic nature; and the enthronement, of the melancholy ego therein.

François-René de Chateaubriand (1768–1848) was born at Saint-Malo in Brittany, within sound of the sea which always
Early Life stirred his imagination and feeling. He came of an ancient and illustrious family. His father was a stern despot, and his mother stood somewhat apart from her children; René's affection was rather for his sister, Lucile, who had a temperament much like his own. These two, in the lonely Château de Combourg, led a strange and melancholy youth, hushed in the presence of their gloomy father, listening to tales of ghosts and to the wind which moaned around the lonely turret. For René, it was a life of hard exercise, followed at night by much solitude and haunted meditation. No wonder that he dates from this epoch his lifelong sadness and his vast creative in-

stinct. " Mon imagination allumée, se propageant sur tous les objets, ne trouvait nulle part assez de nourriture et aurait dévoré la terre et le ciel." He was sent away to school and became a good student in late adolescence. After considering several careers, he was suddenly put into the army by his father, presented at court and to certain lights of the old régime; Malesherbes, the former minister, advised the journey to America which Chateaubriand undertook in 1791. He traveled from the seaboard cities to Niagara and probably to the Ohio, but he never saw the primeval southern forests which made his works so famous. Returning to France, he was drawn into a conventional marriage, then emigrated and played his part courageously as a soldier of the royal camp. Wounded and ill, disillusioned and desperate, he sought refuge in England, where he lived for eight years. At London, he was at first poverty-stricken and on the verge of suicide. Becoming acquainted with English country life, he had an idyllic affair with the daughter of a pastor. Finally he met Fontanes, a sympathetic critic and counselor, who with Joubert later, was largely instrumental in advancing Chateaubriand's literary career. He returned to Paris, and the publication of *Atala* (1801) was followed by the *Génie du Christianisme* in the next year. This was at the time when Napoleon's " Concordat " aimed at reconciling France and the Catholic Church, a circumstance which assured to Chateaubriand and his *Génie* a brilliant success. From now on he is the lion of the salons, he lives but little with his wife, and he becomes distinguished as statesman, ambassador, and the foremost literary figure of his age.

It was the perpetual desire for fresh conquests that led Chateaubriand into politics. For a time he had the favor of Napoleon, but soon broke with him and became a stanch legitimist. He was the chief promoter of the Christian and monarchical tendency which centered around the Restoration of 1815 and affected the earlier Romanticists, for example, Lamartine. Having made a splendid trip to the Orient, having won the devotion of duchesses and the ear of the public, it seems that at last Chateaubriand might have been happy. But his haughty spirit soon found defects in the new monarchy. Under whatever dynasty, it was Chateaubriand's nature to be

Political Career

always in the opposition. Yet he was made ambassador, for short intervals, to Rome, to Berlin and to London; in England he lived in sumptuous contrast to his former poverty. As minister of foreign affairs, he threw his country into a brief war with Spain (1824). On the advent of the bourgeois monarchy of Louis-Philippe (1830), Chateaubriand withdrew from political life and henceforth reigned in the salon of Mme Récamier. Here he was viewed as a social and literary oracle, dominating and often disdaining the younger generation of writers. He prepared his final attitude by writing his *Mémoires d'outre-tombe* and by arranging for his burial in a little island near Saint-Malo, where his lonely tomb still confronts the sea.

This agitated life contained features of grandeur, but was darkened by Chateaubriand's constant melancholy, egotism and **Character** *ennui.* " J'ai baillé ma vie," as he bitterly said, because his imperious imagination always outstripped reality. His perpetual longings for the unattainable brought into French literature the so-called *mal de René.* He was too intense, too self-centered and haughty. His pride devoured everything, leading to disgust with action, with affection, with glory and finally with himself. But his egotism rides above the wreck, not only permeating his Memoirs, but making him the chief hero of his other works. " Il n'y a que Chateaubriand dans l'œuvre de Chateaubriand." With the exceptions of the principle of honor and the Catholic religion, he affects to consider life an utter void and he enjoys a perverse satisfaction in the spectacle of human ruins and illusions. Thus it is not surprising that Chateaubriand represents primarily the literature of escape, and that his splendid gifts adorn the presentation of far-off civilizations, whether in the East or in the West.

The Western influence, dating from his four months' stay in America, appears in *Atala, René* and *Les Natchez;* the **Western** Eastern, in which may be included much of Cha-**Inspiration** teaubriand's treatment of Christianity, is visible in the *Génie du Christianisme* and conspicuous in the *Itinéraire de Paris à Jérusalem* and the prose epic, *Les Martyrs.* With the partial exception of the *Génie* and of his Memoirs, all of Chateaubriand's important works deal either with the Orient or with the Occident. In the latter field he found more novelty and

exhibited more strength. He had composed, by 1800, a huge
manuscript volume, describing his trip to America and the
Indian tribe of the Natchez; for during the years of fighting
and exile, his visions of American vastness and his embellish-
ment of Indian maidens had grown apace. He was ready now
to extract from this manuscript such episodes as
"Atala" *Atala* and *René*. *Atala* (1801) is probably the
most perfect of his works in its harmonious construction, the
interest and charm of its characters, the high values of its
scenery and style. It has a peculiar attraction for Americans,
since it is the first work of French genius in which the scene is
laid wholly in this country. Chateaubriand's accounts of the
savannahs and forests of the old Louisiana territory have long
been famous; and the flora and fauna which he exhibits in his
luxuriant images and descriptions were according to the recorded
documentation of the time. The same may be said of his general
use of local color and local customs. As regards character,
he adds the new note of " psychological exoticism " (Chinard),
or the absorbing depiction of modern struggles against a primitive background. But it may be admitted that his savages are
rather too " good Indians " to be probable. The heroine, Atala,
has been brought up by a Christian mother. Her lover, Chactas,
later becomes half-civilized. As a young warrior, he was taken
prisoner by a hostile tribe of which Atala was a member; she
rescues him and flees with him into the forest; but she cannot
marry him because of a vow made to her dying mother. The
conflict in her mind, the love-passages in the forest, crowned by
the death and burial of Atala, are very impressive and recall
in places *Manon Lescaut*. Underlying the story are deep currents of emotion which break out in extreme Romanticism: as
where Chactas expresses a desire to clasp his beloved and
soar with her through the débris of the world and eternity; and
elsewhere the author declares: " Les grandes passions sont
solitaires et les transporter au désert c'est les rendre à leur
empire." This is Rousseauism, with more emphasis on wider
spaces and the wildest desires. The style, as usual with Chateaubriand, is majestic and melancholy. The grave cadences
of his prose seem naturally allied with this tale of " old unhappy
far-off things," with the sweep of great expanses and eternal

passions. The descriptions of nature are both accurate and picturesque, and *Atala* worthily opens the nineteenth century as the first masterpiece of French eloquence after Rousseau.

Another tragic story of the West was first published as a part of the *Génie du Christianisme*. *René* (1802) is but a brief episode, yet its influence upon both the form and **" René "** sentiment of Romantic fiction was very great. The hero is another Chateaubriand, an ill-fated young Frenchman, who can find happiness neither in the civilization of Europe nor beyond the sea. He cannot live with his devoted Indian wife, and he relates to Chactas, now grown old, the melancholy history of his sentimental experiences. These include poignant memories of childhood, the affection of an unfortunate sister, travels and adventures in the "stormy ocean of the world," attempts at suicide and finally the plunge into the American wilderness. The *mal de René* consists in the perpetual disappointment which confronts insatiable desires, whether concerning the sympathy of women, the consolation of Nature, or the venture of life as a whole. The *mal* is not wholly new, but the personal intensity of Chateaubriand gives it fresh poignancy. " Mon cœur est naturellement pétri d'ennui et de misère." He finds existence only a shifting abyss and he calls on the longed-for storms to sweep him into unknown climes. By a sort of cosmic fallacy, the greater aspects of Nature are associated with man's demonic heart, whose movements are compared with the rising and sinking of the Mississippi's floods. The following passage may well illustrate Chateaubriand's dangerous charm:

> Je descendais dans la vallée, je m'élevais sur la montagne, appelant de toute la force de mes désirs l'idéal objet d'une flamme future; je l'embrassais dans les vents, je croyais l'entendre dans les gémissements du fleuve; tout était ce fantôme imaginaire, et les astres dans les cieux, et le principe même de vie dans l'univers.

It is to be noted that the author is perfectly aware of his Romantic excesses; Chactas concludes with the safe moral: " Il n'y a de bonheur que dans les voies communes."

From his manuscript volume of Americana, Chateaubriand drew later the long epic narrative of *Les Natchez* (1826). The subject is the massacre of the French colony of the Natchez in 1727, with which is interwoven the story of the Indian adventures and loves of René and their tragic termination. **"Les Natchez"** Plot and probability are hampered by Chateaubriand's insistence on certain stock devices of the epic form (cf. *Les Martyrs*): invocations, apparitions, enumerations of tribes and troops, and particularly the intervention of angels and Indian gods in battles. Apart from this absurdity, the author again follows fact as regards both the central subject and the use of local and historical color. The characters offer interesting cases of exotic sentiments and conflicts. An older and more despairing René, who has been adopted by the Natchez, is observed in his ebb and flow from the savage to the civilized life, and back again. He is loved by Celuta, whom he weds through gratitude, and this bronzed heroine alternates between sentiment and duty — for René is supposed to have betrayed her tribe. The real traitor, Ondouré, and René's blood-brother, Outougamiz, are conventional figures of the epic. More individual and pleasing is the maiden Mila, whose naïve feeling for René is well portrayed. The story ends in a general catastrophe of violence, suicide and murder.

The work which marks the transition from the Western to the Eastern influence is the *Génie du Christianisme* (1802). **"Le Génie du Christianisme"** This book stands at the center of Chateaubriand's system, whether as regards religion or art, forces which he here tries to amalgamate. He defends the " genius " of Christianity in maintaining that this faith has been productive of greater results, in literature and the arts, than are found in the ancient pagan masterpieces. The *Génie* represents a revolution in criticism and aesthetics; it breaks with the tradition of the Renaissance; it is rather hostile to the eighteenth century; it prefers the medieval and the Gothic, and aims at reviving the historic past of France; it is Romantic rather than Classical or philosophic in spirit; it argues for the " beau idéal " or the principle of an artistic choice in nature; and it establishes the *moi* as the main source of inspiration: " On ne peint bien que son propre cœur et la meilleure partie du génie se compose de souvenirs."

Chateaubriand believes that Christianity has developed the soul of man and made literature and the arts expressive of a

higher spiritual truth than was possible in the pagan " chaos."
This holds even for writers like Racine and Voltaire, whose best
The
Argument
characters — Phèdre and Lusignan — are Christian
in spite of themselves. The chief beauties of a
" bizarre " product like the *Divine Comedy*, thinks Chateaubriand, also spring from Christianity. Milton is better appreciated by this critic than by any French writer hitherto. The
Bible itself is discussed and praised as a literary monument.
Yet Chateaubriand shows a wise moderation in esteeming the
truth and taste of the best ancients, like Vergil. Again, Christianity is associated with the idea of solitude in nature. The
nymphs and fauns have vanished, " pour rendre aux grottes leur
silence et aux boix leurs rêveries." The divine immensities of the
deserts and of the American forests are now capable of a vaster
inspiration. So modern descriptive poetry, of which Chateaubriand gives a faulty sketch, should be superior to the ancient.
Also the modern Christian epic, using its own supernatural
machinery, is better than the pagan variety. This support of
the *merveilleux chrétien*, challenging Boileau's Classical principles, is exemplified by the practice of Milton as well as of Dante
and produced unfortunate results in Chateaubriand's own work.
With regard to prose literature, it is not surprising that he rejects " la philosophie," in favor of the more orthodox seventeenth
century. As regards the fine arts, rather superficially treated,
it is notable that he dwells on the religious side of Gothic
architecture, which is linked with his passion for the past. There
is a picturesque chapter on ruins, the " poétique des morts," which
always attracted his interest. The Madonnas of the Italians
and the orations of Bossuet are also cases in point, and the
general conclusion is: " Que l'incrédulité est la principale cause
de la décadence du goût et du génie."

But Chateaubriand's logic is not so serried as it may appear
from the above presentation. He is more occupied with present-
Defects and
Merits
ing plausible sentiments or series of glittering
tableaux, often done in his handsomest bravura style.
The *Génie* has been called a religious museum. Christian truth,
declares one critic, can do without art and uses a sterner apolo-
getic, as with Pascal. Just as Mme de Staël had a weakness for
the pleasures of melancholy, so Chateaubriand indulges in the

pleasures of Christianity. He inaugurates, for France, the aesthetic view of religion, which has been so prominent since. But
his book represents a strong and, at its time, a necessary reaction. Eighteenth-century skepticism had fallen into des-
iccation and materialism. It was the right moment for religious revival. Chateaubriand's influence was felt on the Biblical
poetry of the Romanticists and on certain writers of the historical
school. His unparalleled prestige was largely based on the
Génie du Christianisme.

The prose epic of *Les Martyrs* (1809) is, as regards its central
subject, a more old-fashioned *Quo Vadis*. It deals with the
Eastern conversions, struggles and martyrdoms of the early
Subjects: Christians under Diocletian. But this frame-work
"Les Martyrs" is extended through the *récit* of Eudore, the hero, to
cover travels and experiences in various Roman provinces, including the Orient. The unity of the story suffers through this
extension. Its illusion, as a work of fiction, is weakened by the
introduction of all the epic machinery of the *merveilleux chrétien*.
The best part of *Les Martyrs* is found in particular characters
and episodes: the charm of Cymodocée, the heathen maiden
whom Eudore loves and converts; the picture of Velléda, the
stormy druidess; and the battle-scenes among the Franks, containing the war-cry of " Pharamond," which incited Thierry to
write his history of the Merovingians.

Whatever his anachronisms, Chateaubriand made wide studies
for *Les Martyrs*, the results of which appear also in *L'Itiné-*
" L'Itiné- *raire de Paris à Jérusalem et de Jérusalem à Paris*
raire " (1811). This work, like *Corinne*, had a great
success as a sort of glorified guide-book; it is written with more
good-humor and is concerned more with everyday life than any
other of Chateaubriand's productions. But it is artistically
composed and well reveals his essential traits. The three high
points in his travels were Sparta, Athens and Jerusalem, and
the treatment of these places is climactic and impressive. The
prevailing mood is that of saturation with the melancholy of
ruins, the sadness of vanished glory, the mobility of human
things amid the immobility of nature. The suavity of Greece is
contrasted with the touching mystery of Calvary, and the religious note is often sounded. The author admits that he is

more interested in monuments than in men. He went forth in the spirit of a crusader and he anticipated Byron by awakening an enthusiasm for the Orient.

This large collection of Memoirs is Chateaubriand's last will and testament. It is a voice speaking " from beyond the tomb," " **Mémoires** to tell the whole truth about the author and his **d'outre-** epoch. Unsuccessful when first published, the **tombe,"** **1848–50** *Mémoires* are now recognized as one of the foremost documents of the Romantic era. They contain all of Chateaubriand, his beauties and defects, his power, egomania and puerilities; they recount the several chief stages in his career, parading what he calls his " triple influence, religieuse, politique et littéraire "; they deal closely with the leading figures and events of his day, giving vivid sketches of Revolutionary types like Mirabeau and a full-length portrait of Napoleon as a despot. But the most fascinating pages of the *Mémoires* are found in the early volumes where Chateaubriand dwells upon his formative years at Combourg, the dreams and yearnings of his adolescence. He thinks that a later visitor to the sacred spot —

> pourra reconnaître le château; mais il cherchera vainement le grand bois: le berceau de mes songes a disparu comme ces songes. Demeuré seul debout sur son rocher, l'antique donjon pleure les chênes, vieux compagnons qui l'environnaient et le protégeaient contre la tempête. Isolé comme lui, j'ai vu comme lui tomber autour de moi la famille qui embellissait mes jours et me prêtait son abri: heureusement ma vie n'est pas bâtie sur la terre aussi solidement que les tours où j'ai passé ma jeunesse, et l'homme résiste moins aux orages que les monuments élevés par ses mains.

There are many such wistful passages; for it is one characteristic of the Memoirs, composed from 1811–41, that they weave back and forth between the emotions of youth and the memories of age. The highest virtues of style are found in the reminiscent preludes to the several Parts into which the work is divided. Its tone, as a whole, is unequal; vigor alternates with triviality, harmony and vision with bitterness and wrath; but throughout there is an effect of reality and passion recalling Saint-Simon. Perhaps this is due to the fact, of which Chateaubriand boasts, that he had actually *lived* what his books describe, whether as traveler, soldier, diplomat or publicist. He was almost the last to live and to write in the grand manner.

Chateaubriand's genius made itself felt through the double force of his morbid charm and his expansive imagination. As **Genius** seen in connection with *René*, the charm has its dangers, but it also has its delights. "Son rôle est d'enchanter." There is a seduction in his sensibility, a lulling sweetness in his melancholy, and a high excellence in his harmonious rhythms and images. Chateaubriand's very egotism has its fascination; the reader substitutes himself for the author and goes through similar moods of yearning, pride, isolation and disillusionment. Again, Chateaubriand was " all compact " of imagination, which quality he expands East and West in the comprehensive fashion of modern art. Hence the marvelously rich pictures of many lands and climes. He pours his soul out upon all that is beautiful in Nature; but he cares little for the souls of other people, he is a poor psychologist. As oracle and leader emeritus, he exercised a great influence upon the Romantic movement. According to Faguet, " il est l'homme qui a renouvelé l'imagination française." For two generations such writers as Lamartine and Hugo, G. Sand and even Flaubert derive much of their earlier manner from Chateaubriand. In our own time, Pierre Loti is his most distinguished literary descendant.

BOOK VI

ROMANTICISM

CHAPTER I

THE ROMANTIC MOVEMENT

THE full flowering of the Romantic Movement took place between 1820, when Lamartine published his *Premières Médita-*
History of *tions,* and 1843, when Hugo's last tragedy failed.
the Period The political history of that period furnishes a significant background to its literary output: the individualism of despots, the royalist hopes and the growing sense of democracy are successively reflected in the work of the Romanticists. After Napoleon, the Restoration of the Bourbons was accomplished by a sharp monarchical reaction. Louis XVIII (1815-24) was at first obliged to grant a Constitutional Charter, with liberal provisions, and the Chamber of Deputies was established. But the returning *émigrés* were very influential and soon a reactionary ministry was formed, combining aristocracy, royalism and strong Catholic sympathies. Censorship of the press and the sway of landowners were restored. These tendencies became more pronounced under the reign of Charles X (1824-30), who wanted to be a despot of the old régime. But France, having had a taste of liberty, was unwilling to submit. Publicists like Chateaubriand and Royer-Collard, professors, journalists and the City of Paris all protested, with the result that the Bourbon monarchy was overthrown in 1830 (" Revolution of July ") ; Louis-Philippe, Duke of Orleans, was made King of the French and the so-called " bourgeois monarchy " began (1830-48). This government, in turn, disgusted many writers, because of its lack of distinction and its addiction to timid compromises.

Each new ruler had brought fresh hope to the younger generations of which the Romanticists were composed. It was a time

of expansive feeling and wide aspirations; but these were followed only too soon by disappointment and weariness when govern-
Social ments and councils did not fulfil their promises.
Background The social atmosphere was full of ferment, there was heard the clash of new and old, of the individual against the many. Hundreds of brilliant youths, abandoning the political arena, turned their talents to literature and art. They were no longer hampered by academic training or the tradition of the salons; they could be fully themselves. The renaissance of poetry and painting — fraternal arts which were now closely connected — the considerable development of journalism, the vogue of the " vie de bohème " and of romantic love-affairs: all this gave opportunities to these restless young men. Currents of dandyism, picturesque costumes or poses, and important foreign influences served to direct or to adorn the new movement.

Romanticism was primarily a revolt against the outworn principles of neo-classicism, as exemplified by the poetasters and
Essential dramatists of the eighteenth century and the
Features beginning of the nineteenth. Soon, however, the movement condemned the methods of Boileau and Racine as well. Consequently it rejected the old rules of versification and of tragedy. But more positive features appear among the chief tenets of Romanticism. It stood for individual liberty, for an expansion of the field of art, for the superiority of imagination and feeling over reason, for a truly poetical revival. In its earlier phase, under the influence of Chateaubriand and Lamartine, it was curiously linked with a political conservatism and a return to the national past. It was also more idealistic before 1830, whereas, after this date disillusionment and pessimism became more prominent in the work of various writers.

Théophile Gautier, an ardent adherent of the Romantic cause, declares that the people of a later day can hardly understand
Inspiration the effervescent enthusiasm of that time. There
and Energy was a new sap of life, an intoxicating atmosphere, an absolute surrender to the poetic ideal. There are many records of the advance of the Romantic army upon Paris, nearly one hundred years ago. Personages of fact and of fiction,

undisciplined egoists like the heroes of Stendhal and of Balzac, followed Napoleon, the "great condottiere," in the direction of lawless and materialistic ambition. But others, like the intimate circle of Hugo, expressed their personalities through emotional experience and intense imaginings, with an outburst of tumultuous revolt and wild creative energy. In their assertion of individual rights, their deification of human love and the fatality of passion, their devotion to the long wonders of immortal beauty, they bring back to France a feeling which had been in abeyance since the days of Ronsard.

The great writers of Romanticism were Lamartine, Hugo, Musset, Vigny, Gautier and George Sand; and, to a lesser extent, **Leaders and** Sainte-Beuve as critic, Dumas *père*, Stendhal and **"Cénacles"** Mérimée. These names together with certain others will occupy us in the following chapters. But there were many minor writers who will here be dealt with briefly in connection with the progress of the movement, the formation of the different groups or *cénacles*. First came the group which rallied around *La Muse Française*. This journal lasted only **"La Muse** two years (1823–24), but it had a significant influence **Française"** upon nascent Romanticism. As in the case of the Pléiade, its founders and chief contributors were seven in number: Alexandre Soumet, Alexandre Guiraud, Emile Deschamps; Hugo and Vigny; Saint-Valry and Desjardins. The "two Alexanders," who were then among the foremost representatives of poetry and drama, were still semi-classical and timid in revolt. They came from Toulouse and they, with others of the group, were crowned by the Académie des Jeux Floraux of that city. Soumet is best known for his tragedy of *Saül*. He had a second-rate derivative talent, but he was then ranked as a demi-god and his prestige considerably aided the *Muse*. Guiraud wrote the prospectus for the journal, a valuable feature of which was the attention it paid to foreign literatures. Emile Deschamps actively launched the publication and furnished a salon for the first *cénacle*. As a poet, Deschamps is credited with a Lamartinian sweetness and grace. Lamartine himself remained apart from the circle. Its two minor adherents need not concern us, but let us note that several of Vigny's best poems appeared in the *Muse;* also five contributions from Hugo, including an interesting review of Scott's *Quentin Durward*. In 1824, the main issues of Romanticism were still confused and vague; Hugo disavowed the term; the new spirit was not yet disentangled from Classicism and royalism. But already it was sufficiently strong to call forth denunciations from academic critics, who, declaring that Romanticism "did not exist," thereby helped to crystallize its existence.

The *Muse* suspended publication, and Soumet passed to the ranks of the enemy. The rest of the group were kept together **The Salon** by Charles Nodier, who received and encouraged **de l'Arsenal,** them in his home at the Arsenal Library. Nodier **1824-27** (see next chapter) was an indolent good-natured dilettante who had in him, it is said, the composition of ten men, including " poet, romancer, historian, bibliophile." He defined Romanticism as " la liberté régie par le goût," a remark which set the tone for his chatty receptions. Lesser lights of the *Muse* and of the Nodier *cénacle* were these: the wild Jules Lefèvre, a Byronist; the witty Ulric Guttinguer; Baour-Lormian, translator of *Ossian;* Chênedollé, a transition poet; and the beautiful Delphine Gay, known as the " Muse de la Patrie," who had the fortune to be admired by Classicists and Romanticists alike.

By 1827, Victor Hugo had attained his poetic majority. In the same year he formed a close friendship with Sainte- **Le Grand** Beuve, and these two constitute the head and front **Cénacle,** of the greatest Romantic *cénacle*. This was known **1827-30** as " le cénacle de Joseph Delorme," such being the pen-name of Sainte-Beuve. In its membership were numbered such familiar names as Vigny, Nodier, Deschamps and Guttinguer; that weird poet, Gérard de Nerval; the enthusiastic Dumas *père*; and the adolescent Musset, who came more casually. The movement now takes on more significance and breadth; it includes painters (Delacroix) as well as poets; it makes the theater its chief stamping-ground; plays like Hugo's *Marion Delorme* are read to large gatherings; more important works are actually produced; and a critical direction is given to Romanticism through the efforts of Sainte-Beuve (see Bk. VIII, Ch. I). With some justice, then, this group has been called " le cénacle de Joseph Delorme." But its creative leader was, of course, Victor Hugo, whose priest-like personality was almost worshiped by his associates. Théophile Gautier, another enthusiastic admirer, was enlisted for the battle of *Hernani* (1830), which marked the definite triumph of the movement. Shortly afterwards the unity of the Romantic school was broken up and the last *cénacle* was dissolved; partly because of the Revolution of July, but more on account of dramatic rivalries and the exaggeration of ideas and egoistic tendencies. The current of production, however, continued until well into the forties.

The severe censorship of Napoleon and some hesitation regarding the "Charter" had much restricted the liberty of the press until about 1820. From then dates the foundation of modern literary journalism, the establishment of important critical reviews. They appear in considerable number between 1820 and 1830. They are mostly short-lived and reflect the confused conflicts of the time; those that are liberal in politics are often reactionary in literature, and vice versa. *La Muse Française* is the most thoroughly Romantic. But *Le Globe* (1824–30) had a wider scope and a vaster influence, and it aimed at liberalism in every sphere. It was founded by Dubois and other disciples of the "trio of the Sorbonne;"[1] the "doctrinaires" were among its contributors, and Sainte-Beuve was its chief critic. These men expand the treatment of literature, in an intelligent and cosmopolitan spirit, to include social and political topics; and the various fields are divided up among expert writers. Romanticism is given ample room in the *Globe,* though few of these intellectuals are sensitive to the more imaginative and artistic values of the new movement. On the other hand, they adopt the formula that "literature is the expression of society," and they show wide cosmopolitan tastes, both of which tendencies proceed from Mme de Staël. If Rousseau is the fountain-head of Romanticism, Chateaubriand is its "Sachem," Lamartine its elder brother, and Mme de Staël its intellectual godmother.[2]

Mme de Staël, indeed, had given currency to the term

Home Influences: Journalism

---

[1] Villemain, Guizot, Cousin; see below, Ch. VII; and for the "doctrinaires", or liberal bourgeois statesmen, see same chapter.

[2] A reference to the preceding Book will make this plain.

"Romantic." Her interest in Italy is responsible for French contacts with the works of Sismondi and Manzoni. But it is **Foreign Influences: Germany** chiefly the increasing vogue of *De l'Allemagne* that makes us realize how Romanticism was a general European movement, with emphasis on the literatures of the North. The Northern inspiration largely replaced the imitation of antiquity. The Germans who influenced the younger French writers are mainly those of the Golden Age, especially Goethe and Schiller. Goethe was long known as " the author of *Werther*," a work which fostered the sentimentalism of Nodier's *nouvelles*, as well as the *mal de siècle* of Constant's *Adolphe* and of Sénancour's *Obermann* (1804) — that " confession monotone et pénétrante." Sainte-Beuve and Musset also wrote confessional novels, partly modeled on *Werther*. *Götz von Berlichingen*, also by Goethe, is a predecessor of the Romantic drama; poems like the *Erlkönig* had some influence on the mysterious and fantastic side of Romanticism; while *Faust*, especially in its sentimental and diabolical aspects, deeply impressed the French imagination. *Faust* was known through many versions, the most remarkable of which is the translation by Gérard de Nerval. About 1830, there are many expressions of an exalted admiration for Goethe, who was viewed as the archetype of the man of genius. Schiller is a good second, particularly as regards the theater. His historical dramas, *Don Carlos*, *Wallenstein*, etc., undoubtedly furnish examples for the Romantic school. The third conspicuous success in France was the *Tales* of Hoffmann. These were admired and imitated, for their fantasy and *diablerie*, by such men as Nodier and Soulié. It was almost entirely the Romantic side of Germany that was appreciated in France. There were two general effects of this influence: German writers gave a considerable impulse to the new currents of poetic liberty; and their works served less as close models than as sources of vigorous inspiration for the French.

It would be impossible to enumerate all the phases of the English influence; four of the capital names must suffice. **England: Shakespeare** Shakespeare furnished much of the argument for the chief Romantic manifesto, Hugo's *Préface de Cromwell*, and his treatment of buffoons and crowds underlies

Hugo's practice in this respect. The translations by Alfred de Vigny, *Shylock* and *Le More de Venise*, were the finest ever made, and the performance of the latter play marked an epoch in the Romantic drama. Dumas *père* declares that *Hamlet* opened to him a new dramatic world and that his own historical "tableaux" owe much to Shakespeare. Musset's woodland fantasies are like delicate echoes of *Twelfth Night* and *As You Like It*. All of this implies that there had been a thorough revolt against the Voltairian attitude towards Shakespeare. Furthermore, two visits of English actors to Paris materially assisted in promoting the Shakespearean vogue.[3]

With this was coupled a vogue of a very different character. The strange fascination which "Ossian" exerted on the French Macpherson's reached its climax in the Napoleonic era. Chateau-"Ossian" briand was his herald, and Mme de Staël made him the Homer of her North. The discovery that "Ossian" derived less from Homer than from Macpherson gradually chilled the French, but the legend of the Bard was not yet dispelled for the men of 1830. He is still a fixed star in the literary firmament, and his nebulous glamour appeals to many amateurs and minor poets. Authoresses like Mme de Genlis and Delphine Gay, long-haired Romanticists like Boulay-Paty and Jules Lefèvre, lead the Caledonian through strange mazes and metamorphoses. The Ossianic atmosphere penetrates a good deal of Lamartine, especially the *Premières Méditations*, inducing a tender feeling for landscape, mingled with the melancholy attached to earthly things. Alfred de Musset also imitates the Bard in several poems. Mistiness and sadness, together with the passion for the past, are what this generation admired in Ossian.

Byron is the most important foreign influence upon French Romanticism. Indeed, by many Byron was regarded as the arch-romanticist of Europe. His person was made the subject of a sinister legend, according to which the poet appeared as a murderer and criminal. For French imitators, he stood as the representative of Satanic revolt, of grandiose nature, of the Orient, of passion ending in cynicism. His works were translated in twenty complete editions from 1820 to 1850. The phases of his influence begin with *Childe Harold*, passing through the

---

[3] More about Shakespeare will be found in Ch. V, below.

rebellious individualism of *Manfred, Lara* and *Cain,* to end with the sensual cynicism of *Don Juan.* Important critical appreciations were written quite early by Nodier, Vigny and Hugo. Then Byronic enthusiasm was fanned to a white heat by the poet's connection with the Grecian cause and by his untimely death. The *Muse Française* " ne peut que chanter et pleurer Byron." Delavigne mingled Byronic and Oriental inspiration in his *Odes Messéniennes;* so did painters like Delacroix and Géricault. Many imitators were variously indebted to the Englishman, including the four chief poets of the era. First, Lamartine declares a warm personal admiration for him. The poem of *Désespoir* owes much of its power to *Manfred,* and in *L'Homme* Lamartine tries at once to glorify Byron and to refute his pessimism. " C'est un ange qui a étudié le diable " — even to the extent of feebly continuing *Childe Harold* in *Le Dernier pèlerinage d'Harold.* Hugo feels the influence especially in *Les Orientales* (*Mazeppa,* etc.) and in some of the melancholy notes of the *Feuilles d'automne.* Vigny imitates Byron in a dozen early poems, and his very notion of the philosophic poem, as found in *Le Déluge* for example, is probably Byronic in source. Similar echoes are found in the sadder poems of Musset, as well as in such of his dreams as express bitterness and revolt. Finally, Gautier's *Albertus* is quite Don Juanesque in character. It is plainly the more passionate, the more melancholy and excessive aspects of French Romanticism that seek their prototype in Byron.

Sir Walter Scott is the father of the French historical novel as regards the picturesque reconstitution of the past. Picturesqueness in description, characterization and dialogue, is **Scott** the triple aspect of the Waverley Novels that carries over into France. Scott's diffused influence reached its apogee about 1820, when he was universally admired. He harmonized with the prevailing vogue of local color and of an antiquarian interest in the past. These characteristics are found, for instance, in Vigny's *Cinq-Mars,* together with Scott's ability to brush in the political background. Balzac's *Chouans* shows picturesqueness in dialogue and costumes, as well as Scott's penetration into epochs and his skill in handling crowds. Mérimée's *Charles IX* and Hugo's *Notre-Dame* represent the farther reaches of the movement. The Waverley Novels likewise promoted a feeling for the past and a care for characteristic detail among such historians as Thierry and Barante. Scott's antiquarianism had a more human appeal than that of Chateaubriand.

It will now appear that there are many aspects to French Romanticism and that it is difficult to summarize the great move-

Qualities ment satisfactorily. Its pervasive force may be centered around its belief in the expansive power of the *individual*. It emphasizes the particular, where Classicism had emphasized the universal. Individual sentiment, passion, genius, are the order of the day; hence lyric poetry is the predominant form. The individual soul rises high in exaltation or it plunges into its own depths with a fresh sense of the mystery of existence; or it goes roaming far from actuality, seeking remoteness in place or time. Associated then with the emotional development of the ego are such major Romantic qualities as idealism, melancholy, liberalism, exoticism and medievalism, together with an expansive treatment of nature and life. Examining these, we find that idealism, which begins as "enthusiasm," is not characteristic of the whole movement and is best illustrated by Lamartine and certain phases of Vigny and Hugo. Many Romanticists are prone to melancholy, due to the failure of their too personal or conflicting ideals. Liberalism was prominent in the political current; it is also found in the literary revolt against Classical subjects, styles and rules; it is connected with the spirit of adventure and personal freedom. How natural for the Romanticist to go far afield for material, to invade the Middle Ages and many distant lands! Hence his predilection for splendid scenery, for local color and the picturesque. Finally, the school expands the Classical conception of the world, to include not only the beautiful but also the "grotesque" and the characteristic; not so much the abstract and universal as the concrete and diversified. The whole approach to art is now through the senses and imagination rather than through the reason. As regards form, these various tendencies appear in a considerable enlargement of the language, admitting specific and colorful terms, in a greater variety of styles, in an anti-classical belief in the "mélange des genres."

That is, comedy and tragedy may be woven together, and lyricism dominates even in drama and fiction. Contrary to the eighteenth century, the emphasis is now less on ideas than on artistic inspiration and processes; a change that will be reflected in our subsequent treatment.

CHAPTER II

IMMEDIATE PREDECESSORS: NODIER, BERANGER, LAMARTINE

IT has been seen that Charles Nodier (1780–1844) was very susceptible to foreign influences and that he served as a leader and enthusiastic comrade of one Romantic group.

Nodier

Sainte-Beuve considers him the type of the generally productive man of letters, who lacked concentration: " Philologue ici, romanesque là, bibliographe et Werthérien, académique et . . . excentrique." Nodier also reflects the stormy uncertainty of his political epoch. He was born at Besançon, educated privately, and went up to Paris for a literary career. But the key-note of his character was a revolutionary Romanticism, and his anti-Napoleonic manifestations soon caused the authorities to banish him to Switzerland and the Jura, where he was " interned " for a number of years. He there developed a taste for nature-studies and philology. Travels in Italy and Illyria completed his literary baggage. He returned to France just in time for the tempests of 1814–15, wrote as journalist under the Restoration, and finally settled down as librarian at the Bibliothèque de l'Arsenal in 1824. Here his talent mellowed, his amiability furthered his reputation, and he was elected to the Academy before his death.

Nodier wrote some charming poetry and some adequate criticism, but the only surviving portion of his work consists of tales that curiously mingle sentiment and fancy.

His Stories

They are laid in remote and romanesque places, they have strong touches of *diablerie* and superstition, they contain Wertherean melancholy, desperate deaths, anti-social sentiments, brigands, fairies, various kinds of madness, mystery and vampires. His earlier works (*Le Peintre de Saltzbourg* and *Les Proscrits*) are mainly sentimental and doleful. The later stories show his adventurous imagination and emphasize the fantastic,

527

an element which, following Hoffmann, Nodier acclimatized in France. The two Illyrian productions, *Jean Sbogar* (1818) and *Smarra* (1820), present respectively a mysterious bandit and the legend of a vampire. They belong to what Nodier himself styled the frantic school ("l'école frénétique"). *Trilby*, which probably furnished the title for Du Maurier's novel, is one of Nodier's most finished and delightful stories. It concerns a goblin or *lutin* who befriends and bewilders a Scotch maiden. *Thérèse Aubert* recalls the days of youthful sentiment, but in a more mature and truly moving fashion. Some of Nodier's best writing was done in his calmer maturity; he was always a master of a certain kind of style, composed of flexible charming sentences and a graceful fancy. He is not strong on characters or composition. He is thoroughly Romantic in sources, subjects and temperament.

Jean-Pierre de Béranger (1780–1857), of bourgeois parentage and habits, belonged to no literary group. He was a *chansonnier*

Béranger and he remains the most notable composer of French popular songs. In 1813 the epicurean poet, Désaugiers, led Béranger to a certain *caveau* or "Rhymers' Club," where the newcomer sang and was well received. His topical and political songs soon had a wide vogue; he is considered to have "enfranchised" the *chanson* in 1817 with his *Dieu des bonnes gens*. Béranger was always close to the popular heart and from now on he aided in promoting the cult of Napoleon among the people. He was prosecuted twice for sedition. Aside from that, Béranger always modestly refused public recognition and led a retiring life. In his old age, his company was valued by such men as Chateaubriand and Lamartine. His excessive prestige in his own era was followed by a strong critical reaction. But he must be credited with having conferred upon the *chanson* all the literary value of which it seems capable.

Béranger wrote at least three different kinds of songs. He began with the old *gaulois* type, free, gay and bacchanalian.

Kinds of Chansons This was the kind affected by Désaugiers, who remained superior to his disciple in gaiety and ease. In Béranger, the epicurean manner seems artificial, though he possesses wit and a certain gallant swing. This style may be illustrated by *Le Roi d'Yvetot*:

Il était un roi d'Yvetot
  Peu connu dans l'histoire,
Se levant tard, se couchant tôt,
  Dormant fort bien sans gloire,
Et couronné par Jeanneton
D'un simple bonnet de coton,
    Dit-on . . .

Béranger really finds himself in the second kind of *chanson,*
where he indulges the liberal and patriotic vein. Barring ephemeral and occasional pieces, the best products of this period
are those where the larger popular sentiments and questions are
treated — such as Napoleon or the " principles of '89 " — and
no discrepancy was felt between the two ideals, since they both
tended to the glory of France. The third division consists of
the songs of Béranger's old age, which are often of a personal
or sentimental cast, exemplified by *Ma Canne* or *L'Adieu.* Some
irony, more of fantasy and revery characterize these last songs,
which are often wholly delightful.

Along with much that is commonplace, Béranger has the instinct for reflecting the human currents and feelings of his
Béranger's period. His muse is essentially patriotic or senti-
Qualities mental. His form is usually simple and direct,
though sometimes the exigencies of the stanza forced him into
obscurities and awkward turns of expression. The new Romanticism did not affect him greatly; his verses are neo-classical,
if anything. It should be remembered that they were intended
primarily to be sung, and the sweep of the rhythm, mounting up
to a well-chosen and memorable refrain, may thus disguise a
certain literary poverty. The sentimental manner may be
illustrated by

    Sois-moi fidèle, ô pauvre habit que j'aime;

the clever refrain by that of *Le Juif errant*:

    Toujours, toujours,
    Tourne la terre où moi je cours;

and political satire by the refrain:

    Chapeau bas! chapeau bas!
    Gloire au marquis de Carabas!

The case of Alphonse de Lamartine (1790–1869) is quite different. His name authentically opens the succession of

Lamartine   great Romantic poets. To his noble and charming figure is attached the triple prestige of poet, idealist and statesman. He was of a versatile, sensitive and thoroughly aristocratic nature. Born at Mâcon, of an excellent patriarchal family, he always clung with a " natural piety " to his early associations. His sensibility and Rousseauistic readings made him a prey to melancholy in his adolescence. This tendency was increased by his unfortunate love-affair with Mme Julie Charles, who became the " Elvire " of Lamartine's inspiration. What saddened the man deepened and purified the poet. The publication of *Les Premières Méditations* (1820) was an event; the work attracted the attention of Talleyrand, and Lamartine was appointed as secretary to the embassy at Naples.

Even in his troubled youth, Lamartine had strong political ambitions. After serving at Naples and at Florence, he wished

His Career   to play a greater rôle at home, and stood for election as deputy. Defeated at first, he was elected in 1831, and this date is a turning-point in his career. Returning from the Orient, he issued a manifesto which announced a progressive and liberal policy. Then he took his seat as an independent and maintained a position of isolation for ten years, during which period he perfected himself as an orator. In 1840, distrustful of the bourgeois ministry, Lamartine came out in the Opposition, declaring frankly his belief in the Revolution of 1789. Eight years later he was the leading figure in another revolution, which he animated by many democratic speeches as well as by his glowing and inaccurate *Histoire des Girondins*. When another Saint-Antoine swept into the Hôtel de Ville in February, 1848, it was Lamartine who time after time restrained the mob by his commanding presence, his courage and his adroit oratory. Adored by the populace, he reached his zenith as minister of foreign affairs and virtually as head of the Provisional Government. Yet in a few months he had lost all his prestige and in the presidential election the fickle people turned from him to the rising star which bore the magic name of Bonaparte. When Bonaparte perpetrated his Coup d'Etat and became Napoleon III, Lamartine was submerged politically. After all his triumphs, he spent an old age of semi-poverty and literary hack-work. He was not a practical politician; in politics as in other matters he remained the idealist. There, too, he sowed the seeds of fine thought and feeling, some of which have flowered in modern democratic France. Yet in spite of his statesmanship and his powers of eloquence, the real enduring contribution of Lamartine was made to French poetry.

The three forces which dominated Lamartine's early life and which constitute the chief inspiration of his poems were nature, **His Inspiration** religion and woman; it may be added that the three are closely associated in his greatest verse. *Le Crucifix*, for instance, in which the beloved emblem passes from the dying to the living, is in memory of the ethereal Elvire, and in *Le Temple* the poet mingles sacred and profane love. Again, his sweethearts are linked with their background in nature. So the bright figure of Graziella, the Italian maiden, is duly portrayed against the brilliant Neapolitan scenery; and the pale shade of Elvire haunts immortally the placid Lac du Bourget. The typical Lamartinian landscape is formed by certain elements which stand almost as symbols of love and revery: the lake, the twilight hour, the stealing moonbeam, the gentle slopes, the tall sad trees. Finally, nature and God, "le roi de la nature," are made one in many Pantheistic poems, especially from *Les Harmonies*. Lamartine's faith is not strictly orthodox. It partakes of a vague religiosity and it concerns itself, none too deeply, with the usual philosophical problems; but it expresses a constant idealism.

Les Premières Méditations (1820) mark the beginning of nineteenth-century poetry. As M. Lanson has demonstrated, **His Works** these lyrics usually have bookish sources (Petrarch, Rousseau, the Bible) and in form they show a continuity with neo-classical tradition rather than a distinct break. Their tremendous vogue was due primarily to the intimacy, the purity and plaintive sincerity of Lamartine's individual voice, which, like that of Rousseau, restored the ring of great emotion to literature. Hence the immediate effect of the volume on the tender-hearted. In spite of the fading influence of time, Lamartine's best stanzas still lie embedded, like perfect crystals, in the memories of many readers. Such are the verses of *L'Isolement*:

> Fleuves, rochers, forêts, solitudes si chères,
> Un seul être vous manque et tout est dépeuplé.

Such is the picture of *L'Automne*:

> Salut, bois couronné d'un reste de verdure. . . .

And such the beauty of *Le Lac*, which perpetuates the memory of Elvire in one of the most famous and sorrowful love-songs in the language:

> Que le vent qui gémit, le roseau qui soupire,
> Que les parfums légers de ton air embaumé,
> Que tout ce qu'on entend, l'on voit ou l'on respire,
> Tout dise: "Ils ont aimé!"

Nothing that characterizes Lamartine is absent from this first volume. *Les Nouvelles Méditations* (1823), published after his marriage to an Englishwoman, partially substitute for the old melancholy a happy love in a sunny landscape; otherwise they prolong the moods and measures of the first collection and have suffered to some extent the common fate of a sequel. Sainte-Beuve says of the second *Méditations* that they constitute a less artistic whole, though several individual pieces show a more sustained breadth and inspiration. The first series has more spontaneity, the second more finish. Among the best-known lyrics here may be mentioned: *Le Crucifix* (to Elvire); the sensuous beauty of *Ischia* and *Chant d'Amour* (to his wife); *Les Préludes* and *Bonaparte* (reflective poems). When Lamartine published *Les Harmonies poétiques et religieuses* (1830), the audience had grown accustomed to the poet's voice. Here he sings mainly of religion, through hymns and prayers, cantatas and invocations. He frequently strikes a bold and rich note — which he is tempted to hold too long. This tendency towards length leads to an increased use of varied rhythms in the same poem. The easy flow sometimes becomes too easy and the memorable effects are fewer in proportion. But there are half-a-dozen unforgotten poems, including the *Hymne de l'enfant* (naïve childish faith), *L'Occident* (solemn and superb

Pantheism), the despairing confession of *Novissima verba* and above all the tribute to Graziella in *Le Premier Regret*:

> Mais pourquoi m'entraîner vers ces scènes passées?
> Laissons le vent gémir et le flot murmurer;
> Revenez, revenez, ô mes tristes pensées!
> Je veux rêver et non pleurer.

After writing this volume, Lamartine turned to politics, and his succeeding publications (for instance, *Les Recueillements* and the prose romance of *Graziella*) are not so significant. An exception must be made for *Jocelyn* (1836). This long narrative poem concerns the frustrated loves of a priest and his companion. It is remarkable for two things: a deeper philosophy than is customary with Lamartine and a splendid treatment of nature in the episode of *Les Laboureurs*. The conception of *Jocelyn*, as of *La Chute d'un ange* (1838), is often epic and symbolical in effect, reminding one of Alfred de Vigny (see Ch. IV, below).

The technical qualities of Lamartine's poetry are, first, a suave harmony, continuing the tradition of Racine and of the **His** eighteenth-century elegists; a fluidity of composi- **Qualities** tion, connected with a preference for floating, soaring objects and images; a softness of tone and outline; and an exposed sensibility, like that of "an Æolian harp." Moreover, his poetry is subjective to a degree unknown in French poetry since the Pléiade. In form, Lamartine stands less for elaborate workmanship than for improvisation and spontaneity. He did not despise revision, but he needed restriction. His poems tend progressively towards a full easy movement, lacking definiteness of contour and containing sometimes negligences and bombast. Often too his muse has an airy insubstantiality, like that of Shelley. But it is seldom that Lamartine fails to affect the reader by the expansive grace of his emotions and the lifting power of his ideals.

CHAPTER III

THE POETS: VICTOR HUGO

As Voltaire dominated the eighteenth century, so does Hugo dominate the nineteenth, and partly for the same reasons: ver-

His Rank satility, longevity (1802–85) and the power of an ever-driving pen. Not only is Hugo the most representative writer of the past century; he is the greatest lyric poet that France ever had, and he possesses one of the master imaginations of the world. The French are proud of him, not so much as the author of *Les Misérables* or of *Hernani*, but because in the writing of poetry he shows amazing powers of vision and expression. But his judgment and balance fall below his creative abilities, and the man is inferior to the poet. The facts of his life and work must be distinguished from the "legend," which he and his admirers carefully fostered.

Victor-Marie Hugo was born at Besançon in 1802. His father was an officer in Napoleon's army and commanded under

Youth Joseph Bonaparte when the latter was made king of Spain. General Hugo took his family with him, and Victor's boyish eyes were filled with the picturesqueness of Italy, the light and splendor of Spain. The latter country left its impress upon many of his works (for example, *Hernani*, *La Légende des siècles*). The Hugo family settled at Paris in 1812, and Victor went in for omnivorous study and much juvenile verse-making. At the age of fourteen he declared: " Je veux être Chateaubriand ou rien." The youthful poet failed of the prize in several Academy competitions, but was later crowned by the Jeux Floraux de Toulouse. He and his brother established a journal — *Le Conservateur littéraire*, (1819–21) — for which Victor wrote voluminously. The journal was well named, for at this period Hugo was conservative in everything, preferring the consecrated literary tradition and manifesting, *à la* Chateaubriand, an ardent royalism and Catholicism. These were also the principles of the Société des Bonnes Lettres, which Victor joined a little later. After his mother's death, a period of discouragement and loneliness propelled Hugo into a swift marriage with the beautiful Adèle Foucher. Marital responsibilities hastened his productivity and he brought out the first volume of *Odes et Ballades* (1822). This publication launched him on his career, talented young friends were grouped around him, and the *cénacle* of the *Muse Française* was formed with Hugo's active collaboration. The youth already impressed these côteries by his grave and priest-like demeanor and by the promise of his genius.

The year 1827 may be regarded as marking Hugo's maturity and his conversion to Romanticism. This year saw the publi-

Career cation of *Cromwell* and its preface; the poet assumed the leadership of the chief Romantic *cénacle;* and his intimate friendship and literary association with Sainte-Beuve was started. In 1830, he is at the height of his young glory, with the victory of *Hernani,* and for ten years thereafter he wields a literary scepter. In this decade numerous plays were performed, four important volumes of verse were published, together with the very successful *Notre-Dame de Paris;* and Hugo was gradually converted to a cautious republicanism. His popularity was increased through his expression of democracy (for example, in *Ruy Blas*), as well as through his exaltation of Napoleon, and fresh côteries surrounded him with dangerous incense. After several applications, he was elected to the Academy in 1841. He suffered a great domestic bereavement through the drowning of his daughter in 1841; he had already broken with Sainte-Beuve for private reasons. He assumed a more prominent rôle politically, and in 1848 he declared for republicanism against Bonaparte. His opposition to the latter led to Hugo's exile and caused an inextinguishable hatred for "Napoléon le petit." The poet was banished first to Brussels, then took up his residence on the Channel Islands, Jersey and Guernsey (1852–70). His life in exile was characterized by virulent attacks on Napoleon III (*Les Châtiments*) and on other French leaders; by an acquaintance with new landscapes and seascapes, which are prominent in *Les Travailleurs de la mer;* and by an unceasing literary productivity, which finds its crown in *La Légende des* *siècles.* Returning to Paris in 1870, Hugo went through the siege and reconstruction, and wrote *L'Année terrible.* He was now a " grand vieillard," who posed in his salon as a demi-god. His last years were filled with a great and growing popularity. France saw in him a hero and prophet who had experienced and reflected her own vicissitudes and who now shed glory on the Republic. In 1875 he was elected senator from Paris; he was fêted widely on his eightieth birthday, and his death in 1885 was made the occasion of an apotheosis. His ashes were laid in the Pantheon amid much pomp and almost universal tribute.

In many respects Hugo deserved his fame. He was an authentic genius and an indefatigable worker. His best writings are **Character** marked by a great imaginative flame and by an understanding of the heart of humanity. But in his own life his heart and his judgment likewise were often submerged by his ego. Friends fell away from him, women suffered from his treatment, no cause could reckon on his support, if his pride or prestige was at stake. His inordinate vanity has been made the subject of many stories; he actually thought that the city of Paris should be renamed in his honor. He loved his country and especially his children; but love, literature and politics became with Hugo occasions for self-aggrandizement, and because of his political veering, the charge has been made that he lacked sincerity both in his life and his works. This is probably too severe, but steadfastness of thought and conduct are scarcely to be expected from Hugo's whirling brain and imagination. He is an echo of ideas rather than an originator. He is not to be greatly loved or trusted, but rather to be admired when properly set on his pedestal. That pedestal consists of nearly fifty volumes, many of which are masterpieces. We shall consider only his poetry in this chapter.[1] The lyrical inspiration with which Hugo began predominated for twenty years and is also conspicuous in his drama during that period.

The volumes of *Odes* (1822–24) and later of *Odes et ballades* **First Fruits** (1826) are far from indicating the true power of Hugo. The odes particularly seem second-rate today in their effete royalism and neo-classicism. These occasional

---

[1] For his drama and fiction, see below, Chapters V and VI.

pieces are full of apostrophies and banalities. The ballads are better poetry, and such a chivalric inspiration as *Le Pas d'armes du roi Jean*, with its skilful swing, announces the author as a virtuoso of rime and rhythm. These qualities and others are conspicuous in *Les Orientales* (1829), where Hugo's muse is decidedly stronger. Deference is shown to the Byronic vogue, and certain poems dealing with Greece and Turkey have a conventional flavor; but those dealing with Spain have kept all their freshness of coloring; in fact, splendid color is the hall-mark of *Les Orientales*. The volume includes such a *tour de force* as *Les Djinns* and the reworking of Byron's *Mazeppa*, with the fine symbol of the poet bound to his genius as Mazeppa was bound to his horse. Great suppleness of rhythm and language are to be found in *Les Orientales*, of which one critic has said, " On est ébloui, mais on n'est pas ému."

More emotion appears in the four volumes of the next decade.. The poet now turns to subjective experience. Also, profiting by **Mature** the advice of Sainte-Beuve, Hugo seems to reveal a **Personal** better taste and less tendency to excess than in any **Poetry** other period. This is certainly true of *Les Feuilles d'automne* (1831), where the treatment is subdued and the themes are personal or concerned with hearth and home. But the poet loses in *éclat* what he gains in sobriety. The " twilight " note of the *Chants du crépuscule* (1835) indicates more melancholy and pensive doubt than is found elsewhere; but there is too much " occasional verse " on very different subjects. Consequently the volume lacks unity. It is noticeable that here Hugo seems less captivated by kings and shows the beginnings of his humanitarian sentiments. His religion had died down. In fact, no great convictions inspire *Les Chants du crépuscule*, though the form is often powerful or graceful. *Les Voix intérieures* (1837) set out to express " cette musique que tout homme a en soi," and the personal voices often mingle with those of Nature at large. There are echoes of her moods, whether compassionate or indifferent, the sound of the sea is heard, and nature and art are prettily compounded in such charming poems as *Le Passé* or *Puisqu'ici-bas toute âme*. The volume is an admirable lyric collection. Finally, *Les Rayons et les Ombres* (1840), in its alternation of happiness and sorrow, also contains many notable poems. There is the famous *Guitare,* with its refrain,

> Le vent qui souffle à travers la montagne
> Me rendra fou!

There is the mournful splendor of *Oceano Nox* and another mingling of art and nature in *La Statue.* Above all, there is Hugo's greatest poem of sentiment, that " pathetic sonata " called *Tristesse d'Olympio.* The theme of this, as in Lamartine's *Lac* and Musset's *Souvenir,* is the revival of love's memory amid associated scenery, and Hugo's solution is that the memory is not preserved in external objects but lives darkling in the human heart —

> C'est toi qui dors dans l'ombre, ô sacré souvenir.

In general, nature is viewed as linked with our emotions and as an educator of humanity. The volume sums up several of the author's previous tendencies, such as the depiction of family life or of landscape, and announces coming tendencies, such as compassionate humanitarianism and satiric indignation.

Les *Châtiments* (1853) fulfil Hugo's declaration —

> Et j'ajoute à ma lyre une corde d'airain.

Written during exile, the book is one long-sustained invective against Napoleon III. On account of its unity, vehemence and

Satire

biting force, this is regarded by many as Hugo's greatest volume of verse. That distinction should rather be reserved for *La Légende des siècles,* but it is true that *Les Châtiments* " enlarge the limits of poetry " and bring into satire a new ardor and imagery. We have here less virtuosity and more direct emotion than is usual with Hugo, because his hatred of the third Napoleon was probably the master-feeling of his public life. *Les Châtiments* present a constant antithesis between the night of the past (usurpations, crime and the degradation of races) and the light of the future (expiation, the restoration of justice, the triumph of human love and of the powers of nature). Much of this appears in *L'Expiation,* the best-known poem in the collection. Its moral is that the great

and
Meditations

Napoleon's ruthlessness is punished less by his own defeats than by the nullity of his successor. This poem contains some of the finest tirades in the language. *Les*

Contemplations (1856) are more serene and constitute a sort of long autobiography. Hugo has now assumed his rôle of *songeur* or seer. He " contemplates " nature (*Pasteurs et troupeaux*), meditates on death, particularly the loss of his daughter, reflects on his own past and still hates his enemies. All his lyric gifts are here in full force and certain of his lyric extravagances: an abuse of enumeration and repetition, a flux of words, or a tendency towards a mere coquettish prettiness (*mignardises,* cf. Rostand's *Musardises*). But his power of apocalyptic vision makes the second part of the volume resemble a darker Revelation of St. John. This soaring away from the known earth into realms of hallucination and immensity is Hugo's greatest feat in *La-Légende des siècles*.

That collection consisted of four volumes, ranging from 1859 to 1883. The earlier volumes are superior to the later. Epic: " La The term " petites épopées " was used as a sub-Légende des title, and the whole work proceeded from the epic siècles " conception of recording the destinies of mankind at various periods and as expressed by various heroes. Vigny had already poetized this idea, which was carried on by Hugo, by the work of Leconte de Lisle and by Heredia's *Trophées*. [2] Apart from the conception, however, Hugo's manner is epic in only a few narratives (*Eviradnus, Ratbert,* etc.) and includes poems of all sorts and sizes. In his survey of the ages, the author shows a preference for remote and god-like periods, and his apocalyptic genius appears riding above the chaos of pre-historic times. The beginnings of creation (*Le Sacre de la femme, La Conscience*); the warfare of Titans and gods (*Le Titan, Le Géant aux dieux*); a superb Naturalistic vision of Pan and his like (*Le Satyre*); the heroics of Roland and of the Cid: these are the subjects that attracted Hugo, who felt an affinity for the gigantic and even the monstrous. He also well portrayed Biblical times, as in the charming idyll of *Booz endormi;* and the ideals of chivalry still stirred him, as in *Aymerillot* and *Eviradnus.* But more civilized aspects of culture, such as Grecian beauty or the modern refinement of France, scarcely inspired him at all. Consequently, *La Légende des siècles* shows great gaps from the historical point of view. Again, Hugo's treatment

[2] See below, Bk. VII, Ch. III.

of history was too simplified in that he saw a clear conflict between good and evil, a perpetual antithesis of " Dieu " and
" Satan." Kings are always odious and tyrannous, whereas
democracy (le peuple) shall be released and justified. Hope is
the vision which shines above the crumbling " wall of the centuries." Hugo, for poetical purposes, puts " legend " side by
side with history and violates accuracy at will; but the historical
coloring is often superb, vivid reconstruction is attained in many
places, the symbols are usually well-chosen, and, above all, the
powers of expression here revealed are unrivaled and almost
inhuman. The poet creates his own mythology in his dealings
with Titans and giants and in the marvelous *Satyre*. A
sinister beauty and a strange force predominate in the work
(*L'Aigle du Casque, Le Parricide*); there is an alternation of the
ideal with the brutal (*L'Epopée du ver*); magnificent invective
shines in *La Vision de Dante,* and a more restrained Renaissance
beauty in *La Rose de l'Infante.* Sometimes there are violences
and absurdities, as in the notion of the Sultan who achieves redemption through succoring a pig. Kings, monsters, children,
gods, animals, criminals and the abounding personality of the
author make the strangest jumble. More and more Hugo dons
the mantle of the prophet and lays down the law to humanity
(cf. *La Fonction du poète*). The thought is often commonplace or
empty, yet it has been said that the hollowest verses are formed
so solidly that they stand upright like richly wrought armor.
The composition of individual poems is excellent. Hugo can
do anything with rhythm, while in language and in metaphor he
opens new horizons. His greatest gifts of imagination and
rhetoric are here revealed in their perfection and even in their
over-perfection and excess.[3]

His imagination declares itself in many ways: in the actual
number and novelty of his images; in his power of sustained
Imagination personification and vision; and particularly in his
myth-making faculty, his evocation of immensity.
In the first place, his images are often striking, novel or freshly
adapted; they are sometimes ugly and they are incessant. Hugo

---

[3] *La Légende* is Hugo's culminating work, but for the sake of completeness there
may be mentioned: *Chansons des rues et des bois* (1865), *L'Art d'être grand'père*
(1877) and *Les Quatre Vents de l'esprit* (1881).

simply saw the world in terms of the imagination, and he has been called " next to Chateaubriand ... the great imagist " of French literature (Babbitt). So we find long successions of figures, the intention being to compare the object to as many other objects as possible. This sometimes leads to a welter of mixed figures, as where Dante is compared first to a mountain, then to an oak and finally to a lion. But at his best Hugo presents hundreds of suitable poetic images, consisting mainly of similes and metaphors. His figures are of the greatest variety, realistic, spiritual, tragic and terrible, or simply charming. The second feature of his imaginative ability is the gift of sustained personification or amplification. This appears in his vision of the Wall (" le mur des siècles "), or in such a poem as *Mazeppa*, where we find a long and appropriate succession of images within the main simile. Bold metamorphoses and many personifications of general ideas (*le Peuple, le Vers, l'Idée*) also occur. There is the recurrent personification of *l'Echafaud*, like the sustained vivification and symbolism of Notre-Dame. Finally, his creative myth-making has already been exemplified in connection with *La Légende* — a new angle of Olympus, a bold entrance of titanic forces, together with the Zodiac, the Word and a comprehensive person called Tout. Hugo constructs fresh figures in " la Déroute " and " les Batailles " of Napoleon. He shows a kind of animism in treating elements as living, thinking forces: " La mer fait des maladresses." Oceans and wars, demi-gods and centuries parade before us, and Hugo's highest visioning does not fall short of sublimity.

To illustrate this power of sublime conception, we may take the poem called *Le Parricide*. King Canute of Denmark has killed his own father. The crime is not discovered, but Canute dies, rises again in his restlessness, wraps himself in a shroud of snow and goes roaming in search of God. Wherever he goes, throughout a strange universe, " a drop of blood falls upon his shroud." This is the recurrent *motif*, like the constant snow in *L'Expiation*. The shroud soon becomes wholly crimson, and Canute in an agony of remorse is driven from the throne of God.

A like sublimity marks Hugo's language at its best. He is the greatest master of poetic style and knows all the resources

of French rhetoric. His language is nearly always grammatical
and syntactical; his faults proceed rather from too much style
Rhetoric   and too much imagination. He had the widest
range in vocabulary of any French poet, totally
outsoaring the Classical restrictions. He adored words:

> Car le mot, c'est le Verbe et le Verbe c'est Dieu.

Above all, he had a preference for the grandiose: for such words
as *immense, sombre, vaste,* for such figures as lions, titans and
the seven wonders of the world. The gigantic runs readily into
the grotesque, and the grotesque into the *goguenard* (*Le Géant
aux dieux*). He also gives a large place to the purely fantastic.
On the other hand, he does not always eschew mere prettiness
and wit. Among his prominent rhetorical devices are the
following: the double substantive (*l'homme-troupeau, la reine-
esclave*) ; the recurrent *motif,* such as the Eye that ever watches
Cain in *La Conscience;* and long enumerations or parallel clauses
beginning with the same word. This last habit, effective at first,
grew upon Hugo until it became a fault of his method, leading
to many repetitions and excrescences. But his inveterate trait,
equally dangerous, is antithesis, the psychological results of
which will be developed elsewhere. Here it may be exemplified
by the title of *Les Rayons et les Ombres* or by the fine Alexandrine from *Booz endormi*:

> Car le jeune homme est beau, mais le vieillard est grand.

Harmless and even appropriate in many cases, this kind of
balance became an obsession with Hugo, leading to monotony
and, often, to a twisting of the truth. Another device, more typically French, is the long *période,* the sustained sweep of sentences in which the effective line or word comes last. This has
analogies with the " surprise ending " of Maupassant and may
be found in *Bivar, Tristesse d'Olympio* (see above) and several
speeches from *Hernani,* ending in " l'échafaud." In the matter
of sonority and tone-color, Hugo is unsurpassed. Witness the
vibrant note, the clashing of dollars and drums in *Les Reîtres*:

> Sonnez, clairons, sonnez, cymbales!
> On entendra siffler les balles. . . .
> Sonnez, rixdales, sonnez, doublons!

Or again, the sinister noise of the yew-trees crushed by the genii (*Les Djinns*):

> Les ifs que leur vol fracasse
> Craquent comme un pin brûlant.

As regards structure, Hugo is a master of exact, harmonious and beautiful composition, whose regularity he knows how to vary at need. Finally, his verse-rhythms show an equal variety and freedom.[4]

It has been seen that Hugo runs to excess; he has the defects of his qualities. But the qualities outweigh the defects — a

His Genius truth which hostile critics hardly consider — and there are dozens of masterpieces in which the artist displays an almost Classic beauty and restraint. Other of his poetic virtues might be mentioned, such as his sensibility and his power of suggestiveness. Through the universality of his genius he exemplifies, indeed, nearly every mode and quality of Romanticism. But rhetoric and imagination are his special forte. His thought lacks depth and coherency: his Naturalism wars with his more orthodox faith in God, in immortality and in the spirit of mankind. His expansive poetic power is the gift that remains unassailable. This gift has influenced and often transported two generations, at home and abroad. Other poets may do this or that, said Théodore de Banville, but, he added, referring to Hugo's Guernsey sojourn,

> The Master's yonder in the Isle.

And in England, Swinburne was one of Hugo's greatest admirers and imitators.

[4] For the Romantic liberation of the Alexandrine, see below, Ch. V.

CHAPTER IV

THE POETS: MUSSET, VIGNY, GAUTIER

OF these three writers, Musset is the most passionate, Vigny the most intellectual, and Gautier the most elaborate and sensuous. Alfred de Musset expresses the direct emotions of love and youth; Alfred de Vigny fathers the " poème philosophique "; Théophile Gautier begins a tendency towards impersonality and incorporates in his work the doctrine of art for art's sake.

The chief event in Alfred de Musset's life (1810–57) was his love-affair with George Sand. As a youth of eighteen he had **Musset** been the *enfant terrible* of Hugo's group, and his early poems show a mingling of Byronic passion with adolescent gaiety and daring. The trip to Italy with George Sand (1833) effectively disposed of the gaiety, and the two writers failed in their signal attempt to carry the Romantic theories into love and life. Their rupture left the stronger nature of the woman almost unharmed, but Musset sank into despair and debauchery, a night relieved only by the composition of a few great poems that immortalize his sorrow. He produced very little during the last ten years of his life. " Que de lumière!" exclaims Sainte-Beuve, " que d'éclipse et d'ombre! "

Musset's poems are to be found today in the two collections of *Premières poésies* (to 1833) and *Poésies nouvelles* (1836–52). **Chief** They range from the youthful abandon of his first **Volumes** volume (*Contes d'Espagne et d'Italie*, 1829), through the cynic gloom of *Rolla*, down to the supreme cry of defeated passion in the famous *Nuits*. The prose *Confession d'un Enfant du siècle* also recounts his love and grief. His poetic dramas will be considered in the next chapter. The *Contes d'Espagne et d'Italie* show Romantic exoticism and the " lure of distance," Romantic swagger and irony (*Don Paez, Mardoche*). Though inferior as a whole to his later work, this volume contains various charming *chansons*, which were always a *forte* with Musset.

544

The *Contes* represent the reckless sparkling dandy that was the poet's first incarnation. As for expression, this is the only volume that freely takes Romantic liberties (*enjambement*, etc.), and even here Musset parodies certain features of the Romantic technique. His break with the school occurred shortly afterwards; he rebelled against the *rime riche* and the rhetorical processes of Hugo's circle; but the narrative poems of *Namouna* and *Rolla* (1833) none the less reflect the exaltation, Don Juanism and disillusionment so characteristic of the period. *Rolla*, or the "last night of a rake," is Musset's longest narrative poem and made his reputation among those who admired Byronic effusions. Up to this point Musset is essentially the poet of youth, and Sainte-Beuve declared him the embodiment of adolescent genius.

He fully became the poet of love in the series always associated with his name: the *Nuit de mai* and the *Nuit de décembre* (1835), which particularly and poignantly recall his heart-affair; the *Nuit d'août* and the *Nuit d'octobre*, which are calmer in tone. Three of these four lyrics consist of dialogues between the poet and his Muse. The latter generally urges recovery from sorrow, the healing effects of time and of work. But the poet retorts — and this is Musset's outstanding creed:

> Après avoir souffert, il faut souffrir encore,
> Il faut aimer sans cesse, après avoir aimé.

The *Souvenir* of 1841 worthily concludes the series in its vehement and beautiful expression of the thought that, though love may be lost, its memory can never perish. Of these masterpieces, *La Nuit de mai* is the most exquisite lyrically, from the swooning beauty of the early strophes to the great figure of the pelican as compared with the poet's heart. Musset's other verse often has this lyric charm, especially audible in such songs as *Adieu Suzon*, *Rappelle-toi* and the *Chanson de Barberine*:

> Beau chevalier qui partez pour la guerre,
> Qu'allez-vous faire
> Si loin de nous?
> J'en vais pleurer, moi qui me laissais dire
> Que mon sourire
> Etait si doux.

The *Stances à la Malibran,* in their insistence on the essential
unity of genius and love, constitute a fine elegy. The
Other Poems *Lettre à Lamartine* pays tribute to that poet's calmer
idealism, contrasted with the *mal romantique* of Musset himself.
Sur la paresse lets the writer, with his usual frankness, tell us a
great deal about his ideas and his habits: his invincible idleness;
his hatred of present-day manners, mediocrity, journalism; his
preference for the gallantry of his ancestors, for living danger-
ously and expansively; and his love of Régnier as the master
of virile satire. The poet's spiritual longings are vaguely expressed in *L'Espoir en Dieu*:

> Malgré moi l'infini me tourmente,

but elsewhere Musset admits his general indifference to politics
and religion. His apprehension of such subjects is quick rather
than profound. He is not a philosopher, not an interpreter of
mankind nor of nature. He is distinguished by a charming fancy
rather than by the greater creative imagination. He is at his
best in " short swallow-flights of song."

The form of this poetry is not perfect. In versification and
expression Musset is too often careless or obscure. Yet his style
Qualities has a natural eloquence. His verse is most distinguished when his emotion is at white heat, and in re-
belling against the *cénacle* he declared that feeling is far more
important than form. His cult of the emotions and senses is
more refined than Gautier's and more idealistic than Byron's.
His great merit is that he sings incomparably of the ardors of
love and the depths of love's despair. His *ennui* and Byronism
are compatible with a passionate sincerity; his eloquence and
harmony are then the direct expression of his feeling; he really
did desire and strive to make romantic love the greatest thing
in life. He lives as the chief exponent and victim of this tendency, which is so marked in his generation. He is also Romantic
in his frank self-confession, his need for individual expansion
and exaltation. He is the poet of personality:

> Mon verre n'est pas grand, mais je bois dans mon verre.

Hence he formed no school and has had no successful imitators.
Like his hero, Rolla, he displays his bruised heart amid the

magnificence of nature and of history; yet we feel that these trappings are not the essential thing. He reflects the exoticism and the medievalism of his epoch — but medieval faith is no longer his:

Je suis venu trop tard dans un monde trop vieux.

He is capable of witty dialogue and of telling stories in verse (*Simone, Silvie*) — but his best story is his own, as related in the *Nuits*. He appeals most deeply to those whose hearts have remained young; yet the sober critic, Taine, concludes his *Littérature anglaise* by an ardent appreciation of Musset. Comparing him to Tennyson, Taine admits that in several respects, the English country gentleman was superior to the fevered Parisian *roué* — "mais j'aime mieux Alfred de Musset que Tennyson." There are many for whom Musset is still singing and who will agree with Taine as to the power and poignancy of his lyric cry.

The poetry of Alfred de Vigny [1] (1797–1863) is more impersonal in expression than that of Musset, but it also springs, **Vigny's** partially at least, from the circumstances of his **Outer Life** inner and outer life. That life consisted of a series of disappointments. Born of a noble family and believing in *noblesse oblige* in every sense, Vigny realized that nobility was at a discount in France. Entering military service he found that career unsatisfactory and recorded his experiences in the collection of stories called *Servitude et grandeur militaires* (1835). Falling in love with the actress Dorval, he was deceived by her and gave vent to his bitterness in the poem on *La Colère de Samson*. Attached quite early to two of the Romantic *cénacles*, he lost faith in the movement and broke with his former comrades; in Sainte-Beuve's famous phrase:

Et Vigny, plus secret,
Comme en sa tour d'ivoire, avant midi rentrait.[2]

He retired, that is, into an intellectual and artistic solitude, and emerged only when duty called him.

---

[1] See also Chs. V and VI, below.

[2] Hence the origin of "the ivory tower" in modern usage; its ancient source is the *turris eburnea* of the Vulgate.

Vigny is then the poet of the inner life. His thought revolves around certain fixed ideas, and the idea, in each poem,
Inner Life is embodied in a concrete imaginative symbol.
and Symbols This process can be illustrated by the principal
titles in Vigny's single volume of poetry.[3]   In the poem already
cited, Samson represents the betrayal of man's strength —

> Et plus ou moins la femme est toujours Dalila.

In *Moïse*, the prophet typifies the loneliness of genius.   In *La
Bouteille à la mer*, the imperishable idea ("la Science") is
symbolized by the message cast overboard in a shipwreck; a
similar devotion to the Idea is found in *L'Esprit pur* and *La
Maison du berger*.   The latter poem suggests, in its title and
content, a retreat into the bosom of nature.   *Le Cor* symbolizes
Roland's heroic death, and *La Mort du loup* teaches silence and
energy.   It is in this fashion that Vigny creates the "poème,"
which may be defined as a short narrative or idyllic poem expressing symbolically a philosophical thought.

The final divisions of his work correspond partly to his
favorite reading (the Bible, Homer, Byron).   The "Livre mys-
His Work tique" includes *Moïse*, *Le Déluge* and *Eloa*, that
story of the angel-maiden who became enamored
of Lucifer.   The "Livre antique" has both a Biblical and a
Homeric subdivision, and the latter class, by extension, includes
Vigny's early idylls (*La Dryade*, etc.).   The "Livre moderne"
is largely historical and more definitely symbolic: it contains
Le Cor, Madame de Soubise, etc.   The fourth and most important division is "Les Destinées," wherein appeared most of
the poems mentioned in the preceding paragraph.   There is a
certain historical progression in the volume and this, together
with the emphasis on human deeds and "destinies," the migra-
tion of the human spirit across the ages, makes Vigny antedate
the *Légende des siècles* and Leconte de Lisle.

The nature of Vigny, proud, sincere, pessimistic and stoical,
Ideas is discreetly revealed in most of his poems; but
the direct personal confession or complaint is hardly
found.   He generalizes from experience, and his tendency is

---

[3] One volume holds his entire verse to-day.   But he published, in order,
Poèmes, 1822; *Eloa*, 1824; *Poèmes antiques et modernes*, 1826; there appeared posthumously *Les Destinées*, 1864, and the prose *Journal d'un poète*, 1867.

towards the abstract. His chief ideas may be now summed up. He believes primarily in the power of thought, whether as scientific knowledge or as the poet's vision. In the latter form, the outer world may serve for symbols, but the inner world contains the enduring reality. Vigny's sensibility is awakened less by the usual human emotions than by the thrill of comprehending and expressing " le Dieu des idées." He can trust no other god but this; his pessimism causes him to doubt the beneficence of Providence and the effective intervention of Christ (*Le Silence, Le Mont des Oliviers*). Vigny believes that man's existence is unjustly ordered and that evil is often triumphant. This melancholy is the essential feature of his philosophy and arises not only from the facts of his life — and his exalted demands upon life — but also from his conception of the poet as necessarily an isolated martyr (cf. *Chatterton*). A stoical silence or energetic labor constitutes the only refuge. Another refuge may appear in Nature, but, closely considered, Nature does not answer the appeal of man (*La Maison du berger*):

> On me dit une mère et je suis une tombe.

For Vigny, the pathetic fallacy is pathetic folly. Therein he differs from such Romanticists as Lamartine. Vigny is almost the first to adopt the scientific attitude that the natural law is non-human and implacable. He is uncertain with regard to love. Delilah is viewed as an "enfant malade," but more usually woman (Eva, Eloa) is idealized and made the symbol of beauty. Man is fated, whether under the ancient or the Christian dispensation (*Les Destinées*) to endless striving and endless failure. Without hope, but with resignation and in silence, he should endure his fate and show compassion towards his kind. Addressing Nature, the poet declares:

> Plus que tout votre règne et que ses splendeurs vaines,
> J'aime la majesté des souffrances humaines.

This message is expressed in language of a singular elevation and sobriety. Vigny's best manner is simple and large, **Style** Classic rather than Romantic. He composed slowly, was not naturally productive, and is at times halting or obscure. Like Lamartine, he had an aristocratic contempt for the writer's trade. But just as Musset's style becomes perfected through warm emotion, so does Vigny's through the cooler but intense processes of thought. With him the idea at its best imposes the proper form. He is, then, the intellectual among the Romanticists, and he reflects the more pessimistic side of the movement with nobility and sincerity. In his technique, his view of nature and his impersonal manner he stands apart from Romanticism; yet a subjective mood or sentiment underlies the majority of his poems, which show Romantic influences also in their exotic, primitive or historical coloring. A grave and melancholy power, a stern idealism, a soldierly view of duty and honor — these things elevate Vigny's poetic expression to a very high level.

The nature and the talent of Théophile Gautier (1811–72) were thoroughly artistic. He cared for nothing but art, he **Gautier** was a painter in his youth, and he developed to a high degree the quality of form in poetry. His admiration for Victor Hugo turned him from painting to poetry and it was at the *première* of *Hernani* that Gautier's pink doublet ("le gilet rouge") symbolized his new fervor as well as his perpetual desire to scandalize the bourgeois. His early poems began to appear (*Poésies*, 1830; *Albertus*, 1832; *La Comédie de la Mort*, 1833). From 1836, Gautier became a galley-slave of journalism, a polygraph who wrote criticism, stories and travels. His appreciation of nature and art was enlarged by visits to various countries, especially by his trip to Spain in 1840. Poetry was still Gautier's chief attachment and in the publication of *Emaux et Camées* (1852), he attained his high-water mark. In person, "le bon Théo" was a sort of sunny Hercules, calm and almost Oriental in appearance, fond of the pleasant externalities of life. He significantly said of himself: "Je suis un homme pour qui le monde extérieur existe."

Gautier's early poetry is violently Romantic. *Albertus* is a free and fantastic narrative poem, dealing with the trans- **Early Poems** formations and orgies of a witch, containing both *macabre* and Don Juanesque elements. Gautier here uses strong words and metaphors and is evidently striving for originality; but his composition of verse is solid and his talent for close description, with analogies to painting, is already prominent. Still more sepulchral in tone is *La Comédie de la Mort*, presenting a hero who is seeking an ideal love through many loves that are not ideal. This is Gautier's farewell to youthful Romanticism; but he also wrote about this time (*Poésies diverses*) some elegies as well as delicate and colorful poems of a more impersonal cast. This tendency is fully re-"Emaux et vealed in *Emaux et Camées,* a volume which must Camées" have been slowly elaborated and which crystallizes a transition in French poetry. From now on the movement is away from the sentimental and the personal towards the impassive and the "Parnassian." [4] Gautier is the man who bridges the two schools; his more morbid Romanticism is reflected by his great admirer, Baudelaire; but his sense of objective form finds its continuation not only in Baudelaire but in the whole Parnassian group.

The very title of *Emaux et Camées* implies delicate workmanship, and the volume as a whole perfectly illustrates Gautier's Theory of artistic standards and processes. His point of de-Art parture, in theory, is *l'art pour l'art;* in practice, the example of other arts, especially painting and sculpture, controls his technique. The theory is indifferent to morality; not eager for emotions or ideas, it is concerned mainly with external beauty. The practice includes, first, the "seeing eye," whether as directed to the larger *tableaux* of nature or to the smaller gems of art; second, the clever hand, exercised in the manipulation of the brush and the chiselling of poetic cameos; and finally, as a consequence of this attitude, frequent *transpositions d'art* — that is, the transportation of pictorial, sculptural and jewel-like effects from art into literature. It is significant that Gautier's favorite subjects are paintings and pastels, obelisks and *pans de mur;* also that his brother poets speak of him in terms of painting and enamelling. *Emaux et Camées* give an impression of slow chiselling and a kind of airy solidity; the poems stand out in relief like massy clouds before a thunder-shower. In this volume Gautier uses octosyllabic quatrains almost entirely, and it goes without saying that his sense of composition, in short pieces, is almost perfect.

[4] See below. Bk. VII, Ch. III.

" Art for Art's sake " is, then, Gautier's special contribution and his war-cry. He is not interested in politics, philosophy

Qualities or religion, but he has enough intelligence to serve his own plastic ends. He also subdues emotion to the purposes of art. Personal incidents and love-affairs are treated, but they are made impersonal and serene. The form is certainly more evident than the feeling, and the form is a close transcription of beautiful reality. Gautier is a great stylist. His poetry has the correctness, limpidity and purity of the best prose — even of his own prose. In either field he possesses a very large vocabulary from which he can draw the choice word for exactness and vividness. His words often have an exotic. or artistically technical coloring. He achieves picturesque brilliancy in landscapes and interiors. His rhythms are subtle and varied, and the same may be said of his images, which are frequent and sustained. In his desire to give the sharp external impression, he anticipates the Imagists of today. In his insistence on beauty as the important content of life and of poetry, he narrows the Romantic formula, but he leads the way for a whole generation of modern French poets, who also usually follow his impersonal and plastic bent. His creed is epitomized in the poem called *L'Art,* of which part has been thus translated by Austin Dobson:

> All passes. Art alone
> > Enduring stays to us;
> The Bust outlasts the throne,
> > The Coin, Tiberius.

> Even the gods must go;
> > Only the lofty Rhyme
> Not countless years o'erthrow, —
> > Not long array of time.

CHAPTER V

THE ROMANTIC DRAMA

THE stage was the first thing affected by the Revolution, and as late as Napoleon, Classical tragedy was still supreme. Bona-
Tenacity of parte reorganized the theaters and established the
Tragedy four houses — the Opéra, the Opéra-Comique, the Comédie-Française and the Odéon — that remain subventioned by the government today. He also fostered the Classical forms because of their reactionary tendency; he wished his Empire to resemble the old monarchy. Talma and other notable tragedians trod the boards in the high Roman fashion, declaiming Corneille, Racine, Voltaire, their feeble imitators and the dilutions of Ducis. Even under the Restoration little visible change appeared until Hugo, though certain popular undercurrents were making for freedom.

We have mentioned the work of Sébastien Mercier,[1] who broke theoretically with Classicism but was too timid in practice.
Predecessors His name should be distinguished from that of
of Népomucène Lemercier, who did just the opposite
Romanticism thing: the latter did not dare to theorize but attempted various innovations, especially in *Pinto* (1800). This play is really a *drame,* written in prose and including the mixture of comic elements. There is little tragic dignity about Lemercier, who suggests Bernard Shaw in his leveling of history to the bourgeois and practical plane. The subject of *Pinto* is akin to that of Hugo's *Ruy Blas.* More directly antecedent to the Romantic drama, however, is the Boulevard melodrama of Pixérecourt and his followers. Pixérecourt (1773–1844) was called the " roi du mélodrame," and no less than thirty thousand representations were accorded to his plays, which were quite lacking in literary value (*Cristophe Colomb, Robinson Crusoë, Cœlina*). But it seems likely that such productions paved the way for Hugo

---

[1] See above, p. 423

in the following respects: the attention paid to scenery and stage-devices, the mingling of comic and tragic elements, and the development of four staple figures of melodrama (*jeune premier*, heroine, heavy villain and grotesque buffoon). By laying a substratum of popularity for the new form, Pixérecourt served Hugo as Hardy had served Corneille. The poets of the twenties are transitional in their sympathies. Alexandre Soumet is vaguely Romantic in aspiration and more definitely so in his use of historical "machines" (for instance, *Jeanne d'Arc*, 1825); but he clings to the Classical rules. So does Casimir Delavigne in such early plays as *Les Vêpres siciliennes* (1819). But Delavigne was the most fashionable poet of his decade, following the Greek vogue in his *Odes messéniennes* and shifting more decidedly towards Byronism and Romanticism in his *Marino Faliero* (1829). The historical coloring of this play, as of *Louis XI* and of *Les Enfants d'Edouard* (Shakespearean), bears witness to the new influences; also Delavigne, though essentially a compromiser, handles the unities with some freedom and introduces Romantic sentiments and temperaments.

Various foreign influences should also be mentioned, such as the interest in German drama, due to Mme de Staël and Schlegel; Fauriel's translations from Manzoni (1823), who was the first Italian to rebel against the unities; and particularly the change in the French attitude towards Shakespeare. This was caused partly by the visits of English actors to Paris. Their second visit (1827–28) was a notable event. Such players as Kean, Kemble, and Miss Smithson took literary Paris by storm. *Hamlet* and *Othello* were especially well received, and these performances affected the production of Dumas *père*, Alfred de Vigny and Victor Hugo.

The last-named writer was the Romantic leader in every field, and it was on the stage that he won the victory for the Romantic

Hugo's Theory   cause. It should be noted that much of this drama is polemic in intention. Hugo threw down the gauntlet in his *Préface* to *Cromwell* (written 1827). This document is considered as the manifesto of the new school. Hugo divides the course of poetry into three great ages, of which the modern is primarily dramatic and culminates in Shakespeare. But the dramatic does not exclude an admixture of the epic or the lyric. The author thus declares for a *mélange des genres* — a famous phrase, more particularly applicable to the mingling of tragic and comic effects conspicuous in the Romantic drama. This combination, together with the juxtaposition of beautiful and ugly, of bad and good, is included in Hugo's "theory of the grotesque," involving an antithesis which he would derive philosophically from the dual nature of man. The grotesque is illustrated in art by Gothic architecture and by Shakespeare's alternations of buffoonery and high tragedy; it is found in nature itself, and Hugo boldly asserts: "Tout ce qui est dans la nature est dans l'art." This phrase expresses the broad Romantic view of both terms, in opposition to the Classic view of *la belle nature*. As regards drama and verse, the revolt is fundamentally against the neo-classical system. The forcible imposition of the unities, whether suitable or not, is characterized as a fetish of mediocrity and of slavish imitators. The only essential unity is that of action, which may well exclude the other two. Hugo also attacks the banal *récit* and insists on the importance of the concrete spectacle, with some use of local color. Like Diderot, he holds that rules are an impediment to genius. He wishes for more liberty in the Alexandrine, for more "characteristic" touches. He believes that verse is still the best vehicle for the serious *drame*: this term, as used by the Romanticists, designates an all-inclusive "tableau of life," especially the elaborate historical drama. *Cromwell* itself is a huge historical hurly-burly, but an impossible play. The real importance of Hugo's manifesto is in the new liberty which it evokes and the new theories which it sets in action.

To make these theories count, there were the enthusiasm and talent of the royally gifted writers of that age — Hugo, Dumas **"Hernani,"** *père*, Musset and Vigny shall be our chief ex-**1830.** amples — ably seconded by admiring groups of artists and minor poets. These groups had the interests of literature at heart, they were inspired by the passion of reform and revolt, and they had gallant leaders. Consequently there was enough to make the atmosphere electric when, on February 25, 1830, the first representation of *Hernani* was staged before the two rival camps. The Classicists protested against every daring *enjambement*, against every realistic or extravagant touch.

But the Romanticists, rallying around the red *gilet* of Gautier, answered with vehement applause, cheering the fresh sweep of action and passion here displayed. For several nights the issue of the battle was in doubt, and then the opposition slowly gave way. The Romantic drama was an accomplished fact.

The innovations effected by *Hernani* appear, first, in violat-ing the rules of the Alexandrine. The play begins with an **Innovations** *enjambement,* or run-over line, of the kind that no Classicist could tolerate; again, many lines discard the set division of the Classical Alexandrine into two equal halves and employ an irregular division into three, frequently unequal periods. For example:

> Qu'est cet homme? Jésus mon Dieu! si j'appelais?

contrasted with the Classical:

> Nuit et jour, en effet, pas à pas, je te suis.

These two features (*enjambement* and " free cesura ") are henceforth characteristic of Romantic versification in general: but it should be remembered that even the Romanticists stick to Classic regularity in about ninety per cent of their verse. The path of freedom is none the less made clear. *Hernani* also offended "lès purs," as they called themselves, by the use of everyday language, by calling a spade a spade on occasion; and by alternating this tendency with gorgeous and even vio-lent epithets and figures. Another novelty in style is the broken movement, due to interruptions or shifts of mood. This gives rise to " moody " dialogue, as it may be termed, unlike the smooth Classic pattern. Again, Classical decorum is violated by the attention paid to objects and concrete action; this is manifest in the stage-directions, which here for the first time become elaborate. The unities, as necessary rules, are forever laid to rest. Henceforth, though many good plays are written within **and** the unities, no good play *must* be so written. **Character-** *Hernani* changes its place and time at will, and has **istics** no compelling unity of action. Part of the time our sympathy is with Hernani, the gloomy bandit, and with his sweetheart, Doña Sol. In another act, we are more concerned with Don Ruy Gomez, the jealous old guardian of the girl.

In Act IV (which is frequently a *hors d'œuvre* in the Romantic drama), we applaud the nobility of Charles V, the newly elected emperor. For a time it appears that Hernani, restored to rank and power by Charles, will win his bride, and a happy ending is indicated. But the vengeance of Ruy Gomez is still to be reckoned with; in Act V he calls the bride and groom to account, with disastrous consequences for all concerned. A famous and typical expression of the Romantic temperament is to be found in Hernani's speech (Act III, scene IV):

> Je suis une force qui va!
> Agent aveugle et sourd de mystères funèbres!
> Une âme de malheur faite avec des ténèbres!
> Où vais-je? je ne sais. Mais je me sens poussé
> D'un souffle impétueux, d'un destin insensé.
> Je descends, je descends, et jamais ne m'arrête.
> Si parfois, haletant, j'ose tourner la tête,
> Une voix me dit: Marche! et l'abîme est profond,
> Et de flamme ou de sang je le vois rouge au fond!
> Cependant, à l'entour de ma course farouche,
> Tout se brise, tout meurt. Malheur à qui me touche!
> Oh! fuis! détourne-toi de mon chemin fatal,
> Hélas! sans le vouloir, je te ferais du mal!

The characters in the play are all Romantic types, moved by strong passions of love or revenge and repeating the typical gestures of melodrama. The removal of the unity of time should allow ample space for character development, but Hugo's psychology, here and elsewhere, is inferior to his lyric gift and intensity. There are fine poetic outbursts in *Hernani*, attended by brilliant *coups de théâtre*. The construction, however, is not sound throughout, and the characters are excessive, theatrical and often untrue to life.

Hugo's other plays may be more briefly considered. *Marion Delorme* (written 1829, produced 1831) is the story of a **Other Plays** courtesan redeemed by love and is the first play of importance to treat that favorite Romantic theme (cf. *La Dame aux camélias*). It is an unpleasant but powerful tragedy, and the two main characters — Marion and her lover Didier — however exaggerated, are impressively presented. The construction of the play would be excellent, were it not marred by the introduction of a burlesque element. *Le Roi* *s'amuse* (1832) was removed from the boards, partly on account of its horror, but mainly because it presents the monarchy, especially Francis I, in no favorable light. The King endeavors to seduce a girl whose father, the King's jester, unwittingly has his own daughter killed instead of the libertine monarch. From this drama, Verdi took the plot of his opera, *Rigoletto*. *Le Roi s'amuse* shows the development of Hugo's democratic sentiments. Passing over minor plays (*Lucrèce Borgia, Marie Tudor* and *Angelo*) — which are in prose and thereby even more melodramatic — we come to *Ruy Blas* (1838). After *Hernani*, this is Hugo's most important play. The two dramas antithetically treat of the rising splendor of the Spanish monarchy and of its gloomy decline. In *Ruy Blas*, the historical presentation of a corrupted court and its usages is very well done. The plot offers a violent contrast in situation. Ruy Blas is a lackey, who through his passion for the Queen rises to high dominion in Spain. He is overthrown partly through the machinations of the villain, Don Salluste, partly because his own character is not equal to his opportunities. The moral seems to be, once a lackey always a lackey. The most interesting personage in the drama is the bohemian Don César de Bazan. The passions are strongly depicted, and the plot is unusually logical and swift. With *Ruy Blas*, Hugo's dramatic glory ended. *Les Burgraves* (1843) was a failure, in spite of its epic quality, and marks the finish of the Romantic drama. As Gautier significantly said: " Il n'y a plus de jeunes gens "; reactionary tastes were in control of writers and public.

Not only did Hugo liberate versification but several of his plays tended also to liberate the minds of the people and to Qualities: serve democracy. Historically, these dramas are Defects and likely to take one-sided views, but they traverse a Merits wide range of countries and periods, at least five countries being represented. A wide free scope in place, time and subject, is an essential feature of the treatment; a new complexity is given to drama, by the expression of things historical, picturesque, physiological, " moody " and concrete; the *caractéristique* offers realistic details about manners and costumes; stage-setting is for the first time fully described; the number of speaking parts is far beyond that of Classic tragedy.

But with all these additions, the Romantic theater remains inferior to the Classical in harmonious artistic worth. The reason is that Hugo's drama is mostly melodrama. We find constant excesses and forced antitheses, whether of language, character or plot. These "fatal" heroes, forever making the same gestures, these suddenly converted kings or lackeys do not give a sense of reality. And the plots, in spite of their fevered movement, frequently lack the solid construction that makes for dramatic probability. There are too many wild flights, too many strange devices and tricks; hiding places, disguises, poniards, sombreros, duels and scaffolds; and grotesque buffoonery is pushed beyond all limits. At the same time, there are scenes, situations and *coups de théâtre* (like the picture-scene in *Hernani*) that are extremely effective; there are tirades that can still sweep an audience off its feet; and always Hugo remains the master of poetic expression, especially in love passages. This is the greatest merit of his drama. With Hugo, whatever is not lyrical is melodramatic.

Alexandre Dumas *père*,[2] in spite of the great vogue of his romances, figures in French literature rather as a dramatist.
Dumas père He wrote mainly in prose, and his plays are of two kinds: the big historical "spectacle," and the more personal drama of Romantic character and passion. He was even more melodramatic than Hugo; he underwent similar foreign influences (Shakespeare and Byron), and he too brought in many lands and epochs. A sort of rivalry is to be noted between Delavigne, Hugo and Dumas; in successive plays one of the trio would strive to outdo the others in strong effects. Dumas had a more consecutive dramatic sense than Hugo, but his plays, lacking all poetic virtue, are often brutal, feverish and crude. Coming after Pixérecourt, he is the first Romanticist to evoke the national past and to "put the memoirs into action," in ways that are picturesque, vivid and violent. Such are the characteristics of *Henri III et sa cour* (1829), a well-conducted play of jealousy and assassination; of *Christine* and her lover Monaldeschi (1830); of *Napoléon Bonaparte* (1831), which begins the series of vast historical *tableaux*. In the same year, Dumas also begins the other kind of drama (personal

---

[2] For his biography and his novels, see Ch. VI, below.

passion) by his remarkable and famous *Antony*. This play carries to an extreme the presentation of the Romantic hero, who is the victim of fatality and an outcast from society. Antony pushes his passion and misanthropy to the point of slaying the woman whom he loved, because in his (and her) distorted view, this is the only way of saving her lost honor. Other historical plays are *Charles VII chez ses grands vassaux, Catherine Howard* and particularly *La Tour de Nesle* (1832). This last has been called a "fantastic evocation of the Middle Ages." It deals with the loves of Marguerite de Bourgogne and Buridan, who pass through all degrees of criminality and excess; murders, dungeons, sorcery, disguises, and an especial emphasis on physical suffering, are characteristic of this play and of the author's melodramatic talent generally. Dumas staged also many successes from the "Babylonian edifice" of his novels — *La Reine Margot, Les Trois Mousquetaires* — huge productions, taking many hours to act. His preference was for historical subjects, which he recreated in the alembic of an imagination both riotous and unrestrained. The best of his plays, well-plotted and grimly powerful, are more widely representative of the *drame* than is the lyrical output of Victor Hugo.

The plays of Musset also fall mainly within two divisions: the play of fancy in the manner of Shakespeare, and the drawing-room comedy in the manner of Marivaux. The

Musset

first kind may be illustrated by *Fantasio* and by *A quoi rêvent les jeunes filles*. Such plays reflect the woodland atmosphere of *As You Like It*, together with a sort of irresponsibility as to time, place and setting; a fanciful charm in the treatment of femininity and in poetic style also suggests Shakespeare. The other type, illustrated by *Il faut qu'une porte soit ouverte ou fermée*, uses the salon atmosphere and shows the wit and delicacy of a more Romantic *marivaudage*. Musset's originality shines through his imitations. The titles of his plays are frequently taken from popular proverbs, which they illustrate in action; hence these dramas are called *comédies-proverbes* (cf. *Il ne faut jurer de rien, La Coupe et les lèvres*)· The *proverbes* are written mainly in prose, though of a poetic cast. Musset's best plays were composed from 1830 to 1840.

Musset wrote for his own satisfaction and for the reading public rather than for the stage. Only a few of his eighteen dramas were acted during his lifetime and are regularly presented to-day. The characteristics of the "closet-drama" are seen in their somewhat archaic style, the rapid changes of scene, the wilful play of fancy rather to the neglect of solid construction, and a tendency to interrupt the action with lyric individualism. *Fantasio* depicts a hero of romantic tempera-

Particular Plays ment who rebels against the commonplace and becomes a buffoon in order to aid a pretty princess. *A quoi rêvent les jeunes filles* is a poetic extravaganza, which derides the "romanesque." *Un Caprice* is also rather anti-romantic in theme; a man has a passing fancy for a woman who sends him back to his wife. *Il ne faut jurer de rien* again presents a charming heroine who convinces a rake that domestic love is best. Other interesting plays are *Barberine* and *Les Caprices de Marianne*. *Lorenzaccio* is a *drame*, in which the chief character is a kind of Hamlet drawn against a Renaissance background. This is considered one of the best historical plays of the period. The best of the *comédies-proverbes* is *On ne badine pas avec l'amour*, with its very significant title. Here we have echoes of the affair with George Sand, not only in the famous speech which declares the elevating power of love, but also in the cold and coquettish figure of the heroine. She rejects the affection of her cousin, Perdican. He begins to console himself with a village girl, the heroine then becomes jealous and seeks to win Perdican back. The play ends with the suicide of the village girl and the tragic separation of the would-be lovers who have "jested."

It is evident that Musset's plays, like his poetry, tend to the Romantic exaltation of love. These dramas frequently have the true "lyrical cry." But the passionate expression of sentiment alternates with the reverse of the medal — a Byronic and cynical attitude (cf. *La Coupe et les lèvres*). Musset is excellent in poetic flights, his dialogue is often witty and appropriate, and he is more competent in the depiction of character — mainly the several varieties of his own character — than any other Romantic dramatist. He understands what makes a dramatic situation. But instead of sticking to the development of the plot he often

prefers to wander irresponsibly in charming and imaginative
bypaths. His plays have a personal and unique attractiveness.

Alfred de Vigny's drama also closely reflects his individual nature. He was first inspired by the English actors
Vigny   to produce certain Shakespearean adaptations
(*Othello*, 1829; *Shylock*, never acted), which
were the best hitherto made in French. In opposition to
the prudery and thinness of Ducis, they convey to a high
degree the spirit, the fulness and the freedom of the original. Vigny also attempted the historical drama in *La
Maréchale d'Ancre* and wrote a graceful salon-comedy in *Quitte
pour la peur*. But his best play, which many think the greatest
play of the Romantic era, is the *drame intime* of *Chatterton*. The
legend of Chatterton, the "marvellous boy," is used to develop
the thesis of the poet-martyr: the possessor of such a talent is
necessarily in discord with ordinary life and must live and die
unhappily. Chatterton is placed in a quiet domestic setting, an
old Quaker and the heroine, Kitty Bell, are kind to him; but there
is a coarse business husband, and the hard world is too much for
the poet. He is mortified by lordly patronage, his manuscripts
are finally rejected, and his love for Kitty cannot be honorably
returned. Therefore he kills himself. The treatment is elevated
and even calm in tone, the sentiment fine and poignant. In presenting the dilemma of the poet-martyr, Vigny gives a new subject to the Romantic theater. He also crystallizes in dramatic
form the main *motif* of his own poetry, the lonely and melancholy
devotion to "l'esprit pur."

Thus the Romantic Drama has to its credit a dozen plays of
considerable strength or charm. It expresses best the surge of
Summary   feeling and of passion. Its poetry is in excess of its
strictly theatrical values. Its powers of characterization are not great and are rather monotonously exercised:
the "fatal" hero is always in revolt, the suffering heroine is
always in love. As drama, the Romantic output is surpassed
both by the Classical and by the Realistic kind. Racine excels
Hugo in well-balanced art, just as Augier excels him in truth
to life. Yet the Romantic drama appears historically as a
necessary bridge between Classicism and Realism. It forever destroyed Classical tragedy, by its establishment of a larger

framework and its abolition of set rules. It anticipates Realism in the attention paid to characteristic and concrete detail, whether in vocabulary, dialogue, description or stage-directions. But of course the spirit of Romanticism is different from that of any other school, and to those who admire the ardors and melancholies of that spirit, the Romantic drama will always appeal.

CHAPTER VI

THE ROMANTIC NOVEL

EITHER the Romanticists were disposed to view nature and society as symbolic of their inner dreams; or else, self-absorbed, they tended to neglect the realities of the outer world. Hence they were usually disqualified as novelists of contemporary French life. They sought refuge in the ivory tower, in the picturesque past, in exotic landscapes or realms of pure fancy, and finally in humanitarian visions. So we may classify four different types of fiction, which at least offered a considerable range of imagination and feeling.

1. The Personal Novel and Stendhal.

The novel of sentiment, issuing from Rousseau, from Mme de Staël and especially from *René*, is dominant at the beginning **The Personal** of the century. Sénancour's *Obermann* (1804) goes **Novel** farther than *René* in its representation of morbid pessimism and an impotent will. Without being a masterpiece, the book contains much sincere thought and feeling; there is almost no outer action. Sénancour's single frustrated love-affair is incorporated in this novel, which presents as its main interest the sufferings of an uneasy and despairing soul. Because of this feature, *Obermann*, in spite of its early date, has been held to anticipate the gloomy decline of Romanticism in the thirties. Two other important autobiographical novels belong to this of an intimate heart-affair, analyzed with great skill and pene- later period. Sainte-Beuve's *Volupté* (1834) is again the record tration. The book lacks emotional appeal, and the hero's egotism and sensual mysticism are not attractive. But Sainte-Beuve frequently attains both scientific precision and a supple artistic expressiveness. *Volupté* thus has affinities with the work of Stendhal; and the hero (Amaury), though a dreamer, believes in the power of action and will. Such attributes are not conspicuous in Musset's *Confession d'un enfant du siècle* (1836), which is turgid with the full Romantic tide of aspiration and despair. It records the fiasco with George Sand and is a lament for unfulfilled love. Sincerity, sensibility and sadness make this book representative of its generation, while the less pleasing " confessional " note goes back to Rousseau. More characteristic of Musset's talent are such charming and melancholy tales as *Frédéric et Bernerette* and *Le Merle blanc*. As personal novels should be mentioned also the *Stello* of Vigny, and much later (1863) the *Dominique* of Fromentin (see Bk. VIII, Ch. III).

The psychological novel, whose chief representative in this period was Stendhal, may be associated with the above. Henri

Stendhal Beyle (1783–1842), who took the pen-name of Stendhal, is one of the most curious and interesting figures of his time. He stands distinctly outside of the main Romantic current and was generally at odds with his French environment. He disliked his own family and his early surroundings at Grenoble, was unhappy in Paris, and much preferred Italy, where he mainly lived after the Restoration. But he took a creditable part in the Napoleonic campaigns; indeed, Napoleon and Byron were his chief heroes. A " romantic hussar," a man of action, he believed in energy, liberty and the development of the passions. Outwardly, Beyle was hard, proud and egotistical; but inwardly he had " too sensitive a heart and too clairvoyant a mind." He was a skeptic and a psychologist, deriving intellectually from the ideologues.[1] His two great passions were war and love, and his eleven heart-affairs are boldly analyzed in his four chief books. *De l'Amour* (1822) consists of a series of notes, almost formless, written in the dry precise style which was habitual with Stendhal. The book divides love into four categories and deals with the effect of each variety upon the several temperaments. Eccentricity and obscurity of statement alternate with remarkable penetration. For instance, we have the famous theory of " crystallization," according to which one's sweetheart becomes the center of the world's beauty and interest; and beauty itself is defined as " la promesse du bonheur." Stendhal's novels amplify the themes here suggested. *Armance*

---

[1] Especially Destutt de Tracy. See above, Bk. IV, Ch. I.

(1827) deals with the failure of two proud sensitive souls to come
to an understanding. Far more important in the history of
fiction is *Le Rouge et le Noir* (1831). The title indicates the
strife between the Napoleonic spirit of the military and the
power of the clergy, whom Stendhal thoroughly hated. The
originality of the book appears both in the manner of treatment
and the character of the hero, Julien Sorel. The latter is no
romantic sentimentalist, but personifies the strong-willed egotistical *arriviste* of the period (cf. Balzac). Julien makes love in
order to further his ambition and slays his first mistress when she
betrays him to his second. The women are modeled upon
Stendhal's intimate acquaintances. Their conduct is open to
the charge of improbability. But in the dissection of motive,
the presentation of ambition, passion and revenge, the book
shows a power which was rare at that time. *La Chartreuse de
Parme* (1839) makes easier reading, is more eventful and picturesque and seems wider in its appeal. Stendhal is now in his
favorite Italy; Italian passions, intrigues and society are excellently depicted. The author's worst fault is usually a kind of
hard tension and aggressiveness, whose effects are less conspicuous here. His *forte* at all times is the minute observation of
"soul-states." In *La Chartreuse de Parme*, he reveled in the
portrayal and analysis of the impulsive duchess, the highwayman
and the unscrupulous hero. Stendhal's heroes are really himself
in various environments, and thus his fiction is linked with the
personal novel. He also wrote *Racine et Shakespeare* (1824), a
paradox on the Romantic revolt, which shows that he hardly
understood the movement. His books were little read in their
own period. He was evidently born out of his due time, and
it is not surprising that he waited (as he prophesied) half a
century for recognition. Then occurred a curious literary revival. Stendhal was claimed and praised both by the Naturalists and the psychologists. Taine, Zola, Bourget, Rod and Hervieu vied in doing him honor or in imitating his processes; and his
influence has become conspicuous on the latter-day analytical
novel.

2. The Historical Novel and Hugo.

We shall see in the next chapter how Romanticism "revolutionized history," how the enthusiastic imaginations of Thierry and of Michelet put life and color into the Middle Ages. But the historians themselves were actually inspired by the Romantic fiction of Chateaubriand and Scott, and the historical novel stands as a dominant literary form for nearly two decades after 1826. This date marks the appearance of the first important example, Alfred de Vigny's *Cinq-Mars,* a romance of the conspiracy under Louis XIII. Through his serious attention to the genre and his abundant documentation — having read some three hundred works in preparation — Vigny really organizes the historical novel after the pattern of Sir Walter Scott: the study of manners and costumes together with character-sketches of the epoch treated. But Vigny's pen is too heavy to create a vivid masterpiece, his figures are obscured by their environment, and the book lacks life and verve. The *milieu* and the historical color are, however, well represented, and thereby Vigny makes the "first evocation of the national past" in Romantic fiction.

Vigny [marginal note]

Mérimée's *Chronique de Charles IX* is a more authentic and vital novel, and there are features in the author's character and career which will help explain this. Prosper Mérimée (1803–1870) was born a Parisian, but with a strain of English blood and English phlegm in his make-up. With his intimate, Stendhal, he shared powers of objectivity and of psychological penetration rare among the Romanticists; archeological researches were also prominent in his mind. He began writing with the so-called *Théâtre de Clara Gazul* (1825), containing plays in imitation of the Spanish drama. The "local color" in this is excellent, as also in another mystification called *La Guzla,* a collection of spurious Illyrian ballads which quite imposed upon the public. Mérimée thus shows his capacity for dealing ironically with Romantic motives. He led for some years the life of a Parisian man of fashion, winning fame not only through the *Chronique* but through the series of *nouvelles* which will be treated in the next section. In 1830 he paid a visit to Spain and formed a lasting association with the family of the

Mérimée [marginal note]

future Empress Eugénie. His heart-affairs culminated in the correspondence known as *Lettres à une inconnue* — " probably his best romance," since here alone do we find adequate feeling. A cultivated man of the world, a student and linguist, Mérimée was appointed Inspector-general of historical monuments, and his archeological preoccupations overflow into his tales. He became an Academician, a promoter of such exotic interests as Russian fiction, and under the Empire he wielded some power as senator and diplomat.

Written during Mérimée's youth, the *Chronique du règne de Charles IX* (1829), represents the artistic flowering of the his-
The torical novel. Proceeding from Scott, as did all of
" Chronique " these writers, Mérimée conserves the famous pictur-
esqueness of description and dialogue which characterize the Waverley Novels; also he uses true historical figures (kings and potentates) mainly as background and concentrates on the en-deavor to depict manners through typical invented figures and vivid scenes. Of the latter, several are imitated from D'Au-bigné's *Les Aventures du Baron de Fœneste* (1630). With sprightliness and ease Mérimée presents successively the German mercenaries, the *raffinés* (dandies) of the epoch, court scenes and various occupations of the sixteenth century. The author's great virtue is that he is a master of brevity, as opposed to the long descriptions of Scott, Hugo and Balzac. Another quality is his impartial objectivity. Relating the strife of Catholics and Protestants at the time of the massacre of St. Bartholomew, Mérimée holds a brief for neither side; he ironi-cally shows how conversions could be involved with personal influences, as where the seductive Diane de Turgis woos Mergy partly in the hope of winning him to Catholicism. The heart-interest is prettily handled, but is left somewhat in the air at the end, with Mérimée's characteristic indifference. The style is beyond praise, terse, witty and finished. Well-written, inter-esting, with excellent characterization and a large amount of historical truth, the *Chronique du règne de Charles IX* remains the most artistically proportioned novel of this kind. But like most of the author's work, it lacks strong emotion.

Victor Hugo introduced, as he wished to do, an epic range and significance into the novel. He shows again his poetic

power of vision, his liking for large symbols and vivifications.
Notre-Dame de Paris (1831), on the picturesque side marvel-
"Notre-Dame ously revives the fifteenth century and makes the
de Paris" Cathedral itself, in all its Gothic elaboration, the
epitome of that century and the hero of the book. The very
bells of the cathedral are animated, the bell-ringer, Quasimodo,
is a "human gargoyle," and the descriptions of Paris at large
are unusually vivid and lifelike. Unfortunately this gift does
not extend to the creation of character, and Hugo's lack of
psychological power was never more conspicuous. There are
no grays or browns on his palette; he silhouettes people in black
and white; and in order to display "the continual antitheses of
God," a character is likely to be black within and white without,
or vice versa (the ugly Quasimodo *versus* the handsome Phoebus).
As for plot, we find many excursions, long descriptions and
melodrama, whether of the improbable or the brutal kind. But
individual scenes and the massed effects of crowds are often
excellent. The style is characteristic of its author, colorful, evocative, very large in vocabulary and in imaginative appeal. This
power of imaginative rendering, of summoning back the swarming life of the Middle Ages, is the best feature of *Notre-Dame*.

A certain interest in the proletariat is discernible in the above
novel and is more conspicuous in *Les Travailleurs de la mer* and
His Social in *Les Misérables*. The former work is a fruit of
Novels Hugo's Guernsey sojourn and depicts the warfare
between human and elemental forces — an epic conception. So
the lonely fisherman, Gilliat, struggles with waves and storms
and is finally involved in the great combat with the octopus.
Les Misérables (1862) was written two decades before it was
published and thus properly belongs to the Romantic era. This
novel, for breadth and massiveness, is Hugo's most imposing
work. It is a "chaos of all genres and subjects," ranging in
tone from the lyric idyll to apocalyptic prose, including humanitarian sentimentalism, pathos, bathos, discussions of *argot* and of
sewers, the battle of Waterloo, politics, and antiquarianism. The
five loosely coördinated books, the episodes, and the interventions
of the author show that he is using the novel less as a form of
art than as a vehicle for his social views. Of his two main ideas,
the first is that embodied in the title: the proletariat (Jean Val-

jean, Fantine) is crushed by organized society, represented by its prejudices and its police; and secondly, Hugo believes that human misery and crime may offer their own expiation, as in the case of Valjean, the ex-convict. The early parts, concerning the redemption of Valjean, are surely the best and the most moving; the great merit of the novel (as in the case of Dickens and of Tolstoy) is in its power of making the reader thrill to the simpler feelings of humanity; for example, the desperation and devotion of Fantine's mother and the idyllic loves of Fantine and Marius. The variety of the *milieux* treated also adds to the range of the social novel. On the other hand, the characters are delineated either superficially or with too much symbolism — Javert as *the* policeman — and the wandering story allows too many improbabilities and coincidences. Hugo conferred upon fiction the two gifts of his imaginative style and his encyclopedic ardor. His last novel, *Quatre-vingt-treize*, is a return to the historical romance. It deals with the Terror, in the Vendée and in Paris, and presents excellent pictures of the Revolution. Hugo's fondness for children reappears, also his animism or the power of endowing external objects with life. Purely as fiction, *Quatre-vingt-treize* ranks among his best work.

Finally, Alexandre Dumas *père* (1802–70) represents the full popular success of the historical novel and also its artistic decadence. Dumas, a mixture of noble and negroid **Dumas père** blood, drew from his father the cult of Napoleonic energy which overflows into his life, his dramas and his novels. Scott and Shakespeare were his literary masters. His dramatic successes (see preceding chapter) launched him on a tide of high living and fast writing which he kept up for forty years. In fiction he was responsible for nearly three hundred substantial volumes, a certain portion being delivered by his " factory " of collaborators. Like Balzac, Dumas carried his imagination into life itself, living fantastically, buying schooners, building a huge palace of " Monte Cristo," which had to be sold for debt. Towards the last he became a poverty-stricken wanderer. He was a strong eupeptic person and put his vigorous vitality into his romances, which otherwise are often improbable, whether as history or fiction. But Dumas' robust treatment, his popularizing genius and his dramatic temperament make him the chief representative of the " cloak-and-sword " novel, which he handles with much narrative skill, especially in dialogue. He gives us the spectacle of a past which cannot have existed as a whole, though many separate traits are historical. His sources were usually the memoir-writers of the various periods; but the memoirs were hastily read and freely adapted by Dumas or his collaborators. His characters are of the simplest types and his style is poor; also he is fond of melodramatic incident and he boldly " fakes " history when he cannot find it; consequently most of his work is below par from the standpoint of literature. Exceptions must be made for the best of the Valois series, for the *Trois Mousquetaires* (1844) and for one or two novels centering around Marie Antoinette. These relics of our youth still stand out alluringly and are still entertaining. It was as an " entertainer " that Dumas became a prey to the *roman-feuilleton*, a newspaper-serial form of publication which hindered the footsteps of Balzac and Sand, and finds its culmination in the wild creations of Eugène Sue (*Les Mystères de Paris, Le Juif errant*). Both Dumas and Sue flourished in the forties, which period then marks the decline of the historical novel proper.

3. Tales and Fantasies.

The master of the *nouvelle*[2] is Mérimée, Romantic in his depiction of exotic scenes and primitive passions. But he is the " Classicist of Romanticism " in his objective coolness and the admirable qualities of his restrained style. Let us consider, among his best works, *Colomba, Carmen* and *La Vénus d'Ille*. The celebrated *Colomba* (1840) remains the most finished example of his art. Already in *Mateo Falcone*, Mérimée had dealt with Corsican passions, but with less direct observation and *vraisemblance*. *Colomba* is remarkable for excellent and not too excessive local color, for the skilful transition to the Corsican point of view, and for the able characterization of Colomba herself. This independent and revengeful girl gradually leads her

---

[2] This term will be used mainly in its modern signification of a long short-story, tending towards the "novelette"; the term *conte* will mean short-story; but at times the earlier meaning of the two words will persist, the *nouvelle* as the more realistic type, the *conte* as suggesting the fantastic or marvellous (*Contes cruels, Contes des mille et une Nuits*)

more civilized brother to the point of slaying their hereditary enemy. Several of the minor characters, especially those without the law, are well sketched. The book is a masterpiece of concise and sustained narrative power. These qualities are not so visible in *Carmen,* which is loosely composed, especially as compared with the dramatic versions. The archeologist who tells the story is not sufficiently alive to the misfortunes of Carmen's besotted lover. But the heroine is amply and powerfully displayed and creates the rôle of the Spanish " vampire." *La Vénus d'Ille* is really a *conte* in its dealing with the fantastic and supernatural world. It springs from the myth of the statue of Venus whom a mortal has unwittingly espoused to his own great detriment. Besides these stories of primitive passions, Mérimée also sponsored the *nouvelle mondaine* in the dandyism and worldly-wiseness of *Le Vase étrusque* and *La double Méprise.* Sangfroid is Mérimée's virtue as well as his fault. Emotion with him is sporadic, but his judicious constraint, together with the ease and elegance of his finished style must place him very high. *Colomba* has been called " un roman dont le seul défaut est d'être aujourd'hui sans défauts."

The "fantastic" school of story-telling, fathered by Nodier's talent, finds its natural leader in Gautier. His early volume,

Gautier *Les Jeunes-France* (1833) combines gaiety, libertinism and irony. He indulges in persiflage against certain Romantic excesses and habitually chooses from the movement only what he needs for his own artistic purposes. In the novel *Mademoiselle de Maupin* (1835) and in *Fortunio,* we are frankly in a pagan wonderland, where morality is in abeyance, and where passion, beauty and wealth are supreme. Two of Gautier's major themes, fantasy and the *macabre,* are found in *La Morte amoureuse,* a superbly constructed story of a wild love that conquers death. The idea of " phantom love " or the dream-mistress is very insistent in this author's tales. It recurs in *Arria Marcella,* in *Omphale, Une Nuit de Cléopâtre,* etc. This reveals Gautier's type of Romanticism. It is the kind that revolts against the mediocre and the ugly aspects of modernity and seeks escape either in exotic lands or the distant past. Such heroes as Fortunio, Gyges and Tiburce (in *La Toison d'Or*) are mouthpieces for the expression of Gautier's dreams and longings, which are sensuous and plastic rather than idealistic. They are voiced, however, not in the more flamboyant manner of Romanticism, but moderately, artistically, with a care for diction and elegant decoration. Gautier is still writing enamels and cameos. *La Jettatura* (1856) might in other hands be full of wild throbs and rhetoric — it is a tale of the evil eye, of lost love and duels and suicide — but it is treated by Gautier in a mild-mannered and somewhat ironic fashion that removes much of its dramatic force. Local color and a choice style are the dominant interests. Similarly, *Le Capitaine Fracasse* (1861–63) belongs to the Romantic era as a historical fantasy. Following Scarron, Gautier resuscitates a band of strolling players, interweaves their fortunes with those of some youthful nobles, and beautifully describes certain features and landmarks of the epoch (Louis XIII), especially the Château de la Misère. *Le Capitaine Fracasse* is for many the most delightful of Gautier's novels; it is akin to the picaresque romance of adventure. His brilliant style, his fine prose rhythm, his sense of color and form, his search for unusual or exotic characters, are more conspicuous than any wealth of ideas or any depth of sensibility.

Gautier and Hugo kept up their Romanticism well into the second half of the century. Two latter-day Romanticists, writers of fantastic tales, are Villiers de l'Isle-Adam (1838–89), author of *Contes cruels, Isis,* etc., and the eccentric Barbey d'Aurevilly (1808–89). The latter achieved striking effects in his best novel, *Le Chevalier des Touches,* and in a collection of stories well named *Les Diaboliques.*

4. George Sand.

Aurore Dupin, who married the Baron Dudevant and is best known by her pen-name of George Sand, led a productive and **Life** variegated life (1804–76). She came of a mixed stock, which on her mother's side had been very irregular in its love-affairs; her paternal grandmother was severe and aristocratic: the girl's youth was divided between the two households, and it is characteristic that she kept her affection for both. Most of her childhood was passed in the ancient and pleasant province of Berry (central France), whither she returned in her old age and where many of her stories are located. Religious phases, a convent education in Paris and much reading of Rousseau were followed by the stultifying marriage of convenience with Dudevant, whom Aurore presently abandoned. But she remained devoted to her two children. She was launched on her literary career partly through the collaboration of Jules Sandeau and through influential friendships. The affair with Musset was preceded and followed by others. But no emotion could permanently upset the deep placidity of George Sand's character, nor interrupt the sequence of her numerous volumes. She traveled abroad about 1836, became interested in the doctrines of 1848, and later retired to her province, where she was known to the neighborhood as " la bonne dame de Nohant." An interesting correspondence with Flaubert belongs to this period; he emphasizes the head and she prefers the heart. Instead of art for art's sake, she upholds " l'art pour le vrai, l'art pour le beau et le bon."

Hers was a big broad nature, amoral or apathetic in certain respects, but capable of much ardor and devotion. George Sand was always in love with somebody or something and the four stages of her productiveness simply vary the object of her affections. The first period (1832–40) is the epoch of *l'amour-passion* (Stendhal's phrase) and marks the creation of her special type, " la femme incomprise." In a series of feverish novels (*Indiana, Lélia, Valentine, Mauprat*), the authoress expresses her violent reaction from her house of bondage and proclaims the rights of free love. Her reputation was made by *Indiana* (1832), which is the first novel to hold forth lyrically on woman's sufferings, and may be taken as typical of the series. A young girl, having married an old man, is attended by two would-be lovers. The one, " Sir Ralph," is her cousin and guardian. Mute, devoted and stolid, he protects her from the selfish passion of the other lover, who is not above courting the Creole maid in lieu of her mistress. When Indiana has gone through countless sufferings and humiliations in the affair, " Sir Ralph " proposes a joint suicide which somehow results in their union instead. The story contains violent scenes and declamations against the cruelty of man. *Lélia* is even stronger

Periods

in the enthroning of Romantic passion. The revolt against marriage expressed in the above novels led to a wider revolt in George Sand's second or socialistic period (1840–48). Having been subjected to diverse strong influences, Lamennais in religion, Proudhon and a certain Michel (de Bourges) in radical politics, she proceeded to mingle utopianism and metaphysics in various novels (for example, *Le Compagnon du Tour de France*). They are not remarkable for strong thought or consistency, but again they show emotion — which is now the love of humanity — and her usual charm of style. This series also includes the interesting *Consuelo*, which is concerned with eighteenth-century history and intrigue. More purely " social " is the communistic and leveling *Meunier d'Angibault*, in which a good deal of property is burned in order that a rich widow may marry an artisan. It is generally conceded that there is too much " thesis " and declamation about George Sand's problem-novels. After the disillusionment of 1848, she returns to her native heath and writes the best stories of country life that the century has produced. She had already shown her ability in this direction by the two idylls, *La Mare au diable* and *François le Champi*. The third period (c. 1848–60) is then filled by her love of outdoor nature and country folk. *La Petite Fadette* illustrates the genre, with the fidelity of its beautiful description and its excellent psychology of simple hearts. Finally, a fourth period (1860–76) is mentioned by some critics and would include later miscellaneous novels. They are love-stories at large and show occasional signs of weariness. Of these, *Nanon* is a tale of the Revolution and *Le Marquis de Villemer* — the best of this period — deals capably with high life.

It will be apparent that George Sand did many things. As opposed to Balzac, she is supposed to represent the "roman idéaliste." Individualistic and passionate at first, she also helps create the social novel in her second period, attains her apogee with her country stories, and writes always with ease and often with eloquence. A tendency to over-idealize or romanticize and a lack of good composition are her worst faults. She was an improviser and admitted that she wrote simply by " turning on the faucet." But at her best she is widely sympathetic and interesting and conveys the sense of life in many ways.

CHAPTER VII

CRITICS AND HISTORIANS

In general, Romanticism met with no formidable opposition, but there were several important writers who stand apart from the main currents of the period. Already under the Empire, a group of critics were marked by their conservative tendencies. Joseph Joubert (1754–1824), a profound and delicate thinker, has been called " the critics' critic," since he won the admiration of Sainte-Beuve, Arnold and others. He led a simple and retired life, devoted mainly to the pleasures of friendship and conversation. In his stormier youth, he was influenced by Diderot and became the lifelong friend of Fontanes; from about 1800 Fontanes and Joubert together were the chief counselors of Chateaubriand. Joubert's single volume of *Pensées* (not published until 1838) is a series of crystallized meditations in the manner of the seventeenth-century *moralistes*. The eighteenth century was severely judged by this Platonic idealist, who preserved a detached and serene soul through all the national upheavals. His literary judgments show true insight, but his form suffers from too much subtlety or too much condensation. Joubert was not really creative, and the future will probably find that he has been overvalued by the past.

The Reactionaries: Joubert

The " Catholic reaction," in which Lamartine and Chateaubriand participated, was headed, in the domain of theology proper, by Joseph de Maistre and the Abbé de Lamennais. The former (1753–1821) was a " grand théoricien théocratique " and the first leader, under Napoleon, to demand the restoration of Catholicism. De Maistre was a semi-foreigner, a Savoyard by birth and residence. He had the career of a magistrate and diplomat. He was strong for the principle of Papal authority, even infallibility (*Du Pape*, 1819), and he became a dominant figure among the Ultramontanes, the group that sought to subordinate the

Joseph de Maistre

Gallican church to the power of Rome. His finest book is the *Soirées de Saint-Pétersbourg* (1821), dialogues dealing with high spiritual problems. They are expressed in a clear logical form which owes much to the eighteenth century, whose principles De Maistre detested. His influence was at its height during the Second Empire and affected the virulent journalist, Veuillot, and the eccentric neo-romanticist, Barbey d'Aurevilly. Of a very different character was Joseph's brother, Xavier de Maistre, who wrote the sentimental and charming *Voyage autour de ma chambre* (1794).

The Abbé de Lamennais (1782–1854), by his ardent and eloquent nature and by his association with Chateaubriand and

Lamennais Lamartine, is more closely linked with literature. Like Chateaubriand, he came of a Breton family and environment and was endowed with certain traits of the " Northern " romantic imagination. A great reader in his youth, he passed through a stage of skepticism and was not ordained priest until 1816. The *Essai sur l'indifférence* (1817–19) attracted much attention, and Lamennais was esteemed one of the Catholic leaders. His chief disciples were Lacordaire and Montalembert. The three writers founded, after the Revolution of July, a progressive journal called *L'Avenir*, which became too liberal in the eyes of the Church. Lamennais was finally condemned by the Pope and lost his power among the orthodox. He had previously published (1834) his *Paroles d'un croyant*, which remain the most individual expression of his fiery faith. Dogmatic and Ultramontane, Lamennais yet represented a fine effort to assimilate Catholic orthodoxy and democratic liberalism, and the effort wholly failed. His endeavor was to spiritualize the Church, working first from the top and then (after 1830) from the bottom. The *Essai sur l'indifférence* develops a theory of " certainty " as regards dogma, using the fallacious basis of universal historic testimony. The *Paroles d'un croyant* consist of highly imaginative parables and visions, written or chanted in a Biblical style. The book resembles its author in its alternation of tenderness and violent ardor, and thereby Lamennais clearly belongs to the Romantic generation.

Under the Restoration, there were three gifted professors and lecturers who exercised a considerable influence upon French youth. This "trio of the Sorbonne" was composed of Villemain in criticism, Cousin in philosophy and Guizot in history. In their several fields, each of these men stood for a new historical method, and all three were liberal-minded. Their eloquence was unsurpassed, while their best books were simply products of their courses. Abel Ville‑ main (1790–1870) emphasized social background and compara‑ tive literature. The value of his *Tableau de la littérature au moyen âge* has faded out since specialists have made a study of medieval documents, but his *Tableau de la littérature fran‑. çaise au XVIIIe siècle* (1828) still keeps its usefulness and in‑ terest. This work helped restore the eighteenth century to its proper place in the history of thought; it offered capital ex‑ amples of "literature as the expression of society"; it used the method of comparisons and cross-influences (particularly from England); and it was written in a style of genuine if old‑ fashioned eloquence. Villemain had taste, judgment and knowl‑ edge. Together with Mme de Staël, he may be credited with founding nineteenth-century criticism.

The Trio of the Sorbonne: Villemain

The talent of Victor Cousin (1792–1867) was less reliable. His life carried out his motto of "il faut paraître"; he was con‑ stantly in evidence as a popular lecturer and edu‑ cator. Appointed professor of philosophy when quite young, he endeavored to fill the gaps in his training by trips to Germany and an enthusiasm for Hegel. His most important volume, *Du Vrai, du Beau et du Bien* (1853) was composed of courses delivered in 1818 and again in 1836. He received many public honors, influenced the mechanics of the French educa‑ tional system, and in his old age wrote a series of admiring volumes on his "amoureuses," such heroines of the seventeenth century as Mme de Longueville and Mme de Sablé. Victor Cousin stands first for a new and significant emphasis on the his‑ tory of philosophy and, secondly, for the doctrine of Eclecticism, or the endeavor to combine into a working creed the best and most plausible portions of past systems. Revolting against the Empiricists (sensationalists), he manufactured an unstable com‑ pound of Plato, Descartes and the German idealists. His eclectic synthesis is superficial and his method faulty. In aesthetics, he again approximates a Platonic idealism, an emotion which is the

Cousin

" pure sentiment of the beautiful and the sublime." More characteristic of his age is the fact that he recognizes the independently creative rôle of the artist, and he is among the first to formulate the doctrine of " art for art's sake." He also belongs to his period by his capacity for feeling and inspiring Romantic enthusiasm and by his lack of deep reflective powers.

François-Pierre-Guillaume Guizot (1787–1874) was a more solid and serious person. A French Protestant by upbringing, **Guizot: the** he preserved throughout life the austerity of that sect. **Man** As teacher, historian and statesman, he was a leader of the " doctrinaires," the moderate liberals who stood as champions of the bourgeoisie and of constitutional monarchy. Guizot was also a distinguished orator and publicist. He entered politics early, occupied various administrative positions after Waterloo, lost and regained his professorial chair and gave his epoch-making courses on civilization, 1828–30. Under Louis-Philippe, Guizot held several portfolios, was made ambassador to England and, joining the Opposition, ranked as minister of foreign affairs and head of the cabinet, 1841–48. In government he believed in the *juste milieu*, repressed democracy pure and simple, and constantly maintained that the upper middle class was the backbone of the nation. Similar views characterize his attitude towards history, which he tended to consider as an adjunct to practical politics.

Nevertheless, Guizot is regarded by many as the greatest of French historians. In opposition to the 'Romantic school (see **His Work** subsequent pages), he headed the political school, " whose object was rather to explain than to narrate, to teach than to paint " (Gooch). Furthermore, Guizot's masterpiece, the *Histoire Générale de la Civilisation en Europe* [1] inaugurated a fresh philosophy of history and revealed its author as the greatest generalizer since Montesquieu. As a universal history, the work is more broadly based than that of Bossuet or even that of Montesquieu; it accepts the theory of Providence, but usually explains events as arising from human and social causes or the structure of governments. Guizot's *forte* is the

---

[1] Published with the accompanying work (*Histoire Générale de la Civilisation en France*) as a *Cours d'Histoire moderne*, in, 1828–30. Guizot also wrote a valuable *Histoire de la Révolution d'Angleterre* (1828); he was a profound admirer of Anglo-Saxon institutions.

exposition of the underlying ideas of an epoch. For instance, he holds that the two main currents of modern civilization are the spirit of free inquiry and the struggle for liberty as warring with the slow centralization of power. Again, Guizot shows how the modern world amalgamated older elements from the Roman Empire, from the establishment of Christianity and Feudalism. The bourgeoisie incorporated the best progressive growth of the Middle Ages, and in the long run " its existence involved representative government." The *Civilisation en France* was intended to develop the thought that France, through her assimilative and radiating energy, exhibits the highest type of intellectual civilization. The lectures were unfortunately suspended before Guizot had passed the early Middle Ages, but he had revealed his ability to study the body politic as an organism and had strongly emphasized the national " unité morale " as rising above the conflict of classes. The author's cold reasoning and his sober style prevent any display of picturesque or dramatic talent. He is not dealing primarily with personalities or with facts in themselves and his books lack color. Sainte-Beuve declared that Guizot made everything too symmetrical and " enchained," and the great critic, after reading the historian, would take down a volume of De Retz's Memoirs to remind himself how history was actually made. But Guizot, by his intellectual quality, by his impartiality and sure erudition, as well as by his establishment of the Société de l'Histoire de France, ranks as the leader of this earlier generation in philosophic history, as Thierry was the master in the narrative kind.

The imaginative qualities which Guizot lacked are to be found, even too abundantly, in the Romantic school of historians.

The Romantic School: Thierry   Michelet was profoundly influenced by the general Romanticism of his period, and Thierry found his vocation through reading Chateaubriand's *Martyrs*. Scott and Chateaubriand, the one in his antiquarianism, the other in his poetizing of the Middle Ages, may be considered the godfathers of this school. Augustin Thierry (1796–1856) must be distinguished from his younger brother, Amédée, who wrote about the Gauls. Thierry began his career as the secretary of the eccentric social philosopher, Henri de Saint-Simon, from whom the historian may have partly derived his sympathy with the masses. An interval of journalism and a systematic study of the sources of French history were followed by the production of two masterpieces, the *Histoire de la conquête de l'Angleterre par les Normands* (1825) and the *Récits des Temps Mérovingiens* (1840). Unlike other historical writers of the time, Thierry was neither a professor nor a politician. His health prevented any active life; from the age of thirty he was blind and partially paralytic; but these handicaps blighted neither his vital enthusiasm nor his capacity for labor. His was a fine character, courageous, simple and ardent. As a writer, he combines a genius for detail with a power to animate the whole record of a faded past. The result is a picturesque restoration of the early Middle Ages, an imaginative and colorful interpretation, which combines a true "intuition" of past sentiments and ideas with an ability to press out the storied life from charters and chronicles. So the Merovingian kings move vividly before our eyes, and the epic of the races takes form in their migrations. Thierry is among the first to emphasize intensive racialism (that fetish of the nineteenth century), and his *Conquête de l'Angleterre* over-stresses the Norman influences on English social life. His narrative gift is excellent, he is a master of proportion in composition and of choice and moderate expression in style. Thierry is the first to put history on a high literary plane.

The Romantic qualities appear in their greatest efflorescence in the work of Jules Michelet, the "Victor Hugo of history." **Michelet** He came of the people and he was right in declaring, "je suis resté peuple." The poverty and privations of his childhood left Michelet, as they left Dickens, with a warm sympathy for the masses and with some distrust of the world of society. As a boy, he sought relief from drudgery in visiting a certain Museum of French history, which gave him the first inspiration for his future work. He succeeded in getting an education and was an avid reader. In 1827 he translated the works of Vico, the Italian philosopher, and was appointed to teach at the Ecole Normale, where his *causeries* were much esteemed. Ten years later he passed to the Collège de France. As a consequence of an attack on the Jesuits he lost his professorial chair; he also lost his post in the national archives, when Napoleon III came into power. Discouraged and embittered against imperialism, Michelet won happiness again through the companionship and collaboration of his devoted second wife. This is the epoch of his travels and of his curious volumes, semi-scientific, semi-mystical, on *L'Oiseau, La Femme, La Bible de l'Humanité*. Michelet always kept something of the feeling and enthusiasm of a child. Susceptible, kind-hearted and thoroughly good, he was rather a solitary, revealing his "wingèd spirit" only to his intimates or in his books.

As for the *Histoire de France*, the composition of this work runs through all his mature life. Three separate parts are to "Histoire de be distinguished: six volumes on the Middle Ages, France" written from 1833–43; then Michelet's sudden leap to the Revolution, 1847–53; finally, the treatment of the intervening period (*Renaissance et Temps modernes*, eleven volumes, 1855–67). The first part is Michelet's most perfect and harmonious work, written before his prejudices and imagination overcame him. His ardent patriotism and his tendency to symbolism made him view medieval France as a living person. His object is the "resurrection of the life of the past as a whole," and he succeeds in this through his gift of sympathetic imagination, applied to the complex of institutions, events and personalities. He believed that a great writer should understand and welcome eagerly "the diverse manifestations of the human spirit" (Monod). The power of vision and expression thus attained is beyond anything in the range of French history hitherto. As Sainte-Beuve says, Michelet makes all other historians seem like compilers. Some of the outstanding features of the work are the famous survey of the French provinces (Michelet was the first to emphasize geographical history); the apotheosis of Joan of Arc as the soul of France; and the full-length depictions of Louis IX and Louis XI. The writer's usual habit is to narrate by a succession of vivid scenes. The second part of the work was undertaken after Michelet's campaign against the Jesuits. It enthrones the Revolution as embodying, especially in its dawn, the hope of a humanity liberated from king and church. The people *en masse* can be viewed as the hero of the epic, and the people can do no wrong, in Michelet's view. At least, the mob spirit and the Terror are attenuated, to the greater glory of Revolutionary principles and ideals. In brilliant *tableaux* (the Convocation of the States-General, the flight to Varennes, etc.) and in prophet-like demeanor, Michelet is rivaled only by Carlyle, whom he also resembles in various errors and faults of proportion. The third part of the *Histoire* shows this great talent in its decline. Bitter attacks on the old régime and the Catholic church, a tendency to credit scandalous memoirs and to over-estimate the small fact as determining history, are scarcely atoned for by the continuance of the author's wonted eloquence and power of depiction. There is too much propaganda and too little care and thought. Michelet here exhales hatred and prejudice, and the four chief objects of his hatred, it has been well said, were priest, king, England and the bourgeoisie.

But at his best, as an interpreter of the Middle Ages, Michelet is incomparable. Page after page contains fire and feeling, **His Talent** knowledge and insight. Like Thierry, he breathes upon musty documents and informs them with life. He was possessed of a " flamme intérieure," which he communicates to ancient ages and to the reader as well. One of his admirers, Monod, declares that Michelet remained the chief fortifying and consoling force in the nation; that after 1830 he was almost the only example of continued Romantic idealism and optimism. He sought the original and striking features of an epoch, and his *Histoire*, in its mobile and fervent style, is most original and inimitable. He was too individual to found a school, but later historians admit their debt to his inspiration and admit his supremacy in the imaginative and emotional revivification of the past. Michelet was primarily an artist, who chose history as his working material.

The work of Thiers and of Mignet, who belonged to the " political " rather than to the Romantic school, may be more **Thiers and** briefly considered. Adolphe Thiers' long and bril-**Mignet** liant career (1797–1877) is closely connected with the destinies of his country. With Mignet, he founded *Le National* and helped expel the Bourbons in 1830. With Guizot, he shared the direction of the doctrinaire policy and alternated with him as leader of the cabinet and of the Opposition under

Louis-Philippe. Thiers was partly responsible for the third Napoleon, but his great opportunity was found in the days of '70–'71, and his patriotic services then were rewarded by his election as the first President of the French Republic. As a historian he is not deep, shows political bias and neglects documentary sources. But his treatment is extremely clear and fresh. The *Histoire de la Révolution française* (1823–27) was for long the most popular work on the subject. It shows a certain political opportunism and fatalism, but it is tolerably impartial and very readable, with its easy luminous style. The *Histoire du Consulat et de l'Empire* (1845–62) is a greater book and remains the most complete account of Napoleon, as it was a considerable factor in the restoration of the Napoleonic cult. Thiers was well equipped and experienced in matters of administration and diplomacy; he made special studies of finance, geography and battle-fields; his chief handicap is externality, a lack of the philosophic power with which Guizot was so abundantly endowed. Thiers' close friend, Mignet (1796–1884) has a higher place as an accurate and thoughtful historian. His *Précis de la Révolution française* (1824) is still useful in its condensed and logical presentation of events. But Mignet is not an accomplished writer. His chief work, the *Succession d'Espagne* and the editing of documents relative to that subject, belongs to history as a science rather than to history as literature.

BOOK VII

REALISM

CHAPTER I

THE TRANSITION: BALZAC

HONORÉ DE BALZAC (1799–1850), in spite of the *de* which he inserted in his name, was of comparatively humble birth. He
Life was of peasant stock on the side of his father, who seems to have endowed Honoré with his strong physique and personality. The mother left him her taste for mystical reading (cf. *Louis Lambert*); also she paid his debts and often nagged him mercilessly. More sympathetic to the lad's ambitions was a sister, Laure, who was among Balzac's first biographers. Though the family was of Southern origin, Honoré was born and spent his youth in the sunny country of Touraine, which he has glowingly celebrated in his fiction (*Le Lys dans la vallée, Contes drôlatiques*), and this environment probably added to his Rabelaisian exuberance. At the Collège Vendôme, near Tours, Balzac passed six years of hot-house discipline and promiscuous hard reading. His health was seriously affected for a time. Then he was sent to Paris, " pour faire son droit "; his law-studies and the notary who directed them appear conspicuously in his novels (*Gobseck, L'Interdiction*). He was finally allowed to take a fling at literature, and we see him (1819) happily installed in the conventional garret and writing enthusiastically to his sister about his career — which he had not yet started. Some years of application resulted in ten melodramatic novels (*Œuvres de jeunesse*); these even Balzac would not sign. Desiring to make money rapidly, he became involved in a printing and publishing concern, which led to financial insolvency (*Illusions perdues, César Birotteau*). The aristocratic Mme de Berny helped rescue him from this predicament and interested him in the epoch of the Revolution.

This was depicted in *Les Chouans* (1829), with which novel Balzac begins the famous series of the *Comédie humaine*.

Les Chouans is significant because it marks the transition from the historical novel to the novel of contemporary manners. When the transition became complete, modern Realism was born. The Realistic tendency is still more pronounced in the early *Scènes de la Vie Privée*, which included such important studies in actual life as *Gobseck* and the *Curé de Tours*. With the appearance of such masterpieces (1833–34) as *Eugénie Grandet, Le Père Goriot* and *La Recherche de l'Absolu*, Balzac's method of work may be considered as established. His enormous productivity has fairly begun. He is henceforth the "anchorite of labor" who toils for months together, from two in the morning all through the day, sustaining himself with black coffee and allowing an occasional holiday for Gargantuan meals and social pleasures. Balzac was well received in certain salons and deigned to pose as a social lion. But he lacked distinction and was never admitted to the Academy. He grew up in the society of the Restoration, which knew all the difficulties of "reconstruction" on a large scale. So his novels present many types of *arrivistes* (Rastignac, Rubempré), who pass through various environments in their search for position and wealth. Owing to his perpetual need of money, Balzac was in changing relations with different publishers and theatrical directors; he also found it wise to change his place of residence frequently, in order to avoid persistent creditors. He had fleeting affairs with various women, but the only true successor to Mme de Berny was a Polish lady, Mme Hanska. This affair began in 1833, was long maintained by scattered meetings and correspondence (*Lettres à l'Etrangère*), caused sudden visits to Switzerland, Italy and the Ukraine, and was consummated in marriage just before the novelist's death. Though it ultimately ruined him, this passion fostered Balzac's talent and productive power. "Etre célèbre et être aimé" were his two most steadfast desires. So we find him absorbing Parisian and provincial life, entertaining strange dreams of wealth, either through Sardinian mines or through dealings with the Great Mogul, becoming an amateur of *bibelots* and collections (*Le Cousin Pons*), constantly binding himself over to publishers and pawning the future for the present. In this respect he resembled Sir Walter Scott, and the practical life of each was damaged by the writer's too liberal imagination. Like others, Balzac contracted to produce *romans-feuilletons* at top speed, and after 1836 the results appear in some instances of hasty composition and style. Yet many of his best works (for example, *César Birotteau*, 1837) were also written rapidly. It has been estimated that he made an average of almost twenty-five thousand francs yearly, and from 1845 his financial position became easier. By then all his efforts were directed toward marrying Mme Hanska and setting up a fine establishment in Paris. Trips to Russia, a long sickness, and disillusionment after marriage, precipitated the end. He died, literally worn out by life and labor, in August, 1850.

By nature, Balzac offers a curious compound of the idealist and the materialist. His powerful imagination, his sanguine **Temperament** dreams of love and happiness, his (Swedenborgian) mysticism tended in the one direction; but his very physical being, his coarseness, his Rabelaisian and middle-class characteristics induced in him much gusto for the real world. By intuition he is a Romantic genius; by his extraordinary and detailed memory for the concrete, he is the founder of the Realistic school. His two chief ideals, love and creative art, were stained by the money-making ambition. Exuberant and even titanic power is his special mark. No such industry and driving force had hitherto appeared in fiction. It led him into eruptions of gaiety and egotism, in which everything had to bend to his will, and in which the world of real people faded away before the huger reality of the *Comédie humaine*. It led him finally into that realm of hallucination and monomania in which he wrote his last imposing novels — *Le Cousin Pons, La Cousine Bette*. Numerous anecdotes show how for Balzac his visions became facts, and it is in the ultimate fusion of the real and the romantic that the secret of his spell resides.

Besides his fiction, Balzac wrote several volumes of plays, articles and miscellanea; but the *Comédie humaine*, the product of **Plan of the "Comédie humaine"** twenty years' labor, stands out as his great achievement. This collection includes about ninety-five separate titles of novels, novelettes and short stories. Over four million words and over two thousand characters, one-fourth

of them " reappearing," were used in this vast scheme. Its central
feature is the endeavor to present completely and concretely the
social life of contemporary France: " completely," because Balzac's idea was to include every social category and most fields
of knowledge; " concretely," because Realism of detail and a close
acquaintance with small bourgeois life were employed to an un-
precedented extent; " contemporary," because the historical novel
of the past is incidental in Balzac's work and he studies chiefly
the modern epochs with which he had personal contact. It is in
these three respects that he expands the novel far beyond the
range attempted by Scott and Hugo. As early as the middle
thirties he had determined his plan of social studies, had chosen
his general title (as a counterpart to Dante's *Divina Commedia*),
and had fixed on the device of reappearing and interlocking characters to mortice together his growing edifice. In the *Avant-
propos* of 1842 he evinces his encyclopedic intention and his view
of society as divisible into species according· to profession and
habitat. At least one-third of his titles (*Le Médecin de Campagne, La Vieille fille, Les Employés*, etc.) indicate this preoccupation with social types, which is further manifest from the
divisions given to the *Comédie*. The first and largest Part is
called " Etudes de Mœurs " and is subdivided into six kinds of
Scènes: those pertaining respectively to the *Vie privée, Vie de
province, Vie Parisienne, Vie. politique, Vie militaire* and the·
Vie de campagne. The second Part is called " Etudes Philosophiques," and the third, " Etudes Analytiques." These include fewer titles and have no subdivisions; the intention here
was more abstract — to deal with the causes and principles
underlying society (*La Recherche de l'Absolu, La Peau de
chagrin, La Physiologie du mariage*). To recur to the first Part,
the various *Scènes* overlap in their content, which is not always
logically subdivided; but Balzac's intention of becoming the
" secretary of society," studied in its chief categories, is here
fulfilled. We may mention a few samples under each·heading.
The *Vie privée* included ultimately the early novelettes dealing
with modest bourgeois life (*La Bourse, La Maison du Chat-
qui-pelote*), together with such fine character studies as *Le
Colonel Chabert* and later full-length novels like *Le Père Goriot*
or *Béatrix*. The *Vie de province* contains Balzac's main attempt,

turgid and sentimental, to depict idealistic love — *Le Lys dans la vallée;* it also has the incomparable *Eugénie Grandet, Pierrette,* the huge fresco of *Illusions perdues,* and others. The titles here cover four French provinces. The *Vie Parisienne* includes a parallel fresco of the metropolis — the *Splendeurs et Misères des courtisanes* — and several novels of intrigue and business. The *Vie politique* has, for instance, *Une Ténébreuse Affaire* (mystery story); the *Vie militaire* has *Les Chouans;* and the *Vie de campagne,* appropriately includes *Les Paysans, Le Médecin de campagne* (ideal doctor) and *Le Curé de village* (ideal priest). The last three *Scènes* embrace fewer titles than the first three, and it was Balzac's intention to enlarge their content. He planned in all one hundred and fifty novels. Several unwritten masterpieces were to gather around his hero Napoleon, and others, judging from the semi-autobiographical novels already mentioned, would undoubtedly have gathered around Balzac himself.

As with his temperament, so we must consider Balzac's work in its Romantic and in its Realistic aspects. The origins of his **Balzac's** Romanticism are not far to seek. The English **Romanticism** " School of Terror " (Maturin and Lewis), the melodrama of Pixérecourt, certain contemporary strains in Hugo or in Sue were not without influence. Balzac's own *Œuvres de jeunesse* (*Argow le Pirate, Jane la Pâle,* etc.), which are fairly voluminous, teem with melodramatic incidents, violent deeds, missing heirs and mysterious characters. Consequently, the *Comédie humaine* contains a revival of Maturin's Melmoth; a gruesome villain like Vautrin; sinister bands like that of the " Thirteen "; piracy in *La Femme de trente ans;* crimes, vendettas and harrowing deaths in many novels. Apart from this *bas-romantisme,* there is also the more legitimate type, to be seen in Balzac's individualism: not only does he exhibit his heart and mind in many passages, but he preaches individualism in the careers of his male and female climbers (Rastignac, de Marsay, Valérie Marneffe). The exaltation of the imagination (*Séraphita, La Peau de chagrin*), of passion (Véronique, Mme de Mortsauf, Esther van Gobseck), of the artistic life (*Gambara, Illusions perdues*) all have their Romantic bias. The delineation of such strong passions, rising to the point of mania, is often fine and stirring; but pathos is not usually Balzac's *forte*. Again, his descriptive processes are often those of the Romantic painter. Except in *Le Lys dans la vallée*, he scarcely treats nature in an idealistic way; nor is he prone to use Catholicism other than as a desirable discipline. This is replaced by the somewhat material and exaggerated mysticism of *Louis Lambert* and *Séraphita*. Exaggeration and excess were, unfortunately, two Romantic temptations to which Balzac fell an easy prey. The thick coloring of his style in " purple passages," the millions of francs with which he suddenly endows his leading characters, the agonizing death-beds, and especially the growing effect of hallucinations in his own mind, the huge mushrooms of many midnights of toil — all these are symptoms of the Romantic fever.

But as a whole the *Comédie humaine* is the earliest and still the most conspicuous monument of French Realism. We may **Realistic** define Realism as the art of representing actuality, **Features** viewed largely from the material standpoint, in a way to produce as closely as possible the impression of truth. What then are the chief Realistic qualities and elements in the work of Balzac? As regards *truth*, it would seem that his deliberate pessimism, his exaggerations in plot and incident, and his use of grandiose monomaniacs as characters, would be " romantic." But his careful verisimilitude gives nevertheless the impression of reality, and we feel that most of the *Comédie humaine* has actually happened. This is undoubtedly because Balzac conceives his novels with an intense and powerful vision. He leans towards *materialism*, which is his second Realistic quality — the emphasis on force, food, money and concrete objects. He especially stressed various material occupations: physical living, which depends upon eating, which depends upon money, which depends upon work in trade or profession. The space given to money and business affairs is among Balzac's most notable features, and his knowledge of this field seems comprehensive. The insistence on material things is also apparent, not only in the long descriptions of furniture and the like, but in the fact that a mere object (a purse, a crucifix) is often made a pivot in the plot. Again, it seems materialistic that so many of his characters have analogies with the animal world. The very idea of social species came to him, as he says, from a comparison " entre l'humanité et l'animalité," and throughout he sustains the comparison and insists upon the resemblance between men and beasts. Allied to this trait is the attention paid to *science*, especially the modifications of character due to environment, topography, physiology or pathology. Certain pseudo-sciences, such as mesmerism, also figure largely. Balzac's " encyclopedic zeal " finds expression in *documentation* and in *breadth of treatment*. Two kinds of documents appear: technical disquisitions by the author, with display of erudition in many fields; or the use of such actual documents as a military proclamation or a business prospectus. Conscientious researches (*enquêtes*) often seem inorganic as regards the story proper, but add to the fullness of background and the sense of reality. The breadth of treatment (Realistic universality) seems to ignore nothing in contemporary life and is conspicuous in Balzac's elaborate introductions. Some tediousness results from such long-winded descriptions and expositions. One finds also a tendency towards mediocrity and triviality of representation, but in this respect Balzac sins less than his successors, and many even believe that he attains his greatest effects in the depiction of mediocre and ordinary lives. He is not so successful in etching true aristocrats and people of refined breeding. He was a Royalist and something of a tuft-hunter, yet his vision of *manifold democracy* is perhaps the best embodiment of the mingled art and truth of the *Comédie humaine*. All in all, he attains a *solidity* of effect, of workmanship, of cumulative power that is simply incomparable. But among his Realistic virtues we can include neither a thoroughly sympathetic heart (such as the Russians have) nor the impartial and impersonal attitude of Flaubert and the later school. Balzac is perpetually intruding himself into the story. The *sociological aspect* already developed, the amount of delineation by classes and types, is the crowning conception of this Realist.

Other features of his method will appear from a consideration of such fictional elements as exposition, plot and character-

Method ization. A Balzacian exposition, like the head of a comet, bulks very large and frequently tries the patience of the reader. Often fifteen or twenty per cent of the whole novel will be devoted to preambles, topographical, socio-historical, biographical or generally descriptive. At times (*Eugénie Grandet, Père Goriot*) this expository manner is logical, progressive and valuable for an understanding of the whole. At other times (throughout the *Médecin de cámpagne* and the *Curé de village*) there are too many unorganized disquisitions. In about one-third of his stories, Balzac uses the method of beginning with action, *in medias res,* and then returns to solid exposition. He uses the first-person form of narration almost as frequently, and both of these devices are evidently intended to vitalize the heavy material.

His plots are rather complex in the conspiracy-novel (*roman-complot*) as well as in the large frescoes, where it is a question of depicting various social groups. The study of many *milieux,* both for their historical value and as influencing character, is very important in his scheme. But when the exhibition of one salient character is the main thing, then the plot tends towards simplification and a progressive accumulation of incidents. The *roman-complot* itself usually revolves around the doing to death of some particular martyr: examples are Cousin Pons, Pierrette and Colonel Chabert. In the character-novel also, the protagonist is often done to death, but rather by his or her own fault; some mischievous mania obsesses and finally destroys the person. Examples are César Birotteau, led astray by his ambitions; Balthazar Claes, whose passion for research ruins his family life and ultimately his whole *morale;* Baron Hulot, disintegrated by libertinism; Goriot, with his excessive paternal devotion. Such plots frequently present grandiose characters, analogous to Shakespeare's passion-ridden heroes, and with Balzac too we may find the " ruling passion strong in death." So the miser Grandet clutches on his death-bed at the golden crucifix, and so Claes ends his illusory search with the cry of " Eureka!" Impressive as these monomaniacs are, solidly as they are built up, they seem less humanly real than the host of more average characters, belonging to every grade, profession and moral stratum, which swarm through the *Comédie humaine.* Balzac often constructs his character around a definite keynote or central personal trait (cf. La Bruyère). Thus César Birotteau is described as a large sanguine son of a peasant, and this rôle he maintains throughout. His costume, his physique, his deeds must correspond to this initial characterization. A similar use of *harmony* is found in most of Balzac's descriptions, whether of person or place, and together with this is found a process of *accumulation* of points along the definite line suggested by the keynote. The " maison Vauquer " breathes an atmosphere of wretched poverty: each room, each article of furniture, the aspect of each boarder must contribute to the total effect. At the same time, each boarder has his or her distinctive individuality, to be reinforced through the details of costume, personal habit, biography and manner of speech. For example, Poiret is a machine and everything about him is mechanical. Small wonder that Balzac needed miles of descriptive matter and that his details — characteristic, causal or cumulative — appear as numerous as stars in the sky!

Most cultivated critics have held that Balzac does not write well, that his style is too cumbersome, materialistic, sometimes **Style and** absurd and pedantic. Lapses of various kinds can **Influence** certainly be found. But granted the nature of his material — and his own nature — it is difficult to see how another medium could be employed. He marches " with huge feet fairly plowing the sand of our desert " (Henry James), and his style labors onward with him. In the best narrative portions it can be swift, unpretentious, direct; when he tries fine writing, he usually and ridiculously fails; but at certain puissant moments, the " efflorescence " of his style rises to heights of delineation and passion. In appropriate figures of speech and in characteristic dialogue, he is not found wanting. Thus his style is as variable as his subject-matter, but it too frequently lacks distinction — just as his depiction of fine women often lacks delicacy. In this, as in other respects, he inaugurates the rule of force and displaces that of beauty.

The influence of Balzac has no limitations or end. He simply transformed fiction and made the modern novel the most comprehensive literary vehicle. Important novelists in many countries have recognized his leadership. Henry James, primarily a psychologist, calls him " the master of us all "; George Moore, though a dilettante, has written a wonderful tribute to the reality of the *Comédie humaine;* as for his Realistic successors, their name is legion throughout Europe and America (see Chapters IV and V, below).   This predominance, together with his expansive and titanic power, goes far towards ranking Balzac as the greatest novelist of all time.

CHAPTER II

AUGIER, DUMAS *FILS* AND HENRY BECQUE

The year which saw the failure of Hugo's *Burgraves* (1843) also saw an attempted revival of Classical tragedy in Ponsard's Ponsard and *Lucrèce*. In this and in more modern subjects, Scribe Ponsard represents, in opposition to Romanticism, the so-called school of " bon sens." But his drama was color-less and short-lived. More important historically was the varied productivity of Eugène Scribe (1791–1861), who occu-pied the post of chief entertainer during the first half of the century. Scribe created the modern *vaudeville*, or light comedy of intrigue, and his mechanical dexterity furnished many of the elements of the " well-made play," whose formula still subsists. Neo-classical comedy, under the Empire, was but a bare skele-ton which Scribe undertook to vitalize by a system which both suspends and complicates the interest; he introduced much in the way of devices, preparations and stage-business. But Scribe scarcely belongs to literature. He was a vulgar author, depict-ing superficially a vulgar bourgeoisie. His characters are sil-houettes, his style crass and incorrect, and his ideals center around money-marriages. His vogue marks the fact that pure tragedy is dead and that comedy, light or serious, will hence-forth occupy itself with clever plots and with contemporary life. Successors to Scribe, under the Second Empire, were Emile Labiche (*Le Voyage de Monsieur Perrichon*, etc., etc.), whose gay talent and fertility found a suitable outlet in the *vaudeville;* and Meilhac and Halévy, who wrote sparkling librettos for Offenbach's operas.

Serious Realistic comedy was undertaken by Emile Augier (1820–89), who owes something to Scribe and to Ponsard. Augier Augier led an even, prosperous life as a Parisian bourgeois of the better sort, and his career was marked by almost unbroken successes with critics and public alike. For a generation his name predominated in the répertoire of the Comédie-Française. He wrote, partly in collaboration, twenty-seven plays, roughly divisible into three groups. The earliest group contains dramas written for the most part in mediocre verse and including fanciful or remote subjects: *La Ciguë* (1844) imitates the antique in the manner of Ponsard; *L'Aventurière* (Padua, sixteenth century) presents already one of Augier's main theses, that the adventuress is the enemy of the family. More significant is *Gabrielle* (1849), which denounces the doctrine of Romantic escape in free love. By sensible arguments the heroine is won back to her husband, whom she thus apostrophises:

> O père de famille, ô *poète*, je t'aime!

The dramatist seems to conceive of poetry as a domestic virtue.

In his second period, Augier establishes himself as a writer of excellent *comédies de mœurs*, a modern though inferior Molière. The famous *Gendre de M. Poirier* (1854) recalls the *Bourgeois Gentilhomme* in the aspirations of its hero, in the blend of sense and humor, and especially in the deft balancing of characters, scenes and forces. The *Mariage d'Olympe*, intended as an answer to the *Dame aux Camélias*, again denounces and punishes the courtesan who has invaded an honorable family. In fact, the family and marriage are now the chief concerns of Augier: a marriage must be properly established (*Ceinture dorée*), or it must be safeguarded (*Poirier*), or it must be broken up, if unsuitable (*Mariage d'Olympe*).

Augier's third period consists mainly of " social comedy," a broader development of the comedy of manners. Either the family is viewed as part of the organism of society or widespread social defects (money-rule, luxury, clericalism and corruption of the press) are portrayed on an ample scale. Luxury and venal love are strongly depicted in *Les Lionnes pauvres; Maître Guérin* presents the unscrupulous man of affairs who always remains within the law; *Les Effrontés* and its sequel, *Le Fils de Giboyer* (1862), deal with political and clerical intrigue and give us a new type in Giboyer, the indurated journalist. Like Figaro, this personage has had a variegated career; he represents the proletariat and a sort of socialism. The dramatist appropriately concluded his career with *Mme Caverlet,* a play concerning divorce, and with *Les Fourchambault* (1878), a large *tableau* of family complications.

In Augier's drama we have something like a less elaborate and more moral *Comédie humaine.* He stages a history of the **His** bourgeoisie under the Second Empire. His social **Qualities** purview covers the new struggle of classes, the questions of patriotism and clericalism, several varieties of the money question, and marriage with all its adjuncts (love, dowry, triangles, children, divorce). His Realism appears in this comprehensiveness, as also in a certain impartiality and impersonality of treatment; in contrast to Dumas *fils,* Augier rarely intervenes with sermons, and events of his own life are apparently not dramatized. His careful massing of background (*Mariage d'Olympe,* etc.,) is again Realistic, and so is the use of small incidents and objects. The characters, many of whom stand on their feet as solid and salient types, are gradually and distinctly built up. Thus Augier is a psychological Realist as well. People like Poirier, Olympe and Vernouillet are not easily forgotten. The ideas of Augier are anti-romantic and sensible from the standpoint of average living. He is never mystical or passionate, he does not understand or employ the grander sweeps of passion, emotion, religion or speculative thought. Unoriginal, sane and healthy, he is a good representative of the best bourgeois spirit as well as of an excellent dramatic tradition. His technique is occasionally conventional in the use of stage tricks, in concèssions regarding the heart-interest and happy endings; but he is rich in situations and scenes, while his gestures and single speeches (*mots de situation*) are often telling. Augier and Dumas *fils* together establish the Realistic drama in their successful endeavor " de porter au théâtre une peinture exacte de l'humanité, et des cas de conscience."

More impassioned and personal than Augier, more of a preacher and a genius was Alexandre Dumas *fils* (1824–1895), who as a **Dumas fils** natural son of his Romantic father would readily turn to dramatic paths. After a rather unhappy boyhood in a boarding-school, he was taken under the wing of the elder Dumas and shown certain varieties of gay life. But having no pronounced taste for dissipation and being considerably

in debt, the son turned to literature and first to novel writing
(*La Dame aux Camélias*, etc.). A dramatic version of this story
started his career as a playwright, which continued until 1887
and included sixteen plays. Dumas *fils* was made an Academician and became quite a figure in society, in spite of frail health.
Among his friends he was noted for his penetrating wit and his
essentially upright character. He took up several social causes,
defending the rights of natural children as well as more liberal
divorce laws. The Naquet divorce bill (1884) was passed
largely through Dumas' influence. In many of his earlier plays,
his own experiences, contemporary events and personages appear,
though with adequate disguise. Two opposing tendencies dominate his later work — good Realistic technique *versus* a moralizing and sermonizing habit which grew on him. Thus an intense
and concrete vision of " l'homme social " wars with the *pièce à
thèse* (the problem-play with a dogmatic solution), which he
virtually creates. His drama is abundantly moral but it seems
risqué and cynical in that he usually deals with the divagations
of love in high life.

It is perhaps unfortunate that Dumas *fils* is still largely known
to the Anglo-Saxon public as the author of " Camille " or *La
Dame aux Camélias* (1852). This play is Romantic
Plays   in theme — a courtesan " rehabilitated " or purified
by a great love — and exhibits a youthful ardor not found elsewhere in Dumas' work. More characteristic of his true manner
is the careful rendering of Marguerite Gautier's *milieu*. Similarly,
in *Le Demi-monde* (1855) all that concerns the shady setting
is masterfully handled, and in this respect Dumas is an initiator.
The heroine, Suzanne d'Ange, is among the first of modern
vampires, and Olivier de Jalin is the author's favorite type of
raisonneur hero. The trick by which the latter deceives and
frustrates Suzanne has been severely criticized. First-hand
knowledge of Parisian life is also found in two subsequent plays,
Le Père prodigue and *Le Fils naturel* — the titles of which are
evidently applicable to the two Dumas. In *La Question d'argent*
(1857), Realistic drama takes a distinct step forward in the
presentation of business affairs and of the unscrupulous millionaire, Jean Giraud. Money is as conspicuous as in Balzac, and
yet the author is at pains to show that it cannot conquer esteem

or love. His disposition to moralize begins to be notable in this play and comes to a climax in *Les Idées de Mme Aubray* (1867), in which theories of Christian charity are placed in opposition to maternal affection. Other plays of this last period are: *L'Ami des femmes*, a complicated diatribe against irresponsible women; *La Femme de Claude*, in which another vampire meets death in the author's "revolver reaction against Romanticism;" *L'Etrangère*, which is good melodrama; *Denise* and *Francillon*, which again display Parisian women in no favorable light.

The fact is that neither Dumas' men nor his women are of heroic mold; the women are usually viewed either as seductive **Characters** perils or as empty-headed playthings; the men are **and** **Character-** weak, selfish and voluptuous. The only type ad- **istics** mired by the author is that of the *raisonneur* — the cynical and clever man of the world, who understands, explains and manipulates the other characters, not usually for his own benefit (René de Charzay, Olivier de Jalin and the hero of *L'Ami des femmes*). But all of these types — pleasure-seekers, feeble parents, hard young men and girls — are set forth with precision and logic. These two qualities are marked in all of Dumas' processes: precision and logic produce the clear-cut effect of his style and appear in his salient epigrams; they also characterize his plot-construction, which is closely knit together and develops like a mathematical demonstration. The plots progress not by Augier's balance of forces, but by straight logic to an inevitable conclusion. The use of "seeds" or preparations and of dove-tailing, cumulative scenes is conspicuous. A certain balance, however, is found in the fact that the sub-plots often doubly illustrate the main theme: two groups of people, respectively more advanced and less advanced in years than the main protagonists, are involved with the same general problem (for example, *La Question d'argent*, *Le Demi-monde*). These several features of Dumas' method are not all Realistic; in fact his logic sometimes operates to the detriment of his Realism, and the same is true of his preachments. For instance, in too many plays a character steps out of the picture to moralize its message; in others, probabilities and persons are forced in order to convey the moral. Characters become more and more mouthpieces of the author and are even allegorical symbols: one man has been dubbed Conscience, one woman is Passion, Olivier de Jalin is Friendship and Mme Aubray the Gospel. Dumas' theory of the " théâtre utile " damaged his dramatic illusion and his artistic verity.

Yet, all in all, he is a convinced and capable Realist, and his dramatic skill and power are often beyond praise. Intensity and vibrant sincerity set him above Augier, whom he also surpasses in imaginative force and feeling. But he is inferior to Augier in breadth of treatment and in poise. Dumas is Realistic in his penetrating and unsparing delineations of Parisian society, the deft natural touches in dialogue and in stage-business, and the slow painstaking reproduction of all that concerns background and the gradual evolution of character. In spite of some fixed ideas and habits, he remains a creative, earnest dramatist of very nearly the first order, essentially French in his subjects and viewpoints, his coruscating wit, psychological insight and knowledge of theatrical resource.

Dumas' most noteworthy successor, after Realism had passed into Naturalism, was Henry Becque (1837–1899). Becque

Becque   goes further than Dumas in the direction of pessimism, in a sort of brutal photography and in sharp concise technique. These are his main qualities, which may have resulted in part from the disappointments of his life: he failed on the Bourse and in journalism, and his plays were not really successful until his name became identified with the Théâtre Antoine (see Bk. IX, Ch. II). *Michel Pauper* (1870) reveals the sources of Becque's pessimistic power. The drama concerns an inventive workman. The effect of his lonely despair in conflict with capitalism is very strong. Certain minor plays preceded *Les Corbeaux* (1882) which is Becque's masterpiece and probably the best play produced by the Naturalistic movement. The Vigneron family is suddenly left without a head and father; the four helpless women are about to be victimized by the birds of prey (lawyer, notary, creditors) who descend upon the house. The chief " corbeau " agrees to defend the women from the other rascals, if the second daughter will marry him; he tells her, " Vous êtes entourée de fripons, mon enfant." The drama gives a great impression of reality, done with contained irony. Becque expresses himself without exaggeration or sympathy; his tone is that of cold disgust. He stands for the " slice of life " theory, according to which the absolute verity of the single scene, with carefully chosen, biting dialogue, is of more importance than the total composition. Finally, in *La Parisienne* (1885), we have a portrait of the light-hearted woman who vibrates from one lover to another, because her first choice behaves too much like a husband. *La Parisienne*, even more than *Les Corbeaux*, represents the perfect " slice of life " with its return at the end to the original situation.

Apart from photography and pessimism, Becque's Naturalism is also seen in the exactness of his ironic " studies," especially in matters of business. Affairs are affairs for him — and he learned them on the Bourse. The influence of money is constantly shown, often in petty ways. His intense though partial vision of reality is heightened by his dramatic short cuts and concentration. He and his school strive for an " integral Realism," the core of a situation or of a character, presented in a condensed dialogue that is bare of ornament. Becque is an artist in ugliness. He has a tragic power that is found neither in Augier nor in Dumas. In technique, he is more Naturalistic than these two men, for he revolts against the devices which they had inherited from Scribe. Henry Becque has been a strong influence upon the younger generation of dramatists (see Bk. IX, Ch. II).

CHAPTER III

THE REACTION IN POETRY:
BAUDELAIRE AND THE PARNASSIANS

THE year 1857 was a notable date in French letters. It was marked by the appearance of Dumas' *Question d'argent,* of **Baudelaire** Flaubert's *Madame Bovary* and of Baudelaire's *Fleurs du mal.* Partly a successor to the Romantic poets, partly in revolt against their doctrines, Charles Baudelaire (1821–67) crowded into his short life the elements of dissipation and of spiritual travail which find intense expression in his single volume of verse. A rebel against domestic restraint, against scholastic discipline, against any respectable career or behavior, he found himself at twenty a dandy of the Latin Quarter, in possession of a small fortune. This he quickly spent. Involved in debts and in an unfortunate *liaison,* he tried art-criticism and journalism, writing up two of the yearly " Salons," and producing at intervals (1856–65) his remarkable translation of Edgar Allan Poe, whose tales he made known to Europe. The publication of the *Fleurs du mal* engaged Baudelaire in a lawsuit which caused a certain scandal. But the poet was honored by his brother artists (Gautier and Banville), and his position seemed secure. Unfortunately, his health was already undermined. He shortly made the mistake of trying to live in Belgium, a country which he found unsympathetic; there he was stricken with paralysis, and he returned to die in Paris.

Baudelaire's strange physiognomy, like that of a shady priest or a seedy actor, was borne out by a wilful singularity in character and behavior. Desiring to astonish, over-fond of mystifications, he was deliberately irregular in costume, language and opinions. Behind his cold and disturbing mask, he indulged tastes for debauchery, wine and hashish; and he sometimes exaggerated his perversity to the point of Satanism. Yet he had strong spiritual reactions and was influenced by an ideal love.

These opposing forces vie with one another throughout the *Fleurs du mal* and are crystallized in the great line:

Dans la brute assoupie un ange se réveille.

A number of these poems had appeared first in the reviews. The title chosen for the volume was meant to " épater le bour-**"Les Fleurs** geois " and is not very suitable; *Spleen et Idéal* (a **du Mal "** sub-title) is more exact. The book has no central plan, except as it depicts the successive soul-states of the author. The essential duality of his nature produces, on the one hand, many evidences of Catholic mysticism: repentance, desire for atonement, appeals to the Lord, a churchly vocabulary and reminiscences, a liking for ritual and hymns; on the other hand, the poetry of revolt finds expression in tributes to Satan or to Cain and in complacent descriptions of debauchery and horrors. Adoration for Madonnas and a pure earthly love are at variance with Realistic impressions of " une horrible Juive," of corpses, of creepy sunsets and of *Les petites Vieilles.* Ennui and spleen, mulattos and cats, " artificial paradises " and other artificialities, white nights, sumptuous imaginings, and fervent solemn religious prostrations, make a curious jangle in Baudelaire's " cracked soul " (*La Cloche fêlée*). But whatever the material, the projection of the poet's inner life is always powerful and intense. His form is masterly and original, while the " new shudder " upon which Hugo congratulated him applies as much to the poetic transcription as to the sinister subjects treated.

The poems are mostly short, comprised within a page or two, and the irregular sonnet form (see *L'Ennemi*) is a favorite. **Formal** This brevity was partly inspired by Poe, who **Merits** also seems responsible for some use of the repetend and the refrain. Baudelaire reacts against the Romantic theories of facile inspiration and effusiveness, and he takes few of the Romantic liberties; he is sparing in his use of *enjambement,* of rich or rare rimes. He employs mainly the Classic mold, into which he pours his unusual substance. His Alexandrines are more full and sonorous than those of any Romantic poet. He is the master of a certain organ-roll, aided by polysyllables, enumerations and a plenitude of effect which has been aptly likened to a Beethoven symphony:

> Je sais que vous gardez une place au poète
> Dans les rangs bienheureux des saintes Légions,
> Et que vous l'invitez à l'éternelle fête
> Des Trônes, des Vertus, des Dominations.

His images are original and readily visualized; we see the woman who sails along like a " beau navire " or the wounded man who lies under a pile of corpses,

> Et qui meurt, sans bouger, dans d'immenses efforts.

Baudelaire also makes an excellent use of antithesis, and his epithets are striking, suggestive and sometimes paradoxical (" aimable pestilence "). He chooses his words with unerring care and artistic restraint. Perhaps his most important quality is a power of concentration and condensation, visible in the total plan of the poem as well as in single verses. Therefore certain of his lines are memorable and of a lapidary perfection —

> La musique souvent me prend comme une mer.
>
> L'empire familier des ténèbres futures.
>
> Les parfums, les couleurs et les sons se répondent.

The last quotation illustrates Baudelaire's conception of sense-transference or of certain correspondences between the arts, a theory which he did not push to the extreme of the later Symbolists (see Bk. IX, Ch. III). His own senses were very keen. His thorough acquaintance with painting and with music, his love for Delacroix and his early appreciation of *Tannhäuser,* will account for such perfect tableaux as *Don Juan aux enfers* and for the orchestral effect already mentioned. Such a couplet as

> Je hais le mouvement qui déplace les lignes
> Et jamais je ne pleure et jamais je ne ris,

indicates an impassivity rebutted by such a prayer as

> Ah! Seigneur, donnez-moi la force et le courage
> De contempler mon cœur et mon corps sans dégoût.

Baudelaire never had this " force and courage." Consequently his poetic expression is limited to a few ideas and to a single deep furrow plowed in the lyric field. But his form and his virtues are Classical, and Baudelaire is already a classic. He was a sufficiently great artist to universalize his personal experience, to subject his reality to a lifting and transmuting power, and thereby to say certain sorrowful things once for all.

Baudelaire represented the decay of Romanticism in his morbidity and taste for extremes; he was like his "maitre impeccable," Gautier, in linking the two major obsessions of death and voluptuousness. Romantic devotion to technique reaches its climax in Théodore de Banville (1823–91), a clever and sometimes a charming manipulator of rimes and rhythms. His numerous volumes, from *Les Cariatides* through the *Trente-six ballades joyeuses*, show facility, verve and a sense of beauty which, however, he is inclined to make an " article de Paris." He is mainly occupied with celebrating lovely ladies in sparkling odes, triolets and other set forms. Banville has dexterity without depth.

Banville

The pressure of the new Realistic forces, particularly as regards science and the objective attitude towards history and nature, impinges on poetry in the work of the Parnassians. The activity of these poets was brought to a focus in the collection called *Le Parnasse contemporain*[1] (1866, 1869 f.) which gave its name to the school. The group started with diverse talents and aims, but with a common desire for faultless artistic workmanship. Some of the early founders (Catulle Mendès, Glatigny, etc.,) never made a profound mark; others began as Parnassians and ended as something else. This was the case with Sully Prudhomme, François Coppée and Verlaine (see Bk. IX, Ch. III). The term " Parnassiens " came to connote an Olympian calm, which these young writers affected; they were averse to Romantic storm, stress and subjectivism; for similar reasons they were also known as " les Impassibles." For a time they all submitted to the influence of a strong chieftain who gave direction and body to the movement.

"La Parnasse"

This leader was Leconte de Lisle (1818–94), who ranks as the foremost poet of his epoch both in thought and in expression. He was of exotic birth, coming from the Ile-de-Bourbon, near Madagascar. Tropical scenery and emotions appear in the few poems that commemorate his youth,

Leconte de Lisle

[1] The name evidently proceeds from Mount Parnassus, the home of the Muses.

during which period he took a long voyage in the East. He was brought up severely, presently sent to France, and compelled to study law at Rennes. Finally he settled in Paris, where he supported himself by teaching and by translations. He was poor and proud, leading a life in which the chief events were extensive studies, volumes of poetry and intercourse with a few friends. After the publication of the first *Parnasse contemporain*, Leconte de Lisle became the head of the group, but before that he had published several of his most distinctive volumes: *Poèmes antiques* (1852), *Poèmes barbares* (1862). He also made excellent translations from Homer, Theocritus and the Greek dramatists, an activity which helped his art rather than his financial status. Official recognition came with his appointment as assistant librarian at the Luxembourg and with his election to the Academy in 1886. He was never widely popular. His last collections were the *Poèmes tragiques* (1884) and the *Derniers poèmes* (1895).

All of these volumes are written in much the same manner and are to be distinguished chiefly by the range of periods which they illustrate. Victor Hugo also was reflecting the trend of the times by subduing emotion and seeking historical subjects. Leconte de Lisle's conception is similar to that of the *Légende des siècles* (which his first volume antedates), in that he records the creeds and destinies of various races and eras, taken in their most expressive types or at their culminating point. But he emphasizes more the element of religious thought, and he often uses the Greek material and manner, which Hugo rarely employs. In his version of the epic of humanity, the Parnassian poet shows a historical rather than an imaginative approach, and he manifests a scientific approach in the wideness and exactness of his knowledge. In fact, he is opposed to the general looseness of the Romanticists, to their exploitation of self, to their sentiment and rose-color, as well as to their interpretation of nature and their ignorance of the sciences. His qualities are the direct contrary of these; and among them we may consider first his objectivity.

His Qualities   Leconte de Lisle puts the least possible of himself into his work. He strives to minimize the expression of personal sentiment, which he regards as a changeable and exaggerated thing. He is after more enduring material. His sonnet, *Les Montreurs,* is a bitter diatribe against those who complacently display their hearts to others. He tells the public:

> Je ne te vendrai pas mon ivresse ou mon mal,
> Je ne livrerai pas ma vie à tes huées,
> Je ne danserai pas sur ton tréteau banal
> Avec tes histrions et tes prostituées.

Yet one may say that there is a note of passion in this very vehemence. But it is true that there are only a few allusions to the poet's own sentiments and then mainly in connection with childhood scenes. This objectivity does not make him impassive about everything. He feels social wrongs as well as the general pains and afflictions of men (*Qaïn*); and especially he feels and answers the call of imperious beauty, whether in humanity or nature:

> Et les mondes encor roulent sous ses pieds blancs.
> (*Hypatie*)

His attitude towards science, in the large sense, is also characteristic and anti-romantic. He dislikes the Romanticists on account of their ignorance. He held that profound knowledge of the past is necessary in order to write about it, and he says that " art and science, too long separated, should now become closely united." But Leconte de Lisle cannot stand modern inventions — the telegraph, the railroads and industrialism. These blight the vision,

> Et nous avons perdu le chemin de Paros.

He seeks only the *spirit* of the cosmos, as studied and revealed in the larger, more imaginative sciences: ethnography, ancient and oriental history, archeology and geography; and the natural sciences too, which he follows in his depiction of animals. In the use of his sources, especially of Greek, Indian and Scandinavian monuments, he shows, together with some poetic license, an admirable understanding and treatment of historical truth. He arranges this to emphasize types, racial traits, general or controlling ideas. But in his revamping of old legends he does

not often indulge in the fanciful reconstruction of the Roman_
ticists. Leconte de Lisle also follows the great natural laws
of science, which agree with his demand for exactness, order
and objectivity. Yet his scientific thought is illuminated by the
proper imagery, the harmony of the verse and the poet's sense
of beauty.

Connected with this tendency would be his attitude towards
Nature, which is also scientific, following Humboldt and Darwin.
He does not view man at all as the center of the universe, and
Nature is not really in sympathy with humanity. Thus the poet
discards anthropomorphism and the pathetic fallacy. But he
admires great natural manifestations, such as storms, jungles
and large animals. His animals, indeed, are represented on
their own basis, often independently of man, a significant
departure from the tradition of the fable. These wolves and
elephants and condors are carved in bold relief, like the
sculpture of Barye. In lonely grandeur they roam the desert
or the jungle. Whether he is dealing with animals or with
natural scenery, this poet has great descriptive power. His de_
piction is full, vivid and accurate. Leconte de Lisle views
nature as unified in essence and origin, under a diversity of
forms. But sometimes the flux of forms impresses him most
and gives rise to his pessimism:

> La Vie antique est faite inépuisablement
> Du tourbillon sans fin des apparences vaines.
>   (*La Maya*)

This metaphysical pessimism is largely Indian in its expression. In presenting religion as the culminating experience of
each race and in giving us symbols of many religions, the poet
realizes that there has been no single stable belief and he asks
to be whirled away towards new gods. After making his appeal
to Maya, the " mirage immortel " of Illusion, he feels so strongly
the constant flux of all beliefs that finally he seeks a negative
Nirvana. With this Oriental pessimism is mixed something of
the Schopenhauer brand, concerning the misery of being born;
and Leconte de Lisle is also utterly out of sympathy with
democracy and modern life. His thought, then, is often sad
and austere.

Equally austere, but of an austere perfection, is his style, and so his final characteristic is formal beauty. For this he goes **His Form** back to the Greeks, but his ideal goddess is a severe Athene rather than a smiling Aphrodite. He is the last link in the Gallo-Greek chain: Ronsard, Racine, Chénier, Leconte de Lisle. His religion of art has produced some of the loftiest of modern poems, of which *Midi* may be especially cited; sculptured verses in the manner of Gautier, though with more gravity and consistency; marble as opposed to intaglio work. Leconte de Lisle's structure is clear and logical. He chooses his words and balances his rhythms to make the picture and the idea salient. The words are notable for their precision, yet they often have also an appropriate metallic sonority and even at times a romantic suggestiveness. This style combines majesty and sadness; it is a march of the dying gods. The poet is not inventive as regards meter, approving the restraint of the crystallized forms. His verse has a durable solidity and splendor, together with a certain coldness. All in all, with his devotion to ideals of beauty, by the new values that he gave to descriptive poetry, and through his piercing natural philosophy, this poet ranks as the leader of his generation. [2]

Leconte de Lisle's most distinguished pupil was José-Maria de Heredia (1842–1905). He too was half a foreigner, born in **Heredia** Cuba of an aristocratic family. His people were descended, on one side, from the original Spanish conquerors, whom Heredia has often celebrated in his verse. He pursued advanced historical studies in Havana and at the Ecole de Chartes, but soon left pure scholarship and became a member of the Parnassian group. He had the manner and breeding of a conqueror, and a brother-poet said that " his neckties were as splendid as his sonnets."

Heredia's single volume, *Les Trophées* (1893), contains about one hundred pieces, many of which had already appeared elsewhere. The great majority of these poems are sonnets. The title was chosen to indicate the " trophies " or the " spoils " of

[2] As a contemporary phenomenon, we may note the Provençal poetry of Frédéric Mistral (1831–1914) and that of his brother-Félibriges — a society for the encouragement of the Provençal muse. The masterpiece of this school is Mistral's *Mireille* (1859), a glowing tale of the South, with an epic flow and a Doric background.

humanity throughout the ages. Here we have again the conception of Hugo or of Leconte de Lisle; Heredia shows the
"Les   learning of the latter rather than the' riotous imagi-
Trophées"   nation of the former. The presentation, of course,
is much condensed; the sonnet form calls for the essential
characteristics of each type considered. The races and epochs
included in Heredia's survey are Greece, Rome, the Middle Ages
and the Renaissance, his favorite period of " Les Conquérants,"
and Old Japan; there is also a final, more personal section on
Nature and Dreams. The poet's sympathies are selected rather
than widespread. He gives us " historical impressions," with a
good deal of externality. He is metallic, sumptuous and strenuous,
and is to be viewed almost entirely from the standpoint of form.

The *Trophées* were dedicated to Leconte de Lisle, whom Heredia follows precisely for the cult of form and impersonality.
He aims at a high, lasting perfection, and he attains effects of
mingled exactness and splendor, pressing the full value from each
word or image. His muse is subtle and complicated, with unexpected revelations. Hence he enjoys the difficulty of the
sonnet, which with him is a condensed but a developed organism,
varied in its functioning, much enlarged in its scope. Each of
his sonnets, it has been said, is " as large as an epic." Heredia
generally employs the regular French form, both in octave and
Artistic   sestet, but he introduces a striking feature in his
Effects   last line, which frequently opens up fresh horizons.
Observe the final touch in *Les Conquérants* or in *Antoine et
Cléopâtre*. New stars dawn in the visions of poet or conqueror,
Antony sees the flight of galleys in Cleopatra's eyes, the Greek
runner seems to fly from his pedestal into the arena, and Pegasus

> Bat le ciel ébloui de ses ailes de flamme.

Heredia has many resources, both of eloquence and of erudition.
He sees things across their historical, mythological or heraldic
trappings, and he is especially strong and suggestive in his diction. The conqueror's dream is called a " rêve héroïque et
brutal " — heroic, because of the knightly adventure involved;
brutal, because gold was the object of his search. Moreover, the
poet perfectly fuses idea and form: he forwards the unity of the
total effect not only through epithet, but through image and

sentiment, through sound and syllables. Like Gautier's, his imagination was essentially plastic, he often uses the terms of the painter, the sculptor or the goldsmith. He celebrates these arts, and his own work could be reproduced by them. Thus among his chief formal characteristics are the sonorous and the pictorial values.

As regards sonority, one critic introduces an article on Heredia by exclaiming, " Fanfares, cymbals, trumpets and Roman horns!" Heredia, whom Gautier congratulated on the sonority of his very name, brings over something of the verbal sumptuousness of his native Spanish tongue. He is a master of rhythm, cadence, consonance. Witness the hard distinctness of *Les Conquérants*, which is full of tone-color and metallic luster, set off against the softer connotations of *Le vieil Orfèvre*. There is also the pictorial quality, especially vivid in *Le Récif de corail* or *La Dogaresse*, which revives a painting by Veronese. In both poems, we have an exceedingly brilliant coloring, arranged in a progression of values or planes. Many sonnets are pictorially descriptive of nature: for instance, those on Japan, the New World or Brittany; and Heredia might seem intoxicated with sounds and colors, were it not that he always gives us the feeling of choice and mastery.

One may ask then, Does this poet deal mainly in sounding brass and tinkling cymbals? By no means. The idea or sentiment is there, though preferably veiled or viewed through external adornment. But it is true that Heredia has not very many ideas. They are few but strong, and individualized by the language in which they are expressed. Heredia speaks largely from the standpoint of a Renaissance humanist who believes in beauty plus force, in the splendor of high moments, in a " spectacular universe," and in man as a fine active animal. This standpoint may be illustrated by the superb cycle on *Antoine et Cléopâtre*. " Impassive " and serene, Heredia is not troubled by the Romantic malady nor tortured by metaphysics. Yet he can express discreetly, as in his Roman Epitaphs, the epicurean melancholy of passing splendors, the " lachrymae rerum " and the sense of ruin. This tenderer note might have been more frequently sounded, for Heredia omits many of our more familiar feelings and yearnings.

CHAPTER IV

REALISTIC FICTION:
FLAUBERT AND MAUPASSANT

In 1848 there had occurred an event whose consequences deeply influenced fiction and the drama. The " Revolution of

History February " resulted in the establishment of the short-lived Second Republic and finally in the Second Empire (1852–70), with Napoleon III, nephew of the great Napoleon, as Emperor. Those who looked forward to a restoration of the imperial glories of France could for a time believe their hopes fulfilled. The new government, though highly centralized, showed constructive tendencies in education, industry and the arts. Paris was splendidly rebuilt as a modern capital, railroads and public works were developed throughout the country, and towards the end of his reign Napoleon showed a willingness to meet certain liberal and democratic desires. Prestige abroad and the glory of French arms were enhanced by the victories in the Crimea (1854–56) and the rescue of Italy from Austria (1859). Yet the swift "débâcle " of the Franco-Prussian war indicated something very wrong in the State. Within a few months, France had lost her European prestige, her armies and Alsace-Lorraine. The disaster of Sedan (Sept. 2, 1870) in which Napoleon surrendered with eighty thousand men, was followed by the fall of Strassburg and Metz. During the siege of Paris, which lasted four months, a Provisional Government was in control. In February, 1871, after Paris had capitulated, the National Assembly appointed Thiers, the historian, as President of the French Republic. Thiers concluded peace with Germany.

Several causes for decay, during the Second Empire, were prominent in the minds of contemporary writers. The chief cause was the presence of too much luxury, tending to materialism in living and to personal and political corruption (treated

612

by Augier, the Goncourts and especially by Zola). Another cause was that the idealism which Lamartine and G. Sand had brought to the movement of 1848 was replaced by the cynicism and doubt which naturally accompany a political reversion (cf. Flaubert's *L'Education sentimentale*). Connected with this was a deterioration in moral tone and in artistic taste, found both in bureaucratic officials and in the " little bourgeoisie," ever bent on declaring itself. The reaction of 1848 found the reading public in a transition phase, weary of Romanticism, assenting to the abolishment of the *roman-feuilleton,* and prepared by Balzac as well as by social conditions for the definite advent of Realism. The tendency towards objective description which declared itself (see preceding chapters) in drama, poetry and painting (for example in Courbet) would naturally find its greatest scope in fiction.

By 1855, we find the term *le réalisme* taking-hold, and critics generally begin to employ it in a depreciatory sense. The word connoted for them the immoral, the brutal or the trivial, and few there are who perceive the significance of the literary method. Almost alone Sainte-Beuve saw its possibilities and favored, though with due reserves, its expansion. But as the movement gained force, through the efforts of Flaubert and his colleagues, conservative critics slowly yield the stronghold of " taste " and admit elements of power and truth in Realism. For a time, however, its productions were not glorious and were easily demolished. A certain Champfleury, an ardent admirer of Balzac, wrote some insipid stories, *Chien-Caillou* and *Les Bourgeois de Molinchart* (1855), which contain petty observations and small-town talk. More talent appears in the work of Ernest Feydeau, who caused good critics to esteem him the rival of Flaubert. Feydeau's brilliant and sensuous *Fanny* (1857) presents the psychological case of a lover who is jealous of a husband; the novel evinces strength in the delineation of passion and of material background. But Feydeau's other work is inferior, his name has not endured, and it is time to come to the true banner-leader of the movement.

Gustave Flaubert offers in his method the concentrated essence of Realism, and in his life (1821–80) a concentrated

devotion to literature. He called himself a " Benedictine of letters," and in his elimination and scorn of everything else, he ap-

Flaubert   pears not only as a zealot of art for art's sake, but
also as a victim of that separation of author and
public which is one of the more lasting and less fortunate legacies
of Romanticism. He was born at Rouen, where he spent his childhood and adolescence. His father was a surgeon of repute, and a
medical environment left its effect on Flaubert's work. His
mother was of Norman blood, which was apparent also in her
son's physique; Gustave had a " viking " exterior, a large frame
and a certain exuberance, especially in his attractive youth.
Among his friends were Louis Bouilhet, the poet; Alfred Le
Poittevin, the uncle of Guy de Maupassant; and Maxime Du
Camp, who was scarcely of a caliber to understand the novelist.
Flaubert was sent to Paris to study law and already showed his
indifference to everything but literature. In his twenties he
wrote various Romantic effusions (*Œuvres de jeunesse*), had two
love-affairs not fortunate in their issue, and became subject
to the intermittent attacks (neurasthenic or epileptic) which
later accentuated his melancholy and pessimism. At twenty-
five he gave up all thought of a large full life and settled near
Rouen, on the family estate of Croisset, to become a laborious
galley-slave of letters. This existence was interrupted only
by a long journey to the Orient, undertaken with Maxime Du
Camp (1849) ; and by later flights to Paris, where he associated
with the Naturalistic group (see next chapter). The gradual
loss of his family and friends, increasing ill-health and the effect
of the Franco-Prussian war, further darkened his middle years;
his declining days were somewhat brightened by the discipleship
of Maupassant and by the generous interest of George Sand,
with whom he maintained a most revealing correspondence.
Otherwise, Flaubert developed a proud, solitary and suspicious
nature, exasperated by ordinary contacts and obsessed by that
hatred of everything " bourgeois," which finally ruled him as
a mania. This was in part an acquired misanthropy, for he
started with a fund of geniality and kindness, which indeed he
always manifested towards his friends and relatives. He had
really a simple soul, thwarted and twisted by excessive theories;
his mind contained only a few ideas, but these dominated him

absolutely. Chief among them were the devotion to beauty in style and the cult of objective and often ugly truth. So the clash of Romanticist and Realist, with their partial fusion in his work, will explain much of Flaubert.

By temperament and taste he was undoubtedly a Romantic, of a violent and exuberant sort: a worshiper of exotic splendor, **Temperament** of the sumptuous past and of lovely phrases and coloring. Hence the voyage to Egypt and the East, with its profound effect upon his imagination; hence his early fondness for Chateaubriand and his sympathies with Gautier; hence his more morbid taste for " le mystérieux, le lugubre, le macabre "; and hence his dislike of mediocrity and his predilection for the ivory tower. But as a late-comer, Flaubert had the sensation of a creed outworn, and he evolved the conscience of a Realist. He incessantly preaches and exemplifies two princi-**and Method** ples: accurate observation or documentation, impersonality in style and treatment. The love of truth actuated his search for the real thing, but the love of beauty still demanded the perfect phrase. So his famous theory of *le mot juste*, the indefatigable hunt for the most exact and expressive word, was paralleled by a more naïve conviction that there was a " pre-established harmony " between beauty and truth in style, that the truest phrase would also be most pleasing to the ear. As regards his methods, Flaubert was a fairly consistent Realist, offering an " arsenal " of technical devices for his followers; but in his subjects, though preferring the Romantic, he alternates regularly between the two extremes. Thus, before undertaking *Madame Bovary*, he wrote his first extravagant and dithyrambic version of the *Tentation de Saint-Antoine* (1847). He read this manuscript to his friends, who advised him to destroy it and take a more " earthly " subject. For seven years then, he toiled patiently on the Realism of *Madame Bovary*, whose appearance, just when conditions were most favorable (1857), soon established Flaubert as the most accomplished and audacious artist of the movement. The publication of the novel also led to a lawsuit in which the author was acquitted of any attempt to scandalize. Severity and truth, indeed, mark the handling of the rather difficult subject — to wit, the dangers of Romanticism for a provincial *bourgeoise*. The stages of Emma

Bovary's decline are clearly marked: her early Romantic readings and dreams; her torpid marriage; the longings aroused by a ball and her sharp judgment of her husband; her Platonic love for Léon, the young clerk; the more criminal affair with Rodolphe, her full flowering, his abandonment, and her long illness; the second affair with Léon, her wasteful expenditures and neglect of home duties; the harrying by creditors and the determination to end it all by suicide. Emma is a living character, completely depicted in enduring colors; and the other personages also live, within their narrow range; the "soft" stupid husband and the talkative apothecary, Homais, represent two ironic aspects of the bourgeois. There is scarcely a sympathetic character in the book; these people are prevailingly foolish or feeble. Although Emma Bovary must incorporate many of his own dreams, the author does not abandon his attitude of severely impersonal detachment. He never shows feeling and scarcely allows himself to have an opinion. This impassive projection of the story and nothing but the story gives to *Madame Bovary* a great Realistic strength — an objectivity and a concentration that Balzac did not usually evince. Other Realistic features are the careful study of the country-town environment; the *justesse* of observation, delineation and diction; the prominence of money difficulties, of physiology and disease; the use of characteristic detail, like the nondescript cap of Charles Bovary; the presentation of the mediocre in character and circumstance. But all of this is lifted and made artistic by Flaubert's perfect sense of style, which will be considered later. *Madame Bovary* is not only a technical marvel, it is also thronged with provincial life and truth. It has been called the French *Middlemarch*, and it remains the greatest novel of the century.

Even during the composition of this masterpiece, Flaubert was haunted by his deeper desire for remote and Romantic magnificence. He turned Eastwards, to realize his "Salammbô" dream, and after six years of assiduous labor and documentation, including a visit to the site of Carthage, he published his gorgeous *Salammbô* (1862). Throughout the packed chapters of this semi-epic, description and archeology run riot, in a festival of color. The historical setting, which lacks interest, is that of the war of the mercenaries against Carthage in the third century before Christ. The story is nominally that of the princess and priestess, Salammbô, the men who loved her, and her mystical consecration to the goddess Tanit. But the thread of action is submerged in archeological details and confusing ·enumerations; as Flaubert admitted, "the pedestal is too large for the statue", and the characters seem effaced and dull. What remains is the evocation of a ruthless period, elaborately revived and described with an amount of painstaking care that shows Flaubert's Realistic conscience still dominant. The author remains hard and cold, but the reader ends by believing that this Carthage thus lived in its cruelty, horror and pomp, with all the complications of its material life — costumes and ceremonies, sieges and superstitions — made plausible and distinct. The glowing reality of the impression is enhanced by the bare tension of a style whose crisp energy wholly accords with the subject. *Salammbô* is a choice tapestry where a thousand details crush and crowd together; it is a mosaic floor paved with pebbles and precious stones; it is at once a *tour de force* and a unique and barbarous monument. But it is a monument of erudition rather than of humanity.

Yet once more Flaubert turned to a modern Realistic subject. Seven years were needed for the composition of *L'Education sentimentale* (1869). This novel is laid around the Revolution of 1848 — again requiring inordinate documentation — and it deals with the loves of a certain Frédéric Moreau. He is supposed to be the masculine counterpart of Emma Bovary. Flaubert acknowledges that the hero is a poor creature and that the structure of the novel is lax and amorphous; but these features are deliberate and anticipate the Naturalistic doctrines of no hero and no plot. Whatever their warrant in the stupider side of life, such characteristics do not make for interest or art. But the ironic and careful presentation of the epoch considered lends weight to *L'Education sentimentale*. The author's pendulum swings back to Romanticism in the final *Tentation de Saint-Antoine* (1874), in which the vision of the saint's more metaphysical temptations gives rise to some superb writing. The alterating currents are found side by side in the volume of *Trois contes* (1877), of which the best

Other Works

and most Realistic story — *Un Cœur simple* — shows more human sympathy than Flaubert usually allowed himself. His hatred of the bourgeois reaches to the point of monomania in the unfinished *Bouvard et Pécuchet*. This work treats the efforts of two retired merchants to find interest in a series of avocations for which they are not suited. Their ventures are described in an extremely technical manner, and again there is no plot.

Except in *Madame Bovary*, Flaubert's composition is not uniformly successful. Elsewhere long passages could be deleted without hurting the composition and to the benefit of the interest. But at his best he illustrates two structural principles which became a part of the heritage of fiction. He condenses and concentrates his data towards a unity of tone and a totality of effect. And he scatters and interweaves the various elements in his narrative (analysis, description, dialogue, history) so as to make them march all together, driving four-in-hand where Balzac had driven tandem. Flaubert called these long complex passages his "tableaux"; striking examples are the scene of the agricultural fair in *Bovary* and the first chapter of *Salammbô*. The presentation from one standpoint, that of the heroine, again helps sustain the unity of the former novel. In both works, Flaubert's style is masterly. Accurate observation leads to appropriate expression. The concrete phrasing tends to a certain "materialization" of sentiment or idea (red cheeks as a sign of love); the figures are suitable to the setting (" ses rêves tombant dans la boue comme des hirondelles blessées "). But beyond such Realistic devices, this style has usually a full richness and beauty that sweep us at once into the presence of a classic. Superb passages, like the sunrise in *Salammbô* or the end of the *Tentation de Saint-Antoine*, reveal Flaubert as the legitimate successor of Chateaubriand in rhetorical perfection. It may be that he lacked the large creative flow, succeeding rather by dint of will and patience. But we cannot forget that Flaubert furnished the best model of Realism to his generation and became the "novelists' novelist." We cannot forget the preeminence of *Madame Bovary* nor the heavy purple splendor of *Salammbô*.

Composition (margin note)

and Style (margin note)

Like Flaubert, Guy de Maupassant (1850–93) was a Norman Realist. He spent his childhood at Etretat, his youth at Rouen, where he preferred fishing and boating to study.

Maupassant He served in the war of 1870, then took a small post at Paris, in the ministry of marine. In 1873, he came under Flaubert's influence and showed himself a docile pupil in this relationship, which lasted seven years. During that period Maupassant was gay, strong, fond of practical jokes (*farces*); he lived an easy-going life; in vacations he returned to his beloved boating. Two things indicate his later development: he prefers savage nature to the crowded waterside resorts; and he publishes a volume of poems (*Des vers*) in which several pieces are strongly Naturalistic. The same tendency appears in *Boule de suif*, which began his career as a story-teller. This tale was published in the collection known as *Les soirées de Médan* (1880), to which Zola, Huysmans and others contributed (see next chapter). After the success of *Boule de suif*, Maupassant decided to devote himself wholly to authorship. A series of stories, novels and journalistic contributions gave him fame and financial ease. Practically all of his work was done during the next decade, which period witnessed a change in the temperament of the writer. Ambition and hard work made him preoccupied, dissipation made him morose; formerly a robust sportsman, he became a " taureau triste "; morbid analysis drove him into pessimism; he dipped into high life with doubtful results; he traveled in Corsica, Algeria and Italy; increasing ill-health sent him to the Riviera, and there, in 1892, he was stricken with madness. He died, probably by his own hand, eighteen months later.

Maupassant's theory of literature owed much to Flaubert, especially as regards the necessity of accurate individualizing observation and the search for the *mot juste*. Flaubert taught him a long patience and how to choose the characteristic aspect of every object — to consider a tree or stone until it became unlike every other tree or stone. With this impersonal observation a certain individualism was bound up, for Flaubert told his pupil that he must possess originality, native or acquired. So we find Maupassant declaring for the " whole truth," but the truth as seen across an individual temperament, which introduces some logic and illusion into the chaos of appearances. Although his artistic attitude seems cold and impartial, Maupassant's fiction is permeated with a definite personal philosophy and derives from the successive phases of his own life. " C'est toujours à des anecdotes ou à des épisodes personnels qu'il demande la matière de ses récits " (Maynial). But while aided by recollection or gossip, Maupassant recorded the deeds of actual people, and while he angered certain Normans through the faithfulness of his observation, his manner is highly impersonal and detached. Let us consider the six divisions of his short-story subjects. These number nearly three hundred titles, and their external range is exactly as wide as the author's experience.

The first division and the largest, including one-fourth of the tales, deals with Normandy, the province which the author **His Stories** knew best as a youth and to which he often returned on vacations. He knew the peasant life, with its meanness, shrewdness and occasional pathos (*Le Petit Fût, Hautot père et fils*); the open air life of hunting and boating (*Les Bécasses, Mouche*); cynical aspects of small-town narrowness (*La Ficelle*). Again, Maupassant's experience of 1870 was from the angle of the countryman who sees his province invaded by the Prussians. A smaller but excellent division of stories contains half-a-dozen masterpieces on that subject (*Boule de suif, Les Prisonniers, L'Aventure de Walter Schnaffs*), together with a few tales of military life in general. Next came the result of Maupassant's contacts with official ministries and with the existence of petty bureaucrats and bourgeois (*En Famille, L'Héritage*). Then Parisian high life (*L'Inutile Beauté*) and fast life, particularly the ruses of women (*Les Epingles, Le Rendezvous, Décoré!*). Travel, especially on the Riviera, furnished some excellent backgrounds (*Champ d'Oliviers, Jules Romain*); Africa and Italy supplied various light loves (*Allouma, Les Sœurs Rondoli*). Finally, there are about forty stories connected with the author's malady; they range from the fantastic and morbid to the insane; the fear of death, Maupassant's chief obsession, becomes complicated with ideas of crime and other hallucinations (*La Peur, Le Horla, Un Fou, Qui sait?, Suicides, La Morte*). A similar progression may be traced in Maupassant's novels, of which the most conspicuous are *Une Vie* (1883), presenting the sad existence of a crushed wife in Normandy; *Bel-Ami* (1885), the Parisian climber in a world of journalism and corruption; *Pierre et Jean* (1888) and *Fort comme la mort*, which are less cynical than previous novels but no less pessimistic in their treatment of the woes of the heart. In Maupassant's work as a whole, the point of view is generally somber or sardonic. He was not a lover of mankind and wore the dark glasses of the professed Naturalist.

It is primarily as a short-story writer that Maupassant excels, and since he is often considered the best modern representative **His Talent** of this genre, his technique should be carefully examined. In actual length, his stories vary a great deal. The *nouvelle* which usually heads the volume (*Monsieur Parent, Yvette*), may run from fifty pages to twice that length. But the more characteristic form is the *conte* which is extremely brief and laconic. Maupassant's point of departure is usually an episode, a " slice of life " chosen to illustrate character or manners. Many of these " facts " were related to him by his mother or his friends. Sometimes he merely tells an anecdote (*Le Verrou*) or outlines a situation (*L'Infirme*); or he draws a sketch (*Un Portrait*) or writes a letter (*La Moustache, Mots d'amour*). The *conte* proper readily becomes improper (*Les Epingles, La Patronne*). At its best, the structure of his works is marked by two things: an economy which gives only the essential elements of character, situation and development; and an onward movement which combines logic with the maximum of simplicity. Hence a dramatic swiftness which is Maupassant's especial gift. Naturalness and simplicity also mark his use of language, which is straightforward and not unusual in vocabulary. Even the titles of his stories are unpretentious and easily forgotten. He disliked the impressionistic over-refined style favored by the Goncourts. His sentences are clear and rapid. His language is sober, often sardonic, with an effect of dry precision. This results from his use of the *mot juste* (noun, verb or adjective), which because it is the characteristic or salient word lends to the style an accent of bold relief in detail or description. To characterize, he chooses the essential trait of costume or setting; and the *trait final* has also its perfect precision and fitness. He is an exponent of the direct *dénoue-*

ment, in which the last paragraph furnishes a dramatic close to the narrative. However, the " surprise ending " is less common in Maupassant than is often believed; it can certainly be found (*La Parure, Le Pain maudit, L'Ami Joseph*), but more frequent is the rounded ending which fulfils our expectations. Some of his stories (for example, *Le Père Milon*), announce the *dénouement* at the beginning. For the sake of vividness, he leans to the first-person form of narration and often uses as a prelude of men's dinner or some casual meeting. The kernel of the story may be some small object, around which the train of events is organized; witness *Le Parapluie, La Ficelle* or *La Parure,* which last has been voted the best short story in existence. Dealing with rudimentary types, Maupassant's psychology is limited, though not insufficient. He appreciates outdoor nature and shows considerable power in describing it. As a Realist, of course, he thoroughly places his tales in terms of material setting, exterior or interior, costumes, habits, and so on. Otherwise, in the type of stories and in the supple dexterity with which he tells them, he resembles La Fontaine and is considered, in fact, the legitimate continuator of the old *conte gaulois.* His Classical qualities are sobriety, balance, sureness of eye and simplicity.

Apparent naturalness, then, is the hall-mark of Maupassant's technique, just as " Naturalism " (see next chapter) stamps his outlook and philosophy. The latter undergoes a progression from a robust sensualism, in which the forces of Nature are accepted, to the pessimistic effect of this materialism on a man who develops mind and heart and who perceives that the joys of this earth are fleeting. Although he over-stresses the depiction of the distasteful and the ignoble, we recognize, towards the end, the presence of a soul in revolt. This may account for the philosophic digressions, which seem to increase in his later work, somewhat to the detriment of narrative unity. Misanthropy, the mental fatigue of his generation, the lack of spiritual comfort or belief, warred against love and the life-force which were " apaisés soudain par l'Eternel Oubli " (*Fort comme la mort*). Death was finally the stronger, and before death came philosophic nihilism and madness.

CHAPTER V

FICTION (CONTINUED):
ZOLA, THE GONCOURTS, DAUDET

It seems best to make between "Realism" and "Naturalism," in their literary significance, a distinction both of time and of degree. The best work of Balzac and of Flaubert stands for the earlier development of Realism; while Zola and his school pushed that doctrine to an extreme and dubbed it *le Naturalisme*. Maupassant belongs rather to this later phase of the movement. Naturalism then is an excessive form of Realism and is usually considered as possessing the following characteristics. First, it allows a still larger variety of subjects, emphasizing the lower and coarser forms of life; it presents this material in a fashion which is often revolting; it rejects ideality, it minimizes heart-interest and plot-interest in favor of "facts" and notations; it magnifies the study of the industries and seeks to apply to fiction the processes of the natural sciences; from these, taken in their application to heredity and environment, it draws its conception of life — deterministic, fatalistic, essentially pessimistic. The laws of brute Nature are viewed as grimly controlling the destinies of helpless and hopeless man. Pessimism is, in fact, widely characteristic of this generation of writers (cf. Flaubert, Leconte de Lisle, Taine), who seem, for the most part, to have exhausted the springs of enthusiasm and sentiment. This "maladie morale," according to Bourget (see Bk. IX, Ch. IV), results especially from the general depression produced by the Franco-Prussian war. The former French gaiety seems to be much obscured, and certainly it is least conspicuous in the powerful but gloomy work of the Naturalists.

The head and front of the Naturalistic school, though he preferred to call it a method rather than a school, was Emile Zola (1840–1902). His father was an Italian engineer who had

623

settled in France; his mother was French. The boy grew up at Aix-en-Provence, then moved with his mother to Paris, where his brief education was of a scientific rather than of a literary character. He knew poverty and the working-classes, from which he presently chose a wife (1870). He did not figure in the war nor in any external events until much later. He led an uneventful, virtuous and sedentary life. For a time he was clerk in the publishing house of Hachette, then went in for journalism and (c. 1880) wrote his critical articles which contain the theory of Naturalism. He acquired a suburban property at Médan, where originated the *Soirées de Médan*, of 1880. This collection contained rather grim stories of the Franco-Prussian war and is regarded as a manifesto of one Naturalistic group (Zola, Maupassant, Huysmans, Paul Alexis, Céard, Hennique). The year 1880 is thus the central year of Naturalism, as 1857 is that of Realism. Zola had already become known through the early volumes of the Rougon-Macquart series. The severe labor and documentation demanded by this series occupied him for twenty-two years (1871–93). He emerged from his semi-obscurity to champion Dreyfus (see Bk. IX, Ch. I) in 1898. His indictment of the military powers (*J'Accuse*) caused Zola to be sentenced to imprisonment, and he sought refuge in England. There and later in Paris he embarked on the series of the *Trois Villes,* followed by the *Quatre Evangiles,* which he did not live to complete. His accidental death (1902) was caused by asphyxiation. He was distinguished for his tenacity, his polemic spirit, his interest in the proletariat and his lack of taste.

Zola

Zola lived largely as a recluse, and he was not an artist; his fiction suffers from these handicaps. He was formidable mainly by his method, which he developed as early as *Thérèse Raquin* (1867). Its principles are laid down in his critical work, especially *Le Roman expérimental* (1880) and *Les Romanciers naturalistes* (1881). He defines art as "un coin de la nature vu à travers un tempérament." The personality of the writer admits variety and clothes the work in individual form — for instance, the Goncourts are allowed their more refined and aristocratic reactions. But the substance is immutable Nature (reality) which provides " human

His Theory

R   .   "L   Foins"

documents." These were studied physiologically and socially by Balzac, and psychologically by Stendhal,[1] who are claimed as the two pedestals of Naturalism. In either case, observation rather than imagination is the novelist's requisite. To this the Naturalist should now add the experimental method of science (derived from Claude Bernard's *Introduction à la Médecine expérimentale,* 1865): that is, he should expose his sensibility to life and he should work, as in a laboratory, upon the events and characters provided by experience. Zola did not perceive that the writer cannot really produce and manipulate his material, as the scientist can; the term " experimental " is then a misnomer, while another distortion of true science is the extent to which Zola relied on the doctrine of heredity throughout the *Rougon-Macquart.*

This huge cycle, consisting of twenty volumes, records the " histoire naturelle et sociale d'une famille sous le second em-**" Les Rougon** pire." The family, originating from a neurasthenic **Macquart "** and a drunkard (*La Fortune des Rougon*), prolongs that double taint through its many members and diverse *milieux.* The *Comédie humaine* evidently inspired this social history, which deals with reappearing names in various " conditions " or ranks in life. But Zola emphasizes the trade or profession less than the hereditary taint, and he adds a strong element of pathological and clinical research. He even composed a genealogical tree, with medico-legal data on each descendant. Also his chief figures are not so much characters as grandiose and symbolic types. Thus " Nana " is the Courtesan, Saccard is the Speculator, Dr. Pascal is the Savant, etc. Among the *milieux* represented are Aix-en-Provence (*La Conquête de Plassans*), the fashionable society of the Empire (*La Curée*), the central markets (*Le Ventre de Paris*), the department-store (*Au Bonheur des Dames*) and the railroads (*La Bête humaine*). *L'Assommoir* (1877), which made Zola's reputation, exhibits the drunkard and the saloon; *La Terre* (1887), his most scandalous production, is a degraded treatment of the peasantry. His best and most powerful novels are *Germinal* (1885), that great study of the mines, and *La Débâcle* (1892), a most vivid and truthful fresco of the Franco-Prussian war.

---

[1] It is questionable whether any of the Naturalists proceeded from Stendhal. Certainly Zola was independent of him.

In all of these works, as in the later series of the Cities and the Evangels, the system is much the same. Zola admits that in_ vention was his weak side. He started not from incidents or personages, but from the desire to depict a certain cross-section of life. This he would study as a specialty, partly through first-hand observation but mainly through monographs. The subjects of which he had personal knowledge, for example, the life of the working classes, are naturally much better handled than such monstrous exaggerations as *La Terre* or such a guide_ book as *Rome*. Having determined his field, he would select his main characters — usually some of the Rougon-Macquart — and compose actual *dossiers* for them, as well as for the subsidiary personages. He would fix them in their main traits and choose for them a certain type of dialogue, preferably coarse; and it is a feature of his style that the same kind of language is usual in the indirect dialogue and even in the psychological analyses of his characters (cf. *L'Assommoir*). The psychology, however, is of the most elementary kind. It has been said that Zola gave a soul to things and withdrew the soul from man. Criminals and morons abound in his pages. "La bête humaine" is his favorite phrase, and the physiological presentation of the Realists is pushed to a frequent and deliberate bestiality. This is occasionally relieved, to be sure, by the idyllic note (*Le Rêve, Le Docteur Pascal*). But Zola's strength is found either in the depiction of grandiose types (see above) or in the equally " epic " vivification of certain huge symbols: the Locomotive, the Mine, the Market, the wounded Forest in *La Débâcle*. These Franken-steins live, agonize and die before our eyes. However Romantic they may be, such creations are wonderfully effective and well-sustained. Zola is strong also in the cumulative treatment " des vastes ensembles matériels et des infinis détails extérieurs " (cf. Balzac). Among these " vastes ensembles " should be empha-sized his unsurpassed handling of crowds, whether the morning procession of laborers, a riotous mob of miners, or the array and confusion of the battle-field. Certain descriptive " tableaux " are equally impressive: the parade of carriages and the conserva-tory in *La Curée*; the intricacies of the vegetable market; even homely domestic interiors (a laundry, a living-room); or the swarming credulity of *Lourdes,* which is the best of the *Trois Villes*.

Zola also deserves credit for the humanitarian faith of his latest trilogy — the attack on race-suicide in *Fécondité* and the apotheosis of labor in *Le Travail*. But these works add nothing of note to his method, which remains the crude presentation of the " masses " as an undigested whole. Zola's style harmonizes with his point of view, in its lack of distinction and its heavy lumbering tread which can become, on occasions, a powerful stride. For good or for evil, the man and his method live in his works; but French life could scarcely have existed in all the darkness with which he has surrounded it. His outlook and his rigid *a priori* system keep him from rendering Nature in the fullest sense.

Edmond de Goncourt (1822–96) and his brother Jules (1830–70) offer an interesting case of literary collaboration. " United by art and blood," they thought and felt in common;
The Goncourts and they lived, suffered and died for literature alone. Of a good family and well educated, they were intensely Parisian and modern. After the death of their mother (1848), the brothers were practically inseparable. Like Gautier, they expected to become painters and therefore undertook picturesque excursions in France and Algeria. But they turned to writing instead and after several false starts, they published *Charles Demailly* (1860) ; this novel and *Manette Salomon* (1867) furnished keen studies of artistic careers thwarted by women. Most of the Goncourts' work was based on personal experiences or those of their acquaintances. They also showed a preference for a refined treatment and for subjects that offered exceptional or pathological interest. Such was the case with *Sœur Philomène* (1861), a " study in ivory " of hospital scenes and of a nun's mysticism; while *Renée Mauperin* (1864), the Goncourts' best book, is a subtle and pathetic delineation of a peculiar " jeune fille moderne." None of these novels were immediately successful; indeed, the work of the brothers was scarcely known to the public under the Empire and has never been popular. They were compensated for this general neglect by the formation of an inner circle — that of the " diners Magny," a restaurant where the Goncourts foregathered with Sainte-Beuve, Gautier, Renan, Daudet and occasionally with Flaubert or Taine. This was not a *cénacle*, because of the separatist and carping tendencies of the group,

as manifest in the later *Journal des Goncourt* (9 vols., 1887–95).

In the meantime, the brothers had founded Naturalism, of the low-life kind, in *Germinie Lacerteux*. This book was published **As** in 1865, before any important work of Zola's, and **Naturalists** deals with the pitiful life and loves of a servant-girl. The clinical sort of Naturalism is demonstrated in *Madame Gervaisais* (1869), which is mainly an analysis of religious hysteria. *Madame Gervaisais* and *Manette Salomon* also exhibit the extreme type of the plotless novel, with its deliberate lack of construction and a preference for detached scenes. Jules de Goncourt died of intellectual over-work in 1870, and for some time his afflicted brother wrote nothing. In 1877, Edmond published *La Fille Elisa*, a' bare and severe monograph on prostitution and the penitentiary. Of his other novels, *La Faustin* depicts the life of the theater and *Les Frères Zemganno* that of the circus. This last is probably Edmond's best novel, since it presents, with genuine sentiment, a pair of brothers who were united like the Goncourts themselves. Feeling is not absent from these novels, several of which (for example, *Renée Mauperin*) have very poignant endings.

The Goncourt brothers were a complicated pair, and accordingly their work is composed of strangely mixed materials. On the one hand, it seems clear that they were the earliest theoreticians (cf. *Idées et Sensations*, 1866) and practitioners of an advanced Naturalism. This is evidenced in their blank fatalistic pessimism, in their materialistic rendering of the external world, in their low-life subjects and their predilection for pathology, and especially in their emphasis on note-taking coupled with direct observation. *Germinie Lacerteux* was the biography of their own servant; hospitals were studied at first-hand, Edmond de Goncourt recorded the phases of his brother's last illness and urged feminine readers to send him their intimate observations, in order to perfect the psychology of *Chérie*. On the other hand, these brothers were essentially artists, and they modified their Realistic attitude by two individual novelties: impressionism and the "écriture artiste." Thus they do not represent Naturalism with Zola's force and single-mindedness.

"Impressionism," of the Goncourt variety, is the endeavor to render the sensations produced by external objects; it largely

proceeds from and appeals to the nerves. Like their compeers
As Artists (Balzac, Flaubert, Daudet), the Goncourts were
"slaves of the lamp." After each protracted
effort, their delicate organizations suffered a collapse and they
fostered their hyperaesthetic acuteness of sensation. "Il n'y a
de bon que les choses exquises," said Edmond. Not only, then,
were they preoccupied with nervous maladies (*Charles Demailly,
Sœur Philomène*), but they sought to convey, impression-
istically, all the vibrant sensations to which they were exposed.
Their vehicle was the "écriture artiste," a new kind of
preciosity, an intensely nervous, jerky style, "qui s'applique
surtout . . . à la sensation réalisée par la phrase, l'épithète rare,
l'adjectif substantif et le verbe substantif, la répétition, le pléo-
nasme et le néologisme." Their rhetoric, which too often dis-
regards syntax, clearness and harmony, tends to become an
"orgy of virtuosity" and aims particularly at picturesque and
colorful descriptions. So their novels became a disorganized
series of *tableautins,* while their point of view is that of the
painter who is most sensitive to the visible world (cf. Gautier).
The art-sense of the brothers was increased by their very Parisian
modernity and their love of *bibelots,* of which they left a considerable collection; also by their revival of the eighteenth
century in a series of volumes [2] which display particularly the
paintings, costumes and furniture of the old régime. Together
with this revival, they should be credited with the introduction
of Japanese art into France. In spite of aesthetic excesses, their
"plastic psychology" and their pictorial style have distinct
values, and the Goncourts remain the best equipped artists of
the Naturalistic movement. Edmond founded the "Académie
Goncourt," as a rallying point for literary rebels. This Academy
has crowned some of the most notable books of recent years.

Less forceful and original than the other Naturalists, but
endowed with more charm and humanity, Alphonse Daudet
Daudet (1840–97) owes much of his reputation to the fact
that he was a thorough "Méridional." He was
born at Nimes, and even in his boyhood his ardent temperament
was touched by the Provençal sun. Neither a Catholic up-

---

[2] *La Femme au dix-huitième siècle* (1862), *L'Art au dix-huitième siècle,* etc.

bringing nor a stricter education later at Lyons could restrain
this turbulent youth, fond of reading, but fonder of playing
truant, and reaching the depth of despair when family em-
barrassments forced him to take a post as usher in a small school
(*Le Petit Chose*). Fortunately, his devoted brother Ernest
summoned him to Paris, where Alphonse was soon leading a
bohemian life and publishing his early verses. He joined the
staff of the *Figaro* and became private secretary to the Duc de
Morny, who acted as prime minister under Napoleon III. A
favorite with Morny, Daudet was allowed restorative excursions
to the Midi and Algeria (*Port Tarascon*). From near Arles, in
the winter of 1864, he brought back the *Lettres de mon Moulin*
(publ. 1869), his first real success. His frail health often sent
him back to the South, where he was on excellent terms with
Mistral and the Provençal group of poets. In 1867, Daudet
married Julie Allard, who made him an excellent wife and helped
his literary development. The writer now bade farewell to
Bohemia. His new seriousness was further confirmed by the
events of 1870–71. Daudet served in the home-guard and declared that the war made a man of him. He wrote certain
recollections of this period (*Contes du lundi*), then passed on
to his great novels and knew " l'ivresse du travail." Like
Flaubert and Balzac, he would often work fifteen hours a day,
a régime that seriously impaired his health. After 1877 he
suffered with violent rheumatism and had to give up the
physical exercises that he formerly loved. But he still kept his
country home, in the valley of Champrosay near Paris, and in
the capital itself Daudet had an interior noted for its delightful
family life and wide hospitality. Frequent visitors were
Flaubert, E. de Goncourt and Turgenev — whom the small boy
of the house called " les géants." Daudet was exemplary in
family relations; he was noted for his kindliness and constant
good humor. He was simple in his tastes, distrusting riches, devoted to books (especially Montaigne), yet sociable and well acquainted with many classes of people. He never separated life
from literature. He defined talent as an " intensité de vie,"
and his own talent surely has this quality. His powers of perception and expression were unusually keen. His career was
helped by good-fortune and by his seductive personality, but

his books were written " avec le suc même de l'arbre humain."

An interlocking but useful classification of Daudet's fiction would distinguish: (1) stories and characters of the Midi; (2) **Three** novels of Parisian manners; (3) partly included **Divisions** in the above, the depiction of the humbler classes. **of his Work** His fiction throughout is either autobiographical or closely based on known people and events. On this account, some of his friends avoided him, and it is said that he did not dare return to Tarascon. " To invent for him was to remember." Memories of his impressionable Provençal youth are embedded in the exquisite *Lettres de mon Moulin,* which contain such gems as *Le Curé de Cucugnan* and *La Mule du Pape.* Fancy is wedded to fact in these brilliant joyous stories, and this note is prolonged in the famous Tartarin series. *Tartarin de Tarascon* (1872) creates the type of the boastful and self-deluded Southerner, still the source of inextinguishable laughter. For once, a sequel was not inferior to its predecessor, and *Tartarin sur les Alpes* (1885) was for long the most popular of Daudet's novels. Finally, *Port-Tarascon* (1890) takes the hero again to Algeria, but shows a decline of the novelist's powers. Tartarin thus remains with Daudet during his whole career. The Southern strain is continued in the main characters — though not in the setting — of *Le Nabab* (1877) and of *Numa Roumestan* (1881), which exhibits, more somberly than Tartarin, the clash between a *méridional* temperament and a Parisian environment. But these two titles properly belong to Daudet's second division, the " grand roman de mœurs." In both of them, certain characters have been identified with actual personages: in the former appears a real " nabob," together with the Duc de Morny, Sarah Bernhardt and others, very thinly disguised; whereas in *Numa Roumestan* we have an ironic depiction of the Provençal deputy who stakes his fortunes against the " homicidal North," and who wins out through native force and buoyancy. This is written in Daudet's final manner and is consequently a more intense and closely knit narrative than *Le Nabab,* which remains, however, one of the largest and most interesting canvases depicting the Second Empire. No one excels Daudet in conveying the Parisian atmosphere, and his ornate " views " of the capital are memorable. Between these two novels he wrote *Les Rois* *en exil* (again with a Parisian background), a title which needs no explanation today. Again, *L'Immortel* (1888) is a satire on the Academy, too bitter for Daudet's kindly nature. The greatest of this group of novels and the best known is *Sapho* (1884), a thorough study of the courtesan, her evil power and her environment, but treated with a decent restraint not usually manifested by the Naturalists.

Several other novels also reflect "les mœurs parisiennes," but they seem more particularly to store the vibrations of the author's own heart attuned to the misfortunes of humble folk. His son tells us that he preferred this class to any other, though he was compassionate towards all suffering and mischance. There is much of both in *Fromont jeune et Risler aîné* (1874), nominally the tale of an industrial partnership, but really concerned with the drama of the wicked Sidonie and her deceived husband; the household of the poverty-stricken Delobelles also comes in for a good share of the interest and offers a parallel with Dickens in the alternation of humor and pathos. *Jack* (1876) deals with other failures and presents particularly the story of an unhappy child (cf. *David Copperfield*). *L'Evangéliste* indignantly attacks the effects of religious proselytizing and mania.

Though influenced by the currents of his time, especially by Naturalism and impressionism, Daudet is not a severe and impartial recorder of the world's woes. He is too **His Talent** sympathetic and emotional wholly to represent scientific Naturalism. He comes nearest it in *Sapho,* and even there his personality shines through the somber picture. Again, Daudet is primarily a *raconteur* who loves to tell a story, and his novels are more fully novels than the so-called fiction of Zola. Daudet knows how to choose and make salient "les dominantes" of character and incident. By interweaving moral and physical qualities he makes his chief characters from the beginning stand out clearly; yet he is rather too fond of the "gag," as when the lazy Delobelle perpetually asserts, "je n'ai pas le droit de renoncer à l'Art." Like Dickens, Daudet overworks pathos, and occasionally the Southern "charm" seems to wear a little thin. But behind all these traits there stand (1) the method of the Realist and (2) the style of the impressionist.

The method appears in his choice of specialized subjects, of ample background and sharply etched foreground; also in his habit of persistent note-taking, a habit which resulted in thousands of perfectly rendered scenes and objects; also in his knowledge of and respect for " la vie " rather than in the bookish kind of documentation; finally, in that very sympathy with the humble which, as Brunetière claims, has been found in Russia and England to be compatible with the best Realism. Nor does this novelist slight the depiction of the more interesting and attractive aspects of life. The artistic side of Daudet and probably his friendship with E. de Goncourt inclined him towards a modified type of impressionism in writing. Just as sensitive as the Goncourts to external objects, he contrives to present them adequately without making them dominate; a favorite device is to make things symbolize a soul-state, as where Désirée Delobelle's thwarted aspirations are typified by the stuffed birds with which she decorates bonnets. Daudet's wingèd style gives the thrill of an individual reaction to reality, but he was able to accomplish this without the elaborate manner and vocabulary of the Goncourts. His language, for all its variety and picturesqueness, is clear and not *recherché;* its movement is more easy and conversational than that of other French Realists. Of them all, Daudet is on many accounts the most acceptable to an Anglo-Saxon public.

BOOK VIII

THE AGE OF SCIENCE AND DOUBT

CHAPTER I

THE CRITICS: SAINTE-BEUVE

ALL the movements of the nineteenth century are mirrored in criticism, a genre which greatly increases in productiveness, **The Course** influence and complexity during this period. A **of Criticism** history of French Criticism would find at least one-half of its material in the last century alone. Like other fields of thought, the genre became definitely historical in approach; later it endeavored to borrow its method from the natural sciences as well. These and other varieties will emerge from a brief sketch of the form. Accepting the formula of "literature as the expression of society," modern criticism was born at the beginning of the century. As already seen, cosmopolitan comparison waxed great with Mme de Staël and was continued by Villemain. The latter placed the individual writer in his historical setting, where Sainte-Beuve more firmly fixes him. This high priest of criticism is Protean in his viewpoints; judicial because of his taste, yet biographical, historical and finally approximating a scientific method. The deterministic philosophy is appropriated by Taine, the evolutionary by Brunetière. Personal impressionism was added by Anatole France and Jules Lemaitre. The chief defenders of the Classical standard were Nisard, Scherer and Brunetière; we shall now consider the first of these three.[1]

The most characteristic work of Désiré Nisard (1806–88), professor and publicist, is comprised in his *Essais* **Nisard** *sur l'école romantique* and in his monumental *Histoire de la littérature française* (1844–61). The former book,

---

[1] For Brunetière, France and Lemaître, see Bk. IX, Ch. IV. Edmond Scherer (1815-89) was a Genevan divine who lost his faith in Calvinism and settled in Paris. He stood apart from the main literary movements, but his *Etudes critiques sur la littérature contemporaine* (1863-95) contain some excellent criticism.

in spite of Nisard's efforts towards fairness, is virtually an indictment of Romanticism, and the latter remained for long the
best exposition and eulogy of the French Classical period.
Nisard maintains that this " époque unique " saw an amalgama-
tion of the French and of the (general) human spirit that can
hardly occur again. He tends to make humanity equivalent to
France, and France equivalent to the Age of Louis XIV. Adopting the " point of perfection " theory,[2] he views everything before
the seventeenth century as a preparation, everything after it as a
decline. Then only did the French genius reach its full powers of
clearness and precision: "l'expression des vérités générales dans
un langage parfait." Then only did the " two antiquities,"
Christian and pagan, move harmoniously together. Nisard holds
by tradition, both because of its disciplinary value and because
tradition alone is the guarantee of lasting literary excellence.
So " for sixty years," says Dowden, " Nisard was a guardian
of the dignity of French letters."

We must go back to the days of Romanticism to understand
Charles-Augustin Sainte-Beuve (1804–69), the greatest and most
Career of   universal of French critics. The successive phases
Sainte-Beuve of his life contributed to form his supple talent and
to provide his manifold interests. Born at Boulogne-sur-Mer,
he was carefully reared by women; as a youth he showed a studious disposition and some religious propensities. These were
promptly submerged in the skeptical air of Paris, whither he went
in 1818. He declared that his intellectual *fond* was derived from
such materialists and free-thinkers as Destutt de Tracy, Lamarck
and Daunou. This tendency was increased by an intermittent
study of medicine, which left in him a leaning towards physiology and positivism. In 1824 he joined the editors of the *Globe*
(see Bk. VI, Ch. I), and for this journal he wrote many of the
articles subsequently collected in the *Premiers lundis*. After
1827 he became intimate with Hugo and identified himself with
Romanticism — the only cause, he tells us, to which he fully surrendered himself and that " by the effect of a charm." The spell
was wrought partly by Victor Hugo, partly by Hugo's wife, and
thus inspired Sainte-Beuve composed his poetry and fiction. He
also gave ancestors to Romanticism in the *Tableau de la poésie*

---

[2] See above, pp. 343 and 416.

française au XVIe siècle (1828), and he ranked as one of the most influential members of the school. But after 1830 he gradually detached himself, breaking with Hugo and passing on to other " conversions." None of these was whole-souled, but for a time he showed an interest in Saint-Simonism, then in the liberal Catholicism of Lamennais and his group. An opposing tendency was encouraged by Sainte-Beuve's connection with Swiss Calvinism; this connection was formed through his friendship with the Oliviers, a young couple whom he visited at Lausanne (1837). Throughout his youth, Sainte-Beuve was subject to moods of religious speculation and feeling, manifest particularly in his letters to the Abbé Barbe; but this influence resulted in no transformation of his life and thought; its most important consequence was the masterly study of the Jansenists in his *Port-Royal* (1840–60).

In the meantime, Sainte-Beuve had become well established as a Parisian and as a critic. He frequented the aristocratic salons of Mme Récamier and others, but he scarcely shone as a man of the world. Although epicurean in his tastes for pleasure, he lived frugally and worked hard. During the two decades of the bourgeois monarchy he was writing for the *Revue de Paris* and the *Revue des deux mondes* most of the articles later collected in the *Portraits contemporains* (1869–71) and the *Portraits littéraires* (1862–64). His reputation was steadily growing, and he was made a member of the Academy in 1844. But when the Revolution of 1848 occurred, Sainte-Beuve found himself ill at ease in Paris and accepted an invitation from Liège, where he delivered lectures on Chateaubriand. The resulting volumes (*Chateaubriand et son groupe littéraire*) mark his final break with Romanticism and his inauguration of a bolder and more judicial critical standard. Returning to Paris, he was soon engaged in writing for periodicals his famous *Causeries du lundi* (1851–62), followed by the *Nouveaux lundis* (publ. 1863–70). These weekly articles practically filled the remainder of his life, for Sainte-Beuve too became an " anchorite of labor," scarcely leaving his task except for participation in the Magny dinners (see p. 627) and for duties connected with two lectureships. He became more political in his outlook, wrote a volume defending the socialist Proudhon, and was made a senator of the Empire

(1864). But he sat in the Opposition and delivered towards the end of his life the boldest speeches of a rather cautious career. Sainte-Beuve was intellectually honest and never sold his pen; but in human relations he was sly and variable, not trustworthy as a friend and not notable for high qualities of heart or soul. He was a mental giant, well-nigh complete in his critical equipment, and his most marked trait was the mobility or curiosity which drew him from one field of inquiry to another. The creative efforts of his youth were also fruitful for his critical career; they gave him unusual insight into the processes of poetry and fiction. But they were not beneficial either to his character or to his reputation.

The fact is that these volumes, whether connected with the author's late adolescence or with the amorous experiences of **Poetry and** his early manhood, are noted for their morbid tone. **Fiction** The *Vie, Poésies et Pensées de Joseph Delorme* (1829) presents a descendant of René and of Adolphe, who is also the *alter ego* and the weaker ego of Sainte-Beuve. The poems constitute a moral autobiography, in their display of self-analysis and of epicurean desires. Certain lyrics develop another strain, an attempted rendering of common life, in the manner of Wordsworth; the volume is the most interesting example of this influence in France. Again, a critical and intellectual note is prominent, especially when the author characterizes his contemporaries (for example, *Promenade, Mes livres*). So the poems have been well summarized as " individualistes et romantiques, originales par le ton démocratique, l'inspiration intime, la tendance critique." *Joseph Delorme*, which at least widened the scope of the lyric, is Sainte-Beuve's most important volume of verse and gives the key to the others. Similar strains are found in the *Consolations* (1830) and the *Pensées d'Août* (1837). His novel, *Volupté* (1834), is according to Sainte-Beuve's own avowal " très peu un roman " and again reflects the experience of a self-indulgent, analytical and weak-willed person. There is much religiosity in this novel; it ends in a conversion in which the writer himself hardly participated.

Sainte-Beuve's critical work is very extensive, amounting to forty-eight volumes. Three main periods of his activity, though with some overlapping, may be indicated. The first (1824–

.1840) is his youthful Romantic period and includes, together with the *Tableau* (see above) and the *Premiers lundis*, many of the earlier articles in the *Portraits littéraires*. The second (c. 1835–1848) represents a more neutral and conservative type of criticism, but remains appreciative rather than judicial. This period includes the various volumes of *Portraits*, written for the two principal reviews and addressed largely to feminine readers. The third period (1848–69) finds Sainte-Beuve in his maturity alike as judicial critic and as historian of literature. Its point of departure is the attack on Chateaubriand, and it embraces the two great series of the *Lundis*.

Criticism: Divisions and Campaigns

The term " Romantic critic " implies both that Sainte-Beuve was romantically disposed and that he became the best critical expositor of the movement. His close association with the Hugos and his own creative efforts made his expression more personal, passionate and rhetorical than was later the case. But the rupture of these ties presently caused him to break with the school, and he admits many variations in judgment due to the rise and fall of his Romantic sympathies. This then is his least impartial period. Yet his keen understanding of the movement will appear from certain examples. Of his four articles on Victor Hugo, the first (1827) established Sainte-Beuve as the critical master of the new school. He points out exactly those merits and defects that posterity has accepted in the case of Hugo. Later the critic congratulates the poet on freeing himself from the preciosity of the early *cénacle* and on attaining wider effects. The novels of Hugo are not impartially considered, nor is Sainte-Beuve fair to Vigny. On the other hand, he excellently sums up Lamartine, admiring his spirituality and limpidity. As late as 1857, Sainte-Beuve wrote a finely reminiscent article on Musset, which carries critic and reader back into the old Romantic atmosphere. The poet's endearing qualities and his tragic fate are dwelt upon almost with a sense of personal loss. This note of personal friendly interest recurs in articles on Hugo, George Sand and others. It is true that Sainte-Beuve was subject to feelings of envy and malice where the Romantic leaders were concerned; but when these feelings were not aroused, he

First Period

was capable of the greatest insight and sympathy. M. Michaut esteems him the panegyrist and interpreter of Romanticism, enthusiastic, but with a taste and a sense of proportion which caused him to make certain reserves. He gave currency to the lyrical ideas and theories of the group, for whom, says the same authority, he served both as a Du Bellay and a Boileau; it was his task to " introduire, légitimer et formuler le romantisme " — and he tried to moderate its excesses as well.

In 1840, Sainte-Beuve published two articles that definitely indicate his abandonment of the Romantic cause. He declares that the essay on La Rochefoucauld "marks the end of this crisis and the return of sounder views." The other article, *Dix ans après en littérature*, amounts to a journalistic summary of what Romanticism had accomplished in the previous decade. A certain bias and impatience appear in his colder reckoning with his former admiration. These " illustrious incurables " lack stability — or else they have simply marked time. Sainte-Beuve further announces that he himself has finally turned from poetry to criticism. This resolution was taken after the failure of the *Pensées d'Août*. As Sainte-Beuve profoundly said:

> Il se trouve, dans les trois quarts des hommes, un poète qui meurt jeune, tandis que l'homme survit.

The "man" and his intelligence are thus chiefly conspicuous in the second phase of Sainte-Beuve's critical productiveness. **Second Period** Here he lays a broad foundation for his biographical method. Indeed, as a Romantic critic he had sought the writer's *moi* in his biography and intimate psychology and was disposed to judge a work according to the individuality of its talent and expression. Now the three series of " Portraits " (*Portraits littéraires, Portraits de Femmes, Portraits contemporains*) exemplify the author's lasting interest in the individual, as well as the constant ripening of his ever-curious mind. Even the *Port-Royal* has been styled a collection of portraits. Sainte-Beuve's curiosity recalls that of Bayle, who was treated in an early article (1835) as a leading representative of the critical spirit. The two men were also alike in their fondness for gossip, their insinuative tactics, their tolerant sense of relativity in human and literary affairs. Sainte-Beuve's manner during this period combines ease and finish, and has an engaging " libre allure." His attitude is more disinterested. After traversing his intermediary " campaigns," in behalf of Lamennais and Saint-Simon, the critic ceases to be a propagandist and becomes a free and impartial voice (1833–37). His essays are concerned somewhat less with aesthetic and more with moral and philosophical questions. Gradually he conceives of a " génie critique," which though remaining primarily portraiture can include philosophical and psychological considerations; which through its universal curiosity and its finished form can itself become " creative," a work of art. The best essays of the forties show Sainte-Beuve established in his own field. At the end of this period he was ready for a new campaign.

A whole book might be written on the relations of Sainte-Beuve and Chateaubriand, and indeed Sainte-Beuve himself has **The** written it. *Chateaubriand et son groupe littéraire,* **Transition** composed in voluntary exile, is mainly an indictment of Romanticism and of its illustrious godfather. Sainte-Beuve now formally assumes the rôle of a judge. He points out why he need no longer listen to the oracle with bated breath. " Il est temps que pour lui la vie critique commence." Sainte-Beuve still considers Chateaubriand an incomparable artist, possessed of an " extraordinary elevation." But the critic assails the pagan passion, the *mal de René,* and a certain insincere rhetoric which strives after glory rather than after truth or virtue. Of this glory the idol is vigorously stripped; and though Sainte-Beuve shows a bourgeois animosity in the act, yet his main desire is to arrive at the truth. Such a desire is expressed in the following pronunciamento, which may be taken as a prelude to the mature excellence of the *Lundis*:

> Dégagé de tout rôle presque de tout lien, observant de près depuis bientôt vingt-cinq ans les choses et les personnages littéraires, n'ayant aucun intérêt à ne pas les voir tels qu'ils sont, je puis dire que je regorge de vérités.

Certain general features of the *Causeries du lundi* and of the *Nouveaux lundis* may at once be predicated. We may now perceive, says Mr. Brownell of Sainte-Beuve, " how thoroughly and in what classic spirit he rationalized his early Romanticism."

He is more thoughtful and less soulful. The eulogies of his early period, as well as the insinuations of his middle years, are less conspicuous. His interpretation deepens and be-

Third Period comes more widely historical. The magisterial hand is always there and usually the judicial mind. Everything that concerns the author and his environment is now taken up, but the man himself is still made the center of Sainte-Beuve's analysis. To this principle he clings throughout his career, though with increasing system and science. Both are visible in an article of 1862 (again on Chateaubriand), which is usually esteemed the most important of Sainte-Beuve's critical manifestoes. Here

Method he links the statement of a thorough biographical and psychological method together with a Naturalistic theory regarding "les familles d'esprits." These families of minds consist of groups who show the same mental heredity (for instance, Horace, Boileau, Pope). The day will come, says the critic, when these species will be determined and grouped, and the result will be a new impetus for psychology and literature. But Sainte-Beuve makes only a limited use of this theory and admits that he is chiefly concerned with composing separate monographs. His method is implicit in the motto, " Tel arbre, tel fruit." As a judge, he cannot reckon with the literary product independently of the producer. Then there follows an inventory of the items that constitute the biographical approach: the individual's race, his family, his early associates, the whole story of his youth; he should be studied in the first flush of success and the first symptoms of decay; his attitude towards religion, nature, women and money, his disciples and enemies, his health and habits should be closely examined. Every writer has an " essential vice," and most of them have a keynote or *faculté maîtresse* which can be summed up in an illuminating phrase. Taine and the Naturalists did much to develop these last two points.

Did Sainte-Beuve himself apply the scheme thus outlined? Not scientifically, not methodically, and not with an effort to use all the above categories on every author discussed. He was always too artistic to let the skeleton show through the flesh. But it has recently been shown that Sainte-Beuve does, in the majority of his articles, select from this program according to the individual case. His view of character-study requires a modified adherence to a system which must have been in his mind long before the article of 1862.

Yet Sainte-Beuve remains an artist in technique and standpoint. It is frequently according to an " acte de goût " rather **Art and** than by any elaborate analysis that he makes or sug-**Truth** gests his judicial decisions. His standards are taste, truth to life, tradition, and artistic logic or unity. The greatest of these are taste and truth. In matters of poetry and form he generally cleaves to aesthetic judgments. By such standards he seeks to tone down the excesses both of the Romantic and of the Naturalistic schools; from the same principle derives his gentle mockery of mere erudition. To acquire a taste, he proposes no formulas, he only prescribes a great variety of reading. He has scarcely any system of aesthetics, but he has an infinite discernment. It is partly this side of him that Matthew Arnold considers when he calls Sainte-Beuve " a perfect critic — a critic of measure, not exuberant; of the center, not provincial; of keen industry and curiosity, with ' truth ' for his motto." Truth was at the core of him, thinks Arnold, and he points out how Sainte-Beuve frankly revised his judgments. This is borne out by many passages, notably by the apostrophe to " Reality " in connection with the Naturalistic school: " Réalité, tu es le fond de la vie!" Though shorn of sentiment and idealism, " je t'accepterai encore ... pauvre et médiocre ... mais prise sur le fait, mais sincère." Not always impartial, Sainte-Beuve is careful about accuracy in matters of detail; and he aims more and more at candor and the whole truth.

But this " myriad-minded " critic is not limited to biography, taste or scientific truth. His vision is ever widening, his insight **Historical** ever deepening. Neither does he remain in the **Approach** judicial mood, he frequently forbears to pronounce his decision. In fact, he tends in the later *Lundis* to become more historical in outlook, and this is the last of his main characteristics. For instance, the individual writer is often placed in his historical period and setting. Villemain had started this practice, but Villemain's figures are shaky in their frame as compared with the dexterous workmanship of Sainte-Beuve. His seventeenth and eighteenth-century studies are particularly good examples of interweaving history and portraiture. His knowledge and sense of relativity make him thoroughly discriminate between the various epochs. Nor is the environment allowed to subdue the individual, as in the deterministic theory of Taine. Also Sainte-Beuve, in his later work, leans more towards the depiction of historical personages — generals, statesmen, great ladies — instead of simply criticizing authors. Finally, he is historical in his growing self-effacement and in his indifference to absolute verdicts.

Many other sides might be taken up: his thorough humanism, emphasized by most of his critical compeers (cf. *Qu'est-ce qu'un classique?* and *De la tradition en littérature*); his

Conclusion

humanity which glows through his humanism and allows tradition to include everything worth while; his dualism of mind and body, his epicurean sympathies, his irony and his light touch; his devotion to literature, which he never deserted for another call; the richness, the delightful diversity and the charm of his treatment. Let us glance at his cosmopolitan range. A collection of one thousand articles will evidently deal with many things besides French literature, though that predominates. Sainte-Beuve welcomed the study of Greek and Latin antiquity, the Middle Ages, the Orient, England and Italy. In any or all of these periods he is occasionally silent regarding the greatest figures, apparently because they are less representative. He is not concerned with elaborate methods of comparative literature, but he throws an impartial light on many writers from Firdusi to Wordsworth. His versatile talent likewise takes toll from religion and science, politics and history. A manifold mind, he has also a manifold style. He held that the critic should not commit himself to any style, but should let it vary with the subject. This subordination and suppleness he practices particularly in the *Lundis*, eschewing the rhetoric of earlier essays, though still effectively using figures and the picturesque. He is fond of quotations, by way of illustrating the author. Occasionally he is too journalistic and diffuse. But his style is generally clear and fresh, without obvious mannerisms, and carrying conviction. Sainte-Beuve's morality and spirituality may be questioned, but rarely his intellectual probity. He was variable, not venal. He holds to the rights of reason and neutrality (not indifference) and advocates for purposes of critical divination an " energetic self-surrender." It is true that he had more ideas than Voltaire, more knowledge and penetration than Arnold. When we add his habitual urbanity and truth-seeking, the orchestration of his composite method, his taste and influence, we must recognize in Sainte-Beuve the greatest of modern critics.

CHAPTER II

THE PHILOSOPHERS: COMTE, TAINE, RENAN

THE struggle between religious faith on the one hand and science or skepticism on the other became a leading issue in Science and the last half of the century. This struggle has Doubt been traced in the development of Sainte-Beuve and suggested in the criticism of Scherer. The latter, like certain English agnostics, preserved a high standard of morality after the loss of his Calvinistic beliefs. In philosophy, a deep influence upon French thought was exerted by the discoveries of Darwin (*Origin of Species*, French translation, 1862) and, to a lesser extent, by the speculations of Mill and Spencer. There appeared a formidable array of scientists, typified by Claude Bernard and his contacts with Realism.[1] New interpretations of natural phenomena prevented, for many minds, belief in Catholicism. As in England (George Eliot, Matthew Arnold), many thinkers could find faith only in " honest doubt." Others sought for various " reconciliations " between the scientific and the religious principle; of these the most remarkable example was Auguste Comte, whose master was Saint-Simon.

Henri de Saint-Simon, a descendant of the memoir-writer and an original social theorist, had two main ideas: that of making a " science générale " or a synthesis of useful knowledge; and that of governing industrial society by a hierarchy of *savants*, the priests of his new Christianity. Both of these ideas were Comte incorporated into the system of Auguste Comte (1798–1857). Comte began as a obscure teacher of mathematics, passed through Saint-Simonism and a severe nervous illness, was given a position at the Ecole Polytechnique, from which he was removed in 1844, and published his notable *Cours de philosophie positive* (6 vols., 1839–42). This earlier part of his life and thought was marked by great diligence, in-

[1] See above, Bk. VII, Ch. V.

tellectual power and a predilection for "positive" facts and ideas. But about 1845 he suffered a change of heart. He had already been separated from his wife, and now he met a Mme de Vaux, whose influence, especially after her death, had a pronounced spiritual effect upon Comte. His mind was turned into channels of mysticism and singularity. His character became more and more difficult. Staunch supporters, such as J. S. Mill and Littré, fell away from him. Both of these men had been active in obtaining subsidies for Comte, who lived largely upon private benefactions during his last years. He published additions to his philosophic theory ("System of Politics," "Catechism," etc.) and became active in the establishment of the College of Positivism and the Religion of Humanity, with himself as high priest. But it is in the earlier *Cours de philosophie positive* that we must look for his most substantial contributions to thought.

Comte participated in the reconstructive and humanitarian movement that characterized the decade before 1848. Such **The Positive** writers as George Sand, Fourier, P. Leroux, **Philosophy** Proudhon and even Michelet were then noted for their ardor in the cause of social regeneration. Comte differs from this group in that he is less utopian and more cautious in his approach to social and political reform. Such reform depends, he held, upon society's beliefs, and therefore a thorough philosophic grounding is the first essential. But this in turn must reckon with all the accretions of modern science, and so the leading idea of Comte's first period was to "transformer la science en philosophie." Positivism, in the earlier sense, means the study of phenomena and their laws; as regards this philosophy, says Mill, Comte is the first who attempted its complete systematization and the scientific extension of it to all objects of human knowledge. But it will occur to the reader that we have already had occasion to use such terms as "positive" and "positivist," especially in connection with eighteenth-century thought. In fact, Comte is a more modern *philosophe*, dependent upon such predecessors as Voltaire and Diderot, Descartes and Leibnitz. He has the great advantage, however, of deeper and more systematic knowledge. The *Cours de philosophie* embraces and synthesizes the exact and the natural sciences as well as history and sociology. Comte's most fertile generalizations are along four main lines. First, the " scale of subordination " of the sciences not only distinguishes between the abstract and the concrete but arranges the former " in an ascending series according to the degree of complexity of their phenomena " (Mill). Secondly, he holds that Sociology tops the scale and requires the use of all the other fields of knowledge. It may be said, then, that Comte was the first to found a sociological method and to emphasize the importance of the nascent science. To this end he made a thorough survey of history, and his third contribution is a philosophy of history which is most enlightening in its consideration of causes and leaders. Finally, he distinguishes between the three phases of humanity's development: the first was Theological with its successive divisions of Fetichism, Polytheism and Monotheism; the second was Metaphysical, where abstract ideas ("the gradual disembodiment of a Fetish ") were still considered as powerful entities; the third is the Positive stage, which, though it does not deny the supernatural, insists on attainable facts and the scientific interpretation thereof. Similarly, each science has at different times gone through the three phases: for example, the passage from alchemy and astrology to their modern counterparts. Comte thus naturally believes in Progress and in the consensus of human efforts towards a better civilization. In his sociology, Comte follows Saint-Simon in declaring for the rule of the Positive *savants* curiously linked with the captains of industry; his insistence on this hierarchy is rather dogmatic. This tendency, as well as self-conceit and a hieratic attitude, becomes conspicuous in his later writings when he turned Positivism into the Religion of Humanity. His point of departure is perfectly just — that it is the service of humanity, the " grand Etre," that chiefly counts. But when he tries to convert this rule of life into a creed, with worship of great men and inspiring women, with set observances, a calendar of saints' days, ritual for private and public prayer, excessive systematizing, and much dealing with mystical numbers, the effort fails and becomes partially ridiculous. This is probably the reason why Positivism, which still exists as a church, has only a limited number of adherents in France. Yet it deeply influenced men like Littré and Taine.

In Brazil, a substantial body of Comtists can still be found. In England, where the movement took root early, its best principles were made known by Mill and G. H. Lewes. Frederic Harrison was its ardent disciple, and its highest endeavor was expressed in George Eliot's beautiful poem of the "Choir Invisible."

Comte was not a good writer and did not have the literary power and interest of Taine, who is likewise primarily a philosopher. Hippolyte Taine (1828–93) was born at Vouziers in the Ardennes; the severity of this country left its mark upon his spirit. His life is mainly a "biographie intellectuelle," and even his correspondence contains little personal detail. He was reared in simple and industrious surroundings, then taken to Paris, where for seven years he was a day pupil at the Collège Bourbon. His reflective disposition declared itself early, together with a tendency towards delicate health. Realizing that his vocation was the study of philosophy, he entered the Ecole Normale (1845) with a brilliant group of fellow-students — Prévost-Paradol, E. About, F. Sarcey. Here Taine amassed much knowledge of metaphysics, history, literature, and later of science. He was refused his diploma (*agrégation*) because of the theological leanings of his judges and was sent to teach in the provinces. As an "intellectual," he reacted against this environment, resigned his position and came back to Paris to take his doctorate and write critical articles. These and his monographs gradually gave him fame, and he was made professor at the Ecole des Beaux-Arts (1864). In the same year appeared his notable *Histoire de la littérature anglaise*. For a time he was able to turn to his favorite philosophical studies, then the war of 1870 precipitated him into another path. As a patriotic monument, a contribution to the recovery of his country, Taine wrote *Les Origines de la France contemporaine*, which occupied him for twenty years. At his death he ranked as one of the foremost critical authorities in France. In character he was gentle and reserved, but his intellect was bold, hard and encyclopedic.

A record of Taine's mental development could be written only by establishing his relations with many thinkers of his own and the preceding period. For example, he drew from Hegel his philosophy of history, from Comte the formula of the *milieu* (see

His Mind   below), and in the English positivists and utilitarians
Taine found material to substantiate his scientific
dogmatism and his philosophic determinism. Receptive of many
elements, his mind yet remains original in its assimilative and
organizing power. There are two distinct sides to his intelligence.
Lemaitre calls him a " poète-logician." On the one hand, as
Taine himself said, " ma forme d'esprit est française et latine."
That is, he had the Classical habit of orderly analysis and clear
expression; this was modernized by the scientific passion for note-
taking and for the "petit fait vrai." On the other hand, he
had a Teutonic imagination and some remains of Romantic
sensibility. His " génie poétique " appears in his faculty for
large creative constructions, in his metaphysical melancholy
and especially in his style, which offers a succession of brilliant
images and metaphors. This double gift allows Taine to appreciate such opposites as German idealism and English common
sense, as well as a poet like Musset and a psychologist like
Stendhal. But it left him with a divided mind and a troubled
soul.

In fact, Taine well exemplifies the conflict between the scientific temper and the demands of our spiritual nature. The former

Philosophy   tendency apparently won thē victory, for Taine
could not rest in skepticism. His attitude towards
" la science " (which he rather confuses with philosophy) is
significant of his whole generation. About 1848, Taine, like
Renan, set up absolute science as an ideal and a faith. This
was confirmed by his career at the Ecole Normale and later by
his specialistic studies in physiology, anatomy, chemistry, sociology, etc. His style, in the sixties, abounds in scientific comparisons and metaphors (cf. George Eliot and Sainte-Beuve).
Finally, he held to the Hegelian idea of the unity of all science,
and thus he came to his great generalization that moral or
human phenomena, like those of the physical world, obey in-
variable laws. This is the doctrine of determinism. Taine even
declared that " vice and virtue are products like sugar and
vitriol " — and are just as susceptible of a qualitative analysis.
He saw the history of literature and literature itself as fields
for psychological investigation. In short, he applied a uni-

versal determinism, and his favorite book *De l'Intelligence*
(1870) gives the doctrine of which his other books are illustrations: he makes all knowledge proceed from the sensations,
and he conceives of nature as the reign of law, which should be
extended to the operations of the mind.   But as early as 1867
Taine had written *De l'Idéal dans l'art* (third volume of *La
Philosophie de l'art*, 1865–69), admitting a hierarchy in moral
and artistic values; and now the effects of the Franco-Prussian
war turned him towards a more moralistic conception of history.
Regrets for a changed Germany, doubts and prayers for a
stricken France combined with an inbred pessimism to leave
him without confidence in modern historical institutions (*Les
Origines*).   Also science seemed no longer the sole panacea, and
in his old age Taine reverted to the social and individual necessity of some form of the Christian belief.

As a whole, however, his work represents rather the deterministic and positive strain.   In literary criticism, he applied too

Criticism   rigidly a set of formulas.   Chief among these are the
doctrine of the " faculté maîtresse " and the famous
theory of " race, milieu et moment."   As early as his *Essai sur
Tite-Live* (1856), Taine is seeking for the master-faculty or the
" trait caractéristique et dominant duquel tout peut se déduire
géométriquement."   In Livy, this dominant trait is found in
the fact that he was an orator who became a historian.   Taine
thus explains many things in Livy's career — but he does not
explain Livy.   Still more categorical is the application of " race,
milieu et moment " in the *Histoire de la littérature anglaise*
(1864 f.).   These three forces are viewed as precedent conditions,
operating on a writer or a school.   *Race* signifies the innate, the
hereditary or racial disposition of the man; *milieu* means environment in the broadest sense, including climate and the atmospheric
pressure of the political or religious creed; *moment* indicates not
only the time of an author's appearance but also the momentum
or " vitesse acquise " in a given direction before he appeared.
The system is evidently too rigid to be applied to English literature, in which tradition counts less than the free play of individual characteristics.   Taine is eternally recurring to the influence of the Anglo-Saxon race, of the Norman Conquest, of the
English soil.   Furthermore, he is hampered by his obsession of the

Ideal Englishman, who is supposed to take on successive incarnations in Chaucer, Shakespeare, Shelley and others. Taine usually preferred English to French institutions. With all its faults, this monument of criticism has justly been called the history of English literature which comes nearest to being literature itself; it is written with a massive brilliance and with a cumulative power in the descriptive and analytical passages; and it contains many interesting ideas and contributions — for example, the studies of *milieu* in connection with the Restoration Drama and with Dickens.[2] Similar qualities are found in the various *Essais de critique et d'histoire*, in the second volume of which (*Nouveaux essais*, 1865) appeared the epoch-making article on Balzac. It would be evident from this article that Taine is by no means lacking in a sense of literary beauties. But he preferred to consider masterpieces as documents or as " signs " of the times. He made his taste and his imagination subserve science. His criticism remains philosophic history, with the qualities and defects of such. The danger is that his philosophic " poise settles into immobility " (Brownell). Therefore Taine is more dogmatic and more ridden by his theories than Sainte-Beuve, from whom many of his principles derive.

Taine's method appears at its height in the treatment of history. Conspicuous here are his constructive ability, the **History** power of piling fact upon fact, and also, unfortunately, the predominance of fixed ideas. The *Origines de la France contemporaine* (1875–94) are composed of successive Parts, on the old monarchy, on the Revolution, on the *Régime moderne* (including Napoleon). Reacting from his experiences of the Commune (1871), the writer pens a strong indictment of the French Revolution, which he considers as a compound of anarchy and Jacobinism from the very start. He writes like a " pessimist in a passion," losing his impartiality and judgment. Here, as in his treatment of Napoleon, Taine allows himself a tone of moral indignation which scarcely agrees with his deterministic theories. Too often he has a case to

---

[2] M. J. J. Jusserand was in his youth an admirer and a disciple of Taine's. His *Histoire littéraire du peuple anglais* (1894–1904) shows certain of Taine's principles more cautiously applied and is more nearly the work of a specialist.

prove, he leaves the straight path of historic induction, and he simplifies too much in applying set formulas to men like Danton, Robespierre and Napoleon himself — that *"condottiere* of the Italian Renaissance." The *Régime moderne* is better in its approximation to historical truth and its analysis of modern institutions. But the *Ancien Régime*, often cited in these pages, is Taine's masterpiece as regards both penetration of the past and philosophic insight. Even here he makes too much of the Classical spirit and its influence upon the Revolution. Yet the author's two main qualities, his faculty of generalizing thought and the sweep and power of his objective, metallic, image-laden style, are most visible in this volume. He uses history, as he had used criticism, for philosophic ends. Thus in three fields Taine is *par excellence* "the philosopher and historian of the realistic and scientific movement." His methods were closely associated with those of the Naturalistic novel. Taine and Renan seem to have been the paramount influences upon the last generation of French writers.

Ernest Renan (1823–92) was less of a logician than Taine and more of a critical historian. His imaginative feeling for the past

Renan

was encouraged by his Breton upbringing; he was always sensitive to Celtic poetry and melancholy. Reared in poverty and in a clerical environment, he became a model boy and student. Attracting the attention of Monseigneur Dupanloup, Renan passed through three seminaries, ending at Saint-Sulpice. The raw youth was inducted successively into a classical education, contemporary literature and German philosophy. The last subject shook his faith, which was completely overthrown by the study of Semitic philology. This became his own special field. His honesty soon compelled him to leave the priesthood, a calling to which he was temperamentally well adapted. In this crisis of his fortunes, Renan was sustained by the devotion of his sister, Henriette, who was in turn his practical guide and his spiritual adviser. He taught in small schools, worked towards his university degrees and formed a fruitful association with Berthelot, the scientist. The young scholar wrote *L'Avenir de la Science* (1849, publ. 1890). This chaotic and enthusiastic book is Renan's earliest profession of the scientific faith and contains several of his pet ideas, especially that the world must be regenerated from the top and that the people should be guided by the *savants* (cf. Saint-Simon and Comte).

Renan was made an *agrégé* of the University and finally a doctor. His thesis on *Averroès et l'Averroïsme* (1852), dealing
His Career with Aristotelian doctrines among the Arabs, already reveals his interest in the origin and evolution of beliefs. He also published his *Histoire générale des langues sémitiques,* and in the following year (1856) he married the niece of Ary Scheffer, the painter. Soon he became known as the writer of charming critical articles — on Marcus Aurelius, on Turgenev and especially the famous *Essai sur la poésie des races celtiques.* The most notable of these articles were collected in the *Essais de morale et de critique* (1859). They show Renan not only as concerned with questions of race — one of his chief preoccupations — but also as passing into his second phase, that of the aesthete, interested alike in moral and in artistic beauty. This
Second Phase side of him was further stimulated by the voyage to Syria and Palestine undertaken in company with his sister, who died abroad. It has been said that Henriette died in order that the *Vie de Jésus* might live. Much of this celebrated book (1863) was written spontaneously in Palestine, away from sources and authorities, and it is not strictly accurate in matters of exegesis and historical fact. But it is a work of genius in its poignancy, its sincerity and in the freshness of its romantic and human charm. Renan reconstructs and rationalizes the past, but he feels " la douceur de cette idylle sans pareille." For the first time the life of Christ was written from a layman's standpoint, so that all might read — and all did. The treatment, skeptical yet sympathetic, appealed to a wide circle of former believers and cultured folk. The book popularized the " higher criticism " of the Bible and gave its author a European celebrity. He was made a Professor in the Collège de France, but noisy manifestations in the lecture-room and on the streets led to his removal. The *Vie de Jésus* was the first volume in the epic series
Third Phase: the Scholar called *Histoire des Origines du Christianisme.* The series also comprises *Les Apôtres, St. Paul, L'Antéchrist,* etc. (1866–81). For each of these volumes, Renan visited the appropriate historic site (Asia Minor or Rome) and

according to the method initiated in the *Vie de Jésus,* he linked
with the religious story such consideration of geography, archeology, politics and the general *milieu* as would give solidity to
the treatment. He carefully used original sources, with a full
sense of their uncertainty, and with much historical tact or power
of divination. This critical penetration is coupled with a gift for
resurrecting ancient civilizations and religions. Renan " gave
a voice to dead races." He and Comte made men realize that the
predominance of past generations over the present is in the ratio
of a hundred to one. Renan's vast knowledge of Oriental languages, races and customs allowed him to introduce many comparisons — perhaps too many — with other religions and with
modern Eastern life. Similar methods were employed in his extensive *Histoire du peuple d'Israël* (1887 f.), which connects with
the previous series in that Israel paved the way for the coming
of Christ. Renan again satisfies his passion for origins by showing how the nomadic tribes of Judea, their warrior-kings and
especially their prophets, prepared the " royaume de Dieu." This
phrase for him meant a devotion to the ideas and ideals which
Christ best represents. Rejecting the divinity of the Messiah,
as well as revelation and miracles, Renan's attitude towards
Christianity remains sympathetic, as opposed to the scoffing
of Voltaire, and is of course based on a much wider historical
knowledge. He valued scholarship chiefly for the light that it
throws on the human spirit. His career was crowned by his election to the French Academy, by his reappointment to the Collège
de France, where he was presently made administrator, and by
the editing of the learned *Corpus Inscriptionum Semiticarum,*
which he preferred to any other of his works.

But in the meantime Renan had entered on his last phase —
which some have called his " dilettanteism." To understand this
Fourth development, we must retrace our steps. Even be-
Phase fore the war of 1870, Renan as a liberal had become
interested in politics and was induced to stand for election as
deputy. He was not elected, however, since his views were too
theoretical for his constituents. The war disillusioned him concerning German idealism, nor was he satisfied with French
democracy; his opinions, expressed in the *Réforme intellectuelle
et morale de la France,* were not well received. Henceforth he

felt himself powerless in the realm of action, and his general disenchantment finds expression in the exquisite but bitter *Dialogues philosophiques* (1876). This form (as in the later *Drames philosophiques*) is well suited to the supple variety and shading of Renan's thought. Certain of his philosophical principles may at this point be summarized. He believes that there is no special Providence but rather an ideal principle in the universe, which may finally evolve into the *royaume de Dieu*. To this end all disinterested forms of effort should collaborate, whether in science, morality or art. Anything else is material and ephemeral. Renan still holds to the idea of an intellectual élite, which shall govern the stupid masses. Machinery, vulgarity and material luxury are among the modern deadly sins; he prefers cloistered study and even pagan art, as is visible in *L'Antéchrist*. More and more he takes the spectacular view of the universe. Thus his final manner is marked by a growing skepticism, an indifference to many issues, and a bewildering habit of self-contradiction. Also his moral tone relaxes and he becomes very indulgent to human weaknesses. All this may be considered dilettanteism, if we remember that Renan himself remained a hard and honest worker and that the dilettante habit of mind became much more pronounced in his disciples.

In his later years, Renan was something of a social oracle and entertainer. He carried into the world the priestly unction **Renan in** which he never lost, his " fleeting " epicureanism and **Retrospect** his smiling disenchantment. Part of his moral biography is conveyed in the *Souvenirs d'enfance et de jeunesse* (1883), in which the author is once more concerned with origins — the origins of Renan. These delightful pages contain not only reminiscences but childhood tales narrated by his mother; they emphasize the Breton influences on his youth, the value of his clerical education, and the story of why he left the priesthood. The sentimental side of Renan appears in the *Souvenirs*, the thoughtful side in the undramatic *Drames philosophiques* (1888). Of these the most significant are *L'Abbesse de Jouarre* and *Le Prêtre de Némi;* the latter concerns a priest of Diana and the evolution of a religious belief. Shakespeare's figures are also reviewed symbolically, and Prospero the thinker becomes reconciled with Caliban, who is democracy. Towards the end, Renan shows more optimistic tendencies as regards both this world and the next. He comes to define life as a " charmante promenade à travers la réalité." His style was graceful, languorous, insinuating, romantic in its subjectivism and sentiment. His originality has been described as a compound of " sincerity and irony, of skepticism mixed with the habit of religious speech." He was one of the leaders of his time, he profoundly affected the modern conception of religious history, and influenced, through his writings and personal magnetism, such men as Bourget and Barrès, Vogüé and Anatole France.

CHAPTER III

MISCELLANEOUS WRITERS

WE shall consider here certain historians, moralists and polygraphs who wrote mainly in the second half of the century.

Quinet Edgar Quinet (1803–75) was primarily a historian. The life-long friend of Michelet, whom he resembled in ardent imagination and idealism, Quinet was by birth-right a Romanticist; but his work extended into the Second Empire and underwent the influences of that period. Through residence and marriage, Quinet became well acquainted with Germany and was among the earlier profound students of German thought (Herder and Niebuhr). He was essentially a mystic, as well as a Republican and a Protestant. His mystical tendencies were first revealed in the prose poem of *Ahasvérus* (1833), a prolonged vision of the divine principle pervading the history of the race. Quinet's constant tendency was to confuse religious and secular history and to view the former as always dominant. His great work, *La Révolution* (1865), maintains that the French Revolution failed because it was not animated by a religious principle and did not establish a new religion. Quinet's violent attacks on Catholicism, particularly on the Jesuits, had caused him to lose his chair at the Collège de France and after the Coup d'Etat of 1851, he went into exile and wrote his *Révolution*. He is also to be credited with smaller historical studies on Roumania and Italy, with another formidable vision of the universe called *La Création* and with a final philosophical testament, *L'Esprit nouveau* (1874). The last two works reveal the influence of English science, particularly of Darwin. Quinet's main idea was that of a divine unity — the Absolute — in every field, whether moral, social or scientific. He confused natural law with the spiritual world. He was less of a reasoner than a seer; he foretold the Great War and the rôle of Germany therein. He was endowed with an exuberant imagination; he was " God-intoxi-

657

cated," like Spinoza; he was eloquent, romantic and versatile, even too versatile. "L'immense M. Quinet," as Veuillot calls him, wrote "immense" prose-poems, but his intellect, though serious and lofty, was not vast enough for the task he assumed.

More rational and convincing is the work of another historian, Count Alexis de Tocqueville (1805–59). Like Montesquieu, who **Tocqueville** greatly influenced his thought, Tocqueville came of a family connected with the magistracy and had a legal education. For a time he was judge at Versailles, then he was sent to the United States on an official mission. The result of his visit was the famous *Démocratie en Amérique* (1835–39), the first thoroughgoing and impartial study of our institutions. After this success, Tocqueville embarked on a political career; he became a deputy and, for a brief interval, minister under Louis Napoleon. But he was not a practical politician and he retired after the Coup d'Etat. Failing health did not allow him to complete *L'Ancien Régime et la Révolution,* of which the first part was published in 1856.

Tocqueville's two books derive from his vision of the necessity of democracies and his desire to check their less fortunate con- **His Works** sequences. As a liberal, an aristocrat and a historian of institutions, Tocqueville seems enlightened and impartial in his approach to the democratic question. "Sa méthode était loyale et scrupuleuse comme son âme . . . Il avait l'intuition du monde moderne" (Faguet). Unlike his brother-historians, he is a cautious generalizer, has no set philosophy of history, and deals even too sparsely with considerations of climate, civilizations and race. Behind these forces he sees Democracy as a still greater force in itself; this he studies in its characteristics, its causes and its results. *La Démocratie en Amérique* was also valuable and novel because it displaced the French Revolution as the main preoccupation of historians and showed how the rule of the people was effected in another country. American democracy was different, was more stable, more conservative and bourgeois than the first French Republic. But Tocqueville did not fail to point out the dangers of democracy, its leveling tendencies, its mass-despotism, the lowering treatment to which it subjects intellect and superiority. His work is a useful counterbalance against "the blaze and whirlwind of Rousseau" (Acton).

L'Ancien Régime is the suitable complement to the preceding volume; it shows, a generation before Taine, how the French passed from the monarchical to the democratic State. Again, Tocqueville's chief contention is a conservative one: that the Revolution did not overthrow everything, that on the contrary it kept and developed one of the notable features of the old régime; to wit, administrative centralization. The Revolution further standardized and regularized government and ruled by a central control which Napoleon carried on. One of Tocqueville's forward-looking ideas is a federation of European democracies, along American lines. He would impose certain " checks " upon Republics and maintain an aristocratic infusion through the representative *corps* (cf. Montesquieu), the separation of administrative and legislative functions and the independence of the judiciary. Tocqueville wrote in a clear well-ordered manner, though his pages are sometimes too thickly strewn with observations and digressions; his type of mind was logical, lucid and conservative.

The predominance of the historical genre throughout the century was forwarded by various governments and ministries. Growth of Historical Study   Under the bourgeois monarchy (Guizot and Thiers), historical study, considered as a " national institution," was thoroughly reorganized. This movement was aided by the foundation of special schools and chairs, by the establishment of learned journals and of great collections. To this day, the section devoted to the " Histoire de France " looms largest in the national libraries. Knowledge of medieval France was particularly encouraged by the Ecole des Chartes (revived in 1829); this school also developed the study of Old French and Celtic philology. Under Napoleon III, much historical research was accomplished through the favor of the Emperor and through the influence of Duruy's ministry (1863–69). The Ecole des Hautes Etudes, founded in 1868, has developed scholarly specialization in many fields, and specialization is the mark of latter-day history. With the exception of Taine and of Renan, great names of assured literary standing are scarcely to be found, but there are several minor historians who deserve consideration.

Fustel de Coulanges may almost be classed among the major prophets. He led the calm life (1830–89) of a scholar and teacher. Influenced chiefly by Montesquieu and by Tocqueville, his works exhibit the importance of institutions and forms of government as well as the continuity of national tra-

Fustel de Coulanges

ditions. *La Cité antique* (1864) had an unusual success as a reconstitution of Roman life under the Republic and as an excellent study of the ancient city in general. Artistically and historically considered, the book is a masterpiece. In proportion, penetration and judgment, it leaves little to be desired. Precise and realistic in his style, Fustel gives life and substance to his theme. Yet much of his reconstruction is conjectural, while his criticism of texts and sources is not sufficiently severe. The writer views religion as the main principle of family life and of the State. He rivals Michelet in his " tableaux d'ensemble " and in his emphasis on the soul of a nation. Fustel's *Histoire des Institutions politiques de l'ancienne France* (1875–92) gave him rank as a notable medievalist. He discounted the effect of the Frankish invasions and insisted on the continued power of Roman institutions. He studied the origins of feudalism, since he wished the new France to conserve the best of its past. In both books, Fustel writes in a sober scientific manner; he has a broad vision and a sure touch; his influence on historical research has been considerable.

Henri Martin's useful and monumental *Histoire de France* (3rd ed., 19 vols., 1837–54), belongs to an earlier generation.

Minor Historians

The work long held its own as a standard national history. A good short history of France, still current in our own time, is that of Victor Duruy, whose rôle as Minister of Public Instruction has been mentioned. Duruy wrote several popular schoolbooks and was considered something of an authority on the Roman Empire (*Histoire Romaine*, 1843–74). Of another caliber is the imposing work of Albert Sorel (1842–1906) on *L'Europe et la Révolution française* (1885–1904). Sorel shows how the Revolutionists became heirs to the foreign policy of the old régime; he recognizes the interplay of foreign opinion and domestic events; and he traces completely the course of the ensuing wars. Judicial, learned and a master of composition, Sorel has won a unique place among the historians of diplomacy. " His book," says Gooch, " is at once the first adequate study of the Revolution as an international event and the fairest judgment

of it as an episode in French history." Finally, Ernest Lavisse
(b. 1842) has written the history of Prussia, but ·is best known
through the *Histoire de France* (18 vols., 1900–1911) due to him
and his collaborators. Written in accordance with present special-
.istic tendencies, this coöperative work has superseded the single-
handed histories and is now considered the standard authority.
Lavisse himself wrote for this History a masterly treatment
of *Louis XIV*.[1] As professor and publicist, he has been active
in remodeling the Sorbonne and in enforcing the ideal that the
proper function of University men is to " créer la science " —
that is, to increase and organize knowledge.

French Catholicism was on the defensive until the end of the
century and was usually associated with extreme reactionary
Moralists: principles. Among the staunchest defenders of the
Veuillot faith was Louis Veuillot (1813–83), a virulent
journalist whose portrait appears in Augier's *Fils de Giboyer*.
Veuillot's reputation as a writer has grown in recent years. He
came of the people, received a scanty popular education and
through a visit to Rome was converted at the age of twenty-five.
He went in for Catholic journalism (*L'Univers*), and for many
years he spent himself in this profession. Upholding the Church
against her various enemies, he was a bitter fighter and a satirist
of contemporary life. He had wit, originality, unequal talent
and poor taste. He became known for his short articles and
mélanges, of which the best-known have been collected in *Les
Libre-penseurs* (1848), *Les Parfums de Rome* and *Les Odeurs de
Paris* (1866), Veuillot's masterpiece. This volume preceeds from
the thesis that while Rome is the spiritual head of the world,
Paris is only its " tête charnelle " and a center of corruption.
The city abounds in the morbid and mortuary odors of decom-
position. Veuillot saw materialism as rampant in social life, in
science and philosophy. So he attacks journalism, the drama,
the salons, democracy and literature, whether Romantic or Realistic. Though Classical in standards, he knew neither restraint
nor good manners, and his style is violent, energetic and often
coarse. He is by turns racy and amusing or sarcastic and intolerant. " He had a marvelous gift of righteous indignation

---

[1] Cf. also (preceding the above) the *Histoire générale du IVe siècle à nos jours*, ed.
Lavisse and Rambaud, 1892–1899.

and vitriolic expression " (Guérard). He also had undoubted sincerity and power. His function was to display his partial view of truth and to manifest his scorn for the Second Empire and the " persecutors " of the Church. He believed that human nature was thoroughly corrupt and, like De Maistre, he held sourly to the principle of dogmatic religious authority.

A more artistic and agreeable writer was Eugène Fromentin (1820–76), painter, traveler and novelist. Fromentin lived his **Fromentin** books and one may almost say he painted them. His pictures of African countries, whether on canvas or on the printed page, are unsurpassed for colorful and exact detail (cf. *Un Eté dans le Sahara*). As a novelist, he shines rather in description than in composition or action. His best-known work is *Dominique* (1863), which is a " roman d'analyse " of the personal sort, in the tradition of *Adolphe*. It is a psychological study of the artistic temperament and of self-sacrifice. The hero falls in love with an old acquaintance but has the strength to renounce his love since she is now a married woman. In its idealism, the novel is reactionary, yet many Realistic devices are used in the technique of description and in the sensory approach to nature. But Fromentin had a pure and classical taste which led him back more and more to the " nature " of the ancients. This may be seen in his art-criticism, for instance, in *Les Maîtres d'autrefois* (1876).

During the last two decades of the century, on both sides of the Atlantic, the book known as " Amiel's Journal " had a con- **Amiel** siderable vogue. Its appearance coincided with the prevailing mood of religious doubt and self-analysis.[2] Henri-Frédéric Amiel (1821–1881) was a disillusioned professor, an introspective thinker, a sensitive and conscientious spirit. He was a Genevan by birth and residence, but European in his outlook. This *Journal intime* (1883–84) offers in many ways an epitome of the century's thought and feeling. It is a diary of the inner life, subtly explaining the writer's sterility and melancholy. It also evidences much penetration into philosophy and literature, and it contains many excellent critical judgments. Other moralists will be treated in connection with the reaction against Realism (see next chapter).

---

[2] Compare Matthew Arnold, Mrs. Ward's *Robert Elsmere*, etc.

BOOK IX

THE END OF THE CENTURY

CHAPTER I

IN FICTION: NATURALISM, PSYCHOLOGY AND OTHER CURRENTS

THE disaster of 1870–71 meant the dethronement of France as the first power in continental Europe. The war left a deep **The Third** mark upon many writers as well as upon the French **Republic** populace. The civil strife of the Commune augmented the feeling of uncertainty and depression. After making peace with Prussia, Thiers conducted his government from Versailles and in the Spring of '71 sent troops against the Communists. There followed a brief and bitter civil war before a stable government was restored. Thiers, as the first President of the Third Republic, was supported by Gambetta, orator and statesman; and for some time the policy of " la revanche " against Germany was in vogue. This included the inauguration of universal service and the maintenance of a large military organization. The French had promptly paid the war-indemnity of five billion francs. Under the Presidency of Marshal MacMahon (1873–79) the constitution of 1875 was promulgated. This divided the National Assembly into two governing bodies, the Chamber of Deputies and the Senate. MacMahon did not agree well with Jules Simon, his minister. Simon and Gambetta were the real powers in France, and the former began the dissensions with the Pope which continued for some time. Grévy was the next President (1879–87), whose chief minister, Jules Ferry, was marked for his anti-clericalism and his efforts in behalf of secular education. The colonial expansion of France in Indo-China (Tonkin), the protectorate of Tunis and the beginnings of the advance into Northern Africa date from 1881. A little later came the popular craze for General Boulanger. The " Boulan-

663

giste " movement, which continued under the Presidency of Sadi Carnot (1887–1904), was finally arrested by the suicide of its leader. The movement was accompanied by much political acrimony, charges of corruption and the exaggerations of shrill partisan journalism — three of the worst features of the Third Republic. They were again manifest in the Panama scandal, which ended in the condemnation of De Lesseps, the chief engineer of the undertaking. A more peaceful attitude towards the Church having been adopted, the Republic was recognized by Leo XIII in 1892. The brief Presidency of Casimir-Périer was followed by that of Félix Faure (1895–1899), who, like his successor, M. Loubet, was a man of the people. In 1896, the Dual Alliance with Russia was officially announced. Under Faure and the Waldeck-Rousseau ministry occurred the famous Dreyfus affair. Captain Dreyfus was condemned to life-imprisonment, in 1895, on charges of betraying military secrets to Germany. Many felt that Dreyfus, as a Jew, had been made a scapegoat, in order to avoid an army scandal. Disinterested efforts were made, notably by Emile Zola and Col. Picquart, to secure a new trial, and many " intellectuals," such as Anatole France, came to the defence of Dreyfus. His second trial (August, 1899) resulted in a milder condemnation, attended by a specific pardon and a general amnesty. Nothing was ever proved against Dreyfus, but the case was used to forment every kind of political and racial passion. Under Loubet (1899–1906), the Paris Exposition of 1900 took place. In matters of education, M. Combes, as minister, accomplished the separation of Church and State. The clerical orders and powers, encouraging aristocratic education and royalist sympathies, had not helped the Republic. Combes broke up and expelled many religious associations, and the law of 1905 made the separation complete. From 1904–07 dates the formation of the Entente Cordiale with England, destined to have such important consequences; by the treaty of 1904 there was achieved an amicable division of spheres of influence in Egypt and Morocco. M. Fallières was made President in 1906, and M. Poincaré in 1913. At the turn of the century, France, in spite of her stationary birth-rate, was fairly prosperous. The condition of the working-classes had improved, while the intellectual life of the country had been forwarded by the establishment of compulsory free education. In 1880–90 secular education came to emphasize the importance of modern subjects, and latterly more place has been given to the proper instruction of women. Young people have taken an increasing interest in athletics. Colonial expansion, especially in Africa and the Orient, revived a taste for adventure and was associated with the literature of exoticism (cf. Loti). The Expositions of 1889 and 1900 showed that while France was participating in the results, good and evil, of modern industrialism, her products still kept a distinction of their own. This interest in *articles de vertu* is reflected in the fiction of Bourget. Connected with the industrial situation was the growth of Socialism, which introduced another strong element into the confusion of political parties and the rapid changes of ministries in France.

Let us now see what was happening in literature, particularly in fiction.

The school of Zola, attacked by Brunetière and others, had lost part of its dominion during the eighties. Five of the master's

Naturalism former adherents, including Paul Margueritte and " J.-H. Rosny," had on the appearance of *La Terre* (1887) signed a protest against Zolaism. The advent of the psychological novel, the passing of scientific positivism and the pressure of a more idealistic current (see below) did not favor Naturalism; about 1900 an " enquête " among a number of writers seemed to establish that the movement was dead. Yet there remains the heritage of Naturalism, particularly as regards the notation of fact and the careful descriptions of *milieux*. Thus the movement did not pass away with Zola but became blended with other movements, especially with the development of the symbolistic and the historical novel.

For example, the sinister figure of Joris-Karl Huysmans (1848–1907) is regarded by some as the most advanced Naturalist, by

Huysmans others as an arch-symbolist and a decadent mystic. Huysmans, who came of Dutch ancestry, was a government employee, a slow but careful writer and a person of unattractive character. He passed through a gradual evolution from materialism to an aesthetic Catholicism which led him to make a retreat among the Trappists and finally to profess conversion. Beginning with a displeasing contribution to the *Soirées de Médan* and with a short grimy study of prostitution (*Marthe*, 1876), Huysmans then became introspective and entered on his psychic pilgrimage with *A Rebours* (1884). The very title of this novel indicates a perversity which the hero, Des Esseintes, exemplifies in his search for rare sensations. He finds them in jewels, perfumes, music, weird paintings and medieval Latin literature. *A Rebours* applies the process of external Naturalism to a morbid inner life. The book influenced Oscar Wilde and the hyperaesthetes. It well illustrates the restless neurasthenia of its author, who goes a step further in *Là-bas* (1891), a "disagreeable medley of modern and medieval nastiness" (Wells). The occult and the sacrilegious, particularly in the form of Satanism, here grip the ailing souls of Durtal and of his creator, Huysmans. *En route* (1895) shows a straighter progression in its penitential tears and its desire for holiness. Finally, *La Cathédrale* and *L'Oblat* carry the writer, if not into true religion, at least towards contemplative peace and aesthetic bliss. Like others, Huysmans seems to have sought for faith as a final sensation. His treatment of these mingled themes is repellent, but his soul-states are apparently sincere and exhaustively studied; he thus offers a typical case of decadence blended with Neo-Catholicism; and his literary talent, shown in a nervous impressionistic style with forceful epithet and metaphor, is very considerable. His novels are weak in composition, he can depict only himself, his taste is contaminated, but his power of picturesque description is almost faultless.

Another student of Catholicism, though from a different standpoint, was Ferdinand Fabre (1827–98). Born and bred in the rude mountains of the Cévennes, trained as a youth **Fabre** for the priesthood, Fabre combines these antecedents in a succession of novels by turns autobiographical, clerical and rustic. As a Realistic delineator of peasantry and clergy, he is a disciple of Balzac, and his masterpiece, *L'Abbé Tigrane* (1873), offers parallels with the *Curé de Tours*. *Les Courbezon* and *Mon Oncle Célestin* are also notable novels. This writer studies the passions of the clergy, their benevolence, ambition and pride. But as a whole Fabre's methods are more blunt than artistic, and he never freed himself from a certain provincialism. The brutal

Naturalism of Octave Mirbeau likewise depicts the priesthood (*L'Abbé Jules*, etc.), as well as other subjects.

There were several writers who began as imitators or comrades of Zola and who ended in quite a different manner. Paul Adam **Paul Adam** (1862–1920) accomplished an interesting evolution from a crude materialism (*Chair molle*) to a sort of symbolism which implied a new conception of the historical novel. This is called by M. Doumic the " roman collectif," since the effort is towards group-psychology, towards depicting the collective soul of an epoch, a crowd, a race. In the series called *Le Temps et la Vie* (1899 f.) Paul Adam vividly portrays the Napoleonic era, and less vividly that of the Restoration and Romanticism. The series consists of four novels: *La Force*, *L'Enfant d'Austerlitz*, *La Ruse* and *Au Soleil de Juillet*. It is in moments of national danger that the soul of a people is truly unified; consequently *La Force* is a fine and stirring novel, showing France as exalted first by self-defensive patriotism and then by the intoxication of Napoleonic glory. The cult of energy and of appetites is well-rendered. *L'Enfant d'Austerlitz*, on the contrary, represents a period (the Restoration) of reaction and confusion, and the novel, which is too involved and comprehensive, suffers from the defects of its subject. The *Soleil de Juillet* gives a massive handling of the Romantic era. The author excels in large frescoes, in descriptive sweep, rather than in psychological penetration or in artistic style. He combines features from Balzac and from Zola, and it is a curious tribute to the former master that Balzacian heroes — Rastignac or De Marsay — appear in the background of Adam's fiction as historical personages.

It was natural that Paul Margueritte (1860–1918) and his brother Victor, sons of a distinguished general in the Franco-**The Margueritte Brothers** Prussian war, should turn to that period for the cycle of novels called *Une Epoque* (1898–1904). This also includes four titles: *Le Désastre, Les Tronçons du Glaive, Les Braves Gens, La Commune*. Like Adam, the Margueritte brothers found that the national soul is stronger in wartime than in reaction: *Le Désastre* lent itself to a more intensive portrayal than did the Prussian occupation (*Les Tronçons du Glaive*) or *La Commune*. The first novel is evidently modeled on Zola's *Débâcle,* and though Zola's gloomy depiction of war remains unrivaled, the morale of *Le Désastre* is of a healthier and more tonic quality. Indeed, this quality is characteristic of the best work of Paul Margueritte, who turned from the vulgar Naturalism of *Pascal Géfosse* (1887), through the psychological delicacy of *La Tourmente* (1893), to the collaborative cycle above-mentioned. Even here the influence of Zola is seen, in the importance given to humble people and particularly in the treatment of crowds — the mob which is alternately childish, curious, criminal or heroic. The scenes of collective life in *La Commune* are very impressive. But as in other historical novels (cf. Flaubert and Adam), the strictly fictional elements of incident and character are unduly minimized by the multitude of historical data. Further examples of the "roman collectif" in cycles will be treated in connection with Barrès and Anatole France (see below).

Another pair of brothers, J. H. and S. J. Boëx, signed with the joint pseudonym of " J.-H. Rosny." They may also be classed J.-H. Rosny among the "neo-realists," in that they approved the protests against Zola and stood, theoretically, for a broader and more idealistic view of humanity. Their work, however, is extremely eclectic and peculiar. It is Naturalistic in *Nell Horn* (1886); a study of London low life and the Salvation Army; it is prehistoric in such weird imaginings as *Vamireh* and *Les Xipehuz,* in which we approach, conjecturally, not only the mammoths but the manners of the antediluvians; it deals with the artistic temperament in *Le Termite,* and with sociology in the two important novels, *Le Bilatéral* (1887) and *Marc Fane* (1888). These two studies emphasize the faith of " J.-H. Rosny " alike in science and in humanity as well as in the evolution of both forces towards a moral ideal. In praise of goodness, the brothers also wrote a trilogy — *Daniel Valgraive* (1891), *L'Impérieuse Bonté* and *L'Indomptée.* Their message tends to forward an altruism which implies not self-sacrifice but true self-development. The work of " J.-H. Rosny " is better in moral and symbolistic intention than in artistic execution; action and drama are neglected, the characters are often pedantic, and the style is full of technical and obscure terms. Poetic and dithyrambic flights of style hardly atone for these deficiencies. Yet the Rosny brothers are important representatives of the " roman social," so conspicuous in our times.

Most of the above writers represent either the symbolistic or the historical wing of Naturalism. In accordance .with modern complexity, the novel took on many other forms **Other Varieties of Fiction** during the past generation. It was by turns idealistic, psychological, impressionistic, as regards direction; as regards material, it was fashionable or idyllic, " regionalist " or exotic, military or ecclesiastical. Idealism as a method is either a Romantic survival or a reaction against too much Realism. It is mainly a survival in the work of Octave Feuillet (1821–90), who began as the inheritor of George Sand's rose-colored mantle. The too-celebrated *Roman d'un Jeune homme pauvre* (1858) exhibits this side of him; a more serious and Realistic vein is found in the tragic *Julia de Trecœur* (1872) and in the grim passions of *Monsieur de Camors*. The title-hero of the latter story is Feuillet's best-drawn masculine character. Feuillet excelled in the portrayal of women's hearts and nerves. Idyllic idealism is the specialty of André Theuriet (1833–1907), who has written considerably of field and forest in the Eastern provinces of France. Theuriet and François Coppée (see Chapter III, below) have a rather bourgeois inspiration and a mildly agreeable talent, which is exercised chiefly in the short-story.

Although the Realistic method, as a whole, had not yet spent its force, the last decades of the century were marked by a **Idealistic Reaction** partial reaction against Naturalism. The leaders in this reaction were such writers as Brunetière, Bourget, Barrès — " the three B's," all of whom became Catholics or Conservatives. The Swiss, Edouard Rod, and the aristocrat, Melchior de Vogüé, may also be classed as sharing in this movement. Edouard Rod (1857–1910) passed his youth in Paris and there he attempted to write Naturalistic fiction; but his true bent was rather towards psychological analysis and the literature of ideas. This " intuitivism " (subjective observation) was encouraged by Rod's appointment to a chair at the University of Geneva. Among his important novels are: *La Course à la mort* (1885), which is introspective and pessimistic; *Le Sens de la Vie* (1899), which is moral and idealistic; *La Vie privée de Michel Teissier* and *L'Ombre s'étend sur la montagne*. A number of Rod's later novels are laid in Switzerland and have a thorough savor of the soil. A volume of criticism, *Les Idées* *morales du temps présent* (1891), furnishes an excellent survey of the period and its chief writers. The Vicomte Melchior de Vogüé (1850–1910), called "the Chateaubriand of the Third Republic," was a traditionalist in taste, religion and politics. The work of Zola and his group could not please such a man; and Vogüé wrote *Le Roman russe* (1886) partly to forward the "bankruptcy" of French Naturalism, partly to exhibit the virtues of Russian fiction, from Pushkin to Tolstoy. Like Brunetière (see Ch. IV, below), Vogüé held that the Russian novelists had a better morality and more humanity than the French. He was unusually well qualified, by long residence and intimate association, to speak for the Russian novel, and his book is at once a psychological study and a critical revelation. It is also exceedingly well written. Among Vogüé's own novels, the most notable is *Les Morts qui parlent* (1899).

There is a certain kinship between the idealistic and the psychological novel, also called the *roman d'analyse*. This kind,

Bourget from the *Princesse de Clèves* through *Dominique*, is clearly in the French tradition. It is not surprising, then, that in the early eighties the public should turn from the externalities of Realism to the work of a man whose prime concern was with what he called "soul-states." Paul Bourget (b. 1852) has accomplished the evolution described by Descartes from a bookish education to the "grand livre du monde," thence to varied travels and finally to the world of inner contemplation. He speaks of his many volumes as "les étapes d'une conscience toujours en marche." Beginning with poetry and criticism (see Ch. IV, below), Bourget soon won a reputation as a society novelist: the success inaugurated by *Cruelle énigme* [1] (1885) was continued in the next few years by *Un crime d'amour* and *André Cornélis*, by *Mensonges* and *Un cœur de femme*. These half-dozen novels express the earlier Bourget, who combines a taste for high life — clubmen, salons, elegance, *bibelots* — with a delicate analytical art. Primarily a psychologist and moralist, he chooses the upper strata of society in order best to study the more leisurely developments of modern love. His charming women — Thérèse de Sauve or Suzanne Moraines — are of a

---

[1] *L'Irréparable* (1883) first revived the psychological novel, but was not so successful.

romantic type, sentimental or sensual, complicated descendants of Emma Bovary. The men subjected to this feminine influence are either weak youths, like André Cornélis, or worldly and corrupt *roués*. Bourget himself is not romantic in his treatment of passion, whose consequences he usually deplores; but the atmosphere of these stories is insidiously relaxing and the author's sensibility is " maladive et souffrante."

A change came over his spirit with the publication of *Le Disciple*, in 1889. Bourget mentally resembles Taine, to whom **His Second** he owed much in his conception of the multiple ego **Stage** and in his dissection of emotion and passion. *Le Disciple* tells the story of a youth who likewise fell under the influence of a great deterministic psychologist, whose principles he applied disastrously in his emotional life. The novel created a storm among the critics and had a pronounced effect upon French youth; it displays all of Bourget's qualities, but it is written in a sterner tone and has more of a moral glow than heretofore. The author, however, was not yet through with dilettanteism and cosmopolitanism — two dangers against which he frequently warned others. As for cosmopolitanism, there followed the artistically fruitful journeys to Italy and England (*Sensations d'Italie*, 1891). Such novels as *Cosmopolis* (1893) and *Une Idylle tragique* (1896) deal with the " floating Laputa," the super-city of world-citizens who take no stable root anywhere. As for dilettanteism, Bourget, with a finger on his own pulse, thus defines the disease:

> C'est une disposition de l'esprit, très intelligente à la fois et très voluptueuse, qui nous incline tour à tour vers les formes diverses de la vie et nous conduit à nous prêter à toutes sans nous donner à aucune.

After the Dreyfus affair, Bourget swung into line with the traditionalists, political and religious. In *L'Etape* (1902), he urges a slower social development of the family, which should not hasten through its stages in the American manner. A growing sympathy with Catholicism is found in *Un Divorce* (1904) and in *Le Démon de Midi* (1915). Bourget has also written numerous volumes of *nouvelles* (*Un Saint, Le Luxe des autres*, etc.). In spite of a heavy style, all of this fiction shows a genuine capacity for the imaginative embodiment of abstract ideas and a gift for the minute dissection of modern types. Moreover, Bourget's construction is fundamentally excellent, and the average reader feels impatient when a good plot is hampered by long-drawn-out descriptions and analyses, often unessential to the story. Yet it is in these analyses that the author's peculiar power resides; he ranks as a moralistic philosopher who "adds another chapter to the science of the soul."

Bourget brought psychology into fashion and influenced the work of Edouard Rod (see above); of Marcel Prévost, the popular novelist (*L'Automne d'une femme, Les Demi-vierges,* **Barrès** etc.); and of Maurice Barrès, during his first period. The last-named has by his intense patriotism doubled his fame within recent years. He was born (1862) in the Vosges mountains and brought up in Lorraine while that province was undergoing its painful Germanization. The strife of the two races made a strong impression on the sensibility of young Barrès; but first he turned to another field of literary expression, namely, the "Cult of the Ego." The trilogy published under this general title includes *Sous l'œil des barbares* (1888), which describes a young man's struggle for self-assertion against the Philistines; *Un homme libre* (1889) also develops a theory of egotistical gymnastics; and *Le Jardin de Bérénice* (1891), less obscurely written, repeats a similar theme, with somewhat more regard for the outer world. At this stage Barrès believed that humanity could become a "beautiful forest" only through the intensive cultivation of each individual tree; therefore let us keep our egos in a state of ardent and extreme exaltation. Dilettanteism and affection are conspicuous in these works, which owe most to the influence of Renan. Against this master Barrès presently turned violently, became an apostle of action and wrote another trilogy or cycle called *Le Roman de l'énergie nationale.* The first in the series, *Les Déracinés* (1897), urges that it is dangerous to uproot men from their province (Lorraine). *L'Appel au soldat* (1900) stands for military patriotism. As early as 1889, Barrès had been elected deputy to the Chamber, whose members he now satirizes in *Leurs figures* (1902). Finally, such works as *Au service de l'Allemagne* and *Colette Baudoche* (1909) plead for the defense of the "Eastern bastions" (like Metz), because

France is the chief representative of modern civilization. The development of the author has thus been from egotism, through " regionalism," to nationalism and ultimately to a view of civilization as a whole. Whether in Lorraine or Paris, for the race or for the nation, he has become a stalwart traditionalist, a leader in the " Ligue des patriotes." From complexity and obscurity he has developed a passion for simplicity, whether in character, plot or ideas (cf. *Colette Baudoche*). Without depreciating the value of his service or of his message, it should be said that many people find the literary temperament of M. Barrès perverse, dogmatic, unduly critical and overbearing. But his style has marked qualities of subtlety or eloquence; he has a gift for description and much ironic power.

M. Julien Viaud (b. 1850) took the pseudonym of " Pierre Loti " and has served most of his life as an officer of the French

Pierre Loti navy. Born at Rochefort on the Charente, of Huguenot ancestry (cf. *Le Roman d'un enfant*, 1890), he passed an unhappy sensitive childhood, and at the age of seventeen embarked on the series of voyages which made his fame. Loti offers the most complete modern example of literary exoticism; his talent is essentially subjective and impressionistic; his power of describing foreign lands, their scenery and total effect, is very remarkable. We may see his gift expand from Oceania to Iceland and from China almost to Peru. First came the anonymous *Aziyadé* (1879), followed by *Rarahu* (1880), otherwise known as *Le Mariage de Loti*, which started his vogue. These two novels were laid respectively in Turkey and in Tahiti, while in " l'étonnant et brûlant" *Roman d'un Spahi* (1881), Loti passes on to Senegambia. He first treats of Brittany and the surrounding seas in *Mon frère Yves* (1883). These earlier novels recount mainly his personal adventures under various disguises; they are filled with sensuous glamour and with primitive sweethearts, " femmes de rêve, créatures à peine ébauchées."

With *Pêcheur d'Islande* (1886), Loti returns to Brittany and gives us his most profoundly human book as well as a compendium of his various gifts. Greater and more impersonal emotions find expression in this idyll of the betrothal and parting of two Breton lovers, the fisherman Yann and " la grave et tendre Gaud."

The fisherman never returns from his voyage to Iceland, and the last part of the book describes the waiting and the mourning of the women left behind. Two of Loti's chief obsessions, the changeable devouring sea and the all-pervasive thought of death, are rendered with power and melancholy. *Madame Chrysan_thème* (1887) deals with Japan and again with exotic love. Later stories, such as *Matelot* and *Fantôme d'Orient*, show a partial repetition of old themes. There is also *Le Livre de la pitié et de la mort* (1891), a significant title, under which most of this author's works might be assembled. With few exceptions, they are not really novels; they constitute rather a succession of pictures and of moods within the experience of the writer. For example, a trip to Palestine was recorded in *La ·Galilée* (1895) and was connected with Loti's unsuccessful endeavor to revive his youthful faith; yet there is religious feeling in *Ramuntcho* (1897), the story of two Basque lovers separated by their different creeds. Near this beautiful Basque country, where the Pyrenees slope to the sea, Loti has established himself in his declining years. Of his later writings, *Les Désenchantées* (1908), concerning the advance of feminism in Turkey, has been the most notable.

Like Chateaubriand, Loti possesses a great and melancholy charm. Like the elder enchanter, the *fin de siècle* wanderer makes us participate in the sense of fleeting joys, of ruins, of inevitable death and endings, the lure and failure of exotic love. Like René, Loti's civilized heroes cannot long abide with the simple savage maidens. With a remnant of religious feeling, Loti also wrote an " Itinerary " from Paris to Jerusalem. He is Romantic in his acute sensibility, his absorption in nature and his absorption of nature into himself. His style, with all its simplicity, has the penetrating and suggestive power of music. He is modern chiefly by virtue of his impressionism, in description and sensation, and by the wide range of his latter-day exoticism. Emotional rather than thoughtful, not elaborate in characterization or plot, his fiction moves us by his capacity for sincerely realizing alien landscapes and alien souls.

Jacques-Anatole Thibault (b. 1844), known to the world as Anatole France, is the foremost living French writer. For half a century his piercing mind and fascinating style have reflected the chief movements of his age. Reared in the Latin quarter, his imaginative boyhood turned naturally to books and dreams. **Anatole** He was educated at the ecclesiastical Collège **France** Stanislas; later he knew Greek beauty and became associated with the Parnassians. Strongly Pagan are the *Poèmes dorés* (1873) and the Parnassian drama of *Les Noces Corinthiennes*. France then passed through the usual stages of devotion to science and dabbling in Realism; but he soon returned to the more characteristic dreaming and beauty-loving which reappear in *Le Crime de Sylvestre Bonnard* (1881). This masterpiece recounts delightfully the self-sacrifice of an old scholar, who protects the granddaughter of his former sweetheart. In the charming *Livre de mon ami* (1885), the author definitely renounces science in behalf of imagination and the pensive fancies of his youth.

Anatole France is an intellectual Epicurean, particularly so in his first period (until 1897). This tendency exists in the **The** works mentioned above and increases through his **Epicurean** revival of fairy tales (*L'Abeille*), of the legendary past (*Baltasar*) and of the historical clash between Christianity and Paganism in *Thaïs* (1890). The beauty-lover is also a scholarly dilettante, and Renan influences him during these years. *Thaïs*, so rich in background and in philosophical reflection, likewise owes something to Flaubert's *Tentation de Saint Antoine*. Dilettanteism is prominent in France's literary criticism, which occupied him (see Ch. IV, below) from 1885–92. He returns to tales and legends in *L'Etui de nacre* (1892), where we find one of his most striking short stories, *Le Procurateur de Judée*. Half of this volume deals with the eighteenth century, which from a double standpoint (see above, p. 372) was peculiarly fitted to attract Anatole France. Irony and skepticism are more conspicuous and Voltaire becomes permanently his master in *La Rôtisserie de la Reine Pédauque* with its companion-volume, *Les Opinions de M. Jérome Coignard* (both of 1893). The former, resembling *Candide*, is an agreeably rambling tale of alchemy, gallantry, anti-clericalism and a genial eighteenth-century abbé. Two studies of Italy show still another side of A. France: in *Le Lys rouge* (1894), he wrote almost his first modern novel; the Florentine background is beautifully described, and it is evident that the author approves the stark passion of the lovers depicted therein. The sensual foundations for his dilettanteism are re-vealed again in *Le Puits de Sainte-Claire*, in which are related more or less churchly legends of the Italian Renaissance. In *Le Jardin d'Epicure* (1894), considered by many his most thoughtful book, France gives us the flower of his epicurean meditations up to date. Currents of pessimism and mordant irony are discernible, but the author stoutly maintains his thesis that wisdom lies in the search for intellectual and sensual pleasures.

Nothing very radical had yet been heard from Anatole France; he was even elected to the Academy through the efforts of con-Satirist **and** servatives in 1896. But a new Anatole arises from **Radical** the pages of the *Histoire contemporaine* and from his participation in the Dreyfus affair. In the latter he came out strongly for Dreyfus; in the former he satirized the tradi-tionalists who opposed that cause; in both, people were surprised to see the scholar and the dweller in the past descend to the strife of the market-place. The *Histoire contemporaine* is an-other modern cycle (see p. 668), including *L'Orme du mail* and *Le Mannequin d'osier* (both of 1897), *L'Anneau d'améthyste* (1899) and *M. Bergeret à Paris* (1901). The last two of these works are particularly concerned with the Dreyfus affair, but they all deal with intrigue, political or amorous, provincial and Parisian; the thin plot revolves around the infidelity of Mme Bergeret or the promotion of a priest; clerics, royalists, militarists and society women are bitterly satirized; there are recurring characters among whom Professor Bergeret is the most notable; he is the mouthpiece for Anatole France, and these mouthpieces (cf. Bonnard and Coignard) are always important for the quality of their thought and style. That the " Affair " practically con-verted our author to socialism is apparent from a number of orations and special pleas (collected in *Vers les temps meilleurs*, 1906). But in literature proper this conversion is less visible. Apart from minor works, his remaining years have been spent in composing imaginative interpretations of history, treated either as fiction or as biography. To the latter class belongs the *Vie de Jeanne d'Arc* (1908, but begun twenty years before). Written in the manner of Renan, beautifully unified in tone, this is a reconstruction, half-sympathetic, half-skeptical, of the heroine's environment and personality. Not thoroughly accurate historically, the work explains the atmosphere and birth of a legend. *L'Ile des Pingouins* (1908) is a satirical allegory, a sketch of humanity's development; it is at times as coarse as Rabelais and as bitter as Swift; often obscure in its references, the book yet contains many flashes of genius. *Les Dieux ont soif* (1912), displaying the excesses of the Terror, seems a paradoxical performance on the part of a believer in the Revolution; several of the characters are strongly etched, and private history is well interwoven with that of the nation. *La Révolte des anges* (1914) is anti-Christian, and *Sur la voie glorieuse* (1915) is anti-German.

The message of Anatole France is too complex to be clear. We doubt whether the dilettante has wholly given way to the reformer; he is still too fond of contradiction and too readily disillusioned. Retaining his sympathy for the proletariat, he " passed the sponge of universal raillery " over Church and State. He who loved legends, historical or religious, for their romantic savor, has also mocked at them for their lack of truth. He who decorated the shrine of love has become preoccupied with its biological function. Only two things has he left standing: his own intellect and his artistic competence. These two gifts, in the form of *esprit* and devotion to beauty, are interwoven with his incomparable personal style.[2] The *esprit* appears as compact wit, as delicate or bitter irony, and as the humor that arises from a paradoxical situation. When the female Penguin is seized and inducted into her first garment, she inquires: " Tombe-t-elle bien?" When M. Bergeret grows philosophical, he never addresses his wife but makes brilliant observations to his dog. Paradox is involved in the humor of *Crainquebille*, in the comedy of *Celui qui épousa une femme muette*, and in the situation of *La Révolte des anges*, where the angels become men of the world and the devils become angels. Every situation is enhanced by the *esprit* so characteristic of this author. As for his beauty-worship, that is the trait with which we began and with which we must end. It is in honor of beauty that he finds his most perfect phrases and that he cherishes the fairest images: the image of

---

[2] Which he defined as a compound of "infinite shades of thought."

Dido wandering in the myrtles with her immortal wound; the image of Thaïs, actress and courtesan —

> Immobile, semblable à une statue, mais promenant autour d'elle le paisible regard de ses yeux de violette, douce et fière, elle donnait à tous le frisson tragique de la beauté.

This ideal beauty lives again in *Le Jardin d'Epicure* and haunts the dreams of Bergeret. It is found in superb Pagan flights of fancy, like the vision of Nectaire (Pan) in *La Révolte des anges*. It quickens many exquisite descriptions of nature, whether in the French provinces, in Italy or in the Orient. It is crystallized in short perfect sentences: " Et sur son beau rire un faune presse une grappe de raisin vermeil." It is the most sincere and the most enduring quality of Anatole France, who in matters of thought is a myriad-minded and skeptical Voltairian, but in matters of art remains a faithful Epicurean.

CHAPTER II

IN DRAMA: THE THREE MOVEMENTS

THE three chief dramatic currents towards the end of the century are Naturalistic, psychological and Romantic. But first we should reckon with the destinies of *la pièce bien faite*, which descended from Scribe to Sardou. The well-made play may be defined as a product of artifice rather than art, dependent on incident and formulas rather than on character-study and truth to life. Victorien Sardou (1831–1908), essentially a theatrical expert, used formulas in the manner of Victor Hugo, stage-tricks in the manner of Mr. Belasco, and stage-setting in an original elaborate manner which has since nearly overpowered the modern theater. Sardou wrote about sixty plays, covering an extremely wide range. Some of his **His Two** dramas are serious, but he shines particularly in light **Specialties** comedy and in the big historical " machine." He began by amusing the Second Empire, whose luxury he loved, with such airy trifles as *Pattes de mouche* (1860) and *Nos bons Villageois* (1866). His masterpiece in *vaudeville* is the sparkling *Divorçons* (1880), which extracts merriment from the possibilities of impending divorce laws (see p. 598). These comedies are marked by fertility of invention and by skill in maintaining the interest of the audience. Sardou is at any rate less superficial than Scribe, and a more serious kind of domestic comedy, as exemplified in *Fernande*, is within his scope. Also, *Rabagas* (1872), usually considered his greatest play, exhibits the political demagogue (probably Gambetta) with humor, power and a large background. In the seventies, the versatile writer began the series of semi-historical melodramas with which his name is most frequently associated. The outstanding ones are *Patrie* (1869), *La Haine* (1874), and the three " Doras," (*Dora, Fédora,* and *Théodora*) of which *Fédora* (1882) saw the triumphal advent of Sarah Bernhardt and *Théodora* (1884) marks the introduction

of elaborate stage-settings and costumes.   In this new departure
Sir Henry Irving followed Sardou.   The story of *La Tosca* (1887)
and, in lighter vein, that of *Madame Sans-Gêne* (1893), are
well known; in the latter play, Réjane gave a great characterization of Napoleon's reckless washerwoman.   Sardou continued to
use historical dramas, dealing with the France of the Revolution,
the Italy of *Dante* and the Spain of the Inquisition (*La Sorcière*,
1903). These plays are full of sensational and spectacular
effects and show much cleverness in construction; but within
they are rather hollow.   The dramatist sometimes mingled his
two specialties of *vaudeville* and *mélo*, as in *La Famille Benoîton*
(1865).   He is a skilled tactician of the stage, a " master-builder
of attractive edifices that are not enduring."

A gentlemanly playwright, Edouard Pailleron (1834–99), also
began activities under the Second Empire; but his most notable

Pailleron   dramas were produced later.   In his graceful well-
written comedies, Pailleron depicts the upper social
strata with worldly knowledge and a light touch.   As regards
structure and devices, Pailleron's plots are " well-made," but he
has more elegance than Scribe and seems rather in the literary
tradition of Beaumarchais and Musset.   *L'Etincelle* (1879)
shows how the " spark " of love may be kindled in a woman's
heart.   *La Souris* (1887) stages a ladies' battle for a lover — an
amiable middle-aged Don Juan who succumbs to the charm of
the *ingénue*.   *Le Monde où l'on s'ennuie* (1881) delicately derides
a coterie of blue-stockings and agreeably demonstrates how love
may be superior to learning.   This is Pailleron's most famous
play and is often considered the best light comedy of the century.
It recalls Molière's *Femmes Savantes*.

1. *Naturalism and the Social Drama.*

Naturalistic drama is closely connected with the so-called
théâtre social, which like the *roman social* aims at the portrayal

The   of sociological problems and *conditions* in all their
" Théâtre   diversity.   Balzac, Augier and Dumas *fils* had
Social."   pointed the way; the road was clear, in the last decades of the century, for a succession of plays which should deal
with love in its social aspects (the family, adultery, divorce);

with the confusion of castes and with such groups as the magistracy, doctors and writers, politicians, teachers, business men; with such problems as heredity, the social evil, race-suicide and political corruption. Dozens of people wrote plays along these lines, for this is the most important type of modern drama; Eugène Brieux is its chief representative. But neither Brieux nor Becque could have obtained full recognition save for the exertions of M. Antoine, who as producer and stage-manager founded the Théâtre-Libre (1887–96) and later the Théâtre-Antoine (1897–1906). The effort of the Théâtre-Libre was four-fold: (1) The suppression of the well-made play; (2) realistic stage-settings, naturalness in elocution and pantomime; (3) attacks on the " commercial " theater, the emphasis on a good *ensemble* rather than "stars," and the endeavor to present new playwrights not favored by the subventioned theaters; (4) hence the launching of novelties and of such foreign writers as Ibsen, Hauptmann and Tolstoy. In 1890–95 most of Ibsen was presented at Paris (Théâtre-Libre, Théâtre de l'Œuvre, etc.) and his influence, whether in the direction of Realism or of Symbolism, was considerable. Other Scandinavians, Russians and Germans counted in similar directions. As a Naturalistic movement, the Théâtre-Libre over-emphasized pathology and crime, grossness and pessimism. It preferred sordidness to Sardou. It produced dramas ranging from poetic symbolism to the *pièce rosse* or " tough " play (Becque and Oscar Méténier). It staged a good deal of Zola's fiction and that of the Goncourts. It was illumined by various lesser lights (Céard, Hennique, Rosny, J. Jullien). And it discovered the majority of contemporary dramatists, including Lavedan, Porto-Riche, Curel and Brieux. The regular stage presently claimed most of Antoine's neophytes.

Eugène Brieux (b. 1858) is a man of the people, acquainted with the seamy side of life and a journalist of experience. A "robust paladin," he evinces a complete sincerity, a good sense of fact, a wide and fair handling of social questions. He is the godson of Dumas *fils*, in his blending of reformatory intentions with dramatic technique, to which he sometimes adds the strong " sliced " scenes of Becque. Critics usually make three divisions in the work of Brieux:

and Antoine

Brieux

I. From *Ménages d'artistes* (1890) through *L'Evasion* (1896), a group containing mostly comedy and satire. *La Couvée* is concerned with the training of children, *L'Engrenage* with political corruption, and *Les Bienfaiteurs* is unfavorable to organized charity. *Blanchette* (1892) made Brieux' reputation (*via* Antoine) and is the best play of this period. It presents strong characters and well-knit scenes. The problem revolves around a heroine who has been too well educated for her destiny. The daughter of a village inn-keeper (le Père Rousset), Blanchette has obtained her teaching diploma, but cannot find a position. She remains at home, waiting, and the conflict of the village *milieu* with her ambitions is excellently set forth. She quarrels with Père Rousset, who sends her forth to her disaster; unable to find suitable work, she descends to the depths in one version of the play, but a more moderate "happy ending" installs her, after many tribulations, as the wife of an inferior. The fault of the situation is attributed to the State, which should provide for its trained educators.

II. The second division runs from *Les Trois filles de M. Dupont* (1897) through *Maternité* (1903). Brieux here waxes militant and more pessimistic, while his dramas become definite studies of various environments and professions (cf. Balzac). For example, *Résultat des courses* is a good presentation of lower-class gambling, *Les Remplaçantes* shows the perils of nurses, *Maternité* is a defence of motherhood. In several of these plays, as in the too-famous *Avariés*, it is evident that discussion and reform are occupying Brieux more than straight dramatics. *Les Trois filles de M. Dupont* is better, in its presentation of "chained" women and their limited destinies. But Brieux' masterpiece is *La Robe rouge* (1900), whose title is indicative of the legal profession. Many varieties of judicial rank and character are here developed. The author depicts the magistracy as over-crowded, poorly paid and open to political manipulations. The plot is truly dramatic: a murder has been committed, and since a culprit must be found (for the benefit of the examining magistrate) a false accusation weighs against a peasant, whose wife is put through the "third degree." These inquisitional scenes are common and extremely forceful in Brieux. The peasant's wife, Yanetta, is compelled to acknowledge a former indiscretion, and the husband, though cleared of the charge of murder, loses his domestic happiness and condemns Yanetta. She obtains poetic justice by killing Mouzon, the instigator of the charge and the villain of the plot. Around this central action, other destinies, especially those of the Vagret family, are developed within the main theme of the hard condition of the magistracy. The play, then, happily combines dramatic interest with the study of a particular class.

III. Beginning approximately with *La Déserteuse* (1904) and not yet ended, Brieux' third period is difficult to characterize. The problem too often overrides the play in this last division; yet a calmer and more optimistic note is heard and somewhat wider social questions are treated. *La Française* (1907) supports by discussion rather than by drama the thesis that the French woman is better behaved than is usually supposed by foreigners. *Simone* is interesting technically, as also in its centering of family solidarity around the child;[1] the same moral is found in *Suzette* and *La Déserteuse*. *La Femme seule* (1913) is good drama and equally good feminism. The heroine tries to gain her own bread and is several times defeated by the rivalry or the gallantry of man (cf. *Blanchette*). *Le Bourgeois aux champs* (1914) is an amusing variation on Flaubert's *Bouvard et Pécuchet;* the townsman comes to grief on his farm and the clash of classes is well portrayed.

Brieux' conscientious sincerity, his moral intentions and the comprehensiveness of his social survey are all to his credit. He is broad-minded and earnest, yet with sufficient humor and understanding of human complexities. It is less certain that he makes the most of his dramatic opportunities. Too often he yields to the impulse to talk or to preach; thus the action lags, and the characters fall heavily into the rôles of puppets or mouthpieces. His language is sometimes rough or ungrammatical, but remains as democratic as his subjects and his sympathies. The atmosphere of ugliness or depression which marks certain plays is inherent in the Naturalistic drama. It is still more conspicuous in the brutal though intense work of Octave Mirbeau (1848–

---

[1] This may be considered Brieux' chief "message," since no less than eight plays emphasize the importance of the child.

1917), novelist and dramatist, who wrote *Les mauvais Bergers* (presenting workmen on a strike) and notably *Les Affaires sont les affaires* (1903). This play is in the straight tradition of the money-drama from *Turcaret* to Becque. In Isidore Lechat, Mirbeau fully depicts that peculiarly nineteenth-century type of the predatory millionaire whom Balzac created and whom Dumas *fils* developed (*La Question d'argent*). This type has become worse morally and the presentation is more acrid in Mirbeau. The characters and the financial intrigues are life-like, so that the play is a masterpiece of grim power. With the exception of Mirbeau, undiluted Naturalism was on the decline before the end of the century; the early protégés of Antoine have mostly scattered in other directions, though the technical innovations of the Théâtre-Libre are not forgotten.

2. *Psychology and the " Triangle."*

The second movement in the contemporary drama may be considered as including whatever emphasizes the analysis of

Hervieu character and the psychology of love. The most distinguished of these psychological dramatists was Paul Hervieu (1857–1915); he was also foremost in the domain of high tragedy. He is an artist in sentiment and expression, a rigorous logician in technique, and better than any other modern he recalls the tragic elevation of Racine. These qualities became evident in *Les Tenailles* (1895), which worthily opened the series of his problem-plays. The title (" The Pincers," cf. *Le Dédale* or " The Labyrinth ") indicates a predicament, and Hervieu is fond of showing characters in the clutch of circumstance or individuals conflicting with the law. In this tense tragedy, the " pincers " of matrimony are applied by a hard husband to grip his wife, when she wishes to divorce him and remarry; they are applied by the wife to grip the husband when, ten years later, she forces him to sustain the burden of herself and of her child by a former lover. In each case, the too moderate divorce laws, as Hervieu considers them, operate not for freedom but to compel the bearing of the yoke. He and Brieux differ widely in their views on divorce.

The dramatic swing of the pendulum and the injustice of the

code are again features of *La Loi de l'homme* (1897), in which Hervieu shows himself a convinced feminist. As a dramatist, he

Chief Plays displays too much *esprit de géométrie*, and *L'Enigme* (1901) has almost the rigor of a mathematical puzzle. This tendency is less apparent in *La Course du flambeau* (1901), probably Hervieu's finest play; the main characters are profoundly depicted, the struggles of maternal love are universalized in the high Classic manner, and there is dramatic economy or exact measuring of the means to the end. The title suggests the theme: that the torch of love goes down the ages, just as the doom of sacrifice descends through the generations. Of the three women concerned, the grandmother is devoted to her daughter, Sabine Revel, who in turn gives up everything for her own daughter: an opportunity for remarriage, her honesty in a money transaction, her mother and finally the daughter herself. It is a poignant, cumulative drama. In *Le Dédale* (1903), Hervieu returns to the triangle and to the difficult situation of French women in the matter of divorce. A woman, *divorcée* for adequate reasons, remarries and is then attracted back to her former husband (cf. *Le Berceau* by Brieux). The child appears again as a great influence and ultimately as the solution of the heroine's entanglement; as for the men, they end by killing each other and disappearing over a cliff — a *dénouement* which has been much criticized. Of Hervieu's subsequent plays, *Le Réveil* (1905) and *Connais-toi* (1909) offer the most psychological interest; they both deal with the subconscious or with the dormant depths of character revealed under stress. Hervieu's logical rigor finally yielded place to a more philosophic charity and a mellower dramatic touch. His style becomes progressively clearer, though still at times over-literary; but his best pages maintain a Classic elegance, precision and harmony. His principal idea is that the law is often unjust to individuals, particularly to women. Hervieu is a convinced feminist and seems to commiserate the plight of his tempest-driven heroines. Like the other amorists, he is mainly concerned with the eternal " triangle " and with its possible geometrical variations. But his treatment is refined and skilful.

Georges de Porto-Riche (b. 1849) is also an analyst of love and like Hervieu is more interested in the development of individual temperaments than in general social laws. He is essentially an artist, who has attained an elegant and harmonious manner.

Porto-Riche Beginning with poetic plays, he was soon adopted by Antoine (*La Chance de Françoise*, produced **1888**) and won his reputation through his most characteristic play, *Amoureuse* (**1891**). The theme of this is the clash between an over-fond wife and a too-busy husband; the latter finally allows a lover to profit from his wife's devotion; yet the marital bond remains too strong to be broken. As in Hervieu, the Nietzschean doctrine of the individual's " right to live " appears in this play. The treatment is in the very personal manner of Porto-Riche, combining subtle psychology, graceful style, witty and characteristic dialogue. Similar qualities appear in *Le Passé* (1897), in which the heroine forgives a Don Juan his infidelities for the sake of his charm. The above are drawing-room plays, whereas *Le vieil Homme* (1911) is more romantic and unusual. In the majority of his dramas Porto-Riche depicts men who are light-o'love, fascinating to women and deliberate liars.

François de Curel (b. 1854), an aristocrat by birth and ideas, is interested in morbid psychology, in strong and strange situa-

Curel tions. He is a poet and a Symbolist and betrays the influence of Ibsen. The majority of his plays were produced by Antoine, beginning with *L'Envers d'une sainte* and *Les Fossiles* (both of 1892). The latter play is a masterpiece, though of a somber and painful kind. A father and his son have loved the same woman, who gives birth to a child, the last of the Chantemelles. The rest of this noble family, in one way or another, sacrifice their lives in order that this child may carry on the name. Aristocrats may be immoral and useless " fossils," but — *noblesse oblige*. The love of nature, particularly of ancestral and immemorial forests, is conspicuous in this play, and the author's general message seems to be that long-rooted natural characteristics will ultimately win out. So in *La Fille sauvage* (1902), the barbarous heroine is civilized only to break out with a more deadly ferocity in the end. In *Le Repas du lion* (1897), an aristocrat who has killed a workman tries to make expiation by a life of humanitarian service; but his natural ego is too strong and leads to his undoing. *La*

Nouvelle idole (produced 1899) presents a doctor whose devotion to science leads to disastrous results. In most of these plays Curel has chosen repellent subjects; he is too contemptuous of dramatic laws and technique; but he has an "imaginative strangeness" all his own, and if he often leaves reality he thereby comes the nearer to romance.

Closer to his own period is Maurice Donnay (b. 1860), who began as a cabaret-artist at the Chat-Noir. His first impor-

Donnay tant play was *Amants* (1895), concerning the formation and the rupture of an "affair" between two typical Parisians. In the majority of his plays, light or serious, Donnay appears as an "apologist for free love" (Chandler), an anti-feminist and a dramatist of considerable ability, especially in the depiction of character. *La Douloureuse, L'autre Danger* and *L'Affranchie* are specimens in this manner. He considers wider social questions in *Oiseaux de passage* (1904), and especially in *Le Retour de Jérusalem* (1903), one of his strongest plays. Here it is a question of a *liaison* between a Jewess who has renounced her faith and an aristocratic Gentile; latent differences make the union unhappy. As a dramatist, Donnay has humor and skill, but he lacks profundity. Unlike the chief

And Others psychologists, Henri Lavedan (b. 1859) and Jules Lemaître (1853–1914) do not sound a sufficiently clear individual note to make a lasting impression. Lemaitre is a critic of charm and penetration (see Ch. IV, below). In the drama, he has, to be sure, won · notable successes: *Le Député Leveau* (1890), on the corruption of politics; *Le Pardon* (1895), on reciprocal forgiveness between unfaithful spouses; *Le Massière* (1905), on the studio-world and middle-aged loves. But on the whole Lemaitre has been too versatile to be a great artist. The same is true of Lavedan, who ranges from the easy cynicism of *Le vieux Marcheur* (1899), through the depravity of the *Marquis de Priola* (1902), to the somewhat deliberate idealism of *Le Duel* (1905). The intense patriotism of *Servir* (1913), is conceived in quite a different tone from the satire of *Le Prince d'Aurec*. Lavedan has a tolerant breadth and has won popularity at the expense of concentration and individuality.

3. Romance.

It has been seen that there were romantic elements in the early work of Porto-Riche and throughout the peculiar dramas **Neo-** of Curel. The graceful fancy of Théodore de Ban-**Romanticism** ville found expression in *Gringoire* (historical) and in *Riquet à la Houppe* (*comédie-féerique*); both plays develop the Hugonian antithesis between an ugly body and a beautiful soul. The more heroic strain of Hugo was revived in *La Fille de Roland* (1875) by Henri de Bornier, a drama containing both poetic and patriotic fire. Bornier, Sardou, Catulle Mendès and François Coppée wrote numerous historical plays, many of which suggest the spirit of romance. Coppée (see next chapter) is at his best in *Pour la Couronne* (1895). A faithless Balkan Prince betrays his country and is slain by his own son; the latter shoulders the blame of the treachery rather than accuse his dead father. The character of Militza, the gipsy girl who loves the hero, is very winning, and some of her speeches are in excellent verse. Romantic also are the majority of the plays of Jean Richepin (b. 1849), whose bohemian soul finds expression in *Le Flibustier* (Breton characters), in *Le Chemineau* (1897) where the hero is a cheerful follower of the open road, and in *Les Truands* (1899), which resuscitates the medieval vagabonds of *Notre-Dame*. Thus Neo-Romanticism has many interesting plays to its credit, and Rostand's *Cyrano de Bergerac* is not an isolated phenomenon.

We must turn aside for a moment to consider the work of the Belgian mystic, Maurice Maeterlinck (b. 1862). For him **Maeterlinck** the spirit of romance " dwelt in a Northern land." Born and educated at Ghent he has passed most of his life on his Flemish estate; but as a youth he brought to Paris a taste for dreamy legends and fairy-tales. Then he came under the influence of the Symbolists and of Shakespeare; his early dramas are all symbolic and his first play, *La Princesse Maleine* (1889), caused him to be hailed as the " Belgian Shakespeare." What we find rather in this work is a brooding sense of mystery, of fatality and of " inexorable death." The feminine villain strangles Maleine and is in turn killed by Prince Hjalmar, who then commits suicide. But the bald plot is never the thing with Maeterlinck, who makes us drink deep of symbolism, moodiness and atmosphere. The whole somber castle gives an environment of terror and suspense. The characters are " strange," obsessed, dominated by the powers of Nature, who vouchsafes only sinister symbols and presentiments. Maeterlinck's pathetic puppets are usually a prey to inconsecutive movements and desires (hence the inconsecutive scenes) and wait passively for the Intruder, Death (cf. *La Mort*, 1913). A number of one-act plays emphasize this attitude. In *L'Intruse* (1890), a family expects the death of one of their number. They do not mention their fear, which is entirely atmospheric, expressed by monotonous question and answer about apparently irrelevant things. But the "frisson de l'invisible" mounts through the increasing uneasiness of the blind grandfather, until the fated end. *Les Aveugles* (1890) further stresses the terrors of the unseen, and *Les Sept Princesses* (1891) is equally " Maeterlinckian " in its fairy-tale background. This vein recurs in *Ariane et Barbebleue*, in the tower-scene of *Aglavaine et Sélysette,* and of course in *L'Oiseau bleu.* Such allegorical and fanciful episodes are quite in line with Maeterlinck's Symbolism, which should now be definitely characterized. Let us choose *Pelléas et Mélisande* (1893), the best-known of the dramas which deal with misty events and people in some uncharted land. This play has quite a distinctive plot, namely the Paolo and Francesca situation. Golaud is the old husband, Pelléas the youthful lover and brother, Mélisande the " strange " young bride. But never did a play sound less "triangular." Passion is only vaguely suggested, and the three love scenes emphasize symbolic values: *Mélisande* loses her marriage ring in a fountain; she lets down her wonderful hair which envelops and delights Pelléas; and reality takes on the spaciousness and poetry of a dream. Similarly, in *Aglavaine et Sélysette* (1896), where it is a question of outgoing and incoming sweetheart, the mild Sélysette will throw herself from a tower to make way for her rival. The symbol is found in the slow sinking of the sun indicating the approach of death; and the dialogue, as elsewhere in Maeterlinck, keeps rhythm with the action. In all these early plays, as also in *Intérieur, La Mort de Tintagiles,* and so on, the emphasis is on subconscious intuition, on silence, terror, death and

what the author called the "static drama." It is to his credit
that he has drawn, psychologically speaking, more progression
and action from this method than might be anticipated. The
style of his prose is indubitably poetic, but the dialogue, in its
wilful simplicity and repetition, sounds too often like an Ollen-
dorff grammar and has lent itself readily to parody. Also, a
certain obscurity of intention and effort must be recognized.
But the author always keeps our imaginations quivering.

It may be that Maeterlinck grew tired of contending with the
difficulties of his peculiar form. At any rate, in 1902, he made
His Second a distinct shift. *Monna Vanna* marks an attempt at
Phase   "legitimate" and fairly plain historical drama. The
enveloping action is that of the fifteenth-century feud between
Florence and Pisa. Guido Colonna commands the Pisans and
the Florentine general, Prinzivalle, insists that Guido's wife shall
give herself to him in order to deliver her fellow-countrymen.
When Vanna comes alone to his tent, he suddenly reveals himself
as an idealistic and respectful lover. Returning to her husband's camp, Vanna cannot convince him of her innocence, finds
him too jealous and egotistical and decides to escape with
Prinzivalle. Barring a certain lack of skill in "preparations,"
the drama is progressive and interesting. But more interesting to
the author is the psychological problem, concerning the "greater
love" of Prinzivalle. The total effect is somewhat bewildering.
Marie Magdeleine (1910) is also more like the conventional
drama and offers a similar problem. The lovely miracle-play of
Sœur Béatrice, a medieval legend, is again more characteristic
of the earlier Maeterlinck, and in *L'Oiseau bleu*, the poet-
dramatist returns to the allegorical field which he has made
peculiarly his own. Two children, Tyltyl and Mytyl go forth
to seek the bird of happiness, which they ultimately find at
home. Their adventures, the symbolic persons and scenes they
meet with are beautifully rendered. It is an optimistic allegory;
the author is no longer oppressed by "nightmares"; and since
there are no impassable barriers to the next world, "il n'y a
pas de morts." The dead live again in our memories. In the
sequel, *Les Fiançailles* (1918), the children have grown up and
are able to cope with Destiny. So the two former bugbears,
Death and Fatality, are finally conquered in Maeterlinck's

widening view. He has also given expression to his philosophy in such books as *Le Trésor des humbles, La Sagesse et la Destinée, La Mort.* But his most individual contribution to latter-day literature is in the misty Romanticism of his symbolic plays.

More in the French Romantic tradition is the work of Edmond Rostand (1868–1918). A man of delicate health and temperament, his life was short and his period of productivity was shorter still. After winning his great success, he was made a member of the Academy (1901) and soon retired to his charming home in the Pyrenees, where he spent practically the remainder of his life. He began with a volume of rather trivial verse (*Les Musardises,* 1890), in which he displays much virtuosity as a rhymester of Banville's school. Of his half-dozen plays, the first three are comparatively slight. In the manner of Musset and recalling the subject of *A quoi rêvent les jeunes filles, Les Romanesques* (1894) has yet a pretty wit and charm of its own. It presents two young people who long for distant loves and adventures. The play is a gentle satire on romance by a Romanticist. A higher poetic note is sounded in *La Princesse lointaine* (1895). This dramatizes the story of Rudel the troubadour, a lover of the Princess of Tripoli, whom he has never seen. As a dying man he sails for Tripoli, where the princess will soothe his last hours. Here Rostand adds a complication to the legend; the troubadour's lady and his best friend fall in love with each other; but they are saved from treachery and the princess finally goes to Rudel. The legend is picturesquely handled, with developments that recall the Tristan story. The play has movement and sentiment. Very sentimental is *La Samaritaine* (1897), in its mingling of earthly and heavenly love. The episode of the Samaritan woman is retold, largely in Biblical language, but with the addition of a good second act, in which Photine proselytizes for Christ.

None of these plays foretold the power and success of *Cyrano de Bergerac — comédie heroïque —* whose first representation (December 28, 1897) was the most notable *première* since that of *Hernani.* Again it seemed that Romantic emotion was conquering Paris. Seasoned critics like Faguet declared that *Cyrano* portended a renaissance of the poetic drama, while others like Lemaître saw in it rather an aftermath and

Rostand (margin note)

" Cyrano " (margin note)

a derivative pseudo-revival, which could not set back the clock of time. Historically, the latter view seems correct; it is also true that Rostand was not greatly original and that he owed a great deal to the devices and inspiration of Hugo and even of Dumas *père*. Nevertheless, *Cyrano* in itself is a splendid Romantic drama and one of the great plays of the century. It is also the author's masterpiece, because here he makes the best union of poetry and dramatics in a subject that was peculiarly well suited to his genius. His own leaning towards the *précieux* and towards purple patches is here justified by the character of his hero and the atmosphere of the period treated. Cyrano is a high-flown lover, a swaggerer and duellist, capable of everything from burlesque to rare self-sacrifice. The central theme, by which Cyrano Quixotically serves the love of another man —

> Je serai ton esprit, tu seras ma beauté —

is boldly and successfully handled. The high moments, such as the balcony-scene, the death of Christian and the autumnal melancholy of the *dénouement*, show a happy blending of sentiment with dramatic power. The historical coloring (c. 1640) is ample and excellent. The play constitutes a harmony within itself and with its author.

L'Aiglon (1900) is not such a masterpiece; it shows a weaker and more confused inspiration; but it does not fail to gain **Other Plays** admiration in many respects. The story of the "eaglet," Napoleon's son who would fain be a Napoleon, offers pathetic and psychological opportunities, which Rostand has certainly seized. On the other hand, the dramatic movement, the swift spontaneous action of *Cyrano*, is lacking. Such a tendency would be natural, granted the hesitant nature of the hero, the cumbering atmosphere of the Austrian court, and the numerous secondary schemes and people. The play remains, none the less, too long, too elaborate, and too monotonous. Brilliant scenes and tirades almost redeem this lack of progression, especially the epic scene on the plain of Wagram, in which the dead battalions come to life before the vision of the young prince. His character, the opposition of dream and action in his nature, remains the best feature of the play.

These two dramas, sponsored and personified respectively by the great Coquelin and by Sarah Bernhardt, had swept Europe and America. People waited eagerly to see what Rostand would do next. As a matter of fact, ten years of silence intervened — and then *Chantecler* appeared (1910).

A plaintive and hectic note had already been audible in *L'Aiglon* and (probably for reasons of health) is exaggerated to the point of peevishness in *Chantecler*. This drama lacks moral and dramatic balance. It symbolizes the pathos of an inner struggle towards beauty and nobility, but this excellent feature is partially marred by the author's failings and conspicuous mannerisms. The *données* include the idea of a cock who not only rules his barnyard but, as poet and prophet, causes the sun to rise with his crowing. He falls in love with a hen-pheasant (the Eternal Feminine), who leads him to the Guinea-hen's " five-o'clock " tea. A blackbird typifies worldly wit, a nightingale the power of song, owls and toads the ugly side of life. Thus the play is a symbolic allegory and has links with Aristophanes, the *Roman du Renard* and La Fontaine. But unlike the last-named, Rostand has not kept the balance between the animal and the human side; his figures are too palpably and too highly human, parading under skins and feathers. Unconvincing on the stage, the play well bears reading and has many fine passages; yet the *esprit* and the tendency to puns which the cock berates in the blackbird, are too conspicuous in the language throughout. *Chantecler* is a mixture of too many different things (allegory, satire, extravaganza), and " nous sommes loin de la verve éclatante et primesautière de *Cyrano*."

Rostand's influence is visible in certain *drames* by Catulle Mendès (*Scarron*, etc.) and in such graceful fairy-comedies as **His Talent** *La Fleur merveilleuse* (1910) by Zamacoïs. But ⸱⸱ Rostand's imitators chiefly serve to show his own superiority. The more obvious elements in his power and appeal are the following: First, a clean and brilliant wit, at its best capable of satiric pungency or of delicious turns of speech; at the worst descending to puns and verbal pyrotechnics. Second, a capacity, largely Hugonian in its origin, for dramatic situations, suspensions and well-combined *coups de théâtre* — examples are the duel in Act I of *Cyrano*, the dramatic shifts

between loyalty and love in Act III of *La Princesse lointaine.*
Third, Rostand's personal response to the quality of idealistic
love and of chivalrous deeds; this underlies the *panache* or
" swagger " of Cyrano and appears in the author's panegyric on
Don Quixote. Finally, a poetic power compact of imagery,
sentiment, admirable phrasing; a power that ranges from a
winning and tender pathos, as in the *finales* of his best plays, to
the superb vision of Wagram in *L'Aiglon* and the lyric sweep of
his balcony scene in *Cyrano.* This talent has left its mark on
many notable single lines as well as on the longer speeches of
Cyrano and the Eaglet — passages that are likely to endure
when the voices of carping critics have ceased forever.

CHAPTER III

IN POETRY: SENTIMENT AND SYMBOLISM

In the last decades of the century, the most notable Parnassian poet was Heredia, whose work has already been treated (Bk. VII, Ch. III). Nearly every writer of verse, men as various as Anatole France, Coppée and Verlaine, began by a volume in the Parnassian manner, which shows the profound influence of this school; yet the revolt against Realism included a revolt against the cold marmoreal perfection of Leconte de Lisle. The chief dissidents among the younger generation were either sentimental poets like Sully Prudhomme and Coppée or the founders of the new school who were known as *les Décadents* or *les Symbolistes.*

Sully Prudhomme (1839–1907) was a youth of delicate health and a meditative disposition. He passed through Parnassus and Sully through an unfortunate love-affair which gave him Prudhomme the better part of his lyrical inspiration. Both influences are found in such early poems as *Les Solitudes* (1869). His best volume is *Les vaines Tendresses* (1875). His growing reputation caused him to be elected to the Academy in 1881. From now on his life was filled with conscientious thought and effort. He published two long semi-didactic poems, *La Justice* (1878) and *Le Bonheur* (1888). He received, in 1901, the Nobel prize for literary excellence.

Not greatly original, Sully Prudhomme is the most representative poet of his period. He reflects the chief lyrical tendencies of the century: sentiment like that of Lamartine, philosophic poems somewhat in the manner of Vigny, statuesque Parnassian imitations and hard brilliant sonnets. He reflects particularly and with great conscientiousness the " age of science and doubt "; the struggle between an ethical spirituality and the unresponsive universe deeply impregnated his thought. His primary poetic qualities are sensibility, tenderness, melancholy; and the philosophic " meditation " tempered with sentiment seems to be his *forte.* Sensibility is the most conspicuous element in his earliest work — *Stances et poèmes* (1865) and *Les Epaves* (published posthumously in 1908). In these volumes the poet sounds the whole gamut of disappointed passion, from direct jealousy and baffled desire, through the mournfulness of memories, down to moving suggestions of the happiness that might have been. Some preciosity and infelicities of expression occur in his first volume, which, however, already gives evidence of great skill in *Le Vase brisé,* his most famous poem. *Les vaines Tendresses* would indicate by its significant title that the poet is seeking a wider and less personal expression of feeling. He philosophizes his emotion in such admirable lyrics as *La Beauté* and *Sur la mort;* but the philosophy remains pessimistic. Similarly the sonnets of *Les Epreuves* are conceived on an objective plane and show a most artistic mingling of thought and sentiment. As for *Les vaines Tendresses,* that volume well illustrates several of Sully Prudhomme's gifts; for example, his artistic use of the refrain in the poem called *Ressemblance;* he cares for a girl or he finds her melancholy-minded or she passes on her way, all because:

> Vous ressemblez à ma jeunesse.

This orderly symmetrical construction, recalling Gautier and much admired by Gautier, is very frequent with Sully Prudhomme. Again, his capacity for composing striking lines and couplets may be illustrated from the same volume:

> Je t'aime en attendant mon éternelle épouse;

or witness the declaration that for the happiness of poets,

> Il leur faut une solitude
> Où voltige un baiser.

Sully Prudhomme's delicacy of treatment is marked throughout his work. This delicacy is often like the brush of a bee's wing or the coloring of a wild flower, as where he demands:

> Comment fais-tu les grands amours,
> Petite ligne de la bouche?

It occasionally runs into over-delicacy or preciosity, for instance, when he declares that he honors in the writer's pen (*la plume*) a recollection of the bird's soaring wing. But he naturally strengthened and sobered his vocabulary as he matured, and his later sonnets show a fine taste in diction and a masterly impulsion in their movement. It is not surprising that the sonnet-form was a favorite with this poet, from *Les Epreuves* through *La Justice* (which is entirely written in sonnets). As Lemaître early pointed out, these sonnets are usually composed upon sustained metaphors (or symbols), with the application splendidly developed.

As with the sonnet, so with Sully Prudhomme's entire work: from the sentiment, he generalizes the idea or the conflict, then **His Ideas** finds the concrete embodiment. Thus his best work seems to lie in those fields where his personal melancholy is swayed to a larger expression and where his spirit comes into grave conscious strife with the ever-waiting problems. For most of us this tendency is best voiced in his lyrics. His two big philosophic poems, or allegories, *La Justice* and *Le Bonheur* deal respectively with the idea that man's moral order may be imposed upon the universe and with the ideal of service as making for the best happiness. The narrative value of these poems is not great, and they are not free from prosing and incoherence; but they contain thought, faith and fine lyrical interludes. The poet's chief message seems to lie in his insistence on the necessity for idealism combined with reverence for natural law. His versification is simple and conservative, claiming none of the later licenses. In thought, feeling and form he can be readily apprehended by Anglo-Saxon readers.

Sentimental poetry is also the province of François Coppée (1842–1908). He was a poor boy and learned in the Latin Quarter **Coppée** that sympathy with humble life which is his outstanding trait. His lean years lasted until after 1870, when a series of dramatic successes made his fame. Coppée was an assiduous playwright and a short-story writer of some note; but his real contributions to literature are in the field of poetry. He too learned technique from the Parnassians, dedicating *Le Reliquaire* (1866) to Leconte de Lisle; then he declared himself in favor of more emotion and warmth than the Parnassians possessed. This warmth is found in the three chief aspects of Coppée's work: love-poetry, stories in verse, and records of humble life. The first kind is illustrated by *Les Intimités*, which gives, in *tableaux,* a fairly complete lover's progress, and by *L'Exilée,* written to a Norwegian girl. The narrative poem of *Olivier* is a kind of *Rolla* brought up to date, and indeed Coppée has much of Musset's sentiment and grace. His love-lyrics show sincerity, charm and simplicity in the midst of complications. Many of his well-known *chansons* (for example, the lines beginning "Vous aurez beau faire et beau dire") belong in this group. His versified tales (*La Tête de la Sultane,* or *La Grève des forgerons)* are numerous and show much skill. But most characteristic of Coppée is the collection called *Les Humbles* (1872), in which the "short and simple annals of the poor" are given sympathetic expression. Coppée here follows the Wordsworthian theory and the example of Sainte-Beuve; but his Parisian scenes are more effective than those of "Joseph Delorme," and his technique is better. It is in line with the Realistic movement that Coppée should dwell on the fortunes of the shabby-genteel, of nursemaids, keepers of *kiosques,* and even of grocers —

       C'était un tout petit épicier de Montrouge.

The bald simplicity of this line suggests Coppée's limitations as a poet.

Impassivity and Parnassian technique were definitely rejected by the "Symbolistes" and the "Décadents," who constitute the **Symbolism** most significant school of the *fin de siècle.* Symbolism in the wider sense, as the concrete embodiment of an idea or emotion, is nothing new in French literature and may be found in the poetry of Vigny and Hugo as well as in the fiction of Daudet. The ultra-modern use of the word has been illustrated in connection with Maeterlinck (see preceding chapter); recent poets are "Symbolistic" in so far as they prefer vague *suggestion* to clear statement and in so far as they suggest mystery and magic by the use of haunting music and shadowy images. It is interesting to note that the Symbolists are mostly of exotic origin (Belgian, American or Greek) and that their effects seem more nearly allied to the spirit of English poetry than to the clear ethos of the French. Wilful impressionism and subjectivity often make their work obscure and artificial; but at its best Symholism added new and rich sensations to latter-day poetry. Protesting against all forms of Realism, preferring the foreign influence of the English Pre-Raphaelites and of Wagner, the school began to be formed shortly after 1870 and reached its apogee about 1885. Its members were then styled *Décadents* by the critics, and Verlaine was willing to adopt the term; but Jean Moréas, a Greek, suggested the nomenclature of " Symbolists," which is more widely inclusive and which has prevailed. Yet historically it seems best to consider the followers of Verlaine as *les Décadents* and the followers of Mallarmé as more narrowly *les Symbolistes*. (The English terms, " Symbolism " and " Symbolists," may be used of the whole movement.) The most important members of the (joint) school were Paul Verlaine as their chief poet and Stéphane Mallarmé as their chief law-giver; men of foreign birth like Moréas, Rodenbach and Verhaeren, Stuart Merrill and Vielé-Griffin; wild men like Arthur Rimbaud, Jules Laforgue and other " poètes maudits "; Gustave Kahn, Henri de Régnier and others still living. Not all of the above poets were consistent Symbolists, and many lesser names could be added to the list. The boundaries in which they moved were naturally elastic. They used certain new journals for their propaganda (*La Renaissance,* later *La Plume,* still later the *Mercure de France*), they included theoreticians like Mallarmé or Gustave Kahn, and they effected a considerable revolution against the laws of French versification. We can consider only a few of the most prominent poets.

Paul Verlaine (1844–1896) was not only the leader among the " Décadents "; he was also the greatest poet of the whole **Verlaine** school, and stands out as a distinct if erratic personality. He was an inspired singer of vagabond emotions, in character an " enfant de Bohème," a person of disorderly life who divided his time between cafés, prisons, and hospitals. He offers strange alternations of sensuality and mysticism. The naïve and winning note in his religious poems would lead us to approve his conversions, except for their ephemeral character. Totally unfitted for domesticity, Verlaine deeply loved his wife, who inspired his best poems of sentiment; but when this *grande passion* reached its end in a separation, he turned to lesser and baser loves, frankly sensual. His head was like that of Socrates

— but Socrates turned into a satyr, worshiping Venus and Bacchus. When drunk, the poet would quarrel with his friends, among whom was the grotesque and sinister figure of Arthur Rimbaud. This ultra-Symbolist had a warping influence upon Verlaine, causing the final rupture with his wife as well as the longest of his imprisonments.

Verlaine, like many others, began with a Parnassian volume, *Poèmes saturniens* (1866). The poetry here is mostly objec-

His Work   tive and descriptive; it also echoes Baudelaire in an ironic " saturnine " note, together with a taste for subtle and morbid (*macabre*) sensations. The distinct chiseling of outlines is in contrast to Verlaine's later manner, which has the deliberate vagueness of Symbolism. A delightful volume of *Fêtes galantes* (1869), after Watteau, incorporates eighteenth-century art and grace. In this stanza from *Clair de lune,* the poet resuscitates the ghosts of the old régime in terms that fit his own vagabond Muse:

> Your soul is as a moonlit landscape fair,
> Peopled with maskers delicate and dim,
> That play on lutes and dance and have an air
> Of being sad in their fantastic trim.

La Bonne Chanson (1870), written in honor of his wife, celebrates the intoxication of their engagement and honeymoon; it repre-sents the transition from objective poetry to personal sentiment. This was Verlaine's favorite volume and has genuine lyric feeling. His *Romances sans paroles* (1874) mark a revolutionary date in the history of Symbolism and reveal a new musical manner —

> De la musique avant toute chose,

and the power of suggestion —

> Car nous voulons la Nuance encor,
> Pas la Couleur, rien que la Nuance.
> (*Art poétique*)

The *Romances* are full of Symbolistic impressionism, an elusive mixture of sensations and moods. Verlaine's double conversion, religious and poetical, is of this period. He became a fervent Catholic, a believer, if not a consistent practitioner. His faith is emotional and mystical rather than intellectual or active;

but it produced some ardent religious outbursts which figure in the "delicate and penetrating" volume called *Sagesse* (1881). His poetry has now become completely Symbolistic (observe the lines beginning "Vous voilà, vous voilà, pauvres bonnes pensées"), and the theory here manifest has been thus summarized: this "versified music . . . would do more than accompany the idea; it would evoke the sensation, the memory and the true correspondence, as a perfume represents . . . visions and images." Baudelaire is evidently behind this doctrine of "Correspondences." But where Baudelaire and Gautier had appealed mainly to the eye, the Symbolists (in a wider sense) appeal primarily to the ear and add the element of haunting melody to French poetics. On this acount and because of its religious values, *Sagesse* is Verlaine's finest volume. *Jadis et naguère* (1884), as the title indicates, is a selection from his various phases and tendencies. It is his last important volume. Thereafter his work becomes more and more "décadent," and need not be considered here.

Lacking any sustained moral sense, Verlaine vibrates from indulgence to repentance and back again; he reacts to real emotion after mere sensation, and records both experiences with equal frankness. His naïve sincerity is a chief trait; also Verlaine is essentially the musical impressionist of his time. Many of his verses have a great charm, due to the personal wayward touch, which is often winning, pure and delightful, freely and appropriately expressed. His charm, his sincerity, his power of harmonious suggestion make Verlaine a true poet. Such a lyric as *L'Heure exquise* conveys all his best qualities:

> La lune blanche
> Luit dans les bois,
> De chaque branche
> Part une voix
> Sous la ramée . . .
>
> O bien-aimée!
>
> L'étang reflète,
> Profond miroir,
> La silhouette
> Du saule noir
> Où le vent pleure.
>
> Rêvons, c'est l'heure.

Un vaste et tendre
Apaisement
Semble descendre
Du firmament
Que l'astre irise . . .

C'est l'heure exquise!

Standing for a spontaneous and most personal expression, Verlaine derives the principle of originality from emotion rather **His Poetics** than from a reasoned art. His *Art poétique*, already quoted, is averse to declamation ("Prends l'élo- quence et tords-lui le cou") and is equally averse to abstract thought and *esprit;* these qualities are merely "littérature"; Verlaine prefers dreamy twilight suggestion to logical statement or composition. So any one of his *Romances* will have a musical rather than a logical unity. His poetics, then, are based on the belief that verse should be rendered extremely supple, in order to reflect directly the soul and the mood. But he and his circle stop short of *le vers libre.* The Alexandrine, however, acquires the greatest possible liberty: the medial and the final caesuras can fall on the most insignificant syllables (including mute *e's*); free *enjambement* and weak rimes put little emphasis on the end of a line; masculine and feminine lines need no longer alternate, and Verlaine affects *l'Impair* or an uneven number of syllables in his verse (cf. Swinburne); he allows assonances, tone-color, onomatopeia and repetends (cf. Poe and the last stanza in *L'Heure exquise*); finally, three-fold divisions (*ter- naires*) are frequent in his Alexandrines.

Verlaine was elected "Prince des Poètes" at the death of Leconte de Lisle (1894); Mallarmé was Verlaine's successor in this title.[1] The latter's rôle was scarcely that of a *chef d'école,* whereas Mallarmé had a really formative influence on many poets. For convenience, however, and in spite of the fact that the same men would sometimes frequent Verlaine's cafés and Mallarmé's "Tuesdays," we may distinguish between the "Verlainiens" and the "Mallarméens." The former would in- clude, according to A. Barre, both the "Mélancoliques" and the

---

[1] At the death of Mallarmé (1898), Léon Dierx was elected "prince," and after him Paul Fort (see Epilogue). The system was usually a voting-contest conducted through various newspapers and magazines.

"Excentriques"; melancholy were Samain, Rodenbach, and Maeterlinck; eccentric or "Poètes maudits" were Corbière, Rimbaud, Jammes and others. All of them were "Décadents," and were not ashamed of the fact.

The only important poet of Verlaine's immediate circle was Arthur Rimbaud (1854?–91), the evil genius of the Verlaine

Rimbaud household. A savage and singular prodigy, he wrote all his poetry in his teens, inflicted himself upon Paris for a few years, then disappeared adventurously into the wilds of Africa. He wrote only a few small volumes — *Une Saison en enfer* ("psychological autobiography") and *Les Illuminations* (prose-poems). His two most notable poems (*Poésies complètes*, 1895) are *Le Bateau ivre*, a sustained metaphor about a wandering bark which suffered from Baudelairian nostalgia; and the famous *Sonnet des voyelles*, which states the doctrine of color in sounds:

A noir, E blanc, I rouge, U vert, O bleu, voyelles . . .

In this notion of tone-color, in his deliberate naïveté and his fantastic eccentricity, Rimbaud is Décadent; but he is nearer the school of Mallarmé (cf. René Ghil) in his partial use of *vers libre*, in his compressed syntax and wilful obscurity, as also in his interesting habit of coördinating closely images and suggestions around one main metaphor.

Francis Jammes (b. 1868), a Méridional and bucolic poet, is the heir of Rimbaud in his emphasis on naïveté; the instinctive **And other** is for him the main source of poetry and truth. **"Décadents"** But he belongs to a more recent and contemporary school in his use of *vers libre* and in his externality. He leaves his "soul" alone to write, in allegory or narrative, of objects, animals and people; of paving-stones, donkeys and humble farmers in the South (cf. *De L'Angélus de l'aube à l'Angélus du soir*, 1898). After his conversion, Jammes writes of Nature as the manifestation of God (*Les Géorgiques chrétiennes*, 1912). Much of his work is realistic, prosaic and dull. More truly poetic is the form of the "Mélancoliques," Albert Samain (1858–1900) and Georges Rodenbach (1855–98), who import into France reminiscences of their Flemish and Belgian origins. Both of these poets are inspired by the dead past, and both strive to fuse intimately their souls with past beauty; in that respect they are Symbolistic, and they are Décadents in the mournful and anemic quality of their utterances. Samain has drawn charming eighteenth-century vignettes, of a delicate fantasy recalling Verlaine's *Fêtes galantes*. Such vignettes are found in *Au Jardin de l'Infante* (1893), which also contains many scenes from the faded grandeur of Spain:

> Mon âme est une infante en robe de parade . . . [2]

But Samain's form is regularly Parnassian (cf. *Aux Flancs du vase*, 1898), and he fills this mold with his plaintive minor strains. Georges Rodenbach lived at Brussels and wrote hauntingly of *Bruges-la-morte*, a prose-work of 1892. Among his poetic volumes are *Le Foyer et les Champs* and *Les Tristesses*. As in the case of Samain, Rodenbach's delicate health left its traces on his " art indubitablement mièvre, fluide et décadent " (Vielé-Griffin).

The leadership which Verlaine rarely asserted was wielded by Stéphane Mallarmé (1842–98), idealist, theorist and professor. Mallarmé taught French in London and English in Paris and the provinces. He had some contact with the Pre-Raphaelites and with the Provençal poets (see p. 609). His conversation and his personal magnetism attracted a number of young men to the cause of Symbolism. Otherwise he led an extremely retiring and self-centered life. Highly cultivated, an aesthete even to the point of publishing a magazine of fashion, his ingrowing talent finally turned to great obscurity and sterility. He published little, mostly in scattered form (collected *Vers et prose*, 1893). *L'Après-Midi d'un faune* was printed in 1876, but had little fame until Debussy's music was supported by Nijinski's dancing. The well-named prose *Divagations* are of 1897.

For Verlaine poetry meant emotion and spontaneity; for Mallarmé it was a conscious art, and its chief substance was intellectual. The Platonic Idea (*la Pensée*) of an emotion, not

---

[2] This is the kind of thing derided in that delightful parody on Symbolism, *Les Déliquescences d'Adoré Floupette* (1885):

> Je voudrais que mon ame fût
> Aussi roide qu'un affût,
> Aussi remplie qu'un vieux fût.

the thing itself, was to be approached and adumbrated. The approach is infinite, the Absolute unattainable, and so Mallarmé, like certain heroes of Balzac's, spoils his work by too much devotion. Poe, whom he translated (*Ulalume*, *Le Corbeau*), and Baudelaire, whom he imitated, encouraged his hyperaesthesia. Despairing of plain words as an adequate medium, Mallarmé, like Verlaine, took refuge in their Symbolic and musical allusiveness. This is the chief point of agreement between the two schools. But Mallarmé, with his thoroughgoing intellect, held that each line of a poem must contribute to the whole symphonic effect: a poem must be an enigma for the vulgar, chamber-music for the initiated; further, the chief Idea or metaphor must be attended by numerous clustering minor images, which chime in with the central theme; and these analogies are, in his later work, crowded together with such compression as to break the molds of syntax and violate every principle of clearness. An example of this last point may be found in the first line of *Le Tombeau d'Edgar Poë*:

> Tel qu'en Lui-même enfin l'éternité le change,
> Le Poète suscite avec un glaive nu
> Son siècle épouvanté de n'avoir pas connu
> Que la mort triomphait dans cette voix étrange.

(The last three lines may partly clarify the first). *L'Après-Midi d'un faune* illustrates the process of adumbrating the Idea. In a manner which recalls Browning's *Caliban upon Setebos*, a faun mutters his postmeridial longings; it is "un rêve de désir longuement raconté," but these are very shadowy desires, the nymphs are not real, and the faun ultimately resolves his dream in music — as Mallarmé would do. Again, the clustered and condensed metaphor, the sustaining symbol of the poem may be illustrated by the following quotation:[3]

> Un cygne d'autrefois se souvient que c'est lui
> Magnifique, mais qui, sans espoir, se délivre
> Pour n'avoir pas chanté la région où vivre
> Quand du stérile hiver a resplendi l'ennui. . . .

In short, the swan, typifying the cold and sterile poet, now regrets his sterility, but still holds high his head. The preference

---

[3] It will be observed that this poet's versification is strictly Parnassian. He takes no liberties in that respect.

for white and glacial images, displayed in this sonnet, is evident also in the dramatic fragment called *Hérodiade;* the heroine has a chilly charm and a cold elaboration not unlike that of Salammbô.

All this abstruseness may seem out of place, but such is the soul of Mallarmé. Like each of his poems, Mallarmé himself offers a fascinating problem. How far will the future justify his belief that a piece of verse may be completely orchestrated? How far can suggestion replace direct speech? The writer, we know, has to struggle with a vulgarized medium, in contrast to the musician. How far is it possible to lift everyday language, Symbolically —

> Donner un sens plus pur aux mots de la tribu,

and by apposition and ellipsis, drown ordinary syntax in order that the ideal Words may emerge?

Mallarmé's theory was clearer and more fertile than his practice. The questions just enounced attracted a whole band of young disciples, who frequented his " Tuesdays "; among these were such poets as Jules Laforgue, Jean Moréas, Gustave Kahn, Henri de Régnier, F. Vielé-Griffin, Paul Claudel and others. Since individualism is characteristic of the movement, it naturally broke up into smaller movements: an " Ecole symbolique et harmoniste " was formed with René Ghil and Stuart Merrill as leaders, and later we find the name of Emile Verhaeren in a " philosophico-instrumentist " group; also Moréas broke loose and established his " Ecole Romane " (1891). More or less connected with the Symbolists were such men as the Comte Robert de Montesquiou (the original of Huysmans' Des Esseintes and, it is said, of the Peacock in Rostand's *Chantecler*); and Léon Dierx (1838–1912), third " Prince des Poètes," whose distinguished and dreamy verses — *Les Lèvres closes, Les Amants* — largely antedate Symbolism and are of a Parnassian cast.

Let us consider a few of these poets. No other Parnassian Symbolist is of the caliber of Mallarmé. But with Gustave Kahn (b. 1859), we reach the theory and practice of *le vers libre,* as it has since so abundantly flourished.

Free Verse

Neither the theories of a certain Della Rocca (a Peruvian) nor the " dislocations " of Rimbaud and others can deprive Kahn of his proper credit: he is the inventor of modern free verse, although his kind of free verse is not quite what Americans understand by the term. Kahn was an enterprising critic and fighter, who founded several reviews and pushed his theories with a will. His point of departure was that the line (*le vers*) consists not of measured syllables, but of metrical units — that is, single words or clauses of varying length. Hence definite line-lengths are unessential. The same principle holds good for the strophe, which should be " ondoyante et libre." Kahn does not wholly abolish mute *e*'s, nor does he abolish rime when rime is convenient; he allows assonanced endings, internal rimes and repetends. The symmetry of verse is gone, but Kahn maintains that its distinctive rhythm and cadence remain; he admits that his free verse borders very closely on prose and that a period of anarchy has begun — because the " rhythme propre " for Kahn may be improper for any one else. His chief volumes illustrate these tendencies. *Les Palais nomades* (1887) is based on the charming idea of open-air dreaming, and the volume has been called " aussi idéalement vagabond que *La Maison du Berger* " (Mendès). Original and abundant metaphors adorn the *Chansons d'amant* (1891) and *La Pluie et le beau temps* (1895). Fresh figures and quick-changing colors decorate *Le Livre d'Images* (1897). This and subsequent volumes contain much of what is now called Imagism. The beginning of a poem entitled *Provence* may illustrate Kahn's Imagism and his free verse:

> C'est une face fine et légère;
> pourtant quelle noblesse vit dans ses traits menus,
> et sa chair est claire,
> non qu'elle évoque aucun aspect floral;
> elle est chair, et elle est claire
> comme de la lumière astrale.

Others now followed on the blazed trail, each in his own peculiar fashion. We may pause with two poets of American **The** birth, but of French upbringing and culture: Francis **Americans** Vielé-Griffin (b. Norfolk, Va., 1864) and Stuart Merrill (1863–1915). Vielé-Griffin, whose free form is clearer than that of Kahn, opposes his fluent verse to the rigidity of the Parnassians. He is a healthy poet, of abundant if facile inspiration and production; his emotions are variously and harmo-

niously expressed. He is one of the leaders of the later Symbolistic or " idéo-réaliste " movement (cf. Jammes, Verhaeren,
Paul Fort). His idea is to celebrate " la Vie," all the way from
children's dances, through the oncoming of Spring in Touraine,
to the revamping of mystical legends. Such are the contents of
Cueille d'avril (1886), of *Joies* and of *Clarté de Vie.* In *La Che-
vauchée d'Yeldis* and *La Légende ailée de Wieland le forgeron*
(1900) the poet's aim has been to embody the soul of ancient
legends in an artful and ultra-modern Symbolism (Mendès).
Vielé-Griffin has also a very personal rhythm, and his free verse
is considered too free, too American, by certain French critics.
The same strictures are passed on Stuart Merrill, who, however,
is less addicted to *vers libre* than is Vielé-Griffin. Both of these
men usually keep rime or near-rime. Merrill tends to rough
rhythms and unequal lines. He began as a complicated melodist,
à la Mallarmé, and his earlier *Les Fastes* (1891) are sonorous
and obscure. *Les Quatres Saisons* (1900) show less " instrumen-
tation " and more breadth of treatment, in their mingling of
Pantheism and sociology. Merrill was known both in New York
and France as a socialist and a reformer. So he too left the
ivory tower of Symbolism for the broader conflicts of life;

The greatest modern Symbolist, the most distinguished French
poet now living, is Henri de Régnier (b. 1864). But he is really
Régnier   an eclectic, a reconciler of the several schools. He
has written both free and Parnassian verse, usually
in a classical spirit, as regards both inspiration and formal beauty.
The final flower of Symbolism, he is also a more gifted and
virile Samain in the complexity of the influences which he has
undergone, taking form in numerous measures and manners. An
aristocrat by birth and persuasion, he has elaborately revived
French history and traditions in *La Cité des Eaux* (Versailles)
and more particularly in his novels.[4] He began as an adherent
of Mallarmé, whose circle he frequented for ten years. The
results appear in such early volumes as *Apaisement* (1886),
Poèmes anciens et romanesques (1890), especially *Tel qu'en
songe* (1892), where we find " une âme hautaine, infiniment mé-
lancolique, éprise de rêve, de mystère et d'idéal . . . ob-
sédée des secrètes correspondances des choses." These are the

---

[4] The majority of these belong to the twentieth century. See Epilogue.

familiar hall-marks of Symbolism. Here we find such titles as *Le Songe de la Forêt* or *Motifs de Légende et de Mélancolie;* here we meet with certain " personnages emblématiques " and capitalized symbols, Cavaliers and Princesses, the Beast and the Sword. In those days Henri de Régnier dwelt in a golden palace " with onyx columns " (Jean de Gourmont), but he showed already a preference for Greek nudes and semi-mythological subjects. His cadenced and restrained *vers libre* is among the best French examples of the style; its rhythm and its harmony are distinct throughout his career. But he uses it less in his second period, which is a return to the Parnassian standard. A " free " versifier has the freedom even to revert to the set form of rime and meter, and perhaps Régnier was the more disposed to do this after he became (1896) the son-in-law of Heredia. At any rate, *Les Jeux rustiques et divins* (1897) and *Les Médailles d'argile* (1900) not only reveal a classical (antique) inspiration but frequently " transpose " the kind of subjects and " triumphs " that Heredia preferred. Often, too, it is not a question of transposition but of straight Parnassian technique, particularly in sonnets. This influence continues in *La Sandale ailée* (1906), but here and subsequently Régnier tends towards a third development, the return to Life, the "idéo-réaliste " or " naturiste " standpoint. So he bids farewell to the Forest of his olden dreams, the Forest which he apostrophizes as:

> Forêt, toi, l'innombrable et pareille à la mer,
> O toi, dont le parfum est, tour à tour, amer,
> Délicieux, farouche et fort, comme la Vie . . .
> Je viens à toi, Forêt, je veux vivre. J'oublie
> Que tu fus autrefois fabuleuse à mes yeux.
> Les héros de mon rêve en ont rejoint les dieux.

Poetry like this, with its elegance and serenity, illustrates the classical, one might almost say the conventional side of Régnier. His larger task was " d'académiser le Symbolisme " —and he was made an Academician in 1911. Thus together with Symbolism, *le vers libre* of the best type was officially recognized. Free verse offers even more dangers in French than in English, because of the slighter tonic accent and the greater peril of dispensing with rime; the results are likely to be quite prosaic, especially where the writer's sense of beauty has become impaired; but the best French *vers-libristes* have kept both rime and their sense of beauty.   All the more credit then to such poets as Régnier, who can pour old wine into new bottles with skill and poetic success.   That great metaphor of the creative instinct called *Le Vase* (from *Les Jeux rustiques et divins*) is a perfect example of verse so free that it soars and yet remains bound to earth by the lightest of traditional fetters.

CHAPTER IV

IN CRITICISM

NINETEENTH-CENTURY criticism, so supple and Protean in its forms, continues to offer a wide variety of standpoints. Among the writers may be distinguished: first, the scientific critics and the historians of literature; secondly, the *critiques d'idées;* thirdly, the *critiques de genres* and the Impressionists.

The contact of modern scientific scholarship with criticism has served to direct the latter more and more towards the careful historical study of literature. As examples of this tendency we cannot neglect the work of Gaston Paris and of M. Gustave Lanson. Gaston Paris (1839–1903), the son of Paulin Paris, was the leading scholar of his generation in the domain of Romance Philology. As professor at the Collège de France and the Ecole des hautes Etudes, as editor, investigator and Academician, he embodied the spirit of disinterested research; he had a thorough knowledge of Old French, a discriminating literary taste and a fine personality. These qualities appear in the *Histoire poétique de Charlemagne* (1865), the study of Villon for the Grands Ecrivains series (1901), and especially in the *Poèmes et légendes du moyen âge* (1900), a subject which the author has done so much to clarify. Paris left no *magnum opus;* his incessant industry and his dispersive intellectual curiosity resulted in many monographs and in establishing him as the authority in all that appertains to Old French. Here he preserved excellently the proportion between the linguistic and the literary side of Romance scholarship. His talent was well balanced, well rounded; in this respect he was a modern humanist, as in the courtesy and charm of his personal power. His influence is still felt in the universities of France and of America. With Paris, then, literary criticism usually concerns itself with philological and historical issues rather than with fixed aesthetic judgments.

711'

Criticism more narrowly scientific was represented, between Taine and Brunetière, by the work of Emile Hennequin (1859–

Hennequin   1888) the author of *La Critique scientifique* (1888) and *Les Ecrivains francisés* (1889). Hennequin was a determinist and an evolutionist. He combated the rigidity of Taine's methods and endeavored to set up a science of " Estho-psychologie," defined as " la science des œuvres d'art en tant que signes." This includes three kinds of analysis: aesthetic, of the work; psychological, of the author; and sociological, of the author's admirers or affinities. It is in the last division that Hennequin crosses swords with Taine, since the former prefers to study an author as a cause rather than as an effect, and since he distrusts Taine's " precedent conditions." But Hennequin is equally rigid in the application of his elaborate analysis to Victor Hugo.

Hennequin was but an episode, and the mantle of scientific criticism really fell from the shoulders of Taine to those of

Brunetière   Brunetière. Ferdinand Brunetière (1849–1906), whose name has been so often cited in these pages, might be taken as an example of his own Law of the Drama — " the spectacle of a *will*, striving towards a goal and conscious of the means which it employs." Like a Cornelian hero he fought obstinately against great handicaps. A youth of delicate physique, he failed as a Lycée teacher, failed to receive his diploma at the Ecole Normale — and later entered the same Ecole Normale and won his way successfully as professor. He wrote articles for the *Revue bleue* and became assistant editor of the *Revue des deux mondes,* then editor-in-chief (1893), and finally a member of the Academy. Then occurred his visit to America and his conversion to Catholicism. As in the case of Matthew Arnold, " literature and dogma " henceforth shared Brunetière's energies. During his whole career, he wrote at least one volume a year, in spite of poor health. He died, worn out by writing and speaking, and exhausted by the activities consequent upon his " dogmatisme successif."

For like Sainte-Beuve, Brunetière made many campaigns, and his battles evolved that combination of learning, conservatism and courage which make up his personality. He first became known for his fight against the Naturalistic school, a series of articles collected in *Le Roman naturaliste* (1883) ; much of his best work is contained in the *Etudes critiques sur la littérature française* (1880–1907) ; his application of evolution to literature is to be found in the several works which constitute the *Evolution des genres* (especially as regards criticism, drama, poetry, 1890–94) ; then followed religious polemics and apologia for several years (*Discours de combat*, 1900) ; finally the incomplete *Histoire de la littérature française classique* (1904 ff.) is his last will and testament, with the exception of an interesting volume on *Honoré de Balzac* (1906).

Brunetière is both Classicist and modern. In the former capacity, he resembles his own characterization of Boileau, as being **As Classicist** essentially a " bourgeois de Paris," brusque, frank, self-confident, dogmatic. The two critics have similiar notions of literature as expressing a practical ideal of human life, of the race-genius and of the author's thought. Both men urge the supremacy of reason, both are good fighters and are capable of strong prejudices. Brunetière was for his generation the most influential judge of contemporary literature, just as Boileau was for the age of Louis XIV. The chief ideals of the latter age were those of Brunetière: not only the standard of *la raison*, but the appeal to universality and the habit of judging as a moralist; his article on the essential qualities of French literature (quoted in the Introduction to this History) dwells on the Classical qualities; it is in the name of humanism that he combats the animal side of Naturalism, and' his love of Classical balance makes him the opponent of all exotic or French excess — Loti, the Pre-Raphaelites, Baudelaire and most modern poetry. Brunetière's critical field is practically limited to French literature, and in that field he seems to escape with a sense of relief from the nineteenth century and gladly returns to the simplicity, order and clearness of his favorite period. The *Histoire de la littérature française classique* is the monument to this side of the man.

Yet in spite of himself he was a modernist in several respects. **As Modern** (1) His style, though to some extent archaic or pedantic, shows also modern preciosity, occasional " dislocations " in the manner of the Goncourts, and notably a scientific vocabulary. (2) He is accessible to the nineteenth-cen-

tury type of French patriotism, in that he dislikes Germany and
doubts the English influence on French literature; he prefers
to maintain the solidarity of national thought and tradition.
(3) Although he combated Naturalism as unideal and unsympathetic, he appreciated the broader kind of Realism, when compounded of good sense and observation. He admires George
Eliot, Daudet and the Russians. It is significant that in the
volume on Balzac, he recants to the extent of viewing *le Naturalisme* as inevitable and as sociologically sound, and that here
he places Balzac at the apex of the genre. (4) He is concerned
with the general questions of his time, particularly those bearing
on moral restlessness and metaphysical struggles. In his early
colorless pessimism as in his later conversion, his development
runs parallel to that of other thinkers in the last two decades
of the century. (5) He adopts evolutionary criticism — that is,
the theory that a genre is like an organism which develops. He
states five problems with regard to genres: their independent
existence; their differentiation; their stability; the influences that
modify them; and their transformation. The principle of (progressive) differentiation assumes the Spencerian definition of
evolution — the advance towards complexity from simplicity.
The modifying influences are mainly adapted from Taine. By
the transformation of genres Brunetière means, for example,
that the lyric prose of Rousseau may develop into the poetry of
the Romantic era. This transformation proceeds according to
the struggle for life and natural selection. Thus, in applying
the principles of Darwin to criticism, Brunetière forges the final
link between nineteenth-century science and literature. In
his illustrations of the process (*Evolution de la poésie lyrique,
Evolution de la critique*), he is concerned mainly with the new
forms in each field and omits historical transitions and considerations. The value of his theory has been much debated
and remains debatable. The French fondness for system-making
caused Brunetière to turn literary genres into living organisms or
" abstractions végétatives, qui ont des troncs et qui poussent
des branches " (Lemaître). It is evident that neither a sonnet
nor an epic has any such organic life. Yet it is true that such
a genre as Classic tragedy will seem to accomplish an evolution
(cf. Brunetière's *Epoques du Théâtre Français*, 1892), because

of the perpetual changes operated on the form and the desire for novelty felt alike by artists and public. On the whole, however, it appears that Brunetière as judicial and Classical critic has left a surer record than Brunetière the evolutionist. We can scarcely doubt the excellent contemporary influence of his high standards both of ideality and of form.

Beginning as a pupil of Brunetière, soon appointed as head professor of French literature at the Sorbonne, M. Gustave

Lanson

Lanson (b. 1857) has long been the chief living authority in his chosen field. He has evolved towards the historical and scientific treatment of literary texts. His early volume on *Bossuet* (1890) revealed a taste that was conservative, Classical and certainly not anti-clerical. His most important work, the *Histoire de la littérature française* (1894, and many subsequent editions) still proposes culture and the savoring of individual authors as the chief aims of literary study. But the historical approach necessarily leads a critic into the development of chains of ideas and chains of influence; and the demonstration of these things is perhaps, for the advanced student, the main value of M. Lanson's *Histoire*. The book abounds in thought, psychological insight, judgment and information. M. Lanson's method becomes more and more scientific in his critical editions of Voltaire's *Lettres philosophiques* and of Lamartine's *Premières méditations*, in which the object is to surround the author exhaustively with possible influences pertaining to his literary environment or background. These are technical monuments,[1] but M. Lanson can also please and inform the general reader with his studies on *Corneille* and *Voltaire* made for the Grands Ecrivains series. This critic does abundant justice to the eighteenth century and shows appreciation of contemporary currents as well (*Hommes et livres*, 1895).

As Professeur d'Eloquence Française at the Sorbonne, Emile Faguet (1847–1916) was also a *critique universitaire*, but his

Critiques d'Idées: Faguet

method is at once more personal and less advanced than that of M. Lanson. He has defined criticism as " un don de vivre d'une infinité de vies étrangères " (cf. Sainte-Beuve and Lemaître), and he has carried into

---

[1] So is the indispensable *Manuel bibliographique de la littérature française moderne*, 1909–14.

his portraits an inexhaustible curiosity and intellectual vigor. His productivity was very large, exceeding forty volumes; in his last years he wrote too freely and too loosely. Apart from his *feuilletons* (*Propos de théâtre*, 5 vols., 1903–10) and from his volumes on Nietzsche and Flaubert, the most valuable contributions of Faguet are his four volumes of *Etudes littéraires* — on the four great centuries, from the sixteenth to the nineteenth — and his *Politiques et moralistes du dix-neuvième siècle* (3 vols. 1891–99). His studies are rather monographs on single authors than *vues d'ensemble*, and he is more of a moralist than a scholar. But he is thoroughgoing, independent, and very capable in the manipulation of ideas. He prefers to deal with thinkers rather than with artists; he sees little in Gautier as compared with Vigny, and he judges Voltaire as superficial when compared with Montesquieu. His lively attack on the *philosophes* (*Dix-huitième siècle*: *Etudes littéraires*, 1890) first made his fame, and throughout he prefers the Classical Age for its abiding qualities, the nineteenth century for its " politicians and moralists." Like Diderot, Faguet combines a shrewd sense of reality with his penchant for ideas, and he is thereby able to avoid excessive " isms " and theories. His style is usually vigorous, witty and lucid.

M. Paul Bourget evinces in criticism the same complex of forces that directed his fiction before 1890.[2] His work is a

Bourget mosaic of influences and yet displays an individual pattern. The heir to Taine's determinism, to Renan's dilettanteism, to Stendhal's method of analysis, Bourget's " *enquête* on the moral maladies of the age " marks the complete penetration of psychology into criticism. The *Essais de psychologie contemporaine* (1883) and the *Nouveaux essais* (1885) reveal first the desire of the author, overwhelmed by his bookish upbringing, to " dégager la Vie de cet amas de livres et d'esquisser un portrait moral de ma génération;" he therefore accepts Taine's principle that literature is a " living psychology " and he seeks to determine the soul-state not only of each writer but of each writer's readers, hence of a whole epoch; he passes in review ten modern *littérateurs*, all of whom suffer from some form of pessimism: Renan and the Goncourts are damaged through their dilettanteism, Stendhal and Turgenev

[2] See above, Ch. I.

through their cosmopolitanism, Baudelaire and Dumas *fils* are affected (variously) by the perversities of modern love, while Flaubert, Leconte de Lisle and Taine show the corroding effects of science on the imagination. Other causes for gloom were the result of the Franco-Prussian war, the general *taedium vitae* and the conflict of democracy with culture.

Certain of these points may be pushed too far, but Bourget's main conclusion — that the generation of the eighties was afflicted by a deep pessimism — is borne out by the facts (see above, especially Bk. VIII, Ch. V). Yet this conclusion is not exactly a moral indictment on the part of Bourget. It is rather his habit to analyze writers " autant qu'ils sont des *signes* " (cf. Taine and Hennequin) of current states of sensibility. It is on the basis of his latter-day currency, which Bourget started, that Stendhal is included among the *fin-de-siècle* writers. A similar practice of applied psychology is found in the more scattered but excellently written collection known as *Etudes et portraits* (1888). A later collection, more polemic in tone, is the *Pages de doctrine et de critique* (1912).

Bourget has pronounced gifts as a critic. His style, of which the essay on Rivarol is a capital example, still marches heavily, but seems more " direct and vibrant " than in his novels. He is both a *sensitif* and a thinker, able to penetrate intimately into his favorite writers. He has a great deal of solid knowledge in several fields, and he shows a corresponding profundity which associates historical and philosophical ideas with literature. He perceives, like Brunetière, the " bankruptcy " of Science and takes refuge in Spencer's Unknowable, which later became for Bourget the domain of faith. The earlier *Essais* represented a sort of " critique confessionelle " (Giraud), because Bourget exhibited his own psychological bias together with that of his generation.

Francisque Sarcey, (1827–99), the most popular and influential dramatic critic of his time, was the Aristotle of the *pièce bien faite*. His *Quarante ans de théâtre* (8 vols. 1900–02)

Sarcey consist of critical *feuilletons*, written mainly for *Le Temps*, and cover dramatic history from the ancients to the Théâtre-Libre. Beginning with a sound knowledge and appreciation of the French Classics, Sarcey came to prefer the drama of

Scribe, of Dumas *fils* and of Sardou. This change was due partly to his subservience to contemporary tastes — he always held that a play existed only in relation to its public — and partly to his overweening interest in technique. For Sarcey, technique ("du théâtre") was much more important than literary merit; therefore he could set up the well-made play as a dramatic absolute. He insists upon the "art of preparations," the unity of impression, much action, and especially the *scène à faire* or the precept that the central situation of the plot must be represented on the stage. Apart from too much emphasis on modernity, Sarcey's good sense, knowledge and insight make him an informing and often a reliable critic.

Less information but a great deal of charm and personality is to be found in the critical writings of Anatole France. The four **The Impres-** volumes of *La Vie littéraire* (written for *Le Temps*, **sionists:** 1888–92) reflect the influences that characterize his **A. France** first period (see Ch. I, above). Previously and indeed throughout his career, France wrote many introductions to French Classics and the like, and these *Notices* (now collected in *Le Génie Latin*, 1913) are more of the orthodox and conventional kind. But his fame is closely connected with *La Vie littéraire*, which represents essentially Impressionistic criticism. "The good critic is he who relates the adventures of his own soul among masterpieces." "Objective criticism has no more existence than objective art." So France talks of himself in connection with Gaston Paris or Renan; we learn little of the Middle Ages or of the Hebrews, but we are entertained by the discursive, wilful, epicurean charm of the irresistible Anatole. Deliberate relativity and dilettanteism are ever-present; yet this critic has underlying standards, mainly of the humanistic and classical order. A diatribe against Zola is followed by a plea for the cultural study of Latin. Maupassant is praised as a Classical Realist, and Florian is appreciated for his reminiscential values. Appreciative criticism is, indeed, chiefly in evidence, and the writer's skepticism is here not bitter but tolerant and kindly. Recognizing the development of the critical spirit in these latter Alexandrian times, France approves the genre of criticism as all-inclusive and as affording scope for "the rarest, the most manifold and varied of intellectual faculties." Certainly his own faculties, enveloped in a gracious personal style and an atmosphere of literary vagabondage, are conspicuous in *La Vie littéraire*.

"Certaine beauté," says Jules Lemaitre, "est un dissolvant." The phrase is significant as denoting a difference between Lemaitre **Lemaître** and his brother-impressionist, France. The former, with all his wit and irony, shows a sturdiness and an intellectual consistency which the latter did not have. Jules Lemaitre (1853–1914) was trained as a scholar and began as a teacher; but he soon drifted into journalism and became known through his amusing *feuilleton* on Renan; he wrote many "Impressions" and was made an Academician in 1895; then he took the conservative (Catholic and militarist) side in the Dreyfus affair and returned to the usual standards in his lauding of public morality, patriotism and Classicism. In his last years he became noted as a graceful lecturer, an activity resulting in the popular and sympathetic volumes on Rousseau, Racine and Chateaubriand.

Lemaitre's chief productions are *Les Contemporains* (7 vols. 1885–99) and *Impressions de Théâtre* (10 vols., 1888 ff.). His purpose is to convey appreciative and interpretative criticism, proceeding by "elective affinities" rather than by reasoning or reference to general ideas. He takes as his motto Sainte-Beuve's sentence comparing the critical spirit to a river which winds through a varied landscape and reflects everything in turn. Fortunately, Lemaître's taste is good, and thereby he is saved from the extreme of dilettanteism. He can accept and admire, temporarily at least, writers as different as Racine and Verlaine, the Realists and Rousseau. Like Taine, he frequently sums up a writer in an illuminating phrase: Banville represents the tight-rope in poetry; the Goncourts are the Siamese twins of literature; Heredia puts the Spanish point of honor into his sonnets. Lemaitre writes with verve, naturalness and a wit which is even more incisive than that of Anatole France. In his latter days he became less of an aesthete and more of a moralist, with "un grand désir de comprendre et le goût de regarder dans l'intérieur des âmes." The sincerity of this desire appears in such a volume as that on *Jean-Jacques Rousseau* (1907). All of Lemaître is readable, much of him is sound, and if Impressionism is only a "refined appetite," yet in this case we may usually trust to the excellence of the palate concerned.

EPILOGUE: PRE-WAR LITERATURE

I

Much of the literature belonging to the pre-war period has been discussed in the preceding Book. There we dealt with the **The Field** elder generation of authors who attained fame before the close of the century. Here it is our aim to treat only the talents that flowered from 1900 to 1914; and it is still too soon to be certain about the majority of these talents. It seems best, then, to discuss fully three illustrious representatives of the age and, as regards the remainder, to indicate the currents and ideals with which they were associated.

The word " ideals " is used advisedly, for it seems clear that a certain animating force, variously directed, has usually upheld **The Tendencies** this generation. To the confused abundance of their production, the terms " *décadence* " and " *fin de siècle* " are no longer appropriate. Writers are, on the one hand mystic and spiritual, on the other active and patriotic. It is not easy to separate the tangled threads of these ideals, but perhaps three chief strands may be discerned. (1) The reaction against Naturalism and Positivism is apparent. An idealistic fervor finds expression in the Intuitive philosophy of M. Bergson and his followers, in the cultivation of the inner life by Rolland and others, and in the mystic or Neo-Catholic revival attempted by Claudel and Péguy. (2) There is the creed of energy and force, which inspires " the daring apostles of Life, those who cultivate movement and liberty rather than art " (Mme Duclaux). This movement is extremely diverse and often incoherent. But its range is visible from the very names of such " petites écoles " as Vitalism, Dynamism, Vorticism, Paroxysm, Futurism. These are all schools of force. Their tendencies are summed up in the work of Emile Verhaeren. (3) The native exponents of energy, under the leadership of Barrès (see Bk. IX, Ch. I), turned their attention to the upbuilding of France.

720

This patriotic zeal has several phases, whether as applied to a depiction of the provinces (Regionalism), to a renewed interest in colonial expansion, or to the development of a solid Nationalism. In its extreme form, Nationalism has been linked with a return to Royalist and Catholic sympathies (*L'Action française*). This movement is usually active and practical.

It seems, indeed, that the general tendency of "les jeunes" has been towards an obstreperous activity, towards "violence and volume" rather than measure and taste. Never **Conflicts** has there been an epoch of greater individual **and** liberty, whether in thought or form. Adventurous **Confusions** talents have sought a cohesion or solidarity which they scarcely found; and in the multitude of "isms" it would appear that every individual is making a private school of his own. For instance, Marinetti (an Italian) and Verhaeren (a Fleming), with their interest in the inventions of a mechanical age, are the only "Futurists" that matter; Verhaeren, again, is the chief "Paroxyst"; Jules Romains is the only luminary of "Unanimism," held important because of its application of crowd-psychology to poetry; Fernand Gregh is the apostle of "Humanism," which reacts against the Parnassians and the Symbolists; while "Naturism" or "l'idéo-réalisme" has a more numerous following, whose endeavor is to "faire tressaillir leurs strophes du grand frisson de la vie." This vehement struggle for individual vitality has rarely attained final or consummate form. The chief organs of the new movements have been the *Mercure de France* and, more recently, the *Nouvelle Revue Française*. But rather than dwell on the more eccentric manifestations, we should cope with the underlying philosophy of the age.

II

In the domain of thought, the transcendental philosophy of M. Henri Bergson (b. 1859) was very influential as it was quite **Bergsonism** characteristic of the pre-war period. The rising generation approved his interest in the forces of life (Vitalism) and his advocacy of instinct rather than intelligence (Intuitionism); especially did his doctrine of Creative

Evolution and the flux harmonize with certain aesthetic tendencies of the new era. Partly deriving from Boutroux and Renouvier, offering parallels with the system of William James, the Bergsonian philosophy is contained in three works of progressive importance. In his doctoral thesis, *Essai sur les données immédiates de la conscience* (1889), M. Bergson is already seeking the depths of the inner life and the foundations of liberty. In *Matière et mémoire* (1896) the author discusses, with the latest scientific evidence, the *rapports* between consciousness and the outer world. The work is definitely idealistic and dualistic in its emphasis on the inertia of matter save as energized by spirit. Finally,[1] *L'Evolution Créatrice* (1907) is the fullest and most alluring statement of M. Bergson's metaphysical attitude. It deals with evolution in general, with the meaning of life, the relations of body and spirit, the contrast of intellect and instinct; it furnishes a criticism of modern philosophical systems and it garbs the whole argument in a style of infinite suggestion, imagery and charm.

Although, according to his disciples, M. Bergson's work is strongly grounded on a manifold knowledge of the sciences, yet **The Intuition of Reality** he is throughout opposed to a wholly scientific or "mechanistic" view of the universe. Thereby he continues the belief in the "bankruptcy of science" which was symptomatic of the century's end.[2] The doctrine of final causes, or the teleological explanation of reality, he finds equally man-made and unsatisfactory. Again, our philosophical difficulties arise partly from the inadequacy and confusion of terms, partly from our mental need to "juxtapose phenomena in space" even when ideas do not occupy space. (This parcelling habit is his chief objection to Spencerian evolution). So the true philosopher must go beyond science, must renounce analytic processes in favor of spontaneous perception, and "accomplish an effort of direct *intuition* which may put him into immediate contact with the real" (Le Roy). The nature and functioning of this transcendental intuition are nowhere clearly indicated in *L'Evolution Créatrice*. Having disposed of space, M. Bergson proceeds to dispose of time. What we usually call facts are not

---

[1] His latest book, *L'Energie spirituelle* (1919) does not fall within our scope.
[2] See above, pp. 665 and 717.

ultimate reality, but reality adapted to practical interests; our practical understanding (cf. Kant) tends to solidify the flux of phenomena and to represent the same in set periods of duration; whereas duration likewise flows continously; in thought and in memory, past melts imperceptibly into present and our tomorrows will soon form a compact whole with our yesterdays. M. Bergson's illustrations of this *continuum* are vivid and his treatment of true duration, as being infinitely vaster than matter, is most impressive.

By spontaneous and immediate intuition, then, the philosopher can apprehend what the scientist cannot: the real nature of the Creative soul, of the vital impulse (*l'élan vital*), of movement Evolution and change. Neo-Darwinism is acceptable as regards variation and adaptability. The next step is to maintain that these processes are not passively undergone, but reflected in our perception and action. Hence it is a *creative* evolution in which we participate; we are in the midst of an " unforeseeable creation of forms." By an act of sympathy the observer installs himself in the bosom of reality, in order to " sentir sa palpitation profonde et sa richesse intérieure " (Le Roy). If we must have concepts, let them be plastic, fluid and living like the living models. So only may philosophy " dilate " and go deeper in its endeavor to transcend its present intellectual status. So only may it reflect reality's double and correlative movement towards unification and plurification (cf. James). Life proceeds largely by dissociation, and Evolution, like an exploding shell, bursts into ever-flying fragments.

The best reality to study is the ego — and there is nothing new about that statement. But his disciples hold that M. Bergson The Inner has enlarged the possibilities of " know thyself " by World showing to what extent the division-making processes of the outer world have crept into the multiple ego. These processes, as obsessions, should be discarded, and we should, as in " pure memory," reach to the inner depths of the individual. Already, in *Matière et mémoire*, the writer had maintained that of the several grades or layers of consciousness, the deepest is independent of mechanistic conceptions. It would seem, then, that spirit may have an independent life; cerebral convolutions and records will not explain the original activities of perception and memory. In our inner life — for example, in a deep passion — it is more a question of intensity than of any quantitative analysis. Spatial and numerical measurements must go. This is the doctrine of the " immanence of thought," closely connected with the creative and poetic instinct; this is the source of moral responsibility and of life itself. And in the joy of becoming one with pure reality, we participate in its essential movement.

This movement is a fundamental principle of the new philos-ophy, for which its founder has suggested the title of the " phi-

A Philo- losophy of change." Change or movement, says M. sophy of Bergson, " is original. Things are derived from move-Change ment." Life is a " continuity of genetic energy," and our part in it is to furnish a certain push or tendency. So we have a moving-picture scenario in which, however, it is not a question of adding movement to the fixed pictures, but of starting with the movement and directing it into scenes or elements of experience. Thus we end with the idea of a reality which *creates* and which is *free*. The destiny of human beings has never been foreordained:

> The world was all before them where to choose . . .

We often forgot our creative rôle and lapsed back into mechanism and the struggle for mere maintenance. Yet man has triumphed; yet our gifts and heritage declare nature's solitary exceptional success. Such is the stirring conclusion of M. Bergson's idealistic philosophy.

It is scarcely our part to judge this doctrine, but even a layman may observe that its chief assumptions repose on nothing but our

Tendencies — or M. Bergson's — intuitive apprehension. The and same may be said as regards the " proof " of the Influence will's freedom, of the separate existence of spirit and its possible immortality. Although the author scarcely mentions religion, there is more of revelation than of reasoning in his synthesis. That is why he has been criticized by such men as J. Benda, who find Bergson's anti-intellectualism out of the French tradition, sentimental and romantic with a German tinge. Yet the majority of young French writers in this period waged war, somewhat indiscriminately, on rationalism, ma-terialism and positivism; there was, as we have stated, a renovation of the "ideal" in various forms; and the popularity of Bergson was partly due to the fact that his speculations are capable of many interpretations and uses. For example, Péguy and Claudel (see below) interpreted Creative Evolution very differently, the one being nearer to Vitalism, the other to Intuitionism. Again, "Impulsionism," the "idéo-réaliste" movement, the divagations of the later Symbolists and *vers-libristes*, all have points in common with the new philosophy, which agrees with the modern emphasis on force as well as on formlessness (the flux). It seems probable that Bergsonism, as a system, reached its peak before the war and is now declining.

Whatever the fate of its message, *L'Evolution Créatrice* will remain a literary landmark because of the fascinating and poetic **Literary** power of its style. It is curious that M. Bergson **Values** should originally have renounced and finally adopted the use of images as symbols of the unspeakable and invisible; for his style is vibrant with convergent metaphors, evocative of a varied reality, supple and flowing in accordance with the thought. It is a style of elaborate harmonies, but of comparative clearness, containing many repetitions; it also contains, like that of Pascal, the *frisson metáphysique*, the sense of vastness and soul-yearning. In this many-textured fabric, subtle psychological analysis alternates with technical illustrations from the positive sciences. Frequent cross-references to the creative arts are found, and although M. Bergson has formulated no system of aesthetics, his influence upon recent aesthetic currents and criticism is indisputable.

Remy de Gourmont (1858–1915) is also a sort of Intuitionist with regard to aesthetic theories. Following Bergson in the **Other** "dissociation des idées," he is led by this analysis **Thinkers** into a corrosive and pernicious immoralism, especially in his poetry and fiction. His criticism (*Promenades littéraires*, 1904–13) is likewise based on a sensual principle, but shows genuine gifts of divination and taste. E. Seillière as a critic is anti-romantic and represents an intellectual imperialism in his speculative thinking. As regards religious idealism, or "le Spiritualisme," E. Schuré (*Les Grands Initiés*, etc.) and C. de Pomairols have been considered as the semi-official heads respectively of the Protestant and the Catholic wings of the revival. The Modernist movement, in the Catholic Church, has mainly a theological significance. Neo-Catholicism, in its more active and patriotic affiliations, was forwarded not only by Barrès and the other " B's " (see above, p. 669), but also by the directors of *L'Action française*,[3] Léon Daudet and especially Charles Maurras. Barrès and Maurras have been the two most effective publicists in connection with the maintenance of Nationalist traditions. These include, not only patriotism, but a return *à la* Chateaubriand, to the principles of " throne and altar." Royalism and Catholicism are considered as safeguarding the nation and as establishing " l'idée de l'ordre." Many young intellectuals and aristocrats have tried thus to reverse the wheel of time; Rolland once inquired of such a juvenile Tory why he should cling to the skirts of his great-grandmother.

III

Romain Rolland (b. 1868) is the second great writer of this period. A native of Clamecy in Burgundy, he has celebrated **Rolland** his province in the attempted Rabelaisianism of *Colas Breugnon* (1919) and has told us of his upbringing in an episode of *Jean-Christophe*. Rolland was, however, educated in Paris, where he formed a friendship with Paul Claudel and an early passion for music, especially that of Wagner. Passing through the Ecole Normale and a period of adolescent storm and stress, he soon demonstrated that his dominant interest would be an intellectual internationalism and a desire to reach a synthesis, a world-philosophy in that direction. The powerful influence of Tolstoy alternated with cosmopolitan contacts in Rome; a visit to Bayreuth was presently followed by an endeavor to reform the French theater towards the standard of Shakespeare (*Théâtre de la Révolution*, acted 1898–1902). Rolland then functioned as professor of the History of Music at the Sorbonne (1903–10); he wrote a *Vie de Beethoven* together with numerous studies on other musicians, past and present. Around 1911 he spent some time in Switzerland, to which

[3] This journal represented the continuation of the anti-Dreyfus agitation. See above, pp. 664.

country he retired during the war. Mme Duclaux finds him more Swiss than Latin in his "intense individualism, his moral earnestness, his lyric love of nature and . . . a scolding tenderness in his voice."

All of this earnestness, this cosmopolitanism, this interest in art and in the life of the mind, was poured into *Jean-Christophe*, "Jean- Christophe" which was first published periodically in Péguy's *Cahiers de la Quinzaine*, 1904–12. This ten-volume work is in several respects the most notable French novel of our generation. First, it uses the form as a "rag-bag" miscellany and is panoramic in its view of civilization. Secondly, it centers around the biography of a musician and offers the most striking recent "case" of the artistic temperament doubling upon itself. In one or the other of these respects, *Jean-Christophe* has had numerous sequels in the cycle-novels of the last decade.[4] And thirdly, the book is written with a thorough-going idealism, which is not rose-colored, which faces facts and rings true by all standards of nobility and sincerity.

The three divisions in the life of Christophe Krafft are his German youth, his Parisian struggles and the epoch of final tempests and subsequent serenity (Switzerland, Italy, Paris). Rolland's biographies of Beethoven, of Michelangelo and of Tolstoy, together with certain episodes in the life of Wagner, furnish some material in the three chief phases of the hero-musician. Cosmopolitanism is then evident as regards both places and people. The work is strongly conceived and constructed; but it could scarcely maintain an equal inspiration throughout its whole course. Among the parts that seem most valuable are the following.[5] The heredity of Christopher is significantly set forth, and his childhood is described with charm (*L'Aube*). The awakening of young love is wonderfully portrayed in the affairs with Sabine the somnolent and Ada the sensuous (*L'Adolescent*). Christopher is now becoming conscious of his creative power and generally of "la force de l'Etre." This leads (in *La Révolte*) to his battles with the German small-town atmosphere and with the sentimentalism that he calls the "mensonge allemand." He breaks with his early associations

[4] For example, in the works of Bennett, Mackenzie, Dreiser, Wassermann, Couperus, and Marcel Proust.
[5] The titles of the individual volumes are given in parentheses.

and suddenly flees to Paris. There, like Wagner, he meets with ill-luck and indifference — and Rolland writes what is really an indictment of the boulevards (*La Foire sur la place*). The novelist excoriates the market-place, the ignorant coteries, the corruptions of fast life, the hyper-feminized literature and society. He appeals from this moribund generation to the forces of Life, even of humble life: during an illness he is nursed by a servant-girl who convinces him that there are workers even in Paris. Then we go back to the family life of the Jeannin (*Antoinette*), the pathetic idyll of the girl who loved Christopher at a distance and who in dying left her brother, Olivier, to be his great friend. These two friends keep house together, and gradually (*Dans la Maison* and *Les Amies*) Christopher comes to know a circle of quiet workers and passes through various experiences, amorous and political. The latter kind bring trouble, namely a riot, the death of Olivier and the forced flight of Christopher from Paris. Prostrated in a Swiss town (Bâle), he recovers only to fall a victim to the most violent of his love-affairs, with the enigmatic and passionate Anna. Finally, he is restored to serenity, meets again his Grazia and loves her ideally (*La Nouvelle Journée*), shows benevolence towards the younger generation and passes away. "Saint Christophe a traversé le fleuve."

His whole life-course, indeed, has been a "river," as Rolland says — not a novel but a huge stream journeying epically through

Criticism   a varied landscape, panoramic in its reflections of many scenes, subjects and experiences. The work also resembles a symphony in its triple division, its recurrent *motifs*, its anticipations and fulfillments. So diverse is the story that different countries have shown distinct preferences for different volumes — France for *La Nouvelle Journée*, America for *Le Buisson ardent*. So the work is uniquely European in its scope and influence. People of many races and types move across the stage, and the characterization is usually excellent. Christopher himself, with his naïveté and blundering, his increasing spiritual force and his growing goodness, is wonderfully handled. He is a sort of Parsifal, a "reiner Thor" who becomes "wise through sympathy." He is a very human genius. The gentler but more subtle Olivier is a worthy foil. Olivier's wife, Jacqueline, in her strenuous demands upon life and love, is one kind of modern woman — and many kinds are represented. The heroines are thoroughly differentiated and analyzed. We remember the chief stages in the story by the names of the women, each representing some aspect of her country: Minne, Sabine and Ada; Antoinette at the opposite pole from Colette Stevens; Grazia, the Beatrice, who inspires an autumnal love. Even to the minor characters, such as Christopher's mother, Rolland gives life and individuality.

The art of *Jean-Christophe* is in the total effect rather than in details. It is not written in a choice style. There are many passages of an eloquent earnestness, but the river runs muddily at times and the language becomes diffuse or slack. There are also slow-moving pages of discussion or didacticism. Part of Christopher's revolt is against too much " art," against an ever-refining dilettanteism; he trusts more to the strong rough currents of an abiding inspiration; he trusts above all to the consoling power of *work* and of *will*:

> Je ne suis pas tout ce qui est (dit la voix de Dieu). Je suis la Vie qui combat le Néant. . . . Je suis le Feu qui brûle dans la Nuit. . . . Je suis le combat éternel. . . . Je suis la Volonté libre qui lutte et brûle éternellement. Lutte et brûle avec moi. . . .

This greatly resembles Bergson. The book preaches a creative energy derived from several sources — first, from the natural, hereditary and intuitive genius of the artist; secondly, from his "long espoir" in spiritual realities; thirdly, from Christopher's enduring strength, a strength of the people, Tolstoyan, embracing poverty, confronting hardship — and triumphing over the market-place.

In Rolland's view an artist should feel and express the " religious conscience " of a people. So a " grand souffle Panthéiste " animates this work — a religious fervor without definite religious dogma. Hence, for all its social satire, *Jean-Christophe* is constructive through its final faith in an emergent " true France " and in the stamina of civilization. Lofty and fine issues, simply accepted, dominate the book; nothing could be farther from the literature of the boulevards. Nor does Rolland have recourse, like Barrès and Bourget, to the traditional supports of Church and State. A greater " wind of

the spirit " now animates humanity, and this is also the message
of *Au-dessus de la Mêlée* (1915), the war-book which has been so
widely misunderstood and which, for all its true patriotism, has
cost Rolland his popularity in France. He will regain it, for in
the long run the judgment of France is just. The name of Rolland
will survive this troubled epoch, steadfastly linked with the cause
of truth-telling and of international idealism. Whatever the fate
of his after-work, *Jean-Christophe* remains a noble task, nobly
accomplished.

In certain other novelists we find likewise an idealistic trend,
but it has been less strongly articulate. The Regionalist move-
Other   ment launched by Barrès is exemplified in the work
Novelists   of M. Henri Bordeaux (*La Neige sur les pas, Les
Yeux qui s'ouvrent*), who deals mainly with the province of Le
Dauphiné; and by M. René Bazin, who in *La Terre qui meurt*
(1899) and *Le Blé qui lève* (1907) presents agricultural or social
problems in central France; *Les Oberlé* (1901) especially gives
M. Bazin's contribution to the literature of Alsace (cf. Barrès,
Lichtenberger, etc.). Bordeaux and Bazin are respectable and
highly moral writers, who emphasize devotion to the family as
well as to the state. More colorful is the depiction of North
Africa in the work of M. Louis Bertrand: *Le Sang des races*,
1899; *Pépète le bien-aimé*, 1904. The historical past of France
has been resuscitated in the novels of Henri de Régnier (*Le bon
Plaisir*, 1902; *Le Passé vivant*, 1905) and in those of Maurice
Maindron, especially *Saint-Cendre* (1902). These men write
with a sensual bias, but with considerable knowledge of the past
and much artistic skill in the presentation. The psychological
novel is continued in *La Vie secrète* (1908) of E. Estaunié and
the *roman passionel* in Mme Marcelle Tinayre's *Maison du péché*
(1902). Yellow-back fiction has also abounded, and the confusion
of the epoch is manifest in the heterogeneity of this form. For
example, the Prix Goncourt has been awarded yearly to a series
of " striking " or eccentric novels; yet none of those published
before 1914 seem likely to survive.

IV

Apart from the later manifestations of Symbolism, French poetry seems to have been at a loss during the early years of the twentieth century. The period of 1900–1905 is a **Poetry** period of poetic anarchy and extravagance. After that date, it is held, the various " isms " settled down to a sort of reconciliation based on their common distrust of the intellect and their common desire for a poetic renaissance in the direction of idealism, spontaneity, creative enthusiasm (cf. Bergson). Their intentions were better than their achievement. In France proper, previous to the war, no commanding presence was felt in poetry. Among the conservatives, at the turn of the century, we find the classical and Petrarchan Muse of Auguste Angellier (*A l'amie perdue*, 1896; *Dans la lumière antique*, 1905–11) and the emotional Vitalism of the Comtesse Mathieu de Noailles (*Le Cœur innombrable*, 1901; *Les Eblouissements*, 1907). Both of these writers are perfectly regular in form. As regards the various new " isms," their divisions and principles have been sufficiently catalogued above (section I). One might mention such manifestoes as Marinetti's " Tuons le Clair de Lune " or J. Romains' poem, *La Vie Unanime* (1908). In form, the New Poetry (Paul Fort, Péguy, Claudel) has pushed *vers libre* to the point where it is polymorphic, closer to rhythmic prose than to verse. Like Verhaeren (see below), most of these writers are Whitmanesque **Paul Fort** in form, content or both. Paul Fort (b. 1872), " prince des poètes " since 1912, has written many volumes of *Ballades françaises*, 1897–1920. These deal partly with the writer's self, but more with historical or contemporary France, in Paris or in the provinces (*Le Roman de Louis XI, Paris sentimental, Ile-de-France*). The style ranges from the familiar language of the streets to a quaint archaic French; and Fort uses various so-called adaptations of the Old French popular verse-forms. Like Jammes, he favors a naïve expression — naïveté has been a frequent pose since Verlaine. There is plenty of life and emotion in this diluted mixture of prose and verse, which is printed like prose, but allows occasional rime or near-rime together with repetends and refrains. Paul

Fort has been called " l'exemplaire le plus curieux du poète à la fois spontané et subtil, naturel et pittoresque, ingénieux et savant, opulent et négligé " (Florian-Parmentier).

Charles Péguy (1873–1914), a self-taught mystic and man of the people, was the founder (1897) of the enterprising *Cahiers de la Quinzaine*, which published Rolland, A. Suarès and others. This poet wrote long Mysteries or semi-epics (*Eve, Le Mystère de la Charité de Jeanne d'Arc*) which emphasize his orthodox faith and his belief in " the grandeur and misery of man and his need of salvation." Péguy's talent is unequal, verbose, sensitive and humane. His rhythmical prose is full of repetitions, incoherencies and dilutions, alternating with passages of high imagery and natural beauty. Péguy was killed early in the Great War and is best known by his stirring and prophetic war-poem:

Péguy

> Heureux ceux qui sont morts pour la terre charnelle,
> Mais pourvu que ce fût dans une juste guerre;
> Heureux ceux qui sont morts pour quatre coins de terre,
> Heureux ceux qui sont morts d'une mort solennelle.
>
> Heureux ceux qui sont morts dans les grandes batailles,
> Couchés dessus le sol à la face de Dieu;
> Heureux ceux qui sont morts sur un dernier haut lieu
> Parmi tout l'appareil des grandes funérailles. . . .

The dominating voice in poetry during this period was that of Emile Verhaeren (1855–1916). But Verhaeren's muse is Belgian rather than purely French. Born and bred in Flanders, he studied at Louvain and joined a literary group at Brussels; he published his first volume, *Les Flamandes*, in 1883. This naturalistic collection is aflame with the colors of Rubens and the riot of the senses. A more mystic and restrained note is sounded in *Les Moines*, 1886. Some maintain that it is in the Flemish character thus to alternate the animal and the spiritual. At any rate, having celebrated with a good deal of violence the attractions of his native soil, Verhaeren passed through a nervous breakdown which found expression in such records of the inner life as *Les Soirs* and *Les Débâcles*. He presently recovered contact with the outer world, married, became interested in Socialism, and began his

Verhaeren

third phase with the publication of *Les Villes tentaculaires* (1895).

This final phase contains the most characteristic poetry of Verhaeren. It is marked by objectivity, expansive power and

His Master-pieces

an interest in the manifold aspects of modern industrial life. It is distinctly a new "Futuristic" poetry that appeared under such well-chosen titles as *Les Forces tumultueuses* (1902), *La Multiple Splendeur* (1906) and *Les Rhythmes souverains* (1910). In all his twenty-odd volumes, Verhaeren has not surpassed this trilogy. In the first-named, the poet sings of such "forces" as art and love, such heroes or types as the warrior, the monk, the orator and the financier. *La Multiple splendeur,* more abstract in its intention, bears witness to the power of ideas, of human speech (*Le Verbe*), of aspiration and even of suffering; but above all it revels in the vitality and violence of Nature, whether as triumphing in the marts of the world or as inextricably mingled, in the springtide, with one's personal life and with the beauty of women. *Les Rhythmes souverains* fully embodies a conception of rhythm to which we shall return. *Les Ailes rouges de la guerre* (posthumous, 1917) contains, together with much powerful invective against the Germans, a large vision of the mighty machinery of war.

The chief point about Verhaeren, and his chief difference from nineteenth-century poets, is that he *accepts* modern life with

The New Poetry

its grime and its glory, with all its industrial and civic manifestations. His muse is intensely democratic and surrenders herself to actuality. Verhaeren too has his Five Towns, overhung with smoke and vibrating to the new music of factories and trades. He perceives that "the town is the future." He imagines Paris or Hamburg as an octopus that drains the force from a whole region (*Les Villes tentaculaires*). His pages throng with a naturalistic and teeming life, whether viewed in a metropolis or in the "beautés fortes et rudes" of his native Flanders. Verhaeren was a man of much travel and experience. His talent was mainly plastic and descriptive in his early volumes, but his range went ever deeper and wider in the new century. He declares that

Toute la vie est dans l'essor,

and he believes in the *élan vital* as creatively as Bergson. That is, he projects himself and his imagination into the heart of the riot, and through this " immanence " he attains a kind of spiritual strength in the midst of materialism. Balzac had the same gift, and like Balzac and Hugo, Verhaeren vivifies, through an animistic process, everything that he touches. He also deals with vast and huge subjects — war and desolation, the sea and great cities — in the epic manner of Hugo. A fervent admirer of " la vie intense et rouge," he believes that the pride of life cannot be conquered by penitence or religion, by Magi or Magdalens:

> Ils ne changeront rien à ce qui fut toujours:
> L'humanité n'a soif que de son propre amour;
> Elle est rude, complexe, ardente; elle est retorse;
> La joie et la bonté sont les fleurs de sa force.

Verhaeren's verse-forms are extremely liberal, without being altogether free. Parnassian in his first volumes, he later uses **Technical** the Romantic Alexandrine, then he tends more and **Values** more to discard the Alexandrine in favor of varied line-lengths within the strophe. This is *vers libre* somewhat as La Fontaine used it; its supple variety is not diminished by the continued use of rime. The rhythm, however, is exceedingly free and unconventional; here is his idea as to the expression of the " universal rhythm: "

> Tel l'exprime — sait-il comment? —
> Qui sent en lui si bellement
> Passer les vivantes idées
> Avec leur pas sonore, avec leur geste clair
> Qu'elles règlent d'elles-mêmes l'élan du vers
> Et les jeux
> Onduleux
> De la rime assouplie ou fermement dardée.
>
> (*Le Verbe*)

Verhaeren is fond of very short lines, alternating with longer ones, and thereby he gives an impression of speed and a dramatic effect. He inherits from the Symbolists the use of suggestion and of onomatopeia:

Mes jours toujours plus lourds s'en vont roulant leur cours.

The clash of consonants and the suggestion of vowels play a considerable part in this poetry (see *La Pluie* and *Le Vent*).

As poetry, his work is uniformly violent and voracious. Like some huge machine, it devours and gives forth again indiscrimi-

A Criticism nately " la vie ample et violente; " it does so with an explosive force that is often too highly charged. We grow weary of hearing the siren shriek. Verhaeren not only makes love violently; he even takes a bath with a loud emphasis. The flight of Pegasus is a headlong riotous flight, and even Christian sacrifice appears as a " fevered violence." Verhaeren laps up voraciously the mixed food-stuff of life and therein he is like Whitman, though he is a far greater artist than Whitman.[6] Allowing for his coarser intoxications, it must be admitted that the chief trilogy of volumes analyzed above show powers of poetic expression unrivaled in our time. A large, supple and well-adapted vocabulary; a dramatic terseness of speech; a gift of imaginative recreation and pantheistic fervor; a resounding energy which often reaches poetic ecstasy — these things make Verhaeren a genuine lyrist, whatever we may think of his message and whatever doubts we may have regarding the " multiple splendor " that he finds in industrialism. Verhaeren's vogue is European in extent, and his influence has been felt on such movements as Futurism, " Paroxysm " and " Unanimism." He is thoroughly representative of the New Poetry, in whatever country that may be taking form — and even where it does not take form. The following extracts (from *Un Soir*) will illustrate his creed; may a future reader know, says Verhaeren —

> Qu'il sache, avec quel violent élan, ma joie
> S'est, à travers les cris, les révoltes, les pleurs,
> Ruée au combat fier et mâle des douleurs,
> *Pour en tirer l'amour, comme on conquiert sa proie.*

[6] The subject of Whitman in France awaits thorough investigation. It does not appear that Verhaeren was consciously influenced by the American poet. Vielé-Griffin, Merrill and Claudel probably were. In all of these writers, as in the case of Péguy, similarities to Whitman can be found, especially as regards rhythm, force, externality, Modernism, the use of enumeration and repetition. The *Leaves of Grass* were first fully translated in 1909, though partial translations had appeared from 1886 on.

J'aime mes yeux fiévreux, ma cervelle, mes nerfs,
Le sang dont vit mon cœur, le cœur dont vit mon torse;
J'aime l'homme et le monde et j'adore la force
Que donne et prend ma force à l'homme et l'univers.

.   .   .   .

Une tendresse énorme emplit l'âpre savoir.

.   .   .   .

Comprenez-vous pourquoi mon vers vous interpelle?
C'est qu'en vos temps quelqu'un d'ardent aura tiré
Du cœur de la nécessité même, le vrai,
Bloc clair, pour y dresser l'entente universelle.

V

The drama is best represented by nineteenth-century writers
(Bk. IX, Ch. II), most of whom continue into the period under
Drama: discussion.   Brieux, Hervieu, Curel, Maeterlinck,
Bernstein   Donnay and Lavedan still dominate the theater.
Secondary to these are the twentieth-century writers, who
express, for the most part, the tastes of the boulevards or the
" littérature du sérail " (Baldensperger). The idealistic current
runs thinnest in the theater, and the too-familiar triangle was not
displaced even by the war. Probably the most notable new
dramatist is M. Henri Bernstein (b. 1876), who perpetuates the
tradition of the play that is ingenious, " well-made " and rather
unreal. He usually presents triangular situations (*Le Détour*,
1902; *Le Bercail*, 1904); his characterization is faulty, since his
audience prefers the effects of melodrama and of long-suspended
scenes (*Le Voleur*, 1906); he occasionally runs closer to the
théâtre d'idées, as in *Israël* (1908). *Samson* (1907) is suitably
" strong " and gives a good portrart of the financier in his corrupt
milieu. More is made of spiritual issues in *L'Assaut* (1912) and
especially in *L'Elévation* (1917), one of the best plays inspired
by the war.

Henri Bataille (1872–1922) began with a flare of poetry which
the market-place presently extinguished. He has been called a
"specialist in the pathology of love " (Chandler), and he often
presents abnormal women (*Maman Colibri*, 1903; *La Vierge*

folle, 1910). Like Bernstein, Bataille gives a large place to action that proceeds from unbridled instincts and **Minor Figures** desires. A romantic inclination is visible in Bataille, while Alfred Capus (b. 1858) has taken life more realistically, but easily and superficially enough, in such comedies as *La Veine, Notre Jeunesse, Les Favorites,* and numerous others. The amusing and rather scandalous *vaudevilles* of the collaborators, R. de Flers and G. de Caillavet, are at any rate witty and well wrought. But in none of these dramatists are we conscious of the richness, the turmoil and the profounder realities of life.

The idealistic movement is to be found elsewhere and particularly in the mystical dramas of M. Paul Claudel (b. 1868). **Claudel** A devout Catholic, a traveler and consul of France in the Orient, M. Claudel has written plays as unusual as his experiences. In his first collected volume (*L'Arbre,* 1901, containing five dramas), he endeavored to infuse a mystic note into modern scenes and situations (as in *La Jeune Fille Violaine* and in *L'Echange*). Conscious of this discrepancy, Claudel later transposed *La Jeune Fille Violaine* into medieval terms and the result is his masterpiece, *L'Annonce faite à Marie* (1912, 1914). This play is like a saint's life in its record of spiritual sweetness and martyrdom. Violaine herself, like the majority of Claudel's heroines, is " living and lovable." But the symbolism of all these dramas and the language in which they are written is wilfully strange and obscure. Claudel's medium is again rhythmic prose, often beautiful in its imagery and melody. For all his depiction of violence and pain, his " âme lumineuse " casts a singular glow upon his best passages and the high moments of his rarefied characters.

Claudel is at once an intuitive mystic and a man of action. Some hold that Intuitivism, as a philosophy of ideals, demands **Conclusion** a practical outlet. The younger generation now had need of both qualities: the cataclysm of 1914 was a test alike of their faith and of their " works." We all know how France endured the test. The literature of the Great War and of the reconstruction period lies beyond our scope; it is too soon to classify and judge the confusion of material. But as we close this long survey, we are impressed anew by three outstanding and abiding features of French Literature: its high artistic standards; the continuity of its course or the fact that its line of march has been almost unbroken since the beginning; and the cumulative power of its traditions, effective even among the iconoclasts. These things have been part of the French record for eight hundred years and they promise well for the future.

THE END

BIBLIOGRAPHY

THE following bibliography is strictly selective. It does not give critical editions of works except where they include valuable literary treatment; such editions can usually be found in the bibliographies to which we refer. As far as possible, we have been guided in our choice by the following considerations:

(1) Preference is given to works in English and French; our aim being to include the most modern treatises and those to which our text is directly indebted; (2) in many cases we lighten the reader's task by mentioning translations of works; (3) the best all-round book or article on a subject is marked with an asterisk; (4) a dagger next to a title refers the reader for commentary to our text; (5) in general, we list books and articles in the order of discussion followed in our text; (6) where the place of publication is *not* mentioned, it is either London or Paris, according as the publication is in English or French; (7) we use certain obvious abbreviations (*Caus. du lundi, Port. litt.,* etc.), and " G. E. F." indicates the *Grands Ecrivains français* series (*Etudes biographiques et littéraires*).

BIBLIOGRAPHIES ON FRENCH LITERATURE:

For the Middle Ages: *G. Paris, *La Littérature française au moyen âge,* 5th edition, 1913; C. Voretzsch, *Einführung in das Studium der altfranzösischen Literatur,* 2nd edition, Halle, 1913.

For the Renaissance: H. Morf, *Geschichte der französischen Literatur im Zeitalter der Renaissance,* 2nd edition, Strassburg, 1914; * G. Lanson, *Manuel bibliographique de la littérature française moderne:* I. *Seizième siècle,* 2nd ed., 1911.

For ensuing periods: * G. Lanson, *Manuel,* vols. II, III, IV and V (supplement and index) 1910–1921; H. P. Thieme, *Guide bibliographique de la littérature française de 1800 à 1906,* 1907; Jassy et Lens, *Les Ressources du travail intellectuel en France,* 1921.

Lorenz et Jordell, *Catalogue de la librairie française* gives monthly subject-lists of new French books and an annual index.

HISTORIES OF FRENCH LITERATURE:

* G. Lanson, † *Histoire de la littérature française,* 16th edition, 1921; F. Brunetière, *Manuel de l'histoire de la littérature française,* 2nd edition, 1899; * Suchier und Birch-Hirschfeld, *Geschichte der französischen Literatur von den ältesten Zeiten bis zur Gegenwart,* 2nd edition, Leipzig and Vienna, 1913; G. Saintsbury, *A Short History of French*

739

Literature 7th edition, 1917; C. H. C. Wright, *A History of French Literature*, New York, 1912; L. Petit de Julleville (editor), *Histoire de la langue et de la littérature française, des origines à 1900*, 8 vols., 1896–1899 (chapters by different authors); * Désiré Nisard, † *Histoire de la littérature française*, 4 vols., 1844–1861 (still the standard exposition from the Classical point of veiw).

HISTORIC AND SOCIAL BACKGROUND OF FRENCH LITERATURE:

* *Histoire de France, depuis les origines jusqu'à la Révolution*, 18 vols. (9 Tomes), edited by † E. Lavisse, 1900-1911; F. Schrader, *Atlas de géographie historique*, (Hachette); L. Hourticq, *Histoire de l'art* (*Collection Ars Una: La France*), Hachette; Kr. Nyrop, *Grammaire historique de la langue française*, 3rd edition, vol. I, Copenhagen, 1914; F. Brunot, *Histoire de la langue française des origines à 1900*, 5 vols., 1905–1916; L. E. Kastner, *History of French Versification*, Oxford, 1903; M. Grammont, * *Petit traité de versification française*, 1908; W. C. Brownell, *French Traits, an essay in Comparative Criticism*, New York, 1902.

INTRODUCTORY CHAPTER:

* F. Brunetière, *Le Caractère essentiel de la littérature française* in his † *Etudes critiques*, 5e série, 1893; G. Paris, Preface to Petit de Julleville, vol. I; G. Lanson, *Caractères généraux de la littérature française* in the *Revue des cours et conférences*, XXI (1912), 5–17; M. Bréal, *Le Langage et les nationalités* in the *Revue des deux mondes*, CVIII (1891), 3e pér.

PART I, BOOK I

CHAPTER I:

G. Paris, Introduction to *La Littérature française;* Petit de Julleville, vols, I and II; Lavisse, *Histoire*, vol. I: Ch.-V. Langlois, *La Vie en France au moyen âge*, 2nd edition, 1911, and *De la Connaissance de la nature et du monde au moyen âge*, 1911; H. O. Taylor, selected chapters from *The Mediaeval Mind*, 3rd edition, 2 vols., New York, 1919.

On the *chansons de geste:*

* W. P. Ker, *Epic and Romance*, 2nd edition, 1908; Pio Rajna, *Le Origini dell'epopea francese*, Florence, 1884; * J. Bédier, *Les Légendes épiques*, 4 vols., 1908-1913; W. P. Shepard, *Chansons de geste and the Homeric Problem* in the *American Journal of Philology,* XLII (1921).

The *Chanson de Roland* has been translated into English by C. S. Moncrieff, *The Song of Roland done into English in the original measure*, 1919; and into Modern French by L. Petit de Julleville, *La Chanson de Roland, traduction nouvelle rhythmée et assonancée*, 1878; for analysis of the poem see Bédier, III.

On the *Pèlerinage de Charlemagne*, see J. Coulet, *Etudes sur l'ancien poème français du Voyage de Charlemagne*, Montpellier, 1907.

On the Southern and Feudal Cycles, see Bédier I and II; for translation of the *Girart de Roussillon*, P. Meyer, *G. de R., chanson de geste traduite pour la première fois*, 1884; *Huon de Bordeaux* can be read either in Lord Berners' English rendering (*Tudor Translations*) or in G. Paris, *Aventures merveilleuses de Huon de Bordeaux*, 1899.

CHAPTER II:

On the lyric, in general:

* A. Jeanroy, *Les Origines de la poésie lyrique en France au moyen âge*, 2nd edition, 1904; G. Paris in the *Mélanges de litt. fr.* 1912, p. 539; J. Bédier in the *Revue des deux mondes*, CXXXV (1896), 4ᵉ pér.; F. Diez, *Die Poesie der Troubadours*, 2nd edition, Leipzig, 1883; E. Faral, *Les Jongleurs en France au moyen âge*, 1910.

On the background of the *esprit courtois*:

E. Lavisse, III, Part I; K. Norgate, *England under the Angevin Kings*, 1887; L. F. Mott, *The System of Courtly Love*, Boston, 1896; * A. Luchaire, *Social France at the Time of Philip Augustus* (English transl.), New York, 1912.

On the romance, in general:

W. P. Ker, op. cit.; M. Wilmotte, *Evolution du roman français aux environs de 1150* (Proceedings of the Académie royale de Belgique), Brussels, 1903; W. A. Nitze in *Romania*, XLIV.

On the Matter of Rome:

G. Saintsbury, *The Flourishing of Romance*, New York, 1897; E. Faral, *Recherches sur les sources latines des contes et des romans courtois*, 1913; P. Meyer, *Alexandre le Grand*, 2 vols., 1886 (text and discussion); K. Young, *Origin and Development of the Story of Troilus and Criseyde*, Chaucer Society, 1908.

On the Matter of Britain:

H. Zimmer, *The Irish Element in Mediaeval Culture*, transl. by J. L. Edmands, New York and London, 1891; G. Paris, *Les Romans de la Table Ronde* in the *Histoire Littéraire de la France*, vol. XXX (1888); W. Foerster, *Kristian von Troyes, Wörterbuch zu seinen sämtlichen Werken*, Halle, 1914 (Introduction); H. Maynadier, *The Arthur of the English Poets*, Boston, 1907.

On the *Tristan*:

G. Paris, *Tristan et Iseut* in the *Revue de Paris*, 1894; J. Bédier, *Le Roman de Tristan*, 1900 (Modern French paraphrase of the story);

*W. Golther, *Tristan und Isolde*, Leipzig, 1907; G. Schoepperle, *Tristan and Isolt*, 2 vols. Frankfort and New York, 1913.

On Crestien de Troyes:

Introductions to Foerster's editions of the *Erec, Cligès, Lancelot* and *Yvain;* G. Paris in the *Mélanges de litt. fr.*, p. 229; M. Borodine, *La femme et l'amour au XIIe siècle d'après les poèmes de Chrétien de Troyes*, 1909. The four romances mentioned have been translated into Modern English by W. W. Comfort, Everyman's Library, and selected translations (including the *Perceval*) will be found in W. W. Newell, *King Arthur and the Table Round*, 2 vols., Boston and New York, 1898.

On the Holy Grail:

A. Nutt, *Studies on the Legend of the Holy Grail*, 1888; W. W. Newell, *The Legend of the Holy Grail*, Cambridge, U. S. A., 1902; W. A. Nitze in the *Publications of the Modern Language Association*, XXIV; *Jessie L. Weston, *The Quest of the Holy Grail*, 1913.

The entire *Perceval* and the *Perlesvaus* were published by Ch. Potvin, 6 vols., Mons, 1866–1871; the *Metrical Joseph* by F. Michel, *Le Roman du St. Graal*, Bordeaux, 1841; the *Prose-Perceval* by J. L. Weston, *Legend of Sir Perceval*, vol. II, 1909, and the entire Grail-Lancelot Cycle by O. Sommer, *The Vulgate Version of the Arthurian Romances*, 7 vols., Washington, 1909–1916. On the last, see F. Lot, *Etude sur le Lancelot en prose*, 1918.

Sebastian Evans has translated the *Perlesvaus* as *The High History of the Holy Graal*, Temple Classics, 2 vols.

The Welsh versions of Arthurian stories have been translated into Modern French by J. Loth, *Les Mabinogion*, 2nd edition, 2 vols., 1913 (see Introduction).

On the *romans d'aventure*:

*G. Gröber, *Grundriss der romanischen Philologie*, vol. II: *Französische Litteratur*, Strassburg, 1902, pp. 523 ff.; Ch.-V. Langlois, *La Société française au XIIIe siècle, d'après dix romans d'aventure*, 3rd edition, 1911.

On the *Châtelaine de Vergi*, see Alice Kemp-Welch, *The Châtelaine of Vergi, done into English* (including an edition of the original prepared by L. Brandin), 1903.

The Cycle of the Wager is treated by G. Paris in *Romania XXXIV*.

On Marie de France:

J. C. Fox in the *English Historical Review* XXV and XXVII; J. Bédier in the *Revue des deux mondes*, CVII (1891), 3 pér.; K. Warnke, ed. *Lais der Marie de France*, 2nd edition, Halle, 1900 (Introduction).

J. L. Weston, *Chief Middle English Poets*, Boston, 1914, gives a Modern English rendering of *Sir Orfeo*. Andrew Lang's translation of *Aucassin et Nicolette* appeared in 1887 (Nutt).

CHAPTER III:

On allegory, in general:

G. Saintsbury, *The Flourishing of Romance and the Rise of Allegory*, 1897; W. A. Neilson, *Origin and Sources of the Court of Love*, in the Harvard Studies and Notes, Boston, 1899; Ch. Oulmont, *Les Débats du clerc et du chevalier dans la littérature poétique du moyen âge*, 1911; E. Faral in *Romania* XLI. For Raoul de Houdenc, see M. Friedwagner, Introduction to *R. von Houdenc, Sämtliche Werke*, 2 vols., Halle, 1897–1909.

On the Romance of the Rose:

Introduction to E. Langlois, ed. *Roman de la Rose*, vol. I, 1914, G. Lanson, *Un écrivain naturaliste du XIIIͤ siècle* (Jean de Meun) in *Revue bleue*, 1894. For Modern English verse-translation of the poem, F. S. Ellis, 3 vols., 1900.

On the *Roman de Renard*:

L. Sudre, *Les Sources du Roman de Renard*, 1893, and G. Paris in the *Mélanges de litt. fr.*, p. 337; * L. Foulet, *Le Roman de Renard* (thèse), 1914, and W. A. Nitze in *Modern Language Notes*, 1915. For Marie de France's *Fables*, see Introduction of the edition of Karl Warnke, Halle, 1898, and his *Quellen des Esope der Marie de France*, Halle, 1900. Also J. Jacobs, *History of the Aesopic Fable*, 1889.

On the medieval drama:

E. K. Chambers, *The Mediaeval Stage*, Oxford, 1903; L. Petit de Julleville, *Les Mystères*, 2 vols., 1880; G. Cohen, *Histoire de la mise en scène dans le théâtre religieux français au moyen âge*, 1886; D. C. Stuart, *The Development of Stage Decoration in the Middle Ages*, (dissertation), New York, 1910; W. Creizenach, *Geschichte des neueren Dramas*, 2nd ed., vol. I, Halle, 1911.

On the *miracle* and the *jeu*:

G. Paris et U. Robert, ed. *Les Miracles de Notre-Dame*, 7 vols., 1876–1883; G. R. Coffman, *A New Theory concerning the Origin of the Miracle Play* (dissertation), Menasha, 1914; O. Rohnström, *Etude sur Jean Bodel*, Upsala, 1900; Henry Guy, *Essai sur la vie et les œuvres littéraires du trouvère Adam de la Hale* (thèse), 1898.

On medieval historians:

*Paris et Jeanroy, *Extraits des chroniqueurs français*, 8th edition, 1912 (Villehardouin, Joinville, Froissart, Commines); E. Estienne, *La vie de St. Thomas, Etude historique, littéraire et philologique*, Nancy, 1883; W. P. Ker, *Froissart* in *Essays on Mediaeval Literature*, 1905; for English translation of Froissart, see Lord Berners, *The Chronicles of Froissart*, ed. by W. P. Ker, 6 vols., 1901–1903; Modern English translations of Villehardouin and Joinville will be found in Everyman's Library.

On didactic literature:

Petit de Julleville, vol. II (article by A. Piaget); *Ch.-V. Langlois, *De la Connaissance de la nature* (above); *Le Bestiaire de Philippe de Thaün*, ed. by E. Walberg, 1900; T. Sundby, *Della vita et delle opere di Brunetto Latini*, Italian translation by R. Renier, Florence, 1884; L. J. Paetow, *The Battle of the Seven Arts by Henri d'Andeli*, edited and translated, Berkeley, 1914. .

On storiology:

*J. Bédier, *Les Fabliaux*, 2nd edition, 1895; G. Paris, *Les Contes orientaux dans la littérature française du moyen âge* in his †*Poésie du moyen âge*, II, 3rd edition, 1906. Killis Campbell, *A Study of the Romance of the Seven Sages* (dissertation), Baltimore, 1898.

BOOK II

Chapter I

General aspects :

E. Lavisse, *Histoire de France*, vols. III and IV; Helen L. Cohen, *The Ballade*, New York, 1895 (dissertation); Otto Ritter, *Die Geschichte der französischen Balladenformen von ihren Anfängen bis zur Mitte des XV Jahrhunderts*, Halle, 1914; *G. Doutrepont, *La Littérature française à la cour des ducs de Bourgogne*, 1909.

On the poets:

Introduction to E. Hoepffner, ed. *Œuvres de Guillaume de Machaut*, vol. I, 1908; the same, *Eustache Deschamps*, 1904; F. Koch, *Leben und Werke der Christine de Pisan*, Goslar, 1885; A. Piaget, *Christine de Pisan et le Roman de la Rose* in the *Etudes romanes dédiées à Gaston Paris*, 1891; G. Joret-Desclosières, *Alain Chartier*, 1897; P. Champion, *La Vie de Charles d'Orléans*, 1911.

CHAPTER II:

A. O. Norton, *Mediaeval Universities*, Cambridge, U. S. A., 1909; G. H. Luquet, *Aristote et l'Université de Paris au XIIIᵉ siècle*, in the Bibliothèque de l'Ecole des Hautes Etudes, 1904; D. H. Carnahan, *The Ad Deum Vadit of Jean Gerson*, in the University of Illinois Studies, Urbana, 1917; E. Bridrey, *Nicole Oresme*, 1906; * L. J. Paetow, *The Arts Course at Mediaeval Universities*, Champagne, 1910.

CHAPTER III:

See Book I, Chapter III; L. Petit de Julleville, *Les Mystères*, 2 vols., 1880; the same, *La Comédie et les mœurs en France au moyen âge*, 1886; E. Picot, *Recueil général de sotties*, 2 vols., 1902–1905; C. Oulmont, *Pierre Gringoire*, 1911; F. E. Schneegans, ed. *Maistre Pierre Pathelin*, Strassburg, 1908; for an excellent English translation, Richard Holbrook, *The Farce of Master Pierre Patelin*, Boston and New York, 1905.

CHAPTER IV:

On Antoine de La Sale:

* J. W. Söderhjelm, *La Nouvelle française au XVᵉ siècle*, 1910; J. Nève, *Antoine de La Sale*, Brussels and Paris, 1903; P. Toldo, *Contributo allo studio della novella francese del XV e XVI secolo*, Rome, 1895; G. Paris in the *Journal des savants*, 1895.

On Villon:

* G. Paris, *François Villon* (G. E. F.), 1901; P. Champion, *François Villon, sa vie et son temps*, 1913; Villon has been excellently translated into English verse by John Payne, 1878.

On Commines:

See the edition of the *Mémoires* by B. de Mandrot, 1901–1903.

PART II

In general:

E. Lavisse, *Histoire*, vol. V, Parts I and II; H. Morf, *Geschichte;* * F. Brunetière, *Histoire de la littérature française classique*, vols. I–III, 1908–1914; A. Tilley, *The Literature of the French Renaissance*, 2 vols., Cambridge 1904; * the same, *The Dawn of the French Renaissance*, Cambridge, 1918 (treats also history and art); J. Burckhardt, *Die Kultur der Renaissance in Italien*, revised by Geiger, 10th edition, 2 vols., Leipzig, 1908 (French and English translations of this); P. Monnier, *Le Quattrocento*, 2nd edition, 2 vols., 1908; * Preserved Smith,

The Age of the Reformation, New York, 1920; Sainte-Beuve, *Tableau historique et critique de la poésie française au XVIe siècle,* 1828–1842; P. de Nolhac, *Pétrarque et l'humanisme,* 2nd edition, 1907; E. Picot, *Les Français italianisants au XVIe siècle,* 2 vols., 1906–1907; * J. E. Spingarn, *A History of Literary Criticism in the Renaissance,* 2nd edition, New York, 1908; C. H. C. Wright, *French Classicism,* Cambridge, U. S. A., 1920; J. Vianey, *Le Pétrarquisme en France au XVIe siècle,* 1909 (for the sonnet, as a form, p. 102 ff.).

BOOK I

CHAPTER I:

H. Guy, *Histoire de la poésie française au XVIe siècle,* vol. I, 1910; the works of Morf, Brunetière and Tilley; L. Delaruelle, *Guillaume Budé,* 1907; H. Chamard, *Les Origines de la poésie française de la Renaissance* (Boccard); Ph. A. Becker, *Jean Lemaire, Der erste humanistische Dichter Frankreichs,* Strassburg, 1893.

CHAPTER II:

Introductory volume to the *Œuvres de Clément Marot,* ed. Guiffrey, vol. I, 1911; O. Douen, *Clément Marot et le Psautier huguenot,* 2 vols., 1878; A. Lefranc, essay on the poet's love-affair in the *Grands écrivains français de la Renaissance,* 1914; C. Ruutz-Rees, *Charles de Sainte-Marthe,* traduit par M. Bonnet, 1914; R. L. Hawkins, *Maistre Charles Fontaine,* Cambridge, U. S. A., 1916; Hélène Harvitt, *Eustorg de Beaulieu,* Lancaster, 1918 (reprinted from the *Romanic Review,* 1914 ff.); H. Molinier, *Mellin de Saint-Gelais,* 1911.

CHAPTER III:

See the *Revue des Etudes Rabelaisiennes,* now the *Revue du Seizième Siècle,* edited by A. Lefranc; R. Millet, *François Rabelais,* (G. E. F.), 1892; * A. Tilley, *François Rabelais* (in English), Philadelphia, 1907; * F. Plattard, *L'Œuvre de Rabelais,* 1910; Introduction to the *Œuvres de François Rabelais,* critical edition by Lefranc and others, 1912 ff.; * W. F. Smith, *Rabelais in his Writings,* Cambridge, 1918; the best English translation of Rabelais is by Urquhart and Motteux, 1708 (frequently reprinted).

W. Walker, *John Calvin,* New York, 1906; H. Hauser, *Etudes sur la Réforme française,* 1910; Introduction to the *Institution de la Religion chrestienne,* ed. by Lefranc, Chatelain and Pannier, 2 vols., 1912–1913.

CHAPTER IV:

W. E. H. Lecky, *Rise and Influence of the Spirit of Rationalism in Europe,* New York, 1886; J. Owen, *Ramus* in *The Skeptics of the*

French Renaissance, 1893; articles on Platonism and Marguerite de Navarre in A. Lefranc, *Grands écrivains français de la Renaissance*, 1914; Mary Robinson, *Marguerite of Angoulême*, 1899; A. Chenevière, *Bonaventure des Périers, sa vie, ses poésies*, 1886; W. A. R. Kerr, *Antoine Héroët's Parfaite Amye* in the *Publications of the Modern Lang. Assoc., XX*; A. Baur, *Maurice Scève et la Renaissance lyonnaise*, 1905; J. Arnoux, *Antoine Héroët, néoplatonicien et poète*, Digne, 1913.

BOOK II

CHAPTER I:

J. E. Spingarn, *Literary Criticism*, Part II; A. Rosenbauer, *Die poetischen Theorien der Plejade nach Ronsard und Du Bellay*, Leipzig, 1895; * P. Villey, *Les Sources italiennes de la Défense et Illustration*, 1908; G. Lanson, *Comment Ronsard invente* in the *Revue universitaire*, 1906; C. Jugé, *Jacques Peletier du Mans*, 1907; G. Pellissier ed. of Vauquelin de la Fresnaie, *L'Art poétique*, 1885; F. Flamini, *Du rôle de Pontus de Tyard dans le Pétrarquisme français* in the *Revue de la Renaissance*, 1901.

CHAPTER II:

* J.-J. Jusserand, *Pierre de Ronsard* (G. E. F.), 1912; Claude Binet, *Discours de la vie de Ronsard*, ed. P. Laumonier, 1911; H. Longnon, *Pierre de Ronsard: les Ancêtres, la Jeunesse*, 1912; P. de Nolhac, *Le dernier amour de Ronsard*, 1914; P. Laumonier, *Ronsard, poète lyrique*, 1909 (thèse); C. H. Page, *Songs and Sonnets of P. de Ronsard* (verse-translation), Boston, 1903.

H. Chamard, *Joachim du Bellay*, 1900; Walter Pater, *Du Bellay* in *The Renaissance*, New York, 1899.

Augé-Chiquet, *Jean-Antoine de Baïf*, 1909; A. van Bever, ed. of Belleau, 1909; J. Favre, *Olivier de Magny*, 1885 (thèse); G. Grente, *Jean Bertaut*, 1903; S. Rocheblave, *Agrippa d'Aubigné* (G. E. F.), 1910; G. Pellissier, *La vie et les œuvres de Du Bartas*, 1882 (thèse); H. Ashton, *Du Bartas en Angleterre*, 1908 (thèse).

CHAPTER III:

* R. Sturel, *Amyot traducteur des Vies Parallèles de Plutarque*, 1909; * E. Dowden, *Michel de Montaigne*, Philadelphia, 1905; Grace Norton, *The Spirit of Montaigne*, Boston, 1908; Paul Stapfer *Montaigne* (G. E. F.), 1895; F. Strowski, *De Montaigne à Pascal*, 1907; * P. Villey, † *Les Sources et l'évolution des Essais de Montaigne*, 2 vols., 1908; J. de Zangroniz, *Montaigne, Amyot et Saliat*, 1906; J. M. Robertson, *Montaigne and Shakespeare*, 1909; the Florio and the Cotton translations have been frequently reprinted; L. Lalanne, *Brantôme, sa vie et ses écrits* (Société de l'Histoire de France), 1896; P. Courteault, *Blaise de Monluc, historien*, 1907.

CHAPTER IV:

Ch. Lenient, *La Satire en France*, 2 vols., 2nd edition, 1866; G. Wenderoth, *E. Pasquiers poetische Theorien und seine Tätigkeit als Literarhistoriker* in Vollmöller's *Romanische Forschungen* XIX; F. Giroux, *La composition de la Satire Ménippée*, Laon, 1904; R. Radouant, *Guillaume du Vair, l'homme et l'orateur*, 1907; P. Bonnefon, *Pierre Charron* in *Montaigne et ses amis*, vol. II, 1897; F. Strowski, *Saint François de Sales*, 1898; Duc de Broglie, *Malherbe* (G. E. F.), 1897; *F. Brunot, *La Doctrine de Malherbe d'après son commentaire sur Desportes*, 1891; M. Souriau, *La Versification de Malherbe*, Poitiers, 1912; L. Arnould, *Honorat de Bueil, seigneur de Racan*, 1901; J. Vianey, *Mathurin Régnier*, 1896; Mario Schiff, *La Fille d'alliance de Montaigne, Marie de Gournay*, 1910; Ch. Garrisson, *Théophile et Paul de Viau, étude historique et littéraire*, 1899.

BOOK III

In general:

E. Lavisse, *Histoire*, V, Parts I and II; G. Hanotaux, *Histoire du Cardinal Richelieu*, 2 vols., 1893–1896; G. Boissier, *L'Académie française sous l'ancien régime*, 1909; Victor Cousin, *La Société française d'après le Grand Cyrus*, 2 vols., 1858; Vial et Denise, *Idées et doctrines littéraires du XVIIe siècle*, 1906.

CHAPTER I:

T. F. Crane, *La Société française au dix-septième siècle*, 2nd ed., 1907; E. Magne, *Voiture et les années de gloire de l'Hôtel de Rambouillet*, 1912; H. Vogler, *Die literargeschichtlichen Kenntnisse und Urteile des J-L. Guez de Balzac*, 1908; Fr. Masson, *Histoire de l'Académie française*, 1913; Brunetière, *Vaugelas et la théorie de l'usage* in the *Revue des deux mondes*, 1901; Abbé Fabre, *Jean Chapelain et nos deux premières Académies*, 1890.

CHAPTER II:

Gustave Reynier, *Le Roman sentimental avant l'Astrée*, 1908; *A. Le Breton, *Le Roman au XVIIe siècle;* *T. F. Crane, ed. of Boileau, *Les Héros de roman*, Boston, 1902; O-C. Reure, *La vie et les œuvres de Honoré d'Urfé*, 1910; W. Küchler, *Zu den Anfängen des psychologischen Romans in Frankreich* in Herrig's *Archiv*, 1909; A. Gasté, *Mlle de Scudéry et le Dialogue des Héros de Roman*, 1902; E. Magne, *Scarron et son milieu*, 1905; *A. Franz, *Das literarische Portrait im Zeitalter Richelieus und Mazarins*, Leipzig, 1905.

CHAPTER III:

E. Faguet, *La Tragédie en France au XVIe siècle*, 1883; G. Lanson, *L'Idée de la tragédie avant Jodelle* in the *Revue d'hist. litt.*, 1904; the same, *Antoine de Montchrétien et la litt. fr. au temps de Henri IV* in *Hommes et livres*, 1895; *the same, *Esquisse d'une histoire de la tragédie française*, New York, 1920; E. Rigal, *De Jodelle à Molière*, 1911; E. Rigal, *Alexander Hardy et le théâtre français à la fin du XVIe siècle*, 1889 (thèse); H. C. Lancaster, *The French Tragi-Comedy* (1551-1628), Baltimore, 1907, (dissertation); J. Marsan, *La Pastorale dramatique en France*, 1905; P. Toldo, *La Comédie française de la Renaissance* in the *Revue d'his. litt.*, 1897 and 1899; E. Dannheisser, *Studien zu Jean de Mairets Leben und Werken*, Ludwigshafen, 1888; the same, *Zur Geschichte der Einheiten in Frankreich* in the *Zeitschr. für franz. Sprache u. Lit.* 1892; Ch. Arnaud, *Etude sur la vie et les œuvres de l'abbé d'Aubignac*, 1887; *La Mémoire de Mahelot*, ed. H. C. Lancaster, 1921 (gives stage-settings, etc).

CHAPTER IV:

* G. Lanson, *Pierre Corneille*, (G. E. F.) 4th ed. 1913; E. Martinenche, *La Comedia espagnole en France*, 1900; E. Faguet, *En lisant Corneille*, 1913; A. Dorchain, *Pierre Corneille*, 1918; E. Picot, *Bibliographie Cornélienne*, 1876 (continued by P. Verdier and E. Pelay, 1908); A. Gasté, *La Querelle du Cid*, 1899; W. A. Nitze, *Corneille's Conception of Character* in *Modern Philology*, 1917-1918; A. Tilley, *From Montaigne to Molière*, 1908 (contains several good chapters on Corneille); H. C. Lancaster, *Pierre Du Ryer*, Washington, 1912; A. L. Stiefel, various articles on Rotrou in the *Zeitschr. für franz, Spr. u. Lit.* 1894-1906; G. Wendt, *Pierre Corneille und Jean Rotrou*, Leipzig, 1910.

CHAPTER V:

A. Fouillée, *Descartes* (G. E. F.), 1893; G. Lanson, *Hommes et livres*, 1895; * F. Brunetière, *Jansénistes et Cartésiens* in the *Etudes critiques*, IVe série; E. S. Haldane, *Descartes, his Life and Times*, 1905; G. J. Brett, *The Philosophy of Gassendi*, 1908; F. Perrens, *Les Libertins*, 2nd ed., 1899; H. Joly, *Malebranche*, 1910.

BOOK IV

CHAPTER I:

Lavisse, *l.c.*; †Voltaire, *Le Siècle de Louis XIV*, 1740 — a convenient modern edition is published by Garnier Frères; R. Doumic, *Saint-Simon: La France de Louis XIV*, 1919; * Wright, *French Classicism*, Chs. VII and VIII; F. Brunetière, *Qu'est-ce qu'un classique?* in his *Hist. de la litt. fr. cl.*, vol. II.

CHAPTER II:

Sainte-Beuve, *Portrait de La Rochefoucauld* in the Garnier publica_ tion of the latter's works; J. Bourdeau, *La Rochefoucauld* (G. E. F.), 1895; R. Grandsaigues d'Hauterive, *Le Pessimisme de La Roche- foucauld*, 1914; Sainte-Beuve, *Causeries du lundi*, vol. V. (on Retz); Mme Duclaux, *Madame de Sévigné*, 1914; E. Angot, *Dames du grand siècle*, 1919; Comte d'Haussonville, *Madame de La Fayette* (G. E. F.), 1891; Duc de Noailles, *Histoire de Mme de Maintenon,* 4 vols., 1848–1858; Saint-René Taillandier, *Madame de Maintenon,* 1920; *G. Lanson, *Choix de Lettres du XVIIᵉ siècle*, 10th ed., 1913 (introduction especially instructive).

CHAPTER III:

K. Mantzius, *Molière, les théâtres, le public et les comédiens de son temps*, 1908; * E. Rigal, *Molière*, 2 vols., 1908; G. Lafenestre, *Molière* (G. E. F.), 1909; B. Matthews, *Molière*, New York, 1910; * M. J. Wolff, *Molière, der Dichter und sein Werk*, Munich, 1910; F. Brunetière, *La philosophie de Molière* in *Etudes critiques*, IVᵉ série; L. Moland, *Molière et la comédie italienne*, 1867; G. Huszar, *Molière et l'Espagne*, 1907; Currier and Gay, *Catalogue of the Molière Collection in the Harvard Library*, Cambridge, U. S. A., 1906; † H. Taine, *La Fontaine et ses fables*, 1853, 3rd edition, 1861; G. Lafenestre, *La Fontaine* (G. E. F.), 1895; G. Michaut, *La Fontaine*, 2 vols., 1913–1914; K. Vossler, *La Fontaine und sein Fabelwerk*, Heidelberg, 1919.

CHAPTER IV:

* Sainte-Beuve, *Port-Royal*, 5th edition, 7 vols. (with an index), 1888–1891; E. Romanes, *The Story of Port-Royal*, 1907; F. Strowski, *Pascal et son temps*, 3 vols., 1907–1909; * E. Boutroux, *Pascal* (G. E. F.), 1900; * Viscount St. Cyres, *Pascal*, 1909 (the best account in English); in regard to the *Pensées*, see also the editions of Havet, 1851, and of Brunschvicg, 1897; * J. Lemaître, *Jean Racine*, 1908 (by far the most interesting discussion of the poet); G. Larroumet, *Jean Racine* (G. E. F.), 1898; F. Brunetière in his *Epoques du théâtre français*, 1892; P. Robert, *La poétique de Racine*, 1890; Dreyfus-Brisac, *Phèdre et Hippolyte ou Racine moraliste*, 1903.

CHAPTER V:

A. Bourgoin, *Les Maîtres de la Critique au XVIIᵉ siècle*, 1887; the same in Petit de Julleville, vol. V, ch. 3; G. Saintsbury, *A History of Criticism*, Edinburgh, 1900–1904, vol. II; * F. Brunetière, *L'Esthétique de Boileau* in *Et. cr.* VIᵉ série; G. Lanson, *Boileau* (G. E. F.), 1892; F. Brunetière, *La Philosophie de Bossuet* in *Et. cr.* Vᵉ série; A. Rébelliau, *Bossuet* (G. E. F.), 1900; the same, *Bossuet, historien du protestantisme*, 1909; * G. Lanson, *Bossuet*, 5th edition,

1901; *E. K. Sanders, *Jacques-Bénigne Bossuet*, 1921; F. Castets, *Bourdaloue, la vie et la prédication d'un religieux au XVII⁰ siècle*, 2 vols., 1901–1904.

PART III

On the eighteenth century in general:

Lanson, *Histoire;* Petit de Julleville, Vol. VI; Sainte-Beuve's essays as indexed in the two *Tables alphabétiques* to his works; more particularly, *A. Villemain, *Tableau de la littérature française au XVIII⁰ siècle*, 4 vols., 1828; H. Hettner, *Literaturgeschichte des achtzehnten Jahrhunderts. Theil II: Geschichte der französischen Literatur*, 5th ed., revised, Brunswick, 1894; †E. Faguet, *Dix-huitième siècle: Etudes littéraires*, 1890 (ff.); J. Barni, *Histoire des Idées morales et politiques en France au XVIII⁰ siècle*, 2 vols., 1865–67; E. Bersot, *Etudes sur le XVIII⁰ siècle*, 2 vols., 1855.

For Bibliography: Lanson, *Manuel*, vol. III; Wright, *History;* L. P. Betz, *La littérature comparée*, 2nd ed., Strassburg, 1904.

BOOK I

CHAPTER I:

*H. Rigault, *Histoire de la Querelle des anciens et des modernes*, 1856 and 1859; H. Gillot, *La Querelle des anciens et des modernes en France* (thèse), Nancy, 1914 (exhaustive as far as Perrault's *Parallèles*); F. Vial and L. Denise, *Idées et doctrines littéraires du XVII⁰ siècle*, 1906.

On the larger question of Progress:

*J. B. Bury, *The Idea of Progress; An Inquiry into its Origin and Growth*, 1920 (widely historical, penetrating, philosophic); J. Delvaille, *Essai sur l'histoire de l'Idée de progrès jusqu'à la fin du XVIII⁰ siècle*, 1910 (limited to France, erudite, detailed); F. Brunetière, *Etudes critiques*, V.

CHAPTER II:

*P. Morillot, *La Bruyère* (G. E. F.), 1904; Sainte-Beuve, *Nouv. lundis*, I and X; L. Prévost-Paradol, *Etudes sur les moralistes français*, 6th ed., 1885.

*G. Boissier, *Saint-Simon* (G. E. F.), 2nd ed., 1899; A. Le Breton, *La Comédie humaine de Saint-Simon*, 1914; Sainte-Beuve, *Caus. du lundi*, III and XV, *Nouv. lundis*, X; Taine, *Essais de critique et d'histoire*, 6th ed., 1892.

J. Lemaître, *Fénelon*, 1910; Paul Janet, *Fénelon*, (G. E. F.), 2nd ed.,

1903; H. Sée, *Les Idées politiques de Fénelon* in the *Revue d'histoire moderne,* 1899.

CHAPTER III:

E. Lavisse, *Histoire de France,* VIII, Part II; * C. Stryienski, *Le Dix-huitième siècle,* 1913 (short and readable); J. B. Perkins, *France under Louis XV,* 6th ed., 2 vols., Boston, 1897.

On social conditions:

* H. Taine, *Les Origines de la France contemporaine. Tome I: L'Ancien régime,* 22nd ed., 1899; V. Du Bled, *La Société française du XVIe au XXe siècle.* Vol. V: *Dix-huitième siècle,* 1905; * M. Roustan, *Les Philosophes et la société française au XVIIIe siècle,* (thèse, 1906), 1911; E. and J. de Goncourt, *La Femme au XVIIIe siècle,* new ed., 1896.

On the ladies of the salons:

Sainte-Beuve, *passim,* especially *Caus. du lundi,* I, II, IV; Petit de Julleville, VI (chapter by Brunel); P.-M. Masson, *Madame de Tencin,* 3rd ed., 1910; P. de Ségur, *Le Royaume de la rue Saint-Honoré, Mme Geoffrin et sa fille,* 1897; Introductions to Mme du Deffand's *Correspondance générale* (ed. Lescure, 2 vols., 1865), and her *Lettres à Horace Walpole* (ed. Mrs. Paget Toynbee, 3 vols., 1912); P. de Ségur, *Julie de Lespinasse,* 6th ed., 1913.

On science and the English influence:

D. Mornet, *Les Sciences de la Nature en France au XVIIIe siècle,* 1911; * J. Texte, *Jean-Jacques Rousseau et les origines du cosmopolitisme littéraire au XVIIIe siècle,* 1895 — English translation, 1899; R. Rosières, *Recherches sur la poésie contemporaine,* 1896 (articles on the English and the German influences). Other bibliography on this subject will be found under Books III and IV, below.

BOOK II

CHAPTER I:

* J. Delvolvé, *Essai sur Pierre Bayle,* 1906 (exhaustive, abstruse, authoritative); for the general reader, * Faguet, *op. cit.,* Sainte-Beuve, *Port. litt.,* I. Brunetière, *Etudes critiques,* V. P. Lenient, *Etude sur Pierre Bayle,* 1855 (still useful); for the specializing student, G. Lanson, *Origines de l'esprit philosophique* in the *Revue des cours et conférences,* 1908–10; H. E. Smith, *The Literary Criticism of Pierre Bayle,* (dissertation), Albany, 1912.

* L. Maigron, *Fontenelle,* 1906; Laborde-Milaà, *Fontenelle* (G. E. F.), 1905.

CHAPTER II:

Villemain, Bersot, Faguet (calls Voltaire " un chaos d'idées claires ");
Brunetière, *Etudes critiques*, I and III, also in *Etudes sur le XVIII*
siècle, 1911 (an incomplete study, minimizes English influences); * G.
Lanson, *Voltaire* (G. E. F.), 2nd ed., 1910 (*multum in parvo*); L.
Crouslé, *La Vie et les œuvres de Voltaire*, 2 vols., 1899 (informative,
but prejudiced against Voltaire); G. Desnoiresterres, *Voltaire et la*
société au dix-huitième siècle, 8 vols., 2nd. ed., 1871–76; J. C. Collins,
Voltaire, Montesquieu and Rousseau in England, 1908; S. G. Tallentyre,
(pseudonym), *The Life of Voltaire*, 2 vols., 1903. See also Bk. III,
Ch. I and Bk. IV, Ch. II.

CHAPTER III:

L. Vian (pseudonym), *Histoire de Montesquieu*, 2nd ed., 1879; * A.
Sorel, *Montesquieu* (G. E. F.), 1887; * J. Dedieu, *Montesquieu* (Grands
Philosophes series), 1913 — also English translation; same author,
Montesquieu et la tradition politique anglaise en France, 1909; Faguet,
Villemain, Brunetière (*Etudes critiques*, IV); Paul Janet, Introduction
to school edition of the *Esprit des lois*, 1887; H. Barckhausen,
Montesquieu, ses idées et ses œuvres, d'après les papiers de La Brède,
1907; E. P. Dargan, *The Aesthetic Doctrine of Montesquieu, its*
Application in his Writings, (dissertation), Baltimore, 1909; J. C.
Collins (see preceding chapter).

CHAPTER IV:

Petit de Julleville, Barni, Villemain; Sainte-Beuve, *Caus. du lundi*,
III (on Vauvenargues and d'Aguesseau) and XV (on St. Pierre); M.
Paléologue, *Vauvenargues* (G. E. F.), 1890; Falconnet, *Notice* on
d'Aguesseau in the latter's *Œuvres*, 2 vols., 1865; * A. Lombard, *L'Abbé*
Du Bos, un initiateur de la pensée moderne (thèse), 1913.

On St. Pierre, see Sainte-Beuve (*supra*), Barni, J. Fabre, *Les Pères*
de la Révolution, and J. Drouet, *L'Abbé de St. Pierre, l'homme et*
l'œuvre, 1912.

On the Memoirs, see Ch. Aubertin, *L'Esprit public au XVIII*e *siècle*,
étude sur les Mémoires, 3rd ed., 1889 (our text follows his divisions);
the excellent condensations of Barrière et Lescure (*Bibliothèque des*
*Mémoires relatifs à l'histoire de France pendant le XVIII*e *siècle*,
37 vols., 1846–81) have been made more valuable by the publication
of a thorough *Table alphabétique* by A. Marquiset, 1913.

On the journals, see Petit de Julleville, VI; also P. Van Tieghem,
L'Année littéraire comme intermédiaire en France des littératures
étrangères, 1917.

BOOK III

CHAPTER I:

* F. Vial and L. Denise, *Idées et doctrines littéraires du XVIIIe siècle*, 1909; * H. Lion, *Les Tragédies et les théories dramatiques de Voltaire* (thèse), 1895; E. Deschanel, *Le Théâtre de Voltaire*, 1886 (emphasizes the *romanesque* element); F. Brunetière, † *Les Epoques du théâtre français*, 1892 (on Voltaire and Crébillon); J.-J. Jusserand, *Shakespeare en France sous l'ancien régime*, 1898 — also English edition, New York, 1899; T. R. Lounsbury, *Shakespeare and Voltaire*, New York, 1902; E. P. Dargan, *Shakespeare and Ducis* in *Modern Philology*, X, (1912).

CHAPTER II:

* C. Lenient, *La Comédie au XVIIIe siècle*, 2 vols., 1888; E. Lintilhac, *Histoire générale du théâtre en France*. Vol. IV: *La Comédie au XVIIIe siècle*, 1909; J. Lemaître, *La Comédie après Molière et le théâtre de Dancourt*, 1882; (for Lesage, see next chapter); G. Larroumet, *Marivaux, sa vie et ses œuvres*, new ed., 1894; G. Deschamps, *Marivaux* (G. E. F.), 1897; L. de Loménie, *Beaumarchais et son temps*, 2 vols., 1856; E. Lintilhac, *Beaumarchais et ses œuvres*, 1887.

G. Lanson, *Nivelle de La Chaussée et la comédie larmoyante*, 2nd ed., 1903; F. Gaiffe, *Etude sur le drame en France au XVIIIe siècle*, 1910 (complete list of *drames*).

CHAPTER III:

* A. Le Breton, *Le Roman au XVIIIe siècle*, 1898; G. Saintsbury, *A History of the French Novel*, vol. I, 1917; L. Claretie, *Lesage, romancier*, 1891 (diffuse); E. Lintilhac, *Lesage* (G. E. F.), 1893; (for Marivaux, see preceding chapter); H. Harrisse, *L'Abbé Prévost, Histoire de sa vie et de ses œuvres*, 1896 (original researches); V. Schroeder, *Un Romancier français au XVIIIe siècle. L'Abbé Prévost; sa vie, ses romans* (thèse), 1898 (based on preceding work, but better adapted to general reader); Sainte-Beuve, *Port. litt.*, I; G. R. Havens, *The Abbé Prévost and English Literature* (Elliott Monographs), Princeton, 1921.

CHAPTER IV:

Poitevin, ed. *Petits poètes français depuis Malherbe jusqu'à nos jours*, 2 vols., 1864 (Anthology, with *Notices*); B. Jullien, *Les Paradoxes littéraires de La Motte*, 1859; P. Dupont, *Houdar de la Motte*, 1898; on minor poets, such as Chaulieu and La Fare, see Sainte-Beuve and Villemain, *passim;* * H. Potez, *L'Elégie en France avant le romantisme*, 1898 (Parny, Bertin, etc.); L. Morel, *James Thomson, sa vie et ses œuvres*, 1895; F. Baldensperger, *Young et ses 'Nuits' en France* in

Etudes d'histoire littéraire, (first series), 1907; E. Faguet, *André Chénier* (G. E. F.), 1902; L. Bertrand, *La Fin du classicisme et le retour à l'antique*, 1898.

BOOK IV

To the general titles given for Book I, add here:

J. Fabre, *Les Pères de la Révolution; de Bayle à Condorcet*, 1910; P. Lanfrey, *L'Eglise et les philosophes au XVIII° siècle*, 2nd ed., 1857; J. P. Belin, *Le Mouvement philosophique de 1748 à 1749*, 2 vols., 1913; F. Rocquain, *L'Esprit révolutionnaire avant la Révolution*, 1878.

BOOK IV

CHAPTER I:

*L. Ducros, *Les Encyclopédistes*, 1900; J. Morley, *Diderot and the Encyclopaedists*, new ed., 2 vols., 1897; J. Rocafort, *Les Doctrines littéraires de l'Encyclopédie ou le Romantisme des encyclopédistes*, 1890; J. Bertrand, *Dalembert* (G. E. F.), 1889; *L. Dimier, *Buffon*, 1919; M. Flourens, *Buffon. Histoire de ses travaux et de ses idées*, 2nd ed., 1850; on the later sensationalists: Lévy-Bruhl, *History of Modern Philosophy in France*, Chicago, 1899; F. Picavet, *Les Idéologues*, 1891.

CHAPTER II:

*G. Pellissier, *Voltaire Philosophe*, 1908; J. Morley, *Voltaire*, new ed., 1903; J. F. Nourrisson, *Voltaire et le Voltairianisme*, 1896 (clerical standpoint); Sainte-Beuve, *passim*. E. Faguet, *La Politique comparée de Montesquieu, Rousseau et Voltaire*, 1902. See also Bk: II, Ch. II.

CHAPTER III:

*L. Ducros, *Diderot, l'homme et l'écrivain*, 1894; J. Morley, *op. cit.*, Ch. I, above; R. L. Cru, *Diderot as a disciple of English Thought* (dissertation), New York, 1913; E. Scherer, *Diderot*, 1880; J. Reinach, *Diderot* (G. E. F.), 1894; R. Hubert, *La Morale de Diderot* in *Revue du XVIII° siècle*, 1915–16; F. Brunetière, *Etudes critiques*, II (on the *Salons*).

BOOK V

CHAPTER I:

On Romanticism, in general:

D. Mornet, *Le Romantisme en France au XVIII° siècle*, 1912; same author, *Le Sentiment de la Nature en France de Rousseau à Bernardin de St. Pierre*, 1907; J. Texte, *op. cit.* (Bk. I, Ch. III); M. B. Finch and E. A. Peers, *The Origins of French Romanticism*, 1920.

* A. Chuquet, *J.-J. Rousseau* (G. E. F.), 5th ed., 1919; Frederika Macdonald, *Jean-Jacques Rousseau, a New Criticism,* 2 vols., 1906 (shows d'Epinay-Grimm conspiracy); J. Lemaître, *Jean-Jacques Rousseau,* 1907 — also * English translation, 1907 (sympathetic and penetrating); H. Beaudouin, *La Vie et les œuvres de J.-J. Rousseau,* 2 vols., 1891; G. Gran, *Jean-Jacques Rousseau* (English translation) N. Y., 1912.

Special phases: Irving Babbitt, *Rousseau and Romanticism*, Boston, 1919 (views Rousseauism as a moral malady; bibliography); E. Faguet, *La Politique comparée,* etc.; * C. E. Vaughan, ed., *The Political Writings of Jean-Jacques Rousseau,* 2 vols., Cambridge, (England), 1915 (a critical edition, with good introduction); E. Champion, *J.-J. Rousseau et la Révolution française,* 1909; P.-M. Masson, *La Religion de J.-J. Rousseau,* 3 vols., 1916.

A. Barine (pseudonym), *Bernardin de St. Pierre* (G. E. F.), 1891.

CHAPTER II:

On the Revolution, see the historians discussed in Books VI and VII; also Carlyle; E. J. Lowell, *Eve of the French Revolution*, new ed., Boston, 1900; A. Rousse, *Mirabeau* (G. E. F.), 2nd ed., 1896.

* Lady Blennerhassett, *Madame de Staël. Her Friends and her Influence in Politics and Literature* (English translation), 3 vols., 1889; A. Sorel, *Madame de Staël* (G. E. F.), 1890; * Sainte-Beuve, *Portraits de femmes* (still unsurpassed as a portrait); M. Souriau, *Les Idées morales de Mme de Staël,* 1910; F. Brunetière, † *Evolution de la critique* and *Etudes critiques,* IV (on the novels); E. Faguet, *Politiques et moralistes* (see below), vol. I — also for Constant; Sainte-Beuve, *Causeries du lundi,* II (on *Adolphe*).

CHAPTER III:

* M. Lescure, *Chateaubriand* (G. E. F.), 2nd, ed., 1901; V. Giraud, *Chateaubriand, études littéraires,* 2nd ed., 1912, and *Nouvelles études sur Chauteaubriand,* 1912; † Sainte-Beuve, *Chateaubriand et son groupe littéraire sous l'Empire,* 2 vols., 1860 (revised ed., 1872); E. Faguet in *Dix-neuvième siècle, études littéraires* (very laudatory). On Chateaubriand's American travels, see J. Bédier, *Etudes critiques,* 1903; G. Chinard, *L'Exotisme américain dans l'œuvre de Chateau-briand,* 1918.

General nineteenth-century authorities:

V. Duruy, *Histoire de France,* new ed., 1891 — Engl. transl., revised and continued to 1919, N. Y., 1920; W. S. Davis, *A History of France,* Boston, 1919 (gives much space to the 19th century); Ch.-V. Langlois,

Manuel de bibliographie historique, 2 parts, 1901–04; G. Vapereau, *Dictionnaire universel des contemporains*, 6th ed., 1893. Petit de Julleville, vols. VII and VIII; * G. Pellissier, *Le Mouvement littéraire au XIXᵉ siécle*, 1889 (ff.) — English translation, 1897; F. Strowski, *Tableau de la littérature française au XIXᵉ siècle*, 1912; E. Gilbert, *Le Roman en France pendant le XIXᵉ siècle*, 5th ed., 1909; B. W. Wells, *A Century of French Fiction*, New York, 1912 (brief mention of many novels); † E. Faguet, *Dix-neuvième siècle; Etudes littéraires*, 1887, and † *Politiques et moralistes du XIXᵉ siècle*, 3 vols., 1891–1900; E. Hatin, *Histoire politique et littéraire de la presse en France*, 8 vols., 1859–61; H. Avenel, *La Presse française depuis 1789 jusqu'à nos jours*, 1900.

Lanson, *Manuel*, IV and Supplement; Thieme, *Guide bibliographique;* G. Vicaire, *Manuel de l'amateur des livres au XIXᵉ siècle*, 7 vols., 1894–1910.

BOOK VI

CHAPTER I:

On general history, see above. — T. Gautier, *Histoire du Romantisme*, 1894; L. Maigron, *Le Romantisme et les mœurs*, 1910; P. Lasserre, *Le Romantisme français*, 2nd ed., 1908 (hostile); Lanson, *Histoire;* F. Vial and L. Denise, *Idées et doctrines littéraires du XIXᵉ siècle* (to 1850), 1918; also (for definitions) G. Michaut, in *Pages de critique et d'histoire littéraire*, 1910; and for qualities, F. Brunetière, *Nouvelles Questions de critique*, 1890 (pp. 189 ff.).

Special phases and influences: C. Des Granges, *La Presse littéraire sous la Restauration, 1815–30*, 1907; L. Séché, *Le Cénacle de la Muse Française*, 1908; same author, *Le Cénacle de Joseph Delorme*, 2 vols., 1912; J. Texte, chapter on foreign relations in Petit de Julleville, VII, also *L'Influence allemande dans le romantisme français* in *Etudes de littérature européenne*, 1898; F. Baldensperger, *Goethe en France: étude de littérature compàrée* (thèse), 1904, also *Esquisse d'une histoire de Shakespeare en France* in *Etudes d'histoire littéraire*, second series, 1912; P. Van Tieghem, *Ossian en France*, 2 vols., 1917; E. Estève, *Byron et le Romantisme français* (thèse), 1907; L. Maigron, *Le Roman historique à l'époque romantique: essai sur l'influence de Walter Scott*, 2nd ed., 1912.

On Nodier: * E. Montégut, *Nos morts contemporains*, I, 1884; Sainte-Beuve, *Port. litt.*, I; L. Séché, *Cénacle de Joseph Delorme;* J. Retinger, *Le Conte fantastique dans le romantisme français;* M. Salomon, *Charles Nodier et le groupe romantique*, 1908.

On Béranger: Sainte-Beuve, *Caus. du lundi*, II and XV; E. Caro, *Poètes et romanciers*, 1888; E. Renan, in *Questions contemporaines*, 1868 (hostile).

On Lamartine: R. Doumic, *Lamartine* (G. E. F.), 1912; * H. R. Whitehouse, *The Life of Lamartine*, 2 vols., Boston, 1918; L. Séché,

Etudes d'histoire romantique: Lamartine de 1816 à 1830, 1905; E. Deschanel, *Lamartine*, 2 vols., 1893; C. de Pomairols, *Lamartine*, 1889; * E. Zyromski, *Lamartine, poète lyrique*, 1898.

CHAPTER III:

First, the thorough-going, but rather unsympathetic series by * E. Biré: *Victor Hugo avant 1830*, 1883; *Victor Hugo après 1830*, 2 vols., 1891 (2nd ed., 1899); and *Victor Hugo après 1852*, 1894; L. Mabilleau, *Victor Hugo* (G. E. F.), 3rd ed., 1902; E. Dupuy, *Victor Hugo, l'homme et le poète*, 1893; C. Renouvier, *Victor Hugo, le poète*, 4th ed., 1902; E. Rigal, *Victor Hugo, poète épique*, 1900; M. Souriau, *Les Idées morales de Victor Hugo*, 1908; and see below, Chs. V and VI, also Bk. VIII, Ch. I (Sainte-Beuve).

CHAPTER IV:

F. Brunetière, *Evolution de la poésie lyrique en France au XIXe siècle*, 2 vols., 1894.

On Musset: A. Barine (pseudonym), *Alfred de Musset* (G. E. F.), 1893; Sainte-Beuve, *Caus. du lundi*, I and XIII; L. Séche, *Alfred de Musset*, 1907.

On Vigny: M. Paléologue, *Alfred de Vigny* (G. E. F.), 1891; L. Dorison, *Alfred de Vigny, poète philosophe*, 1892; F. Baldensperger, *Alfred de Vigny, contribution à sa biographie intellectuelle*, 1912.

On Gautier: E. Richet, *Théophile Gautier, l'homme, la vie et l'œuvre*, 1893; M. Ducamp, *Théophile Gautier* (G. E. F.), 1890; Sainte-Beuve, *Nouv. lundis*, V and VI.

CHAPTER V:

* P. Nebout, *Le Drame romantique*, 1897; P. Ginisty, *Le Mélodrame*, 1910; on Delavigne, Sainte-Beuve, *Port. contemp.*, V, and J. Lemaître, *Impressions de théâtre*, III; M. Souriau, *La Préface de Cromwell de Victor Hugo* (critical edition), 1897; P. and V. Glachant, *Essai critique sur le théâtre de Victor Hugo*, 2 vols., 1902–03; H. Parigot, *Le Drame d'Alexandre Dumas*, 1898; L. Lafoscade, *Le Théâtre d'Alfred de Musset*, 1901; E. Fricke, *Der Einfluss Shakespeares auf Alfred de Mussets Dramen*, Bâle, 1901; E. Sakellaridès, *Alfred de Vigny, auteur dramatique*, 1902.

CHAPTER VI:

Wells, Gilbert, Maigron, etc. (see above); A. Le Breton, *Le Roman français au dix-neuvième siècle avant Balzac*, 1901; * J. Merlant, *Le Roman personnel de Rousseau à Fromentin*, 1905; † E. Rod, *Stendhal* (G. E. F.), 1892; A. Chuquet, *Stendhal-Beyle*, 1902; A. Filon, *Mérimée* (G. E. F.), 1898; F. Brunetière et ses élèves (Cavenel, Dimoff, etc.), *Victor Hugo*, 2 vols., 2nd ed., 1906; * R. L. Stevenson, *Victor Hugo's*

Romances in *Familiar Studies of Men and Books*, 1882 f.; H. Parigot, *Alexandre Dumas père* (G. E. F.), 1901, and *Alexandre Dumas et l'histoire* in the *Revue de Paris*, 1902; R. Doumic, *George Sand, dix conférences*, 1909 (English translation, 1910); * W. Karénine, *George Sand, sa vie et ses œuvres*, 3 vols., 1899–1912. On Vigny, Gautier and Hugo, see also preceding chapters.

CHAPTER VII:

On the critics: * I. Babbitt, *Masters of Modern French Criticism*, Boston, 1912; † F. Brunetière, *Evolution des genres: Evolution de la critique*, 5th ed., 1910; E. Faguet in Petit de Julleville, VII; G. Saintsbury, *A History of Criticism and Literary Taste in Europe*, Vol. III: *Modern Criticism*, Edinburgh, 1904; Sainte-Beuve, *Caus. du lundi*, I (Joubert, Montalembert, Lacordaire), and *Port. litt.*, II (Joubert, Joseph de Maistre); A. Beaunier, *La Jeunesse de Joseph Joubert*, 1918 (dispels legend); also M. Arnold, *Essays in Criticism*, I, 1889 (Joubert), and Babbitt, *op. cit.*; Paul Janet, *Victor Cousin et son œuvre* (G. E. F.), 1885; Barthélemy Saint-Hilaire, *Victor Cousin, sa vie et sa correspondance*, 3 vols., 1895.

On the Catholic revival: * A. Guérard, *French Prophets of Yesterday*, 1913; Sainte-Beuve (see preceding paragraph); on Lamennais, Sainte-Beuve, *Port. contemp.*, I and Faguet, *Pol. et mor.*, III.

On the historians: * G. P. Gooch, *History and Historians in the Nineteenth Century*, 2nd ed., 1913 (excellent); * C. Jullian, Introduction to *Extraits des historiens français du XIXᵉ siècle*, 1897; A. Bardoux, *Guizot*, 1894; also Sainte-Beuve, *Caus. du lundi*, I and Faguet, *Pol. et mor.*, I; F. Valentin, *Augustin Thierry*, 1895; also Faguet, *Pol. et mor.*, III and E. Renan, *Essais de morale et de critique*, 1859; G. Monod, *Jules Michelet*, 1875; Faguet, *Dix-neuvième siècle*; J. Simon, *Mignet, Michelet, Henri Martin*, 1890; P. de Rémusat, *Adolphe Thiers* (G. E. F.), 1889 and Sainte-Beuve, *Port. contemp*, IV.

BOOK VII

General Authorities:

G. Pellissier, *Le Mouvement littéraire contemporain*, 2nd ed., 1902; † F. Brunetière, *Le Roman naturaliste*, 1883; David-Sauvageot, *Le Réalisme et le naturalisme*, 1889; L. Desprez, *L'Evolution naturaliste*, 1884; † E. Zola, *Les Romanciers naturalistes*, 1881; † E. Scherer, *Etudes critiques sur la littérature contemporaine*, 10 vols., 1863–95; † J. Lemaître, *Les Contemporains*, 7 vols., 1885–99; 8th vol. (posthumous), 1918.

CHAPTER I:

* A. Le Breton, *Balzac, l'homme et l'œuvre*, 1905; * H. Taine, *Balzac*, in *Nouveaux essais de critique et d'histoire*, 1865 — also English translation of the same essay by L. O'Rourke, New York, 1906; Sainte-Beuve, *Caus. du lundi*, II; † F. Brunetière, *Honoré de Balzac*, 1906 — also English translation.

Chiefly biographical: F. Lawton, *Balzac*, 1910; J. H. Floyd, *Women in the Life of Balzac*, New York, 1921; G. Hanotaux and G. Vicaire, *La Jeunesse de Balzac; Balzac Imprimeur*, new ed., 1922.

Special phases: * Spoelberch de Lovenjoul, *Histoire des œuvres de Balzac*, 1879 (3rd ed., 1888); same author, *Autour de Honoré de Balzac*, 1897; M. Barrière, *L'Œuvre de Balzac*, 1890 (useful summaries of stories); Cerfberr et Christophe, *Répertoire de la Comédie humaine*, 1887.

CHAPTER II:

* H. Parigot, *Le Théâtre d'hier*, 1893; C. Lenient, *La Comédie en France au XIX⁰ siècle*, 2 vols., 1898; † F. Sarcey, *Quarante ans de théâtre*, 8 vols., 1900–02; † J. Lemaître, *Impressions de théâtre*, 10 vols., 1888–98; B. Matthews, *French Dramatists of the Nineteenth Century*, 4th ed., New York, 1895; J. J. Weiss, *Le Théâtre et les mœurs*, 1889; * H. Gaillard de Champris, *Emile Augier et la comédie sociale*, 1910; P. Morillot, *Emile Augier*, Grenoble, 1901; R. Doumic, *De Scribe à Ibsen*, 1893; A. Filon, *De Dumas à Rostand*, 1898.

CHAPTER III:

Brunetière, *Evolution de la poésie lyrique;* T. Gautier, *Etude sur la poésie française, 1830–68* (publ. in *Histoire du Romantisme*, 1874); C. Mendès, *Le Mouvement poétique français de 1867 à 1900* (*Rapport* followed by *Dictionnaire*), 1903.

On Baudelaire: * C. Mauclair, *Charles Baudelaire, sa vie, son art, sa légende*, 1917; T. Gautier, Preface to the *Fleurs du mal*, Lévy ed., 1868 f.; C. Asselineau, *Charles Baudelaire, sa vie et son œuvre*, 1879 (partial); J. Huneker, in *Egoists*, New York, 1909.

On Banville: Sainte-Beuve, *Caus. du lundi*, XIV, and Lemaître, *Contemporains*, I.

On Leconte de Lisle: Jean Dornis (pseudonym), *Essai sur Leconte de Lisle*, 1909; * G. Deschamps, *La Vie et les livres*, II, 1895; J. Vianey, *Les Sources de Leconte de Lisle*, Montpellier, 1907.

On Heredia: Lemaître, *Contemporains*, II; Faguet, *Propos litt.*, III, 1905; J. Richepin in the *Journal de l'Université des Annales*, II (April, 1908); E. Langevin, *José-Maria de Heredia*, 1907 (source-studies).

C. A. Downer, *Frédéric Mistral*, New York, 1901.

CHAPTER IV:

See above, General Authorities; Gilbert, Wells, Brunetière; * E. Faguet, *Flaubert*, (G. E. F.), 1899 — Engl. transl., 1914; R. Dumesnil, *Flaubert, son hérédité, son milieu, sa méthode*, 1905; R. Descharmes, *Flaubert, sa vie, son caractère et ses idées avant 1857* (thèse), 1909; Elliott Monographs, I–IV, Baltimore and Paris, 1914–17; L. Bertrand, *Gustave Flaubert*, 1912; Sainte-Beuve, *Caus. du lundi*, XIII, and *Nouv. lundis*, IV; also (on Feydeau), *Caus. du lundi*, XIV and XV; A. Riddell, *Flaubert and Maupassant, a Literary Relationship* (dissertation), Chicago, 1920; * E. Maynial, *La Vie et l'œuvre de Guy de Maupassant*, 1907; J. Lemaître, *Contemporains*, I.

CHAPTER V:

B. Schmidt, *Le Groupe des romanciers naturalistes*, Carlsruhe, 1903; C. Brun, *Le Roman social en France au XIXᵉ siècle*, 1910.

† E. Zola, *Le Roman expérimental*, 1880; * E. Lepelletier, *Emile Zola, sa vie, son œuvre*, 1909; Brunetière, *op. cit.*; Scherer, *Etudes sur la litt. contemp.*, VII; J. Lemaître, *Contemporains*, I; † A. France, *La Vie littéraire*, I and III; H. James, *Notes on Novelists*, New York, 1916 (Balzac, Flaubert, Zola).

The *Journal des Goncourt*, 9 vols., 1887–96; A. Delzant, *Les Goncourt*, 1889; J. Lemaître, *Contemporains*, III.

Léon Daudet, *Alphonse Daudet*, 1898; Brunetière and Schmidt; G. A. Ratti, *Les Idées morales et littéraires d'Alphonse Daudet d'après ses œuvres*, 1911.

BOOK VIII

CHAPTER I:

* I. Babbitt, *op. cit.* and Brunetière, *Evolution de la critique;* E. Scherer, *Etudes critiques*, I, 1863; G. M. Harper, *Charles-Augustin Sainte-Beuve*, Philadelphia, 1909 (chiefly biography and portraiture); L. Séché, *Sainte-Beuve*, 2 vols., 1904; * G. Michaut, *Sainte-Beuve avant les "Lundis,"* Paris and Fribourg, 1903 (very full up to 1850); L. MacClintock, *Sainte-Beuve's Critical Theory and Practice after 1849* (dissertation), Chicago, 1920 (supplementary to the preceding); G. Saintsbury, *op. cit.*

CHAPTER II:

On St. Simon and Comte: * G. Weill, *L'Ecole saint-simonienne, son histoire, son influence jusqu'à nos jours*, 1896; Lévy-Bruhl, *La Philosophie d'Auguste Comte*, 1900; * J. S. Mill, *The Positive Philosophy of Auguste Comte*, New York, 1887.

On Taine: * V. Giraud, *Essai sur Taine: son œuvre, son influence*, 4th ed., 1909; same author, *Maîtres d'autrefois et d'aujourd'hui*, 1913

(Sainte-Beuve, Taine, Brunetière, etc.);   A. Laborde-Milaà, *Hippolyte Taine, essai d'une biographie intellectuelle*, 1909; G. Monod, *Renan, Taine, Michelet*, 3rd ed., 1895.

On Renan: * L. F. Mott, *Ernest Renan*, New York, 1921 (the fullest biography); M. J. Darmesteter (Mme Duclaux), *La Vie d'Ernest Renan*, 1898; G. Deschamps, *La Vie et les livres*, II, 1895; R. Allier, *La Philosophie d'Ernest Renan*, 1905; G. Paris, *Penseurs et poètes*, 1896.

CHAPTER III:

On Quinet; Faguet, *Politiques et Moralistes*, II; on the minor historians: Gooch, Jullien, etc. (see above, Bk. VI, Ch. VII); on Tocqueville: Faguet, *Pol. et Mor.*, III, and P. Marcel, *Essai politique sur Alexis de Tocqueville*, 1910. On Lavisse: R. Doumic, *Portraits d'Ecrivains*, II, 1909; on Quinet, the church and Veuillot: A. Guérard, *op. cit.* (Bk. VI, Ch. VII); also L. Dimier, *Veuillot*, 1912.

On Amiel: Scherer, *Etudes critiques*, VIII, and Mrs. Humphry Ward's Introduction to her English translation, 1885; on Fromentin: Merlant, *op. cit.*, and M. Wilmotte, *Etudes critiques sur la tradition littéraire en France*, I, 1909.

BOOK IX

General authorities on the *fin de siècle*:

* G. Hanotaux, *Histoire de la France contemporaine*, 4 vols., 1903–08; W. S. Davis, *History of France*; J. E. C. Bodley, *France*, 1898; G. Pellissier, *L'Affaire Dreyfus et la littérature française* in *Etudes de litt. et de morale contemporaines*, 1905; Mme Juliette Adam, *Mémoires*, 7 vols., 1902–1910.

J. Huret, *Enquête sur l'évolution littéraire*, 1891 (interviews with prominent writers); † P. Bourget, *Essais de psychologie contemporaine*, 2 vols., 1883; definitive edition, 2 vols., 1901; G. Pellissier, *Le Mouvement littéraire contemporain*, 1901; * V. Giraud, *Les Maîtres de l'heure*, 2 vols., 1912–14 (Rod, Vogüé, Bourget, Loti, etc.); Sansot-Orland, etc., editors, *Les Célébrités d'aujourd'hui*, numerous small volumes since 1903.

CHAPTER I:

G. Coquiot, *Le vrai J.-K. Huysmans*, 1912; Remy de Gourmont, *Promenades littéraires*, I and III, 1904, 1909; H. Schöffler, *Die Stellung Huysmans im französischen Roman* (dissertation), Leipzig, 1911; Havelock Ellis in *Affirmations*, 2nd ed., Boston, 1916 (Zola and Huysmans). R. P. Bowen, *The Novels of Ferdinand Fabre*, Boston, 1918. On the later Naturalists, see Wells and Gilbert; also, on the Margueritte brothers: R. Doumic, *Etudes sur la littérature française*, III, 1895; on J.-H. Rosny: Pellissier, *Nouveaux essais de litt. contemp.*, 1895; on the idealists and Bourget, see Giraud, *Maîtres de l'heure;* on Bourget and Loti: R. Doumic, *Portraits d'Ecrivains,* II, 1909. G. Michaut, *Anatole France, étude psychologique,* 1913; L. P. Shanks, *Anatole France,* Chicago, 1919.

CHAPTER II:

*A. Benoist, *Le Théâtre d'aujourd'hui,* 2 vols., 1911–12; *F. W. Chandler, *The Contemporary Drama of France,* Boston, 1920; A. E. Sorel, *Essais de psychologie contemporaine;* R. Doumic, *Le Théâtre nouveau,* 1908 (mainly critiques of *premières*); A. Kahn, *Le Théâtre social en France de 1870 à nos jours,* (thèse), 1907; anon., *Le Théâtre Libre,* 1900 (program and achievements of the first three years); *A. Thalasso, *Le Théâtre Libre,* 1909 (fuller history and *répertoire*); W. H. Scheifley, *Brieux and Contemporary French Society,* New York, 1917; H. Burkhardt, *Studien zu Paul Hervieu* (dissertation), Zurich, 1917; R. Le Brun, *François de Curel,* 1905; A. Van Bever, *Maurice Maeterlinck,* 1904; J. Haraszti, *Edmond Rostand,* 1913.

CHAPTER III:

*E. Zyromski, *Sully Prudhomme,* 1907; C. Hémon, *La Philosophie de Sully Prudhomme,* 1907; G. Paris, in *Penseurs et poètes,* 1896. M. de Lescure, *François Coppée, l'homme, la vie et l'œuvre,* 1889; also A. France, *La Vie littéraire,* I and III.

C. Mendès, *Rapport* (see Bk. VII, Ch. III); *A. Barre, *Le Symbolisme. Essai historique . . . suivi d'une Bibliographie,* 1911 (extensive and authoritative); A. Symons, *The Symbolist Movement in Literature,* revised edition, New York, 1919; Amy Lowell, *Six French Poets,* 2nd ed., New York, 1916 (Verhaeren, Samain, R. de Gourmont, Régnier, Jammes, Fort; diffuse criticism; translations); A. Retté, *Le Symbolisme, anecdotes et souvenirs,* 1903; Mme Anne Osmont, *Le Mouvement symboliste,* 1917; E. Raynaud, *La Mêlée symboliste 1870–1890,* 1918; T. de Visan, *L'Attitude du lyrisme contemporain,* 1911; G. Walch, ed., *Anthologie des poètes français contemporains,* 3 vols., 1919 (with *Notices*); G. Kahn, *Symbolistes et décadents,* 1902.

C. Morice, *Paul Verlaine, l'homme et l'œuvre,* 1888; *E. Lepelletier, *Paul Verlaine, sa vie, son œuvre,* 1907 — English translation, 1909. On Mallarmé: J. Lemaître, *Contemporains,* IV, and see paragraph above. On the Americans: T. B. Rudmose-Brown, *French Literary Studies,* 1918. On Samain: L. Bocquet, *Albert Samain, sa vie et son œuvre,* 1905. On Régnier: Jean de Gourmont, *Henri de Régnier et son œuvre, 1908.*

CHAPTER IV:

J. Bédier, *Hommage à Gaston Paris,* 1904; H. Behrens, *Francisque Sarceys Theaterkritik* (dissertation) Greifswald, 1911; Giraud, *Maîtres de l'heure* (on Faguet, Bourget, Brunetière, France, Lemaître); R.

Doumic, *Ecrivains d'aujourd'hui,* 1894 (on Brunetière, Bourget, Faguet, Lemaître); E. Faguet, *Ferdinand Brunetière,* 1911.

EPILOGUE:

W. L. George, *France in the Twentieth Century,* 1908; *Le Larousse Mensuel,* 1910–20 (for dates and facts); * M. Braunschvig, *Notre littérature étudiée dans les textes,* Vol. II, 1921 (lists of important books, 1850–1920), G. Casella and E. Gaubert, *La nouvelle littérature, 1895–1905,* 2nd ed., 1906; F. Baldensperger, *L'Avant-guerre dans la littérature française, 1900–1914,* 1919; E. Henriot, *A Quoi rêvent les jeunes gens,* 1913 (another *enquête* on the various "isms"); Florian-Parmentier, *Histoire de la littérature française de 1815 à nos jours,* no date (1914); Mme Duclaux, *Twentieth-Century French Writers,* New York, 1920.

On Bergson and his influence: E. Le Roy, *Une Philosophie nouvelle, M. Henri Bergson* in the *Revue des deux mondes,* VII (1912) 6e pér. — also English translation, London and New York, 1913; H. W. Carr, *The Philosophy of Change; a Study . . . of the Philosophy of Bergson,* 1914; G. Turquet-Milnes, *Some Modern French Writers,* 1921.

On Rolland: Mme Duclaux (above); P. Seippel, *Romain Rolland, l'homme et l'œuvre,* 1913; S. Zweig, *Romain Rolland* — English translation, New York, 1921.

On the poets and mystics: Amy Lowell and T. de Visan (see Bk. IX, Ch. III); G. Duhamel, *Les Poètes et la poésie,* 1912–13; same author, *Paul Claudel,* 1919; P. M. Jones, *Whitman in France* in *Modern Language Review,* X (1915); S. Zweig, *Emile Verhaeren* — English translation, Boston, 1914; H. Potez (on Verhaeren) in the *Revue de Paris,* 1910; Remy de Gourmont, *Promenades littéraires,* 5 vols., 1904–14.

* A. Schinz, *French Literature of the Great War,* New York, 1920.

INDEX OF NAMES

INDEX OF NAMES

Italic figures indicate the chief references. Italicized *titles* are, as a rule, anonymous. Historical characters are usually omitted, unless they present literary interest. Credit for compiling this index is mainly due to Messrs. W. D. Trautman and Louis Allen, students in the Romance Department of the University of Chicago.

Lightning Source UK Ltd.
Milton Keynes UK
UKHW020847110119
335238UK00009B/966/P